TIMELINES OF THE 20TH CENTURY

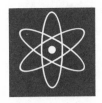

TIMELINES OF THE 20TH CENTURY

A CHRONOLOGY OF 7,500 KEY EVENTS, DISCOVERIES, AND PEOPLE THAT SHAPED OUR CENTURY

David Brownstone and Irene Franck

Little, Brown and Company

Boston   New York   Toronto   London

First Paperback Edition

Library of Congress Cataloging-in-Publication Data

Brownstone, David M.
    Timelines of the 20th century : a chronology of 7,500
key events, discoveries, and people that shaped our century / David Brownstone and Irene
Franck. — 1st ed.
        p.   cm.
    Includes index.
    ISBN 0-316-11406-5 (hc)   0-316-11501-0 (pb)
    1. History, Modern — 20th century — Chronology.   I. Franck, Irene M.
II. Title.
D422.B76   1996
909.82′02′02 — dc20   95-35200

10   9   8   7   6   5   4   3   2   1

Q-KP

Published simultaneously in Canada by Little, Brown & Company
(Canada) Limited

Printed in the United States of America

PREFACE

This is a very wide-ranging and diverse sort of book, with a good deal to offer almost anybody who picks it up and leafs through it. That is as it should be; by any standard you might like to apply, this has been the most extraordinary century in human history, with enough to engage, horrify, uplift, interest — and, for that matter, entertain — anyone with a spark of life and a bit of curiosity.

Our century has been the century of blood and tears, and at the same time a century of scientific breakthroughs that have vastly changed human experience and possibilities. We have been through two bloody world wars, ending with Hiroshima and Nagasaki; scores of revolutions and civil wars; and genocidal attacks on the Jews of the Holocaust, as well as on Cambodians, Gypsies, Armenians, and Rwandans, among others. We have developed nuclear, biological, and chemical weapons that threaten all life on earth, and have gone a long way toward poisoning the planet. All of that will be found in the book, along with three Gandhis, three Roosevelts, Lenin, Hitler, Stalin, Mao, King, four Kennedys, Eisenhower, Churchill, Thatcher, de Gaulle, two Bhuttos, and all the other movers and shakers of the century, right up to Bill Clinton, Bob Dole, Boris Yeltsin, and all of today's major leaders — and two Sarajevos, Pearl Harbor, the New Deal, the Cold War, the civil rights and women's movements, and a good deal more as well.

To some, the scientific and technological side provides only new horrors. But it also provides much of the hope for the future — for now we stand on the edge of space and on the eve of the age of genetic transformation, and have conquered many diseases and greatly lengthened life spans, although we now face new diseases and new public health problems. This has been the first century of the age of flight, and we have gone all the way from the Wright brothers to *Voyager II,* now headed out beyond the solar system into the galaxy. It has also been the time of the double helix, which gave us the secret of life. Here you will find Einstein, Freud, Salk, Hawking, the Curies, and the Leakeys, along with the theory of relativity, the *Kitty Hawk,* antibiotics, nuclear fission, the moon landing, organ transplants, black holes, radio, television, the computer, the Internet, and the immense worldwide communications and information network that is transforming all societies and bringing the whole world into our homes.

All fascinating stuff, and for its diversity alone enormously entertaining to look at, compare, see relationships. To this we have added a century-long look at humanity's culture, including a very wide range of people and their works, drawn from film, literature, theater, music, dance, broadcasting, and the visual arts. Here you will find Picasso, Chaplin, Monroe, *The Wizard of Oz, Wild Strawberries, Waiting for Godot,* the Beatles, bebop, Bogart,

"Stardust," "Bridge Over Troubled Water," *Madame Butterfly,* Nijinsky, Brando, Pavarotti, *Ulysses, Schindler's List, Doctor Zhivago,* Puccini, Madonna, Garbo, *Howl, A Streetcar Named Desire, E.T.,* and very much more — in aggregate both a basic list of key people, works, and movements and at the same time a vastly entertaining look at the culture of our time.

We have also included a very considerable potpourri of other material, drawn from economic, social, and everyday life, for this book would not be complete without such people and matters as Margaret Sanger and the fight for birth control, "Shoeless Joe" Jackson and the Black Sox scandal, the Lindbergh kidnapping, the Manson murders, *Brown v. Board of Education, Roe v. Wade,* the Model T, Kleenex, cellular phones, the San Francisco Earthquake, and Pan Am 103, along with Joe Montana, Jim Thorpe, Jackie Joyner-Kersee, Martina Navratilova, Babe Ruth, and O. J. Simpson, as both football star and murder case defendant.

To capture the whole sweep of our times and set it all in a comparative context, so that readers can find and link events, people, discoveries, works, and ideas across the whole range of human activity, *Timelines of the 20th Century* is organized into four major classifications: Politics and War; Science, Technology, and Medicine; Arts and Literature; and Social, Economic, and Everyday Life. Each classification occupies its own vertical column, with the four columns running from left to right across each two-page spread, so that readers may view events and people in all areas of human endeavor in any given year. The book starts in 1900 and runs through the end of 1994, a total of 95 years.

Timelines of the 20th Century is designed to be a browsable, entertaining, and comprehensive look at the whole history of our time. It is also an indispensable first place to look for students and others researching the key events of the century — for anyone who wants a clear, precise answer to the question, "When did it happen?"

The book is also easy to use. Readers can reach into it directly by year or through its extensive index — or can simply pick it up and browse in whatever era and area takes their fancy. Running heads on each page provide the year and mark the columns by subject. We have kept abbreviations to a minimum, primarily b. for born and d. for died.

Our thanks to our editors, Tracy Brown, Mary South, and Catherine Crawford, copy editor Barbara Jatkola; and to the Little, Brown production staff. Thanks also to Mary Racette, for her help in gathering and organizing the material, and as always to librarians throughout the northeastern library network, in particular to the staff of the Chappaqua Library — Director Mark Hasskarl; the expert reference staff, including Martha Alcott, Teresa Cullen, Sue Farber, Carolyn Jones, Jane Peyraud, Paula Peyraud, Mary Platt, and Carolyn Reznick; and the circulation staff, including Marilyn Coleman, Lois Siwicki, and Jane McKean — for fulfilling our wide-ranging research needs.

David Brownstone
Irene Franck
Chappaqua, New York

TIMELINES OF THE 20TH CENTURY

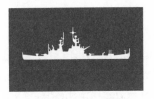

Beginning the modern African anticolonial movement, African-American leader W. E. B. Du Bois and other African-American and African-Caribbean leaders met in London, organizing the first of the six Pan-African Congresses that would ultimately eventuate in a continent-wide body of independent African states.

The British Labour Representation Committee was formed (Feb.) by a coalition of organizations that included the Fabian Society, the Independent Labour Party, and the trade unions (1900-1906); it was the forerunner of the Labour Party.

In China, Boxer rebels besieged foreign legations in Beijing (Peking) (June) and were quickly joined by Manchu government forces; Manchu dowager empress Tz'u Hsi declared war on the foreign powers (June 21). Multinational foreign forces took Tientsin by storm (July 23), fought their way to Beijing (Aug. 4-14), lifted the siege there, and then took, burned, and looted the city (Aug. 14). After Russian forces overran Manchuria (Oct.), China surrendered, ending the Boxer Rebellion and the war between China and its occupying foreign armies.

Irish Republican activist Maud Gonne founded the Daughters of Ireland (Inghindhe Na Eireann).

In South Africa, the tide turned in the Boer War, as greatly superior British forces led by Field Marshal Frederick Sleigh relieved besieged Kimberley (Feb. 15), Ladysmith (Feb. 28), and Mafeking (May 17-18) and went on to invade the Transvaal, taking Johannesburg (May 31) and Pretoria (June 5). Boer forces then mounted a guerrilla campaign, with early success.

The first Nobel Peace Prize was shared by Red Cross founder Henri Dunant and economist Frédéric Passy.

American forces of 90,000 to 100,000, led by General Arthur MacArthur, defeated the forces of the new Philippine republic, led by President Emilio Aguinaldo.

European imperial penetration of Africa continued, as French forces took the northern Sahara and Chad.

German physicist Max Planck theorized that energy exists not continuously, but in discrete units, called *quanta* (Latin for "units"), signaling the beginning of modern physics; from this he would develop the quantum theory, laying the basis for work by Albert Einstein and others.

The human voice was first transmitted by radio (Dec.), to a receiver a mile away, by American electrical engineer Reginald Aubrey Fessenden.

Heading an investigative commission in Havana, Cuba, American physician Walter Reed confirmed that yellow fever was mosquito-borne and therefore possible to eradicate; Reed also found that it was caused by a virus (1901). Two commission members died of the disease's effects — Jesse William Lazear immediately, James Carroll a few years later — having deliberately infected themselves.

French physicist Antoine-Henri Becquerel, discoverer of radiation (1896), recognized that particles in beta rays were electrons and also theorized that radioactivity might result from the transformation of one kind of atom into another. French physicist Paul Ulrich Villard discovered gamma rays, a previously unknown type of radiation.

Different types of human blood were distinguished by Austrian physician Karl Landsteiner, who initially discovered types A, B, and O, then AB (1902). Because blood types are generally incompatible (causing clumping that blocks blood vessels), previous blood transfusions had sometimes been deadly, and some countries banned them.

German count Ferdinand von Zeppelin built the first rigid airship, the cigar-shaped dirigible (zeppelin), filled with a lighter-than-air gas.

Theodore Dreiser wrote his first novel, *Sister Carrie,* a powerfully realistic work that was suppressed by its publishers for its "immorality" and was not available in the United States until 1912, although it was available abroad. William Wyler directed a film version, *Carrie* (1952).

The David Belasco–John Luther Long play *Madame Butterfly* opened in New York; the story of Japanese geisha Cho-Cho-San, who commits suicide after her American lover betrays her, was the basis for the 1904 Giacomo Puccini opera and also figured in the 1988 play *M. Butterfly.*

Giacomo Puccini's opera *Tosca,* based on the 1887 Victorien Sardou play, opened in Rome, with Hericlea Darclée in the title role.

Joseph Conrad published the novel *Lord Jim,* exploring the theme of the moral and physical disintegration of some European colonizers in the southern world who were experiencing what would later be called "culture shock."

L. Frank Baum published the classic children's novel *The Wonderful Wizard of Oz,* the first of his 14 "Oz" books. He was to adapt it into the 1903 theater musical, and it would become the 1939 film classic.

Marthe Rioton created the title role in Gustave Charpentier's opera *Louise,* which opened in Paris accompanied by considerable controversy for its espousal of feminist themes.

Beatrix Potter privately published the first of her children's books, the extraordinarily popular classic *The Tale of Peter Rabbit,* which she had written in 1893 and sent to a sick child.

Colette began her five-novel "Claudine" series with *Claudine at School.*

The population of the earth was estimated at 1.61 billion; it would more than triple by 1994.

The Ellis Island immigration station in New York harbor reopened; it had been destroyed by fire the day after its original opening (1892) and then rebuilt. The main American immigration station, the "Island of Tears" would become the gateway for 10 million new Americans.

The new Automobile Club of America sponsored the first automobile show, in New York's Madison Square Garden; at that time, some 8,000 cars were registered in the United States. Oldsmobiles were produced using mass-production methods that prefigured Henry Ford's later assembly lines.

Millions of visitors attended the Paris Universal Exhibition. Among the innovations they experienced were a "rolling pavement" and an early "Cineorama" with 10 projectors displaying film images on a circular screen.

World heavyweight boxing champion Jim Jeffries successfully defended his title, knocking out challenger James J. Corbett in the 23d round of their New York championship fight.

Eastman Kodak introduced the Brownie camera, making photography easy and inexpensive enough for virtually everyone.

The United States officially adopted the "gold standard," with the gold dollar becoming its standard unit of currency, as it had been in fact for two decades.

At the Paris Olympics, France led the way with 29 gold medals. Women were allowed to compete for the first time; they had been barred from the first modern games (Athens, 1896).

b. Ayatollah Ruhollah Khomeini (Ruhollah Kendi) (1900-1989), Islamic fundamentalist cleric; leader of the 1979 Iranian Revolution.

b. Heinrich Himmler (1900-1945), Nazi leader; head of the SS and the Gestapo, operator of the German concentration camp system, and one of the most notable mass murderers of the century.

b. Vijaya Lakshmi Pandit (Madame Pandit) (1900-1991), Indian diplomat; a key figure in the Congress Party and the sister of Jawaharlal Nehru, she would be the first woman to become president of the United Nations General Assembly (1953-1954).

b. Adlai Ewing Stevenson (1900-1965), American politician; twice Democratic presidential candidate (1952; 1956).

b. Camille Chamoun (1900-1987), Lebanese Maronite Christian politician; president of Lebanon (1952-1958).

b. Hastings Kamuzu Banda (1900-), Malawi independence movement leader; effectively head of state from 1961.

b. Louis Mountbatten (1900-1979), British naval officer; a great-grandson of Queen Victoria, he would be the last viceroy of India.

b. Helen Gahagan Douglas (1900-1980), American actress and congresswoman.

b. Martin Bormann (1900- ?), chief personal assistant to Adolf Hitler, who probably escaped to South America after World War II.

d. Karl Konstantin Albrecht Leonhard von Blumenthal (1810-1900), Prussian field marshal; a leading figure during the Franco-Prussian War (1870-1871).

d. Samory Touré (ca. 1835-1900), West African general long at war with French colonial forces (1889-1898); he ultimately died in exile.

Wilbur and Orville Wright were flying gliders (engineless aircraft) off the sandy dunes at Kill Devil Hills, near Kitty Hawk, North Carolina, where they would later fly the first airplane (1903).

Three European botanists — Hugo De Vries from the Netherlands, Karl Correns from Germany, and Erich von Seysenegg from Austria — independently rediscovered the basic laws of heredity that had been worked out decades before by Gregor Mendel but then ignored.

Russian-American chemist Moses Gomberg identified the first "free radicals," extremely active compounds later known to be destructive in the body.

Danish physician Niels Ryberg Finsen discovered that ultraviolet (UV) rays kill germs; UV lamps were used (by 1904) to sterilize hospital rooms and later also vaccines, blood plasma, and body tissues.

British engineers built the first powered, armored vehicle, used for carrying supplies in the Boer War.

Danish inventor Valdemar Poulsen obtained a U.S. patent for recording with a magnetized wire, but magnetic tape recording would not come into practical use until World War II.

German physicist Friedrich Ernst Dorn discovered radon, a naturally occurring, odorless, colorless, radioactive gas, only decades later understood as a major source of cancer-causing radiation in homes.

Italian physicist Guglielmo Marconi patented an invention allowing wireless telegraphy stations to operate on different wavelengths without interference.

Edmond Rostand's play *L'Aiglon* opened in Paris; Sarah Bernhardt created the role of Napoleon's son.

Georges Méliès created the pioneering, highly experimental film *One Man Band,* innovatively working with multiple exposures.

b. Spencer Tracy (1900-1967), American film star of Hollywood's golden age and beyond.

b. Aaron Copland (1900-1990), who would create classic compositions on American folk, jazz, and popular themes.

b. Helen Hayes (Brown) (1900-1994), American actress.

b. Kurt Weill (1900-1950), German composer of the Weimar period and later a leading American composer for the theater.

b. Louise Nevelson (Louise Berliawsky) (1900-1988), American modernist sculptor.

b. Luis Buñuel (1900-1983), innovative Spanish film director and writer.

b. Madeleine Renaud (1900–1994), French actress.

b. Dorothy Arzner (1900-1979), American feminist film director, writer, and editor.

b. Margaret Mitchell (1900-1949), who in 1936 would publish her only novel, *Gone With the Wind.*

b. Tyrone Guthrie (1900-1971), British director and actor.

b. George Seferis (Georgios Seferiades) (1900-1971), Greek poet.

In baseball, the American League was formed; it was not recognized by the older National League until 1903.

Tennis's Davis Cup competitions began between teams from the United States and Britain for a cup offered by champion Dwight F. Davis; other countries would join the competition in later years.

The German liner *Kaiser Wilhelm der Grosse* caught fire in the port of Hoboken, New Jersey (June 30), with flames spreading to other ships and the dock; 326 people died.

Berliner Gramophone, later Victor Records, introduced its trademark dog listening to a record and the slogan "His Master's Voice."

The vacuum cleaner was invented by Britain's Hubert Cecil Booth.

The paper clip was developed by Danish-German inventor Johann Vaaler.

A Gulf Coast hurricane destroyed much of Galveston, Texas (Sept. 8), killing at least 6,000 people.

In Scofield, Utah, an explosion caused a mine tunnel to collapse (May 1), killing 200 people.

b. Erich Fromm (1900-1980), German-American psychoanalyst and social critic.

d. Friedrich Wilhelm Nietzsche (1844-1900), German philosopher and poet whose construct of the superman *(Übermensch)* would be taken up by the Nazis with murderous intent and effect.

1900 cont.

German mathematician David Hilbert challenged his colleagues to explore new directions by setting out 23 unsolved mathematical problems.

b. (Jean) Frédéric Joliot-Curie (1900-1958), French physicist.

b. Wolfgang Pauli (1900-1958), Austrian-American physicist.

1901

d. Victoria (1819-1901), queen of England (1837-1901) during the high noon of the British Empire.

President William McKinley was assassinated by anarchist Leon Czolgosz at the Buffalo Pan-American Exposition (Sept. 6; he died on Sept. 16). He was succeeded by Vice President Theodore Roosevelt, who continued and expanded American imperial penetration into the Caribbean and the Pacific but made a major set of turns toward trust-busting, conservation, and consumer protection, themes that were to become central concerns later in the century.

Unable to contain continuing Boer guerrilla resistance, British forces in South Africa forced large numbers of Boer noncombatants into concentration camps. Many died of disease developed through starvation and lack of medical care, providing the world with a foretaste of multiple horrors yet to come.

Manchu control of China was greatly weakened by the punitive Boxer Protocol (Sept. 7), the peace treaty forced on China by its victorious foreign occupiers after the Boxer Rebellion. At the direction of President Theodore Roosevelt, Chinese indemnities paid to the United States were used to create U.S. scholarships for Chinese students, many of whom became leaders of the Chinese republic.

American forces took Philippine republic president Emilio Aguinaldo prisoner (Mar. 23), ending major

Italian physicist Guglielmo Marconi sent the first transatlantic wireless telegraphy signal — the letter *S* tapped in Morse code — from St. John's, Newfoundland, to Poldhu, Cornwall, England (Dec. 12). Previously, many people had thought that radio waves could carry no farther than 100 to 200 miles.

German physicist Karl Ferdinand Braun introduced crystal detectors to generate, detect, and amplify radio signals; the detectors were used in radios ("crystal sets") into the 1920s, when they were replaced by electron tubes.

Building on work by Christiaan Eijkman, his predecessor as a medical officer in the Dutch East Indies, Gerrit Grijns first recognized that disease could be caused by lack of a specific substance in the diet (in this case, beriberi, caused by lack of vitamin B_1, or thiamine).

Pierre and Marie Curie measured the amount of heat energy emitted by radium, an early indication of the tremendous energy resource that existed in the atom and would be tapped in the 20th century.

Adrenaline, the hormone that orchestrates the body's response to danger, was discovered by Japanese-American chemist Jokichi Takamine and independently by Thomas Bell.

1900 cont.

d. Oscar Wilde (1854-1900), celebrated Irish playwright; his life was cut short by his imprisonment in Britain for his homosexual preference.

1901

Thomas Mann published his seminal first novel, *Buddenbrooks,* a powerful work that began his exploration of the destruction of the artist and art in a decaying German society, in this instance together with a German family's fall from affluence, cohesion, and rationality.

Konstantin Stanislavsky produced Anton Chekhov's play *The Three Sisters* at the Moscow Art Theater; a landmark in the history of the Russian theater and, from the early 1920s, a major addition to the world repertory.

Pablo Picasso began his "blue period," characterized by pervasively blue representational work and subjects drawn from the underside of life (1901-1904), as in his superb *Woman Ironing* (1904).

H. G. Wells published his prophetic science fiction novel *The First Men on the Moon,* anticipating by almost seven decades astronaut Neil Armstrong's July 20, 1969, "one small step for a man, one giant leap for mankind."

Edward Elgar composed the first of his five patriotic marches, collectively titled *Pomp and Circumstance* (1901-1930), his homage to the worldwide British imperial state, then seemingly at the height of its power. Part of his first *Pomp and Circumstance* march became the anthem "The Land of Hope and Glory."

Financier J. Pierpont Morgan organized the United States Steel Corporation, further developing his financial and business empire, which included the Morgan investment banking firm, railroads, shipping lines, and other massive holdings. U.S. Steel, then the world's largest company, included the Carnegie Steel Company, other steelmaking facilities, ore producers, and a Great Lakes shipping line; it was capitalized by Morgan at $1.4 billion, far more than its intrinsic worth at the start.

The federal government bought Indian treaty lands in Oklahoma and then opened the newly acquired land to settlement on a "first-come, first-claimed" basis, in the Oklahoma Land Rush.

Ex–baseball player Connie Mack (Cornelius Alexander McGillicuddy) became manager (later owner) of the Philadelphia Athletics (1901-1954) of the American League; he would lead his team to nine league pennants and five World Series championships.

Steel manufacturer and philanthropist Andrew Carnegie donated more than $5 million to fund the New York City public library system; after sale of his steel company to Morgan, he would devote the rest of his life to philanthropy.

The historic Spindletop oil well blew in, near Beaumont, Texas, beginning a series of discoveries that

Philippine resistance, though Philippine and Moro Islamic forces continued to fight separate guerrilla actions.

The Commonwealth of Australia was founded, composed of the former British colonies of New South Wales, Queensland, South Australia, Tasmania, Victoria, and Western Australia, which then became Australian states.

Ashanti forces unsuccessfully besieged Kumasi (Apr.-July), held by the British, and were then decisively defeated (Nov.), ending the third and last Ashanti War, their country becoming a British protectorate.

The Japanese militarist and imperialist Black Dragon Society was founded.

The Socialist Labor Party and the Social Democratic Party of America merged to form the Socialist Party of the United States, led by Eugene V. Debs.

b. Hirohito (1901-1989), emperor of Japan (1926-1989).

b. Sukarno (1901-1970), Indonesian independence movement leader; the first president of Indonesia (1949-1966).

b. Eisaku Sato (1901-1975), Japanese prime minister (1964-1972) and leading anti–nuclear proliferation campaigner.

b. Fulgencio Batista y Zalvidar (1901-1973), Cuban soldier and politician whose dictatorship (1952-1959) was toppled by Fidel Castro.

b. Gheorghe Gheorghiu-Dej (1901-1965), Romanian communist politician.

b. Mustafa al-Barzani (1901-1979), leader of the Iraqi portion of the Kurdish national movement.

b. Oliver Edmund Clubb (1901-1989), American diplomat and author.

b. Souvanna Phouma (1901-1984), Laotian politician; head of government (1951-1958; 1959-1975).

Dutch botanist Hugo De Vries first reported that genetic changes sometimes occur spontaneously, calling them *mutations*.

French chemist Victor Grignard discovered a series of magnesium compounds (Grignard reagents) that would be widely used as catalysts in experiments involving organic compounds.

Belgian naturalist Maurice Maeterlinck (better known as a poet and playwright) published his classic *The Life of the Bee*.

A new species of mammal, the okapi, was discovered in Africa.

Element 63, europium, was discovered by French chemist Eugène-Anatole Demarçay.

In America, Thaddeus Cahill developed the electric typewriter, and Miller Reese Huchinson developed the electric hearing aid, the Acousticon.

The first Nobel Prizes in science were awarded. The award for physiology or medicine went to German bacteriologist Emil von Behring for his discovery of the diphtheria antitoxin, the award for physics went to German physicist Wilhelm Roentgen for his discovery of X rays, and the award for chemistry went to Dutch physical chemist Jacobus van't Hoff for his work on chemical dynamics in weak solutions.

b. Ernest Orlando Lawrence (1901-1958), American physicist.

b. Linus Carl Pauling (1901-1994), American chemist.

b. Enrico Fermi (1901-1954), Italian-American nuclear physicist.

Ethel Barrymore opened in New York in Clyde Fitch's play *Captain Jinks of the Horse Marines*; it was her first starring role, in a career that would last more than half a century.

Rudyard Kipling published the novel *Kim*, the story of his orphan-protagonist's travels through India with a Tibetan mystic, a vehicle for Kipling's observations of Indian life as seen through British imperial eyes.

French poet René Prudhomme was awarded the first Nobel Prize for literature.

b. Louis "Satchmo" Armstrong (1901-1971), American trumpeter, cornetist, singer, and bandleader; a seminal figure in American jazz.

b. Marlene Dietrich (1901-1992), German actress and singer; a film star of Hollywood's golden age.

b. André Malraux (1901-1976), French writer who would write *Man's Fate* (1933).

b. Gary Cooper (Frank James Cooper) (1901-1961), American film star.

b. Alberto Giacometti (1901-1966), Swiss sculptor and painter.

b. (William) Clark Gable (1901-1960), American film star of Hollywood's golden age.

b. Jascha Heifetz (1901-1987), Russian-American violinist; for more than six decades, one of the world's leading soloists.

b. Zora Neale Hurston (1901-1960), African-American writer and folklorist.

b. Irene Dunne (1901-1990), American film star of Hollywood's golden age.

would make the United States one of the world's largest oil producers.

U.S. president Theodore Roosevelt sparked enormous controversy among American racists for dining with African-American educator Booker T. Washington.

Robert F. Scott and others, including his compatriot Ernest Henry Shackleton, began an expedition to Antarctica, ultimately cut short by sickness (1901-1904).

b. Roy Wilkins (1901-1981), African-American civil rights leader who would become head of the National Association for the Advancement of Colored People (NAACP) (1955-1977).

b. Harry Bridges (1901-1990), Australian-American labor leader.

b. Edith Clara Summerskill (1901-1980), British physician, women's rights advocate, socialist, and politician.

b. Chic (Murat Bernard) Young (1901-1973), American cartoonist.

b. George Horace Gallup (1901-1984), American public opinion poll expert.

1901 cont.

b. Tage Erlander (1901-1985), Swedish Social Democratic Party leader and premier (1946-1969).

b. Werner Karl Heisenberg (1901-1976), German physicist.

b. René Jules Dubos (1901-1982), French-American bacteriologist and ecologist.

b. Margaret Mead (1901-1978), American anthropologist.

1902

General war threatened in the Balkans, as Macedonian insurgents, supported by Bulgaria, rebelled against Turkish rule; although war was averted by Great Power mediation, the run-up to war in the Balkans continued.

Unrest developed further in southern Russia as economic hardship and calls for democracy grew; the run-up to the 1905 revolution continued.

American imperial expansion continued in the Caribbean; the Dominican Republic became an American protectorate.

Britain and Japan signed mutual assistance pacts, helping clear the way for Japanese expansion in east Asia; Japan prepared to attack Russia.

The U.S. Congress once again extended the Chinese Exclusion Act, first passed in 1882.

The Arabian Civil War began (1902-1925) with successful attacks by Ibn Saud's forces in the Nejd area of southern Arabia.

British and German naval forces seized the small Venezuelan naval main force and blockaded Venezuela, as the two countries escalated their demands for allegedly overdue compensation payments stemming from the 1899 seizure of foreign-owned railroads and other assets.

The Republic of Cuba nominally became an independent state; it remained a de facto American protectorate until 1934.

In Britain, physicists Ernest Rutherford and Frederick Soddy recognized that radioactivity results from emissions as an unstable atom decays into a more stable one (1902-1903); the time for decay of half of a given amount was called its *half-life*.

British mathematician Bertrand Russell uncovered an internal contradiction — the "great paradox" — in symbolic logic, essentially that the set that includes all sets cannot contain itself. This undercut attempts to base all mathematics on formal logic, notably by Russell himself and by Gottlob Frege, whose massive *Basic Laws of Arithmetic* was then in publication.

Austrian neurologist Sigmund Freud invited Alfred Adler and three others to meet with him weekly; the resulting Psychological Wednesday Circle, which would grow to include Carl Jung and others, was the basis for the Vienna Psycho-Analytical Society (1908), later the International Psycho-Analytical Association (1910).

French meteorologist Léon-Philippe Teisserenc de Bort theorized that the atmosphere consisted of two layers, the lower *troposphere* and the higher, cooler *stratosphere*. British mathematician Oliver Heaviside and American electrical engineer Arthur E. Kennelly independently predicted the existence of an electrically

1901 cont.

b. Louis Kahn (1901-1974), who would emerge as a leading American architect in the mid-1950s.

b. Walt (Walter Elias) Disney (1901-1966), American film animator.

1902

Alfred Stieglitz and Edward Steichen led in the creation of New York's Photo-Secession Group, central to the development of the art of photography.

At the Moscow Art Theater, Konstantin Stanislavsky produced Maxim Gorky's play *The Lower Depths,* set at the bottom of czarist Russian society.

Cathleen ni Houlihan, a play by William Butler Yeats and Lady Gregory, opened in Dublin; Maud Gonne created the title role.

Claude Debussy's opera *Pelléas et Mélisande* premiered in Paris; Mary Garden created Mélisande and Jean Périer was Pelléas.

Pioneer French filmmaker Georges Méliès created *A Trip to the Moon (Le Voyage dans la Lune)*; its 30 scenes and more than 800 feet of film make it, to many, the world's first feature film, although Alice Guy-Blaché's *Passion* (also 1902) also has been called the first feature film.

Arthur Conan Doyle published his classic Sherlock Holmes tale *The Hound of the Baskervilles.*

Enrico Caruso became the first major recording star, with 10 records for the Victor company, including his signature aria "Vesti la giubba" from *Pagliacci,* later the first million-selling classical record (1907).

A strike by the United Mine Workers ended after the anthracite coal mine operators agreed to accept arbitration. Their earlier refusal to do so had resulted in popular support for the miners and antitrust actions in general.

The Newlands Reclamation Act, fostered by conservation-minded U.S. president Theodore Roosevelt, provided for the proceeds of federal western land sales to be used to establish western irrigation networks.

The Teddy bear was developed by Russian-American Morris Mitchom; named after U.S. president Theodore Roosevelt, it became an enduring tradition. Germany's Richard Steiff also produced a small stuffed toy bear.

The Tournament of Roses in Pasadena, California, sponsored its first postseason football game; it would become the Rose Bowl, a New Year's tradition.

Fannie Farmer founded her famous Miss Farmer School of Cookery, stressing nutritional meals; her popular cookbook would come from this experience.

Italy passed its first laws protecting women and children, following a campaign initiated by the Milan socialist newspaper *Avanti!* (1897) and adopted by the Unione Femminile (Female Union) (1901).

The Treaty of Vereeniging ended the Boer War (May 31) with Boer capitulation to the British.

A major rising in Angola was defeated by the Portuguese.

b. Georgi Maksimilianovich Malenkov (1902-1988), Soviet communist politician who would briefly succeed Joseph Stalin as leader of the Soviet Union (1953-1955).

b. Alva Reimer Myrdal (1902-1986), Swedish teacher, social planner, politician, diplomat, and peace activist who would become a Nobel Peace Prize winner (1982).

b. Jacques Philippe Leclerc (1902-1947), French general who would lead Free French armored forces into Paris (1944).

b. Mitsuo Fuchida (1902-1976), Japanese naval air officer who would command attacking planes at Pearl Harbor (1941).

b. Thomas Edmund Dewey (1902-1971), American politician.

d. Elizabeth Cady Stanton (1815-1902), American activist; a central figure in the worldwide women's rights movement; author of the Declaration of Sentiments and Resolutions at the historic Seneca Falls women's rights convention (1848), which she and Lucretia Mott organized, and the Declaration of the Rights of Women (1876). She was the founder and first president of the National Woman Suffrage Association (1869) and the National American Woman Suffrage Association (1890).

d. Cecil Rhodes (1853-1902), British financier; founder of the British South Africa Company (1889) and South African prime minister (1890-1896).

charged layer in the upper atmosphere, the *ionosphere* (discovered in 1924).

British biologist William Bateson demonstrated that the basic laws of genetics apply to animals as well as plants. American geneticist Walter Stanborough Sutton proposed that genetic material was located in chromosomes.

British physiologists Ernest Starling and William Maddock Bayliss discovered secretin, the first of a class of "chemical messengers" that Starling later dubbed hormones (1904), which orchestrate bodily functions.

French physiologist Charles-Robert Richet identified anaphylaxis, a severe allergic reaction that can lead to shock and death.

Prototype armed, armored, powered vehicles — forerunners of tanks — were built and exhibited in Britain and France, then Austria (1904).

American zoologist Clarence McClung theorized that a single chromosome — the X chromosome — determines a person's sex.

The first polygraph machine (lie detector), still controversial late in the century, was invented by Scottish cardiologist James Mackenzie.

The intravenous anesthetic Veronal was developed by German biochemist Emil Hermann Fischer.

Indanthrene blue (indanthrone), the first synthetic dye, was developed by James Morton.

Rayon (cellulose ester) was developed by American Arthur D. Little.

Henry James published the novel *The Wings of the Dove*.

German writer Theodor Mommsen was awarded the Nobel Prize for literature.

b. (James) Langston Hughes (1902-1967), leading African-American writer.

b. Richard Rodgers (1902-1979), leading American composer for the musical theater.

b. John Steinbeck (1902-1968), American author who would write *The Grapes of Wrath* (1939) and much more.

b. William Wyler (1902-1981), German-American Hollywood director whose classics would include *The Best Years of Our Lives* (1946).

b. Vittorio De Sica (1902-1974), Italian director and actor who would create *Shoeshine* (1946) and *The Bicycle Thief* (1947).

b. Ansel Easton Adams (1902-1984), photographer of the American West.

b. Marcel Lajos Breuer (1902-1981), Hungarian architect and designer who would become a leading modernist.

b. Ralph Richardson (1902-1983), celebrated British actor.

b. Stevie (Florence Margaret) Smith (1902-1971), British writer and illustrator.

d. Emile Zola (1840-1902), leading French novelist, short story writer, and critic; a major figure in 19th-century literature.

Jane Addams published *Democracy and Social Ethics*, her notable work on the relationship between democracy and social justice.

Glenn Hammond Curtiss established a factory to put engines on bicycles and set several land speed records on the resulting motorcycle (1905; 1907).

John J. McGraw, dubbed "Little Napoleon," became manager of baseball's New York Giants of the National League; over 3 decades, his team would win 10 league pennants and 3 World Series.

President Theodore Roosevelt appointed Oliver Wendell Holmes to the U.S. Supreme Court, where Holmes emerged as a major figure (1902-1935).

American psychologist and philosopher William James published *The Varieties of Religious Experience*, treating religious belief and experience as aspects of reality.

After the government failed to issue a warning, 30,000 people were killed when Mount Pelée erupted (May 8), destroying the city of Saint-Pierre, Martinique.

Danish explorer Knud Rasmussen led the first of his many expeditions to study Greenland and the culture of its people.

The Bureau of the Census became a permanent U.S. agency.

The lawn mower was introduced by Britain's James Edward Ransome.

The split skirt for women riding horseback, adopted by Mrs. Adolph Ladenburg at Saratoga, New York, drew charges of immodesty.

b. Fernand Braudel (1902-1985), French historian.

b. Karl Raimund Popper (1902-1994), Austrian-British philosopher of science.

1902 cont.

The air conditioner was introduced by American Willis Carrier.

b. Barbara McClintock (1902-1992), American geneticist.

b. Paul Adrien Maurice Dirac (1902-1984), British mathematical physicist.

1903

A dissident group led by Vladimir Illich Lenin emerged within the Russian Social-Democratic Workers' Party, calling itself Bolshevik (majority) because it had won intraparty votes on several disputed issues, although it was, in fact, a minority. The Bolsheviks were to split off into their own party (1912) and go on to take power in the 1917 October Revolution.

Aiming to use anti-Semitism to divert antigovernment unrest, the Russian government encouraged anti-Jewish attacks; beginning with spring attacks at Kishinev, Bessarabia (Moldova), the massive pogroms resulted in the murder of an estimated 50,000 Jews; the pogroms did not slow the onset of the 1905 revolution but did greatly speed the emigration to America already under way.

Sponsored by the United States, Panama revolted, winning independence from Colombia, then becoming a de facto American protectorate.

Cuba accepted the American-dictated Platt Amendment, establishing its de facto status as an American protectorate, including a continuing American military presence on Cuban territory, most notably at Guantanamo, which continued to be a major American base into the mid-1990s.

Emmeline and Christabel Pankhurst founded the militant Women's Social and Political Union (WSPU), which was to become the leading organization of the British woman suffrage movement.

Americans Wilbur and Orville Wright flew the first engine-powered, heavier-than-air machine, *Flyer I (Kitty Hawk),* at Kill Devil Hills, near Kitty Hawk, North Carolina (Dec. 17), a major event in human history. The first flight (120 feet) lasted 12 seconds. By 1905, the Wrights' *Flyer III* would stay aloft for nearly an hour.

Marie Curie, Pierre Curie, and Antoine-Henri Becquerel shared the Nobel Prize for physics for their work on radioactivity. Marie Curie was the first woman to receive a Nobel Prize, the first of her two. Pierre Curie declined France's Legion of Honor because it was awarded to men only.

Danish veterinarian Carl Oluf Jensen theorized that tissue and organ transplants, which had been attempted for centuries, failed because the body's immune system rejected them.

Dutch physiologist Willem Einthoven developed the string galvanometer, an early electrocardiograph.

After observing that X rays inhibit the growth of tumors, German surgeon George Perthes proposed that they could be used to treat cancers.

1902 cont.

d. Albert Bierstadt (1830-1902), American landscape painter, notably of the Hudson River valley and Western subjects.

d. Frank Norris (1870-1902), American novelist; a leading naturalist who often wrote on populist themes.

d. John Henry Twachtman (1853-1902), American impressionist painter.

b. Charles Augustus Lindbergh (1902-1974), American aviator and inventor.

b. Menachem Mendel Schneerson (1902-1994), grand rabbi of the Lubavich Hasidim.

b. Bobby (Robert Tyre) Jones (1902-1971), American amateur golfer.

1903

Edwin S. Porter made the landmark silent film *The Great Train Robbery*; it was simultaneously the first American feature film and the first Western.

Alfred Stieglitz founded the magazine *Camera Work* (1903-1917).

Henry James published *The Ambassadors*, set among American expatriates in Paris.

Hayim Nachman Bialik memorialized the victims of the Kishinev massacres in his poem "City of Slaughter."

Scott Joplin composed the first ragtime opera, *A Guest of Honor*.

Jack London published the novel *The Call of the Wild*, set in the Klondike; his protagonists are John Thornton and the dog Buck; Clark Gable would star in the 1935 film version.

Kate Douglas Wiggin published her popular children's book *Rebecca of Sunnybrook Farm*.

Australians adopted the Marie Cowan–A. B. Patterson song "Waltzing Matilda" as their unofficial national anthem.

Samuel Butler's bitterly satirical, semiautobiographical novel *The Way of All Flesh* was published posthumously.

U.S. president Theodore Roosevelt began America's National Wildlife Refuge System with his executive order declaring off-limits Florida's Pelican Island, home of egrets, herons, and other birds imperiled by the use of feathers for hats. Ninety years later, the American system of wildlife refuges would cover nearly 90 million acres.

Baseball's National League and American League held the first postseason championships — the World Series. The Boston Red Sox (Stockings) of the new American League (1900) won the eight-game series five to three over the National League's Pittsburgh Pirates. The two leagues also formed a national commission to oversee baseball.

A backstage fire at Chicago's Iroquois Theater (Dec. 30) generated heavy smoke; 602 people died from smoke inhalation or trampling during the panic that followed, as many exits were unmarked or blocked. In reaction, many cities passed new fire codes for theaters, including fireproof stage materials and more — and more clearly marked — exits.

Under the inspiration of British town planner Ebenezer Howard, the first garden city — a planned community of independent homes with private grounds and communal public

British Indian forces led by Francis Younghusband fought their way to Lhasa, forcing India-Tibet border concessions from the Tibetan government.

French colonial forces in Algeria attacked Moroccan border forces, beginning the long French penetration of Morocco.

A joint British-American commission settled outstanding Canadian and American Alaska border claims, largely in favor of the Americans.

British colonial forces in the process of acquiring Nigeria piecemeal took Kano and Sokoto.

b. Habib Bourguiba (1903-   ), Tunisian national leader (1934-1987); the first premier (1956) and then president (1956-1987) of independent Tunisia.

b. Galeazzo Ciano (1903-1944), Italian fascist politician who would become Benito Mussolini's son-in-law and foreign minister; he would ultimately be executed for treason.

b. Miguel Alemán Valdés (1903-1983), Mexican lawyer and politician; president of Mexico (1946-1952).

b. Ramón Magsaysay (1903-1957), Philippines president (1953-1957).

b. Tunku Abdul Rahman (1903-1990), Malaysian lawyer and politician.

Russian physicist Konstantin Eduardovich Tsiolkovsky published some notable articles on rockets, space flight, and space colonies, proposing the use of space suits, space stations, and liquid oxygen.

Germans Emil Hermann Fischer and Emil von Behring introduced barbiturate drugs.

b. John (Janos) von Neumann (1903-1957), Hungarian-American mathematician.

b. John Vincent Atanasoff (1903-1995), American physicist who would build the first fully electronic computer (1942).

b. Louis Seymour Bazett Leakey (1903-1972), British anthropologist and paleontologist.

b. Konrad Zacharias Lorenz (1903-1989), Austrian zoologist and psychiatrist.

b. Bruno Bettelheim (1903-1990), Austrian-American child psychologist.

Wassily Kandinsky painted his emblematic *The Blue Rider*.

Victor Herbert's operetta *Babes in Toyland* opened in New York.

Norwegian writer Bjørnstjerne Bjørnson was awarded the Nobel Prize for literature.

b. George Orwell (Eric Arthur Blair) (1903-1950), British author who would write *Animal Farm* (1945) and *1984* (1949).

b. (Jocelyn) Barbara Hepworth (1903-1975), British sculptor.

b. Nicolai Cherkassov (1903-1966), Soviet stage and screen star.

b. Georges Simenon (1903-1989), Belgian-French writer who would become a prolific novelist; creator of Inspector Maigret.

b. Mark Rothko (Marcus Rothkovich) (1903-1970), American abstract impressionist painter.

b. Countee Cullen (1903-1946), American writer; a leader of the Harlem Renaissance.

b. Rudolf Serkin (1903-1991), Austrian-American pianist.

b. Aram Khachaturian (1903-1978), Armenian composer.

d. James McNeill Whistler (1834-1903), American artist, long resident in Britain; one of the leading artists of the late 19th century.

d. Paul Gauguin (1848-1903), French painter; a leading postimpressionist, long resident in Tahiti.

land — was built at Letchworth, Hertfordshire, England. Others would be built later, notably after World War II.

Dorothea Douglass became a dominant figure in women's tennis, winning her first of seven singles titles at Wimbledon (1903; 1904; 1906; 1910; 1911; 1913; 1914); after the break during World War I, she would return to the finals (1919; 1920) but lose.

Helen Keller published *The Story of My Life*, describing how she overcame the twin handicaps of blindness and deafness to become a nationally known figure.

Roald Amundsen first sailed the Northwest Passage, from the Atlantic to the Pacific Oceans north of North America, in his sloop *Gjöa* (1903-1906).

Henry Ford organized the Ford Motor Company, introducing his Model A automobile.

W. E. B. Du Bois published *The Souls of Black Folk*, a central work of the 20th-century African-American freedom movement.

A member of Henry Ford's auto racing team, Barney (Berna Eli) Oldfield, became the first man to drive a mile in under a minute.

Charlotte Perkins Gilman published her classic study of women's roles *The Home: Its Work and Influence*.

b. Lou (Henry Louis) Gehrig (1903-1941), American baseball player.

b. Simone Weil (1903-1943), French writer, philosopher, and educator.

d. Calamity Jane (Martha Jane Cannary Burke) (1852-1903), American frontierswoman who toured with Buffalo Bill's Wild West Show.

Japanese forces began the Russo-Japanese War (1904-1905) with a disabling surprise torpedo boat attack on the Russian Far Eastern Fleet at anchor in Port Arthur (Feb. 8), presaging a rather similar attack at Pearl Harbor (1941); the Japanese then besieged Port Arthur. Attacking Japanese forces landed at Chemulpo (Inchon), swiftly moved north, defeated Russian forces on the Yalu River (May 1), and took Korea and most of Manchuria, forcing Russian forces to withdraw to Mukden.

Incumbent Republican U.S. president Theodore Roosevelt won election to a full presidential term, defeating Democratic challenger Alton B. Parker.

As the European alliances that were to go into World War I settled into place, the Anglo-French Entente Cordiale (Apr. 8) made Egypt a British and Morocco a French sphere of influence, also settling several other conflicting Anglo-French colonial claims. Britain and France were to oppose Germany in Africa on many occasions during the decade that followed, as the run-up to World War I accelerated.

Hereros and Hottentots began a major, ultimately failed insurrection against the German occupiers of German Southwest Africa (Namibia) (1904-1908). Insurrections against the Germans also failed in the Cameroons and German East Africa.

U.S.-Panama treaty established the Canal Zone, the 10-mile-wide strip of U.S.-administered land from sea to sea across Panama on which the Panama Canal would be built.

Uruguayan liberal Colorado government forces led by president José Batlle de Ordóñez defeated the conservative Blanco insurrection led by Aparicio Sarava (Jan.-Sept.).

Carrie Chapman Catt and Susan B. Anthony founded the International Woman Suffrage Alliance (IWSA); Catt was first president (1904-1923).

As physics and chemistry became ever more closely intertwined, British physicist Joseph John Thomson, discoverer of the electron (1897), proposed a "plum-pudding model" of atomic structure, with negatively charged electrons embedded in a positively charged sphere. Japanese physicist Hantaro Nagaoka suggested that a ring of electrons surrounded a positive nucleus, an idea widely rejected as impossible, while German chemist Richard Wilhelm Heinrich Abegg theorized that chemical reactions resulted from electrons being exchanged between atoms.

British electrical engineer John Ambrose Fleming developed the diode, a tube with two electrodes (a cathode and an anode) able to detect electromagnetic radiation, making possible the development of radio.

Russian physiologist Ivan Pavlov received the Nobel Prize for physiology or medicine for his pioneering work in animal behavior, focusing on patterns of learned responses to given stimuli (conditioned reflexes), a type of learning he called *conditioning*, as in the classic case of a dog salivating at the ring of a bell, if the ring has previously been associated with food. This laid the basis for the behaviorist school of psychology.

Sigmund Freud published his landmark work *The Psychopathology of Everyday Life.*

The *Diamond Sutra*, the oldest known complete printed book (ca. 868), was discovered at the Cave of the Thousand Buddhas, near Dunhuang, China, and was brought out of China by Hungarian-British archaeologist Marc Aurel Stein, along with numerous other books and antiquities.

Konstantin Stanislavsky produced Anton Chekhov's play *The Cherry Orchard* at the Moscow Art Theater; the last of Chekhov's four great plays, and another major addition to the world repertory, this study of a decaying aristocracy prefigured the revolutionary changes that were to transform Russia.

William Butler Yeats, Lady Gregory, and John Millington Synge led in the establishment of Dublin's Abbey Theatre, which would become the main force in the development of the Irish theater.

Giacomo Puccini's opera *Madame Butterfly,* based on the 1900 David Belasco–John Luther Long play, opened in Milan, with Rosina Storchio in the title role.

Henry James published *The Golden Bowl,* his final completed novel, once again examining American-European personal and cultural interplay in a story about Americans in Europe.

Romain Rolland published the first volume of his massive 10-volume fictional biography, *Jean Christophe* (1904-1912), set in a decaying Europe about to destroy itself in the Great War.

Wladyslaw Reymont began publication of *The Peasants* (1904-1909), his classic work on Polish rural life.

George M. Cohan's songs "Give My Regards to Broadway" and "The Yankee Doodle Boy" were introduced in his musical *Little Johnny Jones.*

The Andrew Sterling–Kerry Mills song "Meet Me in St. Louis" was sparked by the fair there; it would inspire the 1944 Judy Garland film.

Provençal poet Frédéric Mistral and Spanish playwright José Echegaray shared the Nobel Prize for literature.

Construction began on the Panama Canal (1904-1913), in a 10-mile-wide strip of land granted by treaty for the purpose. The American effort, under chief engineer George Washington Goethals (1907-1913), would succeed where earlier French attempts had failed partly because mosquito-eradication plans developed by William Crawford Gorgas largely ended the threat of yellow fever, and also malaria.

Investigative journalist Ida Tarbell published her trailblazing antimonopoly *History of the Standard Oil Company.* Lincoln Steffens published *The Shame of the Cities,* on corruption in city government. They and others would come to be called *muckrakers,* so dubbed by U.S. president Theodore Roosevelt (1906).

The Louisiana Purchase Exposition — the St. Louis Fair — was held in St. Louis, Missouri. Coinciding with it was the third modern Olympics, with the United States being the lead country, winning 21 gold medals.

In *Northern Securities v. United States,* a landmark antitrust case, the U.S. Supreme Court ordered the breakup of the Northern Securities Company, a massive railroad holding company controlled by J. Pierpont Morgan and James J. Hill. The decision was a major victory for the antitrust policies of President Theodore Roosevelt.

A notable early "skyscraper," the 22-story Flatiron Building — named for its triangular shape — was built in New York City (1902-1904).

Cy (Denton T.) Young pitched the first perfect game in professional baseball (May 5), allowing no member of the opposing team to reach first base.

Baseball's second World Series was scratched because John J. McGraw, manager of the National League pennant-winning New York Giants, refused

b. Deng Xiaoping (T'eng Hsiao-ping) (1904-), Chinese leader; he was to become a Communist in France in the 1920s, return to China, and fight throughout the Chinese Civil War; he would ultimately emerge as the leader of the People's Republic of China.

b. Lal Bahadur Shastri (1904-1966), Indian politician who would become a leader of the Congress Party, its general secretary (1951), and ultimately prime minister (1964-1966), succeeding Jawaharlal Nehru.

b. Ralph Johnson Bunche (1904-1971), trailblazing African-American diplomat who would win the 1950 Nobel Peace Prize.

b. Keith Jacka Holyoake (1904-1983), New Zealand politician; prime minister (1957; 1960-1972).

d. Joseph (Hinmahton-Yahlaktit; "Thunder-Rolling-Over-the-Mountains") (ca. 1840-1904), Nez Percé chief who had led his people in their ultimately failed flight to Canada (1877).

d. Theodor Herzl (1860-1904), chief founder of the Zionist movement and first president of the Congress of Zionist Organizations (1897-1904).

d. James Longstreet (1821-1904), American Confederate general.

German engineer Christian Hülsmeyer patented the first radar (radio detecting and ranging), using the reflection of radio waves to locate objects; not developed for decades, radar would figure prominently in World War II.

Dutch astronomer Jacobus Cornelis Kapteyn discovered two great streams of stars moving in opposite directions, only later understood to be the rotating movement of the Milky Way galaxy (1926).

American astronomer Charles Dillon Perrine discovered a sixth satellite of Jupiter, Himalia, then a seventh (1905), Elara.

British biochemist Arthur Harden discovered the first coenzyme, a small compound necessary for other, larger enzymes to work.

French scientist Leon Guillet developed stainless steel, although he did not recognize the value of its resistance to corrosion.

German-American inventor Emile Berliner developed the flat phonograph record, which would replace the wax cylinders then used.

The caterpillar (crawling) tractor was invented by American Benjamin Holt and Britons David Roberts and Ruston Hornsby.

A patent for color television was filed in Germany.

b. J. (Julius) Robert Oppenheimer (1904-1967), American nuclear physicist.

b. B. F. (Burrhus Frederic) Skinner (1904-1990), American psychologist.

b. George Gamow (1904-1968), Russian-American physicist.

b. Charles Richard Drew (1904-1950), African-American physician.

b. John Gielgud (1904-), British actor and director; he would be one of the leading theater figures of the century.

b. George Balanchine (Georgi Melitonovich Balanchivadze) (1904-1983), Russian-American dancer, choreographer, and ballet director.

b. Vladimir Samoylovich Horowitz (1904–1989), Soviet-American pianist.

b. Pablo Neruda (Ricardo Neftali Reyes Basualto) (1904-1973), Chilean poet; one of the century's major Spanish-language poets.

b. Cary Grant (Archibald Alexander Leach) (1904-1986), British-born actor who would for half a century be a Hollywood star.

b. Bing (Harry Lillis) Crosby (1904-1977), American singer and actor; a major figure in popular music.

b. Glenn Miller (1904-1944), American bandleader and trombonist; he would die in a World War II plane crash.

b. Graham Greene (1904-1991), leading British writer.

b. Isaac Bashevis Singer (1904-1991), Jewish-Polish-American writer.

b. Salvador Dali (1904-1989), experimental Spanish painter.

b. Fats (Thomas Wright) Waller (1904-1943), American jazz composer and musician.

b. Frederick William Ashton (1904-1988), British dancer, choreographer, and ballet director.

to compete against the American League's Boston Red Sox (Stockings). The Series would not be called off again until 1994.

Steel magnate and philanthropist Andrew Carnegie established a "hero fund" for people who endangered or lost their lives during attempts to rescue others.

A fungus was inadvertently imported to the United States on Chinese chestnut trees; during the century, it would kill virtually all American chestnut trees, some up to 600 years old.

Fire aboard the excursion steamer *General Slocum* (June 15), on the East River off Manhattan, killed 1,031 people.

Helen Keller, blind and deaf from age 19 months, graduated from Radcliffe College cum laude, aided by teacher-interpreter Annie Sullivan.

U.S. president Theodore Roosevelt began receiving instruction in the Japanese martial art of jujitsu, which then became widely popular.

The first segment of the New York City subway system opened, between the Brooklyn Bridge and 145th Street at Broadway.

The ice cream cone was invented at the St. Louis Fair, reportedly when an unnamed young woman folded a cookie wafer around her ice cream sandwich to keep it from dripping.

b. John Joseph Sirica (1904-1992), chief judge in America's Watergate trials (1973-1975).

On Bloody Sunday (Jan. 19), Russian troops at St. Petersburg's Winter Palace killed more than 100 peaceful petitioners led by priest Georgy Gapon; massive demonstrations and violence flared throughout the country in response to the atrocity. A mutiny on the Black Sea Fleet battleship *Potemkin* (June) brought intensified actions, and Soviets (Councils) began to form throughout the country. The Russian czar responded with the establishment of a toothless Duma (Aug.) and then with the October Manifesto, promising many reforms. By year's end, the sailors' insurrection at Sevastopol and the Moscow insurrection had been crushed, and the revolution had waned.

Port Arthur surrendered to the Japanese (Jan. 2). Japanese forces also defeated the Russians at Mukden (Feb. 21-Mar. 10); this decisive land battle of the war involved 600,000 combatants. At Tsushima (May 27), Japanese naval forces destroyed the obsolete Russian Baltic Fleet, which had sailed around the world to meet them, sinking all of its eight battleships and seven of eight cruisers, with a Japanese loss of three torpedo boats. President Theodore Roosevelt mediated the Treaty of Portsmouth (New Hampshire), which gave Japan Port Arthur and half of Sakhalin Island, forced Russian withdrawal from Manchuria, and made Korea a Japanese sphere of influence.

Anti-Jewish pogroms intensified in southern Russia; at least 1,000 Jews were killed in Odessa.

Edward Grey became British foreign secretary (1905-1916), then building the alliance that went to war in 1914. It was Grey who in 1914 would say, "The lamps are going out all over Europe; we shall not see them lit again in our lifetime."

As the run-up to World War I continued, German forces landed in Tangier in support of Moroccan resistance to the French, precipitating a crisis that threatened to develop into a general European war.

Albert Einstein proposed his special theory of relativity, including the famous equation $E = mc^2$ (energy equals mass times the speed of light squared), positing the interconvertibility of mass and energy. This involved the recognition that measurements of time, space, and motion vary in relation to a particular frame of reference and that, as a system approaches the speed of light, basic changes occur, such as mass increasing and clocks slowing. Einstein also explained the photoelectric effect, basic to television and radar, using Max Planck's quantum theory, and explained Brownian motion, the movement of molecules in liquid, for some providing the first proof of the existence of atoms.

Sigmund Freud published *Three Essays on the Theory of Sexuality,* introducing controversial notions about children's sexual desires toward a parent of the opposite sex, and also *Jokes and Their Relation to the Unconscious.*

French surgeon Alexis Carrel, working in America, developed techniques for suturing (sewing together) blood vessels, an advance that made possible heart surgery and organ transplantation.

Danish astronomer Ejnar Hertzsprung first recognized the relationship between brightness and star types (1905-1907), fundamental to stellar evolution theory.

American geneticist Nettie Maria Stevens discovered that chromosomes are paired.

German bacteriologists Fritz R. Schaudinn and P. Erich Hoffmann discovered the microorganism *Spirocheta pallida,* which causes syphilis, a widespread venereal disease that is often fatal if untreated.

Blanche Bates created the title role in David Belasco's play *The Girl of the Golden West,* ultimately riding off into the sunset with her reformed outlaw hero; it would be the basis for Giacomo Puccini's opera (1910).

Fritz Bleyl, Eric Heckel, Ludwig Kirchner, Max Pechstein, Emil Nolde, and Karl Schmidt-Rottluff were some of the early expressionists who exhibited together in Die Brücke (The Bridge) group (1905-1913).

Pablo Picasso began his "rose period" (1905-1906).

Edward Steichen's studio rooms at 291 Fifth Avenue were converted into the Little Galleries of the Photo-Secession (1905-1917), where he, Alfred Stieglitz, and others showed photography to be an art form, also introducing European artists such as Pablo Picasso to Americans and American artists such as Georgia O'Keeffe. Steichen also produced his photograph *Flatiron Building* and many other classic photographs.

Maude Adams created the title role in James M. Barrie's play *Peter Pan,* based on his novel *The Little White Bird* (1902); Mary Martin would re-create the role in the 1954 Broadway musical.

George Bernard Shaw's play *Man and Superman* opened in London.

Richard Strauss's operetta *Salomé,* based on Oscar Wilde's play (1893), opened in Dresden.

Lewis Hine's American immigration photos included *Ellis Island Madonna* and *Albanian Woman with Headcloth.*

Franz Lehár's operetta *The Merry Widow* premiered in Vienna.

Edith Wharton published her satirical novel *The House of Mirth.*

Western Federation of Miners leader William D. Haywood and Socialist Party leaders Eugene V. Debs and Daniel de Leon founded the syndicalist, direct-action Industrial Workers of the World (IWW), popularly called the Wobblies.

Eleanor Roosevelt, niece of U.S. president Theodore Roosevelt, married her cousin, Franklin Delano Roosevelt, beginning a partnership that would ultimately generate the New Deal and a tremendous flow of social legislation, and take the United States through the Great Depression and World War II.

Herbert Austin founded his automobile manufacturing firm in Longbridge, England; his most famous model would be the Austin Seven (baby Austin) of the 1920s.

Major rule changes in American football included allowing the forward pass and disallowing some dangerous plays.

The first Rotary Club was founded, in Chicago by Paul Percy Harris, so called because meetings were held at members' homes, in rotation; the organization would become national (by 1910) and later international.

The *Ladies' Home Journal* disclosed that a popular babies' teething medication, Mrs. Winslow's Soothing Syrup, contained morphine.

A yellow fever epidemic in New Orleans, Louisiana, ended after a federal mosquito-eradication campaign; of some 3,000 cases, approximately 400 people died.

American May G. Sutton became the first non-British tennis player to win a Wimbledon singles title; she would win again in 1907.

Charles Evans Hughes headed a New York State commission investigating waste and corruption in

Bertha von Suttner received the Nobel Peace Prize, the first woman given the award, founded largely in response to her book on pacifism (1889).

Christian-Muslim fighting grew in the Baku oil fields, prefiguring the Armenian-Azerbaijani wars that would later in the century engulf the two former Soviet republics.

Sinn Fein became the political party of the Irish Republican movement.

Norway peacefully seceded from Sweden by action of the Norwegian parliament, followed by a verifying plebiscite.

Russian grand duke Sergei Alexandrovich was assassinated in Moscow.

Crete won its independence from Turkey.

India's Congress Party (Indian National Congress) sharply criticized the British partition of Bengal.

b. Dag Hammarskjöld (1905-1961), Swedish diplomat; the second secretary-general of the United Nations (1953-1961).

b. Mohammed Abdullah (1905-1982), Kashmiri independence leader known as the "Lion of Kashmir."

b. Wladyslaw Gomulka (1905-1982), Polish communist politician.

d. John Hay (1838-1905), U.S. secretary of state (1898-1905); he had been the chief architect of President Theodore Roosevelt's Open Door policy toward China.

American astronomer Percival Lowell predicted that a new planet would be found beyond Neptune; Pluto would be discovered in 1930.

The first artificial joint was developed by J. B. Murphy for a patient with an arthritic hip; other "replacement parts" would be developed throughout the century, with ever more sophisticated materials.

The first formal tests of human intelligence, originally to identify children who were mentally retarded, were developed by French psychologist Alfred Binet, assisted by his student Théodore Simon.

American physician and bacteriologist Anna Wessel Williams developed a method of diagnosing rabies in the laboratory.

German chemist Richard Willstätter began his work detailing the structure of chlorophyll (1905-1913).

The German navy developed the U-boat (submarine).

The dial telephone was invented by American Almon Brown Strowger.

American John C. Dunton developed a jukebox offering 24 selections.

German physician and bacteriologist Robert Koch was awarded the Nobel Prize for physiology or medicine for his pioneering work on tuberculosis.

b. Emilio Segrè (1905-), Italian-American physicist who would codiscover technetium (1937), astatine (1940), and the antiproton (1955); he would settle in the United States after being ousted by the Fascists (1938).

Polish novelist Henryk Sienkiewicz was awarded the Nobel Prize for literature.

b. Greta Garbo (Greta Louise Gustafsson) (1905-1990), Swedish actress; a star of Hollywood's golden age.

b. Henry Fonda (1905-1982), American actor who would be a film star for more than five decades.

b. Jean-Paul Sartre (1905-1980), French writer and philosopher who would become identified with existentialism.

b. Lillian Hellman (1905-1984), leading American playwright.

b. Claudette Colbert (Claudette Lily Chauchoin) (1905-), American film star of Hollywood's golden age.

b. Mikhail Sholokhov (1905-1984), Soviet writer who would win the 1965 Nobel Prize for literature.

b. C. P. (Charles Percy) Snow (1905-1980), who would emerge as a leading British novelist in the 1950s.

b. Elias Canetti (1905-1994), Bulgarian-born writer, long resident in Britain; he would win the 1981 Nobel Prize for literature.

b. Myrna Loy (Myrna Adele Williams) (1905-1993), American film star of Hollywood's golden age.

b. Harold Arlen (Hyman Arluck) (1905-1986), American songwriter.

b. Michael Tippett (1905-), British composer.

b. Robert Penn Warren (1905-1989), American writer and critic.

the life insurance industry, leading to reform legislation; he would later become U.S. Supreme Court Chief Justice (1930-1941).

As the automobile gradually moved into everyday life, America's Bell Odometer invented a device to measure a car's mileage, Britain's Thorpe & Salter developed the speedometer, and London's City and Suburban Electric Carriage Company built the first multistory car park.

Elsie de Wolfe established herself as a major decorator with her interior design of the Colony Club, New York City's first club for women.

Owen Patrick Smith of South Dakota established greyhound racing, with dogs chasing a stuffed rabbit around a circular track.

b. Raymond Claude Aron (1905-1983), French philosopher, writer, historian, and sociologist.

b. Howard Robert Hughes (1905-1976), American entrepreneur, aviator, and film producer.

b. Christian Dior (1905-1957), French fashion designer.

b. Helen Pennell Joseph (1905–1992), White South African antiapartheid crusader.

1905 cont.

b. Ashley Montagu (Montague Francis) (1905-), British-American anthropologist who would be noted for his writings on such controversial topics as race, sexual equality, and human aggression.

1906

d. Susan B. Anthony (1820-1906), American activist; with her lifelong collaborator Elizabeth Cady Stanton, a founder of the worldwide women's rights movement at the Seneca Falls Convention (1848); Stanton originated and led what was the ultimately successful fight for the 19th Amendment to the U.S. Constitution (1920) (known as the Woman Suffrage or Anthony Amendment), winning women the vote.

India's Congress Party, spurred by the British partition of Bengal, moved from a request for greater participation in British Indian political life to the much stronger demand for home rule, beginning the long process that would ultimately lead to independence.

In South Africa, Mohandas (later Mahatma) Gandhi organized his first satyagraha (nonviolence) campaign (1906-1913), which won substantial gains. In the same year, British forces defeated a final Zulu insurrection.

The all-India Moslem League was founded; in the 1930s, led by Mohammad Ali Jinnah, it would become a mass political organization and the leading force in the campaign that resulted in the partition of India and the creation of Pakistan.

The British Labour Party was founded (Feb.) by several moderate British socialist organizations, including the Fabian Society, the Independent Labour Party, and the trade union movement.

In the wake of the failed 1905 revolution, the Russian government, led by newly appointed premier Pyotr Stolypin, established a reign of terror aimed at destroying

American electrical engineer Lee De Forest developed the triode (audion), a three-element electron tube that could generate, detect, and amplify electrical signals; for decades, it would be basic to all electronics, including radar, cathode-ray tubes, and early computers.

Reginald Aubrey Fessenden broadcast the first radio program, of voice and music (Dec. 24), from Brant Rock, Massachusetts; his listeners included shipboard wireless operators and a few land-based amateurs.

German physical chemist Walther Hermann Nernst formulated the theory that a temperature of absolute zero could never be reached; his explanation was the heat theorem, or the third law of thermodynamics.

German physicist Karl Ferdinand Braun discovered that he could change the path of electrons in a cathode-ray tube using a magnetic field, a discovery basic to television.

British biochemist Frederick G. Hopkins posited that some specific substances in food were required for human health, calling them "accessory food factors," later named vitamins (1912).

German neurologist-pathologist Alois Alzheimer identified Alzheimer's disease, involving the progressive loss of intellectual functioning.

1905 cont.

d. Henry Irving (1838-1905), leading British actor-manager and playwright; long associated with Ellen Terry.

d. Jules Verne (1828-1905), prophetic French science fiction author whose work helped create the genre.

1906

Pablo Picasso painted his landmark, unfinished cubist work *Les Demoiselles d'Avignon* (1906-1907), the central work of the central movement in early-20th-century European art, in which he, Georges Braque, and others made the historic move beyond three-dimensional forms toward new uses and syntheses of forms, colors, and materials.

Upton Sinclair published his novel *The Jungle,* a searing exposé of meatpacking industry practices and a classic in the American "muckraking" tradition, forerunner of later-20th-century investigative journalism. President Theodore Roosevelt and other reformers used the work to help push through the pioneering Pure Food and Drug Act.

Martin Andersen Nexö began publication of his four-part novel *Pelle the Conqueror* (1906-1910), set in the underside of Danish life. Max von Sydow would create the role of Pelle's father in Bille August's 1988 film version.

John Galsworthy published his first novel, *A Man of Property,* the beginning of his multivolume *The Forsyte Saga,* which began as a trilogy (1906-1921); he then generated several further volumes, the entire work becoming the basis for a 26-part British Broadcasting Corporation (BBC) series (1967).

Isaac Albéniz began the 12 piano works in his *Iberian Suite* (1906-1909), which would become by far his best-known work.

Congressional passage of the Pure Food and Drug Act and the Meat Inspection Act provided major federal consumer protection, largely in response to exposés by muckrakers, while the Hepburn Act provided the Interstate Commerce Commission (ICC) with expanded federal regulatory authority; all were victories for progressive U.S. president Theodore Roosevelt.

A massive San Francisco earthquake (Apr. 18), along the San Andreas Fault, estimated later at a strength of 8.3 on the Richter scale, killed 700 to 800 people and destroyed much of the city.

In a highly publicized case, wealthy Harry Kendall Thaw murdered architect Stanford White in the rooftop theater-restaurant of New York City's Madison Square Garden (June 25) after his wife, Evelyn Nesbit Thaw, said White had seduced her before her marriage to Thaw. Thaw was institutionalized; Nesbit continued her stage career.

Alva J. Fisher developed an electric washing machine, the Thor.

Devil's Tower, in Wyoming, was named America's first national monument.

Louis Blériot founded the first French airplane factory.

Oscar S. Straus was appointed U.S. secretary of commerce and labor; he was the first Jewish cabinet member.

the revolutionary movement. The new Duma, convened in May, was dissolved by the czar in July.

Cuba again was occupied by American forces (1906-1909); U.S. secretary of war William Howard Taft also became provisional governor of Cuba.

The threat of a general European war receded, as Germany recognized French claims on Morocco at the multinational Algeciras Conference. France continued to attack Morocco.

Alfred Dreyfus was exonerated and his French army captaincy reinstated, formally ending a dispute that with its anti-Semitic aspects had convulsed France from his arrest (1894) until his pardon (1900).

Britain launched the first of its Dreadnaught class of battleships, a major step in the intensifying arms race that would eventuate in World War I.

Guatemala was at war with El Salvador and Honduras (May-July); the war ended with the issues unresolved.

Theodore Roosevelt was awarded the Nobel Peace Prize.

b. Leonid Ilyich Brezhnev (1906-1982), Soviet leader; Communist Party general secretary and Soviet president (1977-1982).

b. Léopold Sédar Senghor (1906-), Senegalese poet and politician; leader of the Senegalese independence movement and first president of the Republic of Senegal (1960-1980).

b. Hsüan T'ung (Henry P'u Yi) (1906-1967), the last Manchu (Ch'ing) emperor of China (1908-1912).

b. Clark McAdams Clifford (1906-), American lawyer, politician, and adviser to four Democratic presidents, starting with Harry S. Truman.

b. Hugh Gaitskell (1906-1963), British Labour politician.

French physicist Bernard Brunhes discovered rocks magnetized in a direction opposite to the earth's magnetic field, later found to have resulted from periodic reversals of the magnetic field.

A massive explosion leveled a huge area in Siberia, near Tunguska, its cause still unknown to scientists.

German bacteriologist August von Wassermann discovered the Wassermann reaction, from which he developed the first blood test for syphilis.

Joseph John Thomson showed that a hydrogen atom has only one electron; he also was awarded the Nobel Prize for physics for his discovery of the electron (1897).

The term *allergy* was introduced to refer to the condition of people who suffer from hay fever or become sick after taking medications.

Swedish-American Gideon Sundback developed a hookless fastener, a prototype zipper.

b. Hans Albrecht Bethe (1906-), German-Jewish-American physicist who would first propose that the energy source of stars was nuclear fusion (1939); he would help develop the atomic bomb but later become an anti–nuclear weapons activist.

b. Grace Brewster Murray Hopper (1906-1992), American mathematician and computer scientist.

b. Maria Goeppert Mayer (1906-1972), German-American nuclear physicist.

b. Kurt Gödel (1906-1978), Austrian-American mathematician.

Italian poet Giosue Carducci was awarded the Nobel Prize for literature.

b. Billy (Samuel) Wilder (1906-), Austrian-American writer, director, and producer.

b. Dmitri Shostakovich (1906-1975), Soviet composer; a central figure in 20th-century music.

b. John Huston (1906-1987), American director, actor, and writer; he would create *The Maltese Falcon* (1941) and much more.

b. Samuel Beckett (1906-1989), multifaceted Irish writer who would become one of the leading playwrights of the century.

b. Philip Johnson (1906-), American architect; a key figure in the development of the International Style and later in postmodernism.

b. Luchino Visconti (1906-1976), Italian director.

b. Roberto Rossellini (1906-1977), Italian director who would create *Open City* (1945) and *Paisan* (1946).

b. Margaret Bourke-White (1906-1971), American photojournalist.

b. Clifford Odets (1906-1963), American playwright.

b. Josephine Baker (1906-1975), African-American and later French singer, dancer, and actress.

d. Henrik Ibsen (1828-1906), Norwegian playwright and poet; a massive figure in the development of modern theater.

d. Paul Cézanne (1839-1906), leading French impressionist; a seminal figure in modern art.

"Permanents" became popular among women after Charles Nestle (Karl Nessler) developed the permanent wave process for curling hair.

Tommy Burns defeated Marvin Hart in a 20-round fight (Feb. 23) in Los Angeles, California, for the world heavyweight boxing title vacated after the retirement of Jim Jeffries (1905).

The Olympics were held in Athens, although many people did not accept this as an official Olympics; France led with 15 gold medals.

The Intercollegiate Athletic Association (from 1910, the National Collegiate Athletic Association) was established to oversee college sports.

A coal dust explosion killed 1,060 people in Courrières, France (Mar. 10).

b. Warren Earl Burger (1906-1995), American lawyer and leading conservative judge; chief justice of the U.S. Supreme Court (1969-1986).

b. Hannah Arendt (1906-1975), German-American political philosopher and writer.

b. William Joseph Brennan, Jr. (1906-), American lawyer and Supreme Court justice (1956-1990).

1906 cont.

b. Adolf Eichmann (1906-1962), Nazi World War II war criminal, ultimately hanged in Israel.

b. José Figueres Ferrer (1906-), Costa Rican socialist politician; twice president of his country (1950-1953; 1970-1974).

b. Sergei Korolev (1906-1966), Soviet aeronautical engineer.

d. Pierre Curie (1859-1906), French chemist who, with his wife, Marie Curie, did key early work on radioactivity. After his accidental death, she succeeded him at the Sorbonne, becoming the university's first woman professor.

1907

The run-up to World War I continued. In St. Petersburg (Aug. 31), Britain and Russia signed agreements creating the Anglo-Russian Entente, settling most outstanding Central Asian sphere-of-influence questions. The Hague Peace Conference failed to in any way impede the escalating European arms race.

French naval and land forces took Casablanca and much of coastal Morocco, then moved inland.

More than 1 million immigrants passed through Ellis Island on their way to new lives in the United States.

Repression intensified in Russia, with hundreds of summary executions by the armed forces; these were met with a wave of assassinations, as Russia continued on the path that would ultimately lead to revolution.

Russia and Japan agreed to partition Manchuria and to make Korea a de facto Japanese protectorate.

Suffragists in several countries went over to militant action, most notably in Britain, where Emmeline and Christabel Pankhurst and Annie Kenney led a suffragist demonstration in Parliament that resulted in continuing clashes with police and scores of arrests.

German colonial forces suppressed a rising in German Southwest Africa.

To secure funds for the Bolsheviks, Joseph Dzhugashvili (Stalin) organized the robbery of the Tiflis state bank.

Inspired by Albert Einstein's special theory of relativity (1905), Russian-German mathematician Hermann Minkowski posited that time is a fourth dimension in the universe, an idea Einstein used in his general theory of relativity (1915).

Russian scientist Boris Rosing proposed that electrical signals could be converted into patterns of light in a cathode-ray tube. English inventor Alan Campbell Swinton independently suggested that such a tube could act as both camera and receiver; such electron-beam scanning would be used in Vladimir Zworykin's early television (1924).

Previously imported from abroad at great expense, nitrates for both fertilizers and explosives were made cheap and readily available after German laboratory chemist Fritz Haber developed a way to "fix" nitrogen from the air by making ammonia in the laboratory, and German industrial chemist Carl Bosch developed the Haber-Bosch process for large-scale production, vital to Germany during World War I.

Reginald Aubrey Fessenden broadcast the first two-way radio-telephone transmission, between Brant Rock, Massachusetts, and Scotland.

d. Paul Laurence Dunbar (1872-1906), African-American poet, novelist, and playwright, often writing on folk themes.

1907

For Anna Pavlova, Mikhail Fokine choreographed the solo *The Dying Swan,* to music from Camille Saint-Saëns's *Carnival of the Animals* (1886). It became a classic of the Russian ballet, and her signature role, at the Maryinsky Theater in St. Petersburg, with the Ballets Russes in Paris, and then on her unceasing world tours with her own company (1913-1931).

Rioting greeted Dublin's Abbey Theatre premiere of John Millington Synge's play *The Playboy of the Western World,* as outraged know-nothings protested Synge's candid view of Irish life and love. Rioting pursued the play on tour as well. The luminous work survived to become recognized as a classic of the Irish theater.

Constantin Brancusi's sculpture *The Prayer* began the process of abstraction that would ultimately produce works such as his celebrated "Bird in Flight" series and the almost equally celebrated *Egg.*

Florenz Ziegfeld presented *Follies of 1907,* the first of his 24 shows, which in 1911 were renamed the *Ziegfeld Follies* (1907-1931).

Georges Méliès produced the first science fiction film version of Jules Verne's *20,000 Leagues Under the Sea.*

Sholem Aleichem began to publish the very popular story series collectively titled *Mottel, the Cantor's Son* (1907-1916).

During the "panic of 1907," a private rescue effort mounted by a group of financiers, led by J. Pierpont Morgan, prevented an American financial crash.

President Theodore Roosevelt and the Japanese government made the informal "Gentlemen's Agreement," providing for restriction of Japanese emigration to the United States and withdrawal of American anti-Japanese laws and regulations. The United States also allowed Japanese and Korean (but not Chinese) men to bring to America brides from their homelands chosen by photographs; more than 41,000 such "picture brides" would come to America (1907-1921).

American lawyer Clarence Darrow won the acquittal of Industrial Workers of the World (IWW) leader William D. ("Big Bill") Haywood, charged with hiring someone to murder Idaho governor Frank Steunenberg.

Italian physician-educator Maria Montessori established the Casa dei Bambini (Children's House) in Rome, the first "Montessori school." There she developed the approaches, popularized in her book *The Montessori Method* (1909), that would transform early childhood education internationally.

Scottish anthropologist James Frazer published the final 12-volume version of *The Golden Bough* (orig. ed. 1890), a seminal work on religion, magic, and folklore (1907-1915).

Turkish forces defeated a Moldavian (Romanian) insurrection; in the course of the rising, revolutionary forces instituted pogroms against Moldavian Jews.

b. Anthony Blunt (1907-1983), British art historian who would be exposed in the mid-1960s as a Soviet spy in British intelligence during World War II, along with his Cambridge schoolmates Kim Philby, Guy Burgess, and Donald MacLean.

b. Pierre Mendès-France (1907-1982), French socialist politician who as premier (1954-1955) would end the Indochina War.

b. Constantine Karamanlis (1907-), Greek politician; premier (1955-1963; 1974-1980) and president (1980-1985).

b. Joaquin Balaguer (1907-), Dominican Republic lawyer and politician; three times president of his country (1960-1961; 1966-1978; 1986-).

b. Takeo Miki (1907-1988), Japanese prime minister (1974-1976).

b. Mohammad Ayub Khan (1907-1974), Pakistani officer; military dictator of Pakistan (1960-1969).

b. François "Papa Doc" Duvalier (1907-1971), Haitian dictator (1957-1971).

b. U Nu (1907-1995), Burmese politician who would become the first prime minister of Burma (1948-1958; 1960-1962).

b. Lin Biao (1907-1971), Chinese Communist politician.

b. Victor Paz Estenssoro (1907-), Bolivian leader who founded the Bolivian Historical Nationalist Revolutionary Movement; he would be president three times (1952-1956; 1960-1964; 1985-1989).

As part of a deliberate search for chemicals to kill disease-causing organisms but not human cells (an approach he dubbed chemotherapy), German chemist-bacteriologist Paul Ehrlich found that a dye, trypan red, killed trypanosomes, the protozoa that cause sleeping sickness.

American chemist Bertram Borden Boltwood proposed that radioactive materials, disintegrating over time, end up as lead and suggested that the rate of uranium disintegration and the proportion of lead in uranium ore might provide a means of dating rocks in the earth.

Element 71, lutetium, was discovered by French chemist Georges Urbain.

Italy's Prince Piero Conti organized the first known use of geothermal energy to produce electricity, using naturally occurring steam to drive a steam engine attached to a generator.

Paul Cornu, Igor Sikorsky, and others built experimental helicopters; some lifted off the ground but crashed.

French chemist Louis Lumière developed color photography.

Albert Abraham Michelson won the Nobel Prize for physics for measuring the speed of light (1878), the first American Nobel Prize winner.

b. Rachel Louise Carson (1907-1964), American ecologist, teacher, and writer.

b. Nikolaas Tinbergen (1907-1988), Dutch-British zoologist.

George Bernard Shaw's satirical American Revolution play *The Devil's Disciple* opened in London; it had played privately in the 1890s.

Joseph Conrad published his novel *The Secret Agent,* about London anarchists; it would be the basis for the 1936 film *Sabotage.*

Henri Matisse painted *The Blue Nude,* which would be among the hits of the New York Armory Show (1913).

Maxim Gorky published *Mother,* his novel about Russian revolutionaries; it would be the basis for the 1926 film and Bertolt Brecht's 1931 play.

Indian-born British writer Rudyard Kipling was awarded the Nobel Prize for literature.

b. Laurence Olivier (1907-1989), British actor, director, and producer; a central figure in the English-speaking theater.

b. John Wayne (Marion Michael Morrison) (1907-1979), prototypical Western film star.

b. W. H. (Wystan Hugh) Auden (1907-1973), British-American poet who would become a world figure.

b. Katharine Hepburn (1907-), American actress whose extraordinary film career would include four best actress Oscars.

b. Peggy Ashcroft (Edith Margaret Emily Ashcroft) (1907-1991), leading British actress.

b. Barbara Stanwyck (Ruby Stevens) (1907-1980), American actress.

b. Cab(ell) Calloway (1907-1994), African-American singer, bandleader, and songwriter.

On its maiden voyage, the *Lusitania,* then the world's largest ship, set an Atlantic record of 5 days 54 minutes between Queenstown (Cobh), Ireland, and New York City, improved to 4 days 15 hours in 1908.

William James published *Pragmatism,* treating moral constructs as matters capable of rational assessment in terms of their results, rather than as matters of religion-based absolutes.

The American "Great White Fleet" of 16 battleships was sent on an around-the-world tour (Dec. 1907-Feb. 1909) to demonstrate that the United States was a naval power.

French philosopher Henri Louis Bergson published *Creative Evolution,* rejecting scientific materialism and proposing that the physical world of science differs from the world of human experience powered by creative drives.

The first Rolls-Royce automobile, the Silver Ghost, was introduced.

The National League's Chicago Cubs won baseball's World Series; three Cubs became widely known for their infield play, and especially their double plays: (Joe) Tinker to (Johnny) Evers to (Frank) Chance.

b. Walter Philip Reuther (1907-1970), American labor leader.

b. Alfred (von Bohlen und Halbach) Krupp (1907-1967), German industrialist.

b. Dietrich Bonhoeffer (1907-1945), German Protestant minister and anti-Nazi leader.

b. Milton Caniff (1907-), American cartoonist.

d. Elizabeth (Cabot) Cary Agassiz (1822-1907), American educator; founder and first president (1893-1903) of Radcliffe College.

1907 cont.

1908

d. Tz'u Hsi (1835-1908), the dowager empress of China (1861-1908); she had ruled as regent but had been de facto ruler of China since the death of Emperor Hs'en Feng (1861). Her period of rule was that of maximum foreign domination of China. She had abdicated earlier in 1908, her abdication sharply signaling the death of the old order and the imminence of revolution in China. She was succeeded by the child emperor Hsüan T'ung (Henry P'u Yi).

Rejecting Serbian claims, Austro-Hungary formally annexed Bosnia-Herzegovina, having occupied it in 1878. A Serbian-Austrian war was narrowly averted, for a little while.

Republican William Howard Taft defeated Democrat William Jennings Bryan to become the 27th president of the United States (1909-1913).

Liberal Party leader Herbert Asquith became British prime minister (1908-1916); he would lead Britain into World War I. All efforts to stem the arms race failed, including face-to-face meetings between Wilhelm II of Germany and Edward VII of Britain, who could not agree even on moderating their naval build-ups.

Dutch colonial forces completed their conquest of Atjeh (Achin) on the island of Sumatra (Indonesia).

The rise of the Young Turk movement forced Sultan Abdul Hamid II to accept a new constitution embodying many democratic reforms.

Ernest Rutherford first recognized the alpha particle as a helium nucleus. He was awarded the Nobel Prize for chemistry for his work on radioactivity and atomic structure.

The chemical sulfanilamide was discovered; only later would it be found to fight bacteria and be widely used as the basis for "sulfa" drugs (1932; 1936).

The Hardy-Weinberg law, used to predict the distribution of genes in large populations, was developed by British mathematician Godfrey Harold Hardy and Wilhelm Weinberg.

Using Albert Einstein's equations on Brownian motion (1905), French physicist Jean-Baptiste Perrin first calculated the diameter of an atom — approximately one hundredth-millionth of a centimeter.

French astronomer Philibert Jacques Melotte discovered an eighth Jupiter satellite, Pasiphaë.

b. Edward Teller (1908-), German-American nuclear physicist who would lead the effort to build the hydrogen bomb (1949-1952).

b. Michael Ellis De Bakey (1908-), American surgeon who would first implant an artificial heart in a patient (1967) and pioneer in using artificial tubes to replace damaged human blood vessels (mid-1950s) and in the surgical opening of blocked heart arteries (1964).

1907 cont.

b. James Michener (1907-), American writer.

b. Alberto Moravia (Alberto Pinchale) (1907-1990), Italian writer; the husband of writer Elsa Morante.

d. Edvard Grieg (1843-1907), Norway's national composer.

1908

E. M. Forster published his celebrated early novel *A Room with a View*, a sensitive, small-scale work illuminating English class structures and the leveling power of love, which wins out in the end. Ruth Prawer Jhabvala adapted the novel into the 1985 James Ivory film.

At St. Petersburg's Maryinsky Theater, Anna Pavlova danced the title role opposite Vaslav Nijinsky in Mikhail Fokine's ballet *Cleopatra*.

H. G. Wells published *The War in the Air*, his prophetic science fiction novel describing what would become all-too-familiar horrors.

Jacob Epstein created his 18 monumental and controversial nude statues on the British Medical Association building.

Some of their work having been rejected by the National Academy of Design, The Eight — Robert Henri, John Sloan, William Glackens, George Luks, Everett Shinn, Arthur Davies, Ernest Lawson, and Maurice Prendergast — known to their detractors as the "Ashcan School," seceded from the academy and exhibited together, becoming the leaders of a new, later-ascendant movement in American art.

Arnold Bennett emerged as a major novelist with *The Old Wives Tale*, set in his native Staffordshire, England, site of much of his subsequent work.

L. M. Montgomery published her novel *Anne of Green Gables*.

The U.S. Supreme Court made several key decisions affecting workers. In *Adair v. United States*, the Court outlawed the practice of forcing workers to sign agreements (yellow-dog contracts) pledging not to join unions on pain of dismissal. In *Loewe v. Lawlor*, the "Danbury Hatters" case, it ruled that a union-organized national boycott was illegal as a conspiracy in restraint of trade. In *Muller v. Oregon*, it ruled that protective laws and regulations for women were constitutional. Various organizations would campaign for minimum wage laws for women workers, with some success, until blocked by a 1923 Court decision.

American boxer Jack Johnson defeated Canadian Tommy Burns for the world heavyweight boxing title, in a 14-round fight in Sydney, Australia; Johnson became the first Black man to hold the title, his story later depicted in the play *The Great White Hope* (1968).

Henry Ford introduced his Model T Ford, the first car for millions of Americans; more than 15 million, all black, would be sold (1908-1927).

The General Motors Company was founded; in the following decade, it would buy, in succession, Buick, Olds, Oakland, Cadillac, and Chevrolet.

The Boy Scout movement was founded in Britain by Robert Baden-Powell and later in America (1910).

The universal distress signal — SOS, in Morse code — was adopted.

1908 cont.

Army dissidents assassinated King Carlos and Prince Manuel of Portugal; Don Manuel, another son of Carlos, succeeded to the throne as Manuel II.

b. Lyndon Baines Johnson (1908-1973), Texas Democratic politician who would succeed to the presidency after the assassination of President John F. Kennedy (1963), becoming the 36th president of the United States (1963-1969).

b. Salvador Allende Gossens (1908-1973), Chilean socialist politician; president (1970-1973) until deposed and assassinated by a military coup.

b. Adam Clayton Powell (1908-1972), African-American politician who would become the first Black member of the New York City Council (1941-1945) and then a long-term member of Congress (1945-1971).

b. Enver Hoxha (1908-1985), Albanian communist politician who would be the hard-line Stalinist leader of his country (1944-1985).

b. Joseph Raymond McCarthy (1908-1957), American politician whose name was to supply a new epithet to the English language.

b. Nelson Aldrich Rockefeller (1908-1979), American Republican politician; grandson of John D. Rockefeller; he would become four-term governor of New York (1958-1973).

b. Roger Tory Peterson (1908-), American ornithologist, illustrator, and nature writer known for his "Field Guides" (from 1934).

b. John Bardeen (1908-1991), American electrical engineer and physicist.

b. Valentin Glushko (1908-1989), Soviet engineer.

b. Willard Frank Libby (1908-1980), American chemist.

James Barrie's play *What Every Woman Knows* opened in London.

Columbia introduced disks (78 rpm) recorded on both sides.

German writer Rudolf Eucken was awarded the Nobel Prize for literature.

b. Bette (Ruth Elizabeth) Davis (1908-1989), American dramatic film star of Hollywood's golden age.

b. Giacomo Manzù (1908-1991), Italian sculptor; he would create the *Portal of Death,* the doors of St. Peter's in Rome (1964).

b. David Oistrakh (1908-1974), Soviet violinist; one of the leading violinists of the century.

b. Herbert von Karajan (1908-1989), Austrian conductor who would become a leading figure in German music.

b. James Stewart (1908-   ), leading American actor.

b. Olivier Messiaen (1908-1992), French composer, teacher, and organist.

b. Michael Redgrave (1908-1985), celebrated British actor.

b. Rex (Reginald Carey) Harrison (1908-1990), British stage and screen star.

b. Richard Nathaniel Wright (1908-1960), African-American writer.

b. Celia Johnson (1908-1982), British stage and screen star.

b. Anna Magnani (1908-1973), Italian actress.

b. William Saroyan (1908-1981), Armenian-American writer.

Bud Fisher introduced the *Mutt and Jeff* comic strip.

German housewife Melitta Bentz invented the Melitta coffee-filtering system.

Glenn Hammond Curtiss won a *Scientific American* prize for flying his airplane *June Bug* more than a kilometer.

Helena Rubinstein opened a London beauty salon, Britain's first.

Locked windows and doors prevented the escape of 173 children and 2 teachers, who died in a fire (Mar. 8) at the Collingwood Elementary School in Cleveland, Ohio.

Massive earthquakes in Sicily and mainland Italy destroyed Messina and nearby areas, killing 100,000 to 150,000 people.

U.S. president Theodore Roosevelt designated most of the Grand Canyon a national monument. Congress would designate the Grand Canyon a national park in 1919.

The *Toonerville Trolley* comic strip began (1908-1955), created by Fontaine Fox.

The U.S. Bureau of Investigation was founded; it later became the Federal Bureau of Investigation (FBI).

b. Thurgood Marshall (1908-1993), African-American civil rights lawyer and U.S. Supreme Court justice.

b. Harry Andrew Blackmun (1908-   ), American lawyer and U.S. Supreme Court justice (1970-1994); a leading Court liberal, most notably for his majority opinion in the abortion case *Roe v. Wade* (1973).

b. Simone de Beauvoir (1908-1986), French writer, philosopher, and feminist.

1908 cont.

1909

The run-up to a general European war continued. Germany accelerated its construction of massive battleships; Britain moved to match and exceed the German build-up. Rival territorial claims in the Balkans continued to threaten an explosive regional war.

Persian rebel forces took Tehran, deposing Shah Mohammed Ali, whom they replaced with his 12-year-old son, Sultan Ahmad. Russian imperial forces took Tabriz. Middle Eastern oil began to be recognized as a great prize; British companies began to extract Iranian oil.

Civil war began in Honduras (1909-1911); revolutionary leader and former president Manuel Bonilla ultimately was again elected to the presidency.

U.S. Navy and Marine forces were sent to Nicaragua in support of the country's Conservative Party, forcing Liberal president José Santos Zelaya out of power.

Main American occupation forces left Cuba, although the country remained a de facto American protectorate and American bases remained.

With army support, the Young Turks took power in Turkey, replacing ruler Abdul Hamid II with a figurehead, Muhammad V.

b. Kwame Nkrumah (Francis Nwia Kofi) (1909-1972), Ghanian politician. President of Ghana (1960-1966).

Croatian seismologist Andrija Mohorovičić first identified the Mohorovicic discontinuity (Moho), a thin boundary layer 5 to 40 kilometers below the earth's surface, marked by sharp changes in the velocity of earthquake waves as they pass through the earth.

Working in Tunisia, French physician Charles-Jean-Henri Nicolle discovered that typhus was spread from person to person by infected body lice and so could be controlled by personal and public hygiene.

French engineer René Lorin developed the theory of jet propulsion, forward motion from the rearward discharge of a fluid or gas, especially from burning fuels; later used in rockets, missiles, and jets.

The first wholly synthetic plastic, Bakelite, was patented by Belgian-American chemist Leo Hendrik Baekeland; it would not be used commercially until 1928.

Russian-American chemist Phoebus Aaron Theodor Levene first discovered and analyzed ribose during his pioneering work on nucleic acids, later — as DNA (deoxyribonucleic acid) and RNA (ribonucleic acid) — found to work together in chromosomes to convey basic genetic information.

d. (Edmund) John Millington Synge (1871-1908), Irish playwright best known for his *Playboy of the Western World* (1907).

d. Nikolay Rimsky-Korsakov (1844-1908), Russian composer.

d. Edward MacDowell (1860-1908), American composer.

b. Simon Wiesenthal (1908-), Austrian-Jewish activist noted for his work tracking down Nazis who committed atrocities against Jews.

b. Edward R. (Roscoe) Murrow (1908-1965), American broadcast journalist.

Sergei Diaghilev founded the Ballets Russes company in Paris (1909-1929), by far the most significant event in the evolution of the worldwide modern ballet theater. There he would work with many of the leading choreographers, dancers, composers, and visual artists of his time to create much of the modern ballet repertory and a large body of landmark premieres and other performances. His opening program (May 18) included the premiere of Mikhail Fokine's Polovetsian dances from Alexander Borodin's *Prince Igor* (1889), with Adolphe Bolm in the title role.

Konstantin Stanislavsky presented Maurice Maeterlinck's play *The Blue Bird* at the Moscow Art Theater; the play also premiered in London. Shirley Temple would star in the most notable of the later film versions (1940).

Richard Strauss's opera *Elektra,* based on the 1903 Hugo von Hofmannsthal play, itself derived from Sophocles, opened in Dresden, with Ernestine Schumann-Heink in the role of Klytemnestra.

Nikolay Rimsky-Korsakov's *Le Coq d'or (The Golden Cockerel)* opened posthumously in Moscow.

Ferenc Molnar's play *Liliom* was produced; it would be the basis for *Carousel,* the 1945 stage musical and 1956 film.

Some 20,000 shirtwaist makers, many of them young immigrant women members of the International Ladies' Garment Workers' Union (ILGWU), organized a successful strike in New York City (1909-1910); some 3,000 of them pledged, "If I turn traitor to the cause I now pledge, may this hand wither from the arm I now raise!"

American explorer Robert E. Peary, African-American Matthew A. Henson, and four Eskimos reached the North Pole (Apr. 6); a former Peary associate, Frederick A. Cook, claimed to have reached the Pole first (1908), but his claim was discredited.

The multiracial National Association for the Advancement of Colored People (NAACP), originally the National Negro Committee, was founded; it would become the largest organization seeking justice and equality for African-Americans.

French aviator Louis Blériot made the first flight over the English Channel (July 25), flying from Calais to Dover in 36 minutes and winning a £1,000 prize offered by Britain's *Daily Mail*.

On his second Antarctic expedition, Ernest Shackleton discovered Mount Erebus and came within 100 miles of the South Pole.

Elizabeth Arden (Florence Nightingale Graham) opened her first beauty salon, on New York's Fifth

1909 cont.

b. U Thant (1909-1974), Burmese diplomat; the third secretary-general of the United Nations (1961-1971).

b. Andrei Andreyevich Gromyko (1909-), Soviet diplomat; Cold War foreign minister (1957-1985).

b. Barry Morris Goldwater (1909-), Arizona Republican senator (1953-1965; 1969-1987) and conservative Republican presidential candidate defeated by Lyndon Johnson in 1964.

b. Juan Bosch Gaviño (1909-), Dominican Republic writer and socialist politician; president of his country (1962-1963) until deposed by a military coup.

d. Hiroboumi Ito (1841-1909), Japanese politician who played a key role in the modernization of Japan; his opposition to the Russo-Japanese War forced him out of power, and he ended his long career as governor of Korea (1905-1906), where he was assassinated by a Korean nationalist.

d. Geronimo (Jerome; Goyathlay) (1829-1909), Chiricahua Apache leader who organized Apache guerrilla bands in northern Mexico and the southwestern United States late in the western Indian Wars.

d. Red Cloud (Mahpiua Luta) (1822-1909), Oglala Sioux general; leader of Native American forces in Red Cloud's War (1866-1868).

The IUD (intrauterine device) for contraception was devised by German physician R. Richter.

Danish botanist Wilhelm Ludvig Johannsen proposed the term *genes* to refer to units of inheritance contained within chromosomes.

Guglielmo Marconi and Karl Ferdinand Braun shared the Nobel Prize for physics for their work in wireless telegraphy.

Halley's comet, among the brightest periodic comets, returned, generating enormous popular interest. Thousands of people feared that its coming would mean the end of the world.

b. Edwin Herbert Land (1909-1991), American inventor who would invent polarized glass (1932), the basis for his Polaroid Corporation, and also the Polaroid Land Camera (1947).

b. Rita Levi-Montalcini (1909-), Italian neurobiologist who would codiscover the nerve growth factor (1954).

b. Virginia Apgar (1909-1974), American physician and anesthesiologist.

1910

Mexican dictator Porfirio Díaz, who had agreed to democratic presidential elections, arrested opposing candidate Francisco Madero, who escaped to organize an insurrection from American exile, beginning the long Mexican Revolution and Civil War (1910-1920), which was to cost an estimated 1 million lives.

At Osawatomie, Kansas, former president Theodore Roosevelt delivered a speech titled "The New Nationalism," calling for greatly strengthened federal regulation

Alfred North Whitehead and his protégé Bertrand Russell published *Principia Mathematica* (1910-1913), a notable attempt to base mathematics on logic, destined for failure by Russell's own "great paradox" (1902) and by Kurt Gödel's "incompletability theorem" (1931).

German chemist-bacteriologist Paul Ehrlich introduced salvarsan (arsphenamine), an arsenic

André Gide published the novel *Strait Is the Gate.*

Swedish novelist Selma Lagerlöf was the first woman to be awarded the Nobel Prize for literature.

b. Jessica Tandy (1909-1994), British-American actress; she would create Blanche Du Bois on stage in *A Streetcar Named Desire* (1947).

b. Eudora Welty (1909-), American writer; much of her work would be set in her native Mississippi.

b. Benny (Benjamin David) Goodman (1909-1986), American jazz clarinetist and bandleader.

b. Ethel Merman (Ethel Zimmerman) (1909-1984), American singer and actress.

b. Gordon Bunshaft (1909-1990), leading American architect.

b. James Agee (1909-1955), American writer and critic.

d. George Meredith (1828-1909), English novelist.

d. Isaac Albéniz (1860-1909), Spanish composer and pianist.

Avenue; she would popularize choosing makeup shades to match skin tone and clothing.

In tennis, Hazel Hotchkiss won the first of what would be three successive women's U.S. singles titles (1909-1911), and William A. Larned won the third of five successive U.S. men's singles titles (1907-1911).

The Lincoln head penny was introduced in the United States, replacing the previous Indian head penny.

A fire at the St. Paul mine in Cherry, Illinois, killed 259 of 279 miners (Nov. 13).

b. Herblock (Herbert Lawrence Block) (1909-), American political cartoonist.

b. Al Capp (1909-1979), American cartoonist.

Wassily Kandinsky painted an untitled, highly abstract watercolor that was later described by some as the first classifiably nonobjective painting, later titled *First Abstract Watercolor.*

E. M. Forster published the novel *Howards End,* set in a rigidly class-conscious Edwardian society soon to experience explosive changes. Ruth Prawer Jhabvala would adapt it for the 1992 James Ivory film.

Radio received a boost in popularity after electronics inventor Lee De Forest broadcast Enrico Caruso singing live from the Metropolitan Opera House. A new U.S. law also required that American passenger ships using American ports must be equipped with radio.

The U.S. Congress passed the Mann ("White Slavery") Act, banning transportation of women across state lines for "immoral purposes."

of business and finance and enhanced social welfare programs, two of the main tenets of what would become his "Bull Moose" presidential platform (1912).

Nebraska Republican representative George Norris led the successful fight to change U.S. House of Representatives rules and thereby curb the power of authoritarian House Speaker "Uncle Joe" Cannon.

d. Edward VII (Albert Edward) (1841-1910), king of Britain and Ireland (1901-1910); he was succeeded by his brother, George V. Edward had had little impact on the train of events that eventuated in world war, although he had made some faltering personal attempts at reconciliation with Germany.

The Union of South Africa was formed. It included the British Cape Colony, Natal, and the former Boer states of Transvaal and Orange Free State.

A Democratic revolution deposed Manuel II, establishing the Portuguese republic (1910-1926).

Eleutherios Venizelos became prime minister of Greece with army support. Venizelos was to lead Greece through the First Balkan War and through World War I on the Allied side.

Japan formally annexed Korea, previously a de facto protectorate, and would hold the country until the end of World War II (1910-1945).

Turkish forces partially defeated a major Albanian insurrection (Apr.-June), but the insurrection continued as a guerrilla war, further weakening Turkish control in the Balkans as the Balkan Wars approached.

In New York City, Harriet Stanton Blatch, daughter of Elizabeth Cady Stanton, organized the first major militant American woman suffrage parade.

Andrew Carnegie used some of the money he had gained from the sale of his steel company to found the Carnegie Endowment for International Peace.

compound that was the first drug to cure syphilis and so called the "magic bullet."

From studies of the fruit fly *Drosophila* (1907-1910), Thomas Hunt Morgan found that genes are lined up in rows on chromosomes, with some characteristics being linked by proximity on the same chromosome, and that some are sex-linked, being on the same chromosome that determines an individual's sex.

American pathologist Francis Peyton Rous recognized that some viruses can cause cancers, a conclusion largely ignored for decades.

Scottish-American astronomer Williamina Fleming discovered "white dwarfs," extremely dense stars late in stellar evolution.

French chemist Georges Claude began to experiment with light produced by electricity passing through "noble gases," the brightest being neon; once fully developed, these gases would be widely used in advertising.

Pollen desensitization treatments were first developed for hay fever sufferers, and asthma was recognized as a type of allergic reaction.

American physician James Bryan Herrick first identified sickle cell anemia, but its cause would not be understood for decades (1949).

The first wireless telegraph message was transmitted between land and an airplane.

b. Dorothy Mary Crowfoot Hodgkin (1910-1994), Egypt-born British chemist.

b. Jacques(-Yves) Cousteau (1910-), French marine explorer, environmentalist, writer, filmmaker, and inventor; codeveloper of the Aqualung (1943) and a leader in the fight to protect Antarctica (1988-1991).

At the Ballets Russes company in Paris, Vaslav Nijinsky and Ida Rubinstein danced the leads in Mikhail Fokine's new ballet *Shéhérazade,* music by Nikolay Rimsky-Korsakov. Tamara Karsavina and Fokine danced the leads in *The Firebird,* choreographed by Fokine to music by Igor Stravinsky.

Giacomo Puccini's opera *The Girl of the Golden West,* based on the 1905 David Belasco play, opened in New York, with Emmy Destinn creating the title role opposite Enrico Caruso. Conducting was Arturo Toscanini, the Metropolitan Opera's principal conductor (1908-1915).

T. S. Eliot, still a Harvard undergraduate, wrote his celebrated poem "The Love Song of J. Alfred Prufrock" (1910-1911; published 1915).

Fyodor Chaliapin created the title role in Jules Massenet's opera *Don Quichotte.*

Italian futurists led by Umberto Boccioni and Giacomo Balla published *Technical Manifesto of the Futurist Painters.*

German writer Paul von Heyse was awarded the Nobel Prize for literature.

b. Galina Ulanova (1910-), Russian ballerina who would become prima ballerina of the Bolshoi Ballet in the 1940s.

b. Akira Kurosawa (1910-), Japanese director and writer; he would become a towering figure in 20th-century cinema.

b. Jean-Louis Barrault (1910-1994), French actor, director, and manager; he would be Deburau on screen in *Children of Paradise* (1945).

b. Eero Saarinen (1910-1961), Finnish-American architect.

A bombing at the *Los Angeles Times* building (Oct. 1) killed 21 people. Union leaders James B. McNamara and his brother, John J. McNamara, were charged and on advice of their attorney, Clarence Darrow, pleaded guilty on a plea bargain; James received a life sentence and John a 15-year sentence.

Danish explorer Knud Rasmussen founded Thule, making it his base for explorations of northern Greenland; it would become a key defense station during World War II, by U.S.-Danish agreement.

In a sensational British murder case, Hawley Harvey Crippen was captured on arriving in Canada (July 31) with his typist, Ethel Le Neve, disguised as his son, after the poisoned remains of Crippen's missing wife were found buried in the cellar of their London home. Crippen was convicted of the murder and hanged; Le Neve was acquitted.

International Women's Day (Mar. 8) began to be observed by various socialist organizations.

Jane Addams published *Twenty Years at Hull House,* a memoir of her days as a pioneer in America's emerging social work movement.

Massive summer forest fires in western North America included the "Great Idaho Fire" (Aug. 10-21) in the Bitterroot Range, which consumed more than 3 million acres, killing 85 people.

W. E. B. Du Bois became editor of *The Crisis* (1910-1934), journal of the National Association for the Advancement of Colored People (NAACP).

Emma Goldman published *Anarchism and Other Essays.*

The *Krazy Kat* comic strip began, created by George Herriman.

1910 cont.

French forces continued their conquest of Morocco, taking much of the southern portion of the country.

d. Julia Ward Howe (1819-1910), American abolitionist, women's rights movement leader, and writer; best known as the author of "Battle Hymn of the Republic" (1862).

b. Jacques Lucien Monod (1910-1976), French biochemist.

d. Elizabeth Blackwell (1821-1910), British-American physician; the first woman to graduate from an American medical school (1849); founder of a New York hospital (1857) and a London medical school for women (1869).

d. Florence Nightingale (1820-1910), British nurse and administrator who laid the basis for modern nursing during the Crimean War.

1911

Armed revolts against the Manchu (Ch'ing) government began at Wuchang, in central China (Oct. 10), spread throughout China, and quickly brought down the Manchus. With the victory of the revolution of 1911, Sun Yat-sen returned from America, becoming the provisional president of the Chinese republic.

At Ciudad Juárez, in Chihuahua, Mexico, Francisco Madero's forces decisively defeated those of dictator Porfirio Díaz (May). With victory, however, came more war, as the revolutionary movement splintered, with Emiliano

During balloon experiments, Austrian-American physicist Victor Hess discovered radiation coming from outer space, later dubbed cosmic rays (1925); radiation was previously thought to originate only from the earth.

Ernest Rutherford, Hans Geiger, and Ernest Marsden developed the first practical model of the atom that placed the positively charged nucleus at the center, later modified by Niels Bohr and others.

b. Jean Genet (1910-1986), French playwright and poet; he would be a leading figure in the "theater of the absurd."

b. Katherine Dunham (1910-), African-American dancer, choreographer, director, and teacher.

b. Sylvia Sidney (Sophia Kosow) (1910-), American actress; she would become the quintessential Depression era American film star.

d. Leo Tolstoy (1828-1910), Russian author of *War and Peace* (1865-1869) and much more.

d. Mark Twain (1835-1910), American writer and world figure.

d. Winslow Homer (1836-1910), celebrated American artist.

d. Marius Petipa (1818-1910), seminal French choreographer and dancer; a major figure in ballet.

Barney (Berna Eli) Oldfield set a land speed record of over 131 miles per hour at Daytona Beach, Florida, driving a Benz automobile.

Glenn Hammond Curtiss became a celebrity and won a $10,000 prize for a then-daring flight from Albany to New York City.

World heavyweight boxing champion Jack Johnson successfully defended his title against ex-champ Jim Jeffries, who had retired with the title (1905).

b. Mother Teresa (Agnes Gonxha Bejaxhiu) (1910-), Yugoslav-born Albanian religious leader who would found the Missionaries of Charity (1950).

b. Joy Gessner Adamson (1910-1980), Austrian conservationist and writer.

b. Abe Fortas (1910-1982), American lawyer and U.S. Supreme Court justice.

d. William James (1842-1910), leading American psychologist and philosopher; elder brother of novelist Henry James.

d. Mary Baker Eddy (1821-1910), American religious leader who founded the Christian Science movement (1876).

Frank Lloyd Wright built Taliesin, his seminal work and Wisconsin home, later to become his architecture school and workshop (1932), as well as a place of pilgrimage in modern architecture.

Vaslav Nijinsky and Tamara Karsavina created the leads in Mikhail Fokine's ballet *La Spectre de la Rose,* music by Carl Maria von Weber. Nijinsky created the title role, opposite Karsavina, in Fokine's *Petrushka,* music by Igor Stravinsky. Both ballets

Fire at New York City's Triangle Shirtwaist Company factory (Mar. 25) killed 146 workers, most of them young immigrant women who were burned or forced to jump to their deaths because the factory's exit doors were barred. A huge public outcry resulted in stronger state fire and antisweatshop laws.

American explorer Hiram Bingham discovered Machu Picchu, the long-lost Inca stronghold high in the Peruvian Andes.

Zapata leading the faction that demanded quick redistribution of the land.

A general European war came closer with the dispatch of the German gunboat *Panther* to the Moroccan port of Agadir, which provoked a second Moroccan crisis; Germany ultimately withdrew. The French attack on Morocco continued, although Moroccan forces for a time besieged French-held Fez.

Italy went to war with weakened Turkey (Sept.), quickly taking Tripoli (Oct.) and much of the rest of Libya.

Winston Churchill became First Lord of the Admiralty (1911-1915); he would leave the cabinet after the disaster at Gallipoli and the Dardanelles (1915).

Still pursuing conflicting imperial interests in southwest Asia and with Mideast oil increasingly seen as a major prize, British forces occupied large portions of southern Persia, while Russian forces did the same in northern Persia.

Victor Berger of Milwaukee became the first American socialist to serve in the U.S. House of Representatives.

Raicho Hiratsuka organized Japan's Bluestocking Society and originated the magazine *Bluestocking (Seito)*.

b. Ronald Wilson Reagan (1911-), 40th president of the United States (1981-1989).

b. Milovan Djilas (1911-1995), Yugoslav communist politician and writer who was his country's leading dissident during the Tito era.

b. Eduardo Frei Montalva (1911-1982), Chilean Catholic liberal; Christian Democratic president of Chile (1964-1970).

b. Georges Pompidou (1911-1974), French politician; premier (1962-1968) and president (1969-1974) of France.

American physicist Robert Millikan measured the charge of an electron, helping to confirm the theories of Max Planck and Albert Einstein.

Austrian psychiatrist Alfred Adler broke with Sigmund Freud over the primacy of sex, the first of Freud's early followers to break away; Adler's approach would make power relations central and introduce the idea of an inferiority complex.

After studying the 1906 San Francisco Earthquake, American geologist Harry Fielding Reid proposed that faults, long thought to have been produced by earthquakes, actually preceded them, with earthquakes resulting as pressure built up along the faults.

Dutch physicist Heike Kamerlingh Onnes discovered superconductivity, the loss of resistance to electricity in certain materials at very low temperatures; a working theory and practical applications of the phenomenon would not come for decades.

Early humanlike fossil remains were found on Piltdown Common, in Sussex, England, by Charles Dawson (1911-1912). Called *Eoanthropus dawsoni* (Dawn Man or Piltdown Man), they would be proved fraudulent in the 1950s; the perpetrator of the hoax remained unknown.

Scottish physicist Charles Wilson invented the cloud chamber, a device for detecting subatomic particles, later improved by others; a basic tool for nuclear physicists.

Arnold Gesell established the Yale Clinic of Child Development, where he did pioneer work on the stages of child growth and development, summarized in the Gesell Development Schedules.

were presented by Sergei Diaghilev's Ballets Russes company.

Franz Marc and Wassily Kandinsky were the leading figures in the highly experimental, largely expressionist Der Blaue Reiter (The Blue Rider) group (1911-1914). Among those also exhibiting with the group in that period were Jean Arp, Paul Klee, and August Macke.

Margarethe Siems created the Marschallin role in Richard Strauss's opera *Der Rosenkavalier (The Knight of the Rose),* libretto by Hugo von Hofmannsthal.

Scott Joplin wrote his folk opera *Treemonisha,* heard in concert in 1915 and staged for the first time in 1975.

Edith Wharton published her novel *Ethan Frome,* set in New England.

Irving Berlin composed his classic song "Alexander's Ragtime Band."

The literary magazine *The Egoist* began publication (1911-1919); it would become a major vehicle for the work of many modern poets, including T. S. Eliot and Ezra Pound.

Belgian writer and naturalist Maurice Maeterlinck was awarded the Nobel Prize for literature.

b. Lucille Ball (1911-1989), American actress and comedian; she would become a world figure in television.

b. Tennessee (Thomas Lanier) Williams (1911-1983), one of the leading American playwrights of the 20th century.

b. William Gerald Golding (1911-1993), British writer noted for his novel *The Lord of the Flies*

Norwegian explorer Roald Amundsen led the first party to reach the South Pole (Dec. 14).

With the revolution in China came the beginning of the end of the practice of foot-binding, wrapping a woman's feet so tightly that the small toes were bent over and the arches often broken, a practice that had crippled many women from at least the 11th century in pursuit of small feet, regarded as sexually attractive.

Baseball great Cy (Denton T.) Young retired after a 21-year career, having set records for number of games won (511) and number of innings pitched (7,356); baseball's annual award for best pitcher would be named for him.

In *Standard Oil Company of New Jersey v. United States,* the massive Standard Oil trust was ordered dissolved, pursuant to antitrust laws; a major victory for trustbusting reformers.

American naturalist John Muir published *My First Summer in the Sierra,* about his years in the Yosemite Valley, which he had successfully campaigned (1880-1890) to have named a national park.

The North Pacific Fur Seal Convention was signed by the United States, Japan, Great Britain, and Russia, saving many species of seals, sea lions, sea otters, and other marine mammals, which had been hunted to near extinction for their skins, though some populations never recovered.

In the first Indianapolis 500-mile automobile race, Ray Harroun won with an average speed of nearly 75 miles per hour.

The electric self-starter for automobiles, invented earlier (1899), began to be used on Cadillacs, gradually eliminating difficult hand cranks.

1911 cont.

b. Hubert Horatio Humphrey (1911-1978), American Democratic politician; four-term senator, vice president, and 1968 presidential candidate.

b. Josef Cyrankiewicz (1911-1989), Polish communist leader.

b. Konstantin Ustinovich Chernenko (1911-1985), the last conservative Communist Party leader of the Soviet Union (1984-1985); after him would come Mikhail Gorbachev and massive change.

b. Bruno Kreisky (1911-1990), Austrian chancellor (1970-1983).

b. Ne Win (Maung Shu Maung) (1911-), Burmese general and military dictator (1958-1960; 1962-1988); a major force in Burma even after the 1988 army coup that formally removed him from power.

d. Benjamin Henry Grierson (1826-1911), American general who after the Civil War commanded the African-American 10th Cavalry (1866-1888) in the American Southwest.

d. Pyotr Stolypin (1862-1911), Russian premier; he was assassinated in Kiev (Sept.).

American aviator Glenn Hammond Curtiss built the first seaplane.

Marie Curie received the Nobel Prize for chemistry for her 1898 codiscovery of elements 88 (radium) and 84 (polonium), making her the first person to win two Nobel Prizes and the first to win two for science; earlier that year, she had been rejected for membership in France's Academy of Science.

b. Luis Walter Alvarez (1911-1988), American physicist.

d. Ellen Swallow Richards (1842-1911), American chemist long associated with the Massachusetts Institute of Technology; its first woman student and teacher and a key founder of home economics and ecology.

d. Williamina Paton Stevens Fleming (1857-1911), Scottish-American astronomer, long associated with the Harvard Observatory, who discovered white dwarfs (1910), 10 novas, and more than 200 variable stars.

d. Alfred Binet (1857-1911), French psychologist who developed the first formal tests of human intelligence (1905).

1912

China's Manchu (Ch'ing) dynasty formally ended with the abdication of child emperor Hsüan T'ung (Henry P'u Yi) (Feb. 12). His forces too weak to rule China, provisional president Sun Yat-sen resigned in favor of Manchu dynasty general Yüan Shih-k'ai, who became the first president of the Chinese republic (1912-1916).

Democrat Woodrow Wilson defeated Republican William Howard Taft and Progressive (Bull Moose)

German geophysicist Alfred Wegener first formally outlined the theory of continental drift, proposing that the continents moved to their current positions after having been, some 200 million years ago, a single continent he called Pangaea. The theory would be ridiculed until the 1960s, when geological evidence and theories began to support it.

(1954); winner of the 1983 Nobel Prize for literature.

b. Czeslaw Milosz (1911-), Polish writer; a leading dissident during the communist period.

b. Ginger Rogers (Virginia Katherine McMath) (1911-1995), American film star of Hollywood's golden age; noted as Fred Astaire's dance partner.

b. Robert Taylor (Spangler Arlington Brugh) (1911-1969), American film star of Hollywood's golden age and beyond.

b. Margaret Sullavan (Margaret Brooke) (1911-1960), American stage and screen star.

b. Marshall McLuhan (1911-1980), Canadian prophet of the new electronic age.

b. Gian Carlo Menotti (1911-), Italian-American composer.

b. Elizabeth Bishop (1911-1979), American poet.

b. Mahalia Jackson (1911-1972), American gospel singer.

d. Gustav Mahler (1860-1911), leading Austrian composer and conductor.

d. Carl Nielsen (1865-1911), Danish composer.

The first downhill ski race was organized by British skier Arnold Lunn, who had earlier organized the Alpine Ski Club (1908).

b. Josh Gibson (1911-1947), leading African-American baseball player.

b. L. Ron (Lafayette Ronald) Hubbard (1911-1986), American writer and founder of the Church of Scientology (1952).

d. Carry Amelia Moore Nation (1846-1911), American temperance activist best known for her hatchet attacks on saloons.

Rabindranath Tagore's work was introduced in the West with the publication of an English translation of his rather mystical poetry collection *Gitanjali,* titled *Song Offerings,* with an introduction by William Butler Yeats. One of India's most prolific lyrical poets and a multifaceted writer, Tagore immediately became a major mystical figure in the West.

On its first voyage, the "unsinkable" British liner *Titanic* sank after colliding with an iceberg off Newfoundland (Apr. 15); 1,500 people died, among them many notables.

d. Robert Falcon Scott (1868-1912), British explorer who led the second party to reach the South Pole (Jan. 17), arriving one month after Roald Amundsen's expedition. Scott and all his party died

Theodore Roosevelt to become the 28th president of the United States (1913-1921). Socialist presidential candidate Eugene V. Debs received more than 900,000 votes, over 6 percent of the vote.

Serbian, Greek, and Bulgarian forces numbering 300,000 to 400,000, their countries allied in the Balkan League, attacked somewhat smaller Turkish forces in Macedonia and Thrace (Oct. 17), beginning the First Balkan War with early successes. At Monastir (Nov. 5), the Serbians defeated and destroyed a Turkish army, and at Salonika (Nov. 9), a Turkish garrison of 20,000 quickly surrendered to the Greeks. But the Bulgarian siege of Constantinople failed (Nov.-Dec.), forcing Bulgarian withdrawal.

Vladimir Illich Lenin founded the Russian Social-Democratic Workers' Party (Bolsheviks), formerly the Bolshevik faction of the Russian Social-Democratic Workers' Party.

The African National Congress (ANC) was founded as a Gandhian nonviolent movement of all people of color seeking to create a multiracial, fully integrated, democratic state in South Africa.

American imperial activity continued in the Caribbean. The U.S. Marines took control of Honduras (Jan.) and Nicaragua (July); both countries became de facto American protectorates.

At Milwaukee, Wisconsin (Oct. 14), would-be assassin John N. Schrank shot and seriously wounded Theodore Roosevelt; quickly captured, Schrank was then permanently institutionalized.

Attacking Italian forces took Libya, Rhodes, and the Dodecanese Islands from weak Turkish forces; presaging what was to come, the Italians used airplanes as bombers for the first time. Italy kept the conquered areas by the terms of the Treaty of Ouchy.

France continued its conquest of Morocco, declaring Morocco a protectorate, although the war had not yet been

From study of Cepheid variables — stars with a regular variation in brightness — American astronomer Henrietta Swan Leavitt established a method for determining the distance of a variable star from its period of variation and its luminosity. This would greatly help astronomers in developing an understanding of the actual size and nature of the universe.

German physicist Max von Laue developed the technique of X-ray crystallography, an invaluable analytical tool, in the process discovering that X rays are a form of electromagnetic radiation.

In a speech before the London Society of Psychical Research, Sigmund Freud made his first major statement on the unconscious as a repository of thoughts repressed by the conscious mind. A key disciple, Carl Jung, published *Psychology of the Unconscious,* soon afterward breaking with Freud over the primacy of sexual drives and early experiences. Jung founded his own school of analytic psychology, focusing on the whole life, including midlife crises, and on universal archetypes.

Max Wertheimer, Wolfgang Köhler, and Kurt Koffka developed the Gestalt approach, stressing that perception must be viewed as a whole (Gestalt), not broken into smaller parts. Later leaving Nazi Germany, Köhler would bring the theory to the United States (1935).

In analyzing atomic behavior, Dutch-American chemist Peter Debye developed equations to predict the movement of molecules considered dipolar (with motion between areas of slight positive charge and slight negative charge), the motion being called *dipole moments.*

British physicist Joseph John Thomson found, in experimenting with neon, that two varieties existed, later recognized as isotopes (1913).

Vaslav Nijinsky choreographed and danced the lead in his highly controversial and later classic ballet *The Afternoon of a Faun (L'après-midi d'un faune)*, set to the Claude Debussy orchestral work (1894) and presented by Sergei Diaghilev's Ballets Russes company. Diaghilev also presented Nijinsky, Tamara Karsavina, and Adolphe Bolm in Mikhail Fokine's ballet *Daphnis and Chloe*, music by Maurice Ravel.

Constantin Brancusi began his celebrated, ultimately highly abstract "Bird in Flight" series with his *Maiastra*, then a representational bird derived from myth.

Marcel Duchamp painted his highly abstract, controversial *Nude Descending a Staircase No. 2*; it became a celebrated work after its enthusiastic reception at New York's Armory Show (1913).

Enrico Guazzoni's Italian silent film epic *Quo Vadis* was the longest film yet shown and the most notable of the several film versions of the 1896 Henryk Sienkiewicz novel.

Gaston Lachaise began his long series of "goddess" nudes (1912-1927) with *Standing Woman*.

James Weldon Johnson published the landmark African-American novel *Autobiography of an Ex-Colored Man*.

Jacob Epstein sculpted the tomb of Oscar Wilde in Paris.

Mack Sennett invented the extraordinarily popular Keystone Kops film comedy group, featuring them in scores of films.

Alexander Archipenko's sculpture *Walking* introduced the concept of inner space by boring holes in what earlier would have been solid figures.

Amy Lowell published her first poetry collection, *A Dome of Many-Coloured Glass*.

in a blizzard on the return trip; his records were later found by a search party (Nov.).

The Industrial Workers of the World (IWW) led 20,000 largely immigrant workers in the successful Lawrence, Massachusetts, textile strike, gaining national support by publicizing the plight of many women and children workers in the mills.

The U.S. Children's Bureau was established, with Julia Lathrop as its first director; its major concerns were child labor, infant and maternal mortality, child care, and the juvenile justice system.

At the Stockholm Olympics, Finnish runner Hannes Kolehmainen took three gold medals — in the cross-country, the 10,000 meters, and the 5,000 meters, the latter a world record; he would later win the marathon at the Antwerp Olympics (1920). Native American athlete Jim Thorpe won the decathlon and pentathlon; his medals were stripped over a controversy about his amateur status, but were later restored (1982).

British aeronautical engineer Thomas Octave Murdoch Sopwith founded his Sopwith Aviation Company, producing a popular series of airplanes named for animals; the Camel would be widely popular as a fighter plane during World War I.

Hadassah, the Women's Zionist Organization of America, was formed by Henrietta Szold and others in New York City to foster Jewish religious and social ideals.

Mount Katmai erupted in southern Alaska, spewing into the sky debris that clouded the northern atmosphere for months, and left the adjoining valley a volcanic wasteland called the Valley of the Ten Thousand Smokes, now part of Katmai National Park and Preserve.

The U.S. Congress passed the Radio Act to regulate broadcasting.

concluded. At Fez, a Moroccan revolt within the French garrison failed (Apr.), as did Moroccan assaults on the city (May).

Outer Mongolia declared itself an independent nation (Nov. 3).

b. Kim Il Sung (Kim Jong Ju) (1912-1994), dictator of the Democratic People's Republic of Korea (1948-1994).

b. (Leonard) James Callaghan (1912-), British Labour politician and prime minister (1976-1979). He would be succeeded by Margaret Thatcher.

b. Vo Nguyen Giap (1912-), North Vietnamese general; commander of besieging forces at Dien Bien Phu (1954) and commander in chief of North Vietnamese troops during the Vietnam War.

b. Kim (Harold Adrian Russell) Philby (1912-1988), Soviet double agent in British intelligence who was to provide one of the most notable spy stories of the century.

b. Archibald Cox (1912-), American lawyer; U.S. solicitor general (1961-1965) and Watergate special prosecutor (1973).

b. Erich Honecker (1912-1994), East German communist leader (1971-1989).

d. Arthur MacArthur (1845-1912), American general; commander of American forces during the Philippine-American War (1899-1901); father of General Douglas MacArthur.

d. George Stuart White (1835-1912), British field marshal; Boer War commander of besieged British forces at Ladysmith (1899-1900).

d. Maresuke Nogi (1843-1912), Japanese general; commander of besieging Japanese forces at Port Arthur (1904-1905) during the Russo-Japanese War.

James B. Murphy developed the first immuno-suppressive drug, designed to minimize the body's rejection of transplants.

Using approaches developed in the Haber-Bosch process (1907), German chemist Friedrich Bergius developed methods of processing oil and coal to form gasoline.

French surgeon Alexis Carrel received the Nobel Prize for physiology or medicine for his work on new methods of suturing blood vessels (1905).

Polish-American biochemist Casimir Funk introduced the term *vitamine* (shortened to *vitamin* in 1920) for vital substances previously called *accessory food factors*.

The first "map" of a chromosome was produced.

b. Alan Mathison Turing (1912-1954), British mathematician and cryptographer; a specialist in computer logic.

b. Glenn Theodore Seaborg (1912-), American nuclear chemist who would discover plutonium (1940) and other elements; he would work with the Manhattan Project during World War II.

b. Wernher Magnus Maximilian von Braun (1912-1977), German-American rocket expert.

d. Wilbur Wright (1867-1912), American inventor who, with his brother Orville, built and flew the first airplane (1903).

José Clemente Orozco created a series of paintings of prostitutes, the *House of Tears*.

Laurette Taylor created the title role in the long-running comedy *Peg o' My Heart* by J. Hartley Manners.

German writer Gerhart Hauptmann was awarded the Nobel Prize for literature.

b. Wendy Hiller (1912-), British stage and screen star; she would create Eliza Doolittle on film in *Pygmalion* (1938).

b. Eugène Ionesco (1912-1994), Romanian-French playwright; a pillar of the "theater of the absurd."

b. Jackson Pollock (1912-1956), leading American abstract impressionist painter.

b. Gene (Eugene Curran) Kelly (1912-), American actor, dancer, singer, and choreographer.

b. John Cheever (1912-1982), leading American writer.

b. Michelangelo Antonioni (1912-), Italian film director and writer.

b. Woody (Woodrow Wilson) Guthrie (1912-1967), American composer and folksinger.

b. Jorge Amado (1912-), Brazilian novelist.

d. August Strindberg (1849-1912), Swedish playwright.

d. Jules Massenet (1842-1912), French composer.

Fashion designer Coco Chanel opened a millinery, her first shop, at Deauville, France, establishing a fashion house in Paris two years later.

The Japanese steamer *Kiche Maru* sank off Japan (Sept. 28), killing 1,000 people.

b. Barbara Wertheim Tuchman (1912-1989), American historian and writer.

b. David Ross Brower (1912-), American environmental activist, most notably as executive director of the Sierra Club (1952-1969).

b. John Paul I (Albino Luciani) (1912-1978), Italian priest and pope (1978).

b. Milton Friedman (1912-), American economist whose laissez-faire and monetarist theories were to provide much of the ideological basis for conservative government leaders late in the century.

b. Julia McWilliams Child (1912-), American cookery teacher and writer noted for her television series *The French Chef* (1963-1973).

b. Ben (William Benjamin) Hogan (1912-), American golfer who would win 62 tournaments, including 3 majors in a single year (1953).

b. Charles Addams (1912-1988), American cartoonist.

Militant confrontations mounted as Emmeline Pankhurst led a series of major Women's Social and Political Union (WSPU) demonstrations for woman suffrage, with mass arrests, the force-feeding of imprisoned women, and increasing violence all placing the question of woman suffrage at the center of British public life, even as war threatened.

Patrick Pearse founded the Irish Volunteers, which three years later would be the small Irish Republican main armed force in the Easter Rising and later would grow into the Irish Republican Army. James Connolly and James Larkin founded the even smaller Irish Citizen Army. In northern Ireland, the Protestant Ulster Volunteers was founded, as both sides prepared for civil war.

Balkan League forces took most of European Turkey (Jan.-May) and besieged Constantinople. Great Power intervention resulted in the Treaty of London (May 30), ending the First Balkan War; Turkey lost nearly all of its European territories to the Balkan League, keeping the Gallipoli peninsula, and the new nation of Albania was established.

Chinese revolutionary forces led by Sun Yat-sen mounted a failed insurrection against the new Chinese republic; Sun fled into Japanese exile (1913-1916).

Victoriano Huerta, who commanded the Mexico City garrison, took power by coup, assassinating President Francisco Madero; the Mexican civil war continued.

As a general European war approached, the Young Turks took power by coup in Turkey, establishing a de facto alliance with Germany.

Boer leader James Hertzog founded South Africa's segregationist National Party.

b. Richard Milhous Nixon (1913-1994), 37th president of the United States (1969-1974) and principal figure in the Watergate scandal, who resigned to avoid impeachment.

Focusing on the simplest element, hydrogen, Danish physicist Niels Bohr proposed a "solar system" model of atomic structure, with electrons circling a nucleus in fixed concentric orbits, or "shells," emitting energy in discrete units as they jump from orbit to orbit.

American psychologist John Broadus Watson published *Psychology as a Behaviorist Views It*, effectively founding the behaviorist school of psychology; rejecting "talking therapy," his scientific approach focused on human actions as observable and measurable responses to stimuli, shaped through training (conditioning) rather than instinct or heredity.

British physicist Henry Gwyn-Jeffreys Moseley identified the connection between chemistry's periodic table and the number of electrons in an atom, the result being that element's atomic number.

British chemist Frederick Soddy recognized that many elements exist in variant forms, called isotopes (Greek for "same place"). Working independently, American chemist Theodore William Richards discovered that lead varies in atomic weight, supporting Soddy's isotope theory.

German physicist Johannes Geiger developed a device, the Geiger counter, to measure radiation by recording energized subatomic particles.

American astronomer Henry Norris Russell independently discovered the relationship between star type and brightness outlined by Ejnar Hertzsprung (1905), developing the Hertzsprung-Russell diagram.

Hungarian-American physician Béla Schick developed the Schick skin test for diphtheria, then a widespread, serious childhood disease.

Marcel Proust published *Swann's Way*, the first volume of his seven-part *Remembrance of Things Past (A la Recherche du temps perdu)* (1913-1927), one of the most highly regarded literary works of the century.

Modern European art scored a massive American triumph at New York's Armory Show, the first and by far the most notable international exhibition to cross the Atlantic. Of 1,600 works exhibited at the 69th Regiment Armory (Feb. 17-Mar. 15), 400 were modern European works, many of them highly abstract, including Marcel Duchamp's *Nude Descending a Staircase No. 2*, the hit of the show.

Sergei Diaghilev's Ballets Russes company presented Vaslav Nijinsky's ballet *The Rite of Spring (Le Sacre du printemps)*, the lead danced by Marie Piltz. The ballet's highly sexual fertility rite, complete with ritual sacrifice, shocked Parisian audiences. Diaghilev also presented *Jeux*, choreographed by Nijinsky to music by Claude Debussy, with Nijinsky, Tamara Karsavina, and Ludmila Shollar dancing the leads.

D. H. Lawrence published the novel *Sons and Lovers*, a major, largely autobiographical work; Dean Stockwell would create the Lawrence role in the 1960 film version.

Willa Cather published her autobiographical novel *O Pioneers!* set on the Nebraska frontier of her youth.

Cass Gilbert designed the 55-story Woolworth Building; the tallest building in the world became one of the magnets that would make New York a world city.

Marcel Duchamp sculpted *Bicycle Wheel*, later described by some as an early — perhaps the first — "kinetic" sculpture.

Charles Ives introduced his orchestral work *The Fourth of July* and his *Holidays Symphony*.

Henry Ford introduced the moving assembly line, a major innovation quickly adopted by many industries worldwide.

Canadian-American explorer Vilhjalmur Stefansson began his five-year stay above the Arctic Circle, living off the land and exploring; he would later advise the U.S. government on Arctic resources and on survival techniques for troops, notably during World War II.

The first Morris cars were produced from the factory founded (1912) by William Morris (later Viscount Nuffield), who had begun building motorcycles and automobiles on his own more than a decade earlier.

Charles Beard and Mary Ritter Beard published *An Economic Interpretation of the Constitution*, central to the development of a materialist and economic determinist interpretation of American history.

George McManus introduced Maggie and Jiggs in the comic strip *Bringing Up Father* (1913-1945).

The 55-story Woolworth Building was built in New York City, becoming for some years the world's tallest building.

The Industrial Workers of the World (IWW) decisively lost the Passaic, New Jersey, textile strike.

An explosion in a Dawson, New Mexico, coal mine killed 263 people (Oct. 22).

Crossword puzzles were introduced in the *New York World*.

b. Rosa Parks (1913-   ), African-American civil rights activist who would generate the Montgomery bus boycott and help spark the modern civil rights movement when she refused to give up her bus seat to a White passenger (1955).

1913 cont.

b. Menachem Begin (1913-1992), Polish-Israeli politician; prime minister of Israel (1977-1983).

b. Willy Brandt (Carl Herbert Frahm) (1913-1992), German politician who was a leading figure in the post–World War II period.

b. Gerald Rudolph Ford (1913-   ), 38th president of the United States (1974-1977).

b. Jacobo Arbenz Guzmán (1913-1971), president of Guatemala (1950-1954) until deposed by a U.S.-backed right-wing coup.

b. Klaus Barbie (1913-1991), Nazi SS officer and war criminal who was tried and sentenced to life imprisonment (1987).

b. William Joseph Casey (1913-1987), American lawyer and politician; head of the Central Intelligence Agency (CIA) (1981-1987).

d. Emily Wilding Davison (1872-1913), a direct-action British feminist who threw herself before the horse of Britain's King George V at the Epsom Derby and was killed, then becoming a martyr.

d. Harriet Tubman (ca. 1821-1913), leading African-American abolitionist who emerged as a major figure as a conductor on the Underground Railroad (1851-1861); later a Union soldier, scout, and nurse.

d. Alfred von Schlieffen (1833-1913), Prussian general; originator of the Schlieffen Plan to take western Europe by invading Belgium and then moving swiftly to take the Channel ports. The main elements of his plan would be followed in World War II, after the Germans had failed by departing from his plan in 1914.

French physicist Charles Fabry discovered evidence of an atmospheric ozone layer, later understood to be beneficial to life on earth by blocking much of the sun's damaging ultraviolet rays.

Giving up a career as an organist, German physician Albert Schweitzer became a medical missionary, working at his hospital and leper colony at Lambaréné, in Gabon (then French Equatorial Africa).

Vitamin A was discovered by American biochemists Elmer McCollum and Marguerite Davis and independently by Thomas B. Osborne and Lafayette B. Mendel.

The Michaelis-Menten equation, developed by German chemists Leonor Michaelis and Maud Lenora Menten, allowed chemists to predict the rate of a chemical reaction spurred by a catalyst, depending on the concentration of the substances involved.

In Egypt, a solar collector measuring more than 13,000 square feet was built to turn water into steam, to run an irrigation pump; an early modern example of using solar energy.

The first plant for converting geothermal energy into electrical power was built in Italy.

German microscope designer Oskar Barnack developed the first miniature camera, the Leica I; it would become commercially available in 1924, setting the standard of 35 mm for picture size.

Igor Sikorsky built the first four-engine airplane, the Bolshoi, the basis for the Ilya Mourametz, Russia's World War I bomber.

The 16th Amendment enabled the U.S. Congress to impose federal income taxes.

E. J. Bellocq produced his *Storyville Portraits* (ca. 1913), of prostitutes in New Orleans.

Rabindranath Tagore, who had burst upon the Western cultural scene only a year earlier, was awarded the Nobel Prize for literature.

b. Albert Camus (1913-1960), Algerian-French writer who would become a massive cultural figure by mid-century.

b. Burt (Burton Stephen) Lancaster (1913-1994), American film star.

b. (Edward) Benjamin Britten (1913-1976), British composer who would become a leading creator of operas, part of a wider body of work.

b. Vivien Leigh (Vivian Mary Hartley) (1913-1967), British stage and screen star; she would be Scarlett O'Hara in *Gone With the Wind* (1939).

b. Tyrone Power (Tyrone Edmund Power, Jr.) (1913-1958), American film star of Hollywood's golden age and beyond.

b. Robert Capa (Andrei Friedmann) (1913-1954), leading American photojournalist who would cover several wars.

b. Mary Martin (1913-1990), leading American musical theater star.

b. William Inge (1913-1973), leading American playwright.

b. Elizabeth Janeway (1913-), American writer and feminist; a key voice in the renewed women's movement, most notably with *Man's World, Woman's Place* (1971).

b. James Riddle Hoffa (1913-1975), American labor leader.

b. Alice Marble (1913-1990), American tennis player.

b. Walt Kelly (1913-1973), American cartoonist.

d. J. (John) Pierpont Morgan (1837-1913), American financier who controlled a massive financial and business empire and was one of the leading art and book collectors of his time; his bequests included the Morgan Library and a substantial art collection to the Metropolitan Museum of Art, both in New York City.

d. Ferdinand de Saussure (1857-1913), Swiss linguist whose focus on language as having an interdependent structure laid the basis for the modern movement of structuralism.

At Sarajevo (June 28), Bosnian nationalists armed by Serbs assassinated Archduke Francis (Franz) Ferdinand, heir to the Austrian throne, generating a set of confrontations that quickly resulted in World War I (1914-1918), a conflagration that was to cost the lives of at least 8 million in the military and 6 million civilians, with at least 21 million more casualties. The Allies would include France, the British Empire, Russia, the United States, Serbia, Italy, Belgium, Greece, Romania, Montenegro, Japan, and Portugal; the Central Powers would include Germany, Austro-Hungary, Turkey, and Bulgaria.

In the west, German forces overran Belgium (Aug. 3-20) and rolled up British and French forces, swiftly moving toward the Channel ports and the splitting of Allied armies, which would have brought them their long-planned quick victory. But the Germans broke their rush to the English Channel, turned toward Paris, and were stopped by French forces on the Marne River (Sept. 4-9), altering the course of world history. Allied and German armies then fought a series of indecisive battles, each unsuccessfully trying to outflank the other. Instead, they raced side by side to the sea, ultimately setting up the twin facing systems of fortifications that were to endure until near the end of the war and result in the loss of millions of lives in bloody, fruitless trench warfare.

In the east, massive Russian forces advancing into East Prussia were decisively defeated by smaller German forces at Tannenberg (Aug. 26-31), the Masurian Lakes (Sept. 9-14), and Lodz (Nov. 11-25), while Austrian and Russian forces fought an inconclusive, costly war on the central European plain. The ebb and flow of the far more fluid war in the east also took millions of lives.

War quickly developed on several other fronts, as well. Austrian and Serbian forces met in Serbia, British and Russian forces engaged the Turks in southwest Asia and North Africa, and British forces attacked German colonial forces in Africa.

Britain was dominant at sea, destroying the German China Squadron off the Chilean coast and largely pen-

Ernest Rutherford discovered the proton, a positively charged atomic particle, for decades thought to be the smallest of such particles and only later understood to be made up of yet-smaller particles, called quarks, which would solve the puzzle of how positively charged protons, which could be expected to repel each other, could form a nucleus.

A liquid core for the earth, analogous to the yolk of a soft-boiled egg, was proposed by German-American geologist Beno Gutenberg, who observed that earthquake waves are refracted in passing through the earth; the line between core and mantle is now called the Gutenberg discontinuity.

French surgeon Alexis Carrel performed the first successful heart operation on a dog, preparing techniques for use on humans.

The "Big Bertha," a giant gun that fired shells weighing nearly a ton, was built at the Skoda Works in Austro-Hungary; it would be used to devastating effect during World War I, notably at Liège and Namur, Belgium.

British biologist Henry Hallett Dale isolated from the ergot fungus a compound he named acetylcholine; he found that it affected nerves, but its nature would only later be understood (1921).

British astronomer Arthur Eddington posited that spiral nebulas were really other galaxies.

Thyroxine, the hormone produced by the thyroid gland, was first isolated as a crystal by American biochemist Edwin C. Kendall.

American astronomer Seth Barnes Nicholson discovered a ninth Jupiter satellite, called Sinope.

George Bernard Shaw's classic play *Pygmalion* opened in London; Mrs. Patrick Campbell created Eliza Doolittle, and Herbert Beerbohm Tree created Henry Higgins. Wendy Hiller and Leslie Howard would re-create the roles in the 1938 film, and Julie Andrews and Rex Harrison in the stage musical version, *My Fair Lady* (1956).

James Joyce began to emerge as a major 20th-century literary figure. His autobiographical novel *Portrait of the Artist as a Young Man* began publication in serial form in *The Egoist* (1914-1915). He also published the classic short story collection *Dubliners.*

Robert Frost became a noted American poet with the publication of his second collection, *North of Boston,* which included "Mending Wall" and "The Death of the Hired Man."

E. M. Forster completed the novel *Maurice* (1913-1914), focusing directly on homosexual themes. With homophobia a very real menace in Britain, he chose not to publish it in his lifetime; it first appeared in 1972.

Pearl White starred in *The Perils of Pauline,* one of the earliest of the immensely popular film serials.

Cecil B. De Mille coproduced and codirected the first film of Jesse Lasky's film company, *The Squaw Man,* starring Dustin Farnum.

Mary Pickford starred in the title role of *Tess of the Storm Country,* directed and shot by Edwin S. Porter.

Sergei Diaghilev's Ballets Russes company danced the definitive version of Mikhail Fokine's 1909 ballet *Le Coq d'or,* music by Nikolay Rimsky-Korsakov.

Blanche Sweet starred in the title role of the film *Judith of Bethulia,* written and directed by D. W. Griffith.

American public health nurse Margaret Sanger coined the term *birth control* and began publishing her landmark 16-page pamphlet *Family Limitation* and the magazine *Woman Rebel.* In a sensational case, her husband, William Sanger, was arrested, tried, and sentenced to 30 days in jail for possession of the pamphlet in defiance of the government ban on disseminating such information.

The first ship passed through the new Panama Canal (Aug. 3), linking the Atlantic and Pacific Oceans and eliminating the costly and difficult sea journey around South America. It had been completed ahead of schedule (1913) by chief engineer George Washington Goethals, who became governor of the Canal Zone (1914-1917).

The last known passenger pigeon, named Martha by her keepers at the Cincinnati Zoo, died (Sept. 1); as recently as the mid-1800s, an estimated 2 billion of these wild pigeons had lived in eastern North America before being extinguished by hunting, disease, and loss of habitat.

During World War I (1914-1918), Marie Curie and her daughter Irène (later Joliot-Curie) established X-ray stations in the field, training young women to take X rays of the wounded.

Russian explorer Boris Vilkitski was only the second person (the first since 1878) to sail the Northeast Passage, north of Eurasia, though he was obliged to halt in place during the winter, completing the journey only after the ice broke up the following spring (1914-1915). Despite its difficulties, this route would be important during World War II.

The Canadian Pacific liner *Empress of Ireland* sank in the St. Lawrence River after colliding with a Norwegian coal ship; 1,024 people died.

The Federal Reserve System, a 12-region American federal central banking system, and the Federal

ning up German naval forces, which would come out for a major engagement only once, at Jutland in 1916. But German submarines and surface raiders made their presence felt and would soon begin the long, crucial Battle of the Atlantic.

American forces took Vera Cruz, Mexico, blocking German arms shipments to the Huerta dictatorship. Civil war continued in Mexico; after Victoriano Huerta had fled the country, Venustiano Carranza's forces took Mexico City (Aug. 15). Fighting continued between Carranza's government forces and the armies of Emiliano Zapata and Francisco (Pancho) Villa.

Mohandas (later Mahatma) Gandhi left South Africa, going home to India to practice law. He would soon emerge as leader of the Indian national movement.

Sun Yat-sen founded the Kuomintang, the Chinese political party that would become the ruling party of the Republic of China (1929-1949).

Britain's Women's Social and Political Union (WSPU), led by Emmeline Pankhurst, abruptly dropped its militant woman suffrage campaign, turning instead to complete support of the war effort, probably in return for a government promise of suffrage after the war.

b. Jiang Qing (Chiang Ch'ing; Luan Shu-meng) (1914-1992), Chinese politician and actress, the third wife of Mao Zedong and the leader of the "Gang of Four."

b. Mohammed Zahir Shah (1914-), the last king of Afghanistan (1933-1973).

b. Yuri Vladimirovich Andropov (1914-1984), Soviet Communist Party general secretary (1982-1984) and president (1983-1984).

d. Jean Jaures (1859-1914), French socialist antiwar leader; assassinated on the eve of World War I by a French nationalist (July 31), greatly impeding French and international socialist opposition to the war.

In his *Behavior: An Introduction to Comparative Psychology*, John Broadus Watson proposed experimenting on animals to establish principles of psychology.

New York City doctors placed Mary Mallon in an institution for the rest of her life (1914-1938); popularly known as "Typhoid Mary," she was a typhoid carrier who was herself immune to the disease. A cook, Mallon had been spreading the disease through food handling since at least 1904, as doctors confirmed in 1907; she had been institutionalized before (1907-1910) but released on her promise not to work as a cook.

German physicist Max von Laue received the Nobel Prize for physics for his discovery of X-ray crystallography (1912).

b. Jonas Edward Salk (1914-1995), American physician and medical researcher who developed the first polio vaccine (1952) and an influenza vaccine (1953).

b. James Alfred Van Allen (1914-), American physicist who predicted the existence of the Van Allen belts (discovered in 1958); a powerful influence on the U.S. space program.

b. Norman Ernest Borlaug (1914-), American plant pathologist and agricultural scientist long associated with the Rockefeller Foundation (1944-1960), working primarily in Mexico; he led in developing the high-yield grains that allowed the Green Revolution from the 1960s.

Edgar Rice Burroughs published the first of his Tarzan novels, *Tarzan of the Apes.*

Giovanni Pastrone wrote, directed, and produced the film *Cabiria,* set in Roman times; a landmark work in the Italian epic style, it would strongly influence other emerging filmmakers, including D. W. Griffith and Cecil B. De Mille.

Julia Sanderson and Donald Brian sang Jerome Kern's first hit song, "They Didn't Believe Me," in the musical *The Girl from Utah,* a landmark work of the American musical theater.

W. C. Handy published the songs "St. Louis Blues" and "Yellow Dog Blues."

b. Alec Guinness (1914-   ), British stage and screen star who would be one of the leading actors of the century.

b. Bernard Malamud (1914-1986), American writer who would focus on American Jewish life.

b. Dylan Thomas (1914-1953), Welsh writer who would become a celebrated lyric poet.

b. John Berryman (1914-1972), American poet.

b. Octavio Paz (1914-   ), Mexican writer, editor, and critic who would become a major figure in Latin American literature.

b. John Richard Hersey (1914-1993), American writer, who would emerge as a major figure with the war novel *A Bell for Adano* (1944).

b. Marguerite Duras (Margaret Donnadieu) (1914-   ), French playwright, filmmaker, and novelist.

d. Ambrose Bierce (1842-1914), American writer, most notably on themes of the American West and for his satirical *Devil's Dictionary* (1906).

Trade Commission (FTC), an antitrust enforcement body, were established.

Louella Parsons began writing her syndicated movie column.

Marcus Garvey founded the Universal Negro Improvement Association (UNIA).

An Eccles, West Virginia, coal mine disaster killed 181 people (Apr. 28).

Red electric traffic lights were introduced by Alfred A. Benesch, of Cleveland, Ohio's Traffic Signal Company.

The cartoon *Felix the Cat* first appeared, created by Jack Sullivan.

The United States held its first national figure skating tournament, in New Haven, Connecticut.

b. Babe (Mildred) Didrikson Zaharias (1914-1956), American athlete.

b. Joe Louis (Joseph Louis Barrow) (1914-1981), American boxer.

b. Barbara Ward (1914-1981), British economist and writer.

b. Thor Heyerdahl (1914-   ), Norwegian ethnologist who would cross the Pacific (1947) and Atlantic (1969) in primitive craft to support the thesis of early seaborne contacts between the Old and New Worlds.

b. Saul Steinberg (1914-   ), American cartoonist and illustrator.

b. Tenzing Norgay (1914-1986), Sherpa mountaineer.

b. Joseph Shuster (1914-1992), American cartoonist.

1914 cont.

d. Daniel De Leon (1852-1914), American Marxist; Socialist Labor Party leader who was a founder of the Industrial Workers of the World (IWW) (1905).

1915

Costly, inconclusive trench warfare brought more than a million casualties on the western front, as neither side was able to make a decisive breakthrough.

In the east, the Russians were again defeated at the Masurian Lakes (Feb. 7-21). The German-Austrian spring offensive scored the massive Torlice-Garnow breakthrough, then smashed the entire Russian front and advanced 300 miles (May-Oct.) to take Warsaw and Vilna. The Germans were the first to use substantial quantities of gas in warfare, in their attack on Bolimov, Poland (Jan. 31). They used it again at Second Ypres (Apr. 22-May 25).

Italy joined the Allies; the long stalemate on the Isonzo River began; it would cost more than 1 million casualties. Serbian forces were smashed by invading German, Austrian, and Bulgarian forces (Oct.).

British forces made the long, failed attack on the Turks at Gallipoli (Feb. 1915-Jan. 1916), while British and Turkish forces fought inconclusively in Mesopotamia, and Russian and Turkish forces fought in the Caucasus.

Armenia rose against the Turks. Hundreds of thousands of Armenians joined Russian forces retreating north, many ultimately settling in Soviet Armenia.

At sea, German submarines pursued the Battle of the Atlantic, sinking large numbers of Allied and neutral ships,

Albert Einstein developed his general theory of relativity (published 1916), expanding on his special theory (1905). Using Hermann Minkowski's idea of time as a fourth dimension (1907), he posited that space and time are not distinct, but merge in a space-time continuum.

French physicist Paul Langevin developed an echo-sounding device for locating underwater objects, later called sonar (sound navigation and ranging). Not ready for practical use until the end of World War I (1918), it was used primarily to locate icebergs but would be important during World War II to locate mines and submarines.

American chemist William Draper Harkins observed that the mass of the helium nucleus is not exactly four times that of hydrogen, but somewhat less, and theorized that if hydrogen could be converted to helium, a large amount of energy would be released. This theory would be confirmed only decades later, as the process of nuclear fusion.

Bell Telephone engineers made the first transatlantic voice telephone call, between Virginia and Paris's Eiffel Tower, using electron tubes recently developed by Lee De Forest; also, the

1914 cont.

d. August Macke (1887-1914), German expressionist painter; a founder of The Blue Rider group; an early casualty of the war.

d. Jacob A. Riis (1849-1914), American documentary photographer and social reformer.

d. John Muir (1838-1914), American nature writer and pioneer conservationist who led the successful campaign (1880-1890) to make Yosemite a national park and founded the Sierra Club (1892).

d. Pope Pius X (Giuseppe Melchiorre Sarto) (1835-1914), Italian priest (1858-1914) and pope (1903-1914); a conservative who stressed tradition and sharply opposed attempts to modernize the Catholic Church. He was later beatified (1951) and canonized (1954).

1915

D. W. Griffith directed and produced the epic film *The Birth of a Nation* — for its sweep and technical advances, a landmark of world cinema; for its overt racism and glorification of the Ku Klux Klan, one of the most controversial American films. Lillian Gish, Mae Marsh, Henry B. Walthall, Ralph Lewis, and Miriam Cooper led a huge cast.

Franz Kafka published "The Metamorphosis," the best known of the three stories he published during his lifetime and a greatly influential work in modern literature.

Kasimir Malevich painted *Black Square,* a geometric work that became the centerpiece of suprematism.

D. H. Lawrence's novel *The Rainbow* created a considerable stir for its sexual frankness, which helped break new ground in Britain.

Susan Glaspell led in the formation of the Provincetown (Massachusetts) Players (1915-1929), the experimental theater group that would become the main producer of Eugene O'Neill's plays, also introducing the work of several other playwrights.

Leo Frank was murdered by an anti-Jewish lynch mob in Marietta, Georgia (Aug. 17). Charged with raping and murdering Mary Phagan, a 14-year-old Atlanta girl (Apr. 26, 1913), Frank had been convicted in a prejudicial atmosphere and on the basis of tainted evidence; his death sentence had been commuted after new evidence was found by detective William J. Burns and also because of a worldwide clemency campaign.

The Ku Klux Klan (KKK) went "national," developing a membership of more than 1.5 million, with substantial new strength in the South and Midwest.

After his ship *Endurance* was crushed by ice, Antarctic explorer Ernest Henry Shackleton led an 800-mile overland trek to a remote whaling station on South Georgia Island.

Philadelphia Phillies baseball pitcher Grover Cleveland Alexander had a season earned run average of 1.22, a record that would stand for more than five decades.

The first American birth control organization, the National Birth Control League (later Voluntary Parenthood League), was founded by Mary Dennett, seeking to legalize dissemination of contraceptive information.

1915 cont.

among them the liner *Lusitania* (May 7), with a loss of 1,198 lives, 128 of them Americans.

American forces took Haiti (July 3), beginning a 19-year occupation of the country. Franklin D. Roosevelt would eventually withdraw the troops (1934), although the United States would continue to dominate Haitian government financial matters until the mid-1940s.

In Mexico, President Venustiano Carranza's forces decisively defeated the forces of Francisco (Pancho) Villa at Celaya (Apr.). Villa retreated north, no longer threatening to take power, while Emiliano Zapata's undefeated forces retreated into southern Mexico.

The American Women's Peace Party was founded, with Jane Addams its first president; it would later develop into the Women's International League for Peace and Freedom.

b. Augusto Pinochet Ugarte (1915-   ), Chilean general who would lead the military coup that overthrew the Allende government and then rule as dictator (1973-1989).

b. Aung San (1915-1947), Burmese politician; leader of the Burmese national movement.

b. Balthazar Vorster (1915-1983), South African National Party leader; prime minister (1966-1978) and president (1979) of South Africa.

b. Yitzhak Shamir (Yitzhak Yzernitzsky) (1915-   ), Israeli politician; a former Stern Gang terrorist chief of operations who became a hard-line Herut Party prime minister (1983-1984; 1986-1992).

b. Moshe Dayan (1915-1981), Israeli soldier and politician.

b. Hu Yaobang (1915-1989), Chinese communist politician and leading reformer in the 1980s.

d. Edith Louisa Cavell (1865-1915), British nurse working in Belgium who was executed as a spy by German occupation forces (Oct. 7).

first trans–North American call was made, between New York and San Francisco.

Austrian-American physician Joseph Goldberger demonstrated that the disease pellagra is a vitamin-deficiency disease.

British bacteriologist Frederick William Twort discovered bacteria-killing viruses, named *bacteriophages* (bacteria eaters) by French-Canadian microbiologist Félix-Hubert D'Hérelle, who discovered them independently (1916-1917).

Chemicals were first deliberately used in the laboratory to induce cancer; the century would see the introduction of many new carcinogenic substances.

After poison gases began to be used on the battlefield, British physicist Hertha Ayrton developed the Ayrton fan to drive away the gases, replacing them with fresh air (ca. 1915).

American biologist Thomas Hunt Morgan published his fundamental work *Theory of the Gene*.

Engineers in Britain's Royal Naval Air Service built an experimental tank, the first model being dubbed "Little Willie."

Germany's Fokker airplanes were the first to have their machine guns synchronized with the propeller.

British physicist William Henry Bragg and his Australian-born son, William Lawrence Bragg, shared the Nobel Prize for physics for work in X-ray crystallography, the only father-and-son pair ever so honored.

b. Fred Hoyle (1915-   ), British astronomer and writer; a key exponent of the "steady state" theory of the universe (1948).

Charlotte Perkins Gilman published the novel *Herland,* in which she created a feminist utopia.

John Buchan published his classic spy thriller *The Thirty-nine Steps,* later to become Alfred Hitchcock's classic film (1935).

Ruth St. Denis and Ted Shawn founded the Denishawn school and dance company (1915-1931), a major force in the development of the modern dance movement.

Virginia Woolf published her first novel, *The Voyage Out.*

Somerset Maugham published *Of Human Bondage,* the basis for three later films (1934; 1946; 1964).

French writer Romain Rolland was awarded the Nobel Prize for literature.

b. Orson Welles (George Orson Welles) (1915-1985), American director, actor, writer, and producer; a major figure in world cinema for *Citizen Kane* (1941) and *The Magnificent Ambersons* (1942).

b. Arthur Miller (1915-), American playwright; his work would include *Death of a Salesman* (1949) and *The Crucible* (1953).

b. Frank (Francis Albert) Sinatra (1915-), American singer and actor; a worldwide celebrity for more than half a century.

b. Ingrid Bergman (1915-1982), Swedish actress; a major international film star after *Casablanca* (1942) and *For Whom the Bell Tolls* (1943).

b. Saul Bellow (1915-), American writer focusing on American Jewish life; winner of the 1976 Nobel Prize for literature.

Coast-to-coast long distance telephone service was inaugurated in the United States.

Jess Willard became heavyweight boxing champion of the world, defeating Jack Johnson in Havana, Cuba.

More than 800 people died when the excursion liner *Eastland* sank while at its Chicago dock (July 24).

Near Gretna, Scotland, 227 people, mostly soldiers, were killed when two trains collided (May 22).

d. Booker T. (Taliaferro) Washington (1856-1915), African-American educator; head of Alabama's Tuskegee Institute, he was an advocate of accommodation and self-help and a major force in the African-American community from the mid-1890s.

d. Joe Hill (Joseph Hillstrom; Joel Hägglund) (1879-1915), Swedish-American Industrial Workers of the World (IWW) activist and labor songwriter who composed "Casey Jones"; he was convicted of murder on flimsy evidence and executed by the state of Utah.

1915 cont.

d. James Keir Hardie (1856-1915), British socialist and trade unionist; a founder of the Labour Party (1906) and his party's first leader in the House of Commons.

d. Porfirio Díaz (1830-1915), a general in the revolutionary army of Benito Juárez; dictator of Mexico (1876-1911).

b. Peter Brian Medawar (1915-1987), Brazilian-born British-Lebanese zoologist.

d. Paul Ehrlich (1854-1915), German chemist and bacteriologist; a pioneer in chemotherapy who developed a cure for syphilis (1910).

d. Henry Gwyn-Jeffreys Moseley (1887-1915), British physicist who linked atomic number to the periodic table (1913); he was killed in action at Gallipoli.

1916

Incumbent Democrat Woodrow Wilson won a second term as U.S. president, defeating Republican Charles Evans Hughes. Wilson's campaign slogan was "He kept us out of war!"

Both sides suffered enormous losses on the western front, the Germans with 1 million casualties in their failed 10-month attack on Verdun (Feb.), and the British and French with 1.25 million casualties in their failed 5-month attack on the Somme (June). The British introduced tanks on the Somme; the Germans introduced phosgene gas at Verdun.

German physicist Arnold Sommerfeld modified the Niels Bohr model of atomic structure (1913), suggesting that elliptical, rather than circular, orbits for electrons would better explain the hydrogen atom.

American naturalist and explorer Roy Chapman Andrews began his series of American Museum of Natural History expeditions to east and central Asia (1916-1930), making many new fossil finds, including the first whole dinosaur eggs.

1915 cont.

b. Elisabeth Schwarzkopf (1915-), German soprano; a leading interpreter of the operas of Mozart and Strauss.

b. Billie Holiday (Eleanora Fagan) (1915-1959), American jazz singer.

b. Edith Piaf (Giovanna Gassion) (1915-1963), French singer; her signature song was "La Vie en Rose."

b. Robert Motherwell (1915-1991), American painter who would be a leading abstract expressionist.

b. Yul Brynner (1915-1985), Russian-American actor and director.

d. Rupert Brooke (1887-1915), British poet; a war casualty; his war writings, *1914 and Other Poems*, were published posthumously (1915).

d. Alexander Nikolayevich Scriabin (1872-1915), Russian composer.

d. J. A. H. (James Augustus Henry) Murray (1837-1915), creator of the *Oxford English Dictionary*.

1916

Expressing their protest against a culture that in 1916 produced a million casualties at Verdun, more than a million more on the Somme, and millions more on other fronts, a few young people in the arts met in Zurich to found the dada movement, an anti-arts-and-literature "scream" against the horrors of the war then tearing their world apart. Among the dadaists, many of whom later became surrealists, were Marcel Duchamp, André Breton, Paul Eluard, Philip Soupalt, Jean Arp, and Max Ernst.

After the failure of Dublin's Easter Rising and the executions that followed, William Butler Yeats pub-

David Sarnoff, of the American Marconi Company, suggested that stations should be established to transmit voice and music to home "radio music box" receivers; his idea would take root, and he would become a major developer of the Radio Corporation of America (RCA) and then the main force behind the establishment of the National Broadcasting Company (NBC).

Margaret Sanger founded the first American birth control clinic, in a largely immigrant community in Brooklyn, New York.

The much more fluid war on the eastern front was at least as costly and also inconclusive, with 2 million to 3 million casualties, most of them coming with Russia's successful Brusilov Offensive (June 4-Sept. 20) against the Austrians in southern Poland and subsequent equally successful German counteroffensives (June-July). Farther south, Romania joined the Allies (Aug. 27) and was quickly defeated by the Germans; Bucharest fell (Dec. 6). Allied and Central Powers forces fought to a stalemate in the Vardar Valley, and the long Italian-Austrian stalemate continued on the Isonzo River.

In southwest Asia, Russian forces scored considerable successes against the Turks in the Caucasus Mountains, while Turkish forces advancing against British and Indian forces in Egypt and Palestine were stopped in the Sinai Peninsula (Aug. 3), with the Allies going over to the offensive late in the year. The Arab Revolt began in Arabia's Hejaz (June 5); Arab forces were led by Hussein Ibn Ali and his son Faisal, later advised by British officer T. E. Lawrence (Lawrence of Arabia).

At sea, German submarines sank a reported 2.2 million tons of Allied shipping. At Jutland (May 31-June 1), the main German and British battle fleets fought the only major sea action of the war, with German forces then fleeing to safety; they did not come out again.

James Connolly of the Irish Citizen Army and Patrick Pearse of the Irish Volunteers led 1,500 to 2,000 lightly armed Irish Republicans in Dublin in the failed Easter Rising (Apr. 24-29). The insurrection was easily defeated by 5,000 well-armed British regulars. Fifteen leaders of the rising, including Connolly and Pearse, were later executed, becoming early martyrs of the Irish War of Independence.

Pancho Villa's forces raided Columbus, New Mexico (Mar. 15), then evaded American forces seeking to find them in northern Mexico (1916-1917).

Turkish government forces committed the mass murder of 1 million to 1.5 million Armenians, forced by the

French surgeon Alexis Carrel and British chemist Henry Dakin developed the Carrel-Dakin treatment for deep wounds, such as those sustained on the battlefield, using a special sterile solution.

In an experiment involving the photoelectric effect, American physicist Robert Millikan confirmed Albert Einstein's theory of that effect (1905) and also Planck's constant, a fundamental value in physics.

British engineers built the first production-model tank, the 30-ton Mark I ("Big Willie"), developed from the 1915 prototype; it was an armed, armored, powered vehicle running on tracks, not wheels (actually mounted on a caterpillar-style tractor). These slow tanks — reportedly so called after their secret developmental code name "water carrier" — saw their first action on September 15 but were not used to notable effect for another year, at Cambrai (Nov. 20, 1917).

Working at Stanford University to revise and further develop Alfred Binet's intelligence tests (1905), American psychologist Lewis M. Terman produced the Stanford-Binet Intelligence Scale, which set the standard for mental testing; a score on the test was called an "intelligence quotient," or IQ. That same year, one of Terman's students, Arthur S. Otis, developed the Otis Group Test of Mental Ability, the first intelligence test designed for group (not just individual) testing. The U.S. Army drew heavily on the Otis test in its Army Alpha Test, which would be given to nearly 2 million recruits before and during American participation in World War I, in the first large-scale use of intelligence testing.

In *The Atom and the Molecule,* Gilbert Newton Lewis introduced the idea that atoms share

lished his elegiac short poem "Easter 1916," prophetically ending with "A terrible beauty is born."

D. W. Griffith made a massive attempt to balance his racist film *The Birth of a Nation* with his classic film *Intolerance,* four related stories deploring bigotry and its accompanying savagery.

Rabindranath Tagore published his novel *The Home and the World,* expressing his complete support for Indian freedom from British imperial domination.

Carl Sandburg emerged as a major figure in American poetry with the publication of his *Chicago Poems.*

James Joyce published his autobiographical *Portrait of the Artist as a Young Man* as a complete novel.

The Provincetown Players presented *Bound East for Cardiff,* the first of Eugene O'Neill's plays to be produced.

John McCormack introduced the extraordinarily popular war song "Roses of Picardy."

W. C. Handy published the song "Beale Street Blues."

Henri Barbusse published *Under Fire,* a strongly antiwar novel based on his own World War I experiences.

The Four Horsemen of the Apocalypse, Vicente Blasco Ibáñez's novel of World War I, was published; it would be the basis for two films (1921; 1961).

Mark Twain's novel *The Mysterious Stranger* was posthumously published.

Luigi Pirandello produced his play *Six Characters in Search of an Author.*

Gustav Holst composed his orchestral work *The Planets.*

Fritz (Frederick Douglass) Pollard, halfback on the Brown University football team, was the first African-American to be named an all-American and to play in the Rose Bowl.

John Dewey published *Democracy in Education;* its espousal of practical experience and rejection of educational authoritarianism would be central to the development of modern teaching practices.

Labor activists Thomas J. Mooney and Warren K. Billings were convicted of bombing the San Francisco Preparedness Day parade (July 22), killing 10 people. Mooney's death sentence was later commuted after a worldwide campaign for clemency, as was Billings's life sentence. Both would be freed in 1939.

U.S. president Woodrow Wilson nominated Louis Brandeis to the Supreme Court; the first Jewish Supreme Court justice (1916-1939), Brandeis was confirmed only after long Senate hearings.

A major epidemic of polio (poliomyelitis, or infantile paralysis) caused over 27,000 cases in the United States alone.

The first radio news report was broadcast.

Marcus Garvey founded the newspaper *Negro World,* the chief organ of the "Back to Africa" movement.

Austrian-Jewish philosopher-theologian Martin Buber founded *Der Jude,* a leading magazine for German-Jewish intellectuals.

b. Walter Leland Cronkite, Jr. (1916-   ), American broadcast journalist who, as chief anchor for CBS television news (1962-1981), would authoritatively interpret the main stories of two decades, in the process becoming the leading newscaster of the day, speaking to American and worldwide audiences.

Turks into concentration camps in the Syrian Desert, where most died of famine and famine-induced disease. This became known as the Armenian Holocaust.

American forces began an eight-year occupation of the Dominican Republic (1916-1924).

Jeanette Pickering Rankin, a Montana Republican, became the first woman to be elected to the House of Representatives (1917-1919).

b. François Mitterrand (1916-), French socialist politician; president of France (1981-1995).

b. Pieter Willem Botha (1916-), South African National Party leader; prime minister (1978-1984) and state president (1984-1989).

b. Sirimavo Ratwatte Bandaranaike (1916-), Sri Lankan politician who would become the world's first woman prime minister (1960-1965; 1970-1977).

b. (James) Harold Wilson (1916-1995), British Labour Party leader and prime minister (1964-1970; 1974-1976).

b. Edward Richard George Heath (1916-), British Conservative prime minister (1970-1974).

b. Eugene Joseph McCarthy (1916-), American politician; liberal Democrat, Minnesota senator (1959-1971), and leading Vietnam War opponent; failed Democratic candidate for the presidential nomination (1968).

d. Roger David Casement (1864-1916), British supporter of Irish nationalism; he was captured while landing from a German submarine after having failed to secure arms for the Easter Rising. He was executed for treason (Aug. 3).

d. Yüan Shih-k'ai (ca. 1859-1916), Chinese general; first president of the Republic of China (1912-1916).

electrons and the corollary rule that the number of electrons in compounds is generally even.

b. Francis Harry Compton Crick (1916-), British molecular biologist who would codiscover the double-helix form taken by the DNA molecule, carrier of basic genetic information (1953).

b. Hans Jürgen Eysenck (1916-), German-British psychologist who would develop behavior therapy, inspired by psychologists such as Ivan Pavlov and John B. Watson, focusing on treating symptoms, as an alternative to psychotherapy, especially Freudian psychoanalysis.

b. Maurice Hugh Frederick Wilkins (1916-), New Zealand–British biophysicist whose work in X-ray crystallography would aid in the discovery of the double-helix structure of DNA (1953).

d. Percival Lowell (1855-1916), American astronomer; founder of Arizona's Lowell Observatory, who predicted the existence of Pluto (1905).

Robert Graves published his first poetry collection, *Over the Brazier*.

Swedish writer Verner von Heidenstam was awarded the Nobel Prize for literature.

b. (Eldred) Gregory Peck (1916-   ), American film star who would become an archetypal American hero, most notably in *Gentleman's Agreement* (1947) and *To Kill a Mockingbird* (1962).

b. Emil Grigoryevich Gilels (1916-1985), Soviet pianist who would emerge as a world figure during the post–World War II period.

b. Yehudi Menuhin (1916-   ), American violinist; one of the century's leading violinists and a revered figure in the world of music.

b. Trevor Howard (1916-1988), British actor.

b. Shirley Jackson (1916-1965), American writer.

d. Enrique Granados (1867-1916), Spanish composer and pianist; killed when his ship was torpedoed by a German submarine; he was returning from the Metropolitan Opera opening of his opera *Goyescas*.

d. Franz Marc (1880-1916), a founder of The Blue Rider group and a leading German expressionist painter; he was killed at Verdun.

d. Henry James (1843-1916), major American novelist and literary figure, long resident in Britain.

d. Jack (John Griffith) London (1876-1916), American writer largely dealing with themes of the sea and the far north.

d. Thomas Eakins (1844-1916), leading American painter.

d. Sholem Aleichem (Solomon Rabinovich) (1859-1916), Jewish-Russian writer; the most popular Yiddish-language writer of his time.

b. Robert Kane (1916-   ), American cartoonist who would create the comic strip *Batman* (1939).

d. James Jerome Hill (1838-1916), American railroad magnate, who with J. Pierpont Morgan controlled much of the U.S. western railway system through their Northern Securities Company, until they were forced to break up the monopoly by a landmark Supreme Court antitrust ruling (1904).

d. Rasputin (Gregory Yefimovich Novykh) (1872-1916), flamboyantly sexual Russian monk and faith healer who was a favorite of Czarina Alexandra; he was openly assassinated by three leading Russian conservatives (Dec. 16).

d. Hetty (Henrietta Rowland Robinson) Green (1834-1916), American financier who was reputedly the richest woman in America at her death.

The United States declared war on Germany (Apr. 6). American warships joined the Allies in the Battle of the Atlantic, while war production accelerated and the American Expeditionary Force (AEF) began arriving in Europe (June). The stalemate continued on the western front; German forces withdrew to the Hindenburg Line (Feb. 23-Apr. 5), there repelling the massive, costly, failed French Nivelle Offensive (Apr. 16-20), which generated major French army mutinies (Apr.-May). British forces also made costly, failed attacks, notably at Passchendaele (Third Ypres) (July 31-Nov. 10) and Cambrai (Nov. 20-Dec. 3).

On the eastern front, the new Russian Provisional Government mounted the failed Kerensky Offensive (July 1-19); Russian armies began to disintegrate as the October Revolution approached.

On the Italian front, the long stalemate on the Isonzo River was broken at Caporetto (Oct. 24-Nov. 12), when German and Italian forces broke through, capturing 275,000. Across the Mediterranean, British forces scored successes against the Turks in Palestine and Mesopotamia. Greece entered the war on the Allied side (June 27), and defeated Romania left the war (Dec.).

German submarines sank more than 6 million tons of Allied shipping, but Allied forces began to win the Battle of the Atlantic, with the introduction of the convoy system (May) and the entry of American naval forces into the war.

In Russia, growing army mutinies and nationwide demonstrations began the February Revolution, forced the abdication of Nicholas II (Mar. 15), and brought the Provisional Government to power, led first by Prince Georgy Lvov and then by Alexander Kerensky. Bolshevik forces in Petrograd stormed the Winter Palace and deposed the Kerensky government in the October Revolution (Nov. 6-7). The Bolsheviks, led by Vladimir Illich Lenin, then took power in many areas. The Russian Civil War began (1917-1922) with Red-White fighting in the Ukraine, which spread throughout the country, accompanied by foreign intervention on the White side and multi-

Taking off from Albert Einstein's equations regarding general relativity, Dutch astronomer Willem de Sitter theorized that the universe was expanding, a startling notion at the time, though within a few years supported by astronomical evidence. Einstein himself had realized that his equations did not fit an unchanging universe but had added a "corrective" factor to fit his preconceived idea of a static universe, making what he later described as the greatest scientific mistake of his life.

German astronomer Karl Schwarzschild predicted the existence of "black holes" as a late stage in the evolution of certain large stars, in which all light, energy, and matter collapse, held by gravitation so intense that space and time are curved.

Albert Einstein observed that specially stimulated molecules emit light of a single color; this observation would be basic to the development of lasers but would not be practically pursued until the 1950s.

On Mount Wilson, near Pasadena, California, American astronomer George Ellery Hale built a 100-inch reflecting telescope, for three decades the largest in the world, which would lead to numerous advances in astronomy.

American microbiologist Alice Evans recognized undulant fever (brucellosis) as a single disease, which could be prevented through the pasteurization of milk. However, her discovery was disregarded for years, since milk "fresh from the cow" was regarded as supremely healthy, and pasteurization would not become widespread until the 1930s.

Dutch-American physical chemist Peter Debye first used powdered crystal solids in X-ray diffraction, a significant advance in chemical

In wartime Paris, all the arts continued to converge: Sergei Diaghilev's Ballets Russes company presented *Parade*, choreographed by Leonid Massine to music by Erik Satie, libretto by Jean Cocteau, and set and costumes by Pablo Picasso; Massine and Maria Chabelska danced the leads.

Sergei Prokofiev composed his first symphony, the *Classical*. The premiere of his opera *The Gambler* (written and composed in 1916), based on Fyodor Dostoevsky's 1866 novel, was canceled as the Russian Revolution developed; the opera would not be produced until 1929.

George M. Cohan introduced his popular war song "Over There."

Hamlin Garland published *A Son of the Middle Border*, the first of his eight linked autobiographical works.

Piet Mondrian, Theo van Doesburg, and other Dutch artists formed a group called De Stijl, also the name of their magazine edited by van Doesburg (1917-1932).

Martin Andersen Nexö began publication of his five-volume novel *Ditte, Daughter of Man* (1917-1921).

The Provincetown Players presented Eugene O'Neill's one-act play *The Long Voyage Home*.

William Butler Yeats published the poetry collection *The Wild Swans at Coole*.

The musical *Oh, Boy!* opened in New York; music was by Jerome Kern and lyrics by P. G. Wodehouse, who cowrote the book with Guy Bolton.

Karl Adolph Gjellerup and Hendrik Pontoppidan, both Danish writers, shared the Nobel Prize for literature.

Margaret Sanger was arrested for disseminating birth control information after she published *What Every Woman Should Know*; the landmark New York State court ruling that resulted established that doctors could legally supply birth control information to their patients.

The U.S. Congress passed the 18th (Prohibition) Amendment (Dec. 18), which then went to the states for ratification.

To help fund the war effort, the U.S. Congress enacted the first federal excess profits tax; it would become a major fund-raising device during World War II. Congress also enacted the Liberty Loan Act, authorizing the issuance of war bonds to the public, done with great success.

The United States for the first time imposed literacy tests as a prerequisite for immigrant admission; the tests had little impact at the time, as wartime conditions had virtually closed the Atlantic to immigrant ships, but they would be, as intended, a massive bar for many immigrants during the postwar period.

The French ammunition ship *Mont Blanc* and the Belgian steamer *Imo* collided in the harbor of Halifax, Nova Scotia (Dec. 6); the resulting explosion killed 1,600 people.

Not one member of baseball's Washington Senators reached first base as Ernie Shore of the Boston Red Sox pitched a perfect game (June 23).

A troop train derailed in the Alps (Dec. 12), near Modane, France, killing 543 people; it was the world's worst railroad disaster to date.

The British warship *Vanguard* exploded in Britain's Scapa Flow (July 9), killing 800 people.

British Theosophist and women's rights campaigner Annie Besant, a force in India's political life and a

ple secession movements. Finland declared its independence from Russia (Dec. 6), and Japanese forces entered the war (Dec.), taking Vladivostok.

British foreign minister Arthur Balfour issued the Balfour Declaration (Nov. 2), supporting, with qualifications, the establishment of a Jewish homeland in Palestine.

The Cheka, the Soviet secret police and internal security organization, was founded (Dec.). It later became the GPU (1922) and OGPU (1923), and would be Joseph Stalin's main mass murder instrument.

In the United States, the Espionage Act of 1917 and the Sedition Act of 1918 together provided the legal basis for the development of a Red Scare and attacks on antiwar and radical dissenters; more than 1,500 people were ultimately prosecuted and hundreds imprisoned. The entire leadership of the Industrial Workers of the World (IWW) was arrested (Nov. 1917); hundreds were convicted of sedition, for opposing American participation in World War I, breaking the power of the IWW, which before the arrests had 50,000 to 100,000 members.

A Cuban revolution was defeated by American troop landings; American forces again occupied Cuba.

Nguyen That Thanh (later Ho Chi Minh) joined the French Socialist Party.

b. John Fitzgerald Kennedy (1917-1963), 35th president of the United States (1961-1963); he would be assassinated in Dallas, Texas (Nov. 22, 1963).

b. Indira Gandhi (1917-1984), who would become Indian prime minister (1966-1977; 1980-1984); the daughter of Jawaharlal Nehru and mother of Rajiv Gandhi.

b. Park Chung Hee (1917-1979), South Korean president (1961-1971) and dictator (1971-1979).

analysis, discovered independently by American physicist Albert Wallace Hull.

Element 91 (protactinium) was discovered by German physical chemist Otto Hahn and Austrian physicist Lise Meitner.

French engineers developed their own tank, the 15-ton Schneider, primarily used for infantry support; this would be the main postwar tank, the model for American and Italian tanks.

b. Barry Commoner (1917-   ), American biologist noted for his work with highly reactive, destructive chemicals called free radicals. Active against nuclear testing, he would be a popular writer and ecologist, a key figure in the developing green movement, and a candidate for president under the green/socialist-oriented Citizens Party (1980).

d. Elizabeth Garrett Anderson (1836-1917), the first licensed woman physician in Britain (1873), who cofounded and ran a medical school (1883) and hospital (1886) for women in London; later Britain's first woman mayor (1908).

d. Ferdinand von Zeppelin (1838-1917), German general and aircraft designer who developed the dirigible, or zeppelin (1900).

b. Anthony Burgess (John Anthony Burgess Wilson) (1917-1993), British writer best known for his satirical novel *A Clockwork Orange* (1962).

b. I. M. (Ieoh Ming) Pei (1917-   ), leading American architect.

b. Dizzy (John Birks) Gillespie (1917-1993), leading American jazz trumpeter and bandleader; a founder of bebop.

b. Carson McCullers (1917-1967), American writer; much of her work would be set in the South.

b. Andrew Wyeth (1917-   ), leading American realist painter.

b. Gwendolyn Brooks (1917-   ), African-American writer who would largely explore the African-American experience.

b. Heinrich Böll (1917-   ), German writer who would be a powerful critic of the Nazi period and of postwar German society.

b. Thelonious Sphere Monk (1917-1982), American pianist and composer.

b. John Lee Hooker (1917-   ), American blues composer, singer, and guitarist.

b. Lena Horne (1917-   ), American singer, actress, and dancer; a pioneering African-American artist on screen and in variety.

b. Robert Lowell (Traill Spence, Jr.) (1917-1977), American poet.

b. Robert Mitchum (1917-   ), American film actor who would emerge as a major dramatic star late in his career.

b. Nat "King" Cole (Nathaniel Adams Coles) (1917-1965), African-American jazz musician; a leading popular singer in the 1950s.

leader of the home rule campaign, became president of the Congress Party (1917-1923); she would disagree with the far more militant independence and civil disobedience movements that would soon develop under the leadership of Mahatma Gandhi and Jawaharlal Nehru.

b. Fannie Lou Hamer (1917-1977), African-American civil rights activist and Mississippi politician who would become a cofounder of the Mississippi Freedom Democratic Party (1964).

b. Helen Gavronsky Suzman (1917-   ), South African political figure; a leading White antiapartheid activist and cofounder of South Africa's Progressive Party (1959).

d. (Maria) Francesca (Xavier) Cabrini (Mother Cabrini) (1850-1917), Italian-born American nun and saint; founder of the Missionary Sisters of the Sacred Heart (1880), she worked with poor immigrants in America (from 1889) and would become the first American saint (1946).

d. Buffalo Bill (William Frederick) Cody (1846-1917), American Western frontiersman, express rider, army scout, buffalo hunter, and (from 1883) proprietor of Buffalo Bill's Wild West Show; he was made a legendary figure by Ned Buntline and other authors and journalists.

d. Emile Durkheim (1858-1917), French sociologist who established some of the fundamental principles for the study of social structures in works such as *The Rules of Sociological Method* (1895).

1917 cont.

b. Oliver Tambo (1917-1993), South African freedom movement leader.

b. Ferdinand Edralin Marcos (1917-1989), Philippine president (1965-1986) and dictator (1971-1986).

b. John Bowden Connally (1917-1993), American politician.

d. Mata Hari (Margaretha Geertruida Zelle) (1876-1917), a Dutch dancer who was convicted and executed as a German spy.

d. Belva Bennett Lockwood (1830-1917), American lawyer, feminist, suffragist, and pacifist; she was the first woman lawyer admitted to practice before the U.S. Supreme Court (1879) and the presidential candidate of the National Equal Rights Party (1884).

1918

Russia formally left the war by the terms of the later-repudiated Treaty of Brest-Litovsk (Mar. 3), losing much of western Russia and the Ukraine and pledging demobilization.

German forces in the west, much reinforced by eastern front forces freed by the Russian collapse, mounted five failed major offensives aimed at breaching Allied fortifications and winning the war. These took place on the Somme River (Mar. 21-Apr. 5), in Flanders (Apr. 9-29), on the Aisne River (May 27-June 6), at Paris (June 9-13), and on the Marne River, where their defeat at Second

Measuring distances using Henrietta Swan Leavitt's method involving Cepheid variable stars (1912) and using observations from the new Mount Wilson telescope, American astronomer Harlow Shapley first described the shape of our Milky Way galaxy, making it clear that our solar system — traditionally seen as the center of the universe — is, in fact, on the fringes of the galaxy, tens of light-years from the center. This would be one of the 20th century's many such correctives to a solar system–centered view.

b. Joan Fontaine (Joan De Havilland) (1917-   ), American film star of the 1940s and 1950s.

b. Ossie Davis (1917-   ), African-American actor, writer, director, and producer; husband of Ruby Dee.

b. Sidney Robert Nolan (1917-1992), leading Australian painter, largely on historical themes.

d. Auguste Rodin (1940-1917), French sculptor; a major figure in 19th-century art.

d. Edgar Degas (1834-1917), a leading French impressionist painter and sculptor noted for his ballet figures.

d. Herbert Beerbohm Tree (1853-1917), British actor-manager who created Henry Higgins in *Pygmalion* (1914).

d. Scott Joplin (1868-1917), American composer and pianist; a central figure in ragtime.

d. Tom Thomson (Thomas John Thompson) (1877-1917), Canada's leading landscape painter; an early member and inspiration of what would be the Group of Seven.

1918

James Joyce attempted to begin serial publication of his masterwork *Ulysses* in *The Little Review,* but several issues of the magazine were seized by the U.S. government as "obscene" for carrying his work, which was banned in the United States until 1933.

Kasimir Malevich painted *Suprematist Composition: White on White,* a geometric work that for many would come to be emblematic of modernism in contemporary painting.

A massive influenza pandemic (1918-1919), the greatest natural disaster of the 20th century, took an estimated 25 million to 50 million lives, as the then largely untreatable influenza was spread to most of the world's inhabited areas, often by and among soldiers and sailors. Probably originating in Asia, the virus was first identified at Fort Riley, Kansas, but was named "Spanish flu" for its severity in Spain. In some places, public and commercial institutions closed for a time, and people wore surgical masks in the streets.

Marne (July 15-Aug. 5) signaled the beginning of the end of the war. Pursuing Allied forces, now including Americans, crossed the Meuse River into the Argonne Forest (Sept. 26) and breached the Hindenburg Line (Sept. 27).

German sailors at Kiel successfully mutinied (Oct. 29), beginning the German Revolution, which quickly forced the abdication of Wilhelm II (Nov. 9) and brought about the Armistice (Nov. 11), effectively ending the war in the west.

On the southern front, Allied forces destroyed the Austrian army at Vittorio Veneto (Oct. 24-Nov. 4), taking 300,000 prisoners and forcing an armistice (Nov. 4). The Allied-Bulgarian armistice had come earlier (Sept. 29), as had the Turkish armistice (Oct. 30).

d. Nicholas II (1868-1918), the last Romanov emperor of Russia (1894-1917), executed with his wife and family by their Bolshevik captors at Yekaterinburg (Sverdlovsk) (July 16).

Civil wars and wars of independence flared throughout Russia. Admiral Alexander Kolchak's White forces in Siberia were aided by intervening Japanese and American forces and by former Czech and Slovak prisoners organized as the Czech Legion, who were fighting their way out to Siberia. White forces came close to taking Moscow. British, French, and American forces took Murmansk and occupied Archangel. French forces took Odessa, in support of White forces in southern Russia. Finnish independence was won with the aid of intervening German forces. Latvia declared itself independent (Nov. 18), beginning the Latvian War of Independence (1918-1920), which would also involve German forces. Lithuania declared itself independent (Feb. 16), beginning the Lithuanian War of Independence (1918-1920); invading Soviet troops were defeated by German forces, which later withdrew. Insurrection also began in the Ukraine, as nationalists led by Simon Petlyura fought Soviet forces, and in Georgia, Armenia, and Azerbaijan; independence for these nations would come only after the collapse of the Soviet empire.

American astronomer Annie Jump Cannon established a star classification system, dividing stars into types on the basis of their spectra, which she would use in her major star catalog (1924); it would remain in use throughout the century.

In a notorious case of scientific fraud, Austrian biologist Paul Kammerer claimed to have proven, through experiments with midwife toads, that acquired characteristics could be inherited; however, the toads were later found to have been colored with India ink, giving false data. Kammerer committed suicide shortly after the fraud was exposed (1926).

Radio moved out of the world of professionals with the development of the superheterodyne receiver by American radio engineer Edwin Howard Armstrong; with it and others that followed, a listener could simply turn a dial to get better reception or to switch from one wavelength to another, making radios appropriate for mass use.

German mathematician Emmy Noether demonstrated that symmetry in physics implies the existence of a conservation law, proving the reverse as well; this would aid in the development of future theories in physics.

French engineers developed the 7.5-ton Renault F.T. tank.

German physicist Max Planck won the Nobel Prize for physics for his fundamental work on quantum theory.

German chemist Fritz Haber won the Nobel Prize for chemistry for his development of a process to "fix" nitrogen by making ammonia (1907).

b. Richard Phillips Feynman (1918-1988), American physicist.

Lytton Strachey published the book *Eminent Victorians*, a bitingly realistic set of short biographies of some of the previously sanctified pillars of British society.

Marcel Proust published *Within a Budding Grove*, the second part of his seven-part *Remembrance of Things Past*.

Alexander Blok published his long poem *The Twelve*, set in St. Petersburg during the Bolshevik Revolution, its protagonists twelve Red Guards; this work was Blok's homage to that revolution.

Booth Tarkington published the novel *The Magnificent Ambersons*, the basis for Orson Welles's classic 1942 film.

Lillian Gish, Robert Harron, and Dorothy Gish starred in *Hearts of the World*, a war story set in Britain and France; D. W. Griffith directed and produced.

The Provincetown Players presented Eugene O'Neill's one-act play *The Moon of the Caribbees*.

Vladimir Mayakovsky premiered his mystery-drama *Mystery-Bouffe*, a celebration of the first anniversary of the Bolshevik Revolution.

George Gershwin composed his first major hit song, "Swanee," sung by Al Jolson on Broadway in the musical *Sinbad*.

Georges Pitoëff choreographed Igor Stravinsky's ballet *L'Histoire du Soldat* (*The Soldier's Tale*).

Irving Berlin's armed forces show *Yip Yip Yaphank* featured Berlin himself singing "Oh, How I Hate to Get Up in the Morning." He also wrote the song "God Bless America" for the show, but it was shelved until 1939, when it emerged to become an unofficial anthem in a second world war.

A powerful typhoon struck Tokyo, killing more than 1,600 people.

In the United States, as millions of men left their jobs to go to war and war production accelerated, millions of women joined the workforce. As soon as the war was over, most women were just as quickly forced out of work, although their work experience would powerfully influence the thinking of many women during the interwar period.

Financier Bernard "Barney" Baruch, later an adviser to many American presidents, became head of the War Industries Board, turning massive American industrial production, already heavily engaged in supplying the Allies, fully toward war production.

Forest fires destroyed Cloquet, Minnesota, and the surrounding communities (Oct. 21), as well as more than 2,000 square miles of forest, killing 559 people.

Knute Rockne became head football coach at Notre Dame University (1918-1931), developing the highly publicized dominant college team of the period, with five undefeated seasons; during his tenure, he would introduce platoon substitution, stress the forward pass, and develop such stars as triple-threat George Gipp and his famed "Four Horsemen" backfield.

Airmail was introduced in the United States, and the federal government issued its first airmail stamps.

British author Marie Stopes published *Married Love* and *Wise Parenthood*, best-selling books that would make her a leading figure in sex and birth control education.

Roald Amundsen traversed the Northeast Passage, the icy seaway north of Eurasia; like Boris Vilkitski before him (1914), he was obliged to winter over before completing his journey.

U.S. president Woodrow Wilson put forward his "Four-teen Points" regarding the coming peace settlement, among them the formation of the League of Nations. He was to pursue his plan with considerable success at the Paris Peace Conference (1919), only to find his position repudiated by the U.S. Senate, which would refuse to join the League of Nations and reject the Treaty of Versailles.

India's Congress Party began to demand full self-determination for India.

The Irish Republican political party Sinn Fein won an electoral majority and formed a new government.

American Socialist Party leader and perennial presidential candidate Eugene V. Debs was imprisoned for his opposition to World War I, receiving a 10-year prison term, commuted in 1921.

Poland and Czechoslovakia became independent states.

Serbia, Montenegro, Croatia, Dalmatia, Bosnia, and Herzegovina united as the new Kingdom of Serbs, Croats, and Slovenes (later Yugoslavia) (Dec.).

American Socialist Victor Berger, indicted for sedition because of his opposition to World War I, was refused his seat in the U.S. House of Representatives.

Equal voting rights for women over 30 were won in Britain.

Haile Selassie I (Ras Tafari) became regent and effectively ruler of Ethiopia (1918-1928).

Japanese feminists founded the activist New Women's Association.

b. Helmut Heinrich Waldemar Schmidt (1918-   ), West German Social Democratic politician; chancellor (1974-1982).

b. Nelson Rolihlahla Mandela (1918-   ), leader of the South African freedom movement.

Giacomo Puccini premiered three one-act operas at New York's Metropolitan Opera: *The Cloak* (*Il Tabarro*), *Sister Angelica* (*Suor Angelica*), and *Gianni Schicchi*.

Willa Cather published *My Antonia*.

b. Ingmar Bergman (1918-   ), Swedish director and writer who was to become a massive figure in film history.

b. Alexander Solzhenitsyn (1918-   ), Russian novelist; a key dissenter of the Soviet period.

b. Ella Fitzgerald (1918-   ), American jazz and popular singer.

b. Jerome Robbins (1918-   ), American dancer and director; a prolific ballet choreographer and a major figure in the musical theater.

b. Leonard Bernstein (1918-1990), American composer, conductor, and pianist; a leading figure in the world of music.

b. William Holden (William Franklin Beedle) (1918-1981), major American film star from the late 1940s.

b. Alan Jay Lerner (1918-1986), leading American writer and lyricist.

b. Muriel Spark (1918-   ), prolific British writer who would become a major figure in the 1960s.

b. Rita Hayworth (Margarita Carmen Cansino) (1918-1987), American dancer; a film star and sex symbol of the 1940s.

b. Robert Preston (Robert Preston Meservey) (1918-1986), versatile American stage and screen star.

b. Susan Hayward (Edythe Marrener) (1918-1975), American actress.

Near Ivanhoe, Indiana, a troop train hit a circus train; 68 people and many animals of the Hagenbeck-Wallace Circus died (June 22).

Five railroad cars derailed in Brooklyn, New York, killing 97 people (Nov. 1).

Roger Baldwin, director of the American Union Against Militarism, was imprisoned as a conscientious objector.

The Canadian coast steamer *Princess Sophia* sank off Alaska, killing 398 people.

Japanese industrialist Konosuke Matsushita founded the Matsushita Electric Industrial Company, building it into a substantial empire.

The Kelvinator, an electric-powered refrigerator, was introduced in the United States, as was the first electric mixer.

The comic strip *Gasoline Alley* was created by Frank O. King.

Red, green, and yellow traffic lights, powered by electricity but manually triggered by an operator, were introduced in New York City.

b. Billy (William Franklin) Graham (1918-   ), fundamentalist Protestant minister who would, as a leading radio and television evangelist, become a worldwide figure in the 1940s, preaching throughout the world, even to huge audiences in the Soviet Union during the Cold War.

1918 cont.

b. Ahmed Ben Bella (1918-   ), Algerian officer and a leader of the Algerian national movement; the first premier of independent Algeria (1962).

b. Anwar al-Sadat (1918-1981), Egyptian president (1970-1981).

b. Gamal Abdel Nasser (1918-1970), leader of the 1952 Egyptian Revolution, premier (1954-1956), and president (1956-1970).

b. Nicolae Ceausescu (1918-1989), Romanian communist dictator (1965-1989).

b. Spiro Theodore Agnew (1918-   ), American lawyer and politician; vice president (1969-1973) who resigned after pleading "no contest" to a charge of income tax evasion.

1919

The Paris Peace Conference (Jan. 18, 1919-Jan. 16, 1920) founded the League of Nations and negotiated several postwar treaties, most notably the Treaty of Versailles with Germany (June 28), which set territorial concessions, as in Poland, Alsace-Lorraine, the Rhineland, and the Saar; broke up Germany's prewar colonial empire; and set massive reparations, all issues that would be used by the Nazis to fan German nationalist sentiment on the road to another world war. The Treaty of Saint-Germain (Sept. 10) dismembered Austria-Hungary and ended the Hapsburg monarchy, while the Treaty of Neuilly (Nov. 27) set Bulgarian territorial losses and reparations.

Red Army successes in southern Russia pushed Anton Denikin's White forces south to the Black Sea, while Alexander Kolchak's White forces were pushed back and then dispersed in Siberia, as the Russian Civil War began to wind down. Red forces were unable to oppose Chinese reoccupation of Outer Mongolia.

American physicist Robert Goddard published his classic rocketry work *A Method of Reaching Extreme Altitudes,* which predicted the coming of space flight. His work would be ridiculed or ignored by many in his lifetime and in his own country but would inspire German rocket researchers, giving them a technological edge during World War II.

During a total solar eclipse, British astronomer Arthur Eddington made observations, including the bending of light by a gravitational field, that helped confirm Albert Einstein's theory of relativity.

Ernest Rutherford reported his success in artificially splitting an atom, by bombarding nitrogen atoms with alpha particles to produce oxygen and hydrogen (1917-1919); further ex-

d. Gustav Klimt (1862-1918), Austrian artist; much of his work was in the art nouveau style.

d. Claude Debussy (1862-1918), leading French composer.

d. Wilfred Owen (1893-1918), British war poet; he died in France.

d. Guillaume Apollinaire (Wilhelm Albert Kostrowitzky) (1880-1918), French writer and critic; a leading surrealist.

d. (Alfred) Joyce Kilmer (1886-1918), American poet; he was killed in action in France.

d. Henry Adams (1838-1918), American writer; the grandson of U.S. president John Quincy Adams.

d. Rubén Darío (Félix Rubén García Sarmiento) (1867-1918), Nicaraguan writer.

Franz Kafka published *In the Penal Colony,* the third of the powerful, extraordinarily influential works published in his lifetime.

In the wake of the Great War, Abel Gance made the antiwar film *J'Accuse,* which was well received throughout war-weary Europe.

James Branch Cabell published *Jurgen,* the second of his group of "Poictesme" novels; it became the very highly publicized object of a major American "obscenity" case, ensuring its and his popularity.

André Breton took the lead in founding the magazine *Littérature.*

John Reed, who had been in Russia during the Bolshevik Revolution, wrote his version of the events in *Ten Days That Shook the World.* Sergei Eisenstein

In baseball's Black Sox scandal, eight players for the favored Chicago White Sox (popularly renamed the Black Sox) were charged with conspiracy to throw the World Series to the Cincinnati Reds. All eight were acquitted (1920), even though some had taken bribes; but all were barred from baseball for life. One was star "Shoeless Joe" Jackson, to whom a young fan memorably said, "Say it ain't so, Joe." In the scandal's wake, Kenesaw Mountain Landis was appointed commissioner of baseball, to ensure the game's integrity.

Nebraska ratified the 18th (Prohibition) Amendment (Jan. 15), completing the ratification process; the amendment would go into effect a year later.

William Z. Foster led 300,000 to 350,000 steelworkers in a massive, failed American Federation of Labor (AFL) strike to organize the steel industry and

d. Rosa Luxemburg (1871-1919) and Karl Liebnecht (1871-1919), both founders of the German Communist Party. Luxemburg was a leading Marxist theoretician and an international socialist and communist movement figure. She and Liebnecht led the quickly failed Spartacist League insurrection in Berlin (Jan.), then were captured and murdered by the right-wing Freikorps militia (Jan. 15). German Communists also established the Bavarian Communist Republic (Apr.), a short-lived communist state that was quickly defeated by the Freikorps.

Sinn Fein declared Ireland independent (Jan. 21) and Eamon De Valera first president of the new country, beginning the Irish War of Independence (1919-1921), a guerrilla war pitting the Irish Republican Army against British and Irish Protestant forces.

Afghanistan, before and during World War I a British protectorate, became an independent state after the assassination of Afghan king Habibullah Khan (Feb.). He was succeeded by his son, Amanullah Khan (1919-1929), who soon after his accession declared a jihad (holy war) against the British, invaded India (May), and was quickly defeated by British Indian forces.

The Arabian Civil War began in the western Arabian Hejaz, pitting Ibn Saud's forces against those of the Hashemite king, Hussein Ibn Ali (1919-1925).

Estonia won its independence, defeating invading Soviet forces with the help of British warships in the Baltic (1918-1919). The Latvian and Lithuanian Wars of Independence continued.

In India, Mahatma Gandhi organized his first satyagraha (nonviolence) campaign (Feb.), stopping for a time after the Amritsar Massacre (Apr. 13), in which British forces commanded by General Reginald Dyer killed at least 379 and wounded 1,200 unarmed Indian demonstrators trapped in the Jillianwalla Bagh, an open plaza. The atrocity enhanced anti-British sentiment throughout India, providing an enormous spur to the Indian independence movement.

periments along these lines in the 1930s would lead to nuclear fission. Rutherford also succeeded Joseph John Thomson as head of the prestigious Cavendish Laboratory.

Frederick Soddy's theory of isotopes (1913) was confirmed by British chemist Francis William Aston, who developed a device called a mass spectrometer to measure the proportion of different isotopes in an element. He found that not only radioactive elements but also common stable elements exist in different forms, or isotopes.

Austrian-German zoologist Karl von Frisch discovered that bees "dance," communicating to other bees information about the location of food.

Introduction to Mathematical Philosophy was published; it had been written by pacifist British mathematician Bertrand Russell while he was imprisoned for six months because of his activities against World War I and for the rights of conscientious objectors.

based his heavily censored 1928 film on Reed's book.

Sergei Diaghilev's Ballets Russes premiered Leonid Massine's *La Boutique fantasque,* with music by Gioacchino Rossini arranged for the ballet by Ottorino Respighi.

Tamara Karsavina and Leonid Massine danced the leads in the Ballets Russes company presentation of Massine's ballet *The Three-Cornered Hat,* music by Manuel de Falla, set and costumes by Pablo Picasso.

Conrad Veidt and Werner Krauss starred in the classic German expressionist film *The Cabinet of Dr. Caligari,* directed by Robert Wiene.

Virginia Woolf published the novel *Night and Day,* using the highly experimental "stream-of-consciousness" technique.

Hermann Hesse published his first major novel, *Demian,* his protagonist the deeply conflicted, self-analytical figure seen as well in his later novels.

Lillian Gish, Richard Barthelmess, and Donald Crisp starred in the film *Broken Blossoms,* written, directed, and produced by D. W. Griffith.

Charles Chaplin, Mary Pickford, Douglas Fairbanks, and D. W. Griffith founded the film company United Artists, which would become a major force in the growing industry.

Ernst Lubitsch produced and directed the German film *Madame Dubarry (Passion),* starring Pola Negri and Emil Jannings.

Ethel Barrymore starred on Broadway in Zoë Akins's play *Déclassé,* a story set in English society.

George White produced the first revue in his series *George White's Scandals* (1919-1926).

win an eight-hour workday (Sept. 1919-Jan. 1920). The industry would not be organized until the 1930s.

A strike of Boston, Massachusetts, police officers was broken by the State Guard, called out by the city administration and Governor Calvin Coolidge. All strikers were dismissed, and Coolidge's national reputation soared.

American boxer Jack (William Harrison) Dempsey won the world heavyweight title (1919-1926), defeating Jess Willard; Dempsey was dubbed the "Manassa Mauler" after his Colorado birthplace.

French tennis player Suzanne Lenglen won her first of six women's singles titles at Wimbledon (1919-1923; 1925).

Glenn Hammond Curtiss opened the first flying school; his NC-4 "flying boat," one of many airplanes built for the U.S. Navy during World War I, made the first transatlantic crossing.

Italian-American financier Charles Ponzi built a financial pyramid on promises to pay investors a 50 percent profit; he did so at first, but from the money paid in by new investors, until the scheme collapsed (1920); Ponzi was sent to prison and later was deported to Italy.

The Radio Corporation of America (RCA) was founded; David Sarnoff, employed there that year, became its general manager (1921), then president (1930), building a major radio and television empire.

British aviator John William Alcock, with Arthur Brown navigating, made the first nonstop transatlantic flight (June 14), flying from Newfoundland to Galway (Ireland) in 16 hours 28 minutes, winning a £10,000 prize offered by Britain's *Daily Mail.* Alcock would die a month later on a flight to Paris, but

1919 cont.

Vladimir Illich Lenin founded the Third, or Communist, International (the Comintern) (1919-1943), consisting of all the world's Communist Parties; it would become an instrument of Soviet foreign policy and an operational means of controlling the world's Communist Parties.

Revolution in Hungary set up the Hungarian Socialist Republic, led by Béla Kun (Mar.). Hungarian forces attacked Czechoslovakia (Mar. 28) but were defeated by Romanian and Czech forces, the Romanians then taking Budapest and destroying the Kun government (Aug. 4).

In Germany, the Workers' Party was founded; it would become the Nazi Party (National Socialist German Workers' Party).

The Communist Party of the United States was founded, as one of two parties that split away from the Socialist Party; both splinters would become a single Communist Party (1920).

In Italy, Gabriele D'Annunzio formed a private military force, taking and briefly holding disputed Fiume in 1921; his force was expelled by the Italian army.

Greek forces prematurely took Smyrna from the Turks and marched unopposed farther into Thrace and Anatolia, expecting major territorial concessions in the postwar period, as did initially occur in 1920.

In *Schenck v. United States,* during the Red Scare of the time, the Supreme Court unanimously affirmed the Sedition Act conviction of an anti–World War I protester for disseminating antiwar leaflets, with Justice Oliver Wendell Holmes creating the "clear and present danger" doctrine.

The pacifist and nonviolent Women's International League for Peace and Freedom (WILPF) was founded; among its leaders were Jane Addams and Emily Greene Balch.

Religious, nonviolent pacifists founded the International Fellowship of Reconciliation (IFOR); its members would include Mahatma Gandhi and Martin Luther King, Jr.

H. L. Mencken published *The American Language,* contending that American English was self-generating and unique, rather than merely being derived from British English, a novel view that many language "purists" sharply resisted.

The Milton Agar–Jack Yellen song "Happy Days Are Here Again" was introduced; it would later be used in the film *Chasing Rainbows* (1930) and be adopted as Franklin D. Roosevelt's campaign song (1932).

Jacinto Benavente's play *The Bonds of Interest* was the first production of New York's Theater Guild; Helen Westley starred opposite Dudley Digges.

Sherwood Anderson published the extremely well received midwestern short story collection *Winesburg, Ohio.*

Walter Gropius emerged as a major figure in the development of modern design as director of the Weimar Bauhaus (1919-1928).

Somerset Maugham published *The Moon and Sixpence,* inspired by the life of Paul Gauguin; it would be the basis for Albert Lewin's 1942 film.

Max Beckman painted his darkly bitter *The Night* in a style emblematic of his own and much other postwar German art.

Elmer Rice's play *Street Scene* opened in New York.

Swiss writer Carl Spitteler was awarded the Nobel Prize for literature.

b. (Jean) Iris Murdoch (1919-   ), British writer and philosopher who would emerge as a major figure with her novel *A Severed Head* (1961).

b. Doris Lessing (1919-), British novelist and short story writer whose work would often explore feminist concerns.

he had helped usher in the age of long-distance flight.

Britain's *R34* airship was the first dirigible to cross the Atlantic.

Herbert Hoover emerged as a major figure in international postwar relief efforts; his humanitarian role would help carry him into the U.S. presidency (1929).

John Maynard Keynes published *The Economic Consequences of Peace,* focusing on the negative consequences of the high war reparations being demanded of Germany.

Marcus Garvey founded the Black Star shipping line, meant to be the cornerstone of his "Back to Africa" movement.

St. Louis Cardinals field manager Branch Rickey developed the "farm system" in baseball, to prepare players for the major leagues.

Swiss theologian Karl Barth published *The Epistle to the Romans,* criticizing Germany's warlike stance.

The International Labor Organization (ILO) was established by the Covenant of the League of Nations; it would become a United Nations agency (1946).

The Permanent Court of International Justice, later the World Court, was established by the Covenant of the League of Nations.

Mary Dennett, head of the Voluntary Parenthood League, led a failed campaign for U.S. congressional passage of the Dennett bill, to legalize dissemination of birth control information (1919-1924).

Scheduled commercial air service began between London and Paris.

Disputing the terms of the Treaty of Versailles as anti-Chinese and pro-Japanese, student demonstrations in Beijing (Peking) (May 4) grew into the nationwide May 4th Movement.

b. Mohammed Reza Shah Pahlevi (1919-1980), shah of Iran (1941-1979); he would be deposed in the Iranian Revolution.

b. Evita Perón (Maria Eva Duarte) (1919-1952), Argentine politician, the wife of dictator Juan Perón.

d. Theodore Roosevelt (1858-1919), 26th president of the United States (1901-1909), who succeeded to the presidency after the assassination of William McKinley (1901). In 1912, he was the unsuccessful presidential candidate of the Progressive (Bull Moose) Party.

d. Emiliano Zapata (1883-1919), Mexican Indian revolutionary leader; assassinated while his forces still held southern Mexico.

d. Georgi Valentinovich Plekhanov (1856-1919), leading moderate Russian Marxist theoretician and politician; a Menshevik leader who returned from exile after the February 1917 revolution and fled into exile again after the Bolshevik Revolution, dying in Finland.

d. Louis Botha (1862-1919), South African Boer War guerrilla general; the first premier of the Union of South Africa (1910-1919).

d. Wilfrid Laurier (1841-1919), Canadian Liberal Party leader who was Canada's first French-Canadian prime minister (1896-1911).

b. J. D. (Jerome David) Salinger (1919-), American writer most noted for *The Catcher in the Rye* (1951).

b. Margot Fonteyn (Peggy Hookam) (1919-1991), who would become the most celebrated of British ballerinas; late in her career, she would often be partnered with Rudolf Nureyev.

b. Pete Seeger (1919-), American folksinger, composer, and instrumentalist; he would survive blacklisting during the McCarthy period to become a world figure in folk music.

b. Vera Lynn (Vera Welch) (1919-), British singer who in World War II became the "Forces Sweetheart" with her signature song "We'll Meet Again."

b. Merce Cunningham (1919-), leading American dancer and choreographer.

b. Sam Wanamaker (1919-1993), American actor who would be blacklisted during the McCarthy period and would become prime mover in the rebuilding of Shakespeare's Globe Theatre.

b. Jennifer Jones (Phyllis Isley) (1919-), American film star.

d. Pierre-Auguste Renoir (1841-1919), French painter; a leading impressionist.

d. Julian Alden Weir (1852-1919), American painter.

d. Leonid Andreyev (1871-1919), Russian writer.

d. Adelina Patti (1843-1919), Italian soprano.

Regular radio broadcasts were begun in The Hague.

b. Jackie (Jack Roosevelt) Robinson (1919-1972), African-American baseball player who would break the color line in major league baseball (1947) and, by so doing, in American major league sports.

b. Edmund Percival Hillary (1919-), New Zealand–born explorer and ambassador who, with Tenzing Norgay, would reach the top of Mount Everest (1953).

d. Andrew Carnegie (1835-1919), Scottish-American industrialist; head of the Carnegie Steel Company, he became a major philanthropist, founding the Carnegie Endowment for International Peace (1910) and the philanthropic Carnegie Corporation (1911), as well as more than 2,500 libraries in the United States, Canada, and Britain.

Poland and Russia were at war (Apr.-Oct.). Initial Polish and Ukrainian successes were reversed by a Soviet counteroffensive, but Polish forces defeated Soviet forces at the decisive Battle of Warsaw (Aug. 16-25), then moved into southern Russia, while Simon Petlyura's nationalist forces took the Ukraine, initiating massive anti-Jewish pogroms. An armistice ended the war (Oct. 12), while the Treaty of Riga (Mar. 18, 1921) provided substantial Polish territorial gains.

Republican Warren G. Harding defeated Democrat James M. Cox to become the 29th president of the United States (1921-1923). Socialist presidential candidate Eugene V. Debs, imprisoned for his opposition to World War I, received more than 900,000 votes.

Bolshevik forces defeated Alexander Kolchak's White army in Siberia and Peter Wrangel's White army in the Crimea, then crossed the Caspian Sea to attack northern Persia.

The 19th (Woman Suffrage) Amendment to the U.S. Constitution, the Anthony Amendment, was ratified, giving women the vote; Tennessee was the necessary 36th state (Aug. 26). Its single-issue fight won, the National American Woman Suffrage Association (NAWSA) dissolved, to be succeeded by the League of Women Voters (LWV).

Ch'en Tu-hsiu and Peking University librarian Li Ta-chao founded the Communist Party of China (CCP) (May).

d. Venustiano Carranza (1859-1920), Mexican president; he was killed by the forces of General Alvaro Obregón during Obregón's successful coup attempt, which ended the Mexican Civil War.

Mahatma Gandhi led another massive Indian satyagraha (nonviolence) campaign.

Mustapha Kemal (Atatürk) formed a new Turkish provisional government, swiftly moving against Greek and allied forces that had occupied large portions of western Turkey, including Constantinople.

American astronomer Vesto Melvin Slipher first observed the "red shift," the apparent movement of starlight toward the red (longer wavelength) end of the electromagnetic spectrum; this was another confirmation of Albert Einstein's general theory of relativity (1915).

British physicist James Jeans first proposed the "steady state" theory, suggesting that the universe is expanding and new matter is continually being created to form new stars and galaxies.

American astronomer Andrew Ellicott Douglass developed a dating system (by 1920) he called dendrochronology, based on observed patterns of tree rings. These records of annual growth vary distinctively year by year, as Douglass had noted over many years of studying evidence of sunspot activity in the American Southwest. Matching patterns from living and dead trees, researchers would be able to establish dates back more than 3,000 years, making it an important archaeological tool.

American physicist Albert Abraham Michelson first measured the diameter of a star, Betelgeuse, using an interferometer, a device he had designed to cancel out ("interfere with") certain lines in rays of light, allowing for measurement.

Based on observations taken at Norwegian weather stations during World War I, father and son meteorologists Vilhelm Friman Koren Bjerknes and Jacob Aall Bonnevie Bjerknes introduced the notion that weather patterns are dominated by warm and cold air masses "battling" along fronts, terminology inspired by the recent war.

American astronomers Harlow Shapley and Heber Doust Curtis were the leading figures in

Eugene O'Neill's first major play, the powerfully realistic New England–set *Beyond the Horizon,* opened in New York, with Edward Arnold and Richard Bennett as two brothers and Helen MacKellar as the woman they both love.

Constantin Brancusi carved the wooden sculpture *Endless Column,* created for Edward Steichen's garden in Paris.

Marcel Proust published *The Guermantes Way,* the third part of his *Remembrance of Things Past.*

Sinclair Lewis emerged as a major American literary figure with the publication of his satirical novel *Main Street,* pillorying midwestern small-town life and attitudes.

Charles S. Gilpin starred in the title role of Eugene O'Neill's play *The Emperor Jones,* a role later identified with Paul Robeson's stage (1925) and screen (1933) portrayals.

Constructivism became a considerable force in modern architectural theory. Vladimir Tatlin created his highly influential constructivist design for the proposed but never built *Monument to the Third International,* and brothers Naum Gabo and Antoine Pevsner published their influential *Realistic Manifesto.*

D. H. Lawrence published the autobiographical novel *Women in Love.* His frankness on sexual matters was still rather shocking to contemporary British society. In 1969, almost half a century later, Glenda Jackson and Alan Bates would star in Ken Russell's film version.

Edith Wharton published *The Age of Innocence,* her Pulitzer Prize–winning satirical novel set in affluent New York society in the 1870s; it would be the basis for the 1993 film.

The population of the earth continued to grow, reaching an estimated 1.85 billion people, even with the massive multiple impacts of world war, famine, and disease.

Fridtjof Nansen, head of Norway's delegation to the League of Nations, headed League and International Red Cross programs (1920-1923) to repatriate prisoners of war and resettle displaced persons, who received a special identity card dubbed a "Nansen passport."

The National Football League was formed by George Halas, founder and later coach of the Chicago Bears, and others; it would become a major force in sports, with its championship Super Bowls (from 1967, with the American Football League) massive events in American life. Jim Thorpe was named president during the league's first year. The league's first Black coach was Fritz (Frederick Douglass) Pollard, at Akron, Ohio.

Baseball player Babe (George Herman) Ruth was traded from the Boston Red Sox to the New York Yankees; the fabled home run hitter would lead the Yankees to seven league pennants and five World Series championships before retiring in 1935.

The Volstead Act, enforcing the 18th (Prohibition) Amendment, went into effect (Jan. 16), and the Prohibition era began (1920-1933).

French boxer Georges Carpentier won the world light heavyweight championship (1920-1922), eventually fighting in all the major boxing divisions, from flyweight to heavyweight; he was credited with attracting many women fans to boxing.

Massive earthquakes in Gansu, China, took the lives of 150,000 to 200,000 people in one of the worst natural disasters of the century.

Regular radio broadcasts were established in Montreal, Canada, and Pittsburgh, Pennsylvania, where

1920 cont.

U.S. attorney general A. Mitchell Palmer conducted the Palmer Raids (Jan. 2), mass arrests of more than 4,000 alleged subversives throughout the country, some of whom, including anarchists Emma Goldman and Alexander Berkman, were deported, though most were not even brought to trial or were acquitted.

Adolf Hitler joined Germany's Workers' Party, later the Nazi Party.

In Germany, Wolfgang Kapp led a failed right-wing German Freikorps coup attempt, the Kapp Putsch.

The storm troopers (SA) organization was founded by Ernst Roehm; its terrorist tactics would later contribute to Nazi victory in Germany.

The paramilitary Haganah was organized by Palestinian Jews; it would become the Israeli army.

The Treaty of Dorpat (Oct.) recognized Finnish and Estonian independence.

The post–World War I Treaty of Trianon (June 4) provided for Hungarian territorial losses and reparations.

The Arab independence movement rising in Iraq was suppressed by British occupation forces (July).

French forces in Syria decisively defeated Faisal's forces, taking Damascus (July) and forcing Faisal into exile.

Hungarian regent Miklós Horthy openly took power as dictator (1920-1944).

South-West Africa (Namibia), formerly German Southwest Africa, became a League of Nations mandate territory under South African control.

Soviet forces withdrew from Latvia by the terms of the Treaty of Riga (Aug.). Latvia became an independent state.

The Treaty of Moscow (July) recognized Lithuanian independence.

a notable debate over the Andromeda nebula, with Shapley arguing that Andromeda was part of or near our own galaxy and Curtis proposing that it was a distant nebula.

Yugoslavian physicist Milutin Milankovich proposed the still-controversial theory that, due to a tilted axis and an eccentric orbit, the earth undergoes a 40,000-year cycle of weather changes, with a 10,000-year spring, summer, fall, and winter, the latter leading to ice ages.

Amateur French mathematician Eugène Olivier Carissan reported his development of the first known successful automated mechanical factoring machine, designed to identify any whole prime numbers (factors) that, if multiplied together, will produce a given number; an early example of "number sieve" technology. Lost after his death (1925), it was rediscovered, in working order, only in the 1990s.

American pathologist George Whipple proved, through experiments with dogs, that a liver diet could be used to treat anemia in animals.

German physical chemist Walther Hermann Nernst received the Nobel Prize for chemistry for his work on thermodynamics, notably the heat theorem (1906).

b. Denton Arthur Cooley (1920-   ), American cardiologist who would do key early work in open-heart surgery, developing a heart-lung bypass machine (1955) and implanting the first artificial heart in a human being (1969).

b. Rosalind Elsie Franklin (1920-1958), British molecular biologist and physical chemist.

d. William Crawford Gorgas (1854-1920), American physician who supervised the mosquito eradication program (1904-1913) that allowed the Panama Canal to be built without widespread yellow fever deaths.

Ernest Hemingway published the novel *A Farewell to Arms,* a love story set on the Italian front during World War I; it would be the basis for the 1930 Laurence Stallings play and two films (1932; 1957).

Jerome Kern's Broadway musical *Sally* starred Marilyn Miller in the title role, singing "Look for the Silver Lining."

Sergei Diaghilev's Ballets Russes presented Leonid Massine's *Pulcinella,* music by Igor Stravinsky, with Tamara Karsavina and Massine dancing the leads.

Czech author Jaroslav Hasek began publication of his four-volume satirical novel *The Good Soldier Schweik* (1920-1923), a monumental attack on bureaucracy.

Fanny Brice introduced her signature song, "My Man," in the *Ziegfeld Follies of 1920.*

Katherine Mansfield published her short story collection *Bliss and Other Stories.*

The landscape artists of Canada's Group of Seven began to exhibit their works together.

Lillian Gish and Richard Barthelmess starred in the film melodrama *Way Down East,* directed and produced by D. W. Griffith.

Sigrid Undset began publication of her trilogy of historical novels, *Kristin Lavransdatter* (1920-1922).

Norwegian writer Knut Hamsun was awarded the Nobel Prize for literature.

b. Federico Fellini (1920-1993), Italian director and screenwriter; a leading figure in world cinema; the husband of Giulietta Masina.

b. Giulietta (Giulia Anna) Masina (1920-1994), Italian actress best known for her Gelsomina in *La*

station KDKA started broadcasting with the returns from the Harding-Cox presidential election.

Roger Baldwin, Jane Addams, and Helen Keller founded the American Civil Liberties Union (ACLU), with Baldwin as the first director (1920-1950).

Marcus Garvey's "Back to Africa" movement flourished; he became provisional president of the African Republic at a New York Universal Negro Improvement Association (UNIA) convention.

The Gotham Book Mart, New York's famous bookstore, was founded by Ida Frances Steloff; for decades, it would be notable for its authors' receptions and for championing books banned elsewhere.

Coco Chanel introduced the chemise dress, most notable of the loose, low-waisted 1920s styles, free of corsets and other constrictions.

The first coast-to-coast airmail flight was made in the United States; the age of commercial flight was fast developing.

b. John Paul II (Karol Wojtyla) (1920-   ), Polish priest and outspoken anticommunist who would become the first Polish pope (1978-   ); one of the leading conservative popes of the century.

b. James Leonard Farmer (1920-   ), American pacifist and civil rights activist; founder of the Congress of Racial Equality (CORE) (1942).

b. Sugar Ray Robinson (Walker Smith) (1920-1989), American boxer.

d. Max Weber (1864-1920), German political economist and social scientist, whose work helped lay the foundation for modern sociology.

d. Robert Edwin Peary (1856-1920), American explorer who, after several failed attempts, led the first party to reach the North Pole (1909).

1920 cont.

The Treaty of Sèvres (Aug. 10) imposed harsh post–World War I conditions on Turkey; the new Turkish provisional government refused to accept the treaty, ultimately going to war and forcing a new treaty.

The kingdom of Serbs, Croats, and Slovenes and Italy renounced their claims to Fiume in the Treaty of Rapallo (Nov. 12), making it a free city.

Woodrow Wilson was awarded the Nobel Peace Prize.

b. Eduardo Mondlane (1920-1969), founder of FRELIMO (Mozambique National Liberation Front) (1962) and its leader early in the Mozambican Revolution.

b. Javier Pérez de Cuéllar (1920-   ), Peruvian diplomat and fifth secretary-general of the United Nations (1982-1992).

b. Farouk I (1920-1965), king of Egypt (1936-1952).

b. Mohammed Siad Barre (1920-1995), Somali dictator (1969-1991).

b. Mujibur Rahman (1920-1975), Bangladesh independence movement leader; the first president of Bangladesh (1971-1975).

d. Alexander Vasilievich Kolchak (1874-1920), Siberian White commander during the Russian Civil War; captured by Bolshevik forces and executed.

1921

Adolf Hitler became leader of the Nazi Party, formerly the Workers' Party.

Italian Blackshirts, a fascist paramilitary militia, began to take control of the streets; a year later, they were to "march" on Rome with Benito Mussolini.

Physician Frederick Banting and physiologist Charles Best, both Canadians, led the team that first extracted insulin and then developed the basic insulin-injection treatment for diabetes (1922). Banting and laboratory head John J. R. Macleod, but not Best, would receive the 1923 Nobel Prize for physiology or medicine.

Strada (1954), directed by her husband, Federico Fellini.

b. Isaac Stern (1920-   ), American violinist who would emerge as one of the world's leading violinists.

b. Ravi Shankar (1920-   ), Indian sitar player and composer who would introduce Indian music to the world.

b. Charlie "Bird" Parker (Charles Christopher Parker, Jr.) (1920-1955), American jazz saxophonist, composer, and bandleader; a founder of bebop.

b. Mickey Rooney (Joe Yule, Jr.) (1920-   ), American stage and screen actor for seven decades; son of vaudeville star Joe Yule.

b. Toshiro Mifune (1920-   ), Japanese actor who would become an international film star in Akira Kurosawa's *Rashomon* (1950).

d. John Silas Reed (1887-1920), American journalist and communist; author of *Ten Days That Shook the World* (1919); he fled into Russian exile to avoid a charge of sedition and died there.

d. Amedeo Modigliani (1884-1920), Italian painter and sculptor.

Marcel Proust published *Cities of the Plain,* the fourth part of his *Remembrance of Things Past.*

Pauline Lord created the title role of the former prostitute in Eugene O'Neill's classic play *Anna Christie,* which quickly became a staple in the world repertory. A year earlier, then titled *Chris Christopherson* and starring Lynn Fontanne, it had failed in

American boxer Jack Dempsey's successful defense of his world heavyweight title against French challenger Georges Carpentier was the first boxing match to draw more than $1 million in gate receipts. Radio became a sports medium with the broadcast of a blow-by-blow live report of the fight, to an audience estimated at 300,000.

1921 cont.

Japanese prime minister Takashi Hara (Hara Kei) (1856-1921) was killed by a right-wing assassin; part of the run-up to the Japanese military dictatorship of the 1930s.

In Shanghai, the Communist Party of China held its first Congress, electing Ch'en Tu-hsiu party head; Mao Zedong was a delegate.

A cease-fire (July 11) ended the Irish War of Independence; Ireland was partitioned between the Irish Free State and Northern Ireland. In the brief civil war that followed (1921-1922), Irish Free State government forces defeated Irish Republican Army elements who refused to accept the peace settlement; some of the latter then continued as guerrilla fighters.

The French-Moroccan war reignited, as Abd el-Krim led Moroccan independence movement forces against the French and Spanish.

Greek forces scored early victories in the Greek-Turkish War, taking substantial parts of western Turkey before being defeated at the Sakkaria River (Aug. 24-Sept. 16).

Mongolia became a de facto Soviet protectorate after being taken from White Russian forces by Soviet and Mongolian forces (June-July).

Nicola Sacco and Bartolomeo Vanzetti, both anarchists and foreign-born Italian-Americans, were convicted of participation in the murders of two people during a 1920 Braintree, Massachusetts, robbery, and sentenced to death; their trial was conducted under conditions of extreme prejudice.

Palestinian Arab leader Haj Amin al Husseini was appointed grand mufti of Jerusalem by the British; Arab-Jewish conflicts intensified.

Red Army units led by Leon Trotsky and General Mikhail Tukhachevsky crushed a rebellion by Bolshevik sailors at the Kronstadt naval base, near St. Petersburg.

Alexander I became king of the Kingdom of Serbs, Croats, and Slovenes (later Yugoslavia), ruling as a constitutional monarch.

The existence of an atomic particle with no electric charge — later named a neutron — was first proposed by William Draper Hawkins; it would be discovered by James Chadwick (1932).

American petroleum geologist Esther Applin proposed that analysis of microfossils could provide information on oil-bearing geological formations. Initially ridiculed, the idea laid the basis for the field of micropaleontology when Applin and others demonstrated its effectiveness (1925).

The magnetron, a microwave-producing electron tube, was developed by American physicist Albert W. Hull; it would be a significant aid in radar during World War II.

French mathematician Emile Borel first suggested the possibility of game theory: mathematical analysis of conflict situations using parlor games as a model, with players trying to maximize gain and minimize loss; later developed by John von Neumann (1928; 1944).

Swiss psychiatrist Carl Jung published *Psychological Types,* positing that individuals could be classified as either introverts or extroverts.

Leaded gasoline, designed to prevent the too-explosive "knocks" that bedeviled automobile engines, was developed by American chemist Thomas Midgley, Jr. Only decades later, when cars became widespread sources of pollutants, would it be realized that the lead was poisoning the environment.

Swiss psychiatrist Hermann Rorschach developed a test using mirror-image inkblots — abstract images that a patient is asked to characterize — as a nonverbal aid to diagnosing a person's psychological condition.

tryouts. It generated two film versions (1923; 1930) and a Broadway musical (1957).

Sergei Prokofiev conducted the Chicago premiere of his opera *The Love for Three Oranges*. Also in Chicago, he played the premiere performance of his *Piano Concerto No. 3*.

Karel Capek introduced the term *robot* in his play *Rossum's Universal Robots (RUR)*, from the Czech word *robota* (slave or forced labor). Robots would become a science fiction staple.

Lottie Gee sang "I'm Just Wild About Harry," music by Eubie Blake and lyrics by Noble Sissle, in *Shuffle Along*, by far the most successful African-American musical of its time and Broadway's first all–African-American musical.

Max Shreck starred in the title role in F. W. Murnau's classic film *Nosferatu, the Vampire*.

Rudolph Valentino starred in George Melford's extraordinarily popular film *The Sheik*. He played the desert prince and romancer opposite Agnes Ayres. Valentino also starred in Rex Ingram's film version of Vicente Blasco Ibáñez's 1916 novel *The Four Horsemen of the Apocalypse*.

Greta Garbo starred opposite Lars Hanson in Mauritz Stiller's classic film *Gösta Berling's Saga*, based on Selma Lagerlöf's novel (1891).

Anita Loos and John Emerson wrote, and Victor Fleming directed, the feminist film *Woman's Place*, starring Constance Talmadge as a political leader.

Fanny Brice introduced "Second Hand Rose" in the *Ziegfeld Follies of 1921*.

French writer Anatole France (Jacques Thibault) was awarded the Nobel Prize for literature.

b. Alicia Alonso (Alicia Ernestina Martinez Hoyo) (1921-), Cuban dancer; long artistic director and prima ballerina of Cuba's national ballet company.

Vladimir Illich Lenin established the Soviet New Economic Policy (NEP) (1921-1928), providing some incentives to develop small-scale consumer goods industries.

Margaret Sanger founded the American Birth Control League (from 1942, the Planned Parenthood Federation of America) to help spread birth control information, establish clinics, and inform women of doctors who were willing to dispense contraceptive devices.

Marie Stopes founded Britain's first birth control clinic, winning a libel suit against one opponent who accused her of a "monstrous crime" in disseminating birth control information.

American tennis player Bill Tilden won the first of his six U.S. men's singles titles (1921-1925; 1929) and also the second of his three singles titles at Wimbledon (1920; 1921; 1930).

German-American linguist and anthropologist Edward Sapir published *Language*, stressing the necessity of studying language within its cultural context; his work helped lay the basis for both structural linguistics and ethnolinguistics.

Emanuel Lasker's record 27-year reign as the world chess champion (1894-1921) came to an end when he lost to Cuban chess master José Raúl Capablanca y Graupera, who would hold the title for 6 years.

Film comedian Roscoe "Fatty" Arbuckle was charged with the rape and death of Hollywood starlet Virginia Rappe, who died from a burst bladder after his Labor Day weekend party; after two hung juries led to mistrials, he was acquitted on a manslaughter charge, but his career was ruined.

Knud Rasmussen was the first to trace the Northwest Passage, from Greenland west to Point Barrow, Alaska, by dogsled (1921-1924).

1921 cont.

In Persia (Iran), General Reza Khan (Shah Reza Pahlevi), commander of the Cossack Brigade, deposed Ahmad Shah and took power by coup.

Socialist Victor Berger, his sedition conviction overturned by the U.S. Supreme Court, again won election to the House of Representatives and this time was seated.

Iraq became a British protectorate, with Faisal installed by the British as king.

b. Alexander Dubček (1921-1992), Slovak communist politician; a leading Czechoslovak reformer who as head of the government would initiate the Prague Spring (1968).

b. Seretse Khama (1921-1980), first president of Botswana (1966-1980).

b. Suharto (1921-   ), Indonesian general; second president of Indonesia (1966-   ).

b. Daniel Berrigan (1921-   ), American Catholic priest and a leading opponent of the Vietnam War.

b. Jean Bédel Bokassa (1921-   ), Central African Republic military dictator (1966-1979).

b. Virgilio Barco Vargas (1921-   ), Colombian politician; president of Colombia (1985-1990).

German-American pharmacologist Otto Loewi discovered that chemicals are produced when nerves, notably the vagus nerve, are stimulated. He isolated such a substance, calling it Vagusstoff, and found that it could, by itself, produce effects normally triggered by nerves. He soon found that the substance was acetylcholine, previously discovered by Henry Dale (1914).

Albert Einstein was awarded the Nobel Prize for physics for his explanation of the photoelectric effect (1905); astonishingly, his work on relativity (1905; 1915) and the momentous equation $E = mc^2$ were not mentioned.

British chemist Frederick Soddy won the Nobel Prize for chemistry for his discovery of isotopes (1913).

b. Andrei Dmitriyevich Sakharov (1921-1989), Soviet nuclear physicist; later a leading dissident.

b. John Herschel Glenn, Jr. (1921-   ), American aviator and astronaut who would be the first American to orbit the earth (1962); a much-decorated pilot in World War II and Korea and a test pilot, he would later be a Democratic senator from Ohio (1974-   ).

1922

Benito Mussolini took power in Italy; he was appointed premier by King Victor Emmanuel III after Fascist Party Blackshirts had "marched" on Rome (Oct. 24), meeting no opposition from the government or army.

The Teapot Dome scandal began; U.S. Secretary of the Interior Albert M. Fall took $400,000 in bribes for leases on federal oil reserves in Teapot Dome, Wyoming, and Elk Hills, California.

British archaeologist Leonard Woolley began his excavations at Ur (1922-1934), in Mesopotamia (southern Iraq), home of the biblical Abraham, revealing for the first time the scale and significance of the Sumerian civilization, which invented writing. He also uncovered evidence for a great flood (ca. 2800 BC), which presumably inspired the Sumerian epic *Gilgamesh,* itself the possible inspiration for the biblical story of Noah and the ark.

1921 cont.

b. Satyajit Ray (1921-1992), Indian director and filmmaker; creator of *Pather Panchali* (1955), *Aparajito* (1956), and *The World of Apu* (1959).

b. Alex Palmer Haley (1921-1992), American writer.

b. Joseph Papp (Joseph Papirovsky) (1921-1991), American producer and director.

b. Simone Signoret (Simone Kaminker) (1921-1985), French actress.

b. Yves Montand (Ivo Livi) (1921-1991), French actor and singer.

b. James Jones (1921-1977), American author.

d. Camille Saint-Saëns (1835-1921), French composer, pianist, and organist.

d. Enrico Caruso (1873-1921), Italian opera star; the leading tenor of his time.

d. Alexander Blok (1880-1921), Russian symbolist poet.

d. Georges Feydeau (1862-1921), French playwright.

More than 1,000 people died when a gas generator explosion in a chemical plant destroyed much of Oppau, Germany (Sept. 21).

Sixteen-year-old Margaret Gorman became the first "Miss America."

British-American psychologist William McDougall published *Is America Safe for Democracy?* which was widely criticized for proposing the superiority of the "Nordic race."

Near Hull, England, a British dirigible broke apart in midair (Aug. 24), killing 62 people.

The steamer *Hong Kong* ran aground off China (Mar. 18), killing 1,000 people.

b. Betty Goldstein Friedan (1921-   ), American feminist; author of *The Feminine Mystique* (1963) and founder and first president of the National Organization for Women (NOW) (1966).

b. Louis Harris (1921-   ), American public-opinion analyst; a leading pollster from the mid-1950s.

d. (Sarah) Emily Davies (1830-1921), British feminist, suffragist, and educator; founder and leader of Henslow House (1867) and its successor, Cambridge's Girton College for women (1874).

1922

James Joyce published the seminal modernist novel *Ulysses,* in which he used the relatively new "stream-of-consciousness" technique, a great deal of richly textured language, and much Greek mythic resonance while exploring the inner journeys of Leopold Bloom and Stephen Dedalus on a single day in Dublin. The book considerably affected the development of the modern novel; it also was banned for "obscenity" in several countries, becoming "legal" in the United States only in 1933.

The British Broadcasting Corporation (BBC) was founded; it later became a public corporation (1927), funded by transmitter and receiver licensing fees, soon broadcasting to Europe and the Commonwealth. As its first general manager, then director (1922-1938), John Reith helped keep the quasi-public BBC independent and set standards of excellence in programming that would have international influence.

Germany became the first major country to recognize the Soviet Union, the countries normalizing relations with the Treaty of Rapallo.

d. Walter Rathenau (1867-1922), German industrialist; foreign minister of the Weimar Republic; assassinated by German rightists (June 24) who had attacked him as a Jew and a communist for his normalization of relations with the Soviet Union.

Oswald Spengler published *The Decline of the West,* calling democracy decadent, urging Germans to end the Weimar Republic, and helping supply the ideological underpinning for fascism.

The Russian Civil War ended with the departure of Japanese forces from Siberia.

In China, Sun Yat-sen reorganized the Kuomintang along Soviet Bolshevik Party lines and with Soviet advisers.

The Turkish counteroffensive led by Mustapha Kemal (Atatürk) routed the Greek army, which fled in disorder to Smyrna; Smyrna was then taken by the Turks (Sept.), who massacred tens of thousands, many of them civilians.

The Irish Free State became an independent nation; it was to become the Republic of Ireland (1937).

d. Michael Collins (1890-1922), Irish Republican leader, chief negotiator of the 1921 peace treaty that ended the Irish War of Independence and partitioned Ireland, and commander of Irish Free State forces in the subsequent Irish Civil War; he died in an ambush (Aug. 22).

American troops left the Rhineland.

Britain, China, France, Japan, Italy, Belgium, the Netherlands, Portugal, and the United States completed the Washington Conference (Nov. 1921-Feb. 1922), signing a group of agreements aimed at setting national boundaries and spheres of influence in east Asia and the Pacific, and also agreeing to limitations on naval force expansion.

British archaeologists Howard Carter and George Herbert, earl of Carnarvon, uncovered the tomb of Tutankhamen (King Tut), dating to the mid-1300s BC, which Carter excavated after Carnarvon's death (1923). Unlike most tombs, which had been largely cleaned out by robbers, Tutankhamen's yielded a storehouse of artifacts, sparking both professional and popular interest in Egyptian archaeology.

To initial derision, German chemist Hermann Staudinger proposed the existence of "macromolecules," now called polymers, composed of smaller molecules linked together in long chains. When heated, the chains disentangle, giving moldability, but retain their chemical bonds, and so their cohesiveness; these are characteristics of both synthetic polymers, such as plastics, and natural polymers, such as silicon.

Russian biochemist Alexander Ivanovich Oparin advanced the controversial theory that life developed spontaneously — without divine intervention — out of nonliving chemical compounds present naturally in the earth's early environment.

In nutritional studies using specially limited diets for animals, American physiologists Herbert McLean Evans and K. S. Bishop discovered evidence of another vitamin, later determined to be vitamin E (1938). Evans also showed that an extract from the pituitary gland induced greater-than-normal growth, early evidence for the existence of the human growth hormone, found in 1956.

Diabetes was first successfully treated by injections of newly extracted insulin (1921).

Scottish bacteriologist Alexander Fleming isolated the human enzyme lysozyme, the first natural bactericide recognized in the human body.

Film documentarian Robert Flaherty wrote, directed, shot, and edited his classic study of Eskimo life, *Nanook of the North,* setting a standard for documentarians throughout the balance of the century.

T. S. Eliot published his long poem *The Waste Land,* a key modernist work, technically and thematically, although its burden of negativism was to be thrown off by the poet himself a few years later with his move to the Anglican faith.

Frank Lloyd Wright completed the Imperial Hotel, Tokyo, designing it to withstand substantial earthquakes.

German novelist Hermann Hesse published *Siddhartha,* his protagonist a mystical Brahmin truth seeker carrying the birth name of the Buddha; the 1973 Conrad Rooks film version starred Shashi Kapoor.

Lillian and Dorothy Gish starred as the sisters severed by fate in D. W. Griffith's film epic *Orphans of the Storm,* set before and during the French Revolution.

Roger Martin du Gard began publication of *The Thibaults* (1922-1940), his massive eight-volume fictional study of two brothers in the Europe that would be destroyed by the Great War.

Sinclair Lewis published the novel *Babbitt,* again satirizing midwestern life and attitudes, this time in the fictional city of Zenith.

Romain Rolland began publication of his seven-volume fictional biography *The Soul Enchanted* (1922-1933).

Helen Menken and George Gaul starred as the ultimately reunited lovers in Austin Strong's drama *Seventh Heaven,* the basis for the 1927 film.

In a sensational, widely publicized case, Reverend Edward Wheeler Hall and Eleanor Mills, a choir singer who was his sexton's wife, were found murdered (Sept. 16), their bodies intertwined and the scene littered with their love letters to each other. Hall's wealthy older wife, Frances Stevens Hall, her two brothers, and a cousin were later acquitted of the crime (1926), leaving the murders unsolved.

North America's sole surviving herd of wood bison, nearly exterminated by hunting, was protected with the establishment of the 17,300-square-mile Wood Buffalo National Park in northern Alberta and the Northwest Territories, Canada.

Ernest Bevin founded and headed the British Transport and General Workers Union (TGWU).

James "Cool Papa" Bell began his career as an outfielder with the African-American St. Louis Stars, that year hitting .417; long after his 25-year career was over, he would be honored by election to the Baseball Hall of Fame (1974).

Coco Chanel introduced her famous perfume Chanel No. 5.

Fridtjof Nansen was awarded the Nobel Peace Prize for his postwar relief work (from 1920); he donated his award money to further relief efforts.

The International Council for Bird Preservation (ICBP) was founded, becoming a key organization in the worldwide fight to protect birds, their migration routes, and their habitats.

Pioneer Alpine skier Arnold Lunn introduced the slalom race to skiing.

The first paid advertisement was broadcast on radio (July 2).

1922 cont.

Egypt nominally became an independent state, though in fact it remained a British protectorate until 1952.

British forces defeated a Kurdish rising in Iraq (1922-1924).

The British imprisoned Mahatma Gandhi (1922-1924), who emerged from prison with considerably diminished influence.

b. Norodom Sihanouk (1922-   ), king of Cambodia (1941-1955), prime minister (1955-1960), president (1960-1970), and again king (1993-   ).

b. Yitzhak Rabin (1922-   ), Israeli general, army chief of staff (1964-1968), and prime minister (1974-1977; 1992-   ); a leading figure in efforts to bring peace to the Middle East.

b. Julius Kambarage Nyerere (1922-   ), Tanzanian independence movement leader; first president of Tanganyika (1962-1964) and then of Tanzania (1964-1985); a leading African statesman.

b. Ahmed Sékou Touré (1922-1984), first president of Guinea (1958-1984).

b. Augustinho Neto (1922-1979), leader of the Popular Movement for the Liberation of Angola (1957-1979) and the People's Republic of Angola (1974-1979).

b. George Stanley McGovern (1922-   ), South Dakota liberal Democratic senator (1963-1981); he was defeated by Richard M. Nixon in the 1972 presidential election.

b. Mark Odum Hatfield (1922-   ), American liberal Republican politician; Oregon governor (1959-1967), U.S. senator (1967-   ), and a leading opponent of the Vietnam War.

b. Tun Abdul Razak (1922-1976), Malaysian lawyer and politician.

d. Christiaan Rudolph De Wet (1854-1922), Boer general during the South African wars with the English, who became commandant general of Free State forces (1900).

Britain's Vickers Company developed the first revolving-turret tank.

The Japanese navy built the first ship designed specifically as an aircraft carrier; the British navy built a similar ship later in the year.

Niels Bohr received the Nobel Prize for physics for his basic model of atomic structure.

b. Christiaan Neelthing Barnard (1922-   ), South African surgeon who would perform the first human heart transplant (1967) and also design artificial heart valves.

d. Alexander Graham Bell (1847-1922), Scottish-American inventor who developed the telephone (1875) and made major improvements in other devices, including the telegraph and phonograph.

Katherine Mansfield published the short story collection *The Garden Party*.

With the completion of Daniel Chester French's monumental statue *Abraham Lincoln* in Washington, D.C., the Lincoln Memorial and the statue quickly became a national shrine.

Rudolph Valentino starred as the doomed bullfighter in the film *Blood and Sand,* becoming a major matinee idol.

Carl Sandburg published his collection of poems *Slabs of the Sunburnt West*.

Duke Ellington formed his jazz orchestra, which would be the model for many others.

Käthe Kollwitz sculpted *Father and Mother* in memory of her son, Peter, killed during World War I.

Spanish playwright Jacinto Benavente y Martínez was awarded the Nobel Prize for literature.

b. Judy Garland (Frances Gumm) (1922-1969), American actress and singer.

b. Alain Resnais (1922-   ), French "new wave" film director best known for his antiwar *Hiroshima, Mon Amour* (1959).

b. Jean-Pierre Rampal (1922-   , French flutist; from 1945, an international star who greatly popularized the flute.

b. Ava Gardner (1922-1990), American film star.

b. Charles Mingus (1922-1979), American jazz composer and bandleader; a leading bassist from the early 1940s.

Continuous hot-strip rolling steel production was developed by John B. Tytus for the American Rolling Mill Company.

b. Charles Schulz (1922-   ), American cartoonist who would create the comic strip *Peanuts* (1950).

b. Daisy Gatson Bates (1922-   ), Little Rock, Arkansas, newspaper publisher and civil rights leader; as president of the Arkansas chapter of the National Association for the Advancement of Colored People (NAACP), she would lead the historic fight to desegregate Little Rock Central High School (1957).

b. Pierre Cardin (1922-   ), French fashion designer noted for his elegant clothes and bright, attention-getting accessories.

b. Thomas Samuel Kuhn (1922-   ), American historian and sociologist of the development of scientific knowledge; best known for *The Structure of Scientific Revolutions* (1962).

d. Ernest Henry Shackleton (1874-1922), British explorer who made four expeditions to Antarctica, dying during the last.

d. Elizabeth Cochrane Seaman (Nellie Bly) (1865-1922), leading American investigative reporter.

d. Northcliffe (Alfred Harmsworth; Lord Northcliffe) (1865-1922), British press baron whose publishing empire included *The Times* of London, the *Daily Mail,* the *Evening Standard*, and much more.

1922 cont.

d. Erich von Falkenhayn (1861-1922), German general; World War I head of the general staff, whose tenure began after the first Battle of the Marne (1914) and ended after Verdun (1916).

1923

President Warren G. Harding died in office (Aug. 2); he was succeeded by Vice President Calvin Coolidge, who became the 30th president of the United States. Coolidge, as governor of Massachusetts, had become a leading figure in the Republican Party after breaking the 1919 Boston Police Strike. His term of office (1923-1929) was to be seriously marred by the Teapot Dome scandal, although he was never accused of having been personally involved.

German failure to pay reparations required by the Treaty of Versailles triggered occupation of the Ruhr by French and British forces.

Nazi forces in Bavaria mounted a failed coup (Nov. 8-11), the Beer Hall Putsch. Adolf Hitler was one of those jailed after the failure of the coup. He wrote the first volume of *Mein Kampf* while in prison.

By the terms of the Treaty of Lausanne and the Straits Convention, which replaced the postwar Treaty of Sèvres (1920), Turkey kept Turkish Armenia, Turkish Kurdistan, control of the Dardenelles, and other territories that had been ceded away in the earlier treaty. Mustapha Kemal became the first president of the Turkish republic (1923-1938).

American physicist Arthur Holly Compton recognized that X rays scattered by light have increased wavelengths (the "Compton effect"). To explain this, he proposed that light, thought to be wavelike, also behaved like a particle, or *photon*. Working independently and theoretically, French physicist Louis de Broglie posited that atomic particles should exhibit wavelike properties. The idea of wave-particle duality would be a key contribution to quantum theory, confirmed in 1927.

Scottish inventor John Logie Baird developed an experimental television with a rotating disk to convert light into electrical impulses; so did American inventor Charles Francis Jenkins.

Using Henrietta Swan Leavitt's observations about Cepheid variables (1912) and the 100-inch Mount Wilson telescope, American astronomer Edwin Powell Hubble resolved the controversy over the Andromeda nebula (1920), showing that it was at least 750,000 light-years away (later found to be much more). This led to the understanding that the

1922 cont.

b. Jason Robards (Jason Nelson Robards, Jr.) (1922-   ), American actor; the son of actor Jason Robards.

b. Kurt Vonnegut (1922-   ), American writer, best known for *Slaughterhouse-Five, or The Children's Crusade* (1969).

d. Marcel Proust (1871-1922), French writer, author of the seminal seven-part *Remembrance of Things Past* (1913-1927).

d. James MacDonald (1873-1922), Canadian northern landscape painter; a member of the Group of Seven.

1923

George Bernard Shaw's play *Saint Joan* premiered at New York's Theater Guild; Winifred Lenihan created the title role.

Robert Frost published his Pulitzer Prize–winning poetry collection *New Hampshire,* which included "Stopping By Woods on a Snowy Evening."

Sergei Diaghilev's Ballets Russes company premiered the ballet *Les Noces,* choreographed by Bronislava Nijinska, music by Igor Stravinsky.

Edna St. Vincent Millay's Pulitzer Prize–winning *The Harp-Weaver and Other Poems* established her as a major American poet.

Lon Chaney starred opposite Patsy Ruth Miller in the title role of the film *The Hunchback of Notre Dame*; Wallace Warsley directed.

Sean O'Casey began his emergence as a major playwright with Dublin's Abbey Theatre production of his first Irish Civil War play, *Shadow of a Gunman.*

A massive earthquake and subsequent fire destroyed most of Tokyo and Yokohama, killing 140,000, in one of the worst disasters of the century (Sept. 1).

In *Adkins v. Children's Hospital,* the U.S. Supreme Court struck down a federal minimum wage law for women workers in the District of Columbia, declaring that such special state protective laws were unconstitutional and, with woman suffrage having been gained, no longer needed.

Margaret Sanger founded the Birth Control Clinical Research Bureau, the first clinic staffed by doctors, to provide contraceptive information and devices such as vaginal diaphragms and lactic acid jelly.

Austrian-Jewish philosopher-theologian Martin Buber published his best-known work, *I and Thou,* exploring the relationships between humans, their world, and their God.

Finnish runner Paavo Nurmi set a new world record for the mile, at 4 minutes 10.4 seconds.

Marcus Garvey's "Back to Africa" movement fell with his personal fortunes, losing much of its

Libya's Senussi people, led by Omar Mukhtar, were at war with Italian occupation forces, which mounted an eight-year genocidal war against the Senussi.

With Soviet advisory assistance, China's Sun Yat-sen founded the Kuomintang's Whampoa Military Academy and began to prepare for the Northern Expedition (1926-1928).

d. Alexander Stambollisky (1879-1923), Bulgarian Agrarian Party prime minister; he was assassinated during a right-wing coup.

General Miguel Primo de Rivera led a military coup in Spain, becoming dictator (1923-1930).

Lithuanian forces occupied Memel, on the Baltic coast and formerly part of Germany.

The Equal Rights Amendment (ERA) was first proposed, by Alice Paul, head of the National Woman's Party.

b. Henry Alfred Kissinger (1923-   ), Nixon administration foreign affairs adviser, U.S. secretary of state (1973-1976), and chief negotiator of American withdrawal from Vietnam (1973).

b. Robert Joseph Dole (1923-   ), Kansas Republican congressman (1961-1969) and senator (1969-   ); unsuccessful presidential nomination candidate (1980; 1988); Senate majority leader (1984-1986); minority leader (1986-1994); and Senate majority leader (1995-   ).

b. Linden Forbes Sampson Burnham (1923-1985), Guyanese politician who would become prime minister (1964-1980) and president of Guyana (1980-1985).

d. Francisco "Pancho" Villa (Doroteo Arango) (1878-1923), Mexican general; a major figure in the Mexican Revolution and Civil War. Though in retirement, he was assassinated.

universe is much larger than previously thought and contains many galaxies, such as Andromeda and our own Milky Way.

Sigmund Freud published *The Ego and the Id*, his fundamental work positing different levels of human consciousness: the unconscious primitive id, the conscious ego, and its "conscience," the superego.

George Dick and Gladys Dick, husband-and-wife partners, identified the streptococcus bacterium that causes scarlet fever and then developed the Dick skin test to diagnose it and a serum to treat it.

Spanish engineer Juan de la Cierva developed the Autogiro, a type of helicopter; after he founded a production company (1926), some Autogiros went into service in Europe and America.

Element 72 (hafnium) was discovered by Hungarian-Swiss chemist Georg Hevesy and Dutch physicist Dirk Coster.

Robert Millikan won the Nobel Prize for physics for his work in measuring the electron (1911).

b. Alan Bartlett Shepard, Jr. (1923-   ), American astronaut who would be the first American in space, aboard *Freedom 7* (1961).

Dudley Digges and Helen Westley starred in Elmer Rice's play *The Adding Machine,* produced by New York's Theater Guild.

Rudolf Klein-Rogge starred in Fritz Lang's classic German film *Dr. Mabuse, the Gambler.*

Khalil Gibran published his mystical work *The Prophet.*

Irish poet and playwright William Butler Yeats was awarded the Nobel Prize for literature.

b. Nadine Gordimer (1923-   ), South African writer who would be awarded the 1991 Nobel Prize for literature.

b. Marcello Mastroianni (1923-   ), Italian actor; an international star in films such as *La Dolce Vita* (1960) and *Yesterday, Today, and Tomorrow* (1963).

b. Dorothy Dandridge (1923-1965), American actress, singer, and dancer; a breakthrough African-American film star.

b. Joseph Heller (1923-   ), American writer best known for his *Catch-22* (1961).

b. Norman Mailer (1923-   ), leading American writer from the publication of his first novel, *The Naked and the Dead* (1945).

b. James Dickey (1923-   ), American poet and novelist.

d. Sarah Bernhardt (1844-1923), French actress; a leading figure of the French- and English-speaking theaters.

d. Katherine Mansfield (Kathleen Beauchamp-Murry) (1888-1923), New Zealand–British writer; with her husband, John Middleton Murry, part of the Bloomsbury Group. Her short story collection *The Dove's Nest* was published in the year of her death.

strength after his conviction and five-year prison sentence for Black Star shipping line stock fraud.

Pentecostal revivalist Aimée Semple McPherson, noted for preaching, faith healing, and "speaking in tongues" at tent revivals across North America, established the permanent Church of the Foursquare Gospel, based near Los Angeles.

The International Criminal Police Organization (INTERPOL) was organized as a worldwide crime control and information agency; most of the nations of the world ultimately joined.

American amateur golfer Bobby Jones won the U.S. Open, his first major tournament, at only 21.

British fashion designer Norman Bishop Hartnell opened his first dress shop, in London; he would be much favored by Britain's royalty through the 1950s.

Henry Robinson Luce and Briton Hadden founded *Time* magazine, the first magazine in what would become a substantial publishing empire.

b. Arthur R. Jensen (1923-   ), American educational psychologist best known for his controversial claim that Blacks are genetically inferior to Whites (1969)

b. (Ian) Robert Maxwell (Jan Ludwig Hoch) (1923-1991), Czech-British publisher and entrepreneur.

d. Vilfredo Frederick Damaso Pareto (1848-1923), Italian economist, sociologist, and mathematician.

d. Vladimir Illich Lenin (Vladimir Illich Ulyanov) (1870-1924), founder of the Bolshevik Party, leader of the Bolshevik Revolution of 1917, and chief 20th-century leader and theoretician of world communism. A struggle for succession began within the Soviet leadership, from which Joseph Stalin would emerge victorious, then going on to build the dictatorship that would cost the Soviet Union some tens of millions of lives.

Incumbent U.S. president Calvin Coolidge defeated Democrat John W. Davis and Progressive Robert M. La Follette, winning a full term.

After an eight-year occupation (1916-1924), American forces were withdrawn from the Dominican Republic.

In Brazil, an armed forces insurrection at São Paulo and a communist rising in the south led by Luis Carlos Prestes were both defeated by government forces. Prestes led the Prestes Column in a long march to Bolivian sanctuary.

Ho Chi Minh became a Comintern agent in China and Southeast Asia (1924-1941).

Ibn Saud's forces took Mecca (Oct. 13), as the long conquest of Arabia neared completion.

With the Fascist assassination of Italian socialist parliamentary figure Giacomo Matteotti, Benito Mussolini mounted intensified attacks on all Italian opponents and dissidents, consolidating his position as dictator.

In China, Chiang Kai-shek became head of the Whampoa Military Academy.

James Hertzog, an ultra-right-wing Afrikaner Boer War general, became National Party prime minister of South Africa (1924-1929).

Peruvian liberal Victor Haya de la Torre, then in Mexican exile, founded and was first head of the American Popular Revolutionary Alliance (APRA) (1924-1979).

In Britain, Winston Churchill became chancellor of the exchequer in Stanley Baldwin's cabinet (1924-1929).

Australian anatomist and physical anthropologist Raymond Dart, working in a cave near Taung, South Africa, discovered a fossilized skull of a species he named *Australopithecus africanus* (South African ape), calling it a "missing link" between humans and apes and proposing that humans developed in Africa. He also posited, from its anatomy, that the being walked on two legs, not four. Dart's theories were ridiculed by many but inspired others, notably Louis Leakey.

Russian-American inventor Vladimir Zworykin developed an electron-beam-scanning television, using a cathode-ray tube, which had less flicker than John Logie Baird's television (1923). Zworykin patented the two basic components of the modern television system: his iconoscope camera tube and kinescope picture tube.

British astronomer Arthur Eddington discovered that a star's luminosity is directly related to its mass and that stars are gaseous, with energy traveling to the surface by radiation, not convection; this work would be basic to the theory of stellar evolution.

British scientists Edward Appleton and M. F. Barnett discovered the ionosphere, an electrically charged atmospheric layer that fosters the transmission of long-distance radio waves; it was called the Heaviside or Kennelly-Heaviside layer, after those who had predicted its existence (1902).

American astronomer Annie Jump Cannon completed *The Henry Draper Catalogue*, classifying more than 200,000 stars, later expanded to 350,000, and laying the groundwork for much 20th-century astronomical research.

The gas chamber, involving the release of lethal gas in a closed box, was first used for an execu-

André Gide published the novel *Corydon,* his highly controversial, very direct attack on homophobia, triggering major attacks on the author and his work.

E. M. Forster published the novel *A Passage to India,* a perceptive exploration of problematic Indian-British cultural, ethnic, and personal relationships; by far his best-known work, it was used by David Lean as the basis for his 1984 film epic.

Paul Robeson and Mary Blair played the troubled interracial couple in Eugene O'Neill's groundbreaking, highly controversial play *All God's Chillun Got Wings,* his very direct attack on American racism.

André Breton published his *Manifesto of Surrealism,* the central work of the emerging movement. He would publish additional surrealist manifestos in 1930 and 1942.

Konstantin Stanislavsky published *My Life in Art,* a central work of the modern theater.

Sara Allgood starred as Juno Boyle opposite Barry Fitzgerald in Dublin's Abbey Theatre production of *Juno and the Paycock,* Sean O'Casey's second Irish Civil War play.

Constantin Brancusi carved the first versions of his sculpture series *The Fish* (1924-1930) and *The Cock* (1924-1949).

Herman Melville's final novel, *Billy Budd, Foretopman,* was published, 35 years after its completion and 33 years after his death.

The Captive, the fifth part of Marcel Proust's *Remembrance of Things Past,* was published posthumously.

Paul Whiteman conducted the New York premiere of George Gershwin's *Rhapsody in Blue.* On Broadway, the George and Ira Gershwin musical *Lady, Be*

In Chicago, Illinois, "thrill killers" Nathan Leopold and Richard Loeb murdered 14-year-old Robert Franks (May 22); Clarence Darrow's pioneering insanity defense would save both from the electric chair. Leopold would eventually be paroled (1958); Loeb would be killed in prison (1926).

American football player Red (Harold) Grange, dubbed the "Galloping Ghost," came to national attention with a five-touchdown performance, as his University of Illinois team upset undefeated Michigan. His turning professional (1925) generated a controversy that eventuated in the college draft system for athletes.

At the Paris Olympics, American swimmer Johnny Weissmuller won gold medals in three events; he would win two more in 1928, later becoming the star of Hollywood's Tarzan films. Finnish runner Paavo Nurmi, the "Flying Finn," won six gold medals — in the 1,500 meters, 3,000 meters, 5,000 meters, and individual and team events in cross-country; three other gold medals, from the 1920 and 1928 Olympics, would later bring his total to nine.

American entrepreneur Clarence Birdseye founded a company to develop his process for producing frozen foods; they would go on sale commercially in 1930, with ready-cooked frozen foods introduced by 1939.

The Dawes Plan, named after American banker Charles Dawes, supplied Germany with nearly 17 billion gold marks in international loans with which to pay World War I reparations; Dawes was awarded the 1925 Nobel Peace Prize.

Scottish educator and psychologist A. S. (Alexander Sutherland) Neill founded the highly experimental Summerhill School, self-governed by students.

Canadian ice-hockey center Howie (Howarth William) Morenz led his Montreal Canadiens to the

The Soviet government created the nominally independent Mongolian People's Republic, in actuality a fully controlled protectorate.

b. George Herbert Walker Bush (1924-   ), 41st president of the United States (1989-1993).

b. James Earl "Jimmy" Carter, Jr. (1924-   ), 39th president of the United States (1977-1981).

b. Apollo Milton Obote (1924-   ), Ugandan independence movement leader; first prime minister of the Ugandan republic (1962-1966) and then president and dictator (1966-1971).

b. Kenneth David Kaunda (1924-   ), Zambian politician, prime minister, and president (1963-1991).

b. Robert Gabriel Mugabe (1924-   ), leader of the Zimbabwe African National Union (ZANU) (1975-   ); first prime minister (1980-1985) and first president (1985-) of the Republic of Zimbabwe.

b. Mario Alberto Nobre Lopez Soares (1924-   ), Portuguese socialist politician; president of Portugal (1986-   ).

b. Mohammad Zia Ul-Haq (1924-1988), Pakistani military dictator (1977-1988).

b. Ahmadou Ahidjo (1924-   ), Cameroon politician; first president of the Republic of Cameroon (1960-1982).

b. Shirley Anita St. Hill Chisholm (1924-   ), African-American Democratic politician; the first Black woman member of the House of Representatives (1969-1983).

d. (Thomas) Woodrow Wilson (1856-1924), 28th president of the United States (1913-1921), whose tenure saw American participation in World War I, the first federal income tax law, and establishment of the Federal Reserve System. He was a primary mover at the Paris Peace Conference of 1919, but the Senate refused to ratify the Treaty of Versailles.

d. Robert Georges Nivelle (1856-1924), French World War I general whose failed, very costly Nivelle Offensive (1917) triggered massive French army mutinies.

tion, at Nevada State Prison in Carson City; it had been developed by Major D. A. Turner of the U.S. Army Medical Corps as a more "humane" alternative to executions than the electric chair (used since 1890) and hanging. During World War II, the Germans would put the gas chamber to horrific use in mass killings.

Indian physicist Satyendra Nath Bose developed statistical approaches for mathematically describing and predicting the actions of subatomic particles (from 1924); with improvements by Albert Einstein, these would be called the Bose-Einstein statistics.

Russian-British biochemist David Keilin theorized that cells contained a substance that absorbed oxygen, calling it *cytochrome.*

Otto Rank published *The Trauma of Birth,* in Paris and then New York, developing a therapy that focused on reliving the birth trauma.

Polish-American Freudian psychoanalyst Helene Deutsch theorized that women were subjugated to the penis, which she regarded as superior to the clitoris in terms of power and pleasure.

Hermann Oberth's influential book *The Rocket into Interplanetary Space* was published, exploring scientific research in space and introducing the idea of escape velocity.

Good! starred Fred and Adele Astaire, introducing the song "Fascinatin' Rhythm"; another song, "The Man I Love," was cut and would become popular later.

Erich von Stroheim's silent film *Greed,* based on Frank Norris's 1899 novel *McTeague,* stared ZaSu Pitts, Gibson Gowland, and Jean Hersholt.

Thomas Mann published the novel *The Magic Mountain,* set in a tuberculosis sanitarium that was a metaphor for pre–World War I European society.

Walter Huston, Mary Morris, and Charles Ellis starred in Eugene O'Neill's classic play *Desire Under the Elms.* A 1958 film version of the Pulitzer Prize–winning play starred Sophia Loren, Anthony Perkins, and Burl Ives.

Gertrude Lawrence introduced "Limehouse Blues" in *Charlot's Revue,* costarring with Beatrice Lillie.

Polish novelist Wladyslaw Reymont was awarded the Nobel Prize for literature.

b. James Arthur Baldwin (1924-1987), leading African-American novelist, playwright, and essayist.

b. Marlon Brando (1924-), American actor who would emerge as a major theater figure upon creating the Stanley Kowalski role in *A Streetcar Named Desire* (1947); he would later create Don Vito Corleone in the film *The Godfather* (1972).

b. Sidney Poitier (1924-), American actor and director; a breakthrough African-American film star.

d. Giacomo Puccini (1858-1924), Italian composer; a leading figure in opera for works such as *Manon Lescaut* (1893), *La Bohème* (1896), *Madame Butterfly* (1904), and *The Girl of the Golden West* (1910).

d. Franz Kafka (1883-1924), Austrian-Czech writer; a major figure in world literature.

first of three Stanley Cup championships (1924; 1930; 1931); his popularity sped expansion of the game in the United States.

British tennis player Kitty (Kathleen) McCane defeated Helen Wills (later Moody) to win the women's singles title at Wimbledon; she would win again as Kitty Godfree (1926).

Disposable paper handkerchiefs — Celluwipes, later called Kleenex — were introduced by Wisconsin's Kimberly-Clark.

Little Orphan Annie was created by cartoonist Harold Gray.

b. William Hubbs Rehnquist (1924-), American lawyer who would be appointed to the U.S. Supreme Court by President Richard M. Nixon (1971); he would become a leading conservative on the Court and would later be appointed chief justice by President Ronald Reagan (1986).

b. William Sloane Coffin, Jr. (1924-), American minister; while Yale University chaplain in the 1960s, he would be a leading anti–Vietnam War protester.

d. Samuel Gompers (1850-1924), founder and first president of the American Federation of Labor (AFL) (1886-1894; 1896-1924); an advocate of craft and economic unionism, he had strongly and rather successfully resisted industrial unionism and highly political unionism, as epitomized by the Industrial Workers of the World (IWW), the Socialist Party, and the European labor and socialist parties.

Antiforeign feeling mounted in China; British troops fired into a Shanghai demonstration, killing 12 Chinese (May 30), and 50 Whampoa Military Academy cadets died in an armed clash with the British and French (June 23). "May 30th Movement" demonstrations flared throughout China (1925-1926).

For his publicly voiced criticism of American air war backwardness, aviator William "Billy" Mitchell was court-martialed and dismissed. His criticism continued, and included a prediction of a Pearl Harbor–like attack.

The Locarno Treaties (Oct. 5-16) provided for continuing demilitarization of the Rhineland and reaffirmed the French- and Belgian-German borders set by the Treaty of Versailles. Germany would later repudiate the treaties (1936), reoccupying the Rhineland.

Ahmed Bey Zogu led a republican revolution in Albania; a republic was established, headed by Zogu (1925-1928).

American forces intervened on the Conservative side against the Liberals in a Nicaraguan civil war.

Druse rebels in southern Syria scored early successes in the first year of the Druse Rebellion (1925-1927).

Kurdish forces, their post–World War I independent state canceled by the Treaty of Lausanne, mounted a failed insurrection in Turkey, then went over to low-level guerrilla war.

The Arabian Civil War ended with the defeat of the Hashemite forces of Hussein Ibn Ali by those of Ibn Saud.

b. Margaret Roberts Thatcher (1925-   ), Britain's first woman prime minister, who would become the longest-serving British prime minister of the century (1979-1990).

b. Robert Francis Kennedy (1925-1968), American politician, brother of President John F. Kennedy and Senator Edward M. Kennedy; he would be assassinated in Los Angeles (June 5, 1968).

Austrian-American physicist Wolfgang Pauli formulated the exclusion principle — that each electron occupies a unique state in an atom. Dutch-American physicists Samuel Goudsmit and George Eugene Uhlenbeck theorized that electrons must have an intrinsic spin, a fundamental understanding.

Australian-British archaeologist Vere Gordon Childe published *The Dawn of European Civilization*, developing the broad outlines of early cultural development in Europe and western Asia (especially in the third and second millennia BC) and helping to lay a scientific basis for archaeology.

American electrical engineer Vannevar Bush began developing the first analog computer (1925-1930). Unlike later digital computers, which use discrete numbers and on-off signals, the analog computer works with continuous variables, such as voltage or temperature. Later versions, called network analyzers or differential analyzers, would be used in settings such as electrical power networks and telephone systems.

The Mid-Atlantic Ridge was discovered by a German expedition using sonar to map the ocean floor; it would give support to the continental drift theory.

German physicist Werner Heisenberg developed matrix algebra, or matrix mechanics, for mathematical work on the quantum theory.

British mathematician Alfred North Whitehead published his widely popular *Science and the Modern World*.

Alice Hamilton, pioneer in industrial medicine, published her landmark *Industrial Poisons in the United States*.

Sergei Eisenstein created his classic film *The Battleship Potemkin,* his view of the sailors' mutiny on the battleship *Potemkin* during Russia's 1905 revolution, noted for the scene showing the massacre on the Odessa steps.

Franz Kafka's landmark novel *The Trial* was published posthumously, although he had instructed his executor to destroy all of his unpublished work.

Louis Armstrong, Lillian Hardin Armstrong, Kid Ory, Johnny Dodds, and Johnny St. Cyr, recording in Chicago as The Hot Five, began to cut their classic jazz recordings (1925-1927).

The Sweet Cheat Gone, part six of Marcel Proust's *Remembrance of Things Past,* was published posthumously.

The art deco style, a commercial version of art moderne, was introduced to wide audiences at the Paris Exposition, bringing modern forms and materials definitively into the popular docorative arts.

Theodore Dreiser published the novel *An American Tragedy,* a bitterly critical look at American society based on the Gillette-Brown murder case. It would generate two film versions (1931; 1951), the latter titled *A Place in the Sun.*

Charles Chaplin wrote, directed, produced, and starred as "The Tramp" in *The Gold Rush.*

Ezra Pound began publication of *The Cantos* (1925-1972), his long, complex, obscure poetic work, unfinished at his death.

F. Scott Fitzgerald published *The Great Gatsby,* his searching look at some newly rich Americans in postwar, pre-Depression Long Island.

Sinclair Lewis published *Arrowsmith,* about a young doctor choosing between money and his ideals in medicine.

In the celebrated Scopes "monkey trial," Tennessee biology teacher John T. Scopes was indicted under state law for teaching evolution rather than literal creationism. Scopes was defended by Clarence Darrow and prosecuted by William Jennings Bryan, who "won" a minor conviction but, as a practical matter, lost the case to Darrow in the public view after massive world media coverage. Bryan died five days after the trial. The film *Inherit the Wind* (1960) fictionally re-created the trial. Christian fundamentalists revived the issue later in the century.

The Ku Klux Klan, which had gained much strength outside the South during the postwar period, mounted a large demonstration in Washington, D.C., with an estimated 40,000 in the line of march.

African-American labor leader A. Philip Randolph organized the Brotherhood of Sleeping Car Porters and was its first president (1925-1968).

British airplane designer Geoffrey De Havilland introduced his famous Moth series of light aircraft.

Factory ships began to be used in whaling; their use would intensify the commercial exploitation of whales, leading some species to the brink of extinction — notably, by the mid-1960s, the blue whale, fin whale, and sei whale.

The Appalachian Trail Conference (ATC) was founded to develop the Appalachian Trail, proposed by one of the founders, Benton MacKaye; after the trail's completion (1937), the ATC would assist the people and organizations that maintained the trail and lands nearby.

Fourteen people died when the U.S. Navy dirigible *Shenandoah* broke up in a storm near Caldwell, Ohio.

b. Malcolm X (Malcolm Little) (1925-1965), Black Muslim leader who would become a national figure

b. Idi Amin (Idi Amin Dada Oumee) (1925-), Ugandan military dictator (1971-1979) whose reign was notable for its multiple brutalities.

b. Anastasio Somoza Debayle (1925-1980), Nicaraguan dictator (1963-1979).

d. Sun Yat-sen (1866-1925), leader of the Chinese Revolution and founder of the Republic of China, who led the revolutionary movement (1894-1911), was the first (provisional) president of the republic (1911-1912), and founded the Kuomintang (1914).

d. William Jennings Bryan (1860-1925), American lawyer, orator, and populist politician; three times a failed presidential candidate (1896; 1900; 1908); a fundamentalist Christian, he died five days after "winning" the Tennessee antievolution Scopes trial. His "Cross of Gold" speech at the 1896 Chicago Democratic National Convention was a landmark in American political oratory.

d. Friedrich Ebert (1871-1925), German socialist politician; first president of the Weimar Republic, from 1919 until his death.

d. Robert Marion La Follette (1855-1925), American reform politician; Wisconsin governor (1900-1906) and senator (1906-1925); as an unsuccessful Progressive Party presidential nominee (1924), he received 5 million votes, though carrying only Wisconsin.

Austrian-American physician Joseph Goldberger isolated vitamin B_2, or riboflavin; it would be synthesized for medical use by 1935.

British physicist Patrick Blackett took the first photographs of an atom disintegrating under bombardment.

American physicist Robert Millikan gave the name *cosmic rays* to radiation from outer space.

Element 75 — named rhenium, after the Rhine River — was discovered by German chemists Walter Noddack and Ida Tacke (later Noddack).

The Vienna Psychoanalytic Institute was founded to foster the theories of Sigmund Freud; Helene Deutsch was director (1925-1933) and Anna Freud secretary (1925-1938).

Harold Ross founded *The New Yorker* magazine; it would become a formative influence in the work of many American writers.

Josephine Baker opened in Paris in *La Revue Nègre,* scoring a smash hit that established her as a star in Europe.

Lon Chaney starred in Rupert Julian's classic film *The Phantom of the Opera.*

Irish-British playwright and critic George Bernard Shaw was awarded the Nobel Prize for literature.

b. Richard Burton (Richard Walter Jenkins) (1925-1984), Welsh-British stage and screen star whose films would include *Becket* (1964) and *Who's Afraid of Virginia Woolf?* (1966).

b. (Mary) Flannery O'Connor (1925-1964), American southern novelist and short story writer.

b. Yukio Mishima (Hiraoka Kimitake) (1925-1970), Japanese writer noted for *The Sailor Who Fell from Grace with the Sea* (1965).

b. Rock Hudson (Roy Scherer) (1925-1985), American actor.

b. Robert Rauschenberg (1925-   ), American pop artist and assemblage maker.

d. John Singer Sargent (1856-1925), American painter, long resident in Britain; a leading 19th-century portraitist, later a muralist.

in the early 1960s; he would be assassinated soon after splitting with the Nation of Islam to found New York's Muslim Mosque (1965).

b. Medgar Wiley Evers (1925-1963), African-American civil rights leader; militant state chairman of the Mississippi National Association for the Advancement of Colored People (NAACP) when murdered by racist Byron De la Beckwith.

b. Frantz Omar Fanon (1925-1961), Martinican Black Marxist theoretician, writer, and psychiatrist who would become best known for *The Wretched of the Earth* (1961), his book advocating leftist peasant revolutions.

In China, Kuomintang forces, at that time including the Communists, drove north from Canton, taking Hankow, Nanking, and Shanghai in the first phase of the Northern Expedition (1926-1928).

In Russia, Joseph Stalin succeeded in removing several of his major rivals from positions of power, including Grigori Zinoviev and Lev Kamenev.

In Morocco, the forces of independence leader Abd el-Krim surrendered to the French and Spanish, ending the Rif War (1921-1926).

Jósef Pilsudski seized power by military coup in Poland (May 12-14), then became de facto dictator (1926-1935).

d. Simon Vasilievich Petlyura (1879-1926), Ukrainian nationalist; he was assassinated in Paris, probably as an act of revenge for his institution of massive pogroms in the Ukraine during the Russian Civil War and Russo-Polish War.

Joseph Goebbels became leader of the Berlin Nazi Party organization.

The Mexican government sharply curtailed Catholic Church privileges in Mexico; government forces repressed a Catholic (Cristero) insurrection (1926-1929).

A military coup in Portugal ended the first Portuguese republic.

Hirohito became emperor of Japan.

b. Elizabeth II (Elizabeth Alexandra Mary) (1926-   ), queen of the United Kingdom (1952-   ).

b. Fidel Castro Ruz (1926-   ), Cuban communist leader; ruler of Cuba beginning in 1959.

b. Valéry Giscard d'Estaing (1926-   ), French conservative politician; president of France (1974-1981).

b. Bob (Harry Robbins) Haldeman (1926-1993), White House chief of staff (1969-1973) who resigned (1973) and was later imprisoned for Watergate-related offenses.

American physicist Robert Goddard launched the first liquid-propellant rocket (Mar. 16), a four-foot missile that reached a height of 200 feet; a key event in the history of flight.

Austrian physicist Erwin Schrödinger developed the Schrödinger wave equation describing the wavelike behavior of subatomic particles; German physicist Max Born contributed a set of equations using probability theory in describing the wave-particle dual existence of atomic particles. With Werner Heisenberg's matrix algebra (1925), these would provide the necessary mathematical underpinning for what would become known as quantum mechanics, vital to 20th-century chemistry and nuclear physics.

John Logie Baird first publicly demonstrated his television.

American physiologist Walter Bradford Cannon coined the term *homeostasis* to refer to the ability of an organism to establish physiological equilibrium through feedback.

American physician George Minot and his assistant, William Murphy, first treated anemia in humans with a diet high in liver.

American biochemist James Batcheller Sumner was the first person to isolate an enzyme (urease) in a crystalline — and therefore nearly pure — form; he confirmed that enzymes are proteins.

Building on Jacobus Kapteyn's observation of star streams moving in opposite directions (1904), Swedish astronomer Bertil Lindblad proposed that the galaxy was rotating, an idea later developed independently by Dutch astronomer Jan Hendrik Oort.

Italian physicist Enrico Fermi developed statistical techniques for describing and predicting

Isaak Babel emerged as a major Soviet literary figure with the publication of his powerful, honest, and very popular short story collection *Red Cavalry,* based on his own Red Army civil war experiences. His honesty was to bring him death in a Soviet prison.

Sean O'Casey's third Irish Civil War play, *The Plough and the Stars,* was produced by the Abbey Theatre in Dublin. The classic work was met by rioting in the streets, protesting O'Casey's honest portrayal of some revolutionaries.

Fritz Lang created his landmark German science fiction film *Metropolis;* his technological nightmare would profoundly influence the work of generations of filmmakers.

After a court fight, Constantin Brancusi's sculpture *Bird in Space* was admitted into the United States as an artwork rather than as a taxable, otherwise unidentifiable imported chunk of metal.

Ernest Hemingway published *The Sun Also Rises,* his romantic novel about young Americans of the interwar "Lost Generation" in Europe.

Eva Le Gallienne founded the Civic Repertory Theater in New York (1926-1933).

George and Ira Gershwin's musical *Oh, Kay!* opened on Broadway, with Gertrude Lawrence singing "Someone to Watch Over Me."

Jelly Roll Morton organized his Red Hot Peppers jazz band.

Carl Sandburg published *Abraham Lincoln: The Prairie Years.*

A. A. Milne created Winnie-the Pooh.

Italian writer Grazia Deledda was awarded the Nobel Prize for literature.

Richard E. Byrd and his copilot Floyd Bennett made the first flight over the North Pole by airplane (May 9); Roald Amundsen, Lincoln Ellsworth, and Umberto Nobile also flew over the North Pole, in a dirigible; both claims were later disputed.

The British Trades Union Congress called a general strike (May 4-12) in support of a miners' union strike. Government troops, police, and large numbers of volunteers quickly broke the general strike; the miners' strike was later defeated (Aug.).

American amateur golfer Bobby Jones won both the British Open and the U.S. Open, becoming the first to hold both titles at once.

American boxer Gene (James Joseph) Tunney upset Jack Dempsey to take the world heavyweight title.

The first woman to swim the English Channel, Gertrude Ederle, set a new record time of 14 hours 39 minutes.

A troop ship on maneuvers in China's Yangtze River exploded and sank (Oct. 16), killing 1,200 people.

Accompanied by enormous and very skeptical media attention, revivalist Aimée Semple McPherson disappeared; she turned up a month later in Mexico, claiming to have been kidnapped, then resumed her touring career.

Helen Wills (later Moody) began to dominate women's tennis, winning 31 titles (1926-1938), including 7 U.S. and a then-record 8 Wimbledon singles titles.

In *Ideal Marriage: Its Physiology and Technique,* Theodor H. Van de Velde openly discussed sexual activity, notably suggesting a focus on foreplay and simultaneous orgasm, a shift in sexual attitudes.

Britain's Morris Motors introduced the MG (Morris Garage).

1926 cont.

b. José Napoleon Duarte Fuentes (1926-1990), president of El Salvador (1984-1989).

b. Lloyd Bentsen (1926-), American lawyer and Texas Democratic politician; vice-presidential candidate (1988) and Clinton administration treasury secretary (1993-1994).

d. Eugene Victor Debs (1855-1926), American labor leader and socialist politician; organizer of the 1894 Pullman Strike and five-time presidential candidate.

d. Felix Edmundovich Dzerzhinsky (1877-1926), organizer and head of the Soviet secret police, named in turn the Cheka, GPU, and OGPU, and later the NKVD and KGB.

d. Aleksei Alekseevich Brusilov (1853-1926), Russian general; a major figure in World War I for the Brusilov Offensive (1916) and the Second Brusilov (Kerensky) Offensive (1917).

d. Joseph Gurney "Uncle Joe" Cannon (1836-1926), Illinois Republican congressman and highly authoritarian Speaker of the House (1903-1911).

the action of subatomic particles with fractional spins, which could not be handled by Bose-Einstein statistics (1924); these were called Fermi-Dirac statistics after contributions from British physicist Paul Dirac.

b. Elisabeth Kubler-Ross (1926-), Swiss-American psychiatrist; a pioneer in supportive care for terminally ill patients and their families; best known for her *On Death and Dying* (1969).

1927

The Chinese Civil War (1927-1949) began with Kuomintang attacks on the Communists and their supporters in Shanghai (Apr. 12) and other cities; in Shanghai, victorious Kuomintang forces executed 5,000 to 6,000 of their opponents in the Shanghai Massacre. At Nanchang (Aug.), Communist forces were defeated in battle; Zhu De (Chu Teh) retreated to western Kiangsi with the remainder of his forces, where he would later establish the Kiangsi Soviet (1931-1934). Mao Zedong organized failed risings — the Autumn Harvest Uprisings — in the Yangtze River valley (Sept.) and then joined Zhu De in Kiangsi. Kuomintang forces defeated Communist forces in Canton (Dec.).

Belgian priest Georges Lemaître first proposed the "big bang" theory, suggesting that the universe began with the explosion of a highly condensed "atom," which he dubbed a *cosmic egg,* containing all mass, and that it has expanded continuously since then.

Canadian paleontologist Davidson Black and others discovered fossil remains of beings Black called *Sinanthropus pekinensis,* or Peking Man, perhaps 250,000 to 500,000 years old, at Zhoukoudian Cave, near Beijing (Peking),

1926 cont.

b. Marilyn Monroe (Norma Jean Mortenson) (1926-1962), American actress; an international film star and sex symbol.

b. Jack Kerouac (1926-1969), American writer who would become the foremost "Beat" novelist.

b. Colleen Dewhurst (1926-1991), American actress; a star in the theater from the late 1940s.

d. Claude Monet (1840-1926), leading French artist; a founder of impressionism.

d. Antonio Gaudí (1852-1926), Spanish architect; creator of Barcelona's landmark church of the Sagrada Familia (1884-1926), unfinished at his death.

d. Rudolph Valentino (Rodolfo Alfonzo Guglielmi) (1895-1926), Italian-American film star and celebrated sex symbol.

d. Mary Cassatt (1845-1926), American impressionist artist.

d. Rainer Maria Rilke (1875-1926), a leading 20th-century German-language poet.

International agreements to assign broadcasting wavelengths to each country's radio stations were reached.

The Book-of-the-Month Club was founded in the United States.

b. Michel Foucault (1926-1984), French philosopher and historian.

b. Ralph David Abernathy (1926-1990), African-American Baptist minister and civil rights movement leader.

d. Annie Oakley (Phoebe Anne Mozee; Moses) (1860-1926), American Western sharpshooter; long a fixture with Buffalo Bill's Wild West Show (1885-1901).

1927

Al Jolson starred in the historic film musical-melodrama *The Jazz Singer*, beginning the sound film era and opening a new period in world cultural history in which the screen forms would come to predominate, a process that was continuing as the next century approached.

Abel Gance created the epic film *Napoleon*, starring Albert Dieudonné; later "lost," it would be reconstructed and reshown in 1979.

American aviator Charles A. Lindbergh was the first to fly solo across the Atlantic (May 20-21), from New York to Paris in *The Spirit of St. Louis*, becoming an enormous world celebrity.

Henry Ford, under great pressure from other public figures, including U.S. presidents Woodrow Wilson and William Howard Taft, and threatened by massive boycotts and lawsuits, finally publicly apologized for the long-running series of anti-Jewish articles in his *Dearborn Independent*.

Chiang Kai-shek married Mei-ling Soong, consolidating his alliance with the powerful Soong family; as Madame Chiang Kai-shek, she became one of the world's best-known women.

In north China, Kuomintang forces defeated the forces of Manchurian warlord Chang Tso-lin.

Joseph Stalin moved closer to absolute power, expelling his chief opponent, Leon Trotsky, from the Communist Party.

After the failure of a worldwide clemency campaign, Nicola Sacco and Bartolomeo Vanzetti were executed by the state of Massachusetts (Aug. 23); they were to be exonerated half a century later.

Following a Senate investigation and a failed Justice Department cover-up, the Supreme Court nullified the Teapot Dome and Elk Hills oil leases, granted by Secretary of the Interior Albert W. Fall in return for $400,000 in bribes.

U.S. president Calvin Coolidge declared that he would not run for reelection in 1928; his successor would be Herbert Hoover.

Nicaraguan Liberal forces led by Augusto César Sandino developed a guerrilla war against the Conservative government and American occupation forces.

The Geneva naval limitation conference, initiated by President Calvin Coolidge and attended only by the United States, Great Britain, and Japan, failed to achieve any substantial agreements.

The Treaty of Tirana recognized formerly independent Albania as an Italian protectorate.

Syria's Druse Rebellion ended with the French defeat of the Druse.

b. Houari Boumedienne (Mohammed Boukharouba) (1927-1978), Algerian national movement leader who would rule Algeria absolutely (1965-1978).

China; the fossils were mysteriously lost during World War II, although casts had been taken.

Werner Heisenberg posited his "uncertainty principle," the revolutionary theory that a body's position and momentum could not be calculated simultaneously with full accuracy: the more accurate the one measurement, the less accurate the other. This troubling notion prompted Albert Einstein's comment, "God may be subtle, but He is not malicious."

American geneticist Hermann Joseph Muller first showed that X rays could cause mutations in genes and began a campaign to alert others, especially those working with radiation, to the danger.

American psychobiologist Curt Paul Richter first described and named the "biological clock" controlling internal biological cycles (biorhythms), which govern various behaviors in living things.

German physicists Fritz London and Walter Heitler developed the theory that chemical bonds result from shared or transferred electrons.

British physicists George Paget Thomson and Alexander Reid, among others, experimentally confirmed the dual wave-particle nature of electrons and other elementary particles posited earlier (1923).

Hungarian-American physicist Eugene Paul Wigner developed the concept of parity in nuclear physics: that is, in nature, there is no distinction between right and left. This theory was later disproved for some circumstances (1956).

The LD_{50} (median lethal dose) test, to find what dose of a substance kills half the test ani-

Time Regained, the seventh and final part of Marcel Proust's *Remembrance of Things Past,* was published posthumously.

Sinclair Lewis published the novel *Elmer Gantry,* set on the seamy side of Christian evangelism; it would be the basis for a 1960 movie.

Show Boat, the Oscar Hammerstein–Jerome Kern musical of Edna Ferber's 1926 novel, opened in New York, starring Howard Marsh, Norma Terriss, Helen Morgan, and Jules Bledsoe, who introduced "Ol' Man River."

Greta Garbo emerged as a Hollywood star opposite John Gilbert in Clarence Brown's *Flesh and the Devil,* the first of the four Garbo-Gilbert films.

Hermann Hesse published the novel *Steppenwolf,* pursuing the theme of artistic alienation in an inimical culture.

Martha Graham founded the School of Contemporary Dance, a central institution in the development of modern dance.

Janet Gaynor and Charles Farrell starred in Frank Borzage's film *Seventh Heaven,* based on the 1922 Austin Strong play.

The Academy of Motion Picture Arts and Sciences was founded, later best known for its Academy Awards (Oscars).

French philosopher Henri Bergson was awarded the Nobel Prize for literature.

b. Günter Grass (1927-), major German writer from the publication of his novel *The Tin Drum* (1959), a powerful satire set in the Nazi period.

b. Mstislav Rostropovich (1927-), leading cellist, pianist, and conductor who defected from the Soviet

New York Yankees baseball star Babe Ruth hit 60 home runs, a record that would not be broken until 1961.

Russian-French chess player Alexander Alekhine (Aleksandr Aleksandrovich Alyokhin) defeated José Raúl Capablanca y Graupera of Cuba for the world championship; he would hold it until his death (1946), except for a two-year period (1935-1937).

Charles Beard and Mary Ritter Beard began publishing their major four-volume work *The Rise of American Civilization* (1927-1939).

German philosopher Martin Heidegger published *Being and Time,* a study of the essence of being.

Japanese Buddhist philosopher Daisetsu Teitaro Suzuki published *Essays in Zen Buddhism* (3 vols., 1927-1934), the first of his works that did much to introduce Zen Buddhism to Westerners.

The Harlem Globetrotters all-Black basketball team was formed, created and coached by British-American social worker Abraham Saperstein in Chicago.

The U.S. Congress passed the second Radio Act to regulate broadcasting.

Marcus Garvey's five-year prison sentence was commuted; he was deported to Jamaica.

b. Althea Gibson (1927-), American tennis star who would become the first African-American player at the American Lawn Tennis Association championships (1950) and the first to win a championship at Britain's Wimbledon (1957).

b. Cesar Estrada Chavez (1927-1993), American farm worker who would, in the late 1960s, organize the United Farm Workers of America.

1927 cont.

b. Olaf Palme (1927-1986), Swedish politician and international peace negotiator.

b. Roy Marcus Cohn (1927-1986), American lawyer; chief assistant to Senator Joseph McCarthy (1953-1954), he would become one of the leading witch-hunters of the McCarthy period and later a powerful, corrupt, and ultimately disbarred corporate lawyer.

b. Ramsey Clark (1927-   ), American lawyer; as U.S. attorney general (1967-1969), a key figure in civil rights law enforcement; the son of Supreme Court justice Tom C. Clark.

b. Raúl Alfonsin Foulkes (1927-   ), Argentine lawyer and politician; president of Argentina (1983-1989).

mals, was developed by J. A. Trevan; used to establish standard medicinal doses, it would become highly controversial with the rise of the animal rights movement (from the 1970s).

German rocket enthusiasts founded the Society for Space Travel; among them was Wernher von Braun, who would by 1931 be leading rocket experiments that would bear fruit in World War II.

Austrian zoologist Karl von Frisch published *The Dancing Bees,* a fundamental work on animal communication.

Karl Landsteiner discovered two more blood groups: M and N.

b. R. D. (Ronald David) Laing (1927-   ), Scottish psychiatrist who would posit that schizophrenia was a reaction to an insane society (1960); a pioneer in communal treatment for schizophrenic patients (1965).

1928

Joseph Stalin took effective power in the Soviet Union, beginning the period of repression that would grow into the Great Purge of the 1930s, which would take the lives of millions. Simultaneously, he began his first Five-Year Plan (1928-1932), which mounted an attack on Soviet family farmers *(kulaks)* and would generate famine, accompanying disease, and the deaths of millions more.

Kuomintang forces completed the Northern Expedition, taking Beijing (Peking), defeating the northern warlords, and uniting much of China under republican rule; the civil war continued.

British physicist Paul Dirac first predicted the existence of antimatter, atomic particles of equal size but opposite electrical charge; specifically, he predicted the existence of the "antielectron," discovered by Carl David Anderson (1932) and named the positron.

(Henry) Havelock Ellis completed the publication of his seven-volume *Studies in the Psychology of Sex* (1897-1928); though branded by the courts a "filthy publication" and for years restricted to physicians, Ellis's work opened discussion of previously taboo topics and

Union (1974), later leading the National Symphony Orchestra in Washington, D.C.

b. Leontyne Price (1927-   ), American soprano; a breakthrough African-American opera star.

b. Marcel Ophüls (1927-   ), German-French director and documentarian; son of Max Ophüls.

b. Neil Simon (1927-   ), prolific American playwright working largely in comedy.

b. Bob Fosse (1927-1987), American dancer, choreographer, and director; a leading figure in dance theater.

b. George C. Scott (1927-   ), American stage and screen actor, director, and producer.

b. Kurt Masur (1927-   ), German conductor who would lead the New York Philharmonic from 1990.

d. Eugène Atget (Jean Eugène August Atget) (1856-1927), pioneering French photographer.

d. Isadora Duncan (1878-1927), American dancer and teacher; a key figure in modern dance.

b. Coretta Scott King (1927-   ), African-American civil rights leader and wife of Reverend Martin Luther King, Jr., who would work with him during his lifetime and afterward develop her own civil rights work.

b. Robert Heron Bork (1927-   ), American lawyer and judge; U.S. solicitor general during the Watergate affair; his 1986 Supreme Court nomination would be rejected by the Senate.

D. H. Lawrence published the novel *Lady Chatterley's Lover;* banned in many countries for its "obscenity," it became an underground classic.

Radclyffe Hall published *The Well of Loneliness,* on lesbian themes; it was banned in many countries as "obscene."

Sergei Eisenstein created the classic film *October (Ten Days That Shook the World),* based on John Reed's 1919 book. Censored by Stalin (he cut out Trotsky), it was first distributed uncensored in 1967.

Jack Dempsey lost his bid to regain the world heavyweight boxing title from Gene Tunney, who had been knocked to the floor but in a controversial "long count" was given an extra four seconds to recover, as the referee delayed the count until Dempsey retired to a neutral corner.

At Lake Okeechobee, in central Florida, flood conditions caused by a hurricane killed 2,000 to 2,500 people (Sept. 16-17).

Norwegian skater Sonja Henie (Henje) won the first of her 3 successive Olympic gold medals for ice-

Republican Herbert Clark Hoover defeated Democrat Alfred E. Smith to become the 31st president of the United States (1929-1933).

Women gained fully equal voting rights in Britain.

d. Alvaro Obregón (1880-1928), Mexican politician who took power by coup (1920), was president (1920-1924), and was later reelected president (1928); he was assassinated.

Ras Tafari, formerly regent, took power openly in Ethiopia, becoming king Haile Selassie I (1928-1930).

Under the Kellogg-Briand Pact (Aug. 27), 62 nations declared their intent to renounce war as an instrument of national policy; a practical nullity, as rising fascism and militarism would bring about a new world war.

b. Che Guevara (Ernesto Guevara de la Serna) (1928-1967), Latin American guerrilla general and theoretician; a major figure in the Cuban Revolution (1956-1959).

b. Hafez al-Assad (1928-   ), Syrian president and dictator (1971-   ).

b. Li Peng (1928-   ), Chinese communist politician; prime minister (1987-   ).

b. Mohammed Hosni Mubarak (1928-   ), Egyptian general who succeeded to the presidency after the assassination of Anwar al-Sadat (1981-   ).

b. Pol Pot (Tol Saut; Saloth Sar) (1928-   ), Cambodian communist; Khmer Rouge leader during and after the Cambodian Civil War and initiator of the Cambodian Holocaust.

b. Walter Frederick Mondale (1928-), American Democratic politician; Wisconsin senator (1964-1977), vice president (1977-1981), and failed Democratic presidential nominee (1984).

b. Mangosuthu Gatsha Buthelezi (1928-), South African Zulu leader; head of the Inkatha movement.

helped lay the foundation for sex education and birth control.

John Logie Baird demonstrated the first working color television and made the first transatlantic television transmission.

Scottish bacteriologist Alexander Fleming accidentally discovered the antibiotic penicillin while searching for another antibacterial substance; it would be refined later (1940).

Vitamin C was discovered and its structure determined by Hungarian-American biochemist Albert Szent-Györgyi and independently by American Charles King, who isolated it from lemon juice (1932).

Hungarian mathematician John von Neumann developed his minimax theory, first fruits of his exploration of the game theory originally proposed by Emile Borel (1921).

German chemists Otto Paul Hermann Diels and Kurt Alder developed a chemical reaction that could readily be used to induce atoms to form a ring; called the Diels-Alder reaction, or diene synthesis, this would be enormously useful to scientists studying organic compounds.

Margaret Mead published *Coming of Age in Samoa,* her exploration of sexual practices in a preindustrial society, which contributed to developing American acceptance of sexual diversity.

J. B. S. Haldane published his popular and influential book *Science and Ethics.*

b. James Dewey Watson (1928-   ), American molecular biologist who would codiscover the

Bertolt Brecht and Kurt Weill created the musical *The Threepenny Opera (Die Dreigroschenoper)*, based on John Gay's *The Beggar's Opera* (1728). Lotte Lenya and Rudolph Forster would star in G. W. Pabst's 1931 film version.

G. W. Pabst's classic film *Pandora's Box*, based on two Franz Wedekind plays, starred Louise Brooks as a free woman.

Luis Buñuel and Salvador Dali collaborated on the landmark short surrealist film *An Andalusian Dog (Un Chien Andalou)*.

Serge Lifar danced the title role in the Ballets Russes production of George Balanchine's *Apollo,* music by Igor Stravinsky.

Lynn Fontanne created the Nina Leeds role in Eugene O'Neill's Pulitzer Prize–winnng play *Strange Interlude.*

Stephen Vincent Benét published his Pulitzer Prize–winning epic poem *John Brown's Body,* on Civil War themes.

Mickey Mouse emerged as a world figure with the release of *Steamboat Willie,* the first cartoon to have a sound track.

Vsevolod Pudovkin created the innovative Russian Civil War epic film *Storm Over Asia (The Heir of Genghis Khan)*, starring Valery Inkishinikov in the title role.

Maria Falconetti starred in the title role of the film *The Passion of Joan of Arc,* written, directed, and produced by Carl Dreyer.

Selma Lagerlöf completed publication of her novel trilogy *The Ring of the Lowenskölds* (1925-1928).

Vladimir Mayakovsky's play *The Bedbug,* a satire of Soviet bureaucracy, contributed to his fall from official favor.

skating (1928; 1932; 1936); she also would be a 10-time world skating champion and later a film actress.

The Food, Drug, and Insecticide Administration supplanted the former Bureau of Chemistry in the Department of Agriculture (1906-1927), taking over the job of overseeing food safety. It would later become the Food and Drug Administration (1931).

Scotch tape (Sellotape) was introduced by Minnesota Mining and Manufacturing.

Plastics, originally Bakelite, first came into commercial use.

The collapse of the St. Francis Dam, in California's Santa Clara Valley, killed 450 to 700 people (Mar. 13).

A firedamp explosion in a Mather, Pennsylvania, mine killed 195 people (May 19).

French chef Georges Auguste Escoffier was the first of his profession to be awarded the French Legion of Honor.

British football (soccer) star Dixie (William Ralph) Dean ended the 1927-28 season with a record 60 goals in 39 matches, many scored with his head.

b. Noam Avram Chomsky (1928-   ), American linguistics scholar who would posit the view that underlying grammatical forms are inborn; also a prominent person of the Left, notably against the Vietnam War.

b. Hans Küng (1928-   ), Swiss theologian; the first notable modern Roman Catholic figure to question the doctrine of papal infallibility (1970).

b. Mary Daly (1928-   ), American radical feminist; a theologian who would lead in the development of spiritual feminism.

1928 cont.

b. Zulfikar Ali Bhutto (1928-1979), Pakistani lawyer and politician; founder of the Pakistan People's Party (1967) and the father of Benazir Bhutto.

b. Ariel Sharon (1928-   ), conservative Israeli politician.

d. Emmeline Pankhurst (1858-1928), cofounder and leader of the Women's Social and Political Union (WSPU) (1903) and head of the militant wing of the British woman suffrage movement.

d. Chang Tso-lin (1873-1928), Manchurian warlord (1913-1928); assassinated, probably by the Japanese; he was succeeded by his son, Chang Hsüeh-liang.

d. Herbert Henry Asquith (1852-1928), British barrister and Liberal prime minister (1908-1916).

d. Douglas Haig (1861-1928), British commander in chief in France (1915-1918); later a controversial figure because of the massive losses suffered by his command, as on the Somme (1916) and at Passchendaele (Third Ypres) (1917).

d. William Dudley "Big Bill" Haywood (1869-1928), leader of the Industrial Workers of the World (IWW) (1905-1928). He died in Soviet exile, having fled the United States in 1921 after a 1918 sedition conviction for opposing American participation in World War I.

double-helix form of the DNA molecule (1953), which bears basic genetic information.

b. Gerald Stanley Hawkins (1928-   ), British astronomer who would suggest that Stonehenge was an ancient observatory (1963).

Ford Madox Ford finished his quartet *Parade's End* (1924-1928).

Mikhail Sholokhov published his Russian tetralogy *The Quiet Don*.

Norwegian novelist Sigrid Undset was awarded the Nobel Prize for literature.

b. Gabriel Garcia Marquez (1928-   ), Colombian novelist and short story writer; a central figure in Latin American literature and winner of the 1982 Nobel Prize for literature.

b. Jeanne Moreau (1928-   ), French actress; from the 1950s, an international film star.

b. Carlos Fuentes (1928-   ), Mexican writer, critic, and diplomat; a leading Latin American literary figure.

b. Maya Angelou (1928-   ), African-American writer; a feminist and civil rights movement leader.

b. Helen Frankenthaler (1928-   ), American painter; a leading abstract expressionist.

d. Ellen Terry (1847-1928), a leading actress of the late-19th-century English theater, long associated with Henry Irving. She was the mother of stage designer Gordon Craig and the aunt of actor John Gielgud.

d. Thomas Hardy (1840-1928), English novelist and poet; a major figure in English literature.

d. Roald Engelbregt Amundsen (1872-1928), Norwegian explorer who led the first party to reach the South Pole (1911); he died searching for a colleague, Umberto Nobile, whose dirigible had crashed near Spitsbergen.

d. Floyd Bennett (1890-1928), American aviator who, with Richard E. Byrd, was the first to fly over the North Pole (1926); he died of pneumonia before a planned flight over the South Pole with Byrd.

d. George Washington Goethals (1858-1928), American army officer and chief engineer (1907-1913) overseeing construction of the Panama Canal, then governor of the Canal Zone (1914-1917).

India's Congress Party, led by Jawaharlal Nehru, began to call for full independence, emerging as the main force in the independence movement.

Heinrich Himmler became head of the Nazi SS (Schutzstaffel; Blackshirts), which would become the Nazi secret police organization and a key instrument of repression and mass murder.

In the Lateran Treaty, the Vatican recognized the Fascist government of Benito Mussolini, which in turn recognized Vatican sovereignty and established Catholicism as the Italian state religion.

Joseph Stalin's government expelled Leon Trotsky from the Soviet Union; he ultimately settled into Mexican exile.

Former secretary of the interior Albert M. Fall was convicted of bribery in the Teapot Dome scandal. Harry F. Sinclair, who had received the Teapot Dome leases, was briefly jailed for contempt of court.

At least 200 people died in Arab-Jewish clashes, as conflict grew in Palestine.

Alexander I canceled Yugoslavia's democratic constitution and ruled as dictator (1929-1934).

The civil war in Afghanistan was won by the forces of Mohammed Nadir Khan, who took Kabul and executed his opponent, Habibullah Ghazi, then becoming Nadir Shah.

The Sunni Islamic fundamentalist Muslim Brotherhood was founded, its main early strength in Egypt; it would become a major center of fundamentalism in the Muslim world.

b. Yasir Arafat (1929-   ), Palestinian independence movement leader; head of the Palestine Liberation Organization (PLO) (1969-   ).

b. Chadli BenJedid (1929-   ), president of Algeria (1979-1992).

Soviet agricultural scientist Trofim Lysenko reported on a way to modify plants so that acquired characteristics would be passed on, counter to the scientifically supported Mendelian view of genetic inheritance. Lysenko's claimed results were unreproducible, but with support from Joseph Stalin, he would (from 1935) purge Soviet science of all researchers who dissented from his views, crippling Soviet genetics and agricultural science for decades.

American astronomer Edwin Hubble proposed that there was a constant relationship between the speed at which a galaxy is traveling away from the earth and its distance from us. Dubbed Hubble's law, and the relationship Hubble's constant, this formulation would be fundamental to 20th-century astronomy.

German psychiatrist Hans Berger developed the electroencephalograph (EEG) (1924-1929) to measure the brain's electrical activity and aberrations, first detecting alpha and beta waves.

Russian-American chemist Phoebus Aaron Theodor Levene discovered deoxyribonucleic acid (DNA), later found to carry basic genetic information; he had earlier discovered ribose (1909).

German surgeon Werner Theodor Otto Forssmann developed the technique of cardiac catheterization, inserting a flexible tube (catheter) into a vein in his own arm and pushing it through until it reached the heart. In clinical use (from 1941), it would allow analysis of heart problems without exploratory surgery.

British archaeologist Leonard Woolley published *Ur of the Chaldees,* describing for wide audiences his discoveries of the Sumerian civilization in ancient Mesopotamia.

Erich Maria Remarque published his first and best-known novel, the antiwar *All Quiet on the Western Front,* which would be the basis of the 1930 film.

Virginia Woolf published her landmark feminist essay collection *A Room of One's Own.*

Serge Lifar and Felia Dubrovska danced the leads in Sergei Diaghilev's Ballets Russes presentation of George Balanchine's *The Prodigal Son,* music by Sergei Prokofiev.

Sinclair Lewis published the novel *Dodsworth,* later adapted by Sidney Howard into a 1934 play and the classic 1936 film.

William Faulkner emerged as a major American novelist, introducing his fictional Yoknapatawpha setting in *Sartoris* and also publishing *The Sound and the Fury.*

Thomas Wolfe came to wide notice with publication of his massive autobiographical first novel, *Look Homeward, Angel.*

Louise Brooks starred as another free woman in G. W. Pabst's film classic *Diary of a Lost Girl.*

Alfred Doblin published the novel *Berlin Alexanderplatz,* set in disintegrating Weimar society.

Peggy Wood and Georges Metaxa starred in Noël Coward's musical *Bitter Sweet;* Wood and Coward introduced "I'll See You Again."

Richard Neutra's Lovell House, in Los Angeles, was a very early American expression of the new International Style.

Vladimir Mayakovsky's *The Bathhouse,* critical of the Stalinist bureaucracy, was to be his final play.

Stocks on the New York Stock Exchange plummeted, most notably on "Black Tuesday" (Oct. 24), precipitating a worldwide Crash, the disastrous Smoot-Hawley tariffs (1930), and the onset of the Great Depression of the 1930s — and in all probability fascism, world war, and the atomic weapon.

American crime leaders meeting in Atlantic City, New Jersey (May), organized the first national crime syndicate; leading participants included Al Capone, Charles "Lucky" Luciano, Frank Costello, and Meyer Lansky.

During a Chicago gang war, Al Capone ordered the execution of six rival gangsters and a bystander in what came to be known as the St. Valentine's Day Massacre (Feb. 14).

American sociologists Robert Staughton Lynd and Helen Merrell Lynd published *Middletown,* a study of middle-class America based on their sociological analyses of Muncie, Indiana.

French historians Marc Bloch and Lucien Febvre founded the magazine *Annales,* stressing wide-ranging, comparative, interdisciplinary work, a central influence on the 20th-century historians of the "Annales" school, most notably Fernand Braudel.

Mary Dennett was indicted and convicted under obscenity laws for disseminating a 1918 sex education article; her conviction was overturned on appeal (1930), with the aid of the American Civil Liberties Union.

German philosopher Martin Heidegger published *Existence and Being,* a fundamental work in existentialism, attacking logic as inadequate to deal with being, nothingness, and existence in general.

Richard E. Byrd, with copilot Bernt Balchen, made the first flight over the South Pole (Nov. 29).

1929 cont.

b. Bob (Robert James Lee) Hawke (1929-   ), Australian Labour politician; prime minister (1983-1991).

b. Sam Nujoma (1929-   ), Namibian independence movement leader; first president of the Southwest Africa People's Organization of Namibia (SWAPO) (1959-   ) and of Namibia (1990-   ).

b. Jacqueline Lee Bouvier Kennedy Onassis (1929-1994), wife of President John F. Kennedy.

d. Ferdinand Foch (1851-1929), French general; a major figure during World War I.

d. Georges Eugene Benjamin Clemenceau ("The Tiger") (1841-1929), French politician; twice premier of France (1906-1909; 1917-1920) and a key figure in the later stages of World War I and at the postwar Paris Peace Conference (1919).

d. Bernhard von Bülow (1849-1929), chancellor of Germany (1900-1909).

d. Victor Louis Berger (1860-1929), American socialist politician; the first socialist to serve in the U.S. House of Representatives (1911).

b. Murray Gell-Mann (1929-   ), American physicist noted for his work on elementary particles (1961) and on quarks as the basic building blocks of matter (1969).

d. Aletta Jacobs (1851-1929), first Dutch woman physician (1879); founder of the world's first birth control clinic (1882).

1930

Kuomintang forces defeated a Communist offensive in central China most decisively at Ch'angsha (July); the Communist army then retreated into western Kiangsi, where they built up the Kiangsi Soviet.

Mahatma Gandhi led a massive anti–salt tax satyagraha (nonviolence) campaign.

American, Japanese, British, French, and Italian naval growth was limited by agreements reached at the London

American zoologist William Beebe and engineer Otis Barton developed the bathysphere, a submersible craft suspended by a cable from a "mother ship" for underwater observations; it would later be replaced by the free-floating, less vulnerable bathyscape (1948).

As predicted by Percival Lowell (1905), a new planet, Pluto, was found beyond Neptune, by

(Albert) Hirschfeld's theater drawings began appearing in the *New York Times*, each containing the name of his daughter, Nina.

German writer Thomas Mann was awarded the Nobel Prize for literature.

b. Audrey Hepburn (1929-1993), Belgian-born British actress and humanitarian.

b. Beverly Sills (Belle Silverman) (1929-   ), American singer and opera director.

b. John James Osborne (1929-1994), British playwright and actor; a prototypical "angry young man" from his play from *Look Back in Anger* (1950).

b. Max von Sydow (1929-   ), Swedish actor; early identified with the films of Ingmar Bergman.

b. Adrienne Rich (1929-   ), American feminist writer.

b. Claes Oldenburg (1929-   ), American pop artist; a leading figure from the late 1950s.

d. Sergei Diaghilev (1872-1929), founder of the Ballets Russes company (1909); a central figure in shaping 20th-century ballet.

In Cleveland, Ohio, fire involving X-ray films caused poisonous gas to spread through the ventilation ducts of the Crile Clinic, killing 125 people (May 15).

Buck Rogers was created by cartoonists Philip Nowlan and Richard Calkins.

Popeye the Sailor was created by cartoonist Elzie Segar.

b. Martin Luther King, Jr. (1929-1968), African-American minister, civil rights leader, and exponent of nonviolence who would become one of the century's leading figures.

d. Wyatt Earp (1848-1929), legendary Western peace officer; he later lived in Los Angeles and, in the 1920s, was a technical adviser on several movies.

Ansel Adams published his first major work, the landmark photo collection *Taos Pueblo,* text by Mary Austin.

Clarence Brown's film version of Eugene O'Neill's *Anna Christie* starred Greta Garbo in the title role; it was her first "talkie."

Worldwide trade dropped precipitously and the Great Depression came on very swiftly after the establishment of high American tariffs under the Smoot-Hawley Tariff Act, followed by retaliatory high tariffs throughout the world.

American golfer Bobby Jones won a Grand Slam: the British and U.S. Opens and the British and U.S. amateur championships; he then retired.

Naval Conference (Jan.-Apr.), but the agreements were never enforced.

As provided by the Locarno Treaties (1925), French and British forces withdrew from the demilitarized Rhineland.

Japanese prime minister Hamaguchi Osachi was the victim of a right-wing assassin; he survived but would die of gunshot wounds in 1931.

Nuri al-Said became the first prime minister and the strongman of independent Iraq (1930-1958).

Rafael Leonidas Trujillo Molina took power as dictator in the Dominican Republic (1930-1961).

Kurdish insurrections failed in Iran (1930) and Iraq (1930-1931); British forces aided the Iraqi government.

David Ben-Gurion founded the socialist Mapai Party.

Haile Selassie I (Ras Tafari) took the title of emperor of Ethiopia (1930-1974).

Getúlio Vargas took power by coup in Brazil, ruling as dictator (1930-1945).

Carol II became king of Romania (1930-1940).

b. James A. Baker III (1930-), American lawyer, politician, and diplomat; White House chief of staff (1981-1985), treasury secretary (1985-1988), and secretary of state (1989-1992).

b. Helmut Kohl (1930-), German Christian Democratic politician; chancellor of West Germany (1982-1990), then of united Germany (1990-).

b. Gaafar Mohammed al-Nimeiry (1930-), Sudanese Muslim fundamentalist officer; leader of a successful coup (1969) who took full power and ruled as military dictator (1971-1985).

American astronomer Clyde William Tombaugh.

American chemist Thomas Midgley, Jr., discovered a stable, nontoxic liquid compound, Freon, for use as a coolant in refrigerators and air conditioners. Only decades later would scientists realize that Freon and other chlorofluorocarbons (CFCs) can deplete the earth's protective ozone layer (by 1974).

American biochemist Edward Doisy and German chemist Adolf Butenandt independently isolated estrone, a female sex hormone.

British engineer Frank Whittle patented a turbojet engine, but it was not tested until 1937 and not used in flight until 1941.

Joseph Rhine founded the Parapsychology Laboratory at Duke University to test claims of extrasensory perception (ESP), a term he coined to include phenomena such as telepathy, clairvoyance, precognition, and psychokinesis.

b. Neil Alden Armstrong (1930-), American aviator and astronaut who would become the first human to walk on the moon (1969).

d. Glenn Hammond Curtiss (1878-1930), American inventor and aviator who made the first flight of more than a kilometer (1908) and developed the first practical seaplane (1911).

d. Harvey Washington Wiley (1844-1930), American chemist; U.S. Department of Agriculture chief (1883-1912) whose "Poison Squad" led the fight against the adulteration of food, analyzing many food additives, often by testing on themselves.

Marlene Dietrich starred as Lola opposite Emil Jannings in Josef von Sternberg's classic film *The Blue Angel,* very loosely based on Heinrich Mann's 1905 novel *The Small Town Tyrant.*

Lew Ayres starred in Lewis Milestone's film version of Erich Maria Remarque's 1929 antiwar novel *All Quiet on the Western Front.*

Grant Wood's *American Gothic,* his starkly realistic painting of a midwestern farm couple, became a signature work of the American Scene movement.

Noël Coward and Gertrude Lawrence starred in Coward's comedy *Private Lives.*

Ludwig Mies van der Rohe became director of the Bauhaus (1930-1933), serving until it was forced to close by the Nazis.

Robert Frost published his Pulitzer Prize–winning *Collected Poems.*

John Gutzon Borglum completed *George Washington,* the first of his four presidential sculptures at Mount Rushmore, South Dakota.

Responding to calls for censorship, Hollywood established the Motion Picture Production Code, spearheaded by Will H. Hays and the so-called Hays Office.

American novelist Sinclair Lewis was awarded the Nobel Prize for literature.

b. Derek Alton Walcott (1930-   ), Caribbean writer and critic who would receive the 1992 Nobel Prize for literature.

b. Chinua Achebe (1930-   ), Nigerian writer seen as a major African literary figure from his first novel, *Things Fall Apart* (1958).

b. Robert Joffrey (Abdullah Jaffa Anver Khan) (1930-1988), American dancer.

American jockey Earl Sande won all three races in the Triple Crown: the Kentucky Derby, Preakness, and Belmont Stakes. Damon Runyon memorialized him in the poem "A Handy Guy Like Sande."

World population reached an estimated 1.9 billion to 2 billion people.

Charles Lindbergh and his wife and copilot, Anne Morrow Lindbergh, set a transcontinental speed record flying across North America.

Britain's National Birth Control Council (later Family Planning Association) was founded by Helena Wright and others, chaired by Gertrude Denman (1930-1954); it would introduce new birth-control methods, such as the intrauterine device (IUD). Wright also published the best-selling *The Sex Factor in Marriage.*

Cyrus Eaton founded the Republic Steel Company.

A fire at the Ohio State Penitentiary (Apr. 21) killed 320 prisoners, who were trapped in their locked cells when guards refused to open the doors until it was too late.

British aviator Amy Johnson made a record-breaking flight from London to Australia (May 5-24, with stops for repairs), winning £10,000 offered by Britain's *Daily Mail.*

German boxer Max Schmeling won the world heavyweight championship after a controversial foul, following a tournament of contenders for the title vacated by the retired Gene Tunney (1929).

British aviator Francis Chichester made the first solo flight by seaplane across the Tasman Sea from New Zealand to Australia. Chichester would later be better known as a yachtsman.

Spanish philosopher José Ortega y Gasset published *The Rebellion of the Masses,* his political analysis

1930 cont.

b. Malcolm Fraser (1930-   ), Australian Liberal Party leader; prime minister (1975-1983).

b. Mobutu Sese Seko (Joseph Désiré Mobutu) (1930-   ), dictator of Congo (later Zaire) (1965-   ).

b. Tom (Thomas Joseph) Mboya (1930-1969), Kenyan politician.

d. Arthur James Balfour (1848-1930), British diplomat and Conservative politician; prime minister (1902-1905); author of the Balfour Declaration (1917) on the establishment of a Jewish homeland in Palestine.

d. William Howard Taft (1857-1930), conservative Republican; 27th president of the United States (1909-1913) and chief justice of the Supreme Court (1921-1930).

1931

Japan's Kwangtung Army used the Mukden Incident (Sept. 18-19) to take Mukden, China, and then all of Manchuria, ignoring ineffective international protests; Japan was to hold Manchuria, renamed Manchukuo, until the end of World War II.

Japanese prime minister Hamaguchi Osachi (1870-1931) was killed by a right-wing assassin; part of the run-up to Japanese military dictatorship.

Avraham Tehomi founded the Irgun Zvai Leumi (National Military Organization) to press for a Jewish-Arab war and a Jewish revolt against British occupation forces in Palestine by all possible means, including terrorism.

A revolution in Spain deposed Alfonso XIII, replacing the monarchy with a Republican government headed by Al-

Austrian-American physicist Wolfgang Pauli first proposed the existence of the neutrino, a chargeless, virtually massless subatomic particle, basing his prediction on a seeming mass-energy imbalance in the atomic structure. Seen as a clue to the origin of the universe, the existence of neutrinos would be confirmed indirectly by the discovery of antineutrinos (1956) but not directly until 1968.

In Gödel's proof (the incompletability theorem), Austrian-American mathematician Kurt Gödel showed that mathematical certainty is impossible, undermining the work of Bertrand Russell, Alfred North Whitehead, and others on mathematical logic.

b. Clint Eastwood (1930-), American actor and director who would emerge as a major film figure.

b. Lorraine Hansberry (1930-1965), African-American playwright, most notably of her first play, *A Raisin in the Sun* (1959).

b. Sean Connery (Thomas Connery) (1930-), British actor known worldwide as James Bond.

b. Andy Warhol (Andrew Warhola) (1930-1987), American artist.

d. Arthur Conan Doyle (1859-1930), British writer best known as the creator of Sherlock Holmes.

d. D. H. (David Herbert) Lawrence (1885-1930), noted British novelist.

d. Vladimir Mayakovsky (1893-1930), Russian poet and playwright; a leading figure of the early Soviet period.

warning of the potential for tyranny, from both the Right and the Left, in a democracy.

W. D. Fard Muhammad founded the Nation of Islam, later better known as the Black Muslims.

Cartoonist Chic Young created the comic strip *Blondie*.

b. Sandra Day O'Connor (1930–), American lawyer, politician, and judge; the first woman appointed to the U.S. Supreme Court (1981).

d. Fridtjof Nansen (1861-1930), Norwegian explorer and oceanographer best known for his work in postwar relief (1920-1923).

The Theater Guild presented Eugene O'Neill's New England trilogy, *Mourning Becomes Electra*, a modern retelling of Aeschylus' *Oresteia*, starring Alla Nazimova, Alice Brady, Earle Larrimore, Lee Baker, and Thomas Chalmers.

William Faulkner published the novel *Sanctuary*, a southern story of rape, prostitution, murder, and finally the lynching of an innocent man.

In Alabama's Scottsboro case (Mar.), nine young African-American men were convicted of raping two young White women aboard a freight train, on concocted evidence, without adequate counsel, and by a prejudiced judge and jury; eight received death sentences and one, a 13-year-old, life imprisonment. A worldwide protest, a new defense on appeal led by Samuel S. Liebowitz, and Supreme Court partial reversals followed. Ultimately, five were imprisoned; all but Haywood Patterson, who died in prison (1952) after escaping and being recaptured, were ultimately paroled or pardoned, the last by Alabama governor George Wallace (1976).

Wiley Post and copilot Harold Gatty made the first around-the-world flight in the airplane *Winnie Mae*, taking 8 days and nearly 16 hours.

calá Zamora; as Right-Left bitterness grew, a sequence of events began that would lead to the Spanish Civil War (1936-1939).

Italian forces concluded their genocidal war against Libya's Senussi people (1923-1931), taking and executing Omar Mukhtar.

In China, Kuomintang armies mounted offensives against the Kiangsi Soviet, with considerable success.

Britain's Statute of Westminster informally recognized the existence of the Commonwealth (British Commonwealth of Nations), which evolved into a 46-nation association of former colonies, headed by the British monarch.

A low-level border war redeveloped on the Bulgarian-Greek border; League of Nations mediation attempted to resolve the conflict.

The Nobel Peace Prize was awarded to Jane Addams and Nicholas Murray Butler.

b. Mikhail Sergeyevich Gorbachev (1931-), Soviet politician; as general secretary of the Communist Party of the Soviet Union (1985-1991) and leader of his country, he would be largely responsible for the end of the Soviet empire and the dismantling of the Soviet system.

b. Boris Nikolayevich Yeltsin (1931-), president of Russia (1990-) who, after Mikhail Gorbachev, would ultimately dissolve the Soviet Union (1991).

d. Hussein Ibn Ali (1853-1931), leader of the Arab Revolt of 1916 and king of the Hejaz (1916-1924); he was the father of Faisal I of Iraq and Abdullah Ibn Husein of Transjordan.

d. Joseph Joffre (1852-1931), French general; commander of French forces at the pivotal First Battle of the Marne (1914) and later French commander in chief (Dec. 1915-Dec. 1916).

Bell Laboratories radio engineer Karl Guthe Jansky discovered radio waves emitted by objects outside the solar system, laying the basis for modern radio astronomy.

Deuterium, an isotope of hydrogen called "heavy hydrogen" (H-2), was discovered by American chemist Harold C. Urey, who also discovered "heavy water," made with deuterium, which would prove to be a key component of nuclear bombs and reactors. Deuterium also would be used as a radioactive tracer in the study of biochemical reactions in living tissue.

American physicist Ernest O. Lawrence developed the cyclotron, the first circular accelerator, an "atom smasher" that uses electromagnetic fields to speed up atomic particles and induce collisions; scientists are able to study particles thrown off as a result of these collisions.

Swiss chemist Paul Karrer and others first synthesized vitamin A, leading to a greater understanding of vitamins in general and the synthesis of others.

Indian-American astronomer Subrahmanyan Chandrasekhar identified the size (the "Chandrasekhar limit") above which a star will continue to collapse late in its evolution through what in less massive suns would be the white dwarf stage into what others would later call the "black hole."

Swiss physicist Auguste Antoine Piccard and Paul Kipfer set a world height record, ascending 52,000 feet in a balloon with Piccard's closed and pressurized aluminum cabin (later adapted for airplanes); feared lost, they became celebrities upon their safe landing.

Boris Karloff starred in the title role of *Frankenstein,* directed by James Whale and based on the 1818 Mary Wollstonecraft Shelley novel.

Harold Clurman, Lee Strasberg, and Cheryl Crawford broke away from New York's Theater Guild to found the left-oriented Group Theater (1931-1941).

Pearl Buck published her very popular Pulitzer Prize–winning novel *The Good Earth.* Luise Rainer would star in Sidney Franklin's 1937 film version.

Ronald Colman and Helen Hayes starred in John Ford's film version of the 1925 Sinclair Lewis novel *Arrowsmith.*

Sylvia Sidney and Phillips Holmes starred in Josef von Sternberg's film version of Theodore Dreiser's 1925 novel *An American Tragedy.*

Charles Chaplin wrote, directed, scored, and starred in *City Lights.*

Hoagy Carmichael published his signature song, "Stardust."

Bela Lugosi starred in the vampire title role in Tod Browning's horror film *Dracula,* based on the 1897 Bram Stoker story.

Fritz Lang's classic film *M* featured Peter Lorre in the role of the serial child murderer.

Lydia Lopokova, Alicia Markova, and Frederick Ashton danced the leads in Ashton's ballet *Façade,* music by William Walton.

Paul Muni starred as the quintessential gangster in the title role of the film *Scarface,* directed by Howard Hawks.

Of Thee I Sing, George and Ira Gershwin's musical based on a book by George S. Kaufman and Morie Ryskind, opened in New York.

New York Yankees slugger Lou Gehrig drove in a record 184 runs.

At 102 stories and 1,250 feet high, New York's Empire State Building became the world's tallest building.

Britain's National Birth Control Council won a campaign to have the government provide birth control information and devices to married couples on health grounds, starting with monthly birth control education sessions in Ealing.

Chicago crime boss Al Capone was sentenced to an 11-year prison term for federal income tax evasion.

Hubert Wilkins, Lincoln Ellsworth, and others explored the Arctic polar regions by submarine.

Canadian entrepreneur Roy Herbert Thomson bought his first radio station, in North Bay, Ontario; his first newspaper, the weekly *Press* in Timmins, Ontario, followed in 1934. They would be the basis for a major British–North American communications empire.

Dick Tracy was created by cartoonist Chester Gould.

b. (Keith) Rupert Murdoch (1931-   ), Australian-American communications magnate who, starting with a single paper, Australia's *Adelaide News* (1952), would build an international empire including newspaper, publishing, film, and television companies.

b. Dan Rather (1931-   ), American television broadcast journalist who would become nationally known for his reporting of President John F. Kennedy's assassination (1963); later CBS White House correspondent (1966-1974) and then CBS Evening News anchor (1981-   ).

1931 cont.

American pathologist Ernest William Goodpasture developed a way to grow virus cultures in eggs, a technique fundamental to the development of vaccines for diseases such as polio and influenza.

Belgian-American chemist Julius Arthur Nieuwland developed a synthetic rubber, called neoprene, which would become important during World War II, when natural rubber supplies were disrupted.

American chemist Linus Carl Pauling theorized that resonance — a state between shared and transferred electrons — exists in stable molecules such as benzene, a concept helpful in predicting chemical structures and reactions.

German chemist Adolf Friedrich Butenandt isolated androsterone, a male sex hormone, and worked out its structure.

d. Albert Abraham Michelson (1852-1931), American physicist who first measured the speed of light (1878) and the diameter of a star, Betelgeuse (1920); the first American Nobel Prize winner (1907).

1932

In his acceptance speech to the Democratic nominating convention, U.S. presidential candidate Franklin Delano Roosevelt coined his New Deal slogan with "I pledge you, I pledge myself, a new deal for the American people."

Chinese protesting the Japanese conquest of Manchuria instituted a national boycott of Japanese goods. Japan re-

British physicist James Chadwick discovered the neutron, an atomic particle with no electric charge, first posited by William Draper Hawkins (1921). Only a decade later, neutrons would be used to force the first nuclear chain reaction (1942).

1931 cont.

Rudolf Besier's play *The Barretts of Wimpole Street* starred Katharine Cornell as Elizabeth Barrett Browning.

Duke Ellington composed "Mood Indigo."

Antoine St.-Exupéry published *Night Flight*.

b. Toni Morrison (Chloe Anthony Wofford) (1931-), African-American writer who would win the 1993 Nobel Prize for literature.

b. John le Carré (David John Cornwell) (1931-), British writer, largely of spy thrillers.

b. Alvin Ailey (1931-1989), African-American dancer, choreographer, and director.

b. James Earl Jones (1931-), leading African-American actor.

b. James Dean (1931-1955), American actor.

d. Anna Pavlova (1882-1931), the foremost Russian ballerina of the early 20th century.

d. Daniel Chester French (1850-1931), American sculptor of the Lincoln Memorial.

d. Arnold Bennett (1867-1931), who emerged as a major British writer with his novel *The Old Wives Tale* (1908).

b. Desmond Mpilo Tutu (1931-), South African minister, freedom movement leader, and Nobel Peace Prize recipient (1984); the first Black Anglican dean (1975) and archbishop (1986); a leading apostle of nonviolence.

d. Knute Kenneth Rockne (1888-1931), Norwegian-American football coach at Notre Dame University (1918-1931), a major force in shaping the game. He died in an airplane crash.

1932

Aldous Huxley published his grimly prophetic satirical novel *Brave New World,* an enduring warning against the excesses of the bureaucratic state and particularly against the perils posed by eugenics, then part of fascist theory and soon to be part of genocidal practice.

Bruno Richard Hauptmann kidnapped 20-month-old Charles A. Lindbergh, Jr., son of aviators Charles and Anne Morrow Lindbergh, from his Hopewell, New Jersey, home (Mar. 1). Hauptmann demanded and received a $50,000 ransom, then murdered the child (found May 12). He ultimately was convicted and executed (Apr. 3, 1936).

sponded by sending an invasion force against Shanghai (Jan. 28-Mar. 8), which ultimately broke through strong Chinese resistance to take the city, forcing the end of the boycott at the price of temporary Japanese withdrawal from China.

d. Takuma Dan (1858-1932), head of the Mitsui company and a key member of Japan's industrial elite (Zaitbatsu), assassinated by nationalists; another step on the way to Japanese military dictatorship.

Japanese democracy died when Prime Minister Inukai Tsuyohi (1855-1932), who had resisted the military, was assassinated by a group of naval officers; the Japanese run-up to militarism, fascism, and war continued essentially unopposed.

Japan installed Hsüan T'ung (Henry P'u Yi), who as a child had been the last Manchu (Ch'ing) emperor of China (1908-1912), as puppet ruler of Manchukuo (Manchuria).

World War I veterans ("bonus marchers") seeking early payment of bonuses due in 1945 demonstrated in Washington, D.C., many of them camping at Anacostia Flats. Ultimately, 5,000 veterans and their families were violently attacked and dispersed and their squatters' camps burned by divisional-strength, battle-ready regular U.S. Army forces with tanks and machine guns, led by Army chief of staff Douglas MacArthur, by order of President Herbert Hoover.

Mahatma Gandhi was again imprisoned by the British; he began his long series of campaigns for India's Untouchables and other poor and oppressed segments of Indian society.

Antonio de Oliviera Salazar took full power as Portugal's fascist dictator (1932-1968).

At Geneva, a wholly unsuccessful World Disarmament Conference convened (1932-1934).

Bolivia and Paraguay went to war over control of the Chaco region (1932-1935). The Bolivians reversed early Paraguayan successes by mid-1932.

German physicist Werner Heisenberg produced a modified model of atomic structure, positing that the newly discovered neutrons and protons together formed the nucleus and introducing the notion of exchange forces, or exchange particles, to hold them together. He also received the Nobel Prize for physics for his uncertainty principle (1927).

American physicist Carl David Anderson discovered the positron (antielectron), the positively charged counterpart of the negatively charged electron, supporting Paul Dirac's theory of antimatter (1928). It also was discovered independently by British physicist Patrick Blackett (1933).

British physicist John Douglas Cockcroft and Irish physicist Ernest Thomas Sinton Walton designed a particle accelerator ("atom smasher") and used it to split an atomic nucleus, bombarding lithium nuclei with speeded-up protons to produce two helium nuclei, in the first human-induced nuclear reaction.

Hungarian physicist Leo Szilard recognized the possibility of a nuclear chain reaction; then an émigré in Britain, he patented his idea, signing it over to the British government. Szilard would be a key figure in the development of nuclear fission, although his approach would in the end prove unworkable, and another would be used (1942).

Searching for disease-fighting drugs, German chemist Gerhard Domagk found the compound Prontosil, which acted against streptococcal infections; its first use in humans was to save his own daughter's life (1935). The active ingredient of Prontosil was later found to be sulfanilamide, the first "sulfa" drug (1936).

Vladimir Zworykin built the first all-electronic television while working for the Radio Corpo-

Erskine Caldwell published the novel *Tobacco Road,* his story of a broken Depression era Georgia farm family.

Jules Romains began publication of *Men of Good Will* (1932-1946), ultimately a set of 27 novels.

Lewis Grassic Gibbon began publication of his four-volume Depression era Scottish novels, *A Scots Quair* (1932-1934).

Philip Johnson and Henry-Russell Hitchcock published *The International Style,* which would strongly influence the introduction of the Bauhaus-developed style into the United States, as would the emigration of leading architects from Nazi Germany.

Adoption of a standard Braille code by the English-speaking nations was a major leap forward for blind readers.

Fredric March starred in the dual title role in Rouben Mamoulian's horror film *Dr. Jekyll and Mr. Hyde,* based on the 1886 Robert Louis Stevenson story.

E. Y. "Yip" Harburg and Jay Gorney's "Brother, Can You Spare a Dime?" was the prototypical Depression song, popularized by Bing Crosby and Rudy Vallee.

Gary Cooper and Helen Hayes starred in Frank Borzage's film version of the 1920 Ernest Hemingway novel *A Farewell to Arms.*

Cole Porter's *The Gay Divorce* starred Claire Luce and Fred Astaire, introducing "Night and Day."

The financial empire of utilities financier and stock manipulator Samuel Insull, seemingly huge on paper, collapsed; he fled abroad, was returned under extradition, and was eventually acquitted under the loose regulatory statutes of the period.

The Norris–La Guardia Anti-Injunction Act made unenforceable "yellow-dog contracts," prior agreements by workers that union membership would lead to dismissal.

American tennis player Helen Hull Jacobs won her first U.S. women's singles title; she would be the first to win four in a row (1932-1935).

Midwestern murderers and armed robbers Bonnie Parker and Clyde Barrow began their brief, highly publicized criminal careers.

A massive earthquake in Gansu, China, took an estimated 70,000 lives.

The Hoover administration established the Reconstruction Finance Corporation (RFC) to make federal loans to Depression-struck large businesses. The agency became a major New Deal vehicle for a wide variety of loans (1933), stressing small business and family farm loans.

The Soviet ship *Sibiriakov* was the first to traverse the Northeast Passage, the ice-clogged seaway north of Eurasia, without wintering over. During World War II, the Russians would field a fleet of icebreakers to keep this Northern Sea Route open for vital supplies from the Allies.

Both a running back and a defensive tackle, Bronko (Bronislau) Nagurski helped his Chicago Bears football team to the national championship, the first of his three titles with them (1932; 1933; 1943).

Britain's first permanent government-sponsored birth control clinic was founded in Plymouth.

In Seville, General José Sanjurjo led a failed Spanish right-wing military insurrection; Right-Left tensions continued to grow in Spain.

A major rising in São Paulo failed to unseat Getúlio Vargas's dictatorship, as Brazilian government forces defeated a large (40,000 to 50,000) but ill-equipped and untrained "Paulista" army, which received little support from other parts of the country.

Oswald Mosley founded the British Union of Fascists, then made a failed attempt to build a Nazi paramilitary street-fighting force in Britain; his minor forces were defeated on the streets of London's largely Jewish East End.

The Republic of Iraq formally became an independent state, with Faisal continuing as king, although it remained a de facto British protectorate through World War II. Further Kurdish risings in Iraq were defeated by Iraqi government forces with British air support.

Eamon De Valera became president of the Irish Free State Executive Council.

Hermann Goering became Nazi head of the Reichstag.

Ibn Saud formally became king of the new nation of Saudi Arabia.

b. Edward (Ted) Moore Kennedy (1932-), American politician, younger brother of John F. Kennedy and Robert F. Kennedy; liberal Massachusetts Democratic senator (1962-).

b. Jacques Chirac (1932-), French conservative politician; premier (1974-1976; 1986-1988) and president (1995-).

b. Mario Cuomo (1932-), American Democratic politician; New York governor (1982-1994) and a leading liberal.

d. Aristide Briand (1862-1932), French politician who was eleven times premier of France; an architect of the Locarno Treaties (1925) and the Kellogg-Briand Pact (1928) and winner of the 1926 Nobel Peace Prize.

ration of America (RCA), after his previous employer, Westinghouse, had condemned the project as "impractical."

German biochemist Hans Adolf Krebs discovered the urea cycle, the series of chemical reactions by which the kidneys produce urine.

American inventor Edwin Land developed polarized glass, using tiny aligned crystals embedded in glass or plastic to polarize light; he would found the Polaroid Corporation (1937) to market his invention, which would be widely used, as in safety glass and sunglasses.

Quinacrine (Atabrin) was developed as a synthetic substitute for quinine in treating malaria; it would become important during World War II, when supplies of naturally derived quinine were disrupted.

b. Dian Fossey (1932-1985), American primatologist.

James T. Farrell published *Young Lonigan,* the first of his "Studs Lonigan" trilogy (1932-1935), set in a 1920s Irish-American slum in Chicago.

The George S. Kaufman–Edna Ferber play *Dinner at Eight* opened.

The Depression song "Let's Have Another Cup of Coffee" was introduced in Irving Berlin's stage musical *Face the Music.*

George Burns and Gracie Allen began their long-running variety show (1932-1950 on radio; 1950-1958 on television); Jack Benny and Mary Livingstone starred in *The Jack Benny Show* (1932-1955).

British novelist and playwright John Galsworthy was awarded the Nobel Prize for literature.

b. Elizabeth Taylor (1932-   ), British-American actress who would become an international film star and major celebrity, and then a leading anti-AIDS activist.

b. Fernando Arrabal (1932-   ), French playwright of Spanish ancestry who would be a leading figure in the "theater of the absurd."

b. François Truffaut (1932-1984), French director and critic; an originator of the "auteur" theory.

b. Peter O'Toole (1932-   ), British film star, most notably in the title role of *Lawrence of Arabia* (1962).

b. Sylvia Plath (1932-1963), American poet and novelist, most of whose feminist-oriented work would be published after her suicide.

b. John Updike (1932-   ), leading American writer.

b. Omar Sharif (Michael Shalhoub) (1932-   ), Lebanese-Egyptian film star, most notably in the title role of *Doctor Zhivago* (1965).

b. Johnny Cash (1932-   ), American country music singer, songwriter, and guitarist.

Greek businessman Aristotle Socrates Onassis bought six Canadian freighters, using them as the basis for one of the world's largest individually owned merchant fleets; he would become one of the world's richest men.

The German dirigibles *Graf Zeppelin* and *Hindenburg* began regular transatlantic service between Frankfurt and the United States or Brazil.

Amelia Earhart flew solo across the Atlantic Ocean, the first woman to do so.

d. Frederick Jackson Turner (1861-1932), American historian whose classic *The Frontier in American History* (1920) was based on earlier work on the significance of the 1890s closing of the frontier.

d. Ivar Kreuger (1880-1932), Swedish industrialist called the "Match King"; he committed suicide when massive frauds were discovered after the financial demise of his worldwide production operations.

1932 cont.

1933

U.S. president Franklin Delano Roosevelt took office (Mar. 4), beginning the New Deal era. The next day, he declared a "bank holiday," closing all U.S. banks to forestall a developing financial crisis (Mar. 6). He made the first of his radio addresses — "fireside chats" — on the new stability of the banking system (Mar. 12); banks began to reopen the next morning.

In the first "hundred days" of FDR's presidency (Mar. 9-June 16; actually 104 days), Congress enacted a massive body of New Deal legislation, including the Agricultural Adjustment Act and the National Industrial Recovery Act, both later ruled unconstitutional; established the Federal Emergency Relief Administration (FERA), the Civilian Conservation Corps (CCC), and the Public Works Administration (PWA); and provided major new mortgage refinancing and business loan vehicles.

Roosevelt sharply changed course in foreign policy; his administration recognized the Soviet Union and introduced the Good Neighbor Policy, rejecting an imperial role in Latin America for the United States.

In *Natural Childbirth,* a term he coined, British obstetrician Grantly Dick-Read outlined his view that "fear tension pain syndrome" is responsible for much of the pain in childbirth. He developed classes to give parents preparatory physical exercises, including special breathing patterns for different stages of labor, and to educate them about what to expect at different stages of birth. His natural childbirth approach, introducing men as "birth partners" in the delivery room and moving away from the use of drugs during childbirth, would become popular in the United States from the 1950s and spawn other such approaches.

Polish-Swiss chemist Tadeusz Reichstein first synthesized vitamin C, as did Walter Norman Haworth, who named it ascorbic acid. As these and other vitamins were synthesized, it became possible to produce them in large amounts as dietary supplements and to eliminate many vitamin-deficiency diseases.

1932 cont.

b. Athol Fugard (1932-   ), South African writer, actor, and director.

b. Christy Brown (1932-1981), Irish poet, novelist, and painter.

d. Augusta, Lady Gregory (1852-1932), Irish playwright; a founder of the Abbey Theatre (1904).

d. Florenz Ziegfeld (1867-1932), creator of the *Ziegfeld Follies* (1907-1931).

d. Hart Crane (Harold Hart Crane) (1899-1932), American poet.

d. John Philip Sousa (1854-1932), American composer.

1933

André Malraux published the novel *Man's Fate (La Condition humaine)*, set in Shanghai during the Shanghai Massacre at the outset of the Chinese Civil War; his protagonist, Kyo, was Communist leader Zhou Enlai, drawn largely from life.

Diego Rivera's major mural *Man at the Crossroads,* which included a portrait of Vladimir Illich Lenin, was created for Rockefeller Center's RCA Building. It was destroyed by its purchasers because of its "radical" content.

Busby Berkeley choreographed the classic film musical *42nd Street,* directed by Lloyd Bacon and starring Warner Baxter, Ruby Keeler, Bebe Daniels, George Brent, Ginger Rogers, and Dick Powell. Almost intact, the film was the basis for the long-running 1980 Broadway hit musical.

Fred Astaire and Ginger Rogers starred in the first of their 10 classic film musicals together, *Flying Down to Rio.*

During the Great Depression, a long drought, coupled with the inability of bankrupt farmers to reseed their land, turned parts of Oklahoma, West Texas, Kansas, and several other states into the Dust Bowl (1933-1939) — its topsoil literally turned to dust and blown away, its farmers turned into the migrant "Okies" of John Steinbeck's novel *The Grapes of Wrath*.

The Federal Deposit Insurance Corporation (FDIC) was established, as provided by the Banking Act of 1933, to provide federal deposit guarantees and so restore Depression era public confidence in the banking system.

The Federal Emergency Relief Administration (FERA) was established; a primary New Deal relief distribution vehicle, through which Harry Hopkins, acting for the new Roosevelt administration, quickly distributed $500 million to the states for immediate relief payments to those most desperately in need.

Adolf Hitler took power in Germany (Feb. 28). Nazi government attacks on dissidents and Jews intensified, and rearmament began as Germany once again took the road toward war. Heinrich Himmler created the Gestapo, the Nazi secret police, and established and directly operated the German concentration camp system, in which an estimated 10 million to 26 million people, at least 6 million of them Jews, would ultimately be murdered. One of the first camps was at Buchenwald, near Weimar, later especially infamous for antihuman medical experiments.

At Miami, Florida, Joseph Zangara failed in his attempt to assassinate President Franklin D. Roosevelt (Feb. 15), but he did wound Chicago mayor Anton J. Cermak, who later died. Zangara was executed.

Britain's Oxford Union adopted the pacifist pledge, "This House will not fight for King and Country"; for all but a few, pacifism soon seemed an inadequate response to fascism and militarism.

Japanese forces from Manchuria took Jehol, in Inner Mongolia, claiming it as part of Manchuria (Jan.-Mar.). Japanese forces also forced the Chinese out of Tientsin.

In China, Kuomintang forces continued to mount "antibandit" campaigns against the Kiangsi Soviet; Communist forces were defeated (by Sept.), and encirclement was almost accomplished.

Forced agricultural collectivization and heavy industry development were continued in the second Soviet Five-Year Plan (1933-1937), while the attack on Soviet family farmers (kulaks) continued, merging with the massacres and mass exiles of Stalin's Great Purge.

José Antonio Primo de Rivera, son of General Miguel Primo de Rivera, founded the Spanish Fascist Party, the Falange, Francisco Franco's key ideological base during the Spanish Civil War.

Republican government forces defeated anarchist insurrections in Barcelona and other Spanish cities (Jan.-Feb.).

The Pap smear, a simple screening test for cervical cancer, was developed by Greek-American cell biologist George Papanicolaou.

American electrical engineer Edwin Armstrong developed the frequency modulation (FM) method of radio transmission.

To explain puzzling results from the bombardment of radioactive materials, German researcher Ida Tacke Noddack first proposed that they resulted from the breakup of the material's nucleus, a process later known as nuclear fission.

Polyethylene was invented by British researchers Reginald Gibson and E. W. Fawcett; it would be available commercially from 1939, in radar and film, later in consumer products such as milk containers and trash cans.

The electron microscope, developed by Ernst Ruska (1928-1933), was sufficiently refined so that, for the first time, it was superior to conventional microscopes. Focusing electron beams on a screen (much as light is focused on a lens), it provided far greater magnification, allowing the study of bacteria, viruses, and living molecules.

Vienna psychiatrist Manfred Sakel first used shock treatment, deliberately induced by insulin, to treat patients. It was the first of many types of "shock" therapies, of dubious use and considerable notoriety.

Albert Einstein left Germany after Adolf Hitler's rise, settling at the Institute for Advanced Studies in Princeton, New Jersey (1933-1955), where he attempted to build a "unified field theory" of the universe.

Erwin Schrödinger and Paul Dirac shared the Nobel Prize for physics for their work on fun-

Gertrude Stein published her autobiography *The Autobiography of Alice B. Toklas*, her best-known work.

Pablo Picasso began the 46 etchings composing *The Sculptor's Studio* (1933-1934).

Vera Brittain published *Testament of Youth*, the first of what would become a three-volume autobiography.

Giacomo Manzù's sculpture *Girl on a Chair* was the first of his long series.

Charles Laughton starred in the title role in Alexander Korda's film *The Private Life of Henry VIII*, with Elsa Lanchester, Binnie Barnes, Merle Oberon, Wendy Barrie, and Everly Gregg as several of his wives.

Claude Rains starred in the title role of James Whale's science fiction film *The Invisible Man*, based on the 1897 H. G. Wells novel.

Ethel Waters, Marilyn Miller, and Clifton Webb starred in Irving Berlin's Broadway musical *As Thousands Cheer*. Waters also sang "Stormy Weather" in *The Cotton Club Parade*.

James Hilton published *Lost Horizon*, in which he created the inner Asian utopia of Shangri-La.

Noël Coward starred in his own ménage à trois play *Design for Living*, opposite Alfred Lunt and Lynn Fontanne; Fredric March, Miriam Hopkins, and Gary Cooper starred in Ernst Lubitsch's screen version.

Merian C. Cooper's classic monster movie *King Kong* featured Fay Wray as the screaming object of the gorilla's desire.

Ray Middleton and Tamara starred on Broadway in Jerome Kern's musical *Roberta*, its most no-

The Tennessee Valley Authority (TVA) began its federally mandated task of bringing cheap power to the huge river valley within the context of a much wider regional planning concept.

Ratification of the 21st Amendment (Dec. 5) ended Prohibition; however, the new American crime syndicate that had developed during the Prohibition era survived.

The Civil Works Administration (CWA) was established (1933-1934), providing temporary work on public projects for millions of unemployed people; a forerunner of the Works Progress Administration (WPA).

The Civilian Conservation Corps (CCC) was established, a Depression era set of work camps for young men, who were fed, housed, and minimally paid for their conservation project work.

The Home Owners Loan Corporation (HOLC) provided some financial stability by making direct federal loans to more than 1 million homeowners, many of them facing imminent foreclosure.

Ibn Saud granted the first Saudi Arabian oil concession, to Standard Oil.

Brooke Hart was kidnapped by Thomas Thurmond and John Holmes (Nov. 22), who were later lynched by a San Jose, California, mob after Hart's body was found in San Francisco Bay.

Charles F. Urschel was kidnapped by George "Machine Gun" Kelly and others in Oklahoma City (July 22) but released after payment of a $200,000 ransom. Kelly and five others were convicted and sentenced to life imprisonment.

The dirigible *Akron* broke up in midair over the Atlantic Ocean, off New Jersey (Apr. 4), killing 73 people.

1933 cont.

Frances Perkins became the first American woman cabinet member, as secretary of labor in the Roosevelt cabinet (1933-1945).

Nadir Shah of Afghanistan was assassinated (Nov. 8); he was succeeded by his son, Mohammed Zahir Shah.

b. (Maria) Corazon Cojuangco Aquino (1933-), Philippine politician; leader of the Philippine Revolution (1986) and president of the Philippines (1986-1992).

b. Michael Stanley Dukakis (1933-), American politician; Democratic governor of Massachusetts (1973-1977; 1983-1991) and unsuccessful presidential candidate (1988).

b. Samora Machel (1933-1986), Mozambican guerrilla leader; the first president of Mozambique (1975-1986).

d. Calvin Coolidge (1872-1933), 30th president of the United States (1923-1929); former Massachusetts Republican governor (1919-1921) and U.S. vice president (1921-1923); he succeeded president Warren G. Harding, who died in office.

d. Faisal (1883-1933), commander of Arab forces during the Arab Revolt of 1916; briefly king of Syria (1920) and British-affiliated king of Iraq (1921-1933). He was the son of Hussein Ibn Ali.

d. Gonnohyoe (Gombë) Yamamoto (1852-1933), Japanese admiral; a founder of the modern Japanese navy and later prime minister (1913-1914; 1923).

d. Morris Hillquit (1869-1933), American socialist lawyer and politician; five times an unsuccessful candidate for Congress from New York.

d. Nikolay Nikolayevich Yudenich (1862-1933), Russian White forces civil war commander in northwest Russia.

damental particles; Schrödinger left Berlin in opposition to the Nazis.

Thomas Hunt Morgan was awarded the Nobel Prize for physiology or medicine for his work in genetics; he was the first native-born American and the first nonphysician so honored.

table song by far the classic "Smoke Gets in Your Eyes."

The antiwar satirical film *Duck Soup* starred the Marx Brothers.

New York's Theater Guild presented Eugene O'Neill's comedy *Ah, Wilderness!* starring Elisha Cook, Jr., and George M. Cohan.

F. Scott Fitzgerald published the novel *Tender Is the Night*.

Russian poet and novelist Ivan Gasse Bunin was awarded the Nobel Prize for literature.

b. Yevgeny Yevtushenko (1933-   ), Russian poet who would become a leading reformer in the 1960s, even opening the question of Soviet anti-Semitism in *Babi Yar* (1961).

b. Andrei Voznesensky (1933-   ), Russian poet whose work, stressing human rather than political themes, would become enormously popular as the Soviet Union moved away from Stalinism in the 1960s.

b. David Malcolm Storey (1933-   ), leading British novelist and playwright from the 1960s.

b. Michael Caine (Maurice Joseph Micklewhite) (1933-   ), British actor who would become a film star in the mid-1960s.

b. Brigitte Bardot (Camille Javal) (1933-   ), French film actress; the "sex kitten" of the 1950s who would later become an environmentalist crusader.

b. Philip Roth (1933-   ), American writer whose work would be largely set in Jewish-American life.

b. Susan Sontag (1933-   ), American writer and film director who would emerge as a major figure

Barney Ross (Barnet David Rosofsky) won both the world lightweight and junior welterweight championships, losing both in 1934, but then regaining the welterweight title (1935-1938).

Elmo Burns Roper, Jr., founded Roper Research Associates, pioneering in modern political polling.

Some American television stations experimented with televising feature films — two hours in the evening daily and in the morning three times a week.

Wiley Post made the first solo around-the-world flight.

b. Jerry Falwell (1933-   ), American fundamentalist Protestant television evangelist who founded the Moral Majority (1979).

b. Ruth Bader Ginsburg (1933-   ), American lawyer and judge; the second woman appointed to the U.S. Supreme Court (1993).

d. Knud Johan Victor Rasmussen (1879-1933), Danish explorer and ethnologist who studied Greenland and Eskimo cultures.

1933 cont.

1934

Adolf Hitler ordered the murders of Ernst Roehm, other SA (storm trooper) leaders, and many other Nazis in the Blood Purge (June 29-30), also called the Night of the Long Knives.

Defeated and nearly encircled in Kiangsi, China, Communist forces embarked on the Long March (1934-1935), a fighting retreat 2,500 to 3,000 miles to Shensi, suffering massive casualties and defections en route; a defining event for Chinese communism.

Stalin's Great Purge (1934-1939) began, its pretext being the murder of Leningrad Communist Party leader Sergei Kirov. Ultimately, it took the lives of millions, including a major portion of the Communists' own party, government, industrial, and military elites, among them Marshal Mikhail Tukhachevsky and most of the Soviet officer corps, greatly missed when the Germans invaded (1941). Most Soviet "Old Bolshevik" leaders and many cultural figures also were murdered, as were many foreign communists who had taken refuge in the Soviet Union.

As Franklin D. Roosevelt's Latin American Good Neighbor Policy went into effect, the United States abrogated

d. Marie (Maria) Sklodowska Curie (1867-1934), Polish-French physicist and chemist noted for her work on radioactivity and the discovery of the elements radium and polonium (1898), originally with her husband, Pierre Curie. She was the first person to receive two Nobel Prizes (1903; 1911), the first to receive two in science, and the first woman Nobel winner. She and her daughter Irène Joliot-Curie were the only mother-daughter Nobel winners; both died of leukemia, probably caused by exposure to radiation.

French physicists Irène and Frédéric Joliot-Curie first artificially induced radioactivity, using bombardment to release particles and transform one element into another. Meanwhile, Italian-American nuclear physicist Enrico Fermi began to bombard uranium atoms with "slow" neutrons, exploring the creation of new elements.

Bulgarian-Swiss astrophysicist Fritz Zwicky and German-American astronomer Walter

with her early essay collection *Against Interpretation* (1966).

b. Willie Nelson (1933-   ), who would become a legendary American singer, songwriter, and guitarist.

d. John Galsworthy (1867-1933), major English writer from the appearance of his first novel, *A Man of Property* (1906), the first work in *The Forsyte Saga*.

d. Georges Braque (1882-1933), a major figure in 20th-century art; with Pablo Picasso, a founder of cubism.

Thomas Mann, now a refugee from Nazi Germany, where his books were being burned, began publication of his massive four-part novel *Joseph and His Brothers* (1934-1942).

Claudette Colbert and Clark Gable starred in Frank Capra's classic film comedy *It Happened One Night,* an early, luminous work of Hollywood's golden age.

Isak Dinesen emerged as a major writer with her short story collection *Seven Gothic Tales.*

José Clemente Orozco's massive murals *An Epic of American Civilization* were installed at Dartmouth College.

Käthe Kollwitz began her powerful eight-lithograph series *Death* (1934-1935), prefiguring the concentration camp images to come.

James Hilton published *Goodbye, Mr. Chips,* the basis for the 1939 and 1969 films.

Robert Flaherty wrote, directed, and shot his classic documentary film *Man of Aran,* exploring the lives of poor fishing families on Aran, off the Irish coast.

In a nontitle fight, German heavyweight boxer Max Schmeling defeated young African-American boxer Joe Louis, using his victory to spread his Nazi Aryan supremacist views; in a rematch, Louis — by then world champion — would dispatch Schmeling in just two minutes.

The Federal Communications Commission (FCC) was established to assign radio wavelengths to stations and regulate broadcasting.

Midwestern bank robber and murderer Charles Arthur "Pretty Boy" Floyd (1901-1934) was killed by Federal Bureau of Investigation (FBI) agents; the death of a former "public enemy number one" drew great pro-FBI media attention.

Murderers and armed robbers Bonnie Parker and Clyde Barrow, who as "Bonnie and Clyde" had become folk heroes (1932-1934), were killed in a police ambush near Giblans, Louisiana (May 23).

Harry Bridges led an International Longshoremen's Association local strike in San Francisco that became the San Francisco General Strike.

1934 cont.

the 1901 Platt Amendment, which had established effective protectorate status for Cuba. American Marines also were withdrawn from Haiti, after a 19-year occupation (1915-1934).

Chancellor Engelbert Dollfuss took power by coup in Austria, setting up a one-party fascist state on the Italian model and defeating a socialist-led rising; he was assassinated by German-supported Austrian Nazis during their failed coup attempt (July 25).

In the wake of the 1929 stock market crash, the U.S. government created the Securities and Exchange Commission (SEC), as authorized by the 1933 and 1934 securities laws, beginning the era of financial industries regulation. President Franklin D. Roosevelt appointed Joseph P. Kennedy — father of President John F. Kennedy and Senators Robert Kennedy and Edward (Ted) Kennedy — to be first head of the New Deal agency.

Clashes on the Ethiopia–Italian Somaliland border presaged the coming Italian invasion of Ethiopia.

French financier Serge Stavisky, a Russian Jew, committed suicide (Jan. 3) after having been accused of bond fraud. The French fascist right used the case to build massive anti-Semitic, antidemocratic fascist demonstrations that threatened to destroy the republic; it did bring down the government, but a centrist coalition saved the Third Republic.

Nicaraguan Liberal Party general Augusto César Sandino (1893-1934) was killed by Conservative government forces while negotiating a cease-fire. Later in the century, Nicaraguan revolutionaries honored him by calling themselves Sandinistas.

b. Jonas Savimbi (1934-), founder of the National Union for the Total Independence of Angola (UNITA) (1966-) and its leader through the balance of the Angolan War of Independence and Civil War.

Baade recognized extremely bright novas as *supernovas*, theorizing that a massive star explodes and then collapses so completely as to form an extremely dense neutron star; this was confirmed in 1968.

Tritium, a radioactive isotope of hydrogen, was discovered by Australian physicist Marcus Laurence Oliphant; it would be used in nuclear fusion, in accelerators, and as a tracer in biological research.

Louis de Broglie coined the term *antiparticle*. Wolfgang Pauli and Victor Weisskopf showed that some nuclear particles have antiparticles.

Hungarian-Swiss chemist Georg Hevesy developed the use of radioactive tracers in plants, later also applied to humans.

Soviet physicist Peter Kapitza first reported on a new, simple technique for producing liquid helium. Long in Britain (1921-1934), he returned home for a visit and was not allowed to leave; special equipment that had been provided for his research at Cambridge University's Cavendish Laboratory was later shipped to him in the Soviet Union.

Ruth Benedict published *Patterns of Culture*, her influential work stressing cultural equality and relativity, specifically through comparison of the Native American Zuñi and Hopi cultures, and stimulating further comparative studies.

Jean Piccard and his wife, American Jeannette Ridon, set a height record at nearly 58,000 feet in Piccard's innovative balloon.

Radio pioneer Lee De Forest demonstrated a new sound system for motion pictures; it would be put into practical use only later.

William Powell and Myrna Loy created the classic Nick and Nora Charles roles in W. S. Van Dyke's film comedy-mystery *The Thin Man,* very loosely based on the 1932 Dashiell Hammett novel.

Sidney Howard's play *Dodsworth,* based on the 1929 Sinclair Lewis novel, starred Walter Huston and Fay Bainter as Sam and Fran Dodsworth; Huston would re-create his role in the 1936 film.

James M. Cain published his powerful first novel, *The Postman Always Rings Twice,* which would be the basis for several films.

Katherine Emery and Anne Revere starred as the teachers destroyed by false charges of lesbianism in Lillian Hellman's first play, *The Children's Hour.*

Robert Graves published his Roman historical novel *I, Claudius,* which would be the basis for a 1977 television series.

Ethel Merman sang the title song and starred in Cole Porter's Broadway musical *Anything Goes;* she also would star in the 1936 film.

Haldor Laxness began publication of his two-volume novel *Independent People* (1934-1935).

Italian playwright and novelist Luigi Pirandello was awarded the Nobel Prize for literature.

b. Wole Soyinka (Akinwande Oluwole Soyinka) (1934-   ), Nigerian playwright and poet; a world figure who would be awarded the 1986 Nobel Prize for literature.

b. Alan Bates (1934-   ), British actor; he would become a stage star as Mick in *The Caretaker* (1960).

b. Judi Dench (Judith Olivia Dench) (1934-   ), British actress who would star in strong classical roles from the late 1950s.

Karl Barth and Martin Niemöller established the Synod of Barmen, a key anti-Nazi church coalition pledging to "trust and obey only Jesus Christ and no other," in the words of its Barmen Declaration.

Mercedes-Benz developed the first diesel-powered car.

Highly publicized midwestern criminal John Dillinger was killed by FBI agents in Chicago (July 22).

At Barrington, Illinois (Nov. 27), FBI agents killed murderer and bank robber George "Baby Face" Nelson.

Streamlined car design was introduced, in the United States with the Chrysler Airflow and in France with the Citroën Traction Avant.

Elijah (Poole) Muhammad succeeded founder W. D. Fard Muhammad as head of the Nation of Islam.

British tennis player Fred Perry won the men's singles titles at Wimbledon (his first of three in a row); at the U.S. Open, where he was defending champion; and at the Australian Open.

Hakodate, Japan, was destroyed by a fire (Mar. 22) that killed 1,500 people.

The American excursion liner *Morro Castle* caught fire and sank off Asbury Park, New Jersey (Sept. 7-8), killing 134 people.

British historian Arnold Joseph Toynbee began publication of his popular 12-volume work *The Study of History* (1934-1961), outlining the rise and fall of civilizations and his ideas of historical progress.

Flash Gordon was created by cartoonist Alex Raymond.

L'il Abner was created by cartoonist Al Capp.

1934 cont.

b. Yakubu Gowon (1934-), Nigerian politician; in power from 1966 to 1975.

d. Alexander I (1888-1934) of Yugoslavia; assassinated by Croatian nationalists at Marseilles, France (Oct. 9). He was succeeded by his 11-year-old son, Peter; Prince Paul ruled as regent (1934-1941).

d. Heihachiro Togo (1848-1934), Japanese admiral; fleet commander at Tsushima (1905) and then naval chief of staff (1905-1909).

d. Paul von Hindenburg (1837-1934), World War I German commander in chief from 1916 and president of the Weimar Republic (1925-1933).

d. Raymond Poincaré (1860-1934), French politician; three times premier (1912-1913; 1922-1924; 1926-1929) and also president (1913-1920).

William Beebe and Otis Barton set a world depth record, descending more than 3,000 feet off Bermuda in their bathysphere.

Roger Tory Peterson published *Field Guide to the Birds,* the first of his many "Field Guides," which became standard pocket references.

b. Carl Sagan (1934-), American astronomer and writer especially known for his interest in space and the possibility of other life in the universe; codeveloper of the nuclear winter theory (1983).

b. Jane (Van Lawick-) Goodall (1934-), British zoologist known for her studies of chimpanzees in East Africa (1960-).

b. Yuri Alekseyevich Gagarin (1934-1968), Soviet astronaut.

b. Robert Arthur Moog (1934-), American inventor who would develop the Moog electronic synthesizer (1964).

1935

Nazi Germany turned decisively toward war, repudiating the disarmament provisions of the Treaty of Versailles. The Saar Valley was reclaimed after residents voted overwhelmingly to return to Germany. Germany moved toward the mass murders of the Holocaust with passage of the anti-Jewish Nuremberg Laws (government decrees), as anti-Jewish persecution mounted.

Italian forces with modern equipment and air support took Ethiopia (Oct. 1935-May 1936), practicing terror bombing of defenseless civilian populations, in a rehearsal for Spain and World War II, ignoring empty League of Nations protests.

Scottish physicist Robert Alexander Watson-Watt developed the first practical aircraft-detecting radar; with later improvements, it would give Britain a significant edge during World War II's Battle of Britain.

American biochemist Edward Calvin Kendall first isolated the hormone cortisone, which would be widely used as an anti-inflammatory medicine, one of more than two dozen cortical hormones he would isolate.

b. Maggie Smith (Margaret Natalie Smith) (1934-), British actress; a notable theater figure from the mid-1960s.

b. Sophia Loren (Sofia Scicolone) (1934-), Italian actress; a sex symbol who would emerge as a leading dramatic actress in the 1960s.

b. Shirley MacLaine (Shirley MacLean Beaty) (1934-), American film star; a powerful dramatic actress from the late 1970s.

b. Joan Didion (1934-), American novelist, essayist, and screenwriter.

d. Edward Elgar (1855-1934), celebrated English composer.

d. Gertrude Stanton Käsebier (1852-1934), leading American photographer; a member of the Photo-Secession.

d. Andrei Bely (1880-1934), Russian writer; a leading symbolist.

d. Arthur Wing Pinero (1855-1934), British playwright.

b. Winnie Nomzano Mandela (1934–); South African freedom movement leader; the wife of Nelson Mandela.

b. Gloria Steinem (1934-), American feminist writer and founding editor of *Ms.* magazine (1971).

b. Ralph Nader (1934-), American lawyer who would become a key leader in the American consumer protection movement.

b. Kate Millett (1934-), American radical feminist, teacher, sculptor, and writer, most notably of *Sexual Politics* (1970).

Todd Duncan and Anne Brown created the title roles in George Gershwin's landmark folk opera *Porgy and Bess*, set in African-American life; based on Dubose Heyward's 1925 novel and the 1927 play.

Clark Gable and Charles Laughton starred as Fletcher Christian and Captain Bligh in Frank Lloyd's film version of *Mutiny on the Bounty*.

Humphrey Bogart was Duke Mantee opposite Leslie Howard and Peggy Conklin in Robert Sherwood's play *The Petrified Forest*.

The trailblazing Social Security Act set up a federally guaranteed benefits system for retirees and survivors that was to grow into a massive federal-state social insurance network.

The National Labor Relations Act (Wagner Act) established the National Labor Relations Board (NLRB), giving it jurisdiction over union certification and many other labor-management matters; it made union organization far easier by prohibiting designated unfair labor practices by employers and providing new safeguards for workers engaged in organization and collective bargaining.

Bulgarian Comintern leader Georgi Dimitrov introduced the Soviet-ordered worldwide "United Front against fascism" policy, occasioned by Soviet fear of resurgent Nazi Germany, fascist Italy, and militarist Japan. Communists everywhere embraced formerly scorned socialists and liberals — until the 1939 Nazi-Soviet Nonaggression Pact brought another "flip-flop."

In France, socialists led in the formation of the Popular Front, a coalition of the Left formed to counter the country's allied fascist and monarchist movements; the Popular Front would take power in 1936.

Ramsay MacDonald resigned as prime minister of Britain's Conservative-dominated coalition government; he was succeeded by Stanley Baldwin (1935-1937), who presided over two years of drift and inaction, as Britain failed to oppose the rise of fascism, offering no opposition to Benito Mussolini's invasion of Ethiopia, Adolf Hitler's march into the Rhineland, or the Italian-and-German-supported fascist rising in Spain.

Chinese Communist Long March survivors headquartered in Yenan, Shensi, beginning the Yenan Period of Chinese communism.

The American Neutrality Act banned the supply of arms or loans to belligerents and withdrew protection from American nationals sailing on the ships of belligerents. The act would function as a major bar to American aid to Spain.

At Baton Rouge, Louisiana (Sept. 8), Louisiana governor and political machine boss Huey Pierce Long (1893-1935) was assassinated by Dr. Carl Weiss, who was then killed by Long's bodyguards.

Clement Attlee became leader of Britain's Labour Party (1935-1955).

Czech foreign minister Eduard Benes succeeded Tomás Masaryk as president of Czechoslovakia (1935-1938); he served until the dismemberment of his country at Munich.

To rate earthquake magnitude, American seismologist Charles F. Richter developed the Richter scale, a nine-point geological scale, with each point 10 times the strength of the previous one.

Canadian-American physicist Arthur Jeffrey Dempster discovered that uranium had two isotopes, the common U-238 and the rare U-235, which would become of vital importance in nuclear fission (1942).

Applying the approach developed by James Batcheller Sumner with enzymes (1926), American biochemist Wendell Meredith Stanley first isolated a living virus (the tobacco mosaic virus) in crystal form.

Austrian-German zoologist Konrad Lorenz described the process of *imprinting*, by which birds attach themselves in early life to a nearby moving being (or even object), generally but not necessarily their mother; a fundamental set of observations in animal behavior, or ethology.

Irène and Frédéric Joliot-Curie received the Nobel Prize for chemistry for their induction of radioactivity (1934).

Japanese physicist Hideki Yukawa developed a theory of the forces operating within an atomic nucleus, which predicted the existence of an unknown nuclear particle, later discovered by Cecil Frank Powell (1947) and named the pi-meson (pion).

Swiss chemist Paul Karrer first synthesized vitamin B_2 (riboflavin), expanding understanding of the whole range of B vitamins.

Danish biochemist (Carl Peter) Henrik Dam discovered vitamin K, found vital to proper clotting of blood.

John Steinbeck published the novel *Tortilla Flat,* set in a Depression era California fishing town.

Maxwell Anderson's verse play *Winterset,* on themes related to the Sacco-Vanzetti case, starred Burgess Meredith, Richard Bennett, and Margo.

Theodore Newton, Elspeth Eric, and Joseph Downing starred in Sidney Kingsley's Depression era melodrama *Dead End.*

Victor McLaglen created the Gyppo Nolan role in John Ford's classic film *The Informer,* based on Liam O'Flaherty's 1925 Irish Revolution novel.

Laura Ingalls Wilder published *Little House on the Prairie,* the basis for the 1974-1983 television series.

The songs "Cheek to Cheek," "Top Hat, White Tie, and Tails," and "Isn't This a Lovely Day?" were introduced by Fred Astaire, starring and dancing opposite Ginger Rogers in Irving Berlin's *Top Hat.*

Leni Riefenstahl created the Nazi propaganda film *The Triumph of the Will,* shot at the 1934 Nuremberg Nazi Party Congress.

Elias Canetti published the novel *The Tower of Babel.*

b. Elvis Presley (1935-1977), American singer and actor who would become an emblematic figure in rock and roll and a world celebrity.

b. Julie Andrews (Julia Elizabeth Welles) (1935-   ), British singer and actress; a star from her Eliza Doolittle in *My Fair Lady* (1956).

b. Bibi Andersson (1935-   ), Swedish actress who would become an international star in Ingmar Bergman's classic 1950s films.

b. Luciano Pavarotti (1935-   ), leading Italian tenor.

The Committee for Industrial Organizations was founded; led by miners' union chief John L. Lewis, it successfully organized steel, auto, and other industrial unions, which later joined in the Congress of Industrial Organizations (CIO).

In *Schecter Poultry Corporation v. United States,* the U.S. Supreme Court declared unconstitutional the main provisions of the National Industrial Recovery Act, crippling the operations of the National Recovery Administration (NRA), which ceased operations (1936).

The Works Progress Administration (WPA) was established; its first head was Harry Hopkins.

Bill Wilson and Bob Smith founded Alcoholics Anonymous (AA), which became a worldwide organization for recovering alcoholics.

George Gallup founded the American Institute of Public Opinion, signaling the massive worldwide development of the public opinion and market research poll.

John Maynard Keynes published his highly influential *The General Theory of Employment, Interest, and Money,* laying the basis for state economic intervention aimed at avoiding the conditions that had led to the Great Depression.

The Red Rock Lakes Migratory Waterfowl Refuge in southern Montana's Centennial Valley was established, in what would be a pioneering and successful effort to save the endangered trumpeter swan.

African-American track athlete Jesse (James Cleveland) Owens came to wide attention when, competing for Ohio State University, he equaled or bettered four world records in just an hour; his broad jump record of 26 feet 8¼ inches would last for a quarter century.

1935 cont.

Reinforced Paraguayan forces decisively defeated Bolivian forces in the Chaco War, ending major engagements.

b. Hussein I (1935-　　), king of Jordan (1952-　　).

b. António Ramalho Eanes (1935-), Portuguese president (1976-1986).

d. Alfred Dreyfus (1859-1935), French army officer whose conviction for treason (1894) had been tainted by anti-Semitism, generating a massive and ultimately successful campaign for his exoneration and reinstatement.

d. Thomas Edward Lawrence ("Lawrence of Arabia") (1883-1935), legendary British desert fighter; an adviser to Faisal during the Arab Revolt (1916) and author of *The Seven Pillars of Wisdom* (1926).

d. John Rushworth Jellicoe (1859-1935), British admiral; World War I Home Fleet commander in chief, fleet commander at Jutland (1916), and first sea lord (1916-1917).

d. Jósef Klemens Pilsudski (1867-1935), Polish general; Soviet-Polish war commander in chief (1920) and Polish dictator (1926-1935).

The male sex hormone testosterone was synthesized by Croatian-Swiss chemist Leopold Ruzicka.

British physicist James Chadwick was awarded the Nobel Prize for physics for his discovery of the neutron (1932).

d. Emmy (Amalie) Noether (1882-1935), German mathematician; a pioneer in noncommutative algebra, whose work on the general theory of ideals and abstract algebra laid the basis for the "Noether school."

b. Woody Allen (Allen Stewart Konigsberg) (1935-), American director, actor, and writer.

b. Carl Andre (1935-), American sculptor; a leading minimalist from the mid-1960s.

d. Gaston Lachaise (1882-1935), French-American sculptor best known for his "earth goddess" nudes.

d. Henri Barbusse (1873-1935), French journalist, novelist, and poet; best known for his antiwar novel *Under Fire* (1916).

d. Alban Berg (1885-1935), Austrian composer; a leading figure in the development of atonal work and serialism.

d. Edwin Arlington Robinson (1869-1935), leading American poet.

d. Kasimir Malevich (1878-1935), Russian painter; the founder of suprematism.

d. Will (William Penn Adair) Rogers (1879-1935), American entertainer, humorist, and film star.

British automobile racer Malcolm Campbell first broke the 300-mile-per-hour land speed record, reaching 301.13 miles per hour.

b. Eldridge Cleaver (1935-), African-American radical civil rights activist and author; later a born-again Christian lecturer.

d. Jane Addams (1860-1935), leading social reformer, peace activist, and civil libertarian; founder of Hull House (1889); cofounder of the Women's International League for Peace and Freedom (1919) and the American Civil Liberties Union (1920); cowinner of the 1931 Nobel Peace Prize.

d. Billy (William Ashley) Sunday (1862-1935), American fundamentalist Christian; a leading revival meeting preacher (from 1896).

d. Georges Auguste Escoffier (1846-1935), French chef who set standards for modern international cuisine, notably at Monte Carlo's Grand Hotel, Lucerne's National Hotel, and London's Savoy and Carlton Hotels.

d. Oliver Wendell Holmes (1841-1935), American scholar, writer, and legal philosopher; as a U.S. Supreme Court justice (1902-1935), the Court's much-quoted "Great Dissenter."

d. Wiley Post (1899-1935), American around-the-world flier; he and comedian Will Rogers, his passenger, died in a plane crash at Point Barrow, Alaska, en route to Asia.

Incumbent Democratic U.S. president Franklin Delano Roosevelt defeated Republican Alfred M. Landon to win a second term (1937-1941) by a landslide, with Landon winning only in Vermont and Maine.

Fascist general Francisco Franco led a military insurrection in Morocco and mainland Spain against Spain's Republican government, with very substantial German and Italian support; Franco took much of southern Spain and began the siege of Madrid (Nov. 1936-Mar. 1939). The republic was supported by the Soviet Union and by Comintern-organized International Brigades and smaller anarchist-organized international volunteer forces, but received no military aid from the Western democracies.

Germany abrogated the Versailles and Locarno treaties, occupying the Rhineland with complete impunity and greatly encouraging further Nazi aggression; a milestone on the road to World War II.

Many government officials were assassinated during a failed right-wing army coup in Tokyo (Feb. 26-28); although many of the rebels were later executed, the action forced Japan even further toward militarism, fascism, and world war.

The Ethiopian city of Addis Ababa fell to invading Italian forces; Italy annexed Ethiopia, as the war effectively ended.

As part of the Great Purge (1934-1939), Moscow "show trials" began (1936; 1937; 1938); these were to destroy much of the Soviet military, civil, and cultural leadership of the time.

At Xian (Sian), in northern China, Chiang Kai-shek was kidnapped and held by his ally, Manchurian warlord Chang Hsüeh-liang (Dec. 12-25), until he agreed to negotiate a truce and develop a united Chinese front against the Japanese, all of which then eventuated.

Léon Blum became premier of France, at the head of the antifascist leftist coalition Popular Front government (1936-1937).

After some years of experiments showing that organs and tissue could be kept alive by *perfusion* (artificial supply of blood or blood substitutes), Alexis Carrel was joined by Charles Lindbergh (better known as an aviator) in developing an external blood-pumping device, called the Lindbergh machine or perfusion pump, to supply blood to the body's organs. With later improvements, this would help make possible open-heart surgery, organ transplants, and artificial hearts.

British mathematician Alan Turing demonstrated that no single method could be used to prove or disprove all logical statements in mathematics; Alonzo Church came to the same conclusion independently.

German-American physicist Erwin Wilhelm Mueller developed the field-emission microscope, the first to show individual atoms, using the image created when electrons are released from a heated needle.

Swiss chemist Daniele Bovet found that sulfanilamide, known since 1908, was the bacteria-fighting compound contained in the "wonder drug" Prontosil (1932). It would be the first of many "sulfa" drugs, the main antibacterial medicines before penicillin began to be widely used (1940s).

German rocket expert Wernher von Braun was made head of a secret government project to develop military rockets; he and other German rocket enthusiasts had already sent a liquid-fuel rocket 1.5 miles into the air (1934). Their Peenemünde research site would be a prime target for Allied bombing during World War II.

While British engineer Frank Whittle was preparing his turbojet engine (patented 1930) for testing, German engineers under Hans von

Charles Chaplin wrote, directed, produced, and starred opposite Paulette Goddard in his notably still-silent film *Modern Times,* his Tramp now a modern everyman beset by modern industrial society.

Dorothea Lange shot the emblematic Depression era still photo *Migrant Mother, Nipomo, California.*

Margaret Mitchell published her only novel, *Gone With the Wind,* on Confederate themes; it won a Pulitzer Prize, became a worldwide best-seller, and was the basis for the 1939 worldwide hit film.

Paul Robeson as Joe sang "Ol' Man River" in James Whale's film version of *Show Boat,* costarring Irene Dunne, Allan Jones, and Helen Morgan.

Robert Capa shot the celebrated Spanish Civil War photo *Death of a Loyalist Soldier,* emblematic of all the wars of a war-torn century.

Walter Huston, Ruth Chatterton, and Mary Astor starred in William Wyler's classic film version of *Dodsworth,* adapted by Sidney Howard from his 1934 play, based on the 1929 Sinclair Lewis novel.

André Malraux published his Spanish Civil War novel *Man's Hope,* based on his own Republican air force experience; he would write and direct the 1945 film.

Carl Sandburg published his long, narrative poem *The People, Yes,* on populist themes.

Constantin Brancusi carved the first version of his long sculpture series *The Seal* (1936-1943).

Konstantin Stanislavsky published *An Actor Prepares,* a "bible" for aspiring actors the world over.

Gary Cooper starred in the title role opposite Jean Arthur in Frank Capra's populist Depression era film fable *Mr. Deeds Goes to Town.*

At the Berlin Olympics, African-American track champion Jesse Owens won four gold medals — in the 100 meters, 200 meters, 4 × 100-meter relay, and long jump — much to the consternation of racist German hosts, notably Adolf Hitler, who left the stadium rather than personally congratulate Owens.

The Volkswagen (people's car) was designed by Ferdinand Porsche, at the request of Germany's Nazi Party, its name reportedly suggested by Hitler himself; widely popular after the war, the model also would be the basis for Porsche's postwar cars (1948).

American tennis player Alice Marble won the first of her four U.S. women's singles championships (1936; 1938-1940), the more remarkable because she had fought her way back after having tuberculosis.

Bruno Richard Hauptmann was executed (Apr. 3) for the kidnapping and murder of 20-month-old Charles A. Lindbergh, Jr. (1932).

Eleanor Roosevelt's new newspaper column, "My Day," became a syndicated, widely read vehicle for her views and those of her husband, Franklin Delano Roosevelt.

In *United States v. Butler,* the U.S. Supreme Court struck down the Agricultural Adjustment Act and its Agricultural Adjustment Administration (AAA) as unconstitutional; Congress moved to accomplish its goals piecemeal, with devices such as subsidies and parity payments, production quotas, and surplus storage.

Walter Reuther of the United Auto Workers led the first sit-down strike; he and his union would take the technique into the pivotal General Motors sit-down strike a year later.

Detroit Catholic priest Charles Edward Coughlin, an anti-Jewish, pro-Nazi publisher and radio broadcaster, began to encounter heavy criticism even

In an attempt to block the rise of fascism in France, the government banned several fascist and monarchist groups, most notably the Croix de Feu (Cross of Fire), which in the early 1930s had come close to toppling the Third Republic.

Germany and Japan signed the Anti-Comintern Pact (Nov. 25), providing mutual support in any war with communist countries; Japan would not honor the pact after Germany invaded the Soviet Union (1941).

A Palestinian Arab general strike developed into the Arab Revolt (1936-1939), simultaneously an Arab-Jewish civil war and an Arab insurrection against British occupying forces.

d. George V (George Frederick Ernest Albert) (1865-1936), king of Great Britain (1910-1936); son of Edward VII and father of Edward VIII, who became the Duke of Windsor, and of George VI.

Succeeding to the British throne, Edward VIII announced his intention to marry Wallis Simpson, an American divorcée (Nov. 16); he was forced to abdicate (Dec. 10) and was succeeded by his brother, George VI, who later made them Duke and Duchess of Windsor.

Greek general Ioannis Metaxas became premier, then taking power as dictator (1936-1941).

Lebanese Maronite Christian leader Pierre Gemayel founded the Phalange Party; he, his party, and its militia would be a powerful force in Lebanon for half a century.

Panama's status as an American protectorate was ended by treaty.

d. Alexander Berkman (1870-1936), American anarchist who was the companion of Emma Goldman. Imprisoned for 14 years after his failed attempt to assassinate industrialist Henry Clay Frick (1892-1906), he was then a leading anarchist until he and Goldman were deported to

Ohain also were developing a jet engine. German engineer Heinrich Focke built a working helicopter.

German scientist Konrad Zuse began building an early computer — the Z_1 electromechanical calculator, the first of several models.

Hungarian-American physicist Eugene Paul Wigner developed mathematical theories describing the absorption of neutrons by atomic nuclei and predicting the likelihood of neutron capture, an approach that would become useful to those working on nuclear fission (from 1939).

American chemist Robert Runnels Williams first synthesized thiamine, or vitamin B_1, allowing scientists to prepare the substance for the treatment of beriberi, caused by lack of thiamine.

American biochemist Wendell Meredith Stanley isolated nucleic acids from the tobacco mosaic virus; Andrei Nikolaevitch Belozersky isolated pure DNA (deoxyribonucleic acid).

Polish-Swiss chemist Tadeusz Reichstein worked out the chemical structure of the hormone cortisone.

British photographer-inventor Arthur Kingston developed the first plastic lenses; meanwhile, in Germany, I. G. Farben developed contact lenses made of Plexiglas.

The Nobel Prize for physics was shared by American physicist Carl David Anderson, discoverer of the positron (1932), and Austrian-American physicist Victor Hess, discoverer of cosmic radiation (1911).

John Gutzon Borglum completed *Thomas Jefferson,* the second of his Mount Rushmore presidential sculptures.

Margot Fonteyn and Robert Helpmann danced the leads in Frederick Ashton's ballet *Apparitions,* music by Franz Liszt, set and costumes by Cecil Beaton.

T. S. Eliot published *Burnt Norton,* the first part of his long, four-part poem *Four Quartets* (1936-1943).

Greta Garbo starred opposite Robert Taylor in the title role of George Cukor's film version of Alexandre Dumas's 1852 novel *Camille.*

Marcel Pagnol completed his trilogy of "Marius" plays, set in Marseilles: *Marius* (1929), *Fanny* (1931), and *César* (1936). Each was the basis for a film (1931; 1931; 1936), and together they were the basis for *Fanny,* a stage musical (1954) and film (1961).

Henry Travers, Josephine Hull, and Frank Wilcox starred in the comedy *You Can't Take It with You* by Moss Hart and George S. Kaufman.

Sergei Prokofiev composed his symphonic story *Peter and the Wolf,* an instant children's classic.

The Richard Rodgers–Lorenz Hart musical *On Your Toes* introduced George Balanchine's ballet *Slaughter on Tenth Avenue.*

American playwright Eugene O'Neill was awarded the Nobel Prize for literature.

b. Vaclav Havel (1936-   ), Czech playwright who would become a leading dissenter and then president of free Czechoslovakia.

b. Mario Vargas Llosa (1936-   ), Peruvian writer who would be a leading Latin American novelist and a failed presidential candidate (1990).

within his own church, as the murderous face of fascism began to fully emerge. His radio broadcasts had been suspended after Franklin D. Roosevelt's electoral victory.

The Rural Electrification Administration (REA) was established, spurring the development of farmers' cooperative power companies.

Vicente Lombardo Toledano founded and became first president (1936-1941) of the Confederation of Mexican Workers (CTM).

British aircraft designer Reginald Joseph Mitchell developed the Spitfire, the main fighter plane for Britain's Royal Air Force during World War II; 22,000 would be built by the end of the war Mitchell died of cancer shortly before the first production models were delivered (1938).

British tennis player Fred Perry won the men's singles titles at Wimbledon (his third in a row) and the U.S. Open (his third in four years).

The British Broadcasting Corporation (BBC) began television broadcasts.

Ty (Tyrus Raymond) Cobb, the "Georgia Peach," became the first player elected to the Baseball Hall of Fame. Among his many records were a career batting average of .367 and 2,244 runs scored.

American bridge expert Charles Goren published *Winning Bridge Made Easy,* the first of his many books, going on to become a widely syndicated columnist and leading player.

Beryl Markham was the first woman to fly solo east-west across the Atlantic.

1936 cont.

the Soviet Union (1919). Disillusioned, both later left the Soviet Union.

d. Edmund Henry Hynman Allenby (1861-1936), British general; Middle East commander from 1917 during World War I.

d. Eleutherios Venizelos (1864-1936), Greek politician; prime minister from 1910 through both Balkan Wars; he took Greece into World War I on the Allied side in 1917 and represented Greece at the Paris Peace Conference (1919). He also was prime minister (1924; 1928-1932).

d. William "Billy" Mitchell (1879-1936), American flying officer who was court-martialed for his outspoken criticism of American air war preparation (1925); he would be posthumously honored for his prophetic vision of the importance of airpower.

d. A. (Alexander) Mitchell Palmer (1872-1936), American lawyer; while U.S. attorney general (1919-1921), he organized the Palmer Raids, a major feature of the Red Scare (1919-1920).

d. Louis McHenry Howe (1870-1936), key political adviser to Franklin D. Roosevelt (1911-1936) and his personal assistant from 1915.

Dutch-American physical chemist Peter Debye received the Nobel Prize for chemistry for his work on dipole moments in molecules (1912).

d. Ivan Petrovich Pavlov (1849-1936), Russian physiologist who laid the basis for modern behaviorism with his work on the type of learning he called *conditioning*, winning a Nobel Prize for physiology or medicine (1904).

1937

A clash between Japanese and Chinese troops at the Marco Polo Bridge, near Beijing (Peking) (July 7), was the Japanese pretext for beginning the Sino-Japanese War (1937-1945). Japanese forces took Shanghai after strong Chinese resistance, and went on to take much of northern China, including Beijing and Nanking, with the Chinese capital moving to Hankow. After taking Nanking, Japanese troops committed the massive set of atrocities that became known as the Rape of Nanking. Japanese forces also attacked Western naval forces on the Yangtze River, sinking the American gunboat *Panay* and creating the "*Panay* incident."

Augmented by German airpower and Italian ground forces, General Francisco Franco's forces continued to be-

British mathematician and logician Alan Turing published a key paper outlining a theoretical "Turing machine" to help analyze and identify which problems were solvable by logical machines, and by mathematics in general, an analysis that helped shape early computers.

Studying photosynthesis, American chemist Melvin Calvin began using radioactive tracers in plants, detailing the series of chemical reactions by which plants use sunlight, carbon dioxide, and water to produce vital nutrients such as proteins, carbohydrates, and fats.

1936 cont.

b. Glenda Jackson (1936-), leading British actress, from her role in *Marat/Sade* (1964).

d. Federico Garcia Lorca (1899-1936), leading Spanish poet and playwright; his life and career would be cut short by Spanish fascists at Granada.

d. Maxim Gorky (Aleksei Maximovich Peshkov) (1868-1936), Russian writer and revolutionary; a major figure in Soviet literature.

d. (Joseph) Rudyard Kipling (1865-1936), leading English writer, largely on Anglo-Indian themes.

d. Ernestine Schumann-Heink (1861-1936), Austrian-American contralto; a leading opera and concert singer.

d. Luigi Pirandello (1867-1936), Italian playwright and novelist.

d. La Argentina (Antonia Mercé) (1890-1936), leading Spanish dancer.

d. Marilyn Miller (Mary Ellen Reynolds) (1898-1936), American singer, dancer, and actress.

British philosopher A. J. Ayer published his first book, *Language, Truth, and Logic,* introducing logical positivism to English-speaking audiences.

Henry and Edsel Ford founded the Ford Foundation; after acquiring massive funds by bequest (1950), the foundation would become a considerable force in American life.

d. (Joseph) Lincoln Steffens (1886-1936), American journalist and "muckraker"; late in his life, a socialist and then a communist.

d. Moritz Schlick (1882-1936), German physicist and philosopher; a key founder of the Vienna Circle, an influential discussion group of logical positivists.

1937

Pablo Picasso painted his landmark *Guernica,* after the terror bombing of the Basque city by Nazi bombers; exhibited at the Paris Exposition, it became an emblematic work of antifascist resistance in a world headed for the nightmare years of World War II.

While war raged in Spain and China and another world war approached, Jean Renoir's classic anti-war film *Grand Illusion,* about the escape of World War I French prisoners of war from German captivity, pleaded the case for transcendent humanity.

Huge floods struck the Mississippi and Ohio River basins (Jan.-Feb.); 200 to 300 people died, 600,000 to 700,000 were evacuated, many towns and even such large cities as Louisville and Cincinnati were flooded, and damage estimates reached half a billion dollars.

The hydrogen-filled German dirigible (zeppelin) *Hindenburg* exploded in flames while being moored at Lakehurst, New Jersey (May 6), killing 36 of the 98 people aboard. The tragedy was one of the first to be reported "live" on radio, creating a massive shock. Regular use of such rigid, hydrogen-filled airships effectively ended, although nonrigid blimps,

siege Madrid and to press forward in northern Spain. Anarchist-Communist fighting in Barcelona (May) somewhat weakened Republican resistance, while German terror bombing, as at Guernica (Apr. 25), was clearly a rehearsal for wars to come. The world's democracies still refused direct aid to Republican Spain; the Soviet Union did send aid but took in payment Spain's entire supply of gold. As Stalin's reign of terror intensified in the Soviet Union, many Soviet officers were withdrawn from Spain to face execution and imprisonment at home, further weakening Republican armed forces.

d. Mikhail Nikolayevich Tukhachevsky (1893-1937), Russian Civil War chief of staff, architect of the Red Army, and leading Soviet modern military strategist; executed on false treason charges, as were most of the Soviet officer corps, an irreparable set of losses that left the Soviet military essentially leaderless in 1941 when the Nazis came, probably at a cost of millions of lives.

President Franklin D. Roosevelt, many of whose New Deal legislative measures had been declared unconstitutional by the U.S. Supreme Court, attempted to "pack" the Court with his supporters, seeking legislation that would have expanded the membership of the Court with his own nominees. After enormous bipartisan opposition developed, the proposed legislation was withdrawn.

Britain's Peel Commission recommended an Arab-Jewish partition of Palestine. Arab world support for the Palestinian Arabs began to gain momentum.

b. Colin Luther Powell (1937-   ), American general; the first African-American head of the Joint Chiefs of Staff (1989-1993).

b. Saddam Hussein (1937-   ), ruler of Iraq (1971-   ) and later formally president (1979-   ).

b. Gary Hart (1937-   ), American politician; Colorado senator (1974-1986) and failed contender for the Democratic presidential nomination (1988).

d. Andrew William Mellon (1855-1937), American banker; conservative Republican treasury secretary

German-British biochemist Hans Adolf Krebs discovered the sequence of chemical reactions by which cells obtain energy; this metabolic sequence was named the citric acid, or Krebs, cycle.

Electroconvulsive therapy (ECT), the use of controlled electrical shocks to cause temporary loss of consciousness in mental patients, was introduced by Italian physicians Ugo Cerlutti and Lucio Bini; though controversial, it was widely used until the advent of tranquilizers.

The first radio telescope, a backyard parabolic-reflector dish approximately 31 feet across, was built by American astronomer Grote Reber, who would use it to lay out the first radio map of the heavens (by 1942).

British plant pathologist Frederick Charles Bawden showed that the tobacco mosaic virus (isolated 1935) is not composed solely of protein, then regarded as the "essence of life," but also contains nucleic acids — RNA and, it was found later, DNA — which carry basic genetic information.

Element 43 (technetium) was the first element formed artificially in the laboratory, by Italian physicist Emilio Segrè and his team. While teaching in California, Segrè would be removed from his University of Palermo (Italy) post by the Fascists (1938); he would then remain in the United States.

American biochemist Conrad Arnold Elvehjem discovered the B vitamins niacin (nicotinic acid) and niacinamide (nicotinamide); lack of B vitamins causes the vitamin-deficiency disease pellagra.

French pharmacologist Daniele Bovet developed the first antihistamine.

Frank Lloyd Wright's Fallingwater, a home at Bear Run, Pennsylvania, became a centerpiece of modern architecture, as did his own home, Taliesin West, at Scottsdale, Arizona.

J. R. R. Tolkien created the fantasy world of Middle Earth and the race of hobbits in his novel *The Hobbit.*

Margaret Bourke-White published *You Have Seen Their Faces,* her celebrated photo-essay on the Depression era South, text by Erskine Caldwell, her husband.

Sylvia Sidney, Joel McCrea, Humphrey Bogart, and the Dead End Kids starred in William Wyler's classic film version of *Dead End;* Lillian Hellman's screenplay was based on the 1935 Sidney Kingsley play.

The first full-length cartoon, *Snow White and the Seven Dwarfs,* became a worldwide hit.

John Gutzon Borglum completed *Abraham Lincoln,* the third of his Mount Rushmore presidential sculptures.

Paul Muni and Luise Rainer starred in Sidney Franklin's film version of Pearl Buck's 1931 novel *The Good Earth.*

John Steinbeck published the novel *Of Mice and Men;* his dramatization starred Broderick Crawford and Wallace Ford.

Carl Orff composed the cantata *Carmina Burana (Songs of Beuren),* the first work of his "Trionfi" trilogy and his best-known work.

Zora Neale Hurston published the novel *Their Eyes Were Watching God.*

French writer Roger Martin du Gard was awarded the Nobel Prize for literature.

filled with nonflammable helium, remained in small-scale use.

d. Amelia Earhart (1897-1937), American aviator; the first woman to fly solo across the Altantic (1932); she and copilot Fred Noonan were mysteriously lost in the western Pacific (July 2) while on an around-the-world flight; some have alleged that she was taken by the Japanese as a spy and then killed.

American boxer Joe Louis defeated James J. Braddock to become world heavyweight champion, the second African-American to hold the title (1937-1949); he would successfully defend it a record 25 times before retiring.

At least 73 people died after taking the drug Elixir Sulfanilamide, sparking passage of the 1938 Federal Food, Drug, and Cosmetic Act, which would be enforced by the Food and Drug Administration (FDA).

In *National Labor Relations Board v. Jones & Laughlin Steel Corporation,* the U.S. Supreme Court declared constitutional the 1935 National Labor Relations Act; trade union organization intensified.

On Memorial Day, Chicago police fired on unionists striking at the Republic Steel Company, killing 10 people in what came to be known as the Memorial Day Massacre.

The United Auto Workers organized General Motors and other auto companies, using sit-down strikes to occupy workplaces, with the support of Michigan governor Frank Murphy, the National Guard, and President Franklin D. Roosevelt. The Supreme Court later held the sit-down strike illegal (1939), but by then union recognition had been won.

Harry Bridges founded and became first president (1937-1977) of the International Longshoremen's and Warehousemen's Union (ILWU), an affiliate of

(1921-1932) through the boom of the 1920s and the Crash of 1929.

d. Antonio Gramsci (1891-1937), Italian left socialist theoretician and a founder of the Italian Communist Party (1921). He was imprisoned by the Fascist government from 1926 until shortly before his death.

d. Elihu Root (1845-1937), American politician; secretary of war (1899-1904), secretary of state (1905-1909), New York Republican senator (1909-1915), and an architect of American imperial policy in the Caribbean, Latin America, and the Pacific.

d. (James) Ramsay MacDonald (1866-1937), British socialist politician; the first Labour Party prime minister (1924). He was Labour prime minister again (1929-1931) and then Labour-Conservative coalition prime minister (1931-1935).

d. Tomás Garrigue Masaryk (1850-1937), Czech independence movement leader from the 1890s until the establishment of independent Czechoslovakia; the first president of his country (1918-1935) and father of Czech diplomat Jan Masaryk.

South African–American microbiologist Max Theiler developed a vaccine against yellow fever.

The nuclear particle called the muon was discovered by American physicist Carl David Anderson, who had also discovered the positron (1932).

Russian-American geneticist Theodosius Dobzhansky's *Genetics and the Origins of Species* showed how variations from mutations allow natural selection to work its evolutionary changes at the molecular level.

For his work on vitamins, Swiss chemist Paul Karrer won the Nobel Prize for chemistry, shared with Walter Norman Haworth of Great Britain.

b. Valentina Vladimirovna Nikolayeva Tereshkova (1937-), Soviet astronaut; the first woman in space (1963).

d. Ernest Rutherford (1871-1937), New Zealand–born British physicist; longtime head of Cambridge University's Cavendish Laboratory who discovered alpha and beta rays (1899); codeveloped the theory that radioactivity results from the transformation of elements (1902-1903); codeveloped a basic atomic model (1911); discovered the proton (1914); and was the first to artificially split an atom (1919).

d. Guglielmo Marconi (1874-1937), Italian physicist and wireless telegraphy pioneer who sent the first transoceanic radio message (1901).

d. Alfred Adler (1870-1937), Austrian psychiatrist who developed the idea of the inferiority complex and its associated striving for superiority to compensate for feelings of inferiority.

b. Vanessa Redgrave (1937-), British actress; one of the leading actresses of her time; daughter of actors Michael Redgrave and Rachel Kempson, sister of Lynn and Corin Redgrave, and mother of actress Natasha Richardson. She would also become a leading figure in British leftist politics.

b. Jack Nicholson (1937-), American actor and director; an international film star, most notably for *One Flew Over the Cuckoo's Nest* (1975).

b. Dustin Hoffman (1937-), American actor who became a major film star in *The Graduate* (1967).

b. Jim (James Maury) Henson (1937-1990), American creator of the Muppets.

b. Bill Cosby (1937-), African-American actor and comedian; a popular figure of the 1980s.

b. Philip Glass (1937-), American composer who would emerge as a major experimental figure in popular music in the 1960s and a leading composer of operas in the 1970s.

b. Robert Redford (Charles Robert Redford, Jr.) (1937-), American actor, director, and producer who would become an international film star in *Butch Cassidy and the Sundance Kid* (1969).

b. Jane Fonda (1937-), American actress; a leading film star of the 1970s and antiwar activist; daughter of Henry Fonda.

d. George Gershwin (1898-1937), American composer; a major figure, most notably for *Rhapsody in Blue* (1924) and *Porgy and Bess* (1935).

d. Bessie Smith (1894-1937), leading American blues singer of the century.

d. Edith Wharton (1861-1937), American writer.

the new Congress of Industrial Organizations (CIO).

New York Supreme Court justice Joseph Force Crater disappeared without a trace (Aug. 6), creating a never-solved mystery.

American auto racer Wilbur Shaw won the first of his three Indianapolis 500 races (1937; 1939; 1940); he would later be president of the Indianapolis Speedway (1945-1954).

The chairlift was developed for use at Dollar Mountain, in Idaho's Sun Valley ski resort; it would be introduced in Europe by 1939.

American wrestler Man Mountain Dean (Frank Simmons Leavitt) retired from professional wrestling after nearly 7,000 matches and more than 30 movies.

At New London, Texas, a natural gas explosion destroyed a school (Mar. 18), killing 413 children and 14 teachers.

Near Patna, India, an express train derailed, killing 107 people (July 16).

b. Bobby Seale (1937-), African-American activist; cofounder of the Black Panther Party (1966).

d. John Davison Rockefeller (1839-1937), American industrialist whose huge Standard Oil of Ohio was dissolved by court order in 1892, and whose successor Standard Oil of New Jersey was dissolved by court order in 1911. He became a philanthropist on a grand scale, as would be his son, John D. Rockefeller, Jr., and his son's children, including New York governor and U S. vice president Nelson Rockefeller.

At Munich (Sept. 29-30), Britain and France, intent on a policy of "appeasement" toward Hitler, allowed Germany to annex large portions of northern Czechoslovakia (the Sudetenland) in return for what British prime minister Neville Chamberlain called a guarantee of "peace for our time," but without Czech consent. Germany would go on to take the rest of Czechoslovakia (Mar. 1939); after Munich, war was certain.

Germany annexed Austria (the Anschluss); Nazi forces moved in entirely unopposed, while the democracies did nothing to impede Nazi aggression, again greatly encouraging further German aggression and accelerating the onset of another world war.

On Crystal Night ("Kristallnacht") (Nov. 9-10), Nazis throughout Germany smashed the windows of, and in many instances destroyed, Jewish homes, synagogues, and businesses, killing many people and imprisoning an estimated 30,000; a major step on the road to genocide.

Japanese forces, though temporarily stopped when the Chinese flooded the Yellow River plain by breaching its dikes (June), took much of central China, also taking Canton to complete their conquest of the south China coast. The temporary capital at Hankow fell in heavy fighting, and the new capital became Chungking, in the southwest.

Congressman Martin Dies organized the Dies Committee, the first witch-hunting House Un-American Activities Committee (HUAC), using the new vehicle to attack President Franklin D. Roosevelt and a host of other targets as "pro-Communist."

Spanish fascist forces stalled on the Ebro River, in northern Spain, failing to take Barcelona; by year's end, Republican forces had been drained by an ill-advised counteroffensive and a slackening of Soviet aid; the end of the Spanish Civil War was near.

Japanese-Soviet conflict flared on the Siberia-Manchuria border; Russian Far Eastern forces repulsed repeated

British engineer G. S. Callendar first posited the greenhouse effect, the warming of the earth's atmosphere as human activities, notably burning of fossil fuels, produce larger amounts of carbon dioxide, which then trap infrared radiation from the sun, much as a greenhouse does.

Chester Floyd Carlson developed xerography, an inexpensive dry process of copying (xero means "dry" in Greek); he patented it (1940) and later licensed it to Xerox and other corporations.

The coelacanth, a type of fish that biologists thought had died out some 70 million years ago, was found off South Africa (Dec. 25); it is believed to have been closely related to the fish that first moved onto land, the ancestor of humans and other land animals.

Cystic fibrosis was first recognized as a distinct disease by American pathologist and pediatrician Dorothy Hansine Andersen, who also developed tests for its diagnosis.

American physicist Katherine Blodgett invented nonreflecting glass; her techniques for depositing a film on glass would be useful in chemistry, biophysics, and solid-state physics.

J. Robert Oppenheimer and George Volkoff predicted the existence of rapidly spinning neutron stars that emit regular bursts (pulses) of radiation. These stars, the remnants of a supernova and later called pulsars, were first discovered in 1967.

Soviet physicist Peter Kapitza announced that he had discovered superfluidity, virtually frictionless flowing of helium at extremely low temperatures, sometimes even flowing upward, against gravity.

Wendy Hiller as Eliza Doolittle and Leslie Howard as Henry Higgins starred in the film version of George Bernard Shaw's *Pygmalion,* directed by Anthony Asquith.

Sergei Eisenstein made the Soviet nationalist film *Alexander Nevsky,* music by Sergei Prokofiev, ending with the Battle on the Ice and the defeat of invading forces by the defending Russian army.

A national panic was inadvertently generated by Orson Welles's *War of the Worlds* radio broadcast, describing an imaginary Martian landing on earth and resultant hostilities, based on the 1898 H. G. Wells novel.

George Orwell published his Spanish Civil War essay collection, *Homage to Catalonia.*

Jean Gabin and Michèlle Morgan starred in Marcel Carné's classic film *Port of Shadows.*

Raymond Massey starred in the title role in Robert Sherwood's play *Abe Lincoln in Illinois.*

Eugene Loring choreographed and danced the lead in the American folk ballet *Billy the Kid,* music by Aaron Copland.

Robert Taylor, Margaret Sullavan, and Franchot Tone starred in Frank Borzage's film version of Erich Maria Remarque's antifascist 1937 novel *Three Comrades,* set in Germany between the wars.

Orson Welles and John Houseman's Mercury Theatre presented Marc Blitzstein's controversial play *The Cradle Will Rock.*

Sybil Thorndike and Emlyn Williams starred in Williams's play *The Corn Is Green.*

Marjorie Kinnan Rawlings published *The Yearling.*

American Donald Budge became the first tennis player to win a grand slam, winning the men's singles titles at the French and Australian Opens and successfully defending his titles at Wimbledon and the U.S. Open.

The Fair Labor Standards Act greatly improved wages and working conditions for those Americans engaged in interstate commerce, introducing the minimum wage, maximum straight-time workweek, overtime pay, sharp restrictions on child labor, and equal pay for equal work for women and regardless of age.

Under the Federal Food, Drug, and Cosmetic Act, the Food and Drug Administration (FDA) greatly expanded the range of products it monitored, to protect public health in areas such as foods, drugs, and product safety.

American federal prosecutors began an unsuccessful 18-year attempt to deport Australian-born longshoremen's union chief Harry Bridges as an alleged communist.

Cincinnati Reds pitcher Johnny Vander Meer pitched an unprecedented two successive no-hit games.

Boxer Henry Jackson Armstrong — called "Hurricane Henry" for his perpetual-motion style — became the only person to hold three world titles simultaneously: the featherweight, welterweight, and lightweight championships.

Jomo Kenyatta published *Facing Mount Kenya,* his classic anthropological study of the Kikuyu people.

Hungarian entrepreneurs Lazlo and George Biro invented the ballpoint pen, which would soon render obsolete the once ubiquitous fountain pen and inkwell.

Japanese attacks on their positions on disputed Changkufeng Hill.

Stalin's third Five-Year Plan (1938-1942) began; it would be cut short by the German invasion of the Soviet Union (1941), as would his continuing Great Purge.

Paraguay took most of the Chaco region and Bolivia won an outlet to the sea by the terms of the Treaty of Buenos Aires, fully settling the Chaco War.

b. John Wesley Dean III (1938-), American lawyer; counsel to President Richard M. Nixon (1970-1973) and a key prosecution witness in the Watergate affair.

b. Manuel Antonio Noriega (1938-), dictator of Panama (1982-1989) and later an American prisoner.

d. Atatürk (Mustapha Kemal) (1881-1938), founder and first president of the Turkish republic (1923-1938) who took the name Atatürk (Father of the Turks) in 1933.

d. Nicolai Ivanovich Bukharin (1888-1938), Soviet communist theoretician; a leader of the Bolshevik Revolution (1917) and a colleague of Lenin's; arrested during Stalin's Great Purge (1937) and executed with many other "Old Bolsheviks" after show trials in Moscow. Bukharin was later "posthumously rehabilitated" by the Soviet government (1988).

d. Vasili Konstantinovich Blücher (1889-1938), Soviet general; as "Galen," an adviser to China's Kuomintang (1924-1927); later commander of the Soviet Far Eastern Army. He was executed during the Great Purge and later "posthumously rehabilitated" by the Soviet government (1957).

d. Gabriele D'Annunzio (1863-1938), Italian Fascist; a writer and nationalist whose private army took disputed Fiume (1919-1921), which was later retaken by the Italian army.

Austrian-American physicist Isidor Isaac Rabi developed ways to accurately measure energy absorbed and released by beams of molecules, called *magnetic resonance*; his work laid the basis for applications such as the atomic clock, the laser, and magnetic resonance imaging.

German engineers developed their formidable tank, the Panzerkampfwagen, which could travel more than 10 times faster than the early British tanks (1916); in various sizes and models, these would prove devastating in concentrated "panzer" units during World War II.

Nylon was introduced by Du Pont; it had been developed by Wallace Hume Carothers (1934). When silk imports were cut off during World War II, it became popular for stockings and clothing.

Russian-American engineer Vladimir Zworykin developed the first practical electronic television, the *iconoscope*, which would be the basis for modern sets, replacing John Logie Baird's mechanical type.

Swiss chemist Paul Karrer first synthesized vitamin E.

The pressurized airplane cabin was introduced with the Boeing 307 Stratoliner.

Germany's Junkers company began developing ejection seats to be used in military aircraft; the first one was tested the following year.

Italian-American nuclear physicist Enrico Fermi was awarded the Nobel Prize for physics for work on bombarding elements with neutrons (1934).

American novelist Pearl Buck was awarded the Nobel Prize for literature.

b. Rudolf Nureyev (Rudolf Hametovich Nureyev) (1938-1993), Russian dancer and choreographer who would become an international ballet star.

b. Liv Ullmann (1938-), Norwegian actress who would emerge as an international film star in several Ingmar Bergman films.

b. Diana Rigg (Enid Diana Elizabeth Rigg) (1938-), British stage and screen actress best known as Emma Peel in television's *The Avengers* (1965-1967).

b. Joyce Carol Oates (1938-), American writer, often on feminist themes, who would emerge as a major novelist in the 1960s.

b. John Guare (1938-), American writer who would become a leading playwright in the 1970s.

b. Morgan Freeman (1938-), leading African-American actor.

d. Konstantin Stanislavsky (Konstantin Sergeivich Alexeyev) (1863-1938), Russian director and actor; one of the towering theater figures of the century.

d. Osip Mandelstam (1891-1938), leading Russian poet imprisoned in 1934 for publishing a poem offensive to the Stalin government; he died in prison.

d. King (Joseph) Oliver (1865-1938), seminal New Orleans jazz figure; a trumpeter, cornetist, bandleader, and composer.

d. Boris Pilnyak (Boris Andreyevich Vogau) (1894-1938), a leading writer of the Soviet period.

d. Feodor Ivanovich Chaliapin (1873-1938), leading Russian bass of the century.

d. James Weldon Johnson (1871-1938), African-American writer; a poet and lyricist.

The British Broadcasting Corporation (BBC) began its noted international foreign-language broadcasts.

Superman was created by cartoonists Jerry Siegel and Joe Shuster.

Two passenger trains collided near Kishinev, Romania (Dec. 25), killing 100 people.

b. Helen Broinowski Caldicott (1938-), Australian pediatrician who would become a leading anti-nuclear activist.

d. Clarence Seward Darrow (1857-1938), American defense lawyer who fought some of the leading cases of the century, including the murder trial of "Big Bill" Haywood (1907), the *Los Angeles Times* bombing trial of the McNamara brothers (1910), the Leopold and Loeb case (1924), and the Scopes evolution "monkey trial" (1925).

d. Benjamin Nathan Cardozo (1870-1938), American lawyer; a leading jurist and legal scholar and a U.S. Supreme Court justice (1932-1938).

d. Elzie Segar (1894-1938), American cartoonist who created *Popeye the Sailor* (1929).

d. Suzanne Lenglen (1899-1938), leading French tennis player; the winner of six Wimbledon titles (1919-1923; 1925).

The fall of Barcelona (Jan. 26) effectively ended the Spanish Civil War. The Republican army disintegrated; France and Britain recognized the fascist government (Feb.); Madrid and Valencia surrendered.

World War II approached. The Germans took what was left of Czechoslovakia (Mar. 10-16) and then took Memel, Lithuania (Mar. 23). German forces set to take the Polish city of Danzig (Gdansk) withdrew after a British ultimatum (Mar.); Britain continued to guarantee Polish independence. Italy annexed its protectorate Albania; Britain and France guaranteed Greek and Romanian independence (Apr.). The Nazi-Soviet Nonaggression Pact (Aug. 23-24), which partitioned Poland and secretly partitioned the Baltic states, directly signaled the imminence of war.

With the Nazi-Soviet pact, many of the world's Communist Parties "flip-flopped," abandoning their focus on antifascism and becoming "pacifist" (in the United States, "isolationist"); disillusioned, many antifascists left the parties.

World War II began (Sept. 1) with the German invasion of Poland; it would cost the lives of 15 million to 17 million people in the military and 25 million to 35 million civilians (including at least 6 million Jews in the Holocaust), with 23 million to 26 million casualties. France and Britain declared war on Germany (Sept. 3), soon followed by Australia, New Zealand, and Canada. The Allies would include the United States, the Soviet Union, Britain, France, China, and many smaller countries; the Axis would include Germany, Japan, Italy, and several smaller countries.

Polish forces were overwhelmed; besieged Warsaw fell (Sept. 27), and formal resistance ended (Nov.); the long guerrilla war began. Soviet forces took eastern Poland (Sept. 17) and then Latvia, Lithuania, and Estonia (Oct. 10), as provided by the Nazi-Soviet pact.

On the western front, the "Phony War" period of inaction began, with Allied armies facing the Germans on the

The term *nuclear fission* was coined by Lise Meitner in a landmark report (written with her nephew, Otto Frisch) on the possibility of splitting the uranium atom to release enormous amounts of energy (Jan.). She developed the theory after analyzing results of experiments she had performed with her long-term collaborator Otto Hahn, before she was forced to leave Nazi Germany (1938). Alerted by his assistant Frisch, Danish-American physicist Niels Bohr immediately described Meitner's report on nuclear fission at an American physics conference. Bohr himself, working with American physicist John Archibald, outlined the liquid-drop model of an atom's nucleus and recognized that the uranium-235 (U-235) isotope would be more fissionable than its more common cousin, U-238, an understanding basic to the development of the atomic bomb.

Concerned about German atomic experiments, Italian-American physicist Enrico Fermi, Hungarian-American nuclear physicist Leo Szilard, and others persuaded Albert Einstein to send President Franklin Roosevelt a letter (Aug. 2), drafted by Szilard, describing the atomic bomb as feasible and urging its development. The United States' Advisory Committee on Uranium, led by Szilard and Fermi, would result (1940); it would later be replaced by the Manhattan Project (1942-1945). Szilard also urged secrecy among American nuclear physicists so that their discoveries would not aid the Germans in a race toward the atomic bomb; this was a major change in the scientific community, which had widely shared information on new theories and discoveries.

The possibility of a nuclear chain reaction — a self-sustaining process of nuclear fission, given a critical mass of fuel — was recognized by others. Frédéric and Irène Joliot-Curie experimented with producing such a reaction, until

Celebrated African-American singer Marian Anderson was denied use of Washington's Constitution Hall, because of her race, by the Daughters of the American Revolution. In response, Eleanor Roosevelt sponsored Anderson's Easter Sunday Lincoln Memorial concert, a musical event attended by 75,000 to 100,000 people and simultaneously a landmark civil rights movement event.

James Joyce published *Finnegans Wake,* his final novel; as with *Ulysses* (1922), it was a major contribution to 20th-century literature.

John Steinbeck published his quintessential Depression era novel *The Grapes of Wrath,* his protagonists the "Okies" migrating to California after their land had blown away.

London's National Gallery was the site of pianist Myra Hess's marathon series of wartime classical concerts; she would become a legendary figure, continuing on through the German bombing campaigns.

British World War II songs included the classic "We'll Meet Again" and "There'll Always Be an England."

W. H. Auden published the poem "September 1, 1939," his lament for a European world again sinking into the darkness of war.

Vivien Leigh as Scarlett O'Hara and Clark Gable as Rhett Butler starred in Victor Fleming's film version of Margaret Mitchell's novel *Gone With the Wind,* which was to become a worldwide hit.

James Stewart starred in the title role in Frank Capra's populist film comedy *Mr. Smith Goes to*

Massive flooding on China's Yangtze River and throughout northern China reportedly killed 500,000 to 1 million people in one of the worst natural disasters of the century.

While the threat of war grew in Europe, and then became a reality, American war production began, and then accelerated, as orders for arms, land vehicles, ships, and all the basic necessities became a flood. The United States began to become the "arsenal of democracy" that would enable Allied armed forces to fight and win a war on many fronts. Only then did the American economy begin to fully recover from the Great Depression.

Crusading Manhattan district attorney Thomas E. Dewey mounted a major attack on national crime syndicate figures, among them Louis "Lepke" Buchalter, head of the syndicate's assassination squad, called by the media "Murder, Incorporated." Lepke surrendered to columnist Walter Winchell, thinking he had a "deal"; instead he was held on a wide range of charges, including murder, and was ultimately executed (1944).

In the United States, the first television sets went on sale to the public, and the first television pictures were transmitted — of an American president, a major league baseball game, and a college football game.

New York Yankees first baseman Lou Gehrig was forced to retire by the onset of the disease that would kill him (1941), amyotrophic lateral sclerosis, later called Lou Gehrig's disease. He had been called the "Iron Horse" for his stamina, playing in 2,130 consecutive major league games.

President Franklin D. Roosevelt opened the New York World's Fair (The World of Tomorrow) (1939-1940); its emblem and dominating structures were the Trylon and the Perisphere. In San Francisco, the Golden Gate International Exposition also opened

1939 cont.

Maginot Line, while German offensive preparations proceeded.

At sea, German surface raiders and submarines were active. The Battle of the Atlantic began with the sinking of the *Athenia* off Ireland (Sept. 3); it was to be followed by more than 250 other Allied ships that year, including the battleship *Royal Oak* and the aircraft carrier *Courageous*. British ships caught and disabled the German pocket battleship *Graf Spee* off Montevideo, Uruguay (Dec. 13); it was then scuttled by its crew.

Despite a formal proclamation of neutrality, the United States immediately began to rearm and covertly to supply the Allies. After the 1939 Neutrality Act authorized arms sales, the United States openly supplied the Allies.

After the Finns refused Soviet military base demands, massive Soviet forces invaded Finland (Nov. 30); in early fighting, they were stopped at the Mannerheim Line, while amphibious landings were thrown back in the south. At Suomussalmi (Dec. 1939-Jan. 1940), 25,000 to 30,000 Soviets were killed, with few Finnish losses.

In a crucial undeclared Manchurian-Soviet border war, General Georgi Zhukov's Far Eastern Red Army forces sharply defeated Japan's Kwangtung Army (May-Sept.); Japan then turned south and east, toward the coming invasion of Indochina and the Pacific war.

Japanese forces effectively completed their conquest of the Chinese coast; Chinese supplies from abroad then came overland through Haiphong, Indochina, and also through Rangoon on the new 700-mile Burma Road. After initial gains, Japanese spring ground offensives were contained by Nationalist and Communist Chinese forces.

Arab-Jewish peace talks at London's St. James Conference did not eventuate, as the parties could not even agree on how to begin talks. The civil war in Palestine was overtaken by World War II.

France fell (1940). They then hid their uranium store and smuggled out of the country their precious "heavy water" so that neither could aid the Germans, and they stayed to fight in the Resistance.

Hans Bethe developed the theory that the energy of the sun and the stars comes from a process of nuclear fusion, in which hydrogen nuclei merge (fuse), producing helium and energy, an understanding that laid the basis for the hydrogen bomb — and held the possibility of a powerful energy source, if it could be controlled.

Swiss chemist Paul Müller found that DDT (dichlorodiphenyltrichloroethane), known since the 19th century, was a powerful insecticide. Regarded as a wonder chemical, DDT was only later recognized as concentrating to toxic levels in the food chain and banned in the United States and many other countries (from 1972).

French-American bacteriologist René Dubos, the first person to deliberately search in the soil for naturally occurring antibiotics, discovered two — tyrocidine and gramicidin — which would be effective against the pneumococcus organism.

Acting as his own test pilot, Igor Sikorsky developed the first practical, mass-produced helicopter, setting the 20th-century standard.

Massachusetts Institute of Technology scientists built an experimental house heated by flat solar collectors on its roof; the technique was not widely used until the 1970s.

Russian-British biochemist David Keilin established that certain minerals were essential to the body in trace amounts.

Washington. He played the young senator who ultimately confounds the seasoned politicians and jaded skeptics.

Judy Garland starred as Dorothy in Victor Fleming's fantasy-musical film *The Wizard of Oz,* based on L. Frank Baum's 1900 novel.

Laurence Olivier as Heathcliff starred opposite Merle Oberon as Cathy in *Wuthering Heights,* William Wyler's celebrated screen version of Emily Brontë's 1847 novel.

Christopher Isherwood published the largely autobiographical novel *Goodbye to Berlin,* set in the Weimar period.

John Gutzon Borglum completed *Theodore Roosevelt,* the fourth of his Mount Rushmore presidential sculptures.

Tallulah Bankhead created the Regina Giddens role in Lillian Hellman's often-bitter southern family drama *The Little Foxes.*

John Wayne starred in John Ford's classic Western *Stagecoach.*

Basil Rathbone began his long film portrayal of Sherlock Holmes, starring in *The Hound of the Baskervilles,* based on the 1902 Arthur Conan Doyle tale, in the first of his 14 Holmes roles (1939-1946).

Greta Garbo starred as the humorless, finally liberated Russian trade delegate in *Ninotchka,* Ernst Lubitsch's Paris-set political satire.

Philip Barry's stage comedy *The Philadelphia Story* starred Katharine Hepburn, Van Heflin, Shirley Booth, and Joseph Cotten; Hepburn would re-create her role on film.

(1939-1940), on an artificial island built for the occasion in San Francisco Bay.

The New York Yankees won their fourth World Series in a row, defeating the Cincinnati Reds in a clean sweep, four games to none.

Pan American Airways began regular transatlantic and transpacific service, flying the famous "Clippers" designed by Igor Sikorsky; the first flight, to Lisbon, Portugal, was made by the *Dixie Clipper* in a little under 24 hours.

A massive earthquake at Erzincan, Turkey, took an estimated 30,000 to 40,000 lives.

American tennis player Alice Marble captured the U.S. and Wimbledon women's singles titles. Bobby Riggs won the U.S. and Wimbledon men's singles titles.

Germany saw two terrible train wrecks (both Dec. 22); the one at Magdeburg killed 125 people; the other, at Friedrichshafen, killed 99.

Labor leader Warren K. Billings was released; he had been sentenced to life imprisonment after the San Francisco Preparedness Day bombing (1916).

Near Lake Maracaibo, Venezuela, an oil refinery fire destroyed the town of Lagunillas (Nov. 14), killing more than 500 people.

New York's Rockefeller Center was formally completed and opened.

Oregon defeated Ohio State in the first National Collegiate Athletic Association (NCAA) postseason college basketball tournament.

Cartoonist Robert Kane created *Batman.*

b. Joaquim Alberto Chissanó (1939-   ), Mozambican general; president of Mozambique (1986-   ).

b. Violeta Barrios de Chamorro (1939-   ), president of Nicaragua (1990-   ).

d. Nadezhda Krupskaya (1869-1939), Bolshevik leader; wife of Vladimir Illich Lenin until his death (1898-1924).

d. Karl Bernhardovich Radek (Karl Sobelsohn) (1885-1939), an "Old Bolshevik" closely associated with Lenin before and during the October Revolution and the Russian Civil War; he died in a Soviet prison but was "posthumously rehabilitated" after Mikhail Gorbachev came to power.

d. Béla Kun (1886-1939), leader of the communist Hungarian Socialist Republic (Mar.-Aug. 1919); executed in the Soviet Union during the Great Purge.

American physicist J. Robert Oppenheimer first calculated the mass required for a star to form a "black hole" in space.

Element 87 (francium) was discovered by French physicist Marguerite Perey.

Germany's Heinkel HE 178 was the first airplane powered by a turbojet engine.

American biochemist Edward Adelbert Doisy isolated vitamin K.

Ernest O. Lawrence received the Nobel Prize for physics for his development of the cyclotron (1931).

d. Sigmund Freud (1856-1939), Viennese neurologist who founded psychoanalysis and developed a multilevel theory of personality (1912; 1923), giving primacy to sex. His followers would spread his ideas widely, especially in the United States.

William Saroyan's play *The Time of Your Life,* set on the San Francisco waterfront, starred Eddie Dowling, Julie Haydon, and Gene Kelly.

Finnish writer Franz Eemil Sillanpää was awarded the Nobel Prize for literature.

b. Francis Ford Coppola (1939-   ), leading American filmmaker, most notably of *The Godfather* (1972).

b. Jane Alexander (Jane Quigley) (1939-   ), leading American actress who would be appointed to head the National Endowment for the Arts in 1993.

b. Margaret Atwood (1939-   ), leading Canadian writer, often on feminist themes.

b. Alan Ayckbourn (1939-   ), leading British playwrite and director.

b. Judy Collins (1939-   ), American folksinger who would be a major folk revival figure in the 1960s.

b. Margaret Drabble (1939-   ), British writer and feminist.

d. William Butler Yeats (1865-1939), Irish poet and playwright; one of the century's leading literary figures and winner of the 1923 Nobel Prize for literature.

d. Douglas Fairbanks (Douglas Elton Ulman) (1883-1939), leading American action silent film star; husband of Mary Pickford.

d. Ford Madox Ford (Ford Madox Hueffer) (1873-1939), British writer, editor, and critic; author of *Parade's End* (1924-1928).

d. Ma Rainey (Gertrude Pridgett) (1886-1939), influential American blues singer.

d. Sidney Coe Howard (1891-1939), American writer; a major playwright from his *They Knew What They Wanted* (1924).

b. Germaine Greer (1939-   ), Australian feminist writer and critic; most notably author of *The Female Eunuch* (1970).

b. Marian Wright Edelman (1939–   ), African-American civil rights leader and social reformer; a leading children's rights advocate who founded and led the Children's Defense Fund (1973-   ).

d. Pope Pius XI (Ambrogio Damiano Achille Ratti) (1857-1939), Italian priest (1879-1939) and pope (1922-1939) who recognized the legitimacy of Italian fascism in the Lateran Treaty (1929) and accepted Nazi curbs on Catholic political action (1933), though later condemning German fascism, communism, and anti-Semitism.

d. Charles Michael Schwab (1862-1939), American industrialist; president of the Carnegie Steel Company (1897-1901), first president of the U.S. Steel Company (1901-1903), and founder and first president of the Bethlehem Steel Company.

Soviet forces broke through the Mannerheim Line (Feb.); Finland capitulated (Mar.), giving the Soviet Union the bases it had demanded.

German forces invaded Denmark and Norway (Apr. 9), quickly occupying Denmark and easily defeating Norwegian forces; Oslo fell (Apr. 10). Allied forces took Narvik (May) but would withdraw after the fall of France.

German forces using armored spearheads and with air superiority attacked France and the Low Countries (May 10), easily going around the Maginot Line. Dutch surrender came in only four days (May 14). In France, German forces made a decisive breakthrough in the Ardennes, near Sedan, and in three days (May 12-15) split the French army, reaching the Channel (May 21) and defeating the Allies. After Belgium surrendered (May 28), the forced British and French evacuation from Dunkirk began (May 28-June 4). Paris fell (June 14), and France surrendered (June 21); the Germans then installed the puppet Vichy government, headed by General Henri Philippe Pétain. French warships in Algeria were sunk or disabled by the British at Mers el-Kabir and Oran; other warships were disabled by their French crews at Alexandria. Charles de Gaulle organized the London-based Free French movement.

Winston Churchill replaced Neville Chamberlain as British prime minister, while Hitler prepared for a cross-Channel invasion of Britain. But necessary German air superiority over the Channel was denied by the Royal Air Force (RAF) in the Battle of Britain (Aug.-Oct.), in which the outnumbered RAF defeated the Luftwaffe in a series of massive battles; the Germans then went over to the ultimately ineffective terror bombing of the Blitz, while Hitler prepared to invade the Soviet Union.

German surface raiders and submarines scored damaging successes in the Battle of the Atlantic. The addition of 50 American destroyers, covertly given in a destroyers-for-bases swap, helped keep the Atlantic lifeline open.

Italy entered the war as a German ally (June 10), quickly besieging Malta. Italian forces in Albania invaded Greece

Karl Landsteiner and Alexander S. Weiner discovered the Rhesus (Rh) factor, a protein found in most people's blood. If blood with the factor (Rh+) is mixed with blood lacking it (Rh–), blood cells can be destroyed. This can be a problem in transfusions or in childbirth (if mother and child are incompatible). Once recognized, testing allowed the danger to be averted.

American physician Charles Richard Drew developed plans for the first large-scale storage of blood plasma in blood banks, supervising the collection of blood in the United States for Britain, by then at war. This was made possible because tests had been developed for incompatibility of blood by type and by the newly discovered Rhesus factor; tests also were developed to screen blood for disease.

American physicists Edwin Mattison McMillan and Philip Hauge Abelson discovered element 93 (neptunium). More important, with Glenn Seaborg, they discovered element 94 (plutonium), finding that the plutonium-239 (PU-239) isotope could be used in nuclear fission; Enrico Fermi would later show how to produce it (1942). Seaborg recognized that these *transuranium elements* — those beyond uranium in the periodic table — were a series, and he would lead teams discovering elements 95 to 102 (1944-1958). Abelson first outlined a "gaseous diffusion" method for producing enriched uranium, which contained more of the rare U-235 isotope required for a nuclear chain reaction.

Work began on development of the atomic bomb, led by Leo Szilard and Enrico Fermi, under the United States' Advisory Committee on Uranium, later succeeded by the Manhattan Project (1942-1945).

German-British physicists Rudolph Ernst Peierls and Otto Frisch (who with his aunt, Lise

Charles Chaplin wrote, directed, and starred in *The Great Dictator,* his caricature of Adolf Hitler capturing some of Hitler's posturing brutality, although the full measure of humanity's worst mass murderer was yet to be revealed.

Henry Fonda and Jane Darwell starred in *The Grapes of Wrath,* John Ford's quintessential film version of John Steinbeck's Depression era novel.

Arthur Koestler published the novel *Darkness at Noon,* an exposé of the show trials of Stalin's Great Purge; his protagonist was an Old Bolshevik forced to make a false confession.

Bird in Flight was Constantin Brancusi's celebrated, highly abstract sculpture, the latest in a long series of increasingly abstract works stretching back to the *Maiastra* (1912).

C. P. Snow published *Strangers and Brothers,* the first in the 11-volume series of novels under that name, all set within the British public and scientific elites.

Katharine Hepburn starred as a leading international journalist opposite Spencer Tracy as her sports reporter husband in *Woman of the Year,* directed by George Stevens. It would be the first of the nine Tracy-Hepburn films and the beginning of their long personal relationship.

Konstantin Sergueyev and Galina Ulanova danced the leads in the Kirov Ballet production of *Romeo and Juliet,* choreographed by Leonid Lavrovsky to the music of Sergei Prokofiev.

Reflecting his own experience as a war correspondent in Spain and his loyalist sympathies, Ernest Hemingway published the Spanish Civil War novel *For Whom the Bell Tolls.*

Richard Wright emerged as a major writer with his novel *Native Son,* a searing look at life in Chicago's South Side African-American community.

The world's population reached an estimated 2.3 billion people, despite the adverse effects of the Great Depression.

President Franklin D. Roosevelt embargoed the shipment of American scrap iron and steel to Japan (Sept.), finally stopping a vitally important source of supply to Japanese war industries; later it was to become clear that much of what had previously been shipped to Japan returned in the form of bombs, guns, ammunition, aircraft, and warships.

As the United States began to build its armed forces in preparation for war, and as American war production accelerated even further, millions of women entered the workforce, in a very wide range of jobs, many of which had been effectively barred before.

Network television debuted in the United States with a broadcast from WRGB, the General Electric station at Schenectady, New York (Feb. 1); 22 other stations went on the air before year's end. The first presidential convention was broadcast, not live but as television pictures of film.

Scoring the largest number of points in any National Football League championship game, the Chicago Bears defeated the Washington Redskins 72–0, by far the largest differential ever between opponents. No other winning team would ever score even 60 points, although the Detroit Lions came close in their 59–14 win over the Cleveland Browns (1957).

The first Social Security checks were paid out; the first check, for $22.54, was part of an initial payout amounting to $75,844.

Celebrated British philosopher Bertrand Russell was denied appointment to the faculty of New York's City College because of his allegedly "radical" views, which did not prevent Harvard University from offering him a position.

University of Michigan senior Tom Harmon won college football's Heisman Trophy; he was a power-

(Oct.) and were decisively defeated by the Greeks (Nov.). British forces massively defeated Italian North African forces in a Western Desert campaign (Dec. 9, 1940-Feb. 7, 1941) that netted 130,000 Italian prisoners, with total British casualties of fewer than 2,000. British bombers sank three Italian battleships at Taranto (Nov. 11).

U.S. president Franklin Delano Roosevelt defeated Republican Wendell Willkie to win an unprecedented third term.

American supplies continued to flow to the Allies, and the United States began to prepare for war with Japan. Congress passed the Selective Service Act (Sept. 16), the country's first peacetime conscription measure. It also passed the Smith Act (Alien Registration Act), requiring the registration and fingerprinting of all aliens and outlawing membership in organizations advocating the overthrow of the government; this act was used against World War II dissenters and later during the McCarthy period.

Japanese forces took Indochina (Sept.), then attacked free China from the south, cutting off a major supply line; little movement occurred in central and north China.

d. Leon Trotsky (Lev Davidovich Bronstein) (1879-1940), Bolshevik leader; founder and commander of the Red Army during the October Revolution; forced into exile after Joseph Stalin's rise to power; he was assassinated by Soviet agents in Mexico City (Aug. 20).

Abraham Stern founded the terrorist Stern Gang (Lehi; Fighters for the Freedom of Israel).

Carol II of Romania was deposed by coup and succeeded by fascist Ion Antonescu; Romania entered the war on the Axis side.

India's Moslem League, headed by Mohammad Ali Jinnah, broke with the Congress Party, demanding formation of the independent Islamic state of Pakistan; seven years later, the bloody partition of India would begin the long series of Indian-Pakistani wars.

Meitner, had first outlined the possibility of nuclear fission with uranium) calculated that a powerful atomic bomb could be built using only 2 to 3 pounds of uranium; Peierls would later work on such a bomb at Los Alamos, New Mexico, as part of the Manhattan Project.

Penicillin was first isolated and refined by Australian-British pathologist Howard Walter Florey and German-British biochemist Ernst Boris Chain, making clinical trials of its effectiveness possible (1941).

DES (diethylstilbestrol), a synthetic estrogen, began to be prescribed for many pregnant women for morning sickness; the U.S. Food and Drug Administration would later ban DES (1971) after children born to women who took it were found to have been adversely affected, most notably daughters developing rare cancers of the reproductive organs.

Lascaux cave and its extraordinary prehistoric paintings, dating from perhaps 16,000 years ago, were found by four boys looking for a dog in France's Dordogne Valley.

New Zealand–born plastic surgeon Archibald Hector McIndoe, head of a burn center in Britain's East Grinstead, developed techniques for treating burns and performing reconstructive surgery, later widely adopted elsewhere to treat pilots and air-raid burn victims.

Working at Columbia Broadcasting System (CBS) laboratories, Peter Goldmark developed a color television; another approach would later become standard.

Element 85 (astatine) was discovered by Italian-American physicist Emilio Segrè and his team.

Aldous Huxley and Jane Murfin adapted Jane Austen's 1813 novel *Pride and Prejudice* for the screen; directed by Robert Z. Leonard, the film starred Laurence Olivier and Greer Garson.

Katharine Hepburn re-created the Tracy Lord role in *The Philadelphia Story*, George Cukor's film version of the 1939 play, costarring James Stewart and Cary Grant.

Reprising his theater role (1938), Raymond Massey played the title role in John Cromwell's film version of *Abe Lincoln in Illinois*.

Walt Disney's landmark film *Fantasia* joined animation to classical music, played by the Philadelphia Orchestra under Leopold Stokowski and enhanced by stereophonic sound (not yet widely used).

Billboard began its hit song charts (July), the first number one being "I'll Never Smile Again," sung by Frank Sinatra with Tommy Dorsey.

b. Joseph Alexandrovich Brodsky (1940-   ), Russian-American poet; a leading Soviet dissenter who would win the 1987 Nobel Prize for literature and become fifth U.S. poet laureate (1991).

b. John Lennon (1940-1980), British guitarist, singer, and songwriter who became a world figure as a member of the Beatles (1958-1970); he was murdered outside his New York City home (Dec. 8, 1980) by deranged Mark David Chapman.

b. Ringo Starr (Richard Starkey) (1940-   ), British drummer and singer; a world figure as a member of the Beatles (1962-1970).

b. Al Pacino (Alfredo Pacino) (1940-   ), American actor who would emerge as a major film star as Michael Corleone in *The Godfather* (1972).

b. Bernardo Bertolucci (1940-   ), leading Italian film director, most notably for the epic *1900* (1976).

ful "triple-threat" player — a runner, passer, and kicker — whose professional career would be short-circuited after one game (1941) by World War II. After the war, the injured, highly decorated Harmon had lost much of his strength and speed, although he would play two professional seasons.

The Canadian ship *St. Roch* was the first to sail west to east on the Northwest Passage, north of North America (1940-1942).

British potter Bernard Howell Leach published *A Potter's Book;* drawing on his experience with Japanese and Chinese as well as European pottery styles, his work influenced successive generations of potters.

Two passenger trains collided near Osaka, Japan (Jan. 29), killing 200 people.

Richard and Maurice McDonald opened a hamburger stand near Pasadena, California; ultimately, it would be developed into the McDonald's chain.

Frederick Handley Page's British aircraft firm built the first 40-seat airplane, the Heracles, for Imperial Airways.

German-American psychoanalyst and social critic Erich Fromm, a refugee from Nazi Germany, wrote his popular work *Escape from Freedom,* on the individual in modern society.

In a major engineering failure, a suspension bridge over the Narrows near Tacoma, Washington, collapsed into Puget Sound (Nov. 7).

b. Pelé (Edson Arantes do Nascimento) (1940-   ), Brazilian soccer player who became an international star, appearing in the World Cup finals four times and leading Brazil to three wins (1958; 1962; 1970); he would score more than 1,200 goals in his career.

1940 cont.

d. Emma Goldman (1869-1940), Lithuanian-American anarchist and women's rights theoretician and activist; one of the leading radicals of her day; expelled from the United States (1919), she died in exile.

d. Neville Chamberlain (1836-1940), British Conservative prime minister (1937-1940) who is best remembered for prophesying "peace for our time" after giving Czechoslovakia to Hitler at Munich (1938) and guaranteeing the onset of World War II.

A much improved electron microscope was developed by physicists James Hillier and Albert Prebus, working under Vladimir Zworykin (1937-1940).

d. Joseph John Thomson (1856-1940), British physicist who discovered the electron (1897) and first developed the "plum-pudding" model of atomic structure (1904). Physicist George Paget Thomson was his son.

1941

German forces invaded Greece and Yugoslavia, quickly taking both countries. In Yugoslavia, Zagreb (Apr. 10), Belgrade (Apr. 12), and Sarajevo (Apr. 15) all fell, with massive Yugolav and minimal German casualties; in Greece, the pattern was the same, with British forces evacuated by sea. Greek and Yugoslav armies surrendered (Apr. 17); guerrilla warfare began. In the Mediterranean, the British defeated Italian naval forces at Cape Matapan (Mar. 28), while German airborne troops took Crete (May 20-31). Rudolph Hess parachuted into Britain with a quickly rejected German peace offer (May) and was imprisoned.

President Franklin Delano Roosevelt signed the order to begin formal development of the atomic bomb (Dec. 6), the day before the Japanese attacked Pearl Harbor.

American physician and blood-bank pioneer Charles Drew became head of the American Red Cross blood donor program. An African-American, his own blood was initially considered unacceptable; that policy was changed, but blood was still racially segregated (appar-

b. Trevor Nunn (1940-   ), leading British theater and film director.

d. Selma Lagerlöf (1859-1940), Swedish writer who won the 1909 Nobel Prize for literature.

d. Vsevolod Meyerhold (1874-1940), Soviet actor and director; an Old Bolshevik who died in a Stalinist prison, a victim of the Great Purge; he would be "posthumously rehabilitated" (1955).

d. Mrs. Patrick Campbell (Beatrice Stella Tanner) (1865-1940), British actress; she played Eliza Doolittle in George Bernard Shaw's *Pygmalion* (1914).

d. Paul Klee (1879-1940), Swiss artist; a leading modernist and member of The Blue Rider group.

d. F. Scott (Francis Scott Key) Fitzgerald (1896-1940), American writer, most notably of the novel *The Great Gatsby* (1925).

d. Lewis Wickes Hine (1874-1940), American photoessayist.

d. Mikhail Bulgakov (1891-1940), leading Soviet writer.

b. Julian Bond (1940-   ), American civil rights movement leader and politician; a founder of the Student Nonviolent Coordinating Committee (SNCC) (1960).

b. Wilma Glodean Rudolph (1940-1994), African-American athlete.

d. Marcus Mosiah Garvey (1887-1940), Jamaican Black nationalist; founder of the American separatist "Back to Africa" movement.

Orson Welles created his masterpiece *Citizen Kane,* immediately recognized as a centerpiece of world cinema. He cowrote the screenplay with Herman J. Mankiewicz and directed, produced, and starred (as a very lightly camouflaged William Randolph Hearst) in the classic work.

Humphrey Bogart created San Francisco detective Sam Spade in *The Maltese Falcon,* costarring Mary Astor, Sydney Greenstreet, and Peter Lorre. John Huston wrote and directed the film, based on Dashiell Hammett's novel (1930).

While the world watched, the people of emblematic, besieged Leningrad held out — fighting, continually restoring fortifications, surviving on scraps and less. The equally emblematic people of London and other British cities survived the German terror bombing of the Blitz, spending many nights in underground or backyard air raid shelters.

War preparations accelerated in America. President Franklin D. Roosevelt established the Office of Price Administration (OPA) (Apr.), headed by Leon Henderson, which would play a massive role in Ameri-

German submarine "wolf packs" sank massive amounts of Allied shipping in the crucial Battle of the Atlantic, and German surface raiders and long-range bombers also were active, all increasingly countered by Allied escort carriers. British ships sank the German battleship *Bismarck* (May 28), while German submarines sank the British aircraft carrier *Ark Royal.* Huge quantities of American supplies flowed across the Atlantic, as American war production grew and quickly became large enough to supply Britain, then Russia, and then the worldwide Allied war effort.

Massive German forces invaded the Soviet Union (June 22), quickly taking Minsk, Smolensk, and Kiev; besieging Leningrad; and taking an estimated 2 million prisoners, 8,000 to 9,000 tanks, and huge ordnance and munitions supplies. But the attack was overtaken by the Russian winter and hardening Soviet resistance, and it stalled on the outskirts of Moscow (Nov.-Dec.); reinforced by Far Eastern forces, Moscow held, and extended German forces retreated before a counteroffensive (Dec.).

With the German invasion of the Soviet Union, the world's Communist Parties once again followed Soviet foreign policy, "flip-flopping" again to resume their earlier antifascism.

In North Africa, German and Italian forces led by General Erwin Rommel mounted an offensive, taking El Agheila (Mar. 24) and besieging Tobruk; at year's end, the British mounted a counteroffensive. British forces took Ethiopia and Eritrea from the Italians and Syria from the Vichy French.

Japanese aircraft destroyed much of the American Pacific Fleet at anchor and more than 250 aircraft, mostly on the ground, at Pearl Harbor, on Oahu, Hawaii (Dec. 7), beginning the Pacific war; the three crucial American carriers were at sea. Germany and Italy also went to war with the United States (Dec. 11). Japanese forces invaded the Philippines (Dec. 8), taking Manila (Dec. 26). They also invaded Malaya (Dec. 8), began the bombardment of Hong Kong (Dec. 8), and took Allied-held islands

ently at the request of the U.S. armed forces), leading Drew to resign in protest.

American electrical engineer Vannevar Bush, who had developed the analog computer (1925-1930), became head of the U.S. Office of Scientific Research and Development (1941-1945). There he directed the application of scientific technology during World War II, from gathering experts to work on the atomic bomb and radar to developing antibiotics such as penicillin.

German scientist Konrad Zuse built his second early computer, the Z_2, using electromagnetic relays, not tubes; data were entered on punched tape.

In what was called the "one-gene, one-enzyme" approach, George Wells Beadle and Edward Lawrie Tatum posited that chemical reactions in the body are governed by specific genes.

Penicillin was tested in clinical trials in Oxford, England; the "wonder drug" was first used on a large scale to treat infections in the Allied armed forces during World War II, saving thousands of lives; it would be widely available to the general public after the war.

Psychoanalyst Karen Horney published theoretical work that rejected Freudian ideas of sexual primacy, including the notion of penis envy, stressing instead environmental triggers for neuroses; expelled from the New York Psychoanalytic Institute, she founded the Association for the Advancement of Psychoanalysis.

French-American physician André Frédéric Cournand and American physician Dickinson W. Richards introduced into clinical use the technique of cardiac catheterization — inser-

Humphrey Bogart created the role of "Mad Dog" Earle, opposite Ida Lupino, in Raoul Walsh's film *High Sierra.*

Lillian Hellman's very timely play *Watch on the Rhine* starred Paul Lukas as the antifascist German refugee and Mady Christians as his American wife; he would reprise his role in the 1943 film.

Dmitri Shostakovich composed his Symphony No. 7, named the "Leningrad" after the besieged city in which he wrote it.

James Agee's text and Walker Evans's photos combined to create the Depression era southern classic *Let Us Now Praise Famous Men.*

James M. Cain published the novel *Mildred Pierce,* pillorying as antifamily an independent woman who aggressively and successfully pursues her career.

Michael Tippett's oratorio *A Child of Our Time* raised profound moral themes in a world plunged into war and genocide.

Anton Dolin and Alicia Markova danced the leads in Mikhail Fokine's final ballet, *Bluebeard,* music by Jacques Offenbach.

Bette Davis created the Regina Giddens role in *The Little Foxes,* William Wyler's film version of the 1939 Lillian Hellman play.

Fredric March starred as the heroic antifascist German refugee in John Cromwell's film *So Ends Our Night,* based on Erich Maria Remarque's novel *Flotsam;* Margaret Sullavan, Glenn Ford, and Erich von Stroheim costarred.

Gary Cooper starred as the populist common man hero opposite Barbara Stanwyck in Frank Capra's classic film Meet *John Doe.*

can life throughout the war, controlling prices and rents and administering rationing. Roosevelt also declared a state of national emergency (May), essentially invoking wartime powers over civilian life. Other newly created war-related federal agencies were the Office of Production Management, headed by former General Motors head William S. Knudsen, and the National Defense Mediation Board. With the onset of war, rationing began and strikes were voluntarily forgone.

As American men moved into the armed forces, women went to work in basic industries; the prototypical "new woman" of the day became "Rosie the Riveter" — for the duration of the war.

Commercial television, authorized by the Federal Communications Commission (FCC), formally began (July 1) with 15 hours of programming from station WNBT in New York City. The Columbia Broadcasting System (CBS) reported the Japanese attack on Pearl Harbor on television, but only six American television stations would remain on the air during World War II.

In response to A. Philip Randolph's threat to lead a march on Washington protesting employment discrimination, U.S. president Franklin D. Roosevelt created, by executive order, the Fair Employment Practices Commission (FEPC), the first federal organization specifically directed at workplace discrimination.

New York Yankees centerfielder and slugger Joe DiMaggio hit safely for a record 56 consecutive games. That same year, Ted Williams hit .406, the last professional baseball player to have a season average above .400.

In *United States v. Darby,* the Supreme Court upheld the Fair Labor Standards Act, and with it the national minimum wage and overtime pay.

throughout the eastern Pacific north of Australia and New Guinea. Japanese aircraft sank the British battleship *Prince of Wales* and battle cruiser *Repulse* off the coast of Malaya (Dec. 10).

With the invasion of the Soviet Union, the Germans accelerated their mass murders of Jews and other captive peoples. By mid-year, the Jewish Holocaust that had begun in Germany in the late 1930s was well under way, and mass murders of Poles, Russians, and other conquered peoples of eastern Europe had begun.

In his State of the Union speech (Jan. 6), U.S. president Franklin D. Roosevelt originated the "Four Freedoms" wartime slogans: freedom of speech and expression, freedom of worship, freedom from want, and freedom from fear of war.

U.S. president Franklin D. Roosevelt and British prime minister Winston Churchill stressed peace, freedom, and self-determination as Allied themes in the Atlantic Charter, proclaimed at their meeting at sea off Newfoundland (Aug. 9-12).

Japanese forces in China functioned largely as an army of occupation. The Kuomintang-Communist truce was threatened by the Kuomintang attack on the Communists' New Fourth Army headquarters (Jan. 6).

Kwangtung Army chief of staff and war minister Hideki Tojo became prime minister of Japan (Oct. 17).

The Palmach, an Israeli commando force, was organized; it fought with the Allies during World War II and later became the elite frontline striking force of the Israeli army.

Ho Chi Minh founded the League for the Independence of Vietnam (Vietminh).

Norodom Sihanouk became king of Cambodia (1941-1955); he would remain a major force in Cambodian life into the mid-1990s.

Victor Paz Estenssoro founded the Bolivian Historical Nationalist Revolutionary Movement; he would be Bo-

tion of a flexible tube (catheter) through the patient's arm and pushing it into the heart — earlier developed by German surgeon Werner Forssmann (1929) — making it possible to learn about heart problems without exploratory surgery.

The British turbojet engine (patented 1930) was first used in flight.

Ukrainian-American biochemist Selman A. Waksman introduced the term *antibiotic*.

The artificial fiber dacron (terylene) was developed by British chemists John Rex Whinfield and J. T. Dickson.

d. Annie Jump Cannon (1863-1941), American astronomer, long associated with the Harvard Observatory (1896-1940), whose star catalogs laid the basis for much 20th-century astronomical research.

d. Arthur John Evans (1851-1941), British archaeologist, long associated with Oxford University's Ashmolean Museum, who excavated Minoan and Mycenaean sites on Crete, especially at Knossos (1898-1935).

d. Frederick Grant Banting (1891-1941), Canadian physician who, with Charles Best, first extracted insulin (1921) and developed the basic treatment for diabetes.

Joseph Kesselring's classic stage comedy *Arsenic and Old Lace* starred Josephine Hull, Jean Adair, and Boris Karloff.

Lady in the Dark, Kurt Weill's musical, with lyrics by Ira Gershwin and book by Moss Hart, starred Gertrude Lawrence.

The Panoram Soundie, a video jukebox, was introduced, playing a song and accompanying black-and-white film.

b. Bob Dylan (Robert Allen Zimmerman) (1941-), American singer and composer; an archetypal countercultural figure in the 1960s.

b. Joan Baez (1941-), American singer and guitarist who would be a leading folksinger and countercultural figure in the 1960s.

b. Julie Christie (1941-), British actress and international film star from her role in *Darling* (1965).

b. Paul Simon (1941-), American folk-rock singer and songwriter; a leading international musical figure from the mid-1960s.

b. (Dorothy) Faye Dunaway (1941-), American actress who would emerge as a film star in *Bonnie and Clyde* (1967).

d. James Joyce (1882-1941), Irish writer; for his final novels, *Ulysses* (1922) and *Finnegans Wake* (1939), a central figure in 20th-century literature.

d. Rabindranath Tagore (1861-1941), leading Indian writer, composer, and painter; a world figure in poetry and winner of the 1913 Nobel Prize for literature.

d. Isaak Emanuilovich Babel (1894-1941), leading Soviet writer; a victim of the Great Purge, he was arrested (1939) and died in prison. He was "posthumously rehabilitated" in the mid-1950s.

The United Auto Workers organized the Ford Motor Company, last of the "Big Three" auto companies to be organized.

Willie Mosconi won the first of his 13 world championships in billiards, dominating the game until his retirement (1956).

Two major new American public works opened: the Grand Coulee Dam in the state of Washington and the Rainbow Bridge, linking the United States and Canada at Niagara Falls.

b. Donna Edna Shalala (1941–), American educational administrator and politician who would become U.S. secretary of health and human services (1993-).

b. Stokely Carmichael (1941-), African-American civil rights activist.

b. Richard Benjamin Speck (1941-1991), American mass murderer.

d. James George Frazer (1854-1941), British anthropologist and classical scholar famed for *The Golden Bough* (1907-1915), his highly influential work on religion, magic, and folklore.

d. Lou (Henry Louis) Gehrig (1903-1941), American baseball player; first baseman and powerful slugger for the New York Yankees (1923-1939); he died of amyotrophic lateral sclerosis, now widely known as Lou Gehrig's disease.

d. Louis Dembitz Brandeis (1856-1941), American lawyer and judge; an independent who was one of the leading liberals and legal theorists of his time; also the first Jewish Supreme Court justice (1916-1939).

d. Emanuel Lasker (1868-1941), German chess player who held the world championship for a record 27 years (1894-1921).

1941 cont.

livia's president three times (1952-1956; 1960-1964; 1985-1989).

b. Jesse Louis Jackson (1941-   ), African-American minister and politician.

b. Oscar Arias Sánchez (1941-   ), Costa Rican economist, president of Costa Rica (1986-1990), and winner of the 1987 Nobel Peace Prize for his plan to end the Nicaraguan Civil War.

d. Ioannis Metaxas (1871-1941), Greek military dictator (1936-1941).

d. Wilhelm II (1859-1941), emperor of Germany (1888-1918); after his 1918 abdication, he went into exile in Holland.

1942

Japanese forces completed their conquest of the Philippines; Bataan (Apr. 9) and Corregidor (May 6) fell; the subsequent Bataan Death March killed many Allied prisoners. Japanese forces also completed their conquest of Malaya (Jan. 31), easily took the British fortress at Singapore (Feb. 8-15), and took Indonesia (Jan.-Mar.). They also attacked New Guinea (Jan.), taking New Britain, the Solomons, and substantial portions of Papua, and invaded Burma (Jan.), taking Lashio (Apr.) and Mandalay (May) and cutting off the Burma Road supply line to China.

The long American counteroffensive began with the bombing of Tokyo and other Japanese cities by carrier-based B-25s led by Lieutenant Colonel James Doolittle (Apr. 18), followed by the sinking of a Japanese carrier in the Battle of the Coral Sea (May 7-8). Off Midway Island

The Manhattan Project (Manhattan District of the Army Corps of Engineers) was established (1942-1945) to build the atomic bomb, employing numerous top scientists, including many European émigrés, and headed by American physicist J. Robert Oppenheimer, working under U.S. Army general Leslie Groves. The nuclear fission approach originally envisioned by Leo Szilard (1932) proved unworkable, but Enrico Fermi led the team that developed an alternative approach, using piled blocks of uranium and graphite — the "atomic pile." In a historic breakthrough that ushered in the nuclear age, Fermi's group, working under a squash court at the University of Chicago, took the key step in the development of the atom bomb: creating the first chain reaction — a

1941 cont.

d. Virginia (Adeline Virginia Stephen) Woolf (1882-1941), British writer; a leading 20th-century feminist and member of the Bloomsbury Group; she committed suicide.

d. Ignacy Jan Paderewski (1860-1941), Polish pianist, composer, and national movement leader; first prime minister of free Poland (1919).

d. Jelly Roll Morton (Ferdinand Joseph La Menthe) (1890-1941), pioneering American jazz composer, pianist, and bandleader.

d. Edwin Stanton Porter (1869-1941), American cinematographer and director, most notably of the landmark film *The Great Train Robbery*.

d. John Gutzon Borglum (1867-1941), American sculptor known for his four Mount Rushmore presidential sculptures (1927-1939).

d. Sherwood Anderson (1876-1941), American short story writer and novelist.

d. Henri Louis Bergson (1859-1941), French philosopher and antimaterialist who proposed the doctrine of creative evolution (1907).

d. Harry Micajah Daugherty (1860-1941), American politician; U.S. attorney general during the Harding administration; he was charged but never convicted of complicity in the Teapot Dome and other corruption scandals of the period.

1942

Albert Camus wrote the enormously influential essay *The Myth of Sisyphus*, further developing and putting a name to the construct of the "absurd," an existential and surreal view of modern society as wholly antihuman and so disorienting as to destroy the possibility of communication, action, and even survival. He also published his novel *The Stranger*.

Humphrey Bogart as Rick and Ingrid Bergman as Ilsa starred in *Casablanca*, the classic Michael Curtiz anti-Nazi romance-thriller, with Paul Henreid, Claude Rains, Conrad Veidt, and Peter Lorre in strong supporting roles. Pianist Dooley Wilson played "As Time Goes By" ("Play it, Sam").

Greer Garson and Walter Pidgeon starred in the very popular William Wyler film *Mrs. Miniver*, about a British family surviving the rigors of war.

The realities imposed by war dominated American economic and social life, as had been so in many other countries since the outbreak of World War II (1939). Millions of women entered or reentered the workforce, as American industry became the huge engine that would ultimately supply the Battle of the Atlantic, the Pacific war, the Eastern Front, and later the invasions of North Africa, southern Europe, and western Europe. Rationing and a pervasive system of production and consumption controls were imposed, regulated by a group of ubiquitous new alphabet agencies. Taxes soared; so did wages and war-derived profits and profiteering.

A major series of polio (poliomyelitis, or infantile paralysis) epidemics, the worst known in history, began in the United States (1942-1953).

(June 4-6), in the decisive naval battle of the Pacific war, the three remaining major American aircraft carriers met and defeated the main Japanese battle fleet, sinking all four of the Japanese navy's major aircraft carriers while losing only the *Yorktown*. American forces then began "island-hopping" invasions across the Pacific, most notably taking Guadalcanal (Aug. 1942-Feb. 1943).

On the Russian front, the Germans again went over to the offensive in the spring and summer, besieging and taking Sevastopol, Veronezh, and Rostov in July. The tide turned at Stalingrad (Aug. 23, 1942-Feb. 2, 1943), with Russian forces ultimately encircling and destroying or capturing the entire German Sixth Army and beginning a series of offensives that would take them to Berlin. In the west, massive Allied bombing of Germany began, as did the Allied build-up in Britain, in preparation for the invasion of Europe. Probing cross-Channel Allied attacks on St. Nazaire and Dieppe failed.

In North Africa, German and Italian forces defeated the British at Bir Hacheim (May 28-June 13), took Tobruk (June 21), and threatened Cairo. They were decisively defeated at El Alamein (Oct. 23-Nov. 4), where a British counteroffensive began. American forces made amphibious landings at Casablanca, Oran, and Algiers.

Allied forces began to win the Battle of the Atlantic; hard-pressed German submarine commanders shifted their attention to the east coast of the Americas.

At the Wannsee Conference (Jan.), the German leadership to some extent formalized the mass murders of Jews, Poles, Soviets, Gypsies, and many others already under way; they called the Jewish Holocaust, in which an estimated 6 million Jews died, the "final solution." At least 2 million Poles and Soviets, most of them Jews, would be murdered by the Germans at the Auschwitz-Birkenau (Oswiçim) concentration camp complex in central Poland, near Cracow (1942-1944); among the many other major German death camps were Belsen, Buchenwald, Dachau, Maidenek, and Treblinka.

self-sustaining process of nuclear fission, given a critical mass of fuel, in this case uranium-235 (U-235) — in the first nuclear reactor (Dec. 2). German efforts to develop nuclear capability, led by Werner Heisenberg and Otto Hahn, were unsuccessful, possibly deliberately sabotaged by Heisenberg.

Edward Teller and Enrico Fermi conceived of a bomb they called the "Super," using nuclear fusion of hydrogen atoms with an atomic bomb as a trigger (by 1942). Teller would lead in developing the hydrogen bomb (1949-1952).

The world's first fully electronic computer, the ABC (Atanasoff-Berry Computer), was completed by American physicist John Vincent Atanasoff, assisted by Clifford E. Berry, after two years of planning (1937-1938) and three years of construction (1939-1942). Atanasoff set many patterns for modern computers, such as using electron tubes as on-off switches, with a binary (two-digit) system for calculations, and separating the computer's memory from the calculating area. Atanasoff obtained no patents, and his work was not fully recognized until 1973.

Wernher von Braun's German rocket development team launched a successful rocket (Dec. 24); regarded as the first true guided missile, carrying its own fuel and oxygen, it reached an altitude of 60 miles.

Using an electron microscope, Italian-American microbiologist Salvador Edward Luria took the first detailed photographs of a virus.

Hooker Chemical Company began dumping chemical waste in Love Canal (1942-1953), near Niagara Falls, New York; it would become the first federally recognized environmental disaster site (1980).

Orson Welles wrote and directed his second classic film, *The Magnificent Ambersons,* based on the 1918 Booth Tarkington novel; Tim Holt, Joseph Cotten, and Dolores Costello starred.

Robert Helpmann and Margot Fonteyn danced the leads in the ballet *Hamlet,* choreographed by Helpmann to the music of Peter Ilich Tchaikovsky.

Agnes De Mille choreographed the ballet *Rodeo,* music by Aaron Copland; it was presented by the Ballets Russes de Monte Carlo company, now in New York rather than in Nazi-occupied Europe.

Thornton Wilder's play *The Skin of Our Teeth* starred Fredric March, Florence Eldridge, Tallulah Bankhead, and Montgomery Clift.

Irving Berlin introduced his war song "This Is the Army, Mr. Jones" in his armed forces show *This Is the Army.*

James Thurber published his story "The Secret Life of Walter Mitty" in his collection *My World and Welcome to It.*

Irving Berlin's song "White Christmas" became a perennial favorite after Bing Crosby introduced it in the film *Holiday Inn.*

b. Barbra (Barbara Joan) Streisand (1942-), American singer, actress, and film director who would be an international popular music figure from the early 1960s.

b. Harrison Ford (1942-), American film star, largely in science fiction and action films.

b. Paul McCartney (1942-), British guitarist, singer, and composer who would become a world figure as a member of the Beatles (1958-1970) and would found the group Wings (1971).

A massive Bay of Bengal cyclone killed an estimated 40,000 people.

Britain's "Beveridge Plan," named after its chief architect, economist William Beveridge, contained the main elements of the social service network that would be introduced by the postwar Labour government, including national health insurance and social security.

James Farmer founded the Congress of Racial Equality (CORE), which emerged as a major American civil rights organization in the 1960s.

Goose (Reese) Tatum, the "clown prince of basketball," became the star attraction of the Harlem Globetrotters (1942-1954), an all-Black touring basketball team.

A fire at Boston's Cocoanut Grove nightclub (Nov. 28) killed 491 people, as inadequate exits made escape impossible and panic spread.

In the world's worst mine disaster, an explosion killed 1,549 people in Honkeiko, Manchuria (Apr. 26).

The British cruiser *Curaçao,* hit by the liner *Queen Mary* off England (Oct. 2), sank, claiming 338 lives.

The Voice of America began broadcasting into Nazi-held Europe.

b. Muhammad Ali (Cassius Marcellus Clay) (1942-), American boxer; a world heavyweight champion known for his power and quickness; a dominant figure from the mid-1960s through the 1970s.

1942 cont.

In Executive Order 9066 (Feb. 19), U.S. president Franklin D. Roosevelt ordered the internment in concentration camps of 110,000 Pacific Coast Japanese-Americans.

India's Congress Party called for immediate British withdrawal from India; the British responded by imprisoning the entire party leadership.

b. Muammar al-Qaddafi (1942-   ), Libyan head of state (1969-   ).

b. Chris (Martin Thembisile) Hani (1942-1993), South African communist; he would be assassinated by right-wing terrorists.

d. James Hertzog (1866-1942), South African Boer War general; founder of the National Party (1913) and prime minister (1924-1929; 1933-1939).

Alfred Kinsey founded the Institute for Sex Research at Indiana University (1942-1956), from there producing his famous reports (1948; 1953), based on extensive personal interviews.

Ashley Montagu published *Man's Most Dangerous Myth: The Fallacy of Race,* the basis for his draft of UNESCO's 1950 "Statement of Race."

d. Franz Boas (1858-1942), German-American anthropologist, much of whose work focused on the cultures of North America's Northwest Coast; stressing the essential equality of all races, his work was often used to combat Nazi and other racist theories in the 1930s and thereafter.

1943

A Soviet winter offensive followed the surrender of 93,000 surviving German Sixth Army soldiers at Stalingrad (Feb. 2). A final German eastern front offensive was stopped at Kursk (July), the most massive armored conflict of World War II, in which Soviet forces with air superiority smashed attacking German forces that included 17 mechanized divisions; the Germans lost 3,000 tanks and 1,400 airplanes. Soviet forces moved to the offensive on all fronts, taking Kiev and Smolensk.

Despite a German victory at Kasserine Pass (Feb. 14-22), superior Allied forces went over to their final offensive in North Africa, taking Bizerte and Tunis; the remaining German-Italian forces, numbering 275,000, surrendered (May).

As part of the top-secret Manhattan Project, headquartered in Los Alamos, New Mexico, a group of physicists under J. Robert Oppenheimer worked on designing and building an atomic bomb. A plant at Oak Ridge, Tennessee, began producing the fissionable uranium isotope (U-235) that would be used in the Hiroshima bomb (1945); the fissionable plutonium isotope (PU-239) used in the other two early bombs (1945) was produced in the University of Chicago reactor (1942).

British mathematician and cryptographer Alan Turing led a team that built an early electronic special-purpose computer, the Colossus, for use in breaking German codes, especially those

b. Martin Scorsese (1942-   ), leading American film director from the 1970s.

b. Jimi Hendrix (1942-1970), American guitarist and singer.

b. Werner Herzog (1942-   ), German filmmaker, writer, director, and producer.

d. Mikhail (Michel) Fokine (1880-1942), Russian dancer and leading choreographer, most notably for his work during the early years of the Ballets Russes company in Paris.

d. John Barrymore (John Sidney Blythe) (1882-1942), one of the leading American dramatic actors of his time.

d. George M. Cohan (1878-1942), American actor-manager, playwright, and songwriter; a noted figure in American musical theater.

d. Grant Wood (1892-1942), American painter; a leading realist of the 1930s.

Alfred Drake, Joan Roberts, and Celeste Holm starred in the Broadway musical *Oklahoma!* by Richard Rodgers and Oscar Hammerstein II, choreography by Agnes De Mille; the trend-setting work sharply changed the course of American musical theater.

Dolores Del Rio and Pedro Armendariz starred in Emilio Fernandez's classic Mexican film *Maria Candelaria*.

In tune with the times, Ralph Bellamy, Skippy Homeier as the young Nazi, and Shirley Booth starred in the play *Tomorrow the World* by James Gow and Arnaud d'Usseau.

Racial tensions grew in many American industrial cities, as newly arrived war workers brought southern racial tensions with them and wartime housing and other shortages caused existing tensions to intensify. Massive race riots struck Detroit (June), where 29 people died and hundreds were injured; the riots were contained by regular U.S. Army forces (Apr.). Race riots also occurred in New York City, Los Angeles, and several other cities.

A "pay-as-you-go" income tax law was adopted for the first time, withholding income taxes at their source, as payroll deductions, a device that would become standard procedure in the United States.

Allied forces invaded Sicily (July 9), taking it in a little over a month; Messina fell (Aug. 17), and the remaining German forces fled to mainland Italy. Benito Mussolini was deposed by the Italian Fascist Grand Council and imprisoned (July 24), but he was later reinstalled by the Germans as a puppet ruler. Allied forces pursued German forces quickly, landing in southernmost Italy (Sept. 3) and at Salerno (Sept. 9), taking southern Italy up to the German Gustav Line (Nov.) after Italy signed an armistice with the Allies (Sept. 7).

Allied bombers intensified their attacks on Germany, beginning "shuttle bombing" from North African bases (June). At Hamburg (July 26-29), firestorms generated by air raids reportedly killed 50,000 people. Successful raids on the Peenamunde rocket base delayed development of the V-1 and V-2 rocket bombs.

Allied forces decisively won the Battle of the Atlantic, as carrier-destroyer "hunter-killer" surface forces sharply cut into German submarine strength.

In the Pacific war, American forces continued to capture Japanese-held islands, among them New Georgia in the Solomons (July-Aug.) and Betio in the Tarawa atoll (Nov. 20-24), also making a major attack on Bougainville in the Solomons (Nov.).

Stalemates continued in China and Burma, with skirmishing between Communist and Kuomintang forces continuing in north China.

After the Germans had sent 400,000 to 450,000 of Warsaw's Jews to death camps, the city's remaining Jews decided to fight to the death against the Germans rather than let themselves be taken; in the Warsaw Ghetto rising (Apr.-May), they fought with a few small arms and little ammunition against well-armed Nazi troops.

At Casablanca (Jan. 14-23), Franklin D. Roosevelt and Winston Churchill met to plan the coming invasions of southern and western Europe; they put forward the call

produced by the Enigma coding machine. Not realizing that the Allies had obtained a copy of the Enigma from Polish partisans, the Germans believed that their codes were unbreakable. The Allied ability to decode German transmissions would give them a decided edge during World War II.

While also working with France's underground Resistance, Jacques Cousteau and Emil Gagnan developed the Aqualung, used by underwater divers; this scuba (self-contained underwater breathing apparatus) gear supplied divers with air under pressure, freeing them from wearing heavy diving suits with lifelines, which could become twisted or cut.

American astronomer Carl K. Seyfert distinguished a particular type of galaxy with a very bright center spot; such galaxies, now understood to be explosively active, were named Seyfert galaxies.

Dutch physician Willem Johan Kolff invented the dialysis machine, which served as a kind of external artificial kidney.

The hallucinogenic properties of LSD (lysergic acid diethylamide) were discovered accidentally by Swiss chemist Albert Hoffman; studied as a possible biochemical trigger for schizophrenia, the psychedelic drug would become popular in the 1960s, before its dangers were fully understood.

Ukrainian-American biochemist Selman A. Waksman discovered the antibiotic streptomycin, which attacks some bacteria not treated effectively with penicillin, though streptomycin itself can be toxic in too-high doses.

Epoxy resins, used as coatings and adhesives, were first developed.

Paul Lukas re-created his stage role opposite Bette Davis in Herman Shumlin's film version of *Watch on the Rhine*; Dashiell Hammett adapted the 1941 Lillian Hellman play.

Ethel Waters, Lena Horne, and Louis Armstrong led an all–African-American cast in the Vincente Minnelli film version of the 1940 theater musical *Cabin in the Sky*.

Gary Cooper, Ingrid Bergman, and Katina Paxinou starred in Sam Wood's film of Ernest Hemingway's novel *For Whom the Bell Tolls*.

Roger Livesey starred as the obsolete British officer in the Michael Powell–Emeric Pressburger film *The Life and Death of Colonel Blimp,* costarring Deborah Kerr and Anton Walbrook. The film generated considerable criticism from those who thought it unpatriotic because of its far-from-glorious protagonist.

John Van Druten's play *The Voice of the Turtle* starred Margaret Sullavan and Elliott Nugent.

Kurt Weill's musical *One Touch of Venus* starred Mary Martin and John Boles.

Erle Stanley Gardner's fictional lawyer Perry Mason began a long run on radio (1943-1955), then television (1956-1966), starring Raymond Burr.

Antoine St.-Exupéry published his novel *The Little Prince*.

b. Catherine Deneuve (Catherine Dorléac) (1943-   ), French actress who would emerge as a film star in *The Umbrellas of Cherbourg* (1963).

b. Joni Mitchell (Roberta Joan Anderson) (1943-   ), Canadian folksinger, composer, and guitarist who would become a leading folk and blues figure in the late 1960s.

As the war progressed and scarce supplies were channeled to the fighting fronts, home front shortages increased and, in response, rationing intensified, with goods such as meat, fat, cheese, and shoes rationed. Meatless Tuesdays and Fridays were instituted.

The U.S. Supreme Court ruled that saluting the flag was constitutionally a voluntary matter and could not be forced upon schoolchildren against their will, ruling in favor of the Jehovah's Witnesses, who had challenged such compulsion.

The United Mine Workers, led by John L. Lewis, refused to join in American labor's wartime no-strike pledge; they struck the mines, which were then seized by the federal government (May 1) and kept running.

The United Nations Relief and Rehabilitation Administration (UNRRA) was established to aid civilians in liberated areas; UNRRA preceded the formation of the United Nations itself. Former New York State governor Herbert H. Lehman was UNRRA's first commissioner (1943-1946), and former New York City mayor Fiorello H. La Guardia was the second (1946).

British-American jockey Johnny Longden won all three races in the Triple Crown: the Kentucky Derby, Preakness, and Belmont Stakes.

German industrialist and Nazi supporter Alfred Krupp took full control of the Krupp manufacturing empire, replacing his father; Krupp interests actively seized plants in occupied countries and employed concentration camp inmates as forced labor.

For some young men, highly publicized "zoot suits" — with big shoulders, narrow waists, and tapered trousers — were the rage; they were greatly deplored as degenerate by many elders. For masses of young people, jazz dancing, in the form of "jitterbugging," was very much "in."

for unconditional surrender, which they would hold to throughout the rest of the war.

At their Quebec (Aug. 14-24) and Cairo (Dec. 3-7) meetings, Roosevelt and Churchill decided upon and planned the cross-Channel European invasion. At Cairo (Nov. 22-26), Roosevelt, Churchill, and China's Chiang Kai-shek discussed the war in the Pacific. At Tehran (Nov. 28-Dec. 1), Roosevelt, Churchill, and the Soviet Union's Joseph Stalin made a series of far-reaching agreements that would greatly affect the shape of the postwar world, including the fate of many of the nations of eastern Europe and southwest Asia and the founding of the United Nations.

Menachem Begin became leader of the Israeli terrorist Irgun Zvai Leumi (National Military Organization).

d. Isoroku Yamamoto (1884-1943), Japanese admiral; Japanese Combined Fleet commander and the chief architect of the Pearl Harbor attack; he was killed when American fighters shot down his aircraft over the Solomon Islands (Apr. 18).

b. Benazir Bhutto (1943-   ), Pakistani political leader; prime minister of Pakistan (1988-1990; 1993-   ) and daughter of Pakistani prime minister Zulfikar Ali Bhutto, who was killed by his country's military (1979).

b. Lech Walesa (1943-   ), Polish political leader; founder of Solidarity (1980) and president of Poland (1990-   ).

b. Stephen William Hawking (1943-   ), British physicist noted for his theoretical work, especially on black holes, and for his best-selling *A Brief History of Time* (1987).

b. Donald Carl Johanson (1943-   ), American physical anthropologist best known for his East African discoveries, described in *Lucy: The Beginnings of Human Kind* (1982).

d. Marc Aurel Stein (1862-1943), Hungarian-British archaeologist and explorer who while studying Asian cultures and history took to the West many cultural artifacts, including the *Diamond Sutra* (1904).

d. David Hilbert (1862-1943), German mathematician best known for his formulation of modern algebraic number theory and his work on space of infinite dimensions (Hilbert space), important to the mathematics of quantum theory.

d. George Washington Carver (1864?-1943), American agricultural research director at Alabama's Tuskegee Institute (1896-1943); he experimented with crops to enrich the soil, such as the peanut and sweet potato, changing agriculture in the American South.

d. Karl Landsteiner (1868-1943), Austrian-American pathologist and physiologist who first recognized that blood comes in types (1900).

b. George Harrison (1943-), British guitarist, singer, songwriter, and producer who would become an international figure as a member of the Beatles (1958-1970).

b. Robert De Niro (1943-), American actor who would become an international film star in the mid-1970s.

b. Janis Joplin (1943-1970), American singer.

b. Jim Morrison (1943-1971), American singer.

d. Beatrix Potter (1866-1943), British children's book writer and illustrator; the creator of Peter Rabbit and several other fictional animals.

d. Conrad Veidt (1893-1943), German actor who emerged as a film star in *The Cabinet of Dr. Caligari* (1919).

d. Fats (Thomas Wright) Waller (1904-1943), American jazz composer, instrumentalist, singer, and bandleader.

d. Sergei Rachmaninoff (1873-1943) , Russian composer, conductor, and pianist; a major figure in 20th-century music.

d. Leslie Howard (Leslie Stainer) (1893-1943), British stage and screen star; he was killed when his Lisbon-to-London flight was downed by German aircraft.

d. Max Reinhardt (Maximilian Goldman) (1873-1943), Austrian actor, director, and producer; the leading figure in the German theater from the early 1900s until he was forced to flee the Nazis.

Near Lumberton, North Carolina, 73 people, many of them servicemen, were killed when a derailed train was struck by another train (Dec. 16).

Nine railroad cars derailed near Philadelphia, Pennsylvania, killing 79 people (Sept. 6).

b. Arthur Robert Ashe, Jr. (1943-1993), American tennis champion; the first African-American to win the men's singles title at the U.S. Open (1968) and Wimbledon (1975); he would become a major figure in the worldwide fight against AIDS.

b. Billie Jean Moffitt King (1943-), American tennis player; a key figure in making women's tennis a major sport and the first sportswoman to win more than $100,000 in a single year (1971).

b. Bobby (Robert James) Fischer (1943-), American chess player who would become a child prodigy, at 15 the youngest grandmaster, and the first American world champion (1972).

b. H. Rap Brown (1943-), African-American civil rights activist.

d. (Martha) Beatrice Potter Webb (1858-1943), British economist; a leading figure in British socialism, many of whose published works were coauthored with her husband, Sidney Webb.

d. Simone Weil (1903-1943), French writer, philosopher, and educator, active with the Free French forces in London.

Soviet forces pursued the retreating Germans on all fronts. Besieged Leningrad was relieved (Jan. 15-19); Odessa (Apr. 10), Sevastopol (May 19), and Minsk (July 3) were retaken, as was western Russia and the Ukraine, with more than 500,000 German prisoners and massive German air, armor, and ordnance losses.

Soviet forces took much of eastern Poland, stopping across the Vistula River from Warsaw (Aug.). Warsaw rose against the Germans, expecting the Soviets to take Warsaw; instead, the lightly armed partisans were massacred by reinforced German forces, surrendering (Oct. 2) while the Soviets waited. Soviet armies took Romania (Aug. 23) and Belgrade (Oct. 20); Budapest was besieged (Nov.). Defeating the Germans in Latvia, Soviet forces pursued them into East Prussia, taking the Baltic coast; 1.5 million Germans were evacuated by sea (Oct. 1944-May 1945).

On June 6, 1944 (D-day), Allied airborne and seaborne invasion forces attacked in Normandy, encountering light resistance on four of five invasion beachheads and substantial resistance on Omaha Beach; leading forces moved off all beaches quickly. Taking Cherbourg (June 27) and breaking through at Avranches (Aug. 1), Allied forces soon liberated Paris (Aug. 25), took Brussels (Sept. 3) and Antwerp (Sept. 4), and pursued the Germans to the Siegfried Line, breached by the American First Army (Oct. 20), which then took Aachen. Seaborne Allied invasion forces landing in southern France (Aug. 15) took Marseilles and Toulon, then moved up the Rhône Valley.

German forces responded with a last, desperate offensive in the Ardennes, the Battle of the Bulge (Dec. 1944-Jan. 1945); 25 German divisions created a 50-mile-deep salient (bulge) but failed to break the Allied line or even to take the besieged and greatly outnumbered American 82nd Airborne and 101st Airborne Divisions at Bastogne. Allied forces retook the offensive, pursuing the Germans to the Rhine.

In Italy, Allied seaborne landings at Anzio were contained in their beachheads (Jan.-May) until the German retreat

Plutonium for atomic bombs began being produced at the Hanford Nuclear Reservation, near Richland, Washington, eventually a 575-square-mile weapons complex. Through at least the late 1960s, plant operators would secretly release radioactive materials into the air, water, and land in amounts equivalent to a major nuclear accident, while reassuring local inhabitants of their safety. In addition, millions of gallons of highly concentrated, increasingly unstable radioactive waste were stored in tanks, creating later concerns about a massive nuclear waste explosion like that at Chelyabinsk (1957 or 1958). Despite federal government commitments, no significant cleanup had begun as late as 1995.

American pediatric cardiologist Helen Taussig diagnosed the congenital heart malformations of "blue babies," causing insufficient oxygen (and blue pallor), retardation, and early death. She and surgeon Alfred Blalock developed and he first performed an operation to correct the defects. Such operations saved many infants' lives and led the way for modern open-heart surgery.

Building on work by Australian immunologist (Frank) MacFarlane Burnet, British-Lebanese zoologist Peter Medawar worked out how a patient's body rejects transplanted tissue or organs, theorizing that the immune system identifies them as foreign and fights them as if they were a disease. This work opened the way to an understanding of the basic mechanism of autoimmune diseases, in which the body mistakenly attacks its own tissues, and to the development of selective immunosuppressive drugs.

Quinine was synthesized by American chemists Robert Burns Woodward and William von Eggers Doering; the methods they developed

Nikolai Cherkassov created the title role in *Ivan the Terrible, Part I,* Sergei Eisenstein's patriotic epic, scored by Sergei Prokofiev. That film won Stalin's approval, but by the time Part II was completed (1946), Eisenstein, often in conflict with the Soviet cultural bureaucracy, would find that Stalin took the not-completely-adulatory portrayal of Ivan as a personal affront. The film was banned, released only in 1958 during the thaw.

Ansel Adams published *Born Free and Equal,* his World War II Manzanar prison camp photos of uprooted Japanese-Americans imprisoned by their own government.

Francis Bacon emerged as a major painter, completing the triptych *Three Studies for Figures at the Base of a Crucifixion,* which like much of his work focused on the most loathsome aspects of the human experience.

Frank Fay created Elwood P. Dowd opposite Josephine Hull, Jane Van Duser, and an imaginary large white rabbit named Harvey in Mary Chase's stage comedy *Harvey;* the 1950 film version would star James Stewart.

Hilda Simms starred opposite Earle Hyman in the American Negro Theater production of *Anna Lucasta* by Philip Yordan.

Karl Shapiro published the poetry collection *V-Letter and Other Poems,* winning a Pulitzer Prize.

Martha Graham choreographed Aaron Copland's folk ballet *Appalachian Spring,* sets by Isamu Noguchi.

Raymond Chandler and Billy Wilder adapted James M. Cain's 1936 novel *Double Indemnity* into the classic Wilder film, starring Barbara Stanwyck and Fred MacMurray as the murderous lover-conspirators and Edward G. Robinson as the tenacious insurance investigator.

The Bretton Woods Conference (July), in New Hampshire, established a postwar economic stabilization plan; it most significantly included a dollar-based international currency agreement that functioned until the late 1960s and was in force until the early 1970s. The conference also established two major international financial institutions, the International Monetary Fund (IMF), which would become a United Nations agency (1947), and the International Bank for Reconstruction and Development, better known as the World Bank, also linked with the United Nations. The World Bank originally focused on the rebuilding of postwar Europe but would soon shift to the economic needs of developing countries, especially as former colonies gained their independence.

Wartime controls continued to dominate American corporate and union life; in an emblematic case, Montgomery Ward chairman Sewell Avery defied a federal order to extend a union contract and ultimately was carried out of his office by U.S. Army forces, his ejection providing one of the most widely circulated news photos of the time.

In *Korematsu v. United States,* the U.S. Supreme Court ruled the racist 1942 executive order that had forced many West Coast Japanese-Americans into concentration camps legal because of wartime necessity. President Gerald R. Ford later apologized; Congress voted reparations (1988), most of which had not been paid by the early 1990s.

Congress enacted the "GI Bill of Rights," providing a wide range of post–World War II benefits for veterans; federally subsidized college educations would be a major boon to veterans during the postwar period.

American golfer Byron Nelson won a still-unbroken record 11 consecutive open titles, winning 13 of the 23 tournaments in which he played.

after Allied forces breached the Gustav Line (May). Rome, proclaimed an open city, fell (June 4).

American and Allied forces continued to "island-hop" across the Pacific, their victories including Kwajalein (Feb. 1); Eniwetok and the Parry Islands (Feb. 17-21), where 2,000 Japanese fought to the death; New Guinea (Apr.-July), where surviving Japanese defenders became guerrilla fighters; Saipan (June 15-July 9), where most of the 25,000 to 30,000 Japanese defenders fought to the death; and Guam (July-Aug.), where most of the 10,000 defenders fought to the death. In the Philippine Sea, off Saipan, Japan lost 3 aircraft carriers and 450 pilots and their aircraft. American forces retook Leyte (Oct.-Dec.). In Leyte Gulf (Oct. 24-25), a massive American armada, then by far the world's strongest naval force, destroyed most of what was left of the Japanese navy, including 4 aircraft carriers, 3 battleships, and 500 airplanes.

Japanese forces in China mounted successful attacks on Allied airfields in eastern China but failed to take Chungking. Japanese, British, and Chinese forces fought inconclusively in Burma.

Incumbent Democratic U.S. president Franklin Delano Roosevelt defeated Republican Thomas E. Dewey, winning an unprecedented fourth term.

At Quebec (Sept. 12-16), Roosevelt and Churchill discussed the coming invasion of Japan, as well as many postwar European matters. At Potsdam (July-Aug.), the Allies settled much of the immediate postwar future of Germany and planned the occupation and German war crimes trials.

At Rastenburg, East Prussia, an officers' plot to assassinate Adolf Hitler (July 20) failed when Colonel Klaus Schenck von Stauffenberg's bomb exploded but did not kill Hitler. Von Stauffenberg was executed, as were a substantial number of other German officers.

Germany introduced rocket missiles into the war; V-1 bombardment of Britain began (June); V-2s began to fall on London and Paris in September.

would then be used to synthesize other extremely complex organic molecules.

An early electromechanical computer, the Mark I (Automatic Sequence Control Calculator), was developed by Howard Aiken (1939-1944), working with IBM; it would be used for some calculations during World War II.

American physicist Glenn Seaborg and his team discovered elements 95 (americium) and 96 (curium).

Canadian-American bacteriologist Oswald Theodore Avery and his colleagues showed that genetic information is carried in DNA (deoxyribonucleic acid), not in protein, as had been widely assumed.

In *What Is Life?* Austrian physicist Erwin Schrödinger described how chemical codes might determine genetic inheritance, inspiring further work on DNA's structure, as by James Watson and Francis Crick (1953).

Norman Borlaug began to work in Mexico under Rockefeller Foundation auspices (1944-1960) to develop the high-yield grains that would lead to the Green Revolution of the 1960s.

Aureomycin, the first tetracycline antibiotic, was discovered by American botanist Benjamin Minge Dugar and others; it was available for medical use by 1948.

Dutch astronomer Hendrik Christoffel van de Hulst theorized that hydrogen atoms in space should emit radiation, a fact that was later confirmed (1951).

Hungarian-American mathematician John von Neumann and German-American economist

The American Ballet Theater presented Jerome Robbins's ballet *Fancy Free*, music by Leonard Bernstein; it would be the basis for the hit Betty Comden–Adolph Green–Bernstein Broadway musical *On the Town* (1944).

Celeste Holm starred as the 19th-century feminist in *Bloomer Girl*, a musical in the style of *Oklahoma!* by Harold Arlen and E. Y. "Yip" Harburg, choreography by Agnes De Mille

Dick Powell created the Philip Marlowe role opposite Claire Trevor in Edward Dmytryk's classic film *Murder My Sweet*; John Paxton adapted Raymond Chandler's 1940 novel *Farewell My Lovely*.

Fredric March starred as the Allied military governor in a Sicilian town in Paul Osborn's wartime comedy *A Bell for Adano*, based on the 1944 John Hersey novel.

Ingrid Bergman was the woman being driven insane, opposite Charles Boyer and Joseph Cotten, in George Cukor's turn-of-the-century dramatic film *Gaslight*, based on Patrick Hamilton's 1938 play.

Joan Fontaine in the title role starred opposite Orson Welles in Robert Stevenson's film based on Charlotte Brontë's 1847 novel *Jane Eyre*.

Lauren Bacall emerged as a star, opposite Humphrey Bogart, in her first film, Howard Hawks's *To Have and Have Not*, based on the 1937 Ernest Hemingway novel, now a World War II anti-Nazi film.

Robert Helpmann choreographed and danced the lead in the Sadler's Wells production of *Miracle in the Gorbals*, music by Arthur Bliss.

Danish poet and novelist Johannes V. Jensen was awarded the Nobel Prize for literature.

At Hartford, Connecticut, the "Big Top" tent of Ringling Brothers–Barnum and Bailey Circus caught fire and collapsed (July 6); 168 people died, most trampled to death.

A storage tank containing highly combustible liquefied natural gas exploded in Cleveland, Ohio (Oct. 20); the resulting fire killed an estimated 125 people, injuring hundreds more, and destroyed 50 city blocks, containing perhaps 300 buildings. Use of liquefied natural gas was largely ended until the 1970s energy crisis.

Teflon — the first nonburning, nonsticking, easy-cleaning lining for pots and pans — was first introduced commercially, the name being short for polytetrafluoroethylene.

More than 800 people died when a typhoon struck major elements of the U.S. Third Fleet off the Philippines; damage to the fleet was severe.

The star of the Montreal Canadiens, Maurice Richard, became the first professional ice-hockey player to score 50 goals in a season (1944-45).

At least 426 people, many of them in sleeping cars, died of carbon monoxide poisoning from fumes after a train stalled in a tunnel near Salerno, Italy (Mar. 2).

At Port Chicago, near San Francisco, 322 people died when two munitions ships collided and exploded (July 17).

A ship caught fire at Bombay, India, setting off an ammunition dump on shore; more than 120 people died, and an estimated 1,000 were injured.

Austrian economist Friedrich von Hayek published the conservative and antistatist *The Road to Serfdom*; his thinking would powerfully affect conservative politicians for much of the balance of the century.

The United States, Britain, China, and the Soviet Union planned the United Nations at the Dumbarton Oaks Conference (Aug.-Oct.) in Washington, D.C.

Stern Gang terrorists assassinated British Middle East administrator Lord Moyne in Cairo.

Women won the right to vote in France.

b. Rajiv Gandhi (1944-1991), Indian prime minister (1984-1989); son and political heir of Indira Gandhi and grandson of Jawaharlal Nehru.

d. Erwin Rommel ("The Desert Fox") (1891-1944), German general; North African and then western European commander at the time of the Normandy invasion. He committed suicide after being sentenced to death for having approved of the Hitler assassination attempt.

d. Galeazzo Ciano (1903-1944), Italian fascist politician; Benito Mussolini's son-in-law and foreign minister; executed for treason after his capture (Jan.).

Oskar Morgenstern published their classic work *Theory of Games and Economic Behavior*.

In *The Psychology of Women*, Helene Deutsch developed and explored ideas on passivity, masochism, narcissism, and the Oedipal conflict in women's psychological development.

Austrian-American child psychologist Bruno Bettelheim became director of the Orthogenic School at the University of Chicago (1944-1973), there working with disturbed children, some thought to be unreachable. Having previously worked with autistic children (from 1932) and been held at Dachau and Buchenwald concentration camps (1938-1939), he had come to America by special petition of Eleanor Roosevelt, among others (1939).

b. Richard Erskine Frere Leakey (1944-   ), British anthropologist and paleontologist who would do key work with his parents, Louis Leakey and Mary Leakey, on the early origins of humans in East Africa; also an influential conservationist.

d. Alexis Carrel (1873-1944), French surgeon working in America who developed new methods of suturing blood vessels (1905), techniques for heart operations in animals (1914), treatments for deep wounds (1916), and the first external blood-pumping machine (1936).

d. Arthur Stanley Eddington (1882-1944), British astronomer who discovered that a star's luminosity is directly related to its mass (1924).

b. Alice Walker (1944-), African-American writer; a leading literary interpreter of the African-American experience.

b. Diana Ross (1944-), American singer and actress who would become an international popular music star in the 1970s.

b. Michael (Kirk) Douglas (1944-), American film star and producer; a major figure from the mid-1980s; the son of Kirk Douglas.

d. Romain Rolland (1866-1944), French writer; a world figure who won the 1915 Nobel Prize for literature.

d. Wassily Kandinsky (1866-1944), Russian painter and teacher; a pioneer of nonobjective work and founder of The Blue Rider group (1911).

d. Edvard Munch (1863-1944), Norwegian painter; a precursor of expressionism who was best known for *The Cry (The Scream)* (1893).

d. Aristide Maillol (1861-1944), French artist best known as the sculptor of many formal, largely ahistorical female nudes.

d. Billy (George William) Bitzer (1872-1944), pioneering American cinematographer who shot *The Birth of a Nation* (1915) and *Intolerance* (1916) during his long association with D. W. Griffith.

d. Glenn Miller (1904-1944), American bandleader and trombonist; he died when his military plane went down over the English Channel.

d. Piet Mondrian (Pieter Cornelis Mondriaan) (1877-1944), Dutch artist; a modernist and cofounder of De Stijl (1917); he worked with color and in geometrical forms.

d. (Hippolyte) Jean Giraudoux (1882-1944), French writer and diplomat; a popular novelist in the 1920s, later a leading playwright.

In Spain's León province, a train wreck inside a tunnel killed 500 people (Jan. 16).

Swedish economist Gunnar Myrdal published *An American Dilemma,* his trend-setting work on American racism.

Near Ogden, Utah, the Pacific Limited train crashed, killing 48 people (Dec. 31).

b. Angela Davis (1944-), African-American philosopher and communist activist, who would be indicted but ultimately acquitted in the 1970 Jonathan Jackson Marin County Courthouse murders; she had been accused of supplying the guns used by Jackson.

d. Ida Minerva Tarbell (1857-1944), American investigative journalist; a pioneering 20th-century "muckraker."

d. Marc Bloch (1886-1944), French historian; a cofounder of the magazine *Annales* (1929), who fought in the French Resistance; he was captured, tortured, and killed by the Germans.

d. Aimée Semple McPherson (1890-1944), Canadian-American preacher who founded the International Church of the Foursquare Gospel (1923); she committed suicide.

d. George Herriman (1881-1944), American cartoonist best known as the creator of *Krazy Kat.*

Soviet armies took Budapest (Feb. 13) and Vienna (Apr. 15) and made the final attack on Germany, taking Berlin by storm (Apr. 22-May 2).

Allied western front armies crossed the Rhine (Mar.); German resistance crumbled in the west. Allied bombing of Dresden (Feb. 13-14) created a firestorm that reportedly killed 100,000 people.

In Italy, Allied forces breached the Gothic Line (Apr. 9-20), as resistance disintegrated. German forces in Italy unconditionally surrendered (Apr. 29).

German forces unconditionally surrendered to American general Walter Bedell Smith, representing Allied commanding general Dwight D. Eisenhower, at Reims (May 7; effective midnight, May 8), which became V-E Day. A second unconditional surrender was made in Berlin (May 8), to Soviet general Georgi Zhukov and British general Arthur Tedder.

In the Pacific, American forces retook the Philippines (Jan.-Aug.); Japanese forces went over to guerrilla resistance. Iwo Jima also was taken (Feb. 19-Mar. 16); most of its 22,000 to 25,000 defenders fought to the death. In a massive action, Okinawa was taken (Apr. 1-June 22); most of its 130,000 to 140,000 defenders fought to the death; losses included 3,000 planes and pilots, many of them suicide bombers (kamikazes), and the superbattleship *Yamoto*. American bombers based in Okinawa began a massive bombing of Japan, in preparation for the coming invasion; 80,000 people reportedly died in the firebombing of Tokyo (Mar. 9-10).

At Yalta (Feb. 4-11), Franklin Roosevelt, Winston Churchill, and Joseph Stalin agreed on some of the shape of the postwar world, and Stalin reaffirmed his promise to make war on Japan upon conclusion of the European war. Many commitments made at Yalta were broken; the Soviet Union was to take much of eastern and central Europe, and the Cold War lay just ahead.

d. Franklin Delano Roosevelt (1882-1945), at Warm Springs, Georgia (Apr. 12); the 32nd president of the

The first atomic bomb was exploded in a test code-named Trinity (July 16), at the Alamogordo Bombing Range, in the New Mexico desert; radioactive fallout was recorded as far east as New England. This and the bomb dropped on Nagasaki (1945) used a plutonium isotope (PU-239), produced by the first nuclear reactor (1942), while the Hiroshima bomb (1945) used a uranium isotope (U-235). Leo Szilard, a key figure in the development of the atomic bomb, organized a petition signed by many nuclear scientists urging President Harry Truman not to drop the bomb, but to warn the Japanese about its dangers. After Hiroshima and Nagasaki, Szilard left nuclear physics (as did a number of others who had helped to build the bomb), turning instead to molecular biology.

Under Atomic Energy Commission auspices, 18 people — without informed consent — were injected with plutonium to allow scientists to trace its path through the body and gauge its effects. As would be uncovered in the 1980s and 1990s, this was just one of hundreds, perhaps thousands, of American nuclear experiments on civilians and armed forces personnel. Similar wide-scale nuclear experiments were conducted in the Soviet Union and probably in several other countries.

High-altitude west-to-east winds across the Pacific Ocean, which had been discovered independently by Japanese (by 1942) and American (by 1944) fliers, were dubbed the *jet stream*. Studied by Swedish-American Carl-Gustaf Arvid Rossby and others, such wind streams were soon recognized as major features of the atmosphere, occurring in wide bands throughout the world, and as key weather factors, knowledge of which would increase the accuracy of weather forecasting.

Abstract expression began to emerge as a major force in American painting, as the painters of the New York School further developed surrealist "automatic painting." Jackson Pollock led in the development of the "drip and splash" automatic painting technique. "Action painting," stressing the process of creation rather than the works created, became a dominant theory.

George Orwell published his novel *Animal Farm*, a satirical attack on the Stalinist bureaucracy and by extension on all the vicious bureaucracies generated by totalitarian governments. Long after the book had become a historical artifact, Orwell's slogan would endure: "All animals are equal, but some animals are more equal than others."

Photojournalist Margaret Bourke-White, then a war correspondent, showed the full truth of Nazi mass murder in her classic photographs of the German death camp at Buchenwald, taken when those still alive were liberated by Allied forces; her unforgettable social document is one of the artistic triumphs of the century of tears.

Roberto Rossellini directed and cowrote a classic Italian neorealist film, the antifascist *Open City*, set in Rome during the German occupation and shot soon after the city's liberation by Allied forces. Aldo Fabrizi, Anna Magnani, and Marcello Paglieri starred.

Arletty as Garance starred opposite Jean-Louis Barrault as Deburau, the great mime, in Marcel Carné's classic film *Children of Paradise (Les Enfants du Paradis)*.

Peter Pears sang the title role in Benjamin Britten's opera *Peter Grimes*, libretto by Montagu Slater. Britten also composed two song cycles for Pears: *Songs and Proverbs of William Blake* and *The Holy Sonnets of John Donne*.

As Allied armies fought their way into Germany, backed by now-enormous American war production, scarce home front supplies became even scarcer; sugar all but disappeared, and electricity was in such short supply that nationwide dimouts (Jan.) and entertainment industry curfews (Feb.) were ordered. With victory in Europe and then victory over Japan, dimouts and curfews were quickly abandoned, controls on civilian goods production largely disappeared, and peacetime industrial reconversion began. By year's end, rationing had ended on gasoline, meat, butter, tires, shoes, and much else. In Europe, supplies began to flow again, but in much more limited fashion, with wartime controls still largely in effect and huge "black markets" springing up throughout the continent.

With the war ended, massive population shifts and other postwar readjustments began in Europe. Millions displaced by war, many of them slave laborers, returned to their home countries; but large numbers did not, many strongly resisting return to the Soviet Union. In Britain, the new Labour government began to implement its long-standing socialist program, strongly resisted by Conservatives, now out of power. In the United States, strikes began; by year's end, there were major strikes in progress in several basic industries, including those at General Motors and General Electric, with many more on the way.

Huge postwar relief and resettlement efforts began, in many countries led by the United Nations Relief and Rehabilitation Administration (UNRRA), with strong efforts developed by privately funded relief organizations. CARE (Cooperative for American Remittance to Europe) was founded, providing a way for individuals to send direct food shipments to Europe — the "CARE package."

In sharp contrast to what happened after World War I, when the United States refused to join the League of Nations, the Senate overwhelmingly (89–2) accepted American entry into the United Nations.

United States (1933-1945), he had taken his country through the Great Depression and nearly through World War II. He died in office and was succeeded by Vice President Harry S. Truman, who made the final decision to use the atomic bomb on Japan.

The American B-26 bomber *Enola Gay* dropped an atomic bomb, the first used in warfare, on Hiroshima, Japan (Aug. 6, at 8:15 AM), killing 70,000 to 80,000 people; 75,000 to 125,000 more subsequently died because of the bombing, some of them decades later, and hundreds of thousands were injured. A second atomic bomb was dropped on Nagasaki (Aug. 9; at 9:30 AM), killing 40,000 to 70,000 people; 50,000 to 100,000 more subsequently died, and hundreds of thousands were injured. For their threat to the survival of humanity and of much other life on earth, these were widely thought to be the most terrible events of a century of tears.

d. Adolf Hitler (1889-1945), head of the Nazi Party (1921-1945) and German dictator (1933-1945), during the latter period becoming directly responsible for the mass murders of tens of millions. He and Eva Braun Hitler (1912-1945) committed suicide in Berlin (Apr. 30).

d. Benito Mussolini (1883-1945), Italian fascist dictator (1922-1945); he was captured and killed by Italian partisans while fleeing before Allied forces (Apr. 28).

The United Nations was founded at the San Francisco Conference (Apr. 25-June 25).

The Labour Party defeated the Conservatives in Britain; Clement Attlee replaced Winston Churchill as prime minister (July).

Soviet Far Eastern forces attacked Japanese forces in Manchuria (Aug. 9-14), ending their attack with the Japanese surrender.

After Hiroshima and Nagasaki, Japan surrendered, on Aug. 15, thereafter known as V-J Day. Formal Japanese surrender documents were signed aboard the American battleship *Missouri* in Tokyo harbor (Sept. 2).

Italian-American microbiologist Salvador Edward Luria and American microbiologist Alfred Day Hershey independently recognized that viruses undergo mutations, previously recorded only in more complex plants and animals. Mutations in viruses such as the common cold and influenza make them hard to combat because antibodies or vaccines developed against one strain may be ineffective against a new strain caused by a mutation.

The herbicide 2,4-D (2,4-dichlorophenoxyacetic acid) was introduced. Long thought to be nontoxic to humans, it would become notorious during the Vietnam War in the defoliant "Agent Orange," a 50-50 mixture of 2,4-D and 2,4,5-T (2,4,5-trichlorophenoxyacetic acid), the latter found to cause cancer and birth defects and banned in 1985.

As World War II reached its end, the United States established a proving ground at White Sands, New Mexico, for rockets, the development of which would proceed intensively; some 100 émigré scientists, including Wernher von Braun, would play an influential role in the development of rockets, both for space use and for armed missiles.

A team led by American chemist Charles DuBois Coryell discovered element 61 (promethium; after the Greek god Prometheus). It had long been sought as the only "blank slot" on chemistry's periodic table between 1 and 96.

The first microwave oven was patented; on sale within two years, these ovens would become extremely popular in the 1980s.

Writing in *Wireless World*, science fiction writer Arthur C. Clark predicted a worldwide satellite communications system, which would come into being two decades later.

Celia Johnson and Trevor Howard starred in David Lean's film *Brief Encounter*, scripted by Noël Coward from his 1936 play *Still Life*.

Ivo Andric published the novels *The Bridge on the Drina, Bosnian Chronicle*, and *The Woman from Sarajevo*, his "Bosnian" trilogy, all written during the course of World War II.

Joan Crawford starred in Michael Curtiz's screen version of the 1941 James M. Cain novel *Mildred Pierce*. Later, her destructive career woman would be seen by many feminists as part of a largely successful attack on the newly independent American woman, as the "boys came home" from war and millions of women were forced out of the working world.

Laurence Olivier directed and starred in his classic film version of Shakespeare's *Henry V*.

Laurette Taylor created the Amanda Wingfield role, opposite Eddie Dowling and Julie Haydon, in Tennessee Williams's play *The Glass Menagerie*; three later screen Amandas would be Gertrude Lawrence (1950), Katharine Hepburn (1973), and Joanne Woodward (1987).

Norman Mailer emerged as a major literary figure with his first novel, *The Naked and the Dead*, based on his World War II experiences.

Roger Livesey and Wendy Hiller starred in the Highlands-set Michael Powell–Emeric Pressburger film *I Know Where I'm Going*.

Sergei Prokofiev composed the opera *War and Peace*; he and Mira Mendelson wrote the libretto, based on Leo Tolstoy's novel (1865-1869).

Arthur Laurents published the novel *Home of the Brave*, attacking anti-Semitism in the U.S. Army.

Jackie (Jack Roosevelt) Robinson was the first African-American baseball player to be signed by a major league club, the Brooklyn Dodgers; after a period in the minor leagues, he would break the major league color line (1947), a historic event with enormous consequences for American society. Branch Rickey, who had in the same year bought a major interest in the club, was the force behind the signing of Robinson and would stay beside him through the very hard years that followed, despite enormous pressure to change his decision.

Millions of American and British women war workers, who had been recruited and eulogized during the war, found themselves quickly displaced by men returning from the war. Even when their jobs were not returned to men who had left them to go to war, many women found themselves pushed out of the workforce — or pushed out of well-paying industrial jobs into marginal low-paying "women's work." Women pursuing careers were widely attacked as "unwomanly" in the sexist atmosphere that characterized the immediate postwar period, with men — and many women — maintaining that "a woman's place is in the home."

The National Broadcasting Company (NBC) put together the landmark first television "network" in the United States, linking New York, Philadelphia, and Schenectady, a precursor of things to come.

The United Nations Food and Agriculture Organization (FAO) was established; during the balance of the century, it would play a significant role in introducing modern farming techniques and tools to the Third World, and in providing drought and disaster relief to many countries.

The United States delegation to the United Nations included Eleanor Roosevelt, no longer the controversial figure she had been in the 1930s but rather the "First Lady of the World." Chairing the UN Commission on Human Rights (1946), she would

1945 cont.

War crimes trials began in Germany. The Nuremberg Trials (Nov. 1945-Oct. 1946) brought death sentences for Nazi war criminals Hermann Goering, Alfred Rosenberg, Julius Streicher, Joachim von Ribbentrop, Hans Frank, Wilhelm Frick, Alfred Jodl, Ernst Kaltenbrunner, Wilhelm Keitel, Fritz Sauckel, Arthur Seyss-Inquart, and Martin Bormann (tried in absentia). Goering committed suicide in prison while awaiting execution; Bormann was never captured; the others were executed. Three other defendants were acquitted, and seven were imprisoned.

Civil war resumed in China after the Japanese surrender, with Communist forces taking much of north China (Aug.) and American marines supporting Kuomintang control of Beijing (Peking) and many north Chinese cities.

The Sixth Pan-African Congress convened at Manchester, England, led by W. E. B. Du Bois, Jomo Kenyatta, Kwame Nkrumah, and other pan-African leaders, many of whom would go on to lead successful anticolonial movements in Africa.

The Indonesian War of Independence began (1945-1949) after Sukarno proclaimed the establishment of the Republic of Indonesia (Aug. 17); British and Dutch forces occupied the country, and Sukarno's forces mounted a guerrilla war.

Yugloslavia became a one-party communist state led by Tito (Josip Broz).

A military coup deposed Brazilian dictator Getúlio Vargas.

Ho Chi Minh became the first president of the Democratic Republic of Vietnam (Sept.).

In northern Iran, Mustafa al-Barzani led a short-lived, Soviet-backed insurrection (1945-1946).

d. Wilhelm Canaris (1887-1945), German armed forces intelligence head and anti-Nazi underground leader; an organizer of the 1944 Hitler assassination attempt; he was executed by the Gestapo.

Soviet physicist Vladimir Iosifovich Veksler proposed the synchrocyclotron, a circular particle accelerator of improved design; it would be built the following year.

Alexander Fleming, Howard Walter Florey, and Ernst Boris Chain shared the Nobel Prize for physiology or medicine for their work in discovering (1928) and isolating and refining (1940) penicillin.

Wolfgang Pauli was awarded the Nobel Prize for physics for his formulation of the exclusion principle (1925).

d. Robert Hutchings Goddard (1882-1945), American physicist and rocketry pioneer who predicted space flight (1919) and launched the first liquid-propellant rocket (1926).

d. Thomas Hunt Morgan (1866-1945), American biologist who laid the foundations for modern genetics.

d. Johannes Hans Wilhelm Geiger (1882-1945), German physicist who developed the Geiger counter to measure radiation (1913).

Gwendolyn Brooks published her first poetry collection, *A Street in Bronzeville,* on African-American themes.

John Steinbeck published his California-set novel *Cannery Row,* about working people in a hard-hit Depression era town.

Ray Milland starred as the alcoholic, opposite Jane Wyman, in Billy Wilder's film *The Lost Weekend,* an early example of the attack on alcoholism that would be a major theme in the second half of the century.

Rex Harrison, Kay Hammond, and Margaret Rutherford starred in David Lean's film comedy *Blithe Spirit,* based on Noël Coward's 1941 play.

The Richard Rodgers–Oscar Hammerstein Broadway musical *Carousel,* based on Ferenc Molnar's 1909 play *Liliom,* starred John Raitt and Jan Clayton.

Chilean poet and teacher Gabriela Mistral (Lucila Godoy Alcayaga) was awarded the Nobel Prize for literature.

b. August Wilson (1945-   ), African-American poet and playwright; a theatrical chronicler of African-American life.

b. Eric Clapton (1945-   ), British guitarist and singer; a leading soloist from the early 1970s.

b. Itzhak Perlman (1945-   ), Israeli violinist who would surmount poliomyelitis to become one of the leading violinists of the century.

b. George Lucas (1945-   ), American screenwriter, director, and producer.

be a prime mover in the adoption of the landmark UN Declaration of Human Rights (1948).

Fluoridation of the water supply was first introduced in the United States to reduce dental decay; its introduction caused a major debate in many communities, with some even calling fluoridation a communist plot to endanger American health.

Occupied Japan, some of its basic industries damaged by American bombing during World War II, began its long run-up to postwar economic power.

Swedish runner Gunder Hägg set the world record for the mile at 4 minutes 1.4 seconds.

Bess Myerson became the first Jewish "Miss America."

In New York City, a B-25 bomber crashed into the Empire State Building (July 28), killing 13 people.

A bomb exploded aboard an American "Liberty ship" off Bari, Italy (Apr. 9), killing 360 people.

A freight train hit a passenger train near Cazadero, Mexico (Feb. 1), killing 100 people, many of them pilgrims.

Bernard Castro introduced his threefold sofa bed, the Castro convertible.

d. Dietrich Bonhoeffer (1907-1945), German Protestant minister and anti-Nazi resistance leader; arrested in 1943, he was murdered by the Nazis after being accused of involvement in the 1944 failed officers' plot to kill Hitler.

d. Joseph Goebbels (1897-1945), Nazi propaganda minister and war criminal who murdered his wife and six children and then committed suicide (May 1).

d. Heinrich Himmler (1900-1945), Nazi SS and Gestapo leader who committed suicide (May 23); he had directly operated the German concentration camps, in which 10 million to 26 million people died, most of them murdered.

d. Pierre Laval (1883-1945), French politician; premier twice in the 1930s (1931; 1935); head of the collaborationist Vichy government during World War II; he was executed for treason (Oct. 15).

d. Vidkun Quisling (1887-1945), Norwegian Nazi puppet government head; he was executed for treason.

b. Bob (Nesta Robert) Marley (1945-1981), Jamaican singer, songwriter, and guitarist who would be a leading figure in reggae.

b. Rod Stewart (1945-), British singer and songwriter; a leading rock music figure from the 1970s.

d. Béla Bartók (1881-1945), Hungarian composer, pianist, and teacher whose large body of work focused on Hungarian ethnic themes.

d. Jerome Kern (1885-1945), American composer; a major musical theater composer, most notably of *Show Boat* (1927).

d. Theodore Dreiser (1871-1945), American writer; a noted realist best known for *An American Tragedy* (1925).

d. Käthe Kollwitz (1867-1945), a leading German artist whose work reflected her populist, pacifist, socialist, and later anti-Nazi views.

d. John McCormack (1884-1945), Irish tenor; one of the leading singers of his time, most notably of opera and Irish popular songs.

d. Ellen Glasgow (1874-1945), American writer, largely on new southern themes.

d. Emily Carr (1871-1945), Canadian painter, largely of Northwest Coast Native American subjects.

d. Franz Werfel (1890-1945), Austrian playwright, poet, and novelist.

d. Paul Valéry (1871-1945), French poet and essayist.

Civil war flared throughout Greece (1946-1949), as communist forces operating out of Yugoslavia and other communist countries took most of northern Greece.

Irgun Zvai Leumi terrorists bombed British targets in Palestine and abroad; among them was the British office wing of Jerusalem's King David Hotel, where terrorists commanded by Menachem Begin, later Israeli prime minister, killed 91 people, including 17 Jews (July 22); the Irgun also bombed the British embassy in Rome.

American-backed Kuomintang forces took much of north China from the Chinese Communists after a truce (Jan.) mediated by General George C. Marshall broke down. In mid-year, as U.S. marines began to withdraw and American supplies dwindled, Communist forces began to regain strength.

The Vietnamese War of Independence began (1946-1954), as guerrilla forces led by Ho Chi Minh (Nguyen That Thanh) fought French colonial forces, beginning a set of colonial, international, and civil wars that would end with the fall of Saigon (Apr. 30, 1975).

The Indonesian War of Independence continued despite the Cheribon Agreement (Nov.) establishing a Republic of Indonesia that was still to be dominated by the Dutch. A three-way war developed, with Islamic insurgents fighting the Dutch and Sukarno's forces.

Trygve Lie of Norway became the first secretary-general of the United Nations (1946-1953); the UN's first General Assembly convened (Jan. 10).

Winston Churchill delivered his "iron curtain" speech at Westminster College, Fulton, Missouri (Mar. 5); a major early Cold War event.

As Indian independence neared, all efforts to create a united India failed; massive Hindu-Muslim rioting escalated into near civil war as Ali Jinnah's Moslem League continued to insist on a two-country solution.

The ENIAC (Electronic Numerical Integrator and Calculator) computer was introduced by John Mauchly and John Presper Eckert. Built largely with funding by the American military (1942-1946), measuring 80 by 8 by 3 feet, weighing 30 tons, and employing 19,000 vacuum-style electron tubes, it originally had to be rewired for each new task, until John von Neumann proposed storing instructions (coded as numbers) as programs (by 1947). The ENIAC was long regarded as the first all-electronic, general-purpose digital computer; even though later (1973) the ABC computer would be recognized as earlier (1942) and as having influenced its design, the ENIAC remained the most influential early computer and was the first with a stored program.

In Operation Crossroads, the U.S. military exploded two atomic bombs in a lagoon off Bikini, a Pacific atoll in the Marshall Islands (July 1; July 25); the inhabitants had been moved elsewhere, but some 42,000 Americans in military service were exposed, many of whom were sickened by the radiation immediately or later in life. These would be the first of some 70 atomic tests on Bikini and nearby Eniwetok (1946-1958), which heavily contaminated islands as far as 200 miles downwind.

An unusual quality of certain subatomic particles was identified independently by Murray Gell-Mann and by T. Nakano and Kasuhiko Nishijima; Gell-Mann later dubbed it *strangeness* (1953).

German-American biologist Max Delbrück and American biologist Alfred Day Hershey discovered, independently, that genetic matter from different viruses could be combined to form a new virus, laying the basis for genetic engineering.

William Wyler directed the classic postwar "coming home" film, *The Best Years of Our Lives,* starring Myrna Loy, Fredric March, Dana Andrews, Teresa Wright, and Harold Russell; Robert Sherwood's screenplay was based on MacKinlay Kantor's 1945 novel.

Roberto Rossellini directed his World War II Partisan movement film *Paisan,* cowritten with Federico Fellini, a postwar celebration of the Italian guerrillas who fought Benito Mussolini's army and then the Germans.

Claude Rains and Vivien Leigh played the title roles in Gabriel Pascal's film version of George Bernard Shaw's *Caesar and Cleopatra.*

Edmund Wilson published the novel *Memoirs of Hecate County,* banned in several jurisdictions for alleged "obscenity" and therefore more easily becoming a best-seller.

Humphrey Bogart played detective Philip Marlowe opposite Lauren Bacall in Howard Hawks's film version of Raymond Chandler's 1939 novel *The Big Sleep.*

John Hersey published *Hiroshima,* his straightforward, shocking story of the nuclear bombing of that city.

The Theater Guild presented Eugene O'Neill's play *The Iceman Cometh,* with James Barton creating the Hickey role in a cast that included Dudley Digges and E. G. Marshall.

Vittorio De Sica made the thematically dark neorealist film *Shoeshine,* about two boys who become petty criminals in wartime Italy and whose lives are ruined in the process, with one ultimately killing the other.

William Carlos Williams began publication of his massive five-volume work *Paterson,* his themes

Major postwar strikes continued to develop in the United States, among them massive coal, steel, and maritime strikes. President Harry S. Truman ended most price and wage controls (Nov.).

Postwar inflation became a grave problem in the United States, as pent-up demand, wartime savings, and higher wages, coupled with aggressive pricing practices, drove prices up rapidly.

The American crime syndicate began to expand into "legitimate" businesses, most notably with the construction of the Flamingo Hotel, the inspiration of New York gangster Bugsy (Benjamin) Siegel, who thought to turn Las Vegas into the major gambling and entertainment center it ultimately would become. Siegel would not live to see it; he was murdered in 1947, probably by his associates. Warren Beatty would play Siegel in the 1991 biofilm *Bugsy.*

Three key United Nations agencies were founded: the United Nations Educational, Scientific, and Cultural Organization (UNESCO), with British biologist and humanist Julian Huxley as its first director general (1946-1948); the United Nations Children's Fund (UNICEF), originally as the UN International Children's Emergency Fund; and the World Court (International Court of Justice), during the interwar period the Permanent Court of International Justice.

U.S. Senator William Fulbright sponsored the Fulbright Act, originating the Fulbright Scholarships exchange program.

American pediatrician Benjamin Spock published *The Common Sense Book of Baby and Child Care,* which became a parents' bible and in the next five decades would outsell every other book except the Bible itself, with more than 30 million copies.

Britain's Labour government initiated the National Health Service, long one of the cornerstones of Labour social policy.

Albania became a one-party communist state (Jan. 11) led by Enver Hoxha.

Jomo Kenyatta returned to Kenya from London; at the head of the Kenya African Union, he became leader of the Kenyan independence movement.

Jordan (Hashemite Kingdom of Jordan), formerly British-administered Transjordan, became an independent state (May 25).

Juan Perón became president and effectively dictator of Argentina (1946-1955); his wife, Maria Eva "Evita" Perón, became a major figure.

Kurdish independence forces led by Mustafa al-Barzani briefly established a Soviet-backed republic in northern Iran but were defeated by Western-backed Iranian forces.

Under considerable American pressure, Soviet forces were withdrawn from Manchuria.

A democratic Hungarian republic was established (Feb. 1); it survived until the spring of 1947, when it was replaced by a Soviet-supported one-party communist government.

A military coup in Haiti (Jan. 11) replaced President Elie Lescot with Dumarsais Estimé.

A military coup in Portugal failed; Antonio de Oliviera Salazar's dictatorship continued.

British nuclear physicist Alan Nunn May was imprisoned for having been a Soviet spy who had passed on atomic secrets.

Lebanese independence was completed; although declared in 1941, only the 1946 withdrawal of French forces made Lebanon an independent state in fact.

The Republic of the Philippines became an independent state (July 4), although the Communist-led Hukbalahap insurrection continued (1946-1954).

American inventor George Devol built a device to control machines — an early form of robot.

Expanding the principle of radar, which detects the position of objects from the reflection of microwave beams, Hungarian scientist Zoltan Lajos Bay achieved the most precise measurement yet of the distance to the moon by bouncing microwaves off it.

American physicist Vincent Joseph Schaefer developed the technique of cloud seeding, dropping crystals of frozen carbon dioxide from an airplane into clouds to cause precipitation. The technique never had widespread application because it worked only when clouds (and the potential for rain) already existed.

Swedish physiologist Ulf Svante von Euler discovered norepinephrine (noradrenaline), a chemical important in the transmission of impulses in the nervous system.

Swiss-American physicist Felix Bloch and American physicist Edward Mills Purcell independently developed the theory that atomic nuclei are tiny whirling magnets that, in a magnetic field, can be lined up to provide information about the substance comprising them; called nuclear magnetic resonance, this would later be put to medical diagnostic use (1973).

Abraham Pais and C. Moller coined the term *lepton* to refer to a class of light subatomic particles not affected by "strong" forces in the atom. They include the electron, muon, tauon, and related neutrinos.

Two General Electric plants began dumping what would eventually be thousands of pounds of highly toxic PCBs (polychlorinated biphenyls) into the upper Hudson River (1946-1977), where they sank to the bottom and

taken from the everyday life around him in his hometown of Paterson, New Jersey (1946-1958).

Irene Dunne as English governess Anna Owens and Rex Harrison as the Siamese king starred in John Cromwell's film *Anna and the King of Siam*, based on Margaret Landon's biography.

James Stewart starred in Frank Capra's classic film *It's a Wonderful Life*, later to become a staple Christmas story on American television, partly because it prematurely lost its copyright protection.

John Mills, Finlay Currie, Valerie Hobson, Jean Simmons, and Alec Guinness starred in David Lean's film version of Charles Dickens's 1860 novel *Great Expectations*.

Robert Penn Warren published the Pulitzer Prize–winning novel *All the King's Men*, on the life of corrupt Louisiana politician Huey Long.

Ethel Merman introduced "There's No Business Like Show Business" as Annie Oakley in Irving Berlin's *Annie Get Your Gun*.

Erich Maria Remarque published his novel *Arch of Triumph*.

German-Swiss writer Hermann Hesse was awarded the Nobel Prize for literature.

b. Steven Spielberg (1946-), American director, writer, and producer who would become a massive figure in film from the 1970s.

b. Candice Bergen (1946-), American actress and photojournalist; daughter of ventriloquist Edgar Bergen; she would become a major figure as television's Murphy Brown.

b. Cher (Cherilyn LaPiere Sarkisian) (1946-), American singer and actress; a worldwide celebrity performer in the 1980s.

The International Whaling Commission was established, reflecting increasing concern over the fate of the great whales; many species were already endangered. In its early days, however, it had little power.

The United Nations established its Commission on Human Rights, chaired by Eleanor Roosevelt.

American boxer Sugar Ray Robinson won the world welterweight title (1946-1951).

Cleveland Indians pitcher Bob Feller achieved a record 348 strikeouts for the season.

In the first National League playoff, the St. Louis Cardinals defeated the Brooklyn Dodgers, two games to none. The Cardinals then went on to win the World Series, defeating the Boston Red Sox four games to three.

Britain's Wildfowl Trust (later the Wildfowl and Wetlands Trust) was founded by environmentalist and painter Peter Scott, son of polar explorer Robert Falcon Scott.

Jean-Paul Sartre published *Existentialism and Humanism*.

Mother Cabrini was declared a Catholic saint for her work with the poor (1889-1917).

The 30- to 50-year sentence of national crime syndicate organizer Charles "Lucky" Luciano was commuted in return for unspecified World War II services; he was deported to Italy.

The steamer *Vitya* sank in Lake Nyasa, Tanganyika (later Tanzania) (Aug. 2), killing 295 people.

An overnight fire at the Winecoff Hotel in Atlanta, Georgia (Dec. 7), killed 119 people.

The prewar French Third Republic (1870-1940) was succeeded by the Fourth Republic (1946-1958).

Syria became an independent state (Apr. 17).

b. Steve Biko (1946-1977), Black South African freedom movement leader who would be murdered by the South African police.

d. Draza Mihajlovic (1893-1946), Yugoslav general; head of the Chetnik anti-Nazi and anti-Communist guerrilla army (1941-1946); he was taken and executed by Tito's Communist partisans.

d. Homma Masaharu (1887-1946), Japanese general and war criminal; commander of forces in the Philippines (1941-1942); he was executed for atrocities committed against prisoners.

d. Tomoyuki Yamashita (1885-1946), Japanese general in Southeast Asia (1941-1942) and the Philippines (1944); he was executed as a war criminal.

d. Ion Antonescu (1880-1946), Romanian fascist dictator (1940-1944) who was a German ally during World War II; he was executed by the postwar Romanian government.

d. Per Albin Hansson (1885-1946), Swedish Social Democratic politician; while premier of Sweden (1932-1946), he was an architect of the Swedish social welfare network.

d. Francisco Largo Caballero (1869-1946), Spanish Republican prime minister (Sept. 1936-May 1937).

began migrating slowly downriver, ultimately polluting the river right down to its mouth, at New York harbor. In the mid-1990s, after years of discussion and a $3 million fine (1976), enormous PCB problems remained.

Soviet physicist Peter Kapitza, who had earlier been prevented from returning to work at Cambridge University and detained in the Soviet Union (1934), was placed under arrest (1946-1953) for refusing to do nuclear weapons work.

Under the Atomic Energy Act, the Atomic Energy Commission (AEC) was established to regulate the development of nuclear weapons and nuclear energy, whether from nuclear fission or nuclear fusion.

Under the direction of Igor Vasilevich Kurchatov, the first Soviet nuclear reactor went into operation.

The first synchrocyclotron was built, in California.

American biochemist Wendell Meredith Stanley, the first to isolate a virus in crystal form (1935), shared the Nobel Prize for chemistry with James B. Sumner and John H. Northrop, who both crystallized enzymes.

American geneticist Hermann J. Muller was awarded the Nobel Prize for physiology or medicine for his work showing that X rays cause genetic mutation (1927).

d. John Logie Baird (1888-1946), Scottish inventor who built an early experimental television (1923), demonstrated the first practical television (1926), and made the first transatlantic television transmission and first color television (both 1928).

b. Dolly Parton (1946-), American country singer, songwriter, and actress; a country music star from the 1970s.

b. Oliver Stone (1946-), American director and writer, who would be a noted cinematic interpreter of the Vietnam War experience.

b. Rainer Werner Fassbinder (1946-1982), German director whose films would reflect his anarchist views.

b. Sylvester Stallone (1946-), American actor, director, and writer who would emerge as an international film star in *Rocky* (1976).

d. Alfred Stieglitz (1864-1946), seminal figure in American photography; the chief founder of the Photo-Secession Group (1902) and of 291, the Little Galleries of the Photo-Secession (1905); publisher of the magazine *Camera Work* (1903-1917). He was the early sponsor and then husband of artist Georgia O'Keeffe.

d. H. G. (Herbert George) Wells (1866-1946), British novelist and essayist best known for his pioneering science fiction novels.

d. Laurette Taylor (Helen Laurette Cooney Taylor) (1884-1946), American stage star, most notably as Peg in *Peg o' My Heart* (1912) and as Amanda Wingfield in *The Glass Menagerie* (1945).

d. (Newton) Booth Tarkington (1869-1946), American novelist and playwright, many of whose works were made into films.

d. Countee Cullen (1903-1946), African-American writer best known for his poetry; a key figure in the 1920s Harlem Renaissance.

d. Gertrude Stein (1874-1946), American experimental poet and playwright; a noted American expatriate in Europe in the interwar period.

A train derailment near Aracaju, Brazil, killed 185 people (Mar. 10).

A United Airlines passenger plane crashed onto a highway after takeoff from New York City's La Guardia airport (May 30); 42 people died.

b. Karen Gay Silkwood (1946-1974), American atomic plant worker who would expose atomic industry safety abuses.

d. John Maynard Keynes (1883-1946), British economist whose work laid much of the theoretical basis for state economic intervention during and after the Great Depression.

d. Jack Johnson (1878-1946), American boxer; the first African-American man to become world heavyweight champion (1908); his story was told in the play *The Great White Hope* (1968).

d. Harlan Fiske Stone (1872-1946), American lawyer; an associate justice of the U.S. Supreme Court (1923-1941) and later chief justice (1941-1946).

d. Harry Lloyd Hopkins (1890-1946), key adviser to U.S. president Franklin D. Roosevelt during the 1930s and World War II; organizer and administrator of many New Deal programs, including the Federal Emergency Relief Administration (FERA) and the Works Projects Administration (WPA); U.S. secretary of commerce (1938-1941).

d. Sidney Hillman (1887-1946), American labor leader; first president of the Amalgamated Clothing Workers of America (1914-1946); a key labor adviser to U.S. president Franklin D. Roosevelt.

1946 cont.

d. James Hopwood Jeans (1877-1946), British mathematician and astronomer who first proposed the "steady state" theory of the universe (1920).

1947

India was partitioned into the two deeply antagonistic independent nations of India and Pakistan (Aug. 15); 500,000 to 1 million people died in the Hindu-Muslim communal rioting, mass murder, and internal migration of 10 million to 18 million people that quickly resulted. Border conflicts began and would continue unabated into the mid-1990s.

After the partition, Kashmir's Hindu ruler took Kashmir into India; a Muslim insurgency began that became an undeclared India-Pakistan War.

As the Cold War intensified, U.S. president Harry S. Truman established the Truman Doctrine (Mar. 12), stating as policy worldwide American opposition to communism and getting from Congress major military and economic aid for Greece and Turkey.

Deepening the confrontation, U.S. secretary of state George C. Marshall instituted the Marshall Plan, providing huge quantities of American economic and military aid to rebuild and strengthen anticommunist European governments. With the arrival of massive American and British aid, including large numbers of military advisers, the tide began to turn in the Greek Civil War.

Writing as Mr. X in *Foreign Affairs*, George Frost Kennan urged "containment" of the Soviet Union, which became basic U.S. Cold War policy.

Witch-hunting became common in American life. President Harry S. Truman initiated "loyalty oaths" for fed-

The technique of radiocarbon dating, using measurement of the radioactive isotope carbon-14, was developed by American chemist Willard Frank Libby. It is possible because C-14 is taken up only by living plants; after the plant's death, C-14 decays, its half-life being 5,700 years. Measurement of the amount remaining allows scientists to date materials back tens of thousands of years. A major contribution to archaeology, anthropology, and paleontology, radiocarbon dating showed that many sites were older than previously thought.

Transistors, made of semiconductors (crystals of metals with special properties), were developed by Bell Laboratories physicists William Shockley, John Bardeen, and Walter Houser Brittain. The basis for solid-state electronics (so called because electrons move through crystals rather than through a vacuum), they would gradually replace cumbersome, heat-producing vacuum tubes in electronic devices.

At the suggestion of John von Neumann, computers first had stored programs, written in "machine language" with special sets of instructions using numerical codes in the binary system.

Hungarian-British physicist and electrical engineer Dennis Gabor first developed the idea of

1946 cont.

d. W. C. Fields (William Claude Dukenfield) (1879-1946), American vaudeville, stage, and screen star; a notable misanthrope.

d. Manuel de Falla (1876-1946), leading Spanish composer.

d. George Arliss (George Augustus Andrews) (1868-1946), British stage and screen actor.

1947

Cheryl Crawford, Robert Lewis, and Elia Kazan founded New York's Actor's Studio, teaching the Konstantin Stanislavsky–based "method," that actors might seek in themselves emotional truth and power in each role. The organization and the method would profoundly influence the course of the world's acting styles for several decades.

Marlon Brando created the Stanley Kowalski role in Tennessee Williams's landmark play *A Streetcar Named Desire,* decisively establishing the Konstantin Stanislavsky–based "method" as a major force in the American theater. Jessica Tandy was Blanche Du Bois; Kim Hunter and Karl Malden costarred.

Ten American film directors and screenwriters — the "Hollywood Ten"— were given one-year jail terms for contempt and then blacklisted after claiming the protection of the First Amendment when refusing to testify before the House Un-American Activities Committee. Witch-hunting quickly became a way of life in the film industry and soon throughout American life.

Arthur Miller emerged as a major American playwright with *All My Sons,* a World War II story starring Ed Begley as Joe Keller and Arthur Kennedy as the son who cannot forgive his father's war profiteering.

Gregory Peck starred as the journalist who discovers the depth and pervasiveness of American

Jackie (Jack Roosevelt) Robinson became the first African-American major league baseball player and simultaneously the first athlete to break the color line in American major professional sports, starring with Branch Rickey's Brooklyn Dodgers (1947-1957).

African-American Willie Earle, accused of murdering a cabdriver, was lynched in Greenville, South Carolina; 26 people were tried and acquitted, although all had admitted being part of the lynch mob.

Shepherds found the first of the writings known as the Dead Sea Scrolls in Qumran Cave, overlooking the Dead Sea, in modern Israel; dating from the mid-1st century AD and earlier, they included copies of biblical works older than any previously known.

Thor Heyerdahl and five companions sailed across the Pacific on a balsa-wood raft; the 101-day voyage was designed to support his hypothesis that some early peoples had crossed to the Americas by sea; his best-selling book on the experience was named for the raft: *Kon-Tiki* (1948).

The General Agreement on Tariffs and Trade (GATT) was established.

American union organization was made far more difficult and strikes far harder to sustain with the

eral employees; these oaths quickly became standard in public and private sector employment.

Americans for Democratic Action (ADA) was founded by liberals seeking to disassociate themselves from communism.

Communist forces continued to gain strength in Manchuria, moving away from guerrilla tactics and into direct positional confrontation with the Kuomintang army.

Democratic government ended in Hungary, as Soviet occupation forces installed a one-party communist government led by Mátyas Rákosi.

European Communist Parties formed the Cominform (Communist Information Bureau) (1947-1956), a major Soviet propaganda organ, which partially replaced the prewar Communist International (Comintern).

The Central Intelligence Agency (CIA) was authorized by the National Security Act, succeeding the wartime Office of Strategic Services (OSS); it would become a massive, often extralegal worldwide intelligence and covert action organization.

Allied occupation forces withdrew from Italy, although American forces remained in disputed Trieste to discourage a Yugoslav takeover.

In anticipation of British withdrawal and the partition of Palestine, the Arab-Israeli guerrilla war intensified in Palestine; neighboring Arab nations also prepared for war.

A Malagasy rising against French colonial forces failed (Jan.-Apr.).

A military coup in Ecuador replaced President José Maria Velasco Ibarra with Colonel Carlos Mancheno (Aug. 23).

The socialist pan-Arab Ba'ath movement organized itself into the Ba'ath Party (Arab Socialist Renaissance Party);

holography, a method of producing three-dimensional photographs or illustrations of objects, obtained by using different patterns of light diffraction from an object. Not practical until 1965, after the development of the laser (1960), holography would be widely used, as on credit cards, because reproduction, and therefore counterfeiting, is difficult.

Edwin Land introduced his Polaroid Land Camera, the first camera to contain both negative film and positive paper, allowing the development of photographs within the camera itself and producing a print in seconds.

Austrian-German zoologist Karl von Frisch discovered that bees use light polarization in the sky to guide themselves in flight.

U.S. Air Force captain Charles Yeager was the first person to break the sound barrier, flying his Bell X-1 jet faster than Mach 1, the speed of sound (Oct. 14), at the barrier creating a shock wave called a sonic boom.

After analyzing infrared light from Mars, Dutch-American astronomer Gerard Peter Kuiper concluded that its atmosphere was mostly carbon dioxide and therefore unable to support life, a possibility many people had entertained for decades (since the 1877 "discovery" of apparent canals).

German-American biochemist Fritz Albert Lipmann discovered coenzyme A, which included one of the B vitamins (pantothenic acid). He showed that it must be present in the diet, since the body requires it for metabolism but cannot manufacture it.

An experimental spy balloon crashed near Roswell, New Mexico, leaving debris including balloons, sensors, and thin metal radar reflec-

anti-Semitism by masquerading as a Jew in Elia Kazan's landmark film *Gentleman's Agreement;* John Garfield, Celeste Holm, Dorothy McGuire, and Anne Revere costarred.

Charles Chaplin wrote, directed, produced, and starred as a serial wife murderer in the film *Monsieur Verdoux,* loosely based on the story of mass murderer Charles Landru; the work moves somewhat uncertainly between satire and sober social comment.

Deborah Kerr, Flora Robson, and Jean Simmons starred as British nuns founding a mission high in the Himalayas in the Michael Powell–Emeric Pressburger film *Black Narcissus.* Based on Rumer Godden's 1939 novel, it also starred David Farrar.

James Michener emerged as a major American writer with his Pulitzer Prize–winning first novel, *Tales of the South Pacific,* the basis for the musical *South Pacific* (1949).

Judith Anderson starred opposite John Gielgud in *Medea,* adapted by Robinson Jeffers from the Euripides tragedy.

Albert Camus published the novel *The Plague.*

Martha Graham choreographed *Night Journey,* music by William Schuman.

A. B. Guthrie published his classic Western exploration novel *The Big Sky;* Kirk Douglas would star in the 1952 Howard Hawks film version.

Benjamin Britten's chamber opera *Albert Herring* was presented at Glyndebourne by Britten's company, the English Opera Group.

E. Y. "Yip" Harburg's musical *Finian's Rainbow* introduced the song "How Are Things in Glocca Morra?" and starred Albert Sharpe, Ella Logan, David Wayne, and Donald Richards.

passage of the Taft-Hartley Act, which reversed by amendment portions of the union-protective Wagner Act (1935) and Norris–La Guardia Act (1932).

Hard-punching American boxer Rocky Graziano (Thomas Rocco Barbella) won the world middleweight championship in the second of three fights against Tony Zale; the 1956 movie *Somebody Up There Likes Me* was based on his autobiography, which also inspired *Rocky* (1976).

French fashion designer Christian Dior introduced his influential first collection, featuring close-fitting tops and full, pleated skirts; dubbed the "New Look," it was widely popular after years of wartime austerity.

Simon Wiesenthal opened the Documentation Center (1947-1951) in Linz, Austria, gathering materials to aid the U.S. Army in prosecuting Nazi war criminals.

The U.S. Federal Insecticide, Fungicide, and Rodenticide Act (FIFRA) was passed, requiring registration numbers and approval for specific uses of pesticides, later amended (1972) to focus more on the public health and environmental consequences of contact with pesticides.

Superdribbler Marques Haynes joined Goose Tatum as a star (1947-1953) of the all-Black basketball team the Harlem Globetrotters.

W. E. B. Du Bois published *The World and Africa.*

Some 1,560 of the 4,000 square miles of Florida's Everglades were placed under federal protection as Everglades National Park.

Approximately 400 people died in a train wreck near Pematangsiantar, Sumatra (Aug. 3).

its greatest early strength was in Syria and later also in Iraq.

b. Hillary Rodham Clinton (1947-   ), American lawyer, women's rights activist, and social reformer; the wife of U.S. President Bill Clinton.

b. Dan (James Danforth) Quayle (1947-   ), Indiana Republican politician; senator (1981-1989) and U.S. vice president (1989-1993).

d. Aung San (1915-1947), leader of the Burmese national movement; the father of Daw Aung San Suu Kyi. Just before Burmese independence was achieved, while prime minister designate, he and five other members of his cabinet were assassinated (July 19).

d. Christian X (1870-1947), king of Denmark (1912-1947) and Iceland (1920-1944); a symbol of World War II resistance to the Nazis.

d. Anton Denikin (1872-1947), Russian Civil War commander of White armies in the Don River region.

d. Stanley Baldwin (1867-1947), three-time Conservative British prime minister (1923; 1924-1929; 1936-1937).

d. Fiorello Henry La Guardia (1882-1947), American Republican politician; incorruptible Depression era reform Fusion mayor of New York City (1933-1945) and director of the United Nations Relief and Rehabilitation Administration (UNRRA) (1946).

d. Haruyoshi Hyakutake (1888-1947), Japanese commanding general on Guadalcanal (1943).

d. Jacques Philippe Leclerc (1902-1947), Free French general who was commander of the French Second Armored Division during the liberation of Paris (1944).

d. Marc Andrew Mitscher (1887-1947), American air admiral who commanded the carrier *Hornet* at Midway (1942) and later commanded the Fast Carrier Task Force.

tors. The Air Force claimed that it was a weather balloon, but many people rejected that explanation; for decades, people who collected information on sightings of unidentified flying objects (UFOs), and who believed that the earth was being visited by beings from other worlds, cited the Roswell debris as the best evidence for extraterrestrial visitations. Only in 1994 did the Air Force acknowledge that the craft was a spy balloon, of a design later abandoned, meant to detect nuclear blasts elsewhere in the world.

The U.S. Air Force started Project Blue Book (1947-1969) to gather and evaluate data on reports of unidentified flying objects (UFOs), otherwise unexplained phenomena in or from the sky.

George Gamow published his popular book *One, Two, Three . . . Infinity.*

The first checkers-playing computer was developed by American engineer Arthur L. Samuel.

Czech-American biochemists Carl Ferdinand Cori and Gerty Cori received the Nobel Prize for physiology or medicine for working out the Cori cycle, the series of chemical reactions by which the body draws energy from carbohydrates; the award was shared with Argentine Bernardo A. Houssay, who studied the pituitary gland.

d. Max Karl Ernst Ludwig Planck (1858-1947), German physicist whose quantum theory (1900) was basic to modern physics.

d. Alfred North Whitehead (1861-1947), British mathematician and philosopher best known for his *Principia Mathematica* (1910-1913), written with Bertrand Russell.

Henry Fonda as the rebel priest of the title, Dolores Del Rio, and Pedro Armendariz starred in John Ford's Mexico-set *The Fugitive.*

Katharine Hepburn and Spencer Tracy starred in *The Sea of Grass,* directed by Elia Kazan and based on Conrad Richter's 1937 novel.

Raymond Massey, Michael Redgrave, Rosalind Russell, and Katina Paxinou starred in Dudley Nichols's screen version of the 1931 Eugene O'Neill trilogy *Mourning Becomes Electra.*

The Alan Jay Lerner–Frederick Loewe Scotland-set fantasy-musical *Brigadoon* starred David Brooks, George Keane, and Marion Bell.

French writer André Gide was awarded the Nobel Prize for literature.

b. Salman Rushdie (1947-   ), British writer; center of a worldwide controversy, he would go into hiding under an Islamic fundamentalist death sentence after the publication of his 1988 book *The Satanic Verses.*

b. Robert Mapplethorpe (1947-1989), leading American photographer and filmmaker, who would die of AIDS.

b. David Mamet (1947-   ), American playwright and director who would become a major playwright in the mid-1970s.

b. Stephen King (1947-   ), American writer who would be a leading horror novelist.

b. Kevin Kline (1947-   ), American stage and screen star from the late 1970s.

b. David Hare (1947-   ), British writer and director; a major playwright from the early 1970s.

An ammunition factory in Cádiz, Spain, exploded (Aug. 18), killing 300 people.

Near Canton, China, a train derailed and plunged into a river, killing 200 people (July 10).

An explosion in a Centralia, Illinois, coal mine killed 111 people (Mar. 25).

b. David Foreman (1947-   ), American radical environmentalist; a founder of the action-oriented organization Earth First! (1980).

b. Hazel Rollins O'Leary (1947–   ), American lawyer who would become U.S. secretary of energy (1993).

b. Kareem Abdul-Jabbar (Lew Alcindor) (1947-   ), American basketball player; the all-time leading scorer in the game, he would play on four national championship professional teams.

b. Petra Kelly (1947–1992), German environmentalist who would become a worldwide "green movement" figure as cofounder of West Germany's Green Party (1979).

d. Henry Ford (1863-1947), American automobile manufacturer; founder of the Ford Motor Company.

d. Josh Gibson (1911-1947), American baseball player; confined to the Negro leagues, he was sometimes called the "Black Babe Ruth." A catcher, he had a career batting average of .423, hitting over .400 in 13 seasons. He died of a brain hemorrhage after developing a brain tumor.

d. Al (Alphonse) Capone (1899-1947), notorious Italian-American gang leader who operated in and around Chicago in the 1920s and 1930s; later imprisoned for tax evasion (1931-1939).

1947 cont.

d. Victor Emmanuel III (1869-1947), king of Italy (1900-1944) who did not oppose Benito Mussolini's Fascist takeover of Italy and cooperated with the Fascists until 1943.

1948

Arab-Israeli civil war began in Palestine; mass Palestinian Arab flight began. The day that British forces withdrew (May 14), the state of Israel was established and the Israeli War of Independence (First Arab-Israeli War) began (May 1948-Jan. 1949). Syrian, Lebanese, Iraqi, Jordanian, and Egyptian forces immediately invaded Israel (May 14-15); all Arab forces except Jordan's Arab Legion, which held most of Jerusalem, were defeated.

Communist forces took Manchuria, decisively defeating and destroying opposing Kuomintang armies at Mukden, then scored a series of major further victories, ending the year with their decisive victory at Hwai Hai (Süchow) (Nov. 1948-Jan. 1949), which cost the Kuomintang 250,000 of 500,000 engaged and effectively ended the war.

d. Mohandas Karamchand Gandhi, known as Mahatma (Great Soul) (1869-1948), Indian independence movement leader; an apostle of nonviolence who was one of the leading world figures of the 20th century; a Hindu extremist assassinated him in New Delhi (Jan. 30).

Democratic incumbent U.S. president Harry S. Truman defeated Republican Thomas E. Dewey, Progressive

Sexual Behavior in the Human Male, the first volume of the "Kinsey Report," was published by Alfred C. Kinsey, Wardell Pomeroy, and Clyde E. Martin; the landmark study revealed American sexual attitudes and practices to be far more diverse than generally acknowledged.

As debate heated up over competing views of the universe's origin, Fred Hoyle, and independently Hermann Bondi and Thomas Gold, revised and popularized the "steady state" theory of the universe first proposed by James Jeans (1920). Meanwhile, George Gamow, Hans Bethe, and Ralph Alpher explored the theoretical underpinnings of the "big bang" theory originally put forth by Georges Lemaître (1927).

Norbert Wiener published *Cybernetics, or Control and Communication in the Animal and the Machine,* coining the term *cybernetics* (from the Greek for "the science of steering ships") for the study of information flow and control in both machine and living communications systems, notably through the use of

1947 cont.

d. Ernst Lubitsch (1892-1947), German actor-director; one of Hollywood's leading comedy directors.

d. Joseph Stella (1877-1947), American painter; a futurist whose notable early work focused on New York City themes.

d. Pierre Bonnard (1867-1947), French painter, illustrator, and set designer; a leading 20th-century colorist.

d. Willa Cather (1873-1947), American writer; a major novelist from the publication of her autobiographical *O Pioneers!* (1913).

1948

South African writer Alan Paton published *Cry, the Beloved Country,* his own cry of protest against racism in his homeland, as the long night of apartheid began.

Alicia Alonso created the role of accused ax murderer Lizzie Borden in Agnes De Mille's ballet *Fall River Legend,* music by Morton Gould.

Andrew Wyeth painted his crippled neighbor, Anna Christina Olson, at rest in an open field, facing a house and a limitless horizon; as *Christina's World,* it was to become his signature work.

Edward G. Robinson and Burt Lancaster starred in Irving Reis's film version of Arthur Miller's 1947 play *All My Sons.*

Humphrey Bogart, Edward G. Robinson, Lauren Bacall, and Lionel Barrymore starred in John Huston's classic film *Key Largo,* based on the 1939 Maxwell Anderson play.

Lamberto Maggiorani starred in Vittorio De Sica's neorealist classic film *The Bicycle Thief.*

The United Nations Commission on Human Rights, chaired by Eleanor Roosevelt, passed the landmark UN Declaration of Human Rights.

The United Nations established the World Health Organization (WHO), which began its massive worldwide contribution to public health.

After more than 20 years in the Negro leagues, sometimes pitching every day for as long as 29 days, Satchel (Leroy Robert) Paige joined the Cleveland Indians — the color bar having been broken the year before — helping them win the World Series.

U.S. president Harry S. Truman sought and was granted an injunction barring a national railroad strike.

The U.S. Supreme Court sharply ruled that the constitutional separation of church and state was a complete bar to religious instruction in public schools.

The Ampex Corporation developed a practical tape recorder, first used in the United States by the Amer-

1948 cont.

Henry A. Wallace, and Dixiecrat J. Strom Thurmond to win a full term (1949-1953). The very closely contested race was prematurely proclaimed a Dewey victory by several newspapers.

Soviet forces blockaded West Berlin (June 22); a massive supply airlift began (June 26), frustrating the blockade; military action, which could have precipitated a third world war, did not develop. The blockade was lifted in May 1949; by the end of the airlift (Sept. 30, 1949), more than 2.3 million tons of supplies had been poured into the city.

With a South African National Party electoral victory, the new government of Prime Minister Daniel Malan (1948-1954) instituted the racist apartheid system, simultaneously mounting a major attack on all dissent and beginning to create the police state that was South Africa for more than four decades.

American diplomat Alger Hiss was charged by Whittaker Chambers with having been a communist spy in the late 1930s. The case (1948-1950), complete with the "pumpkin papers" (microfilms Chambers said were hidden in a pumpkin), became a witch-hunting period cause célèbre.

Burma became an independent state; its first prime minister was U Nu. Multiple insurgencies began, some of which continued through the mid-1990s.

Civil war in Colombia escalated into an extremely costly Liberal-Conservative government guerrilla war (La Violencia) that took 200,000 to 300,000 lives (1948-1958).

Communist-led Chinese-Malayan forces began a guerrilla insurrection against British occupation forces; it grew into the Malayan Civil War (1948-1960), ultimately won by British and Malayan government forces.

Soviet-backed Czech Communists took power, ending Czech democracy by coup.

feedback. His exploration of the problems faced by humans in an automated society gave his work an audience far beyond technical specialists.

German-American physicist Maria Goeppert Mayer developed the shell theory of nuclear structure, in particular showing how the number of protons or neutrons affects an atom's properties and stability. German physicist Hans Daniel Jensen independently developed a similar theory.

Peter Goldmark invented the long-playing record (33⅓ revolutions per minute, or rpm), allowing the recording of longer, unbroken stretches of music.

B. F. Skinner published *Walden Two,* his controversial novel about the use of behavioral engineering to induce individuals to act for the good of their group rather than in disruptive ways.

A 200-inch telescope, then the world's largest, was built on California's Mount Palomar. It would be later known as the Hale telescope after its designer, American astronomer George Ellery Hale, who had built the 100-inch Mount Wilson telescope in 1917.

The hormone cortisone (compound E) was first successfully used to treat rheumatoid arthritis by American physician Philip Showalter Hench; it would become commercially available the following year.

Swiss physicist Auguste Piccard developed the bathyscaphe, a free-floating submersible using the pressurized cabin he had developed for balloon flight. From the 1950s, others would modify it for long-term underwater use, including Piccard's son Jacques and Jacques Cousteau, who would add jet propulsion.

Humphrey Bogart, Walter Huston, and Tim Holt starred as the prospectors in John Huston's classic film version of *The Treasure of the Sierra Madre*, B. Traven's 1935 novel.

Jerzy Andrzejewski published *Ashes and Diamonds*, his World War II Polish Resistance movement story; the celebrated 1958 film version would be directed by Andrzej Wajda.

John Ford's classic Western *Fort Apache*, the first film in his "Cavalry Trilogy," starred Henry Fonda, John Wayne, and Shirley Temple.

Moira Shearer created the title role in the ballet *Cinderella*, choreographed by Frederick Ashton, music by Sergei Prokofiev.

Tennessee Williams's play *Summer and Smoke* starred Margaret Phillips as Alma and Tod Andrews. Geraldine Page would provide the definitive Alma in the 1952 revival of the play.

Nicholas Magallanes and Maria Tallchief danced the leads in George Balanchine's ballet *Orpheus*, music by Igor Stravinsky, sets by Isamu Noguchi.

William Faulkner published the novel *Intruder in the Dust*, an antiracism story about an African-American man falsely accused of murder in the South.

Olivia de Havilland starred as the woman being driven mad in an insane asylum in *The Snake Pit*, directed by Anatole Litvak; the film spurred movements for reform of the treatment of the mentally ill.

Cole Porter's musical *Kiss Me, Kate*, very loosely based on Shakespeare's *The Taming of the Shrew*, starred Alfred Drake and Patricia Morison. Howard Keel and Kathryn Grayson would star in the 1953 film version.

ican Broadcasting Corporation (ABC) for *The Bing Crosby Show*.

A massive Ecuadoran earthquake centered near Pelileo, in the foothills of the Andes, killed an estimated 4,500 to 5,000 people.

The U.S. Congress attempted to counter one aspect of persistent inflation by extending rent control for another year, but inflation was generally perceived to be a major problem.

American figure skater Dick (Richard Totten) Button became the first person to simultaneously hold the Olympic, World, European, North American, and U.S. men's figure skating titles; he would retain the world title for five consecutive years (1948-1952) before turning professional.

American golfer Ben Hogan won 11 tournaments, including the U.S. Open; it was the first of his four U.S. Open wins (1948; 1950; 1951; 1953).

American tennis player Louise Brough won the first of her four Wimbledon women's singles titles (1948-1950; 1955).

Discounted and discouraged because she was 30 ("too old") and the mother of two, Dutch track star Fanny (Francina) Blankers-Koen won a then-record four gold medals at the London Olympics: in the 100 meters, 200 meters, 80-meter hurdles, and 400-meter relay.

The youngest member of the American track team, Bob Mathias, won the first of his two Olympic gold medals in the grueling decathlon (1948; 1952).

Following the death of world chess champion Alexander Alekhine, Soviet grandmaster Mikhail Botvinnik won the world title (1948-1957).

Mother Teresa began her work in India, founding a Calcutta school to work with the poor.

1948 cont.

d. Eduard Benes (1884-1948), president of democratic Czechoslovakia (1935-1938; 1945-1948); he had resigned after the Communist coup.

d. Jan Masaryk (1886-1948), Czech foreign minister (1945-1948) and son of Tomás Masaryk; he had stayed on in opposition after the Communist takeover of his country and fell or was pushed out of a window in Prague.

Yugoslavia left the Soviet bloc, pursuing an independent course; the Cominform expelled Yugoslavia. Denied their Yugoslav bases and supplies, Greek Communist forces weakened and were driven back by strengthened government forces.

The Karen War of Independence (1948-1950) began in Burma.

A military coup in Jamaica (Oct.) replaced President José Bustamante with General Manuel Odria (1948-1956).

(Sri Lanka) became an independent state and Commonwealth member (Feb. 4).

The Republic of Korea (South Korea) became an independent state (Aug. 15). The Democratic People's Republic of Korea (North Korea) also became an independent state (Sept. 9).

d. Folke Bernadotte (1895-1948), Swedish diplomat who was murdered by Stern Gang terrorists while chief United Nations mediator in Palestine.

d. Mohammad Ali Jinnah (1876-1948), leader of India's Moslem League, architect of the Indian Partition, and founder of Pakistan; the country's first governor-general.

d. Hidecki Tojo (1884-1948), Japanese general and prime minister (Oct. 1941-1944); he was executed as a war criminal.

d. Heitaro Kimura (1888-1948), Japanese general who was commander in Burma (1944); he was executed for

The U.S. Bureau of National Standards built the first atomic clock, using oscillations of the ammonia molecule to keep time.

American geneticist George Snell identified certain histocompatibility genes involved in an organism's rejection of tissue perceived as foreign; this was another step on the road to successful organ and tissue transplants.

American microbiologist John Franklin Enders developed methods for growing viruses in the laboratory involving the use of penicillin to kill contaminating bacteria, leaving the "pure" virus; this technique would be vital to the search for cures for viral diseases, notably polio (1952).

American physicist Richard Feynman developed the theory of quantum electrodynamics, on the behavior and interactions of electrons; it would be basic to further developments in the field. Julian Schwinger and Shinichiro Tomonaga were working along similar lines.

Chester Carlson's xerographic process was first publicly demonstrated.

France's first nuclear reactor was completed; a key figure in the project was Frédéric Joliot-Curie.

The flexible Rogallo wing, used in hang gliders, was patented by husband-and-wife team Gertrude and Francis Rogallo.

Dutch-American astronomer Gerard Peter Kuiper discovered a fifth satellite of Uranus, named Miranda.

Swiss chemist Paul Müller won the Nobel Prize for physiology or medicine for his recognition that DDT (dichlorodiphenyltrichloroethane)

Jane Wyman as the abused deaf-mute young woman starred opposite Lew Ayres and Stephen McNally in *Johnny Belinda,* directed by Jean Negulesco and based on the 1940 Elmer Harris play.

Burt Tillstrom began his long-running children's television series *Kukla, Fran and Ollie,* a puppet show that featured Fran Allison (1948-1957; 1961-1962; 1969-1971).

Irwin Shaw emerged as a major American novelist with the publication of his World War II novel *The Young Lions.*

Laurence Olivier directed and starred in his film version of Shakespeare's *Hamlet.*

Maxwell Anderson's blank verse play *Anne of the Thousand Days* starred Joyce Redman in the title role as Anne Boleyn, opposite Rex Harrison as Henry VIII.

Pete Seeger, Lee Hays, Ronnie Gilbert, and Fred Hellerman founded the Weavers, a seminal American folksinging quartet.

Moira Shearer acted and danced the lead as the mesmerized ballet dancer in the Michael Powell–Emeric Pressburger film *The Red Shoes;* Anton Walbrook and Marius Goring costarred.

American-British poet and critic T. S. Eliot was awarded the Nobel Prize for literature.

b. Mikhail Baryshnikov (1948-   ), Soviet dancer, actor, and artistic director; after his defection (1974), a world figure in ballet.

b. Andrew Lloyd Webber (1948-   ), British composer; a major figure in the musical theater from the 1970s.

b. Richard Dreyfuss (1948-   ), American actor who would emerge as a major Hollywood star in the mid-1970s.

Australian cricketer Donald George Bradman retired with a career (1927-1948) total of 28,067 runs, averaging more than 95 per match.

Britain's National Health Service, initiated by the Labour government in 1946, was made fully operational.

New York City's Idlewild Airport opened; then the world's largest airport, it was later renamed after assassinated U.S. president John F. Kennedy.

The I. G. Farben chemical plant at Ludwigshafen, West Germany, exploded in flames (July 28), killing 183 people.

The International Union for Conservation of Nature and Natural Resources (later IUCN — The World Conservation Union) was founded, becoming a key international organization, notably in monitoring international agreements; its members included dozens of nations, government agencies, and environmental organizations.

The steamboat *Kiangya,* filled with refugees in the East China Sea off Shanghai, exploded and sank (Dec. 3), killing 1,100 people.

Economist Paul A. (Anthony) Samuelson published his textbook *Economics,* which became the world's most widely used economics text.

d. Babe (George Herman) Ruth (1895-1948), American baseball player; both a pitcher and a powerful hitter, he was one of the greatest to play the game. His record of 714 home runs stood until 1974 and his single-season 60 home run record until 1961.

d. Charles Evans Hughes (1862-1948), American Republican politician and judge; New York State governor (1907-1910), U.S. Supreme Court justice (1910-1916), defeated Republican presidential candidate (1916), and Supreme Court chief justice (1930-1941).

1948 cont.

his brutality toward prisoners during the building of the Thailand-Burma railroad.

d. Iwane Matsui (1878-1948), Japanese commander in China during the Rape of Nanking; he was executed as a war criminal.

d. John Joseph "Blackjack" Pershing (1860-1948), commander of American forces in France during World War I and the first American General of the Army.

d. Feng Yu-hsiang ("The Christian General") (1882-1948), north China warlord; a major figure during the 1920s until his defeat by Kuomintang forces in 1930.

d. Walther von Brauchitsch (1881-1948), German field marshal and commander in chief (1938-1941).

was a powerful insecticide; its dangers had not yet been recognized.

d. Orville Wright (1871-1948), American inventor who, with his brother Wilbur, built and flew the first engine-powered airplane (1903).

d. Ruth Fulton Benedict (1887-1948), American anthropologist whose best-known work was *Patterns of Culture* (1934).

1949

An Egyptian-Israeli cease-fire (Jan. 7) effectively ended the Israeli War of Independence (First Arab-Israeli War); no peace treaty was signed, more than 1 million Palestinian Arab refugees had fled to neighboring countries, and decades of Arab-Israeli armed conflict were still ahead.

The Chinese Civil War ended with Communist victory; Beijing (Peking), Nanking, and then all of China, were taken as the Kuomintang army disintegrated. The People's Republic of China began (Oct. 1).

The first Soviet atomic bomb was detonated, beginning the "balance of terror" that was to characterize the four decades of Cold War that followed.

A United Nations–mediated cease-fire preceded the partition of Kashmir between India and Pakistan along the existing battlefront, ending the undeclared Kashmir war; unrest flaring into border clashes and guerrilla insurgency were to continue into the mid-1990s.

The first two-stage rocket — a small rocket atop an expropriated German V-2 rocket — was launched at America's White Sands proving ground, reaching 240 miles high. Another American rocket proving ground was established at Cape Canaveral, Florida.

American astronomer Fred Lawrence Whipple posited the "dirty snowball" theory of comets — that they are formed primarily of ice and grit, with perhaps a rocky core — which would later be confirmed (1985).

American biochemist Linus Pauling established that the cause of sickle cell anemia (discovered 1910) was abnormal hemoglobin (the oxygen-carrying molecule in blood), produced by a defective gene. Later geneticists would find that the defective gene had survived through many generations because it gave its carriers some protection against malaria.

1948 cont.

d. D. W. (David Lewelyn Wark) Griffith (1875-1948), a key figure in cinema history whose films included the epics *The Birth of a Nation* (1915), *Intolerance* (1916), and *Orphans of the Storm* (1922).

d. Antonin Artaud (1896-1948), French writer, actor, and producer whose construct of the "theater of cruelty" prefigured what some critics would dub the "theater of the absurd."

d. Sergei Eisenstein (1898-1948), Soviet film director; a world figure whose films included *The Battleship Potemkin* (1925), *October (Ten Days That Shook the World)* (1928), and *Alexander Nevsky* (1938).

d. Claude McKay (1890-1948), Jamaican-American poet, novelist, and short story writer; a leader of the 1920s Harlem Renaissance.

d. Charles Austin Beard (1874-1948), American historian; coauthor of *An Economic Interpretation of the Constitution* (1913) and several other major works in American history.

1949

"Big Brother is watching you!" was the central phrase and image provided by George Orwell in the celebrated antistatist novel *1984*, his bitter, sober, influential warning about the massive dangers inherent in the creation of the unchecked bureaucratic state.

Bertolt Brecht and Helene Wiegel founded East Germany's Berliner Ensemble, which became one of the world's leading theater companies; they had left the United States after Brecht's 1947 appearance before the House Un-American Activities Committee.

Arthur Miller's landmark play *Death of a Salesman* starred Lee J. Cobb in the Willy Loman role, Mildred Dunnock, Cameron Mitchell, and Arthur Kennedy.

Orson Welles starred as Harry Lime opposite Joseph Cotten and Trevor Howard in Carol Reed's classic

As the Cold War intensified and fear of atomic war with the Soviet Union grew, anticommunist hysteria spread in the United States. Federal Bureau of Investigation (FBI) and private loyalty investigations became common, atomic scientists were routinely suspected of espionage, and blacklisting grew in the entertainment and other industries.

A nationwide steel strike over pensions shut down the American steel industry for six weeks, ending with a substantial victory for the United Steelworkers of America.

A massive Ecuadoran earthquake killed an estimated 6,000 people, leaving 100,000 homeless.

Simone de Beauvoir published *The Second Sex,* which would become a central work for the soon-to-emerge mid-century worldwide women's movement.

American troops left China, and U.S. military aid to the Republican government was ended, accompanied by U.S. State Department charges of Chinese Nationalist government corruption.

An Indonesian-Dutch cease-fire (May 7) ended the Indonesian War of Independence; Dutch forces withdrew during the balance of the year. Sukarno became the first president of Indonesia (1949-1966).

Greek government forces decisively defeated Communist insurgents, taking Mount Grammos and effectively ending the civil war. Communist forces continued to wage a low-level guerrilla war.

In his annual message to Congress, President Harry S. Truman put forward the "Fair Deal" slogan to describe his domestic program, calling it a successor to Franklin D. Roosevelt's New Deal; few of his proposals eventuated.

Eleven Western European countries founded the Council of Europe, which focused largely on the area of human rights.

The Federal Republic of Germany (West Germany) became an independent state (May 23), as did the German Democratic Republic (East Germany) (Oct. 7), completing the postwar partition of Germany.

The run-up to the Algerian War of Independence began, as Algerian independence movement forces moved into low-level guerrilla actions against French colonial forces.

With the signing of the North Atlantic Treaty (Apr. 4), NATO (North Atlantic Treaty Organization) was founded; its members were Belgium, Canada, Denmark, France, Iceland, Italy, Luxembourg, the Netherlands, Norway, Portugal, the United Kingdom, and the United States. Later members included Germany, Greece, Spain, and Turkey.

In Peru, American Popular Revolutionary Alliance (APRA) leader Victor Haya de la Torre, his party out-

The Organization of Behavior by Donald O. Hebb posited that the "firing" of neurons across synapses builds up sets of neural connections that form memory.

American biochemist William Cumming Rose established that of some 20 amino acids known, 8 are vital to human health and so are called the essential amino acids.

Australian immunologist (Frank) MacFarlane Burnet posited that embryos do not reject foreign tissue, presumably because of an undeveloped immune system, and that, once an organism is exposed to foreign tissue in the embryonic stage, the organism does not develop antibodies to it and so does not reject it. Work by British-Lebanese zoologist Peter Medawar would confirm this.

Nystatin, the first safe fungicide, was developed by American chemist Rachel Fuller Brown and and American mycologist Elizabeth Hazen; it would be widely used to fight infections such as athlete's foot and mildew damage to books and paintings.

Dorothy Crowfoot Hodgkin first established the structure of penicillin, using an early computer, allowing it to be synthesized.

Dutch-American astronomer Gerard Peter Kuiper discovered a second satellite for Neptune, named Nereid.

Elements 97 (berkelium) and 98 (californium) were discovered by scientists at the University of California at Berkeley.

German astronomer Walter Baade discovered the asteroid Icarus, with an orbit that takes it within 17 million miles of the sun.

postwar film *The Third Man*, screenplay by Graham Greene. Anton Karas's music included the "Harry Lime Theme."

Robert Motherwell painted his first *Elegy to the Spanish Republic;* he would paint almost 150 works in the series.

Broderick Crawford starred as a lightly fictionalized Huey Long in Robert Rossen's film version of Robert Penn Warren's 1946 novel *All the King's Men.*

Philip Johnson established himself as a leading American architect; his home in New Canaan, Connecticut — the Glass Box — became a centerpiece of the International Style.

The Richard Rodgers–Oscar Hammerstein Broadway musical *South Pacific,* based on James Michener's 1947 *Tales of the South Pacific,* starred Mary Martin as Nellie Forbush and Ezio Pinza as Emile de Becque.

Gwendolyn Brooks published her Pulitzer Prize–winning poetry collection *Annie Allen.*

John Wayne starred in *She Wore a Yellow Ribbon,* the second film in John Ford's "Cavalry Trilogy."

Nelson Algren published the novel *The Man with the Golden Arm,* his realistic study of the life of a "junkie"; Frank Sinatra would play the role in Otto Preminger's 1955 film.

The Weavers popularized the song "If I Had a Hammer," written by two of the group's members, Pete Seeger and Lee Hays.

Shirley Jackson published her story collection *The Lottery.*

Another kind of seminal mid-century work on the condition of women was the United Nations Convention for the Suppression of the Traffic in Persons and of the Exploitation of the Prostitution of Others.

The National Basketball Association was formed; as its first president (1949-1963), Maurice Podoloff helped build basketball into a major American sport.

World heavyweight champion Joe Louis retired from boxing, having successfully defended his title against a record 25 challenges, 4 of them from previous heavyweight champions, over nearly 12 years (1937-1949).

The marathon American Telephone and Telegraph antitrust suit began, as the federal government attempted to force the utility to divest itself of the Western Electric Company, its captive manufacturing subsidiary.

The number of television receivers in use in the United States topped 1 million.

A fire spread from river docks into Chungking, China (Sept. 2), killing 1,700 people.

American golfer Sam Snead won the U.S. Masters and PGA tournaments.

Anna Louise Strong, formerly thought to be a strong American supporter of the Soviet Union, was accused of espionage and deported from the Soviet Union.

Builder William Levitt created his prototypical Long Island postwar suburban community, Levittown, with each house exactly like the next.

The Chinese liner *Taiping* collided with a coal ship (Jan. 27) and sank in the South China Sea, killing 600 people.

lawed by the military, took refuge in Lima's Colombian embassy (1949-1954), until he was free to go into exile.

Investment banker and former U.S. cabinet member James Vincent Forrestal (1892-1949) committed suicide (May); he had recently resigned as secretary of defense (Mar.).

The Soviet bloc Council for Mutual Economic Assistance (COMECON) was founded.

d. Georgi Mikhailovich Dimitrov (1882-1949), Bulgarian Communist; the Nazis had unsuccessfully accused him of setting the Reichstag fire in 1933. He headed the Comintern (1934-1943) and took power in Bulgaria after the war (1945-1949).

Margaret Mead published *Male and Female,* on the determination of gender roles by social and biological factors.

d. Edward Lee Thorndike (1874-1949), American psychologist known for his studies of human intelligence and learning methods. In early work with animals, he developed now-standard experiments such as the maze and the puzzle box, widely used in behavioral studies.

d. Harry Stack Sullivan (1892-1949), American psychiatrist who pioneered in group therapy, seeing mental problems as resulting from interpersonal relations rather than inner causes.

Carol Channing introduced "Diamonds Are a Girl's Best Friend" in the Jule Styne–Leo Robin play *Gentlemen Prefer Blondes.*

American novelist William Faulkner was awarded the Nobel Prize for literature.

b. Bruce Springsteen (1949-), American singer and songwriter who would be a world figure in rock from the mid-1970s.

b. Meryl Streep (Mary Louise Streep) (1949-), American actress who would be an international film star from the late 1970s.

b. Bonnie Raitt (1949-), American singer, composer, and guitarist; a major folk and blues figure from the early 1970s.

d. Bill "Bojangles" Robinson (Luther Robinson) (1878-1949), African-American dancer, actor, and variety entertainer, one of the world's leading tap dancers.

d. Richard Strauss (1864-1949), German composer and conductor; a major figure in 20th-century opera and a highly controversial political figure because of his ties with the Nazis.

d. José Clemente Orozco (1883-1949), leading Mexican painter.

d. Leadbelly (Huddie Ledbetter) (1889-1949), leading American southern blues singer, composer, and instrumentalist.

d. Margaret Mitchell (1900-1949), American writer who became a worldwide celebrity after the publication of her only novel, *Gone With the Wind* (1936).

An express train derailed near Nowy Dwor, Poland, killing more than 200 people (Oct. 22).

The Canadian Great Lakes cruise ship *Noronic* caught fire and sank at dock (Sept. 17), killing 128 people.

Fernand Braudel published *The Mediterranean and the Mediterranean World in the Age of Philip II,* a key work of the Annales school of history, written without notes and research material while he was a German prisoner of war during World War II.

b. John Anthony Curry (1949-1994), British ice skater and dancer.

d. Stephen Samuel Wise (1874-1949), American Reform Jewish rabbi, antifascist, and Zionist leader; first president of the World Jewish Congress (1936-1949).

North Korea attacked South Korea (June 25), beginning the Korean War (1950-1953); the invaders quickly took Seoul, the South Korean capital. Predominantly American United Nations forces intervened (June 30), stopped the advance, and ultimately turned the tide, crushing the North Koreans between forces landed at Inchon (150 miles north) and the southern UN army. UN–South Korean forces retook Seoul, took Pyongyang, and then moved toward the Yalu River, the China–North Korea border. Massive Chinese forces entered the war (Nov. 25), with a force of almost 200,000 quickly pushing UN–South Korean forces back to a front north of Seoul (Dec.) and forcing evacuation of an estimated 100,000 military personnel and 100,000 civilians from Hungnam by sea.

National Guard forces defeated a Puerto Rican rising led by Pedro Albizu Campos (Oct. 30). Puerto Rican nationalists Oscar Collazo and Griselio Torresola tried to assassinate President Harry S. Truman, unsuccessfully attacking Blair House in Washington, D.C. (Nov. 1).

French foreign minister Robert Schuman proposed the establishment of a European coal and steel common market, beginning the development of the European Community (EC).

Chinese forces marched into Tibet effectively unopposed; small-scale guerrilla resistance developed; the Dalai Lama continued to rule, essentially as a Chinese figurehead.

Civil war began in Laos as a factional struggle between Communist and Royal Laotian forces within the Vietnamese independence movement then fighting the French.

Congress passed the anticommunist McCarran Internal Security Act over U.S. president Harry S. Truman's veto; the McCarthy period law set drastic curbs on the legal rights of those accused of being communists.

Alger Hiss was convicted of perjury and subsequently imprisoned for almost four years.

Radioimmunoassay, a powerful medical diagnostic technique using radioactive particles to track drugs, enzymes, and other substances in minute amounts in the body, was developed by nuclear physicist Rosalyn Yalow and internist Solomon A. Berson.

The technique of radiocarbon dating was adapted for medical use by German-American biochemist Konrad Emil Bloch, who used forms of carbon, notably radioactive C-14, to trace the development of cholesterol molecules in the body.

Ashley Montagu drafted UNESCO's "Statement of Race," the first formal statement on the topic from UNESCO (United Nations Educational, Social, and Cultural Organization).

Building on the earlier checkers-playing computer (1947), American mathematician Claude Elwood Shannon developed a design for a chess-playing computer; these computers would be built and become increasingly complex, even challenging world-class chess champions.

Dutch astronomer Jan Hendrik Oort suggested that some billions of comets exist together beyond the sun, remnants of the original planets' formation, with individual comets occasionally being drawn into the solar system. This Oort cloud was theorized as explaining why comets have not long since disappeared.

German-born Danish-American psychoanalyst Erik Erikson published *Childhood and Society*, a key work outlining his view of life's developmental stages, each centered on a crisis to be resolved.

The first computer-generated 24-hour weather predictions were produced on the ENIAC, pro-

Bette Davis created the Margot Channing role opposite Anne Baxter in the theater story *All About Eve*, costarring George Sanders, Celeste Holm, Gary Merrill, and Hugh Marlowe; Joseph Mankiewicz wrote and directed the film.

Silent screen star Gloria Swanson made a tremendous comeback as the faded, long-retired silent screen star in Billy Wilder's classic film *Sunset Boulevard*, costarring William Holden and Erich von Stroheim.

John Hersey published the novel *The Wall*, his account of the defiant, doomed 1943 Warsaw Ghetto rising against the Nazis.

The landmark film *Rashomon* marked the emergence of Akira Kurosawa as a world figure and of Japanese films as a force in world cinema.

Langston Hughes published *Simple Speaks His Mind*, the first of his five "Simple" short story collections, all set in African-American life.

Nicholas Magallanes and Melissa Hayden danced the leads in Frederick Ashton's ballet *Illuminations*, music by Benjamin Britten, set and costumes by Cecil Beaton.

Silvano Mangano emerged as an international star opposite Vittorio Gassman in Giuseppe de Santis's starkly realistic film *Bitter Rice*, set among women workers in the Po Valley.

John Wayne starred in the classic Western *Rio Grande*, the final film in John Ford's "Cavalry Trilogy."

Judy Holliday reprised her Billie Dawn role in George Cukor's film version of Garson Kanin's 1946 play *Born Yesterday*, costarring Broderick Crawford and William Holden.

Despite the tremendously adverse impact of World War II, world populations continued to grow, reaching an estimated 2.5 billion to 2.6 billion people.

Althea Gibson became the first African-American to play at the American Lawn Tennis Association championships, helped greatly by Alice Marble's *American Lawn Tennis* article excoriating tennis's "de facto color line."

In response to a threatened railroad strike, U.S. president Harry S. Truman called out the U.S. Army, which seized the railway system; the unions then canceled the strike.

At Colombo, (Sri Lanka), Commonwealth foreign ministers agreed on the "Colombo Plan," a massive development aid plan for Asia and the Pacific; they were later joined by the United States and Japan.

In Boston, a robbery at the Brink's armored car company's North Terminal Garage (Jan. 17) yielded $2.7 million, receiving national publicity; all 11 bandits were ultimately captured.

George Metesky, dubbed the "Mad Bomber," began planting the first of what would become 30 bombs over eight years in crowded New York City public places, injuring some people and terrorizing the city.

American golfer Ben Hogan won the U.S. Open, despite having been so severely injured in an automobile accident (1949) that doctors predicted he would never play again.

In their first year in the National Football League, the Cleveland Browns won their first of three championships under quarterback Otto Graham and founder-coach Paul Brown (1950; 1954; 1955).

Maurice Herzog led the French team that reached the top of the Himalayan peak Annapurna (June 3), at 26,502 feet the highest peak yet scaled and the first over 26,000 feet.

Passage of the South African Suppression of Communism Act further strengthened the South African police state.

Senator Joseph McCarthy began his witch-hunting career (Feb. 9) by falsely charging that there were 205 card-carrying Communists in the State Department. Among McCarthy's nost notable acts was his false accusation that Asian scholar and diplomat Owen Lattimore was a Soviet spy. Though exonerated by the Senate, Lattimore was indicted for perjury (1952); all charges were later withdrawn (1955).

Vietnamese forces defeated the French in northern Indochina and the Mekong River delta; French forces retreated to the Red River delta.

Nuclear physicist Klaus Fuchs was exposed as a Soviet atom spy (1943-1950); he had worked at Los Alamos (1944-1945) and then at Britain's Harwell atomic energy facility.

Karen insurgents lost central Burma to government forces, ending the main portion of the Karen War of Independence; decades of low-level Karen guerrilla insurgency began.

The Senate's Kefauver Committee held highly publicized hearings on the extent of the penetration of organized crime into Amercan life, with no resulting indictments. Senator Estes Kefauver became a national figure in the process, but he was unable to win the Democratic presidential nomination.

A military coup (Apr.) replaced Haitian president Dumarsais Estimé with Colonel Paul Magloire.

Ralph Bunche was awarded the Nobel Peace Prize for his work as chief United Nations mediator for Palestine.

Walter Ulbricht began his long tenure as Soviet-backed leader of East Germany (1950-1971).

d. Jan Christiaan Smuts (1870-1950), South African Boer general who became a founder of South Africa; he was

grammed by John von Neumann, working with a team of meteorologists.

Magnetic tape was being used for scientific data with the UNIVAC computer then in development, and more generally with computers from 1956.

The first embryo transplants were performed, on cattle; various techniques developed with animals would later be used in treating infertility in humans.

Russian-American astronomer Immanuel Velikovsky published *Worlds in Collision*, his controversial work about cosmic collisions with the earth.

Cyclamate, an artificial sweetener, was developed.

Austrian-American child psychologist Bruno Bettelheim published *Love Is Not Enough: The Treatment of Emotionally Disturbed Children.*

Edward Calvin Kendall, Tadeusz Reichstein, and Philip Showalter Hench shared the Nobel Prize for physiology or medicine for their work with cortisone.

d. Charles Richard Drew (1904-1950), African-American physician who developed modern blood banks (1940), but withdrew as head of the American Red Cross blood donor program in protest over racial segregation of blood (1941).

Nevil Shute published the novel *A Town Like Alice,* set in a Japanese World War II prison camp and then in postwar rural Australia.

Sidney Blackmer created the alcoholic Doc Delaney opposite Shirley Booth in William Inge's play *Come Back Little Sheba.*

The Member of the Wedding, Carson McCullers's play based on her 1946 novel, starred Julie Harris and Ethel Waters.

"Goodnight Irene" became a number one hit and a signature song for the Weavers; words and music by Leadbelly (with John Lomax).

Bertrand Russell was awarded the Nobel Prize for literature.

b. Stevie Wonder (Steveland Judkins Morris) (1950-(Sept. 17)), American composer, instrumentalist, and singer who would surmount lifelong blindness to become a world music figure and leading social reformer.

d. George Bernard Shaw (1856-1950), multifaceted British writer, critic, and social reformer; a world figure in the theater for more than 40 plays, many of them continuing staples in the world repertory. He was also a leading British socialist and a major figure in the Fabian Society.

d. George Orwell (Eric Arthur Blair) (1903-1950), British writer who emerged as a major writer of social protest in the 1930s and became a world figure with the novels *Animal Farm* (1945) and *1984* (1949).

d. Vaslav Nijinsky (1890-1950), Russian dancer and choreographer; the most acclaimed male dancer of the early 20th century, at St. Petersburg's Maryinsky Theater and then in Sergei Diaghilev's Ballets Russes company in Paris (1909-1914), his career cut short by mental illness.

British jockey Gordon Richards became the first jockey to win 4,000 races (May 4).

Californian Florence Chadwick set a new English Channel record, swimming the Channel in 13 hours 20 minutes.

Former world heavyweight boxing champion Joe Louis lost a comeback attempt to Ezzard Charles.

Contact lenses, small corrective lenses that fit directly over the iris of the eye, came into use; they had been conceived as early as 1887 by German physician Adolf Eugen Fick, but glass proved irritating and development awaited improvements in plastics.

Mother Teresa founded the worldwide Missionaries of Charity order.

The Brooklyn-Battery tunnel under New York harbor opened; it was then the world's longest tunnel.

Credit cards began to be introduced; the Diners Club was founded, its card the forerunner of a revolution in debt creation.

In the United States, the National Council of the Churches of Christ was founded.

Pierre Cardin left the house of Christian Dior to found his own Paris fashion house, noted for elegant clothes and bright accessories.

Pope Pius XII announced a new Catholic Church dogma: the bodily Assumption of the Blessed Virgin Mary.

Reverend Billy Graham founded his Billy Graham Evangelistic Association, the basis for the widely attended evangelizing meetings he would hold for decades throughout the world.

Roger Baldwin became chairman of the American Civil Liberties Union (ACLU) (1950-1955).

twice prime minister of South Africa (1919-1924; 1939-1948).

d. Léon Blum (1872-1950), French politician; the Popular Front premier of France (1936-1937; 1938), the first socialist and first Jew to hold the post.

d. William Lyon Mackenzie King (1874-1950), Canadian Liberal prime minister (1921-1926; 1926-1930; 1935-1948) who developed Canadian economic and political independence from Britain and the United States, though strongly allied with both during World War II.

d. Hap (Henry Harley) Arnold (1886-1950), American general; World War II Army Air Corps commander.

d. Peter Fraser (1884-1950), New Zealand socialist politician; Labour Party prime minister (1940-1949).

d. Al Jolson (Asa Yoelson) (1886-1950), American singer and actor; a star in vaudeville and on Broadway; his leading role in the first "talkie," *The Jazz Singer* (1927), began a new era.

d. Kurt Weill (1900-1950), multifaceted German composer best known as a leading theater musical composer in Weimar Germany, where he collaborated with Bertolt Brecht, and later in the United States.

d. Walter Huston (Walter Houghston) (1884-1950), Canadian-American vaudeville, stage, and screen star; the father of director John Huston and grandfather of actress Anjelica Huston.

d. Emil Jannings (Theodor Friedrich Emil Janenz) (1884-1950), German stage and screen star, most notably for *The Blue Angel* (1930), and a leading Nazi cultural figure.

d. Eliel Saarinen (1873-1950), leading Finnish and then American architect, from 1938 partnered with his son, Eero Saarinen.

d. Bibhuti Bhusan Banerji (1894-1950), Indian writer best known for the novels *Pather Panchali* (1928) and *Aparajito* (1932).

d. Edgar Rice Burroughs (1875-1950), American writer; the creator of Tarzan in *Tarzan of the Apes* (1914).

d. Edna St. Vincent Millay (1892-1950), leading American poet.

The United Nations established the UN Relief and Works Agency for Palestine Refugees (UNRWA), which became the primary international aid vehicle for Palestinian refugees.

Regular color television broadcasting began in America.

Peanuts was created by cartoonist Charles Schulz.

L. Ron Hubbard published *Dianetics: The Modern Science of Mental Health,* which became the "bible" of his Church of Scientology.

Two commuter trains collided in Richmond Hill, New York, killing 79 people (Nov. 22).

Chinese and North Korean forces launched a New Year's Day offensive that took Seoul; Allied forces retook the city and established a new front north of it. General Douglas MacArthur, who had publicly demanded the right to bomb Chinese Manchurian bases, was dismissed for insubordination by President Harry S. Truman. Peace negotiations began (July) and became very serious at Panmunjon (Nov.).

Convicted of having transmitted atomic secrets as spies for the Soviet Union, Americans Ethel Greenglass Rosenberg and Julius Rosenberg were sentenced to death by Judge Irving R. Kaufman; a worldwide, ultimately failed campaign for clemency began.

Ho Chi Minh's guerrilla armies, in alliance with the Pathet Lao and Khmer Rouge, took control of much of the countryside in Indochina; the French puppet government led by Bao Dai won little support.

In *Dennis v. United States,* the Supreme Court upheld the legality of the Smith Alien Registration Act of 1940, and therefore the convictions of 11 American Communist leaders, effectively outlawing the U.S. Communist Party.

Mohammed Mossadeq led the Iranian National Front Party to power, then quickly instituted major social and economic changes, among them the nationalization of the oil industry, until then under British control; a period of recurrent crises began.

Soviet spies Guy Burgess and Donald MacLean, who with Kim Philby were principals in one of the most notable spy stories of the century, fled from Britain to the Soviet Union.

The 22nd Amendment to the U.S. Constitution was ratified; the "two-term amendment" provided that no U.S. president could serve more than two terms or more than two years of an unexpired term and one full term. Franklin D. Roosevelt was the first and last president to serve more than two terms.

The U.S. government began nuclear testing at the Nevada Test Site, approximately 75 miles northwest of Las Vegas, conducting more than 100 open-air explosions at the site (1951-1958). Far from being warned or evacuated, inhabitants in the area, numbering some 100,000, were reassured that there was no danger. In fact, large areas were contaminated by heavy radioactive fallout downwind, for distances up to 200 miles, causing widespread radiation-connected illnesses (not publicly acknowledged by the government) in the region for decades. After 1958, nuclear tests were conducted underground, although some radioactive clouds were "vented" into the air. Later legal actions for compensation by "downwinders" and others would fail, as the U.S. Supreme Court ruled that the federal government was immune to suits relating to the tests. The cast and crew of the 1956 film *The Conqueror,* including John Wayne, were among the best-known people who were exposed to — and probable victims of — this radiation (1954).

The first computer available for commercial use and not individually built for special purposes was the UNIVAC (Universal Automatic Computer), designed by John Mauchly and John Presper Eckert, creators of the ENIAC (1946); it introduced storage of data on magnetic tape.

American geneticist Barbara McClintock first reported her discovery that genetic fragments are transposable, as her experiments from the 1930s had shown. Her ideas, which would later win her a Nobel Prize for physiology or medicine (1983), were so sharply ridiculed that she ceased publishing for decades.

American physicist Edward Mills Purcell confirmed Hendrik van de Hulst's prediction

J. D. Salinger published his novel *The Catcher in the Rye;* Holden Caulfield's struggle to "find himself" became an archetypal quest for many increasingly alienated young people in the 1950s and 1960s.

Jean Renoir's film *The River* was set in a British community on the banks of the Ganges; based on a Rumer Godden novel, it was made in India, shot by Renoir's nephew, Claude Renoir, and starred Patricia Walters, Nora Swinburne, Esmond Knight, Radha, and Suprova Mukerjee.

Marlon Brando re-created his Stanley Kowalski role, opposite Vivien Leigh as Blanche Du Bois, in Elia Kazan's film version of Tennessee Williams's 1947 play *A Streetcar Named Desire.*

Alec Guinness starred as the mild-mannered clerk who plans the robbery of his own bank in Charles Crichton's classic film comedy *The Lavender Hill Mob.*

Gene Kelly and Leslie Caron starred in Vincente Minnelli's classic film musical *An American in Paris.*

Humphrey Bogart and Katharine Hepburn starred in John Huston's film *The African Queen,* set in East Africa in World War I; James Agee's film script was based on C. S. Forester's 1935 novel.

Gertrude Lawrence as Anna and Yul Brynner as the Siamese king created the leading roles in the Richard Rodgers–Oscar Hammerstein musical *The King and I.*

James Jones emerged as a major writer with his first novel, *From Here to Eternity,* set in Hawaii just before Pearl Harbor; Burt Lancaster and Deborah Kerr would star in the 1953 film.

Lucille Ball began her long run in the title role of television's *I Love Lucy* (1951-1957), emerging as a world-renowned comedian.

Though banning on-site religious instruction in schools as unconstitutional, the U.S. Supreme Court ruled that releasing children for outside religious instruction was constitutional; "released time" laws were adopted in several states.

Flooding along the long Missouri River caused enormous damage; if estimates of $1 billion were correct, it was the costliest American flood to date.

The United Nations established the office of the UN High Commissioner for Refugees (UNHCR) as the main UN refugee aid organization, succeeding the UN Relief and Rehabilitation Administration (UNRRA) and the International Refugee Organization (IRO).

Direct long-distance dialing began to be fully introduced, as American Telephone and Telegraph tested coast-to-coast direct-dialing telephone service.

The American television networks also became nationwide, beginning coast-to-coast broadcasting. The number of television receivers in use in the United States topped 10 million.

Althea Gibson became the first African-American tennis player to play at Wimbledon, reaching the quarterfinals.

Argentine auto racer Juan Manuel Fangio became world driving champion, a title he would later hold for four straight years (1954-1957).

Sugar Ray Robinson, who had for five years been world welterweight champion, defeated Jake Lamotta to take the world middleweight title for the first of five times.

German industrialist Alfred Krupp, imprisoned after Nuremberg for his Nazi activities, was released on American recommendation to help rebuild German industry.

1951 cont.

Winston Churchill again served as British prime minister (Oct. 1951-Apr. 1953).

A military coup replaced Panamanian president Arnulfo Arias with Vice President Alcibiades Arosmena (May).

A military coup led by General Hugo Ballívian blocked the installation of elected Bolivian president Victor Paz Estenssoro.

d. Abdullah Ibn Hussein (1882-1951), the first king of independent Transjordan (1946-1951); he was assassinated in Jerusalem (July 20) and succeeded by his son Tallal.

d. Ali Khan Liaquat (1895-1951), Pakistan's first prime minister (1947-1951); he was assassinated while in office (Oct.).

The Organization of American States (OAS) was founded, its membership including most of the nations of the Americas, although Cuba was excluded from active membership in 1962.

Libya became an independent state (Dec. 24).

Oman became an independent state, although it was still a de facto British protectorate until the mid-1970s.

d. Arthur Hendrick Vandenberg (1884-1951), Michigan Republican senator (1928-1951); a pre–World War II isolationist who became a key internationalist and United Nations supporter during the postwar period as a UN delegate and chairman of the Senate Foreign Relations Committee (1946-1948).

d. Ernest Bevin (1881-1951), founder and head of the British Transport and General Workers Union (TGWU) (1922) and foreign secretary in the first post–World War II Labour government (1945-1951).

d. Henri Philippe Pétain (1856-1951), French general; a World War I hero who became French premier (June 1940), heading the World War II collaborationist Vichy

(1944) that hydrogen atoms in space emit detectable radiation; this discovery allowed scientists to identify interstellar atoms by their characteristic wavelengths, or "fingerprints," and so to "see" galactic shapes, confirming the theory that our own Milky Way galaxy has the characteristic spiral-armed shape.

American nuclear physicists developed the breeder reactor, so named because, during operation, it creates, out of ordinary uranium-238, more fissionable fuel (U-235) than it uses; a major advance, given the rarity of the U-235 isotope.

Cholesterol and cortisone were first synthesized by American chemist Robert Burns Woodward.

American physicist Lyman Spitzer, Jr., built a device called a *stellarator,* hoping to use it to learn how to harness nuclear fusion (like that powering stars and hydrogen bombs) for human use. His Soviet counterparts worked with a device called a *Tokamak,* but more than four decades later, their goal remained unattained.

Edwin Way Teale published the first of four nature books that would take him 70,000 to 80,000 miles through the American seasons: *North with the Spring* (1951), *Autumn Across America* (1956), *Journey into Summer* (1960), and his Pulitzer Prize–winning *Wandering Through Winter* (1963).

Rachel Carson published her best-selling *The Sea Around Us.*

Nikolaas Tinbergen published *The Study of Instinct,* a key work on animal behavior.

American physicist John Bardeen developed a theoretical explanation of superconductivity, discovered four decades earlier (1911).

Ossip Zadkine's bronze sculpture *The Destroyed City* memorialized the victims of the 1940 German terror bombing of the Dutch city of Rotterdam, a nonmilitary target.

Peter Pears created the title role in Benjamin Britten's opera *Billy Budd*, adapted by E. M. Forster and Eric Crozier from Herman Melville's novel (1924; unpublished at his 1891 death).

Tennessee Williams's play *The Rose Tattoo* starred Maureen Stapleton and Eli Wallach.

Herman Wouk emerged as a popular novelist with his maritime court-martial novel *The Caine Mutiny*; it would be the basis for his own 1953 play.

Julian Beck and Judith Malina founded the highly experimental theater company The Living Theater.

Gian Carlo Menotti's opera *Amahl and the Night Visitors* premiered on television (Dec. 24).

Swedish novelist Pär Lagerkvist was awarded the Nobel Prize for literature.

b. Sting (Gordon Matthew Sumner) (1951-), British singer, songwriter, bassist, and actor; a leading popular singer from the 1970s.

d. Sinclair Lewis (Harry Sinclair Lewis) (1885-1951), American writer; a major figure from the publication of his novel *Main Street* (1920) and the first American winner of the Nobel Prize for literature (1930).

d. André Gide (1869-1951), major French writer who won the 1947 Nobel Prize for literature.

d. Fanny Brice (Fanny Borach) (1891-1951), American singer and actress; a musical theater star from her appearance in Florenz Ziegfeld's *Follies of 1910*.

Golfer Betsy Rawls won the first of her four U.S. Open championships (1951; 1953; 1957; 1960).

Joe Louis, who had retired after 12 years as heavyweight champion (1937-1949), was defeated by Rocky Marciano (Rocco Marchegiano) in his third and last comeback attempt.

The Los Angeles Rams won the National Football League championship, led by Elroy Leon Hirsch, the league's leading receiver, dubbed "Crazylegs" for his elusiveness.

Three separate air crashes occurred in Elizabeth, New Jersey, killing 56 people (Dec. 16), 29 people (Jan. 22, 1952), and 33 people (Feb. 11, 1952).

A commuter train crashed through a temporary overpass in Woodbridge, New Jersey, killing 85 people (Feb. 6).

An explosion in a West Frankfort, Illinois, coal mine killed 119 people (Dec. 21).

German-American theologian Paul Tillich began publication of *Systematic Theology* (3 vols., 1951-1963), his major attempt to answer through Christian belief the questions being raised by mid-20th-century existentialists.

American Protestant minister Norman Vincent Peale published his best-selling *The Power of Positive Thinking*.

b. Randy Shilts (1951-1994), American journalist.

d. Charles Gates Dawes (1865-1951), American banker and politician whose Dawes Plan (1924) brought Germany loans with which to pay World War I reparations and brought Dawes the 1925 Nobel Peace Prize. He was Calvin Coolidge's vice president (1925-1929).

1951 cont.

government; after French liberation, he received a death sentence, which Charles de Gaulle had commuted to life imprisonment.

d. Joseph Benedict Chifley (1885-1951), Australian Labour politician; minister for reconstruction and redevelopment (1942-1945) and prime minister (1945-1949).

d. Karl Gustaf Emil Mannerheim (1867-1951), commander of Finnish forces during the Finnish War of Independence (1918) and the Soviet-Finnish War (1939-1940); president of Finland (1944-1946).

d. Maksim Maksimovich Litvinov (1876-1951), Soviet diplomat, foreign minister (1930-1939), and ambassador to the United States (1941-1943).

d. Mikhail Markovich Borodin (1884-1951), Russian communist who had been chief Comintern representative in China and adviser to Sun Yat-sen and the Kuomintang (1923-1927); he died in Siberia, having been imprisoned there in Joseph Stalin's anti-Jewish purge (1949).

Glenn Seaborg and Edwin McMillan were awarded the Nobel Prize for chemistry for their discovery of new elements, most notably plutonium (1940).

Irish physicist Ernest Thomas Sinton Walton and British physicist John Douglas Cockcroft won the Nobel Prize for physics for first experimentally splitting an atom with their particle accelerator (1932).

South African–American microbiologist Max Theiler won the Nobel Prize for medicine or physiology for his yellow fever vaccine (1937).

b. Sally Kristen Ride (1951-   ), American astrophysicist and astronaut; the first American woman in space (1983).

1952

Republican Dwight D. Eisenhower defeated Democrat Adlai Stevenson to become the 34th president of the United States (1953-1961).

d. George VI (Albert Frederick Arthur George) (1895-1952), king of the United Kingdom (1936-1952); he was succeeded by his daughter Elizabeth II.

In Egypt, Farouk I was deposed by a coup led by Gamal Abdel Nasser (June 23); General Mohammed Naguib was the first premier of the Egyptian republic.

Greek Cypriot forces began a guerrilla war against British occupying forces on Cyprus, calling for union (enosis) with Greece; they simultaneously made terrorist attacks on Turkish Cypriots (1952-1959).

Jonas Salk announced his discovery of a vaccine against polio (poliomyelitis, or infantile paralysis), while an epidemic was raging across the United States, with more than 47,000 cases that year alone. It would be used experimentally (1953) and then put into mass use (1954).

The first hydrogen bomb, which used an atomic bomb to trigger a nuclear fusion device, was exploded at Eniwetok (Nov. 1); its development had been led by Edward Teller (1949-1952), who had broken bitterly with J. Robert Oppenheimer, leader of the atomic bomb development (1942-1945), after Oppenheimer advised against developing the H-bomb. Elements 99 (einsteinium) and 100 (fermium),

1951 cont.

d. Robert J. Flaherty (1884-1951), American documentary filmmaker noted for *Nanook of the North* (1922) and *Man of Aran* (1934).

d. Arnold Schoenberg (1874-1951), Austrian composer whose seminal work with atonality and the 12-tone chromatic scale deeply influenced the course of modern music.

d. John Sloan (1871-1951), American artist; a realist and member of The Eight, whose work was drawn largely from New York life.

d. Artur Schnabel (1882-1951), Austrian pianist and composer; one of the leading pianists of the century.

d. Sergei Koussevitsky (1874-1951), Russian composer and conductor; a major figure in American music from the mid-1930s.

d. Cecil B. De Mille (1881-1951), American director, screenwriter, and producer; a leading film figure for more than four decades.

d. Ludwig Josef Johann Wittgenstein (1889-1951), Austrian-British philosopher, long associated with Cambridge University, whose works were fundamental to modern philosophical explorations. His *Philosophical Investigations* was published posthumously (1953).

d. William Randolph Hearst (1863-1951), American publisher who owned a massive communications empire; a conservative who was a chief architect of the Spanish-American War and later an isolationist. He also was an art collector, housing his collection at San Simeon, his California castle. Orson Welles played a thinly veiled Hearst in his classic film *Citizen Kane* (1941).

d. Lincoln Ellsworth (1880-1951), American explorer and engineer who was among the first to fly over the North Pole (1926) and the South Pole (1935), explored the Arctic by submarine (1931), and funded and led many other expeditions, notably in the Peruvian Andes and Antarctica (1933-1939).

1952

The Diary of a Young Girl was published posthumously in English translation; the wartime journal had been written by Anne Frank while hiding, with her family, in Nazi-occupied Amsterdam before her murder in a German death camp (1944). Published originally in Dutch (1947), it would be the basis for a 1955 play and a 1959 film.

Charles Chaplin wrote, composed the score for, directed, produced, and starred in *Limelight*, a sentimental youth-and-age film that was boycotted by American witch-hunters, as Chaplin had by then been attacked as a communist. The film industry even refused to let the work be considered in voting for the Academy Awards. Chaplin and his *Limelight*

The Eisenhower-Nixon presidential campaign was the first to be reported on live television. The UNIVAC computer was first used, by CBS, to make network television predictions about the presidential election.

At the Helsinki Olympics, Czech long-distance runner Emil Zátopek won a notable trio of gold medals: in the 5,000 meters, 10,000 meters, and marathon.

Debuting at Wimbledon, American tennis star Maureen Connolly won the first of three successive singles titles there (1952-1954).

Beginning with the BOAC De Havilland DH 106 Comet, jet planes were put into commercial service.

An insurrection in Bolivia (Apr. 8-11) deposed General Hugo Ballívian, bringing elected president Victor Paz Estenssoro to power; 2,000 to 3,000 people died.

Kenya's mostly Kikuyu Mau Mau Society began an ultimately defeated guerrilla war of independence against British colonial forces (1952-1956).

Maronite Christian forces took power by coup in Lebanon, replacing the Muslim-led government of Bishara al-Khouri with that of Camille Chamoun.

The European Coal and Steel Community (ECSC) was established; as provided by the 1951 Paris Treaty, its coal and steel common market began the processes that would eventuate in the European Community.

The United Nations began its decades-long condemnation of apartheid and the South African police state.

Tunisian independence forces led by Habib Bourguiba began a guerrilla war of independence against French colonial forces (1952-1955).

Fulgencio Batista y Zaldivar seized power by coup in Cuba, ruling as dictator (1952-1958). He would later flee from Fidel Castro's forces (Jan. 1, 1959).

Hussein, grandson of Abdullah Ibn Hussein of Jordan, took the throne after his father, Tallal, was declared mentally incompetent.

Radio Free Europe was established, funded by the United States and broadcasting to Eastern Europe.

The All-Union Communist Party (Bolsheviks) renamed itself the Communist Party of the Soviet Union.

d. Chaim Weizmann (1874-1952), Zionist leader during the interwar period and the first elected president of Israel (1948-1952).

d. Charles Marie Photius Maurras (1868-1952), French fascist and founder of the Action Française (1899); he

named after the two noted physicists, were discovered during analysis of results from hydrogen bomb explosions.

A partial meltdown of a nuclear reactor core occurred at Canada's experimental installation at Chalk River, Ontario (Dec. 2), creating a million gallons of radioactive water; the first recorded nuclear accident.

British physician Douglas Bevis developed amniocentesis, a prenatal test for genetic problems; widely used, especially for women over 35 or those with a family history of genetic disorders, it would spur the development of genetic counseling.

U.S. Navy scientist Grace Murray Hopper developed the first computer compiler, which automated the writing of repetitive machine instructions.

American physician and anesthesiologist Virginia Apgar developed the Newborn Scoring System, yielding an Apgar score, an emergency checklist for quickly assessing a newborn's medical condition.

In a pioneer sex-change operation, a Danish medical team led by Christian Hamburger transformed George Jorgenson into Christine Jorgenson, using hormone treatments and surgery (1950-1952).

Michael Ventris and John Chadwick deciphered Linear B, a Mycenaean script uncovered on Crete during excavations led by Arthur Evans, identifying it as an archaic form of Greek.

Britain exploded its first atomic bomb, on the Monte Bello Islands, off western Australia (Oct. 3).

score were later "rehabilitated," winning a special Academy Award in 1972.

Gary Cooper starred as an archetypal, incorruptible, ultimately invulnerable American Western lawman in Fred Zinnemann's classic film *High Noon*; deserted by his town, he faces and defeats his (and their) enemies, throws away his badge, and moves on.

Gene Kelly, Donald O'Connor, and Debbie Reynolds starred in the film musical *Singin' in the Rain,* directed by Kelly and Stanley Donen.

Ralph Ellison emerged as a major African-American writer with the publication of his only novel, *The Invisible Man.*

The International Style made a major American breakthrough, as Gordon Bunshaft began constructing New York's glass-walled Lever House.

In Marseilles, Le Corbusier began his innovative—some said brutalist—concrete high-rise structure Unité d'Habitation.

Archibald MacLeish published his Pulitzer Prize–winning *Collected Poems.*

Vittorio De Sica's film *Umberto D,* the story of a terminally poor old man and his dog in postwar Italy, starred Carlo Battisti.

French novelist François Mauriac was awarded the Nobel Prize for literature.

b. Anjelica Huston (1952-   ), American film star; the daughter of John Huston and granddaughter of Walter Huston.

b. Robin Williams (1952-   ), American actor and comedian who would become a film star in the 1980s.

David Brower became executive director of the Sierra Club (1952-1969), making it a leading group in the international green movement.

American golfer Ben Hogan won both America's Masters tournament and the U.S. Open, where he was defending champion.

American swimmer Florence Chadwick set a new speed record, swimming from Catalina Island to mainland California.

American writer and religious leader L. Ron Hubbard founded the Church of Scientology, whose members used a lie-detector-like device, called an "auditor," to try to increase control over their minds.

American pole-vaulter Bob Richards won the first of his record two successive Olympic gold medals in the event (1952; 1956).

Still world champion, Dick Button won his second men's figure skating Olympic gold medal, then turned professional.

During night maneuvers in the Atlantic Ocean, the U.S. carrier *Wasp* and the minesweeper *Hobson* collided (Apr. 26), killing 176 people.

Two passenger trains collided in Rio de Janeiro, Brazil, killing 119 people (Mar. 4).

In Middlesex, England, two express trains hit a commuter train derailed in a station, killing 112 people (Oct. 8).

d. John Dewey (1859-1952), American educator and philosopher; an influential advocate of liberal and humanist educational practices; often called the founder of the "progressive education" movement.

d. Maria Montessori (1870-1952), Italian educator and physician who became a pioneering worldwide

1952 cont.

was imprisoned for life for his World War II collaboration with the Nazis.

d. Harold LeClaire Ickes (1874-1952), American politician; a Republican progressive who became a key figure in Franklin D. Roosevelt's New Deal.

d. Evita Perón (Maria Eva Duarte) (1919-1952), wife and partner of dictator Juan Perón; a major figure in Argentine political life.

d. Stafford Cripps (1889-1952), British radical socialist politician, World War II ambassador to the Soviet Union (1940), and a leading member of the Churchill wartime and Attlee postwar cabinets.

American psychologist William Charles Dement discovered REM sleep, characterized by rapid eye movement (REM) and rising heartbeat, blood pressure, and breathing rate, a time possibly linked with dreaming.

British biochemist Rosalind Franklin took X-ray diffraction photographs of the genetic material DNA, showing its structure to be helical (like a twisting ladder), a key understanding that led to James Watson's and Francis Crick's elucidation of DNA's structure (1953).

British archaeologist Kathleen Kenyon began her excavations of Jericho, in Jordan (1952-1958), uncovering a city 9,000 or more years old, one of the oldest cities known.

The bubble chamber, used for tracking the path of subatomic particles, was developed by American physicist Donald Glaser.

Joseph Wood Krutch published the best known of his nature books, *The Desert Year,* on his life in the desert near Tucson, Arizona.

German physician Albert Schweitzer was awarded the Nobel Peace Prize for his medical missionary work in Africa.

1953

Joseph Stalin began a new Soviet purge. In the "doctors' plot," nine Soviet doctors, six of them Jewish, were charged with and "confessed" to murdering Andrei Zhdanov (1948) and to conspiring to murder many other leaders. Two of the doctors would die in prison before Stalin himself died; all were later exonerated by secret police chief Lavrenti Beria before his own death.

d. Joseph Stalin (Joseph Vissarionovich Dzhugashvili) (1879-1953), Soviet dictator (1928-1953) and builder of a police state that took the lives of tens of millions of

The structure of DNA, the genetic material that carries the "codes" for human inheritance, was first worked out by America's James Watson and Britain's Francis Crick, building on work by British researchers Rosalind Franklin, notably her X-ray crystallography, and Maurice Wilkins. Other researchers would later show how the twisting, ladderlike, double-helix structure is used in DNA's self-replication.

d. Knut Hamsun (Knud Pedersen Hamsund) (1859-1952), Norwegian writer who won the 1920 Nobel Prize for literature.

d. Gertrude Lawrence (Alexandra Lawrence-Klasen) (1898-1952), British actress, a star in musical theater; she became ill and died during the Broadway run of *The King and I.*

d. Paul Eluard (Eugene Grindel) (1895-1952), French poet; after World War I, a founder of surrealism; a major figure in French literature.

d. (James) Fletcher Henderson (1897-1952), American jazz pianist, composer, bandleader, and arranger.

d. Ferenc Molnar (1878-1952), Hungarian writer best known for plays such as *Liliom* (1909) and *The Good Fairy* (1934).

figure in early childhood education from her establishment of the Casa dei Bambini (Children's House) (1907).

d. Philip Murray (1886-1952), American labor leader; president of the Congress of Industrial Organizations (CIO) (1940-1952) and first president of the United Steelworkers of America (1942-1952).

d. Sven Hedin (1865-1952), Swedish explorer who traveled widely in Central Asia, rediscovering many sites along the old Silk Road.

d. Benedetto Croce (1866-1952), Italian historian and humanist philosopher; an antifascist who helped return Italy to democracy.

d. William Green (1873-1952), American labor leader; the second president of the American Federation of Labor (AFL) (1924-1952); in the 1930s, he unsuccessfully opposed the formation and development of the powerful Congress of Industrial Organizations (CIO).

Samuel Beckett's landmark play *Waiting for Godot* became a central work of modernist 20th-century "absurdism," bringing the theme of alienation in an inimical world fully into the theater, in what some critics dubbed the "theater of the absurd." Beckett would translate his French play into English for its 1955 London debut.

Arthur Miller's classic American play *The Crucible* — an anti–witch-hunting play set during the Salem witch trials, but also directed at the witch-

Anticommunist hysteria peaked in American life, as vigilante groups picketed "subversive" films, including Charles Chaplin comedies, and attacked librarians for carrying "subversive" books on their shelves, including, of all things, J. D. Salinger's *The Catcher in the Rye;* neighbors turned on "subversive" neighbors. Roy Cohn and David Schine, assistants of witch-hunting senator Joseph McCarthy, became a highly publicized "antisubversive" traveling team, attacking, among others, U.S. Army libraries abroad for stocking "subversive" books.

people. After his death (Mar. 5) and while a power struggle over the succession continued, a Soviet "thaw" began, which repudiated the worst excesses of the Stalin period; hundreds of thousands of prisoners were released, and many others were "posthumously rehabilitated."

d. Lavrenti Pavlovich Beria (1899-1953), Soviet secret police chief; he was executed during the power struggle that followed the death of Joseph Stalin.

An American- and British-backed Iranian coup was defeated by the Mossadeq government; Shah Mohammed Reza Pahlevi fled into exile (Aug.). The shah was reinstalled by a military coup that deposed Mossadeq, who was then imprisoned, dying in house arrest (1967).

Peace talks broke down in Korea; hostilities recommenced (June). The war ended with a lasting armistice (July 27) that established the cease-fire line between North and South Korea as a new border.

Americans Ethel Greenglass Rosenberg and Julius Rosenberg were executed as Soviet spies after all appeals for clemency had been rejected.

Mohammed Abdullah, the "Lion of Kashmir," was imprisoned (1953-1973) after leading the Kashmiri movement for independence from India.

Fidel Castro Ruz led a small group of revolutionaries in a failed attack on Cuba's Moncada barracks (July 26); he was captured and imprisoned, but later released in an amnesty (1955).

Soviet East German occupation forces suppressed antigovernment rioting in East Berlin that spread throughout East Germany (June 16-17).

Swedish diplomat Dag Hammarskjöld became the second secretary-general of the United Nations (1953-1961).

Yugoslav forces clashed with Italian, American, and British forces at disputed Trieste (Aug. 29-31). Tensions

Harold Urey and Stanley Miller sent an electrical charge through a chemical "stew" and successfully produced amino acids, in a landmark experiment showing how life might have emerged from naturally occurring compounds on earth, as predicted by Alexander Oparin (1922).

Building on the earlier external mechanical blood-pumping machine (the Lindbergh pump) (1936), John H. Gibbon, Jr., developed a heart-lung machine, using it to keep his patient Cecelia Bavolek alive during heart surgery.

Secret British nuclear weapons tests began at the Maralinga test range in southern Australia (1953-1963). The Native Australian (Aboriginal) inhabitants were moved from the immediate area during the test years, but many others nearby were exposed to radiation, as were the evacuees after they began to return (mid-1980s), generating compensation claims against the British government, which had made ineffective cleanup attempts (1967). Nuclear tests also were conducted at the Emu test range and on the Monte Bello Islands and at Christmas Island in the South Pacific.

Alfred C. Kinsey, Wardell Pomeroy, Clyde E. Martin, and Paul H. Gebhardt published *Sexual Behavior in the Human Female*, the second volume of the landmark "Kinsey Report" on American sexual attitudes and practices, transforming understanding of women's sexuality.

In a major cause célèbre, American physicist J. Robert Oppenheimer, who had led the Manhattan Project to build the atomic bomb (1942-1945) and then chaired the Atomic Energy Commission's Advisory Committee (1946-1952), found his security clearance withdrawn, on the grounds of alleged left-wing sympathies and friends, no actual security breach having

hunts of the McCarthy period, then at its peak — starred Beatrice Straight, Arthur Kennedy, Walter Hampden, and E. G. Marshall.

James Baldwin emerged as a major African-American writer with his autobiographical first novel, *Go Tell It on the Mountain.*

Alan Ladd starred as the unwilling gunfighter in the title role of George Stevens's classic Western *Shane;* Van Heflin, Jean Arthur, and Brandon de Wilde costarred.

Benjamin Britten's opera *Gloriana* opened at Covent Garden, part of a gala celebrating the coronation of Queen Elizabeth II. The work was set late in the reign of Elizabeth I, who was treated as human, with faults and virtues, to the dismay of some 20th-century royalists and music critics.

Burt Lancaster and Deborah Kerr starred in Fred Zinnemann's film version of James Jones's 1951 novel *From Here to Eternity,* set in Hawaii before the Japanese attack on Pearl Harbor.

Pablo Picasso created the ceramic *Three Doves,* which became an emblem of worldwide peace movements. His 1949 dove had been the official emblem of the left political Paris Peace Congress.

Jack Hawkins, Donald Sinden, and Denholm Elliott starred in the World War II Battle of the Atlantic sea film *The Cruel Sea,* directed by Charles Frend.

Ralph Meeker created the Harold Carter role in William Inge's Kansas-set play *Picnic,* opposite Janice Rule, Kim Stanley, Eileen Heckart, and Peggy Conklin as the women whose lives he affects.

Deborah Kerr as the older woman and John Kerr as the somewhat troubled boy starred in Robert Anderson's play *Tea and Sympathy.*

But McCarthyism began to be seen as having gone too far, and with the end of the Korean War and the advent of a somewhat less paranoid Soviet regime after the death of Joseph Stalin, the American atmosphere changed; witch-hunting began to be directly opposed in the broadcast media, notably by Edward R. Murrow; in Congress; and then by the exceedingly powerful military.

President Dwight D. Eisenhower appointed California governor Earl Warren to be chief justice of the U.S. Supreme Court (1953-1969), beginning one of the Court's most activist — and most liberal — eras.

The Council of Europe founded the European Court of Human Rights and the European Commission of Human Rights.

The New York Yankees won their fifth World Series in a row, defeating the Brooklyn Dodgers four games to two; it was their fourth World Series win over the Dodgers in seven years. The Dodgers would finally defeat the Yankees in the 1955 World Series.

In Kansas City, Missouri, Bonnie Brown Heady and Carl Austin Hall kidnapped six-year-old Bobby Greenlease, who was found dead (Oct. 7) after a $600,000 ransom had been paid. The two were quickly captured, pleaded guilty, and executed (Dec. 18); $300,000 was later recovered.

Edmund Hillary and Tenzing Norgay were the first to reach the top of Mount Everest (May 29), the world's highest mountain, target of numerous 20th-century expeditions; Norgay had almost reached it with another climber the year before.

American golfer Ben Hogan had an unprecedented sweep of three major golf tournaments: the U.S. Open (for the third time in succession), America's Masters tournament, and the British Open.

abated with a settlement (Dec. 5) that provided for the pullback of both sides and the evacuation of the Americans and British.

General Gustavo Rojas Pinilla took power by coup in Colombia, ruling as dictator (1953-1957).

British forces deposed Guyana's elected left-leaning prime minister, Cheddi Jagan (Oct.).

Ramón Magsaysay became president of the Philippines (1953-1957).

Syrian government forces defeated a Druze insurrection (Dec. 1953-Feb. 1954).

Vijaya Lakshmi Pandit became the first woman president of the United Nations General Assembly (1953-1954).

d. Ibn Saud (Abd al-Aziz Ibn Saud) (1880-1953), king of Saudi Arabia, who extended his control to all of Saudi Arabia in a series of civil wars (1902-1925), then formally became king (1932-1953).

d. Karl Rudolph Gerd von Runstedt (1875-1953), German general; commander in chief in western Europe at the time of the Allied invasion.

d. Klement Gottwald (1896-1953), the first communist president of Czechoslovakia (1948-1953).

d. Maud Gonne (MacBride) (1866-1953), Irish Republican leader and actress; founder of the Daughters of Ireland (1900); best known by far through the love poems of William Butler Yeats, her rejected suitor.

d. Carol II (1893-1953), king of Romania (1930-1940).

d. Robert Alphonso Taft (1889-1953), Ohio Republican senator (1939-1953) and son of President William Howard Taft; a leading conservative, he staunchly opposed Franklin D. Roosevelt's New Deal and was a key pre–World War II isolationist; later coauthor of the Taft-Hartley Act (1947).

been charged. Oppenheimer's position had been weakened because he had advised against building the hydrogen bomb (1949), making an enemy of H-bomb supporter Edward Teller, who testified against him.

American physicists Maurice Ewing and Bruce Charles Heezen discovered rifts in the earth's crust, initially along the mountain range beneath the Atlantic Ocean, most obvious near land, as where the Red Sea splits Africa and Arabia.

American inventor Robert H. Abplanalp developed the aluminum spray can, powered by Freon, only later found to attack the ozone layer.

American physicist Murray Gell-Mann demonstrated that certain atomic particles have a property he called *strangeness*.

Jacques Piccard, son of bathyscaphe inventor Auguste Piccard, built the bathyscaphe *Trieste*, setting a world depth record of more than 10,000 feet.

Jonas Salk, developer of the first polio vaccine, also developed a vaccine against influenza.

British archaeologist Mortimer Wheeler published *The Indus Civilization*, describing his work uncovering the Indus Valley's Bronze Age civilizations, notably at Harappa and Mohenjo-Daro.

American physician Robert Wallace Wilkins found that reserpine, which he had been using to treat high blood pressure (from 1950), was a powerful tranquilizer, the first drug of its kind.

German chemist Hermann Staudinger won the Nobel Prize for chemistry for his work on "macromolecules," or polymers (1922).

Eli Wallach, Frank Silvera, Jo Van Fleet, and Martin Balsam starred in Tennessee Williams's play *Camino Real*.

Howard Hawks directed the film version of the 1926 Anita Loos–John Emerson comedy *Gentlemen Prefer Blondes*, starring Marilyn Monroe and Jane Russell.

Leslie Caron starred as the orphan, opposite Jean-Pierre Aumont and Mel Ferrer, in Charles Walters's film musical *Lili*, set in the world of the circus.

Rod Steiger created the title role, opposite Nancy Marchand, in Paddy Chayevsky's television film *Marty*.

William Holden starred in *Stalag 17*, Billy Wilder's film of the 1951 play.

Dylan Thomas wrote the play *Under Milk Wood*, the basis for the 1973 film.

British political leader and writer Winston Churchill was awarded the Nobel Prize for literature.

b. Jay Olcutt Sanders (1953-   ), American actor who would emerge as a film star in the 1990s.

d. Sergei Prokofiev (1891-1953), prolific and wide-ranging Russian composer and pianist; a leading figure in 20th-century music.

d. Eugene O'Neill (1888-1953), leading playwright of the American and world theaters; he won the 1936 Nobel Prize for literature.

d. Dylan Thomas (1914-1953), leading Welsh lyric poet and playwright whose life and career were greatly damaged by alcoholism.

d. Francis Picabia (1879-1953), French painter; successively an impressionist, cubist, leading dadaist, and leading surrealist.

Rocky Marciano defeated "Jersey Joe" Walcott to become the world heavyweight champion; he would defend his title six times (1953-1956), retiring undefeated, the only heavyweight champion never to have lost a professional fight.

Malcolm Little, who had converted to the Nation of Islam (Black Muslim) faith while in prison, changed his name to Malcolm X, shedding a surname he thought linked to slavery, and became an active Black Muslim leader.

An explosion and fire aboard the U.S. aircraft carrier *Leyte* killed 37 people.

Australian tennis player Kenneth Rosewall won the Australian and French men's singles titles at 19, the youngest player to do so.

At Newport, Rhode Island, Jacqueline Lee Bouvier married Massachusetts senator John Fitzgerald Kennedy.

The British Vickers Viscount turboprop, a propeller-driven airplane with a turbine engine, went into commercial service.

Two express trains collided near Sakvice, Czechoslovakia, killing 103 people (Dec. 24).

Near Wairoa, New Zealand, a train derailed into a river at a bridge washout, killing 166 people (Dec. 24).

A Scotland–Northern Ireland ferry sank in rough seas in the North Channel (Jan. 31), killing 133 people.

A U.S. C-124 transport plane crashed near Tokyo, Japan (June 18), killing 129 servicemen.

I. F. (Isadore Feinstein) Stone established *I. F. Stone's Weekly*, a Washington newsletter noted for its investigative journalism for the next two decades.

1953 cont.

d. Robert Ferdinand Wagner (1877-1953), four-time New York Democratic senator (1927-1949); a key New Deal figure who introduced the National Labor Relations Act (Wagner Act), the Social Security Act, and several other major pieces of legislation.

d. Robert Andrews Millikan (1868-1953), American physicist who first measured the charge of an electron (1911) and gave the name *cosmic rays* to outer-space radiation (1925).

d. Edwin Powell Hubble (1889-1953), American astronomer who put forth Hubble's law (1929) and identified many nebulas.

1954

North Vietnamese forces besieged and took the French fortress town of Dien Bien Phu (Mar.-May) and its 16,000-strong garrison, the decisive victory effectively ending the Indochina War. The terms of the French–North Vietnamese Geneva Accords on Vietnam (July) provided for French withdrawal and partition of the country into North and South Vietnam. North Vietnamese guerrilla units (Viet Cong) began a guerrilla war in South Vietnam, beginning the Vietnamese Civil War (1954-1975).

In 36 days of televised hearings, the methods and inhumanity of witch-hunting senator Joseph R. McCarthy were fully exposed by U.S. Army counsel Joseph R. Welch at the Army-McCarthy hearings (Apr.-May). In December, the full Senate censured McCarthy, whose political end was then in clear view.

National Liberation Front (FLN) forces operating out of Tunisian bases attacked French forces in Algeria, beginning the Algerian War of Independence (1954-1962).

The United States developed intercontinental ballistic missiles (ICBMs), making the destruction of humanity by nuclear war an immediate and very real threat.

The first successful kidney transplant was performed by a Harvard medical team, led by Joseph E. Murray; previous attempts, often using a pig or dog kidney, had been made since the early 1900s.

The cast and crew of the film *The Conqueror* (released 1956) were exposed to radiation during their three-month filming in St. George, Utah, downwind from the Nevada Test Site. Damage from the exposure was recognized only decades later by survivors and their families, after almost a quarter of the 200 people on the film had died of cancer, including Dick Powell (1963), Agnes Moorhead (1963), Susan Hayward (1975), and John Wayne (1979), prompting one unnamed atomic energy official to say later, "Please, God, don't let us have killed John Wayne."

The Soviet military detonated an atomic bomb in the air near Totskoye (Sept. 14), in the southern Urals, deliberately exposing some 45,000

d. Maude Adams (1872-1953), American actress best known for her creation of the title role in James M. Barrie's *Peter Pan* (1905).

d. John Marin (1870-1953), leading 20th-century American painter, most notably as a watercolorist.

d. Marjorie Kinnan Rawlings (1896-1953), American writer best known for the novel *The Yearling* (1938).

d. Vladimir Tatlin (1885-1953), Russian artist and architect; a leading exponent of constructivism.

d. Vsevolod Pudovkin (1893-1953), Soviet director, writer, and actor; best known for his film *Mother* (1926).

National League umpire Bill Klem became the first umpire voted into the Baseball Hall of Fame.

d. Frederick Moore Vinson (1890-1953), Kentucky Democratic politician; appointed by U.S. president Harry S. Truman to be chief justice of the Supreme Court (1946-1953).

d. Jim (James Francis) Thorpe (1888-1953), Native American athlete who won the decathlon and pentathlon at the 1912 Olympics; later a professional football and baseball player. Burt Lancaster played him in a 1951 film.

Federico Fellini's classic film *La Strada* starred Giulietta Masina as Gelsomina, opposite Anthony Quinn as Zampano and Richard Basehart as The Fool.

Akira Kurosawa's *The Seven Samurai* was a martial story about samurai hired to defend a 16th-century Japanese village beset by bandits; it would be the basis for John Sturges's *The Magnificent Seven* (1960).

J. R. R. Tolkien published the fantasy novels *The Fellowship of the Ring* and *The Two Towers*, the first two parts of his trilogy "The Lord of the Rings."

Louis Kahn emerged as a major American architect with his first major work, New Haven's Yale Art Gallery.

Marlon Brando starred in Elia Kazan's film *On the Waterfront,* costarring Eva Marie Saint, Karl Malden, Lee J. Cobb, and Rod Steiger.

Charles Laughton, John Mills, and Brenda De Banzie starred in *Hobson's Choice,* directed, cowritten, and produced by David Lean.

In the landmark *Brown v. Board of Education of Topeka* decision, Chief Justice Earl Warren, writing for a unanimous U.S. Supreme Court, outlawed school segregation as unconstitutional, scrapping the earlier "separate but equal" standard and beginning a new period in American education and civil rights.

British runner Roger Bannister was the first person to run the mile in under 4 minutes, setting a time of 3 minutes 59.4 seconds (May 6); he retired later that year to pursue a career in medicine.

Large-scale vaccination with the Salk polio vaccine began; it ended a major series of polio epidemics in the United States (1942-1953) and laid the basis for control of the disease worldwide.

South Korean minister Sun Myung Moon founded the Unification Church, with its highly visible corps of young converts, who became known as "Moonies."

American-backed Philippine government forces ended the main Hukbalahap insurgency; low-level guerrilla actions continued.

An American-backed military coup deposed Guatemalan president Jacobo Arbenz Guzmán and installed Carlos Castillo Armas (June), beginning the long guerrilla civil war that would continue into the 1990s.

Chinese forces defeated a major rising in Tibet.

Gamal Abdel Nasser took full power in Egypt, becoming prime minister.

General Alfredo Stroessner took power by military coup in Paraguay, beginning his long dictatorship (1954-1989).

In South Africa, the National Party's racist leader, Johannes Gerhardus Strijdom, became prime minister (1954-1958).

d. Alcide De Gasperi (1881-1954), Italian politician; an anti-Fascist, organizer of the then-illegal Christian Democratic Party during World War II, and the first postwar premier of democratic Italy (1945-1953).

d. Andrei Yanuarievich Vishinsky (1883-1954), Soviet lawyer and politician; chief prosecutor at the Great Purge show trials of the 1930s and foreign minister (1953-1954).

d. Getúlio Dornelles Vargas (1883-1954), Brazilian politician; dictator (1930-1945) and democratically elected president (1950-1954); faced with a threatened army coup, he committed suicide.

d. Heinz Guderian (1888-1954), German armored forces general whose panzer spearheads led the Polish invasion (1939) and the breakthrough in France (1940).

Soviet soldiers and many thousands of civilians to radiation. When a film of the soldiers' day-long exercises was revealed in a Finnish documentary (1991), then in *Pravda,* only 1,000 soldiers were still alive.

In a test code-named Castle-Bravo, the U.S. military exploded a hydrogen bomb at Bikini (Mar. 1). Although Bikini had previously been evacuated (1946), fallout badly contaminated other islands, notably Rongelap, 100 miles away; many of its inhabitants were later evacuated.

Chlorpromazine (Thorazine), a synthetic tranquilizer, was first used, to control anxiety and lessen hallucinations; it and other tranquilizers would revolutionize the treatment of mental patients, soon replacing shock treatments for most patients.

Some whooping cranes, thought to have been extinct from the early 1940s, were found in Canada; they would be bred in captivity and released into the wild, in a successful American-Canadian effort.

American physicist Charles Hard Townes led the team that built the first maser (microwave amplification by stimulated emission of radiation), using intense beams of radio waves. Masers are used in atomic clocks and also to measure astronomical distance (1981).

The world's first nuclear submarine, the *Nautilus,* was launched (Jan.); U.S. admiral Hyman Rickover had been its main proponent.

The Soviet Union put into operation the first nuclear reactor designed to produce power for public use (June); others quickly followed in Britain, the United States, and elsewhere.

Joseph Papp founded the New York Theater Workshop, the forerunner of the New York Shakespeare Festival.

Lotte Lenya starred as Pirate Jenny in Marc Blitzstein's translation and remake of the 1928 Bertolt Brecht–Kurt Weill musical *The Threepenny Opera*.

British writer William Golding published his chilling novel *The Lord of the Flies*.

Harold Rome's stage musical *Fanny,* based on Marcel Pagnol's "Marius" trilogy (1929; 1931; 1936), starred Ezio Pinza, Walter Slezak, and Florence Henderson.

Patty McCormack starred as the psychopathic child in Maxwell Anderson's play *The Bad Seed*.

French novelist Françoise Sagan published her best-selling *Bonjour Tristesse*.

American writer Ernest Hemingway was awarded the Nobel Prize for literature.

d. Charles Ives (1874-1954), leading American modernist composer, often drawing upon folk and popular themes.

d. Henri Matisse (1869-1954), French painter, sculptor, and graphic artist; a leading 20th-century artist.

d. Martin Andersen Nexö (1869-1954), Danish writer best known for his four-volume novel *Pelle the Conqueror* (1906-1910).

d. Robert Capa (Andrei Friedmann) (1913-1954), American photographer; killed by a land mine while covering the Indochina War.

d. Colette (Sidonie Gabrielle Colette) (1873-1954), French novelist and short story writer best known for her "Claudine" series (1900-1903).

Three massive hurricanes — Carol, Edna, and Hazel (Aug.-Oct.) — struck the North American Atlantic coast, taking 300 lives in the United States and Canada.

Environmentalists, most notably the Caribbean Conservation Corporation, began intensive multinational efforts to save the endangered green sea turtle, leading to the establishment of the world's largest green sea turtle refuge at Tortuguero Beach, Costa Rica.

The Japanese ferry *Toya Maru* sank in Tsugaru Strait, off Japan (Sept. 26), killing 1,172 people.

British flat-racing jockey Lester Keith Pigott won his first of what would be a record 9 Derbys and 29 Classics.

The Atomic Energy Commission (AEC) first allowed private companies to work in atomic research and production, under government supervision and regulation.

The Boeing 707 was introduced to commercial air service.

A train plunged off a bridge near Hyderabad, India, killing 137 people (Sept. 28).

d. Robert Houghwout Jackson (1892-1954), U.S. attorney general (1940-1941), Supreme Court justice (1941-1954), and chief U.S. prosecutor at the Nuremberg Trials (1945-1946).

1954 cont.

Russian-American physicist George Gamow posited that nucleic acids in the genetic material DNA work in sets of three.

British zoologist and science historian Joseph Needham began publication of his monumental *Science and Civilization in China* (1954-   ).

d. Enrico Fermi (1901-1954), Italian-American nuclear physicist whose team built the first nuclear reactor and produced the first chain reaction (1942), leading to the atomic bomb.

d. Alan Mathison Turing (1912-1954), British mathematician and cryptographer who built an early computer for code-breaking (1943).

1955

Completing the power struggle that had started with the death of Joseph Stalin (1953), Communist Party leader Nikita Khrushchev defeated Georgi Malenkov and took full power as premier of the Soviet Union.

American president Dwight D. Eisenhower and Soviet premier Nikita Khrushchev met at the "Geneva summit," the first such post–World War II superpower meeting (July).

U.S. secretary of state John Foster Dulles stated the concept of "massive retaliation" in the event of a nuclear war; this became basic American Cold War policy.

The United States and the People's Republic of China confronted each other over the issue of Formosa (Taiwan). China demanded that American protection of the Kuomintang government be withdrawn, and the U.S. Senate overwhelmingly authorized President Dwight D. Eisenhower to use force if necessary to defend the island.

At the Bandung (Indonesia) Conference (Apr.), 29 African and Asian nations declared themselves united

The first birth control pill, containing synthesized estrogen and other hormones, was developed by American biologist Gregory Pincus (1951-1955); designed to interrupt a woman's monthly reproductive cycle, preventing conception, it would make possible the sexual revolution of the 1960s. By 1968, adverse side effects such as blood clots were recognized, but other studies would show beneficial side effects.

Dorothy Crowfoot Hodgkin, using a computer, first worked out the complex structure of vitamin B_{12} (cyanocobalamin), which she had first photographed by X-ray crystallography (1948); the substance itself was quickly isolated by others.

Soviet astronomer Viktor Amazaspovich Ambartsumian theorized, from radio observations, that the Cygnus galaxy was exploding, contrary to its serene and static appearance.

American cardiologist Denton Cooley developed a widely used heart-lung bypass machine.

1954 cont.

d. J. (John) Rosamond Johnson (1873-1954), leading African-American composer.

1955

Boris Pasternak wrote the classic Russian Revolution and Civil War novel *Doctor Zhivago,* a key work in Soviet literature and history; banned in his country, it was first published in Italy (1957).

The Family of Man exhibition was mounted at New York's Museum of Modern Art by Edward Steichen, the museum's director of photography.

Ingmar Bergman's classic farce *Smiles of a Summer Night* starred Gunnar Björnstrand, Ulla Jacobsson, Harriet Andersson, and Eva Dahlbeck.

British novelist J. R. R. Tolkien published *The Return of the King,* the last part of the trilogy "The Lord of the Rings."

Susan Strasberg as Anne Frank starred opposite Joseph Schildkraut in the play *The Diary of Anne Frank,* by Frances Goodrich and Albert Hackett; it was based on Frank's diary.

Van Heflin starred as Eddie Carbone, opposite Gloria Marlowe and Richard Davalos, in Arthur Miller's play *A View from the Bridge.*

After Rosa Parks was arrested for refusing to move to the back of a bus in Montgomery, Alabama (Dec. 1), Martin Luther King, Jr., and Ralph D. Abernathy organized the successful 381-day Montgomery bus boycott, desegregating the buses and beginning the modern American civil rights movement.

Emmett Till, a 14-year-old African-American, was lynched in Le Flore County, Mississippi (Aug. 13), apparently for whistling at a White woman; two of his alleged murderers were acquitted by an all-White jury. His lynching became a key issue of the new civil rights movement.

The American Federation of Labor (AFL) and the Congress of Industrial Organizations (CIO) merged into the AFL-CIO, healing the split over industrial unionism that dated to the mid-1930s and had led to the organization of the CIO. George Meany became its president (1955-1979).

Disneyland opened in Anaheim, California; it would quickly become the world's most notable amusement park.

against racism and colonialism and nonaligned as regarded the Cold War.

Civil war began in Sudan between government forces dominated by the Muslims of the north and the Christian and animist Black Africans of the south; war would continue into the mid-1990s.

Ngo Dinh Diem took power in South Vietnam, ruling as military dictator (1955-1963). As French forces began to withdraw, American aid to the South Vietnamese government began to flow, beginning the process of engagement that would result in the Vietnam War.

On Winston Churchill's retirement, Foreign Secretary Anthony Eden succeeded him as Britain's Conservative prime minister (1955-1957).

Argentine dictator Juan Perón fled into exile after being deposed by a military coup.

Juscelino Kubitschek became the elected president of Brazil (1955-1961), succeeding dictator Getúlio Vargas; Kubitschek embarked on a massive — and very expensive — public works program, including the building of Brasília.

The Soviet Union established the Soviet bloc Warsaw Pact (Warsaw Treaty Organization), a military alliance that included the Soviet Union, Bulgaria, Czechoslovakia, the German Democratic Republic (East Germany), Hungary, Poland, and Romania.

West Germany and the Soviet Union established diplomatic relations, an innovative move on the part of the West Germans at the height of the Cold War.

d. Cordell Hull (1871-1955), American politician and diplomat; secretary of state (1933-1944); he was awarded the 1945 Nobel Peace Prize.

British engineer Christopher Cockerell patented the hovercraft (hydrofoil), a type of vehicle designed to generate an air "cushion," allowing it to travel over land or water.

Italian-American physicist Emilio Segrè and American physicist Owen Chamberlain discovered the antiproton; they would share the 1959 Nobel Prize for physics.

American astronomer Kenneth Linn Franklin first detected radio waves emitted from Jupiter, the first such emissions found from a planet.

Synthetic diamonds were first successfully produced from carbon atoms combined at extremely high temperatures and pressures.

American astronomer George Howard Herbig discovered the first "newborn" stars in a previously well-explored region of the Orion nebula.

Element 101 was discovered by Glenn Seaborg and others; it was named mendelevium in honor of Dmitri Mendeleyev, developer of chemistry's periodic table.

An Idaho Falls, Idaho, nuclear breeder reactor went temporarily out of control (Nov.).

d. Albert Einstein (1879-1955), German-Swiss-American physicist who developed the revolutionary concept of relativity (1905; 1915), effectively providing a new view of the universe. An anti-Nazi, he urged development of the atomic bomb (1939), fearing that the Germans would do so first, but later worked for peace and to ban nuclear weapons.

Ben Gazzara, Shelley Winters, Anthony Franciosa, and Joey Silvera starred in *A Hatful of Rain*, Michael V. Gazzo's powerful and pioneering drama on the evils of drug addiction.

MacKinlay Kantor published the Pulitzer Prize–winning novel *Andersonville,* set in the notorious Confederate prison camp.

Pather Panchali was the first film in Satyajit Ray's "Apu" trilogy.

Tennessee Williams's play *Cat on a Hot Tin Roof,* about a decadent, vicious southern family, starred Burl Ives as Big Daddy, Barbara Bel Geddes, and Ben Gazzara.

Vladimir Nabokov published the novel *Lolita,* about a 12-year-old girl in a sexual relationship with a man; the book became a best-seller after it had been banned in several jurisdictions for its "obscenity."

Marian Anderson made her decades-overdue debut at the Metropolitan Opera, the first African-American artist to sing there.

Nikos Kazantakis published his novel *The Last Temptation of Christ.*

Icelandic writer Haldor Laxness was awarded the Nobel Prize for literature.

d. James Agee (1909-1955), American novelist, essayist, screenwriter, and film critic; noted for his essay, with Walker Evans's photos, in *Let Us Now Praise Famous Men* (1941).

d. James Dean (1931-1955), American actor who had, in the year of his death, become a film star in Nicholas Ray's *Rebel Without a Cause,* a symbol of alienated youth.

A bomb placed in luggage by a passenger's son caused a plane to explode near Longmont, Colorado (Nov. 1), killing all 44 people aboard.

Cristóbal Balenciaga, long known for his loose-fitting clothes, introduced the tunic dress.

German-American philosopher Herbert Marcuse published *Eros and Civilization,* on repression of the individual by society, especially under capitalism.

Near Guadalajara, Mexico, a train derailed into a ravine, killing 300 people (Apr. 3).

d. José Ortega y Gasset (1883-1955), Spanish philosopher who was self-exiled in the early Franco years; best known for his political work *The Rebellion of the Masses* (1930).

d. Mary McLeod Bethune (1875-1955), African-American educator; founder of Bethune-Cookman College (1923) and the National Organization of Negro Women (1935); a chief adviser to Franklin D. Roosevelt and Eleanor Roosevelt on African-American matters.

d. Walter Francis White (1893-1955), African-American leader; executive secretary of the National Association for the Advancement of Colored People (NAACP) (1931-1955).

d. Ely Culbertson (1891-1955), American bridge player who formalized the game's bidding system, publicized in his "Blue Book" and his magazine *The Bridge World;* he helped build the game's popularity.

d. Pierre Teilhard de Chardin (1881-1955), French paleontologist and theologian who developed the view that humans and the whole universe are evolving toward spiritual unity, ideas suppressed by his Jesuit order until after his death.

1955 cont.

1956

Incumbent Republican president Dwight D. Eisenhower won a second term (1957-1961), again defeating Democrat Adlai Stevenson.

After Gamal Abdel Nasser nationalized the Suez Canal (July 26), Britain, France, and Israel decided to take the canal, generating the Sinai-Suez War (Second Arab-Israeli War) (Oct. 29-Nov. 6). Israeli forces attacked and defeated Egyptian forces (Oct. 29-Nov. 5), while British and French forces attacked Port Said (Nov. 5-6). U.S. objections reversed the course of events, forcing the withdrawal of Allied forces and replacement of them with a United Nations peacekeeping force (1956-1967).

Nikita Khrushchev detailed the crimes of the Stalin period in his "secret speech" to the 20th Congress of the Soviet Communist Party (Feb.), triggering an enormous storm in the world communist movement. The Soviet "thaw" accelerated, defections occurred throughout the world, demonstrations and armed insurrections flared in the communist world, and Western European "Eurocommunists" began to develop post-Stalinist independent programs.

A Hungarian insurrection (Oct. 23-24) briefly ended Communist rule; Soviet troops withdrew, and the new Imre Nagy government began to make major changes, including withdrawal from the Warsaw Pact, which was unacceptable to the Soviets. Communist Party head János Kádár formed a new Soviet-backed government (Nov. 1). Soviet troops returned (Nov. 4) and quickly suppressed the rebellion, taking Nagy, whom they executed (1958); 100,000 to 200,000 people fled Hungary.

Dartmouth College was the site of a meeting of early computer experts, marking the beginning of intensive efforts to develop "artificial intelligence," still a major goal and still far from achievement in the 1990s. Their work would highlight the enormous complexity and flexibility of the human brain they were attempting to duplicate, especially in the handling of imprecise or incomplete data, and would have practical applications in areas such as robotics and medical diagnostics.

Albert Sabin developed a new polio vaccine based on live, but weakened, viruses. Cheaper to make and easier to store than the Salk vaccine, it could be given orally and offered lifetime immunity. It soon became the vaccine of choice for use around the world.

After physicist Martin Block suggested that right and left are not always equal in the universe, Chinese-American nuclear physicists Tsung-Dao Lee and Chen Ning Yang proposed that the principle of parity (1927) does not apply to particles in weak interaction and described experiments to test the hypothesis, which were carried out by a team led by Chien-Shiung Wu (Madame Wu). Lee and Yang shared the 1957 Nobel Prize for physics.

American physicists Frederick Reines and Clyde Lorrain Cowan discovered atomic particles called antineutrinos, further evidence that neutrinos (posited by Wolfgang Pauli in 1931)

1955 cont.

d. Charlie "Bird" Parker (Charles Christopher Parker, Jr.) (1920-1955), American jazz saxophonist, composer, and bandleader; a creator of bebop.

d. Fernand Léger (1881-1955), French painter, designer, and filmmaker; an early cubist.

d. Matthew Alexander Henson (1866-1955), African-American explorer who joined Robert Peary on the first successful expedition to the North Pole (1909) and on several other polar expeditions.

1956

Ingmar Bergman's classic film *The Seventh Seal,* dealing with the intertwined themes of life and death, starred Max von Sydow, Bengt Ekerot, Gunnar Björnstrand, Bibi Andersson, and Nils Poppe.

Julie Andrews as Eliza Doolittle and Rex Harrison as Henry Higgins starred in the Alan Jay Lerner–Frederick Loewe musical *My Fair Lady,* based on George Bernard Shaw's *Pygmalion* (1914); Moss Hart directed.

Giulietta Masina starred in the title role as the unconquerable Roman prostitute in Federico Fellini's film classic *The Nights of Cabiria.*

Singing such hit songs as "Love Me Tender" and "Hound Dog," Elvis Presley emerged as an international rock-and-roll star.

Allen Ginsberg was acclaimed as a major "Beat" poet with his first poetry collection, *Howl and Other Poems.*

Eugene O'Neill's autobiographical play *Long Day's Journey into Night* starred Fredric March, Florence Eldridge, Jason Robards, Jr., and Dean Stockwell.

John Osborne's play *Look Back in Anger* introduced Jimmy Porter, the prototype of Britain's new "angry young man." Richard Burton starred in the play and in the 1958 Tony Richardson film.

Gregory Peck as an incorruptible advertising man starred in the title role opposite Fredric March in

American sociologist C. Wright Mills published *The Power Elite,* describing the United States as wholly dominated by several intertwining elites; his theories were strongly supported by many American radicals of the 1960s.

The International Finance Corporation (IFC) was founded to channel investment funds into the Third World; the multinational investment bank became a United Nations agency in 1957.

President Dwight D. Eisenhower appointed Judge William J. Brennan to the U.S. Supreme Court (1956-1990); he was to become a leading Court liberal.

The Italian liner *Andrea Doria* sank after colliding with the Swedish liner *Stockholm* in fog off Nantucket Island (July 26); 52 people died.

The Montreal Canadiens, with star goalkeeper Jacques Plante, won their first of five consecutive Stanley Cup championships (1956-1960).

American discus thrower Al Oerter won the first of his four consecutive Olympic gold medals, each performance bettering the one before (1956; 1960; 1964; 1968).

Austrian skier Toni Sailer became the first man to take gold medals in all three Olympic Alpine events: the downhill, slalom, and giant slalom.

Baseball star Mickey Mantle won the first of his three Most Valuable Player Awards (1956; 1957; 1962).

Large demonstrations in Poland ("Polish October") brought down the government, which was replaced by the somewhat more moderate government of Wladyslaw Gomulka.

Mao Zedong encouraged the growth of dissent in China, beginning his Hundred Flowers Campaign (1956-1957) with "Let one hundred flowers bloom, and a hundred schools of thought contend." Dissent did appear, and massive repression quickly followed.

American military advisers began to move into South Vietnam in increasing numbers as French forces completed their withdrawal and South Vietnamese forces began to lose the civil war; the run-up to the Vietnam War began.

Fidel Castro landed in Cuba (Dec. 2) at the head of a small band of revolutionaries; defeated by government forces, they retreated into the Sierra Maestra to build a guerrilla army.

Full-scale war enveloped Algeria, and National Liberation Front (FLN) forces operated throughout the country.

Federal Bureau of Investigation head J. Edgar Hoover began the Cointelpro operation, a massive, illegal counterintelligence operation directed against dissidents, which included illegal wiretapping, kidnapping, burglary, and other illegal acts.

Tunisia's guerrilla war of independence ended with French withdrawal. Tunisia became an independent nation (Mar. 20), its first president being national movement leader Habib Bourguiba (1957-1987).

Angolan anticolonial forces organized the Popular Movement for the Liberation of Angola (MPLA), which would later go over to armed insurrection (1961).

British forces in Cyprus exiled Makarios III, Greek Orthodox archbishop of Cyprus and Cypriot national leader.

did indeed exist, although they had not yet been directly identified.

Human growth hormone, made by the pituitary gland, was isolated by Chinese-American biochemist Choh Hao Li, who worked out the structure of both it and the hormone ACTH (adrenocorticotropic hormone).

Computer programming languages came into use to help programmers with the task of writing instructions for the machines. An IBM team led by John Backus developed FORTRAN (formula translation).

The introduction of tranquilizers (1953; 1954) had an immediate effect on the number of people in mental hospitals; in the United States, that number fell for the first time in years. However, critics charged that patients were being drugged not to help them, but to make them easier to care for.

Videotape recorders were first developed, although they would not become widespread among consumers until the 1980s.

Bette Nesmith (later Graham) invented a liquid used to paint over typing errors, called "Mistake Out" and later "Liquid Paper."

Werner Forssmann, André Frédéric Cournand, and Dickinson W. Richards shared the Nobel Prize for physiology or medicine for their work on heart catheterization (1929; 1941).

John Bardeen, William Bradford Shockley, and Walter Houser Brittain won the Nobel Prize for physics for their development of the transistor. Bardeen would win another in 1972.

d. Irène Joliot-Curie (1897-1956), French physicist, daughter of Marie and Pierre Curie,

Nunnally Johnson's *The Man in the Gray Flannel Suit*, adapted by Johnson from Sloan Wilson's 1955 novel.

Ingrid Bergman starred in the title role as the last of the Romanovs in Anatole Litvak's film *Anastasia*, costarring Yul Brynner and Helen Hayes.

Aparajito was the second film in Satyajit Ray's "Apu" trilogy.

Simone de Beauvoir published the novel *The Mandarins*, about Jean-Paul Sartre, Albert Camus, herself, and other leaders of the existentialist movement.

Marilyn Monroe and Don Murray starred in *Bus Stop*, the Joshua Logan film version of the 1955 William Inge play.

Deborah Kerr as Anna and Yul Brynner as the Siamese king starred in Walter Lang's film version of *The King and I*.

Ludwig Mies van der Rohe began New York's Seagram Building, an International Style centerpiece (1956-1958).

Richard Wilbur published his Pulitzer Prize–winning poetry collection *Things of This World*.

Rosalind Russell starred in the title role in the Jerome Lawrence–Robert E. Lee comedy *Auntie Mame*.

Spanish poet Juan Ramón Jiménez was awarded the Nobel Prize for literature.

d. Bertolt Brecht (Eugen Berthold Friedrich Brecht) (1898-1956), German writer; one of the leading playwrights of the 20th century.

d. A. A. (Alan Alexander) Milne (1881-1956), British writer; creator of Christopher Robin and Winnie-the-Pooh (1926).

By defeating Archie Moore, Floyd Patterson won the world heavyweight boxing title vacated by the retired Rocky Marciano.

Dynamite carried in seven parked army trucks exploded in Cali, Colombia (Aug. 7), killing at least 1,000 people and destroying the city center.

Two planes collided in clear daylight over the Grand Canyon, in Arizona, killing 128 people (June 30).

A fire and explosion in a Marcinelle, Belgium, coal mine killed 263 people (Aug. 5).

Near Mahbubnagar, India, a bridge collapsed under a train, sending 120 people to their deaths (Sept. 2).

b. Anita Faye Hill (1956-), American lawyer and law professor whose explosive confrontation with U.S. Supreme Court nominee Clarence Thomas (1991) would rivet world attention on the issue of sexual harassment and revitalize the American women's rights movement.

b. Joe Montana (Joseph C. Montana, Jr.) (1956-), American football player, perhaps the greatest quarterback to play the game. He would lead the San Francisco 49ers to four championships, two after potentially career-ending back surgery (1986).

b. Larry Joe Bird (1956-), American basketball player; three-time national champion with the Boston Celtics; an outstanding forward who, with friendly rival Earvin "Magic" Johnson, would greatly increase the sport's popularity during the 1980s.

b. Martina Navratilova (1956–), Czech-American tennis champion; one of the leading players in the history of the game, whose records would include nine women's singles titles at Wimbledon.

d. Thomas John Watson (1874-1956), American computer industry pioneer who led International

1956 cont.

Sudan became an independent republic (Jan. 1); the civil war continued.

d. Alben William Barkley (1877-1956), American lawyer and politician; a Kentucky Democrat who as majority leader of the Senate (1937-1947) was a major New Deal figure. After being vice president in the Truman administration (1949-1953), he was reelected to the Senate, dying in office.

d. Anastasio Somoza Garcia (1896-1956), dictator of Nicaragua (1933-1956); he was assassinated; his son, Luis Somoza Debayle, then became dictator (1956-1963).

d. Ernest Joseph King (1878-1956), American admiral; World War II chief of naval operations and fleet commander; chief naval adviser to President Franklin D. Roosevelt.

d. Juan Negrín (1894-1956), the last Spanish Republican prime minister; later prime minister of the Republican government-in-exile.

d. Pietro Badoglio (1871-1956), Italian officer who succeeded Benito Mussolini as premier of Italy (1943) and signed an armistice with the Allies (Sept. 7, 1943).

and wife of Frédéric Joliot-Curie; the Joliot-Curies were the first to induce artifical radioactivity (1934); like her mother, Irène died of leukemia, probably caused by working with radioactive materials.

d. Frederick Soddy (1877-1956), British chemist who codeveloped the theory that radioactivity results during the transformation of one element to another (1902); he also discovered isotopes (1913).

d. Alfred Charles Kinsey (1894-1956), American zoologist and sex researcher; founder of the Institute for Sex Research (1942-1956), where he prepared the "Kinsey Reports" (1948; 1953).

1957

The Soviet Union developed long-range intercontinental ballistic missiles (ICBMs), further intensifying the Cold War "balance of terror."

President Dwight D. Eisenhower declared the Eisenhower Doctrine (Jan. 5), emphasizing direct U.S. military confrontation with the Soviet Union and promising American support, including direct armed intervention if necessary, on behalf of any Middle Eastern countries attacked by the Soviet Union and its clients and allies.

François "Papa Doc" Duvalier was elected president of Haiti, then quickly became dictator (1957-1971) with the aid of his secret police, the Tontons Macoutes.

The Soviet Union launched the first artificial satellite into orbit around the earth (Oct. 4), beginning the "space race." The 184-pound *Sputnik 1,* built by Valentin Glushko, was sent aloft by a converted intercontinental ballistic missile (ICBM); it orbited the earth every 96 minutes, with a maximum height of 584 miles, until early 1958, when it burned up on reentering the earth's atmosphere. *Sputnik 2* (Nov. 3) carried Laika, the first dog in space. Other Sputnik flights followed, some also with animals aboard, testing various life-support and reentry systems. Earlier in

d. Bela Lugosi (Bela Blasco) (1882-1956), Hungarian-American actor who created Dracula on Broadway (1927) and on film (1931).

d. Jackson Pollock (1912-1956), American abstract expressionist; a pioneer proponent of the "drip and splash" and "action painting" techniques.

d. Alexander Korda (Sándor Laszlo Korda) (1893-1956), leading Hungarian-British film director and producer from the mid-1930s.

d. Mistinguett (Jean-Marie Bourgeois) (1875-1956), French singer and comedian; a Paris music hall star.

d. Alexander Dovzhenko (1894-1956), Soviet film director, most notably of *Earth,* set in the Ukraine (1930).

Business Machines (IBM), in his time the world's largest computer company. He was succeeded by his son, Thomas J. Watson, Jr. (1956-1979).

d. Hiram Bingham (1875-1956), American explorer and politician who rediscovered Machu Picchu (1911).

d. Babe (Mildred) Didrikson Zaharias (1914-1956), American athlete, successful in several sports, but best known as a golfer.

Akira Kurosawa created *The Throne of Blood,* his Japanese-language film version of *Macbeth,* starring Toshiro Mifune and Izuzu Yamada.

Alec Guinness, William Holden, Jack Hawkins, and Sessue Hayakawa starred in David Lean's World War II film *The Bridge on the River Kwai,* set in a Japanese prison camp and based on the 1952 Pierre Boulle novel.

Ingmar Bergman wrote and directed his film classic *Wild Strawberries,* starring Victor Sjostrom, Ingrid Thulin, and Bibi Andersson.

Martin Luther King, Jr., Ralph Abernathy, and other leaders founded the Southern Christian Leadership Conference (SCLC); headed by King until his 1968 assassination, and then by Abernathy, it would become the key organization of the civil rights movement.

Coach Red (Arnold Jacob) Auerbach guided his Boston Celtics team, led by Bob Cousy, Bill Russell, and Bill Sharman, to the National Basketball Association championship, their first of an astonishing 9 in the next 10 years (1957; 1959-1966).

In *Watkins v. United States,* the Supreme Court struck down the conviction of a witness seeking Fifth Amendment protection before the House Un-American Activities Committee, sharply attacking witch-hunting and bringing the McCarthy period effectively to a close.

In *Yates v. United States,* the Supreme Court struck down the Smith Act convictions of 14 Communists, making it far more difficult to use the Smith Act to prosecute dissenters.

Albanian Communist dictator and hard-line Stalinist Enver Hoxha broke with Nikita Khrushchev's post-Stalinist Soviet government, then moved toward China (1957-1977).

A notable Soviet "posthumous rehabilitation" was that of Soviet general Vasili Konstantinovich Blücher, executed in 1938.

Indonesia disputed Dutch title to West Irian (Netherlands New Guinea); guerrilla attacks began on Dutch forces.

The Republic of Ghana became an independent state and Commonwealth member (Mar. 6), led by Prime Minister Kwame Nkrumah; it was composed of the former British colonies of Gold Coast and British Togoland.

Soviet intelligence colonel Rudolph Abel was imprisoned; he had operated a Soviet espionage network in the United States (1948-1957) and was later exchanged for U-2 spy plane pilot Francis Gary Powers (1962).

Canadian diplomat Lester Pearson was awarded the Nobel Peace Prize for his role in resolving the Suez Crisis.

Milovan Djilas published *The New Class* abroad while imprisoned for his dissident views in Yugoslavia (1956-1961).

Tunku Abdul Rahman became the first prime minister of independent Malaya (1957-1963).

1957, Soviet engineers had launched their first ICBM.

The International Geophysical Year (IGY) (July 1957-Dec. 1958) saw unprecedented cooperation among some 30,000 scientists from more than 70 nations in studying the earth and space. As a direct result, an international agreement (1959) was reached to set aside the continent of Antarctica as a demilitarized area for scientific research.

A massive explosion of buried nuclear waste, with the release of radioactive gases, occurred at Chelyabinsk (Dec. 1957 or Jan. 1958), a Soviet plutonium-producing complex near Kyshtym, in the Urals. At least 400 square miles were contaminated, an unknown number of people were killed or irradiated, and some towns were permanently evacuated. Kept secret, the disaster was first revealed by Soviet dissident Zhores Medvedev (1976) and confirmed by Soviet scientists (1988) and by the Russian government after the revolution (1991).

During and after a nuclear reactor core fire in Britain's Windscale (later Sellafield) plutonium-producing plant (Oct. 7-12), radioactive iodine and polonium were released into the environment, including the Irish Sea, although the government would, until 1978, maintain that only a minor amount of radioactivity had been discharged. Large areas around the plant in northwest England (Cumbria) were contaminated, and livestock in the immediate area were destroyed, as were more than 500,000 gallons of milk. At least 30 cancer deaths — and perhaps as many as 1,000 — were linked with the accident.

Britain detonated its first hydrogen bomb (May 15).

Jack Kerouac published his seminal "Beat Generation" autobiographical novel *On the Road.*

Laurence Olivier created the Archie Rice role opposite Joan Plowright in John Osborne's play *The Entertainer.*

Nevil Shute published his powerful, Australia-set novel *On the Beach,* postulating the end of life on earth as a result of a nuclear war.

Chita Rivera, Carol Lawrence, and Larry Kert starred in the Leonard Bernstein–Stephen Sondheim Broadway musical *West Side Story,* a modern retelling of Shakespeare's *Romeo and Juliet.*

James Agee's autobiographical novel *A Death in the Family* was posthumously published, winning a Pulitzer Prize.

Lawrence Durrell published *Justine,* the first part of his "Alexandria Quartet."

John Cheever emerged as a major literary figure with the publication of his National Book Award–winning novel *The Wapshot Chronicle.*

Nunnally Johnson wrote, directed, and produced the film *The Three Faces of Eve,* starring Joanne Woodward as a woman afflicted with multiple personalities.

Octavio Paz published the long poem *Sun Stone,* its 584 lines symbolically matching the 584 lines of the Aztec calendar.

The New York City Ballet presented George Balanchine's *Agon,* music by Igor Stravinsky.

"76 Trombones" was introduced by Robert Preston, starring opposite Barbara Cook in Meredith Willson's stage musical *The Music Man;* it would be the basis for a 1962 film.

Fullback Jim Brown began his professional football career with the Cleveland Browns (1957-1966); the National Football League's leading rusher for eight of those seasons, he set several new records, among them career touchdowns (126), not broken until 1994, and career rushing yards (12,312) and total career yards (15,549), which stood until 1984.

In *Roth v. United States,* the U.S. Supreme Court attempted to define obscenity, ruling it outside the protection of the First Amendment, thereby allowing criminal prosecutions for alleged obscenity.

James Hoffa's powerful International Brotherhood of Teamsters was expelled from the AFL-CIO for massive corruption; the union continued to grow and accumulate money and power.

Mass murderer Charles Starkweather, accompanied by 14-year-old Carol Ann Fugate, killed 11 people (Dec.), including 3 in Fugate's family. He was electrocuted (1959); she was sentenced to life imprisonment and later paroled (1977). Their killing spree was depicted in the movie *Badlands* (1973).

More than 500 people died in a series of chemical explosions in Texas City, Texas (Apr. 15-16). The French freighter *Grandcamp* caught fire in the harbor, and its ammonium nitrate fertilizer cargo exploded, setting off further explosions at a nearby chemical plant that destroyed most of the city center. Later that night, another fertilizer freighter, the *High Flyer,* also exploded, causing even more damage.

New York State Police made a highly publicized raid (Nov. 14) on the Apalachin Conference, a national organized crime meeting at the home of Joseph Barbara, Sr., at Apalachin, New York, arresting 58; no substantial convictions resulted.

The Asian flu (influenza) pandemic (1957-1958) affected tens of millions of people, even more than the 1918-1919 pandemic; but more people survived be-

d. Friedrich Paulus (1890-1957), German general; commander of the defeated Sixth Army at Stalingrad (1943).

d. Haakon VII, king of Norway (1872-1957); a World War II symbol of anti-Nazi resistance as head of the Norwegian government-in-exile.

d. James Middleton Cox (1870-1957), American Democratic politician; twice governor of Ohio (1913-1915; 1917-1921) and unsuccessful Democratic presidential candidate (1920); his vice-presidential running mate was Franklin D. Roosevelt.

d. Joseph Raymond McCarthy (1908-1957), American politician; Wisconsin senator (1947-1957) and the leading witch-hunter of his time (Feb. 1950-Apr. 1954); his opponents coined the new epithet "McCarthyism."

d. Miklós Horthy (1868-1957), Hungarian dictator (1920-1944); a Hitler ally during the 1930s and World War II.

d. Ramón Magsaysay (1903-1957), president of the Philippines (1953-1957); he died in office, in an aircraft accident.

Dutch-American physician Willem J. Kolff developed an artificial heart that, implanted in a dog, kept the animal alive for 90 minutes; 25 years later, a refined heart, designed by Kolff and Robert Jarvik, would be implanted in a human being (1982).

A new sleeping pill, thalidomide, began to be prescribed in Great Britain and Germany, and experimentally elsewhere; it would later be recognized as causing birth defects when taken by pregnant women.

The largest radio telescope yet, 250 feet across, was completed at Britain's Jodrell Bank Experimental Station; though not intended for the purpose, it tracked *Sputnik 1* on its landmark earth orbit.

British astronomers Fred Hoyle, Margaret Burbidge, Geoffrey Burbidge, and William Fowler formulated a theory about how elements could be produced in the interior of stars.

Interferon, a virus-fighting protein naturally produced by the body, was discovered by Alick Isaacs and Jean Lindemann.

The World Health Organization (WHO) adopted the Sabin polio vaccine (1956) for use throughout the world.

d. John (Janos) von Neumann (1903-1957), Hungarian-American mathematician who made major contributions in mathematics (in von Neumann algebras), physics, game theory, and computer science.

d. Vere Gordon Childe (1892-1957), Australian-British archaeologist who helped bring archaeology into the social and natural sciences and sketched the broad outlines of early cultural development in works such as *The Dawn of European Civilization* (1925).

St.-John Perse (Alexis St.-Léger Léger) published his poems *Seamarks*.

French writer Albert Camus was awarded the Nobel Prize for literature.

d. Constantin Brancusi (1876-1957), leading Romanian sculptor, whose long move from figurative to highly abstract work was emblematic of the move to modernism in the visual arts.

d. Arturo Toscanini (1887-1957), Italian conductor; a major figure in 20th-century music.

d. Diego Rivera (1886-1957), Mexican painter; one of the century's leading muralists.

d. Gabriela Mistral (Lucila Godoy Alcayaga) (1889-1957), Chilean poet; a leading Latin American poet from the publication of her collection *Desolation* (1922); winner of the 1945 Nobel Prize for literature.

d. Humphrey (DeForest) Bogart (1899-1957), American actor; one of the leading film stars of the century.

d. Jean Sibelius (1865-1957), Finnish national composer; a world figure in music; best known for his *Finlandia* (1899).

d. Nikos Kazantzakis (1883-1957), Greek writer, most notably of the epic poem *The Odyssey: A Modern Sequel* (1938) and the novels *Zorba the Greek* (1946) and *The Last Temptation of Christ* (1955).

d. Sholem Asch (1887-1957), Jewish-American writer; a major figure in 20th-century Jewish literature.

d. James Whale (1896-1957), British film director, most notably of *Frankenstein* (1931).

cause antibiotics now existed to treat secondary infections.

Cristóbal Balenciaga introduced the chemise, dubbed the "sack."

Noam Chomsky published his controversial *Syntactic Structures*, which proposed that grammar was inborn and that specific human languages were developed from an underlying "generative" grammar.

The International Atomic Energy Agency (IAEA), loosely associated with the United Nations, was founded to foster peaceful uses of nuclear energy and help stop the spread of nuclear weapons.

Near Montgomery, Pakistan, a stalled oil train exploded after being hit by an express train, killing at least 250 people (Sept. 29).

At least 175 people died when a train derailed into a ravine near Kendal, Jamaica (Sept. 1).

Two commuter trains collided in fog near St. John's, England, killing 92 people (Dec. 4).

d. Richard Evelyn Byrd (1888-1957), American naval aviator and explorer who made the first flights over the North Pole (1926) and the South Pole (1929), also leading several other expeditions to Antarctica.

d. Christian Dior (1905-1957), French fashion designer noted for his postwar "New Look" designs. He was succeeded by Yves St. Laurent.

Algerian independence forces established a government-in-exile in Tunis while penetrating the strongly defended French Algerian-Tunisian border. Jacques Massu led a French officers' revolt in Algiers, civil war came close in France, and the Fourth Republic fell. Charles de Gaulle became premier of France (June 1), suppressed the Algerian officers' revolt, and developed the constitution of the Fifth Republic, which would replace the Fourth Republic. He also began negotiations with the National Liberation Front (FLN), offering Algerian self-determination and releasing some imprisoned FLN leaders.

Fidel Castro's small guerrilla army came out of the Sierra Maestra (Oct.), taking Cuba quickly and easily.

Lebanese Muslim and leftist Christian forces mounted a major rising against the Maronite Christian government led by Camille Chamoun. Approximately 14,000 American forces intervened (July) to stop the civil war and mediated a compromise settlement; the Americans were then withdrawn (Oct.).

Mao Zedong's ultimately failed "Great Leap Forward" industrialization campaign began (1958-1961). It would massively fail, with great damage to the Chinese economy. The campaign featured mass production of sub-quality industrial goods — especially steel in backyard furnaces — that proved entirely unsuitable for modern industrial development.

A military-backed Venezuelan revolution deposed the Marcos Pérez Jiménez military dictatorship; Rómulo Betancourt became the democratically elected president.

Iraqi prime minister and strongman Nuri al-Said and Faisal II were assassinated during a Ba'ath Party army coup led by General Abdul Karim Kassem, which established a republic.

The British Campaign for Nuclear Disarmament (CND) was founded; its first chair was Bertrand Russell.

U.S. presidential aide Sherman Adams, a former governor of New Hampshire, resigned after being accused of tak-

The first American artificial satellite, *Explorer 1,* was launched (Jan. 31), with a modified V-2 rocket as a booster. Observations from it and succeeding U.S. and Soviet satellites showed two wide bands of radioactive particles circling the earth, later recognized as responsible for auroras; this magnetosphere was named the Van Allen belts after American physicist James Van Allen, who had predicted their existence.

The American satellite *Vanguard* was launched (Mar. 17), yielding observations that the earth is not perfectly round, but bulges somewhat at the equator.

The National Aeronautics and Space Administration (NASA) was created to oversee the U.S. space program (Oct. 1), replacing the earlier, research-oriented National Advisory Committee on Aeronautics (NACA). Development was centered at the U.S. Army Ballistic Missile Arsenal in Huntsville, Alabama, but flights were launched from Cape Canaveral (Cape Kennedy 1963-1973), Florida, and coordinated from the Johnson Space Center in Houston, Texas; landings were at Cape Canaveral or Edwards Air Force Base in California.

The first pacemaker, a small electrical device designed to stimulate regular pumping action in the heart, was implanted in a human's chest. External counterparts had been developed from the 1930s; the internal pacemaker was made possible by miniaturization of batteries and transistors in the early 1950s.

Belgian-French anthropologist Claude Gustave Lévi-Strauss published his *Structural Anthropology* (2 vols., 1958; 1973), focusing on underlying commonalities among different cultures, as part of a movement called Structuralism.

John Lennon, Paul McCartney, George Harrison, and Pete Best formed the Beatles (1958-1970); Ringo Starr would become the group's drummer after Best and a fifth member, Stuart Sutcliffe, left the group (1962). The Liverpudlians would transform popular music.

Chinua Achebe emerged as a major literary figure with the publication of his first novel, *Things Fall Apart*.

Eugene O'Neill's play *A Touch of the Poet* was posthumously produced, five years after his death; starring were Kim Stanley, Eric Portman, Helen Hayes, and Betty Field.

Ralph Bellamy starred as Franklin D. Roosevelt in Dore Schary's play *Sunrise at Campobello*. Mary Fickett played Eleanor Roosevelt, who helps take Franklin through his crippling encounter with polio.

Jorge Amado published the novel *Gabriela, Clove and Cinnamon*, which established him as a popular novelist on the world scene.

Leslie Caron starred in the Alan Jay Lerner–Frederick Loewe film musical *Gigi*, based on the 1945 Colette novel; Maurice Chevalier, Louis Jourdan, and Hermione Gingold costarred, and Vincente Minnelli directed.

Margot Fonteyn danced the title role in Frederick Ashton's ballet *Ondine*, music by Hans Werner Henze.

Reflecting the vastly changed mores of a new time, Shelagh Delaney's play *A Taste of Honey* dealt with the problems of a single, White, pregnant woman; the Black sailor who is the child's father; and the gay friend the mother relies on most.

Spencer Tracy starred in the title role in Preston Sturges's film *The Old Man and the Sea*, based on Ernest Hemingway's 1952 story.

Bill Russell of the Boston Celtics won the first of his five National Basketball Association Most Valuable Player Awards (1958; 1961-1963; 1965).

Brazilian soccer star Pelé, then 17, led his Brazilian national team to victory at the World Cup, his first of three with them (1958; 1962; 1970).

During the International Geophysical Year (July 1957-Dec. 1958), British geologist-explorer Vivian Fuchs led the first overland crossing of Antarctica, supported by supply bases established by a team under New Zealand explorer Edmund Hillary, which in the process became the third party to reach the South Pole (Jan. 4), this one traveling by tractor.

Golfer Mickey Wright won the first of her four U.S. Open championships (1958; 1959; 1961; 1964).

African-American tennis star Althea Gibson won her second successive Wimbledon and U.S. Open championships.

The American nuclear submarine *Nautilus* was the first ship to sail under the North Pole.

The Baltimore Colts defeated the New York Giants in sudden-death overtime to win the National Football League championship.

The Brooklyn Dodgers moved to Los Angeles, and the New York Giants moved to San Francisco. Both moves helped make baseball an even more "national" sport, further signaling the emergence of California as a massive factor in American life.

The first United Nations Law of the Sea Conference was held; it would eventually result in the Convention on the Law of the Sea (1982).

Yves St. Laurent, in his first independent collection, introduced the "little girl" look.

ing gifts from his friend Bernard Goldfine, including a vicuña coat, although Adams was exonerated of all wrongdoing by Congress and fully defended by President Dwight D. Eisenhower.

Robert Welch founded the ultraconservative John Birch Society, which in the early 1960s attracted an estimated 100,000 members; its extremism, which included charges that several American presidents had been communist agents, was ultimately self-isolating and self-destructing.

A Burmese army coup deposed Prime Minister U Nu, replacing him with General Ne Win (Maung Shu Maung).

Egypt and Syria formally merged as the United Arab Republic (1958-1961), though no real merger occurred.

General Ibraham Abboud took power by coup in Sudan (Nov. 17).

The Republic of Guinea became independent; independence movement leader Ahmed Sékou Touré became the first president of the one-party state (1958-1984).

The Republic of Niger became an independent state (Aug. 3).

The European Economic Community (EEC) and the European Atomic Energy Community (Euratom) were created, as provided by the 1957 Treaty of Rome; they would later become parts of the European Community.

d. Claire Chennault (1890-1958), American military aviator; adviser to Chiang Kai-shek in the late 1930s, founder of the Flying Tigers (1941), and American Air Force commander in China (1942-1945).

d. Imre Nagy (1896-1958), leader of the Hungarian Revolution (1956), for which he was executed.

d. Johannes Gerhardus Strijdom (1893-1958), South African politician; leader of the racist National Party and prime minister (1954-1958).

St. Joseph's Hospice opened in London, a pioneering institution designed to house terminally ill patients in a homelike setting, with painkillers as needed. Developed in reaction to excess technological intervention, the hospice movement would spread worldwide.

Element 102 was found and named nobelium, for Alfred Nobel.

In a second nuclear accident at Canada's experimental Chalk River reactor, a defective fuel rod overheated (May 23).

d. Wolfgang Pauli (1900-1958), Austrian-American physicist who stated the exclusion principle (1925) and predicted the neutrino (1930).

d. (Jean) Frédéric Joliot-Curie (1900-1958), French physicist; husband of Irène Joliot-Curie, whom he met when both were assistants to her mother, Marie Curie. The Joliot-Curies were the first to artificially induce radioactivity (1934), and he later led France's nuclear development program.

d. Ernest Orlando Lawrence (1901-1958), American physicist who developed the cyclotron (1931); a key figure in nuclear research.

d. Rosalind Elsie Franklin (1920-1958), British molecular biologist and physical chemist whose X-ray photographs of chromosomes were crucial to James Watson and Francis Crick's elucidation of DNA's structure (1953), although her contribution was initially unacknowledged.

d. John Broadus Watson (1878-1958), American psychologist who founded the school of psychology called behaviorism (1913).

Alvin Ailey founded the American Dance Theater.

Andrzej Wajda directed the screen version of Jerzy Andrzejewski's World War II novel *Ashes and Diamonds*.

Laurence Harvey and Simone Signoret starred in *Room at the Top*, Jack Clayton's film from John Braine's 1957 novel.

Boris Pasternak was awarded the Nobel Prize for literature but was barred from accepting it by the Soviet government, which also had banned his novel *Doctor Zhivago*.

b. Michael Jackson (1958-), American singer who would become an international popular music star from the late 1970s.

b. Madonna (Madonna Louise Ciccone) (1958-), American singer and actress; a music star and worldwide celebrity from the 1980s.

b. Daniel Day-Lewis (1958-), Irish actor; an international film star from the 1980s, most notably as Christy Brown in *My Left Foot* (1989).

d. Ralph Vaughan Williams (1872-1958), noted British composer who often worked with folk and early church themes.

d. Big Bill (William Lee Conley) Broonzy (1893-1958), American blues singer and guitarist; a leading blues singer from the late 1930s.

d. Ronald Colman (1891-1958), British actor; an international silent and sound film star, as in *Arrowsmith* (1931), *Lost Horizon* (1937), and *A Double Life* (1948).

d. Doris Humphrey (1895-1958), leading American dancer, choreographer, and teacher; cofounder of the Humphrey-Weidman school and company (1928-1944).

John Kenneth Galbraith published *The Affluent Society*, an economic analysis and social commentary on American overconsumption and underinvestment in social service areas.

A typhoon (Ida) struck central Honshu, Japan, killing at least 700 people.

The five-mile-long Mackinac Bridge opened; connecting Michigan's Upper Peninsula to the rest of the state, it included the world's longest suspension bridge.

The Brussels World's Fair opened, with exhibits from 51 countries.

A Dutch KLM Super Constellation crashed into the Atlantic Ocean off Ireland (Aug. 14); 99 people died.

d. Pope Pius XII (Eugenio Pacelli) (1876-1958), Italian priest (1899-1958) and pope (1939-1958); he had maintained Vatican neutrality during World War II and was thought by many to have taken minimal action to oppose the Nazi mass murder of Jews, Gypsies, Poles, Russians, and others. A powerful influence in postwar Italian politics, he strongly supported the Christian Democratic Party. He was succeeded by Italian cardinal Angelo Giuseppe Roncali, who became Pope John XXIII (1958-1963).

d. Marie Charlotte Carmichael Stopes (1880-1958), British geologist, botanist, and geographer most noted as an advocate of sex education and birth control, on which she wrote several popular books.

d. G. E. (George Edward) Moore (1873-1958), British philosopher who led a revolt against philosophical problems divorced from the real world; best known for his influence on the Bloomsbury Group.

1958 cont.

1959

Charles de Gaulle became the first president of France's Fifth Republic (1959-1969); he quickly moved to stabilize the French economy and end the Algerian war.

Dictator Fulgencio Batista fled Cuba (Jan. 1); Fidel Castro's forces entered Havana unopposed (Jan. 8). After taking power in Cuba, Castro became dictator and began the process of turning Cuba into a one-party state.

Fatah (al-Fatah), the Palestine Liberation Movement, was founded. It was led by Yasir Arafat (1959-   ), who would take it into guerrilla warfare (1965), and it later became the center of the Palestine Liberation Organization (PLO) (1969).

Full-scale civil war developed in Cyprus; war between Greece and Turkey seemed imminent but was averted; the independent state of Cyprus emerged (formal independence came in 1960), with Greek Orthodox bishop and Cypriot independence movement leader Makarios III its first president (1959-1977).

In Rwanda, then administered by Belgium, the Hutu majority successfully rose against the governing Tutsi minority. Hutu rule would be affirmed by the 1960 and 1961 elections.

Working in East Africa, notably in Olduvai Gorge, in Tanzania, Louis and Mary Leakey discovered hominid remains perhaps 2 million years old, named *Homo habilis* for the shaped stone tools used by the species, intermediate between early *Australopithecus* and *Homo erectus*, or modern humans. This was the first of their many discoveries that would push human beginnings much farther back in time than previously thought.

The extraordinary scientific cooperation of the International Geophysical Year (July 1957 Dec. 1958) was extended with the 12-nation, 30-year Antarctic Treaty (Dec.; effective 1961-1991), making the region south of 60 degrees latitude a cooperative, demilitarized, nuclear test–free multinational laboratory; 27 other countries later joined the treaty; territorial claims were deferred until the treaty's expiration.

The Soviet Union began to launch its Lunik moon probes. *Lunik 1* went astray and eventually went into orbit around the sun. *Lunik 2* was the first to reach the moon, making a "hard" (crash) landing on its surface (Sept. 14).

d. W. C. (William Christopher) Handy (1873-1958), leading African-American musician and composer; the creator of many classic blues tunes, such as "St. Louis Blues" (1914) and "Beale Street Blues" (1916).

d. Edward Weston (1886-1958), American photographer, most notably of California landscapes and seascapes.

d. Tyrone Power (Tyrone Edmund Power, Jr.) (1913-1958), American actor in action films and later in dramatic roles.

Gregory Peck, Ava Gardner, Fred Astaire, and Anthony Perkins starred in Stanley Kramer's *On the Beach,* based on the 1957 Nevil Shute novel. The film, made at the height of the Cold War, is set in an Australia that is the last, failing outpost of life on earth after a nuclear war. It was a chilling warning of what could be in store for humanity.

Alain Resnais directed and Marguerite Duras wrote the film *Hiroshima Mon Amour,* set in post–atomic bomb Hiroshima; Emmanuele Riva and Eiji Okada starred.

Max von Sydow played the title role as the touring 19th-century illusionist in Ingmar Bergman's classic film *The Magician;* Ingrid Thulin and Gunnar Björnstrand costarred.

Anne Bancroft as teacher Annie Sullivan starred opposite Patty Duke as Helen Keller in William Gibson's play *The Miracle Worker;* both would reprise their roles in the 1962 film.

Billy Wilder's classic 1920s comedy film *Some Like It Hot* starred Marilyn Monroe as "all-girl-band" singer Honey, opposite Tony Curtis and Jack Lemmon as musicians in drag on the run from the mob.

Arkansas governor Orval Faubus led unsuccessful attempts to block the integration of Little Rock schools; ultimately, the federal courts ruled unconstitutional state laws allowing them to be closed to effect segregation, and the public schools were reopened (Aug.) despite racist demonstrations.

A massive United Steelworkers of America strike shut down America's basic steel industry (July 15-Nov. 7); it was ultimately stopped by a federal injunction.

An International Longshoremen's Association strike that closed Atlantic and Gulf Coast ports (Oct. 1-8) was stopped by a federal injunction.

United Mine Workers (UMW) leader Joseph Yablonski and his wife and daughter were killed (Dec. 31); UMW president W. A. "Tony" Boyle and others were later convicted of the murders.

Grand jury and congressional investigations exposed the "fixing" of many popular American television quiz shows, most notably with the confession of *$64,000 Question* winner Charles Van Doren, later portrayed in the movie *Quiz Show* (1994).

1959 cont.

In Southeast Asia, the Central Intelligence Agency (CIA) began operating its covert air force, Air America.

North Vietnamese forces opened the Ho Chi Minh Trail through Laos and Cambodia to South Vietnam.

An army revolt failed in Mosul, Iraq (Mar.), as did a wide-scale insurrection in the Kirkuk region (July).

Following a failed Tibetan revolt against the Chinese, the (14th) Dalai Lama went into exile in northern India.

The Southwest Africa People's Organization of Namibia (SWAPO) was founded; it would become the chief Namibian independence movement vehicle, later going over to armed insurrecion (1966).

British multilateral nuclear disarmament advocate Philip Noel-Baker was awarded the Nobel Peace Prize.

d. Daniel François Malan (1874-1959), South African Afrikaner politician; as National Party prime minister (1948-1954), he was the chief architect of the racist system of apartheid.

d. George Catlett Marshall (1880-1959), U.S. Army chief of staff (1939-1945); a five-star general and General of the Army (from 1944); as secretary of state (1947-1949), he developed the Marshall Plan (1947).

d. John Foster Dulles (1888-1959), American lawyer and diplomat; secretary of state (1953-1959) and a major Cold War figure, who brought "brinkmanship" into the language by advocating taking the United States to the "brink" of war as a means of negotiation. His doctrine of "massive retaliation" with nuclear weapons became enduring Cold War policy.

d. William Frederick Halsey, Jr. (1882-1959), American admiral; commander of South Pacific forces (1942-1944) and commander of the Third Fleet (1944-1945).

Lunik 3 took the first photographs of the moon's far side on a flyby (Oct. 4). These space probes confirmed the existence of a solar wind, sprays of charged particles emitted by the sun in all directions, as posited by American physicist Eugene Newman Parker (1958).

The U.S. satellite *Vanguard 2* (launched Feb. 17) transmitted the first television photographs of cloud cover — in effect becoming the first weather station in space. The U.S. satellite *Explorer 6* (launched Aug. 7) transmitted the first television picture of the earth from space.

Grace Murray Hopper developed COBOL, the first computer programming language designed for business use.

Water destined for the Aral Sea, then the world's fourth-largest inland sea, began to be diverted through canals and irrigation projects, part of the Soviet Union's agricultural policy in what are now Kazakhstan and Uzbekistan. Within three decades, the Aral Sea would be one-third its original size and so heavily salinized that much of its marine and coastal life had been destroyed, and the deltas of the rivers feeding it had become salt deserts.

British engineer Francis Thomas Bacon developed the first practical fuel cells, most notably used in the U.S. space program to provide power, heat, and, incidentally, clean drinking water.

Naturalist Gerald Durrell founded the Jersey Wildlife Preservation Trust, doing pioneering work on captive breeding of species facing extinction; forerunner of Wildlife Preservation Trust International (1973).

W. Russell and R. Burch published *The Principles of Humane Experimental Technique*, out-

Geraldine Page and Paul Newman starred in Tennessee Williams's play *Sweet Bird of Youth,* set in a corrupt southern town.

Lorraine Hansberry emerged as a major playwright with *A Raisin in the Sun,* set in Chicago African-American life; Claudia McNeil, Sidney Poitier, Ruby Dee, and Diana Sands starred.

Jean-Luc Godard emerged as a major French director with his "new wave" film *Breathless,* starring Jean-Paul Belmondo and Jean Seberg.

The Richard Rodgers–Oscar Hammerstein stage musical *The Sound of Music,* about the flight of the Trapp Family Singers from the Nazis, starred Mary Martin and Theodore Bikel.

Edward Durell Stone designed the Museum of Modern Art in New York City.

Ethel Merman starred in the Stephen Sondheim–Jule Styne musical *Gypsy,* based on Gypsy Rose Lee's autobiography.

Italian poet and and translator Salvatore Quasimodo was awarded the Nobel Prize for literature.

d. Frank Lloyd Wright (1867-1959), American architect; a world figure in 20th-century architecture.

d. Olga Knipper (1870-1959), Russian actress; a leading player in Konstantin Stanislavsky's Moscow Art Theater; among the roles she created were those of Masha in *The Three Sisters* and Elena in *Uncle Vanya,* both plays by her husband Anton Chekhov.

d. Billie Holiday (Eleanora Fagan) (1915-1959), leading African-American jazz singer.

d. Jacob Epstein (1880-1959), one of the leading British sculptors of the century.

The Boston Celtics, coached by Red Auerbach, defeated the Los Angeles Lakers to win the National Basketball Association championship; it was the first of a record-breaking eight consecutive titles (1959-1966); they also would come back after a year to win two more titles (1968-1969).

The St. Lawrence Seaway was opened; the major Canadian-American waterway, connecting the Atlantic Ocean with the Great Lakes, for the first time allowed oceangoing ships to sail into the North American heartland.

The Xerox Corporation, which had licensed Chester Carlson's xerographic process, introduced the first xerographic copier for commercial use; it would quickly revolutionize paper handling around the world.

After the National Football League refused Lamar Hunt's bid for an expansion franchise, he was instrumental in founding the competing American Football League.

The hovercraft (hydrofoil), a type of air-cushion vehicle, first crossed the English Channel, going into regular service later (1968).

American jockey Willie Shoemaker won both the Kentucky Derby and the Belmont Stakes, two of the three races comprising the Triple Crown.

Hurricane Vera (Sept.) killed 4,500 on Japan's Honshu Island.

An American Airlines Electra crashed in New York City's East River (Feb. 3), killing 65 people.

Floyd Patterson lost the world heavyweight boxing title to Ingemar Johansson but regained it in a rematch (1960).

1959 cont.

d. William Joseph "Wild Bill" Donovan (1883-1959), American intelligence officer; from the mid-1930s, creator of what became the World War II Office of Strategic Services (OSS) and later the Central Intelligence Agency (CIA).

lining the "three R's": reduce the number of animals used in a test, refine tests to decrease pain, and replace animal tests with alternative nonanimal tests where possible.

American medical researcher Harry Eagle developed Eagle's growth medium, a substance that allows mammalian (including human) cells to be grown in a laboratory, essential for much modern research.

Fuel partly melted in a Santa Susana, California, nuclear plant after a cooling system malfunctioned (July 24).

1960

Massachusetts Democratic senator John Fitzgerald Kennedy defeated Republican Richard M. Nixon, in a very close contest that featured the first televised presidential debates, to become the 35th president of the United States (1961-1963); he was the first Catholic president.

Congo (Zaire), formerly the Belgian Congo, became an independent state (June 30); civil war began (1960-1967). Moise Tshombe led the Katanga secession (July 11). President Joseph Kasavubu responded by asking for a United Nations peacekeeping force, quickly approved by the Security Council (July 14), which would stay until 1964. Army commander Joseph Mobutu took power in an army coup (Sept.); Prime Minister Patrice Lumumba fled to establish a Soviet-backed rival government in Stanleyville.

American geologist Henry H. Hess first posited that the seafloor was expanding. This idea, later modified by British geophysicists F. J. Vine and D. H. Matthews (1963) and confirmed by studies of magnetic reversals alongside ocean rifts, would lead to the theory of plate tectonics — that the earth is composed of some 20 moving plates of crust — and would finally end ridicule of the continental drift theory (1912).

American physicist Theodore Harold Maiman developed the first working laser (light amplification by stimulated emission of radiation; also called an optical maser), a device that produces an intensely concentrated beam of light. It would be widely used in medicine and in many other areas, including holography, high-

d. Ethel Barrymore (Edith Blythe) (1879-1959), American actress who emerged as a stage star in *Captain Jinks of the Horse Marines* (1901); the sister of John and Lionel Barrymore.

d. Bernard Berenson (1865-1959), American art critic and historian, long resident in Italy; a leading Italian Renaissance art historian and authenticator.

d. Maxwell Anderson (1888-1959), leading American playwright, from *What Price Glory?* (1924), cowritten with Laurence Stallings.

d. Sidney Bechet (1897-1959), American saxophonist, clarinetist, and bandleader; a leading jazz figure of the 1920s and 1930s.

d. Wanda Landowska (1879-1959), Polish harpsichordist; the leading 20th-century player and teacher of the instrument.

d. Preston Sturges (Edmond P. Biden) (1898-1959), American playwright, screenwriter, and director.

Montreal Canadiens star Jacques Plante introduced regular use of the protective face mask for hockey goalkeepers.

The number of television receivers in use in the United States topped 50 million.

Vince Lombardi took over as coach and general manager of professional football's Green Bay Packers, building them into one of the strongest teams of the era.

b. Earvin "Magic" Johnson, Jr. (1959-), American basketball player; a national college champion (1979) and five-time professional champion with the Los Angeles Lakers; the first big man to dominate as a point guard; with friendly rival Larry Bird largely responsible for basketball's increased popularity during the 1980s.

Ingmar Bergman's film classic *The Virgin Spring,* a story of rape, murder, and revenge set in medieval Sweden, starred Max von Sydow, Birgitta Pettersson, Birgitta Valberg, and Gunnel Lindblom.

Marcello Mastroianni starred in Federico Fellini's classic film *La Dolce Vita,* set in pleasure-seeking, decadent Roman society — and by extension in the empty, high-profile international subculture of the "beautiful people" of that day.

Ansel Adams published the photo collection *This Is the American Earth,* a call for preservation of America's natural heritage; text by Nancy Newhall.

Burt Lancaster in the title role as a shady evangelist, Jean Simmons as a sincere evangelist, and Shirley

The population of the earth began to surge; it was estimated at 3 billion to 3.1 billion, nearly 90 percent more than the 1.61 billion in 1900.

The U.S. Congress enacted the Civil Rights Act (May); though greatly watered down after a filibuster mounted by southern racists, it laid the legal basis for massive changes to come, including equal voting rights and campaigns for desegregation of public facilities. Lunch counter sit-ins began, with a successful desegregation campaign in Greensboro, North Carolina (Feb.).

Racist rioting in New Orleans failed to block the integration of the city's public schools.

1960 cont.

In the highly publicized "U-2 incident," an American U-2 spy plane was downed in Soviet airspace (May 1); its pilot, Francis Gary Powers, was captured and jailed as a spy.

South African police killed 67 and wounded 200 unarmed demonstrators at Sharpeville, near Johannesburg (Mar. 21); after the Sharpeville Massacre, the African National Congress (ANC) abandoned nonviolence, moving over to guerrilla war. British and worldwide condemnation further isolated South Africa.

The army of France's Fifth Republic suppressed a rising of French colonists in Algeria.

After a miltary coup, elected president José Maria Lemus of El Salvador was replaced by Colonel Cesar Yanes Urias (Oct. 26), beginning the long period of guerrilla insurgency that would grow into civil war.

Israeli agents in Buenos Aires captured German war criminal Adolf Eichmann; he would be tried and executed (1962).

Kurdish forces in Iraq, led by Mustafa al-Barzani, began a long insurrection (1960-1970; 1974-).

The Organization of Petroleum Exporting Countries (OPEC) was founded; the cartel's membership included most of the developing world's oil-producing nations.

In Laos, the Pathet Lao insurgency became a full-scale civil war after the Kong Le military coup.

The European Free Trade Association (EFTA) was established, originally as a British-led counterweight to the growing economic strength of the European Community.

At a founding meeting in Chicago, Students for a Democratic Society (SDS) was organized, originally as a reformist group.

In Pakistan, Mohammad Ayub Khan took power by coup, becoming military dictator (1960-1969).

resolution mapping, fiber-optic networks, industrial welding, and biological research.

An 11th-century Viking settlement was uncovered at L'Anse Aux Meadows, in northern Newfoundland, by Helge Ingstad and George Decker; it confirmed pre-Columbian Norse settlements in North America.

American astronomers Allan Rex Sandage and Thomas Matthews discovered quasars, extremely bright objects with a starlike appearance, originally called radio star or quasi-stellar objects (QSOs).

R. D. Laing published *The Divided Self*, outlining his view that schizophrenia is a reaction to an insane society; he developed the approach of treating mental patients in small groups in sheltered, homelike settings. His theories would remain controversial, but his communal treatment, pioneered in London (from 1965), would spread widely.

Jane Goodall began her work (1960-) studying chimpanzees at the Gombe Stream Game Preserve in Tanzania (then Tanganyika), encouraged to do so by Louis Leakey. She would be joined (1962) by Dutch photographer Hugo Van Lawick, later her husband, whose photographs would help to make her a worldwide celebrity.

The first communications satellite (COMSAT), *Echo*, was launched (Aug.); it "passively" transmitted sounds and pictures, unlike later satellites, which would be able to receive, amplify, and transmit radio, television, and telephone signals worldwide.

The world's first weather satellite, *TIROS 1* (Television and Infra-Red Observation Satellite), went into service (Apr. 1), joined some

Jones starred in Richard Brooks's film version of the 1927 Sinclair Lewis novel *Elmer Gantry.*

Harold Pinter emerged as a major playwright with *The Caretaker,* in that period seen as a central work of the "theater of the absurd."

Harper Lee published the novel *To Kill a Mockingbird,* about life in a small southern town, told through the eyes of two young children of a White lawyer defending a Black man unjustly accused of rape.

Jerzy Andrzejewski published the novel *The Inquisitors,* a major contribution to the literature of dissent in Soviet-dominated Poland.

Laurence Olivier starred in the title role, opposite Anthony Quinn as Henry II, in the English-language production of Jean Anouilh's *Becket.*

John Updike emerged as a major American novelist with his second novel, *Rabbit, Run,* the first in his series of "Rabbit" novels.

Paul Scofield starred as intransigent churchman Thomas More in Robert Bolt's play *A Man for All Seasons,* about the dispute between More and Britain's Henry VIII.

Stanley Kramer's film version of the 1955 Jerome Lawrence–Robert E. Lee play *Inherit the Wind,* about the 1925 Scopes "monkey trial" in Tennessee, starred Spencer Tracy as Clarence Darrow, Fredric March as a Bible-pounding William Jennings Bryan, and Gene Kelly as H. L. Mencken, all very lightly disguised.

Alvin Ailey choreographed *Revelations;* it was presented by and became the signature work of his dance company.

Benjamin Britten's opera *A Midsummer Night's Dream,* based on Shakespeare's play, opened at the

Birth control pills, developed by Gregory Pincus (1955), first went on the market; they would help revolutionize sexual activity in the coming years.

Despite a nationwide clemency campaign, which included several widely read books, Caryl Chessman was executed in California (May 2), a stay of execution coming moments too late. He had been convicted of robbery, kidnapping, and rape (but not murder) and sentenced to death (1948) but had maintained his innocence of all charges and gained several previous stays of execution.

In the payola scandal, many disc jockeys were exposed as having received payoffs to plug certain records on the air; many were charged under a new antipayola law.

Two jets, approaching different New York City airports in a snowstorm, collided in midair (Dec. 16); 133 people died, 5 of them on the ground.

Wilt Chamberlain won the first of his four National Basketball Association Most Valuable Player Awards (1960; 1966-1968).

American fundamentalist minister Pat (Marion Gordon) Robertson became the first television evangelist, hosting the *700 Club.*

Unimation, founded in the United States by George Devol and Joe Engelberger, was the first firm to make and sell industrial robots.

American track star Rafer Lewis Johnson received a world record 8,683 points in the decathlon trials leading up to the Rome Olympics, where he took the gold medal in the event.

Ethiopian runner Abebe Bikila won the 26-mile marathon at the 1960 Rome Olympics, gaining wide attention for running barefoot; he would be the first man ever to win two Olympic marathons (1960; 1964).

1960 cont.

The Quebec separatist movement developed, led by Quebec premier Jean Lesage (1960-1966).

In Sri Lanka, Sirimavo Bandaranaike became the world's first woman prime minister (1960-1965; 1970-1977); she succeeded her assassinated husband, Solomon Bandaranaike.

African National Congress (ANC) president Albert Luthuli was awarded the Nobel Peace Prize.

The Republic of Senegal became an independent nation; its first president (1960-1980) was poet and independence movement leader Léopold Senghor.

The Republic of the Congo, formerly the French Middle Congo colony and autonomous since 1958, became an independent state (Aug. 15).

The Central African Republic became an independent country; its first president was David Dacko (1960-1966), who established a one-party state.

Chad (Republic of Chad) became an independent state (Aug. 11); its first president was N'Garta (François) Tombalbaye (1960-1975), who developed a one-party state.

The Federal Republic of Nigeria became an independent state and Commonwealth member (Oct. 1).

Gabon, formerly part of French Equatorial Africa, became an independent state (Aug. 17); Léon M'ba was its first president (1960-1968).

The Independent Republic of Dahomey was established (Aug. 1).

Ivory Coast became an independent state; its first president, who headed a one-party state, was Felix Houphoüt-Boigny.

Madagascar became an independent state (June 30).

months later by *TIROS 2*. They and their successors would become indispensable aids in weather forecasting, especially in tracking hurricanes and other violent storms.

Austrian-British biochemist Max Ferdinand Perutz determined the structure of the oxygen-carrying blood factor hemoglobin; he would share the 1962 Nobel Prize for chemistry with his former student, Briton John Cowdery Kendrew, who worked out the structure of myoglobin.

France exploded its first atomic bomb, at Reggane, in what was then French Algeria (Feb. 13).

Transistors had become so miniaturized that they began to be combined into integrated circuits, etched on thin chips of silicon or another semiconducting material. Even these would grow ever smaller, so that within decades, thousands might be etched on a single microchip.

Jacques Piccard and U.S. Navy lieutenant Don Walsh set a world depth record of more than 35,000 feet, descending to the floor of the Pacific Ocean in a bathyscape.

Chlorophyll was synthesized by American chemist Robert Burns Woodward.

American physicist Donald Glaser won the Nobel Prize for physics for his development of the bubble chamber (1952).

Australian immunologist (Frank) MacFarlane Burnet and British-Lebanese zoologist Peter Medawar shared the Nobel Prize for physiology or medicine for their work on the mechanism of transplant rejection (1944).

Aldeburgh Festival, libretto by Britten and Peter Pears.

Alec Guinness and John Mills starred as competing Scottish military officers in Ronald Neame's film *Tunes of Glory*.

Dean Stockwell, Trevor Howard, and Wendy Hiller starred in Jack Cardiff's film version of D. H. Lawrence's 1913 novel *Sons and Lovers*.

Very much in tune with the times was Charles Strouse's trailblazing Broadway rock musical *Bye Bye Birdie*, starring Dick Gautier, Dick Van Dyke, and Chita Rivera.

Tad Mosel's play *All the Way Home* starred Pat Hingle and Colleen Dewhurst; it was based on James Agee's 1957 novel, *A Death in the Family*.

Phyllis McGinley published the Pulitzer Prize–winning poetry collection *Times Three: Selected Verse from Three Decades*.

French poet and diplomat Alexis Saint-Léger Léger (pen name St.-John Perse) was awarded the Nobel Prize for literature.

b. Kenneth Branagh (1960-   ), British actor and director who would emerge as a leading figure on stage and screen in the 1980s.

d. Albert Camus (1913-1960), French writer and essayist; a central 20th-century figure whose formulation of the "absurd" powerfully influenced the development of the arts and literature.

d. Boris Leonidovich Pasternak (1890-1960), Russian poet and novelist best known for his novel *Doctor Zhivago* (1955). He was awarded the 1958 Nobel Prize for literature but was forced to refuse it.

d. (William) Clark Gable (1901-1960), American film star of Hollywood's golden age and beyond,

Wilma Rudolph became the first American woman to win three Olympic gold medals: the 100 meters, 200 meters, and 400-meter relay.

British flat-racing jockey Lester Keith Pigott was named Britain's champion jockey for the first of what would be 11 times (1960; 1964-1971; 1981; 1982).

British yachtsman Francis Chichester made the first of his three solo transatlantic voyages (1960; 1962; 1964).

Former United Mine Workers president W. A. "Tony" Boyle was convicted of responsibility for the December 31, 1959, murders of rival Joseph Yablonski and his family.

Joy Adamson published *Born Free*, about training the tame lion cub Elsa to return to the wild.

The American submarine *Skate* was the first ship to surface at the North Pole.

The U.S. nuclear-powered submarine *Triton* was the first vessel to travel around the world underwater.

The Dallas Cowboys football team was founded, coached from the start by Tom Landry.

The U.S. Federal Hazardous Substances Act was passed, requiring warning labels, including first aid instructions, on consumer products containing hazardous substances.

In Coalbrook, South Africa, 417 miners trapped by rockfalls died of methane poisoning (Jan. 21).

A C-46 chartered plane carrying California Polytechnic State University's football team crashed on takeoff in fog near Toledo, Ohio, killing 22 people (Oct. 29).

1960 cont.

Mauritania became an independent state (Nov. 28).

The Republic of Mali became an independent state (June 20).

Somalia became an independent state (July 1).

Togo, formerly French Togoland, became an independent state (Apr. 27).

The Republic of Upper Volta, a former French colony that had achieved autonomy in 1959, became an independent state; it was later renamed Burkina Faso (1984).

d. Aneurin "Nye" Bevan, (1897-1960), Welsh coal miner; Labour member of Parliament (1929-1960), leader of the left wing of the Labour Party from the mid-1930s, and husband of Jennie Lee; as minister of health (1946), he introduced the National Health Service.

d. Joseph Nye Welch (1890-1960), lawyer for the U.S. Army in the Army-McCarthy hearings (1954), whose exposure of McCarthy before a worldwide television audience contributed greatly to McCarthy's quick decline and the end of that witch-hunting period.

Two dogs were sent into space in a Soviet spacecraft, which returned safely to earth.

Willard Frank Libby won the Nobel Prize for chemistry for his development of radiocarbon dating (1947).

d. Max Theodor Felix von Laue (1879-1960), German physicist who developed the technique of X-ray crystallography (1912).

d. (Charles) Leonard Woolley (1880-1960), British archaeologist noted for his excavations in the Middle East, especially at Ur (1922-1934).

d. Roy Chapman Andrews (1884-1960), American explorer, naturalist, and writer, long associated with the American Museum of Natural History, who led many Asian expeditions searching for plants and animals, live and extinct (1916-1930).

1961

Katangese forces, aided by mercenaries, scored early successes over United Nations peacekeeping forces in the Congo (Zaire) (Sept.), but reinforced UN forces successfully counterattacked, taking Elizabethville (Dec.). Former Congo prime minister Patrice Lumumba was murdered by Moise Tshombe's forces while a prisoner in Katanga.

Yuri Gagarin became the first human to orbit the earth (Apr. 12), on a 1.8-hour flight in the *Vostok 1*, the first of a series of Soviet spacecraft built under the direction of Sergei Korolev. A later flight (Aug. 6), with cosmonaut Gherman Stepanovich Titov, lasted a full day and circled the earth 17 times.

1960 cont.

most notably as Rhett Butler in *Gone With the Wind* (1939).

d. Oscar Hammerstein II (1895-1960), American lyricist and librettist; a major figure in the American musical theater, most notably for his nine collaborations with Richard Rodgers, among them *Oklahoma!* (1943), *South Pacific* (1949), and *The Sound of Music* (1959).

d. Margaret Sullavan (Margaret Brooke) (1911-1960), leading American stage and screen dramatic actress; she committed suicide.

d. Richard Nathaniel Wright (1908-1960), leading African-American writer from the novel *Native Son* (1940).

d. Mack Sennett (Michael Sinnott) (1880-1960), American actor and director; the leading comedy director and producer of the early silent film era; creator of the Keystone Kops.

d. J. P. (John Philips) Marquand (1893-1960), American writer who emerged as a major novelist with *The Late George Apley* (1937).

d. Nevil Shute (Nevil Shute Norway) (1899-1960), British writer noted for the novels *A Town Like Alice* (1950) and *On the Beach* (1957).

d. Zora Neale Hurston (1901-1960), African-American writer and folklorist.

American journalist William L. Shirer, who had reported from Europe on the rise of Nazism during the 1930s, published his massive *The Rise and Fall of the Third Reich*.

Two trains collided near Pardubice, Czechoslovakia (Nov. 14), killing 110 people.

The munitions cargo of the French freighter *La Coubre* exploded in the port of Havana, Cuba (Mar. 4), killing more than 100 people.

d. Emily Post (1873-1960), American arbiter of "good manners," most notably in her *Etiquette: The Blue Book of Social Usage* (1922).

d. Lewis Bernstein Namier (1888-1960), Polish-British historian who developed a new school of history focused on the collection and analysis of massive amounts of data, as in his work on 18th-century British politics.

1961

Yevgeny Yevtushenko's poem *Babi Yar* memorialized the World War II German massacres of Soviet Jews at Babi Yar, near Kiev, simultaneously taking up the long anti-Semitic history of the Soviet government and opening a major issue in the post-Stalin Soviet Union.

The Congress of Racial Equality (CORE) organized the nonviolent "freedom rides" campaign (May), seeking to desegregate southern public transportation and related facilities. They were almost everywhere met by racist violence, and federal enforcement was needed to complete desegregation.

d. Dag Hammarskjöld (1905-1961), Swedish diplomat; second secretary-general of the United Nations (1953-1961); he died in an aircraft accident, while on a peace-keeping mission to the Congo (Zaire). He was posthumously awarded the 1961 Nobel Peace Prize.

Soviet-controlled East Germany closed the East Berlin–West Berlin border with the Berlin Wall, built overnight (Aug. 12), creating a highly visible artifact of the Cold War.

American-supported Cuban exiles made a failed attempt to invade Cuba (Apr. 17), landing at the Bahia de los Cochinos (Bay of Pigs). Promised American air support and an expected Cuban insurrection did not materialize; 90 people died, and the balance of the invasion force of 1,200 to 1,500 were captured, most of them later traded for medical supplies and food.

A failed French army mutiny in Algeria (July) was led by General Raoul Salan, who then directed terrorist Secret Army Organization (OAS) actions in France and Algeria from abroad.

American aid to Vietnam expanded further; President John F. Kennedy sent General Maxwell D. Taylor to Vietnam and increased the number of American advisers and the flow of supplies.

Cuban-backed Nicaraguan Sandinista guerrillas began the guerrilla insurgency that would become the long Nicaraguan Civil War.

d. Rafael Leonidas Trujillo Molina (1891-1961), Dominican Republic dictator (1930-1961); he was assassinated during an attempted military coup that began a period of unrest that included the 1965-1966 civil war.

General Park Chung Hee took power by military coup in South Korea (May 16).

Neutralist Burmese diplomat U Thant became the third secretary-general of the United Nations (1961-1971).

Alan Shepard became the first American to fly in space (May 5), making a suborbital flight in *Freedom 7,* a U.S. Mercury spacecraft. He was followed by Virgil (Gus) Grissom, launched aboard the *Liberty Bell 7,* another Mercury craft, in a suborbital flight (July 21).

U.S. president John F. Kennedy promised to land humans on the moon within a decade; that goal would be reached two years early (1969). The NASA (National Aeronautics and Space Administration) Spacecraft Center (from 1973 the Johnson Space Center) was established as NASA's mission control for space flights.

The drug thalidomide was recognized as causing serious birth defects, especially gross malformations (1961-1962); among the first to recognize and warn of the danger was American pediatrician Helen Taussig. Years of lawsuits followed, after which some parents of "thalidomide babies" won settlements from governments and drug companies. In some countries, notably the United States, laws relating to the testing and safety of drugs were revised to avoid such disasters in the future.

Murray Gell-Mann developed a scheme for classifying subatomic particles, proposing that they exist in families. As a result of his theory, he and others were able to predict the existence of particles not yet known, which he called *quarks* (from a phrase in James Joyce's *Finnegans Wake*), each paired with an anti-quark and some (controversially) with fractional charges. Israeli physicist Yuval Ne'emen independently developed similar particle groupings.

During the Mohole Project (1961-1966), the American research ship *Glomar Challenger* tried to bring up samples of the Moho (Mo-

Claudia McNeil, Sidney Poitier, Ruby Dee, and Diana Sands re-created their stage roles in Daniel Petrie's film version of Lorraine Hansberry's 1959 play *A Raisin in the Sun*.

Joseph Heller published his very popular first novel *Catch-22*, a satire of American army life so effective as to add the term "catch-22" to the language.

Rudolf Nureyev defected to the West while appearing with the Kirov Ballet in Paris; from 1962, he would often be partnered with Margot Fonteyn.

Stanley Kramer's Nazi war crimes film *Judgment at Nuremberg* starred Spencer Tracy as the American judge, Burt Lancaster as a German judge on trial, Marlene Dietrich, Maximilian Schell, and Richard Widmark.

The Royal Shakespeare Company was founded, originally as the Stratford-on-Avon Shakespeare Memorial Theater. Peter Hall was its first director (1961-1968).

Vittorio De Sica's film *Two Women*, based on Alberto Moravia's 1957 novel, starred Sophia Loren, Raf Vallone, and Jean-Paul Belmondo.

Iris Murdoch emerged as a major novelist with *A Severed Head*.

Jerome Robbins and Robert Wise codirected the film version of the 1957 Leonard Bernstein–Stephen Sondheim musical *West Side Story*, starring Natalie Wood, Russ Tamblyn, Rita Moreno, Richard Beymer, and George Chakiris.

V. S. Naipaul published his Trinidad-set *A House for Mr. Biswas*.

John le Carré created British agent George Smiley and his world in the spy novel *Call for the Dead*.

James Farmer, who had founded CORE (1942), became its national director (1961-1966).

Amnesty International was founded, becoming the world's leading human rights organization, working to free prisoners of conscience, improve their conditions of imprisonment, end the use of torture, and help their families.

New York Yankees outfielder Roger Maris hit 61 home runs, breaking Babe Ruth's 1927 record.

The first industrial robot, built by George Devol and Joe Engelberger's firm Unimation, was installed at a General Motors plant in New Jersey.

The Peace Corps was established, as proposed by U.S. president John F. Kennedy during the 1960 presidential campaign; volunteers were sent throughout the world to work on educational and development projects.

Michel Foucault published *Madness and Civilization*, his notable exploration of society and insanity as a form of social deviance.

Simon Wiesenthal founded the Jewish Documentation Center (Wiesenthal Center) in Vienna, Austria, headquarters of a worldwide effort to trace Nazi war criminals and bring them to justice.

A circus tent fire set by a disgruntled employee killed 323 people, most of them children, and injured an estimated 800 at Niterói, near Rio de Janeiro, Brazil (Dec. 17).

A Sabena 707 crashed near the Brussels, Belgium, airport, killing 73 people, including 18 American figure skaters en route to a competition (Feb. 15).

A. J. (Anthony Joseph) Foyt won the Indianapolis 500, his first of four (1961; 1964; 1967; 1977).

The Popular Movement for the Liberation of Angola (MLPA) went over to armed insurrection against Portuguese colonial forces in Angola, beginning the Angolan War of Independence (1961-1975) and the Angolan Civil War (1975-   ).

Kuwait became an independent nation (June 19); British opposition stopped a planned Iraqi takeover of the oil-rich new country.

U.S. president John F. Kennedy initiated the inter-American Alliance for Progress initiative (Mar.); its promised joinder of major U.S. investment funds to Latin American capital did not materialize.

President Tito of Yugoslavia initiated a 25-nation meeting of nonaligned states in Belgrade (Sept.), founding the Nonaligned Movement, referring to the Cold War; it was to grow into a 108-nation, largely Third World organization focusing on anticolonial and economic issues.

The Republic of South Africa was established, as that country withdrew from the Commonwealth.

Goa was taken by Indian forces (Dec. 18), ending Portuguese rule.

Cameroon (Republic of Cameroon) became an independent state (Oct. 1).

Sierra Leone became an independent state and Commonwealth member (Apr. 27).

Tanganyika became an independent state.

The Republic of Rwanda became an independent state (Jan. 28).

d. Emily Greene Balch (1867-1961), American pacifist; founder and first secretary of the Women's International League for Peace and Freedom (1919) and corecipient of the 1946 Nobel Peace Prize.

d. Samuel Taliaferro Rayburn (1882-1961), Texas Democratic politician; longtime congressman (1913-1961),

horovicic discontinuity) first discovered in 1909. The exploration became too expensive and was abandoned, but techniques developed there were used in deep-sea oil and gas drilling.

Dutch-American physician Willem J. Kolff invented a balloon pump used in the aorta during heart attacks to aid circulation.

Soviet nuclear physicist Andrei Sakharov publicly protested against the Soviet Union's atmospheric testing of nuclear weapons, sparking wider calls for a nuclear test–ban treaty.

The strongest form of malaria parasite was found to be developing resistance to chloroquine, commonly used to treat malaria. This would be but one of many drug-resistant forms of disease discovered in the coming decades.

Three atomic plant workers were killed after a steam explosion in the overheated core of an Idaho Falls, Idaho, nuclear reactor (Jan. 3). These would be the only deaths directly linked to nuclear accidents in the United States until 1986.

Electronic watches made their first appearance, using a battery to keep vibrating a miniature tuning fork, which measured the time; these battery-operated models would increasingly replace mainspring watches.

Element 103 was discovered by A. Ghiorso and others; it was named lawrencium, after Ernest O. Lawrence.

Melvin Calvin received the Nobel Prize for chemistry for his work on the chemical reactions involved in photosynthesis (1937-1945).

Ossie Davis starred as Purlie Victorious Judson in his play *Purlie Victorious,* a satirical look at modern small-town Georgia; Ruby Dee, Godfrey Cambridge, Sorrell Brooke, and Alan Alda costarred.

Audrey Hepburn as Holly Golightly starred opposite George Peppard in Blake Edwards's film version of the 1958 Truman Capote novel *Breakfast at Tiffany's.*

Muriel Spark published the novel *The Prime of Miss Jean Brodie,* her protagonist an offbeat, quite extraordinary Edinburgh teacher.

Rita Tushingham starred in *A Taste of Honey,* Shelagh Delaney's adaptation of her own 1958 play into the Tony Richardson film.

Yugoslav writer Ivo Andric was awarded the Nobel Prize for literature.

d. Ernest Miller Hemingway (1899-1961), American writer; a world literary figure from the 1920s; winner of the 1954 Nobel Prize for literature; he committed suicide.

d. Gary Cooper (Frank James Cooper) (1901-1961), leading American film star of Hollywood's golden age and beyond.

d. Barry Fitzgerald (William Joseph Shields) (1888-1961), Irish actor; a leading figure in Dublin's Abbey Theatre, later a character actor in Hollywood.

d. (Samuel) Dashiell Hammett (1894-1961), archetypal American mystery writer; creator of the Continental Op, Sam Spade, and Nick and Nora Charles.

d. Eero Saarinen (1910-1961), Finnish-American architect; early partnered with his father Eliel Saarinen (1938-1950).

d. George S. (Simon) Kaufman (1889-1961), prolific American playwright, often in collaboration with

Soviet high jumper Valeri Brumel was the first person to jump 7 feet 4 inches, a record he would push to 7 feet 5 inches (1962) and 7 feet 5¾ inches (1963), then taking the Olympic gold medal (1964).

French fashion designer André Courrèges founded his own Paris fashion house; he would popularize trousers for women and knee-length skirts worn with high boots.

The World Wildlife Fund (World Wide Fund for Nature) was founded, becoming a key international conservation organization, working especially to preserve natural habitats and to halt trade in endangered wild animals.

d. Emily Greene Balch (1867-1961), American pacifist and social reformer whose central work was in immigration, child welfare reform, and pacifist movements; she was first secretary of the Women's International League for Peace and Freedom and recipient of the 1946 Nobel Peace Prize.

d. Dorothy Thompson (1893-1961), American journalist and antifascist who emerged as a major figure while reporting on the rise of fascism in Germany (1924-1934).

d. Frantz Omar Fanon (1925-1961), Martinican Black Marxist theoretician, psychiatrist, writer, and revolutionary; author of *The Wretched of the Earth* (1961).

1961 cont.

most notably during the New Deal era, when he was a key legislative ally of Franklin D. Roosevelt; he was House Speaker for 17 years.

d. William Zebulon Foster (1881-1961), leader of the failed American steel strike (1919), three-time presidential candidate of the U.S. Communist Party (1924; 1928; 1932), and chair of the U.S. Communist Party (1945-1957).

d. Erwin Schrödinger (1887-1961), Austrian physicist who developed the Schrödinger wave equation (1926), basic to quantum theory.

d. Lee De Forest (1873-1961), electrical engineer and inventor; a pioneer in wireless telegraphy and radio, he developed the triode electron tube (1906), basic to electronics.

d. Carl Gustav Jung (1875-1961), Swiss psychiatrist and key 20th-century psychoanalyst who, after publishing *Psychology of the Unconscious* (1912), broke with Sigmund Freud and developed his own school of analytic psychology.

d. Arnold Lucius Gesell (1880-1961), American child psychologist and physician; founder-director (1911-1948) of the Yale Clinic of Child Development, who outlined the stages of normal child growth and development, called the Gesell Development Schedules.

d. Henri Edouard Prosper Breuil (1877-1961), French priest and archaeologist known for his work studying, analyzing, and photographing Paleolithic cave paintings.

1962

Thermonuclear war was seriously threatened during the Cuban Missile Crisis (Oct. 22-Dec. 2). President John F. Kennedy responded to the placement of Soviet missiles and bombers by blockading Cuba, demanding removal of all offensive weapons, and stating that the United States would go to war if Cuba used nuclear weapons on any Western Hemisphere country (Oct. 22). Soviet forces went on maximum worldwide alert, as American forces moved toward invasion of Cuba (Oct. 23). President Kennedy and Soviet premier Nikita Khrushchev then negotiated unconditional Soviet withdrawal and the dismantling of missile-launching sites.

Rachel Carson published *Silent Spring*, widely publicizing fears about chemical pollution of the environment, especially the concentration of pesticides such as DDT in the food chain; a key work in the development of worldwide ecological and green movements.

After the tragic effects of thalidomide (1961-1962), the Federal Food, Drug, and Cosmetic Act (1938) was amended to require more stringent testing of possible new drugs, rules that would be criticized as cumbersome later, during the AIDS crisis of the 1980s and beyond.

others, including Marc Connelly, Edna Ferber, and Moss Hart.

d. James Thurber (1894-1961), American writer and artist; many of his satirical illustrations and prose pieces were originally written for *The New Yorker.*

d. Anna Mary Robertson Moses ("Grandma Moses") (1860-1961), American primitive artist who began painting in her 70s and was recognized as a major figure in her 80s.

d. Max Weber (1881-1961), Russian-American painter and sculptor who helped introduce cubism and fauvism to America.

d. Augustus John (1876-1961), leading British painter.

Gregory Peck created the classic role of small-town southern lawyer Atticus Finch in *To Kill a Mockingbird,* defending Brock Peters as an African-American falsely accused of rape. The story is told largely through the eyes of Finch's children. Robert Mulligan's film version of the 1960 Harper Lee novel was as timely as the year's headlines.

Ingmar Bergman's classic film *Through a Glass, Darkly* starred Harriet Andersson as the recently released schizophrenic, Gunnar Björnstrand, Max von Sydow, and Lars Passgard.

Pope John XXIII convened the Second Vatican Council (Vatican II) (1962-1965), which engaged in a deep, precedent-shattering reevaluation of the Catholic Church and ultimately restated church attitudes on matters such as religious liberty and ecumenism, condemned anti-Semitism, and greatly reformed many practices, introducing national languages and contemporary music.

U.S. president John F. Kennedy federalized Mississippi National Guard troops to protect the Supreme Court–ordered enrollment of African-American James Meredith in the University of Mississippi

A French–National Liberation Front (FLN) cease-fire ended the Algerian War of Independence (Mar.); an FLN–Secret Army Organization (OAS) cease-fire substantially ended OAS terrorism. Algeria became an independent nation (July 3), with FLN leader Ahmed Ben Bella as its first premier.

Nelson Mandela, then a deputy vice president of the African National Congress (ANC), who had gone from nonviolence to violent revolution after the Sharpeville Massacre (1960), was convicted of sabotage and jailed; in 1990, he would emerge from prison the leader of the successful South African national movement.

The long, extraordinarily costly Ethiopian-Eritrean War (1962-1991) began after Ethiopia canceled Eritrean autonomy within the Ethiopian-Eritrean federation, in effect since 1952.

A Chinese-Indian border war flared (Oct.-Nov.); it ended with Chinese victory and a unilateral Chinese cease-fire declaration (Nov. 21); Indian opposition ended.

Civil war began in Rwanda (1962-1963), as Tutsi military forces tried to gain control of the new country after the majority Hutus had won control in free elections.

Civil war began in Yemen (1962-1970). Backed by Egyptian forces, which ultimately numbered 60,000 to 80,000, rebel forces established the Free Yemen Republic (Sept.), while Saudi Arabia supported the monarchy.

Anti–nuclear weapons crusader Linus Pauling was awarded the Nobel Peace Prize; he had also won a 1954 Nobel Prize in chemistry.

General Ne Win (Maung Shu Maung) again took power by military coup in Burma; he would hold power for almost three decades (1962-1988).

In *Baker v. Carr,* the U.S. Supreme Court outlawed discriminatory electoral apportionment practices, forcing reapportionment throughout the country and opening the way for the election of many minority candidates.

John Glenn became the first American to go into orbit around the earth, aboard the Mercury spacecraft *Friendship 7* (Feb. 20) in a five-hour, three-orbit flight.

The *Mariner 2* was the first successful U.S. space probe, passing near Venus (Dec. 14) and transmitting data en route (until Jan. 3, 1963).

Telstar, the first "active" communications satellite — able to receive, amplify, and transmit radio waves, not just reflect them — was launched at Cape Canaveral, Florida (July 10). Using it, the first transatlantic television broadcasts were made, both in black-and-white and in color, linking the United States with Britain and France. Later, multiple satellites in a worldwide Intelsat system (1964) would make possible full two-way communication, helping to shape what Marshall McLuhan would call a "global village."

The first of America's OSO (Orbiting Solar Observatory) research and observation satellites was launched (Mar. 7), designed to record solar data and transmit it on command.

The magnetic disk was introduced for the storage and retrieval of computer data; on such "hard disks," information was stored in circular tracks that could be accessed quickly, without passing over all the data in sequence, as was necessary with magnetic tape. With improvements, hard disks would be able to hold massive amounts of data, greatly expanding what was possible with computers.

American historian and sociologist Thomas Kuhn published *The Structure of Scientific Revolutions,* positing that scientists work with a shared body of scientific approaches and understandings (which he called a *paradigm*), such as those deriving from the theories of

Alexander Solzhenitsyn published his classic work on the Soviet Gulag, *One Day in the Life of Ivan Denisovich*.

Dmitri Shostakovich composed his Thirteenth *(Babi Yar)* Symphony, set around five Yevgeny Yevtushenko poems, including his landmark 1961 poem *Babi Yar*.

Peter O'Toole starred in the title role in David Lean's film epic *Lawrence of Arabia*, based on *The Seven Pillars of Wisdom*, T. E. Lawrence's 1926 account of his role in the World War I Arab Revolt; Alec Guinness and Omar Sharif costarred.

Anthony Burgess emerged as a major British novelist with *A Clockwork Orange*, his bitterly satirical novel about a violent, statist, near-future British society.

Claes Oldenburg created his "soft sculpture" *Two Cheeseburgers with Everything (Dual Hamburgers)*.

Henry Fonda starred as the incorruptible presidential nominee in Otto Preminger's film *Advise and Consent*, based on the 1959 Allen Drury novel.

Sean Connery created Agent 007 in the first James Bond film, *Dr. No*.

Dudley Moore, Peter Cook, and Jonathan Miller starred in the offbeat revue *Beyond the Fringe*.

Mick Jagger, Keith Richards, Bill Wyman, Charlie Watts, and Brian Jones organized the Rolling Stones.

Uta Hagen and Arthur Hill starred in Edward Albee's play *Who's Afraid of Virginia Woolf?*

Katherine Anne Porter published the novel *Ship of Fools*, set at sea in the shadow of the Nazi rise to power; it would be the basis of the 1965 film.

(Sept.) and to end anti–civil rights rioting that killed two and injured many.

In New Orleans, the scene of massive antidesegration rioting, all segregation in Catholic schools was ended by church action.

In *Engel v. Vitale*, the U.S. Supreme Court declared unconstitutional a compulsory New York school prayer.

Albert De Salvo, known as the "Boston Strangler," would sexually assault and murder 13 women (1962-1964) before being caught. He would later be stabbed to death in prison (1973).

An Iranian earthquake killed more than 12,000 people (Sept.).

American golfer Jack Nicklaus won the first of his four U.S. Open championships (1962; 1967; 1972; 1986).

Australian Rod (Rodney George) Laver won tennis's grand slam, taking the men's singles titles at Wimbledon and at the U.S., Australian, and French Opens, and helping Australia to win the Davis Cup. He then turned professional.

American historian Barbara Tuchman published *The Guns of August*, her best-seller about World War I.

Brazil won its second successive World Cup, defeating Czechoslovakia three goals to one.

U.S. president John F. Kennedy appointed former football star Byron Raymond "Whizzer" White to the Supreme Court.

Sonny (Charles) Liston won the world heavyweight boxing title by knocking out Floyd Patterson in the first round.

The Laotian Civil War was halted by an internationally mediated peace agreement, but fighting soon resumed, becoming intertwined with the growing Vietnam War as the North Vietnamese used Laotian supply routes and fought in Laos as Pathet Lao allies, while U.S. supplies and air support went to the Laotian government.

A Students for a Democratic Society (SDS) meeting at Port Huron, Michigan, announced the Port Huron Statement, moving the SDS from a reformist to a revolutionary stance.

In Peru, American Popular Revolutionary Alliance (APRA) leader Victor Haya de la Torre won the presidential election but was denied the presidency by his longtime antagonists, the Peruvian military.

An Indonesian-backed anti-Dutch guerrilla war began in Netherlands New Guinea (Feb.), forcing Dutch withdrawal (Aug.); an Indonesian-backed guerrilla insurrection in Brunei (Dec.) was defeated by the British.

Mozambican independence leader Eduardo Mondlane founded FRELIMO (Mozambique National Liberation Front), which two years later would begin the long war of independence.

Uganda became an independent state and Commonwealth member (Oct. 9); its first prime minister was independence movement leader Milton Obote.

The National Front for the Liberation of Angola (FNLA) was founded by Holden Roberto; its guerrilla forces entered the Angolan War of Independence.

Trinidad and Tobago became an independent nation and Commonwealth member, led by independence movement leader Eric Williams as prime minister (1962-1981).

U-2 spy plane pilot Francis Gary Powers was exchanged for Soviet spy Rudolph Abel.

Burundi became an independent state (July 1).

Isaac Newton or Albert Einstein, and that a scientific revolution occurs when experimental results cannot be reconciled with the existing paradigm, leading to a "crisis of confidence" and causing it to be overthrown.

The Minuteman I, the first American solid-fuel system intercontinental ballistic missile, was deployed; the first Soviet counterpart was developed in 1969 and the French in 1971.

In *Animal Dispersion in Relation to Social Behaviour*, British ethologist Vero Copner Wynne-Edwards controversially proposed that natural selection may operate not only on individuals within a group but also on groups within an environment.

British molecular biologist Francis Crick, American molecular biologist James D. Watson, and New Zealand–British biophysicist Maurice Wilkins shared the Nobel Prize for physiology or medicine for their work on the structure of DNA (1953). Rosalind Franklin, whose work in X-ray crystallography provided key data but was initially unrecognized, had died and so could not have shared the award.

d. Niels Henrik David Bohr (1885-1962), Danish physicist who created the basic model of atomic structure (1913).

d. Andrew Ellicott Douglass (1867-1962), American astronomer who developed the tree-dating system dendrochronology (by 1920).

d. Arthur Holly Compton (1892-1962), American physicist who first recognized the Compton effect and posited the existence of the photon (1923), later studying cosmic rays and, during World War II, working to synthesize plutonium for the atomic bomb.

Zero Mostel, blacklisted in Hollywood, continued to pursue his stage career, starring in Stephen Sondheim's musical *A Funny Thing Happened on the Way to the Forum.*

The Loneliness of the Long Distance Runner, Tony Richardson's film version of Alan Sillitoe's 1959 story of alienated youth, starred Tom Courtenay, Michael Redgrave, James Bolam, and Alec McCowen.

Doris Lessing published her novel *The Golden Notebook.*

American writer John Steinbeck was awarded the Nobel Prize for literature.

b. Jodie Foster (1962-   ), American actress and director; a child actress in television and films, then a film star from the late 1980s.

b. Garth Brooks (1962-   ), a leading American country singer.

b. Tom Cruise (Thomas Cruise Mapother IV) (1962-   ), American actor who would become a film star in the 1980s.

d. Marilyn Monroe (Norma Jean Mortenson) (1926-1962), American film star whose substantial aptitude for light comedy was overwhelmed by her status as the world's leading sex symbol; she apparently committed suicide.

d. William Faulkner (William Harrison Falkner) (1897-1962), American writer; a celebrated world figure from the late 1920s; winner of the 1949 Nobel Prize for literature.

d. Hermann Hesse (1877-1962), German-Swiss writer; a world figure from the publication of the novel *Demian* (1919) and winner of the 1946 Nobel Prize for literature.

The Boston Celtics won the National Basketball Association championship, defeating the Los Angeles Lakers four games to three. They were to defeat the Lakers for the title seven times in nine years.

The New York Yankees defeated the San Francisco Giants in the World Series, four games to three. It was the Yankees' 17th World Series win in 27 years, a dominance unparalleled in the history of baseball. The Yankees would not win the World Series again until 1977.

Walter Cronkite became chief television anchor at CBS (1962-1981), emerging as the most influential television newscaster of his time.

Wilt Chamberlain became the first professional basketball player to score 100 points in a game (Mar. 2), against the New York Knicks.

An Air France 707 crashed on takeoff from Paris, France (June 3), killing 130 people, many from Atlanta, Georgia.

In Saarland, West Germany, an explosion in a coal mine killed 298 people (Feb. 7).

An American Airlines 707 crashed into the bay after takeoff from New York City's Kennedy airport (Mar. 1), killing 95 people and destroying 20 artworks by Arshile Gorky.

An Air France 707 crashed near Grande-Terre, Guadeloupe, West Indies (June 22), killing all 113 people aboard.

Near Tokyo, Japan, a commuter and freight train collided and were then hit by an express train (May 3); 163 people died.

b. Jackie (Jacqueline) Joyner-Kersee (1962–   ), American track-and-field champion who would become one of the world's leading athletes as holder of

1962 cont.

Western Samoa became an independent state and Commonwealth member (Jan. 1).

d. (Anna) Eleanor Roosevelt (1884-1962), American social reformer; a leading Democratic liberal who became a world figure as the wife and "eyes and ears" of President Franklin Delano Roosevelt, and later on her own, perhaps most notably as initiator and successful sponsor of the United Nations Declaration of Human Rights (1948).

d. Adolf Eichmann (1906-1962), Nazi SS official; a war criminal who was captured by Israeli intelligence in Buenos Aires (1960) and was tried and hanged in Israel (May 31).

d. Auguste Antoine Piccard (1884-1962), Swiss physicist who, with his twin brother, Jean Félix Piccard, studied the atmosphere and ocean; he set a world height record (1931) in a self-designed balloon with a pressurized cabin, later adopted for airplanes and for use in his bathyscaphe (1948).

d. Charles William Beebe (1877-1962), American biologist and nature writer long associated with the New York Zoological Gardens (Bronx Zoo); a pioneer ocean explorer who helped develop the bathysphere (1930) and set a world depth record (1934).

1963

d. John Fitzgerald Kennedy (1917-1963), 35th president of the United States (1961-1963); assassinated in Dallas, Texas (Nov. 22) by Lee Harvey Oswald, whether or not in concert with others a matter of considerable dispute. He was succeeded by Vice President Lyndon Baines Johnson. Two days later (Nov. 24), while in police custody, Oswald was assassinated by Jack Ruby.

An American-backed military coup deposed South Vietnamese dictator Ngo Dinh Diem (Nov. 1); he and his brother, Ngo Dinh Nhu, head of the secret police, were

The first successful liver transplant was performed by a University of Colorado team led by Thomas E. Starzl.

British astronomer Gerald Hawkins suggested that Stonehenge, a huge circle of standing stones (ca. 1900-1400 BC) on England's Salisbury Plain, was an ancient observatory, originally aligned with solar and lunar eclipses, a view outlined in *Stonehenge Decoded* (1965). The controversial idea gained supporters as other early observatories were found around

1962 cont.

d. Isak Dinesen (Karen Christence Dinesen Blixen) (1885-1962), Danish writer, long resident in Africa; a major figure from the publication of her short story collection *Seven Gothic Tales* (1934).

d. Bruno Walter (Bruno Walter Schlesinger) (1876-1962), leading German conductor; a Jewish refugee in the United States from 1941.

d. Charles Laughton (1899-1962), British-American actor who became a film star in *The Private Life of Henry VIII* (1933).

d. Fritz Kreisler (1875-1962), Austrian-American violinist; a very popular concert and recording artist early in the century.

d. Robinson Jeffers (1887-1962), American poet and dramatist; a major figure from the publication of his *Tamar and Other Poems* (1924).

d. Kirsten Flagstad (1895-1962), Norwegian singer; the leading Wagnerian soprano of the late interwar period.

d. e. e. cummings (Edward Estlin Cummings) (1894-1962), American writer; a leading modernist and sometimes stylistically eccentric poet.

several major heptathlon records, among them six of the seven over-7,000-point heptathlon performances on record.

d. Vilhjalmur Stefansson (1879-1962), Canadian-American explorer of Icelandic descent noted for his Arctic explorations, especially his five-year stay (1913-1918) above the Arctic Circle. He also advised Pan American Airways on polar routes (1932-1945).

1963

Bob Dylan emerged as a major folk-rock singer and songwriter, and as a leading antiwar figure, issuing several classic 1960s songs, including his emblematic "The Times They Are a-Changin'," "Blowin' in the Wind," and "Masters of War."

Philip Johnson designed the New York State Theater at Lincoln Center, his use of historic American forms signaling a major break with the International Style and with modernism.

Martin Luther King, Jr., led a desegregation campaign in Birmingham, Alabama (Apr.-Sept.); Eugene "Bull" Connor's police responded with dogs, water hoses, and beatings, jailing more than 2,000 people. Bombings of civil rights offices (May 11) brought rioting and then federal troops. Four African-American children were murdered in the bombing of the Sixteenth Street Baptist Church (Sept. 15).

Martin Luther King, Jr., delivered his "I Have a Dream" speech at the Lincoln Memorial (Aug. 18) to 250,000 people at the "March on Washington,"

1963 cont.

executed. General Duong Van Minh led the military junta that took power.

In Rwanda, Hutu government forces massacred 10,000 to 15,000 defeated Tutsis, sending 200,000 more into exile (1963-1964).

In the Congo (Zaire), United Nations forces completed their defeat of Katangese secession forces (Dec.); Moise Tshombe went into exile.

Greek-Turkish fighting intensified on Cyprus, growing into civil war (1963-1964).

Student demonstrators at New York's Columbia University occupied several campus buildings for six days (Apr.), until the university administration called in city police to evict them, with hundreds of arrests.

The American-Soviet Hot Line Agreement set up a direct emergency line between the leaders of the two powers, in an attempt to minimize the danger of nuclear war.

The Guinea-Bissau War of Independence (1963-1974) began, as Amilcar Cabral led the African Party for the Independence of Guinea and Cape Verde (PAIGC) into a guerrilla war against the Portuguese.

The Soviet-American-British Nuclear Test Ban Treaty banned atmospheric, underwater, and outer-space testing of nuclear weapons, but permitted underground testing.

A Ba'ath Party (Arab Socialist Renaissance Party) coup won control of Syria; Hafez al-Assad, a coup leader, became air force commander.

Anastasio Somoza Debayle became dictator of Nicaragua (1963-1979), succeeding his brother, Luis; both were the sons of earlier dictator Anastasio Somoza Garcia (1933-1956).

A Dominican Republic military coup deposed elected president Juan Bosch Gaviño.

the world, spawning the new field of paleo-astronomy.

The Glen Canyon Dam was completed on the Colorado River, creating a 180-mile-long reservoir 16 miles upstream from Grand Canyon National Park. It was controversial from the start because of damage to the Grand Canyon's fragile ecology, especially with sometimes massive releases of water after the reservoir was filled (1980); many environmentalists have worked to have the dam removed.

Austrian zoologist and psychiatrist Konrad Lorenz published *On Aggression*, exploring his controversial view that some human behavior, notably aggression, is inherited.

The Lascaux cave and its prehistoric paintings were closed to the public, as many of the paintings had begun to deteriorate from human contact. Photographs and copies, like those made by Henri Breuil, remained as public records.

Quasars, originally thought to be close astronomical neighbors, were found by California Institute of Technology astronomers Maarten Schmidt and Jesse Greenstein to be some of the most distant objects known, and therefore possible sources of information on conditions near the beginning of the universe.

Valentina Tereshkova became the first woman in space, piloting the *Vostok 6* Soviet spacecraft (June 16); she orbited the earth 48 times in a 71-hour flight.

The world's largest single radio telescope, 1,000 feet in diameter, was put into operation at Arecibo, Puerto Rico.

Vela Hotel, a series of U.S. military satellites designed to detect nuclear explosions, was in use (from 1963).

Albert Finney starred in the title role in Tony Richardson's film version of Henry Fielding's 1749 novel *Tom Jones,* costarring Susannah York, Hugh Griffith, Edith Evans, Joyce Redman, and Joan Greenwood.

Catherine Deneuve emerged as an international film star in Jacques Demy's *The Umbrellas of Cherbourg.*

David Alfaro Siqueiros began his massive mural *The March of Humanity in Latin America* (1963-1969).

Harold Pinter wrote the screenplay for Joseph Losey's film *The Servant,* starring Dirk Bogarde in the title role opposite James Fox as his doomed "master."

John le Carré published the Cold War espionage-and-disillusion novel *The Spy Who Came In from the Cold.*

Marcello Mastroianni starred as the filmmaker in Federico Fellini's autobiographical film *8½.*

Luchino Visconti's film *The Leopard* starred Burt Lancaster, Alain Delon, and Claudia Cardinale.

Morris Carnovsky made the first of his three appearances as King Lear at the American Shakespeare Theater (1963; 1965; 1975).

The Stuttgart Ballet presented Kenneth MacMillan's ballet *Las Hermanas,* based on Federico García Lorca's *House of Bernardo Alba.*

Tom Courtenay in the title role starred opposite Julie Christie and Mona Washbourne in John Schlesinger's film *Billy Liar,* adapted by Keith Waterhouse and Willis Hall from their 1960 play.

Hello, Dolly! was Michael Stewart's musical adaptation of Thornton Wilder's 1955 play *The Match-*

which marked the high point of the American civil rights movement.

Alabama segregationist governor George Wallace (1963-1967) made his "stand in the schoolhouse door" in a failed attempt to block African-American registration at the University of Alabama (June); National Guard troops federalized by U.S. president John F. Kennedy guaranteed registration there and throughout the state.

d. Medgar Wiley Evers (1925-1963), African-American civil rights leader who was state chairman of the National Association for the Advancement of Colored People (NAACP); he was murdered at his home in Jackson, Mississippi (June 12). Not until 1994 would White supremacist Byron De la Beckwith be convicted of the murder.

Betty Friedan published *The Feminine Mystique,* a central work that helped trigger the revival of the worldwide women's rights movement.

In *Reynold v. Sims,* the U.S. Supreme Court applied the "one man, one vote" doctrine to the House of Representatives and all state legislative offices; the antidiscrimination ruling forced massive national redistricting of electoral district lines.

The President's Commission on the Status of Women issued the landmark report *American Women,* recommending a series of major equal employment, equal pay, and equal educational opportunities initiatives, with greatly enhanced government help for working mothers.

The "Kennedy Round" of General Agreement on Tariffs and Trade (GATT) negotiations began (1963-1967).

After a malfunction of the U.S. nuclear submarine *Thresher,* its hull collapsed (Apr. 10), killing 129 people in the Atlantic Ocean off New Hampshire.

d. Abdul Karim Kassem (1914-1963), Iraqi premier; he was killed during a military coup.

Malaya, Sarawak, Sabah, and Singapore formed Malaysia (Sept. 16), from which Singapore later withdrew (1965).

Soviet spy Kim Philby escaped from Britain to the Soviet Union.

The Federation for the Liberation of Quebec engaged in a series of bombings and other acts of terrorism, largely in Montreal.

The Organization of African Unity (OAU) was founded; it included most African nations, with the conspicuous exception of racist South Africa.

The United States set up an extensive "early warning" radar system in Greenland, England, and Alaska for detecting intercontinental ballistic missiles (ICBMs).

British secretary of war John Profumo resigned after a highly publicized sex-and-state-secrets scandal stemming from his relationship with Christine Keeler, who was simultaneously sleeping with a Soviet diplomat.

The Republic of Kenya became an independent state (Dec. 12).

The Republic of the Gambia became an independent state and Commonwealth member (Feb. 18).

d. Abd el-Krim (1892-1963), Moroccan leader; founder of the Rif Republic (1921) during the Rif War (1921-1926); defeated, he was imprisoned by the French (1926-1947), then escaped to Cairo, where he died, an anticolonial icon in the Arab and Third worlds.

d. Herbert Henry Lehman (1878-1963), American investment banker and liberal Democratic politician; New York governor (1933-1943), first director of the United Nations Relief and Rehabilitation Administration

The Atomic Energy Committee gave J. Robert Oppenheimer the Fermi Award, a move interpreted as a tacit apology for having denied him security clearance (1953).

For their independent work on the shell theory of nuclear structure (1948), German-American physicist Maria Goeppert Mayer and German physicist Hans Daniel Jensen shared the Nobel Prize for physics with Hungarian-American physicist Eugene P. Wigner, for his work on neutron absorption (1936).

Linus Pauling was awarded the Nobel Peace Prize for his campaign against nuclear testing, becoming only the second person (after Marie Curie) to win two Nobel Prizes.

d. Jean Félix Piccard (1884-1963), Swiss-American chemist and aeronautical engineer who, with his twin brother, Auguste Antoine Piccard, was noted for studies of the atmosphere and ocean, setting a world height record in an innovative balloon of his own design (1934).

d. Theodore von Kármán (1881-1963), Hungarian-American aeronautical engineer and physicist, long associated with the California Institute of Technology, whose mathematical analyses were key to the development of supersonic flight and rockets.

maker, starring Carol Channing in the title role as Dolly Levi; it would be the basis for a 1969 film.

Hits from the emerging Beatles included "She Loves You" and "I Want to Hold Your Hand" by John Lennon and Paul McCartney.

Tyrone Guthrie founded Minneapolis's Guthrie Theater; it would become a leading American regional repertory theater.

Greek poet and diplomat George Seferis was awarded the Nobel Prize for literature.

b. Whitney Houston (1963-), African-American singer; a star from her first album, *Whitney Houston* (1986).

d. Aldous Leonard Huxley (1894-1963), leading British writer from the publication of his novel *Crome Yellow* (1921).

d. Georges Braque (1882-1963), French painter; early in the century, with Pablo Picasso, a founder of cubism.

d. Robert Frost (1874-1963), leading American poet on New England themes; a major literary figure from his collection *North of Boston* (1914).

d. Edith Piaf (Giovanna Gassion) (1915-1963), French popular singer best known for "La Vie en Rose," her signature song.

d. William Carlos Williams (1883-1963), American writer best known as a poet, notably for his five-volume *Paterson* (1946-1958).

d. Jean Cocteau (1899-1963), French writer, filmmaker, and painter; best known for his autobiographical *Opium* (1930).

d. Clifford Odets (1906-1963), American writer; a leading political playwright of the 1930s; a major figure in the Group Theater.

In *Gideon v. Wainwright,* the U.S. Supreme Court affirmed the constitutional right to counsel of indigent state criminal defendants as a matter of equality before the law.

Arthur Ashe became the first African-American tennis player named to America's Davis Cup team.

Australian tennis player Margaret Smith Court won the women's singles title at Wimbledon, her first of three there (1963; 1965; 1970).

James Baldwin published *The Fire Next Time,* essays powerfully supporting the civil rights movement and warning of greater violence to come.

The great salad oil swindle was exposed. From the late 1950s, commodities-futures buyer Anthony (Tino) De Angelis and his firm traded and borrowed on huge amounts of nonexistent salad oil. After the fraud was exposed, De Angelis was convicted and imprisoned, and his firm went bankrupt, as did two other commodity brokerage firms.

The Netherlands' Philips Corporation introduced cassettes for music-quality audiotapes; these would become widely popular in succeeding decades with the development of pocket-size tape players.

d. John XXIII (Angelo Giuseppe Roncali) (1881-1963), Italian priest and pope (1958-1963) who introduced massive changes into the Roman Catholic Church; his accomplishments included several major encyclicals, including *Pacem in Terris,* and the convening of Vatican II (1962-1965). He was succeeded by Italian cardinal Giovanni Battista Montini, who became Pope Paul VI (1963-1978).

d. W. E. B. (William Edward Burghardt) Du Bois (1868-1963), American organizer, teacher, historian, and writer; one of the leading African-Americans of his time.

1963 cont.

(UNRRA) (1943-1946), and New York senator (1949-1956).

d. Hugh Gaitskell (1906-1963), British Labour Party leader (1955-1963).

1964

Incumbent liberal Democrat Lyndon B. Johnson massively defeated conservative Arizona senator Barry Goldwater for the U.S. presidency, winning his first and only full term in office (1965-1969). Goldwater, strongly supported by the most conservative and self-isolating elements of his party, had defeated liberal New York governor Nelson Rockefeller for the Republican presidential nomination.

Congress enacted the Tonkin Gulf Resolution (Aug. 7), making it possible for President Lyndon B. Johnson to commit major American forces to the Vietnam War; the resolution followed two reported and later widely questioned attacks on American vessels by North Vietnamese torpedo boats in the Gulf of Tonkin.

Leonid Brezhnev succeeded Nikita Khrushchev as general secretary of the Soviet Communist Party (1964-1982).

President Lyndon B. Johnson introduced his "Great Society" slogan and a host of major social welfare proposals in a Madison Square Garden speech (Oct. 31).

After the departure of United Nations peacekeeping forces (June 30), Soviet- and Cuban-supported Christophate Gbenye's forces took much of the northeastern Congo (Zaire) and many European hostages; Belgian paratroopers rescued 1,600 to 1,700 hostages at Stanleyville (Nov. 25-27).

At the Berkeley campus of the University of California, a college administration ban on the distribution of political material generated off campus grew into a much wider

The first successful lung transplant was performed by a University of Mississippi (Jackson) team led by James D. Hardy.

The surgeon general's report on smoking and health included the first official U.S. government warning on the dangers of smoking, especially the risks of lung cancer; it was the first of many such warnings, which would later be printed on cigarette packs.

Murray Gell-Mann theorized that quarks, subatomic particles with fractional charges existing in various "flavors," were the fundamental building blocks of matter. He, Richard Feynman, and, independently, George Zweig originally proposed three quarks, to which Sheldon Lee Glashow added a proposed fourth, with a property he called "charm."

The global satellite communications system Intelsat (International Telecommunications Satellite Organization) was founded, originally by 11 nations, the U.S. arm being Comsat (Communications Satellite Corporation); it would grow to more than 100 member countries, with multiple satellites allowing two-way communications.

American and Soviet researchers independently discovered element 104, which the Soviets called kurchatonium (after their nuclear physicist Igor Vasilyevich Kurchatov) and the Amer-

1963 cont.

d. Paul Hindemith (1895-1963), German composer; a leading figure in 20th-century music.

d. Sylvia Plath (1932-1963), American poet and novelist; most of her poetry was published posthumously; her only novel, the semiautobiographical *The Bell Jar,* appeared in the year of her suicide.

1964

With the nearly disastrous 1962 Cuban Missile Crisis so recent a memory, Stanley Kubrick's classic anti–nuclear war comedy *Dr. Strangelove, or How I Learned to Stop Worrying and Love the Bomb* struck a chord heard worldwide. Kubrick cowrote, directed, and produced the film, which starred Peter Sellers (in three roles), George C. Scott, and Sterling Hayden.

Richard Brook directed the Royal Shakespeare Company production of Peter Weiss's play *Marat/Sade,* starring Patrick Magee, Ian Richardson, and Glenda Jackson, who emerged as a star as Charlotte Corday, a role she would reprise in the 1966 film.

Richard Burton as unswerving churchman Thomas à Becket starred opposite Peter O'Toole as Henry II in *Becket,* Peter Glenville's film version of the 1959 Jean Anouilh play.

Russian poet Anna Akhmatova, long silenced under Stalinism, published *Requiem,* her elegy to the millions who were murdered by the Soviet state during the Stalin period; it was one of the central artistic and social documents of the late Soviet period.

The Beatles made their first film, their classic *A Hard Day's Night,* title song by John Lennon and Paul McCartney, directed by Richard Lester. They also made their wildly successful first American tour, becoming world celebrities with a number one hit, "Can't Buy Me Love."

In the most important American civil rights legislation of the 20th century, the Civil Rights Act of 1964 outlawed workplace and public place discriminatory practices based on race, color, sex (though not sexual orientation), religion, or national origin; set equal voting standards; attacked educational discrimination; and provided enforcement mechanisms. The Equal Employment Opportunity Commission (EEOC) it established would enforce a wide range of other antidiscrimination laws.

Civil rights workers James Chaney, Andrew Goodman, and Michael Schwerner were murdered in Neshoba County, Mississippi (June 21). No local murder charges were ever filed, but seven Ku Klux Klan members were later convicted of conspiracy. The killings inspired the film *Mississippi Burning* (1988).

In *Heart of Atlanta Motel, Inc. v. United States,* the U.S. Supreme Court outlawed discrimination in all facilities serving interstate travelers.

American civil rights leader Martin Luther King, Jr., was awarded the Nobel Peace Prize.

Congress passed the Wilderness Act, establishing the National Wilderness Preservation System, starting with 9 million acres of federal wilderness that had been managed as "wild and primitive" since 1924. In this wilderness, the act would ban some activities, such as logging, dams, and permanent development, while allowing others, such as hiking, camping, fish-

confrontation with the emerging New Left on a series of Vietnam War–related issues, then grew into the nationwide antiwar Berkeley Free Speech Movement (1964-1965).

Fannie Lou Hamer, Charles Evers, and Hodding Carter III led in the formation of the Mississippi Freedom Democratic Party, which challenged racist Mississippi regular Democratic Party delegates to the Democratic National Convention.

The 24th Amendment to the U.S. Constitution outlawed the poll tax, used since the post–Civil War Reconstruction period to bar southern African-Americans from voting.

Labour Party leader Harold Wilson became Britain's prime minister (1964-1970; 1974-1976).

Jomo Kenyatta became the first president of Kenya (1964-1978).

The Mozambique National Liberation Front (FRELIMO) mounted a guerrilla war of independence against Portuguese colonial forces (1964-1974).

A military coup deposed elected Bolivian president Victor Paz Estenssoro (Nov.); generals René Barrientos Ortuño and Alfredo Ovando Candía became copresidents of the new military government.

Elected Brazilian president João Goulart (Mar.) was deposed by a military coup; Marshal Humberto de Alencar Castello Branco headed the new military government.

Haitian dictator François "Papa Doc" Duvalier declared himself president for life.

The Palestine Liberation Organization (PLO) was founded.

The Republic of Malawi became an independent state and Commonwealth member (July 6); Hastings Banda

icans rutherfordium (after Ernest Rutherford, head of Britain's Cavendish Laboratory).

American surgeon Michael De Bakey did key early work in surgically opening blocked heart arteries, leading to the development of the coronary bypass operation (1967).

The Moog synthesizer, the first true electronic synthesizer, developed by American inventor Robert Arthur Moog, was introduced by Moog, Buchla and Synket.

China began testing nuclear weapons, exploding an atomic bomb at a test site in the Lop Nor desert, in western Xinjiang province (Oct. 16).

The first three-person crew was launched into space aboard the Soviet spacecraft *Voskhod 1* (Oct. 12).

Various U.S. Ranger spacecraft were launched, photographing the moon; *Ranger 7* made a "hard" (crash) landing on its surface.

The U.S. Bureau of National Standards developed a more accurate atomic clock, using cesium-133; its oscillations were adopted as the new international standard "atomic second."

Harlow Shapley published *The View from a Distant Star,* a work popularizing new understandings in astronomy.

Dorothy Crowfoot Hodgkin won the Nobel Prize for chemistry for her use of X-ray crystallography and computers to analyze large organic molecules.

German-American biochemist Konrad Emil Bloch received the Nobel Prize for medicine or physiology for his pioneering work on radioactive tracers in the body (1950).

Giacomo Manzù completed the doors of Rome's St. Peter's, calling the work *Portal of Death*.

Henry Fonda, Walter Matthau, and Larry Hagman starred in the very sober anti–nuclear war drama *Fail-Safe*, directed by Sidney Lumet.

Jason Robards, Jr., and Barbara Loden starred in Arthur Miller's play *After the Fall*; Loden portrayed an actress who commits suicide, thought by many to represent Miller's former wife, Marilyn Monroe.

Barbra Streisand became a major star in the title role of *Funny Girl*, Jule Styne's musical about Fanny Brice, costarring Sidney Chaplin.

Robert Indiana decorated Philip Johnson's New York Pavilion at the New York World's Fair with his huge pop art poster *EAT*.

Zero Mostel starred in Jerry Bock's Broadway musical *Fiddler on the Roof*, based on Sholem Aleichem's *Tevye's Daughters*.

Burt Lancaster as the rebel general starred opposite Kirk Douglas and Fredric March in John Frankenheimer's *Seven Days in May*, a film about an attempted military coup.

Robert Lowell published his poems *For the Union Dead*.

Irene Worth starred opposite John Gielgud in Edward Albee's absurdist, rather opaque play *Tiny Alice*.

Michael Cacoyannis directed the film *Zorba the Greek*, starring Anthony Quinn in the title role, opposite Alan Bates and Lila Kedrova; based on the 1946 Nikos Kazantzakis novel.

Roger Daltrey, Pete Townshend, Keith Moon, and John Entwhistle founded the Who.

ing, scientific studies, and — more controversially — hunting, mining, and livestock grazing, the focus of attack by many environmentalists.

The Land and Water Conservation Fund Act (amended 1986) established a fund to purchase or lease land, under land trusts or conservation easements, to protect an area's environment, generally in or near national parks.

In *New York Times Company v. Sullivan*, the U.S. Supreme Court ruled that a public official alleging libel must prove "actual malice."

U.S. president Lyndon B. Johnson initiated the "War on Poverty," developing programs such as the Job Corps, Head Start, and VISTA and establishing the Office of Economic Opportunity.

The University of California at Los Angeles basketball team, coached by John Wooden, defeated Duke University to win the National Collegiate Athletic Association (NCAA) Division I title (effectively the national college championship); Wooden-coached UCLA teams would go on to win 9 more national championships in the next 11 years.

At the Tokyo Olympics, American swimmer Don Schollander became the first swimmer ever to win four Olympic gold medals: for the 400- and 800-meter relays, 400-meter freestyle (a world record), and 100-meter freestyle (an Olympic record).

Barefoot Ethiopian runner Abebe Bikila became the first man ever to win two Olympic marathons, taking his second at Tokyo.

British automobile racer Donald Malcolm Campbell set a new land speed record of over 403 miles per hour and a new water speed record of over 276 miles per hour in a hydroplane, which he would die trying to better (1967); his father, Malcolm, had broken the 300-mile-per-hour land record (1935).

was its first prime minister (1964-1966) and then president (1966-1994).

Tanganyika, Zanzibar, and Pemba merged into the United Republic of Tanzania (Apr. 26), led by Tanganyikan independence movement leader Julius Kambarage Nyerere (1964-1985).

Zambia (formerly Northern Rhodesia) became an independent state (Oct. 24), led by independence movement leader Kenneth Kaunda, who became president (1964-1991).

Malta became an independent state and Commonwealth member.

d. Jawaharlal Nehru (1889-1964), Indian Congress Party leader; the first prime minister of independent India (1947-1964). He was the father of Indira Gandhi, brother of Madame Vijaya Pandit, and grandfather of Rajiv Gandhi.

d. Douglas MacArthur (1880-1964), American World War II commanding general in the Philippines and southwest Pacific and Korean War commander until dismissed by President Harry S. Truman (Apr. 1951); he was the son of General Arthur MacArthur.

d. Emilio Aguinaldo (1869-1964), leader of Philippine forces during the Philippine War of Independence (1898) and president of the first Philippine Republic (1899-1901), until his capture by American forces.

d. Herbert Clark Hoover (1874-1964), the 31st president of the United States (1929-1933).

d. Nancy Langhorne Astor (1879-1964), American-born British right-wing politician; a leader of the pro-appeasement Cliveden Set in the 1930s; she was the first woman member of Parliament (1919-1945).

d. Palmiro Togliatti (1893-1964), leader of the Italian Communist Party (1926-1964).

d. Leo Szilard (1867-1964), Hungarian-American nuclear physicist who, after fleeing Germany (1933), sparked and helped lead American development of the atomic bomb (1939-1945). He later organized a scientists' petition against dropping the bomb on Japan without warning (1945). After Hiroshima and Nagasaki, he worked for demilitarization and international control of nuclear technology, leaving nuclear physics for molecular biology.

d. Rachel Louise Carson (1907-1964), American ecologist, teacher, and writer best known for her books *The Sea Around Us* (1951) and *Silent Spring* (1962), fundamental to later ecological and green movements.

d. Alfred Blalock (1899-1964), American surgeon who first performed the operation that corrected heart defects in blue babies (1944), saving many infants and laying the basis for open-heart surgery.

d. J. B. S. (John Burdon Sanderson) Haldane (1897-1964), British geneticist who did key work in population genetics and evolution; also a popular and influential writer, known for his *Science and Ethics* (1928).

d. Norbert Wiener (1894-1964), American mathematician who developed the theory of cybernetics and the use of feedback to control communications systems, as outlined in his *Cybernetics, or Control and Communication in the Animal and the Machine* (1948).

Tom Courtenay and Dirk Bogarde starred in Joseph Losey's antiwar film *King and Country.*

Andy Warhol produced *Shot Red Marilyn,* his silk screen image of Marilyn Monroe, one of the most famous "pop art" works.

French writer and philosopher Jean-Paul Sartre was awarded the Nobel Prize for literature but declined it.

d. Sean O'Casey (John Casey) (1880-1964), Irish playwright; a world figure in 20th-century theater for his Irish Civil War plays *Shadow of a Gunman* (1923) and *Juno and the Paycock* (1924), and for his Easter Rising play, *The Plough and the Stars* (1926).

d. Cole Porter (1893-1964), American composer and lyricist; a leading figure in the musical theater and very popular songwriter.

d. Alexander Archipenko (1887-1964), Russian sculptor; a leading modernist who became an early cubist, explorer of the concept of inner space, and user of new materials.

d. (Mary) Flannery O'Connor (1925-1964), American novelist and poet, much of whose work is set in Georgia.

d. Eddie Cantor (Edward Israel Iskowitz) (1892-1964), American musical theater and film star; a leading singer and comedian.

d. Edith Sitwell (1887-1964), British poet and critic; a leading experimentalist of the interwar period.

Cassius Clay defeated Sonny Liston to become world heavyweight boxing champion; joining the Black Muslims, Clay changed his name to Muhammad Ali.

In a case that shocked the nation, young Kitty Genovese was killed on the streets of New York (Mar. 13), but not one of the people who heard her screaming for 35 minutes called the police or came to her aid.

Australian tennis player Rod Laver won the first of his five world men's singles titles as a professional (1964-1967; 1970); he also would win the men's doubles title twice (1965; 1967).

A passenger train derailed near Custoias, Portugal (July 26); 94 people died.

At Jervis Bay, New South Wales, Australia, 82 people died when the destroyer *Voyager* collided with the aircraft carrier *Melbourne.*

During the unloading of the Egyptian ship *Star of Alexandria* at Bône, Algeria, its munitions cargo exploded (July 23), killing 100 people.

d. Beaverbrook (William Maxwell Aitken; Lord Beaverbrook) (1879-1964), Canadian financier who became a powerful British Conservative press baron and politician.

d. Harold Hitz Burton (1888-1964), American lawyer, politician, and conservative U.S. Supreme Court justice (1945-1958).

American bombing and harbor mining began in Vietnam, and massive American forces arrived, totaling more than 150,000 by year's end, as the Vietnam War began (1965-1973).

Civil war in the Dominican Republic pitted the forces of Juan Bosch Gaviño, the elected president deposed by a military coup (1963), against the Dominican military. American forces totaling 21,000 intervened on behalf of the military; they were later replaced by United Nations peacekeeping forces (Apr. 1965-June 1966).

In Indonesia, government-backed massacres of 200,000 to 300,000 people followed a failed Communist coup.

Pakistani armored forces and aircraft unsuccessfully attacked Indian Kashmir (Sept. 1). Indian forces counterattacked and also responded with successful attacks in the Punjab. United Nations mediation brought a cease-fire (Sept. 27) that ended the India-Pakistan War.

The Voting Rights Act of 1965 enfranchised many southern African-Americans by outlawing discriminatory "tests" used to disenfranchise them, helping lay the basis for the emergence of a major new African-American electorate and body of elected officials.

Congo (Zaire) president Joseph Kasavubu was deposed; General Mobutu Sese Seko (Joseph Mobutu) took power (Nov. 25).

Fatah (Palestine Liberation Movement), led by Yasir Arafat, went over to guerrilla war against Israel, mounting cross-border attacks from bases in neighboring Arab countries.

Ian Smith became prime minister of Southern Rhodesia (1965-1979), leading the ultimately failed effort to preserve White minority rule in what would become Zimbabwe; Southern Rhodesia seceded from Britain, becoming the independent nation of Rhodesia (Nov.).

Houari Boumedienne took power in Algeria by coup, imprisoning former leader Ahmed Ben Bella.

Aleksei Leonov became the first astronaut to take a space walk, outside the Soviet spacecraft *Voskhod 2* (Mar. 18); like other early space-walkers, he wore a space suit and was tethered to his craft.

The Soviet spacecraft *Venera 3* crashed onto Venus, becoming the first spacecraft to reach another planet.

In the new Gemini series of U.S. spacecraft (1965-1966), the Americans sent their first two-person crew into space, Virgil (Gus) Grissom and John Young, aboard *Gemini 3;* had their first space walk, by Edward Higgins White II, from *Gemini 4* (June 3); and completed the first rendezvous in space, with *Gemini 6* and *Gemini 7* (Dec. 15).

The U.S. spacecraft *Mariner 4* (launched Nov. 28, 1964) flew by Mars (July 14), sending back new information about the planet that revealed moonlike craters but no sign of canals, which had been posited (1877), giving rise to the notion that Mars held not only life but also civilization.

The U.S. space probes *Ranger 8* and *Ranger 9* photographed and crash-landed on the moon, with *Ranger 7* producing more than 17,000 photographs.

France became the third nation to move into space, launching its first satellite, *A-1* (Nov. 26).

The Intelsat satellite *Early Bird (Intelsat 1)* was launched (Apr. 6), the first communications satellite for commercial purposes and the first piece of the worldwide Intelsat satellite communications system.

Bell Laboratories scientists Arno H. Penzias and Robert W. Wilson detected background

Omar Sharif starred in the title role opposite Julie Christie as Lara in David Lean's epic film *Doctor Zhivago,* adapted by Robert Bolt from Boris Pasternak's 1955 novel, set in World War I, the Russian Revolution, and the Russian Civil War.

Giulietta Masina starred in the title role in Federico Fellini's *Juliet of the Spirits,* his fantasy-filled exploration of the inner world of a woman in personal crisis.

Henry Moore sculpted his massive *Reclining Figure* at New York City's Lincoln Center.

Julie Christie, Dirk Bogarde, and Laurence Harvey starred in John Schlesinger's film *Darling,* set by writer Frederic Raphael among the "beautiful people" of trendy London.

Alex Haley and Malcolm X published *The Autobiography of Malcolm X,* which would be the basis for Spike Lee's 1992 film biography.

Jerry Garcia, Bob Wier, Ron McKernan, Phil Lesh, and Bill Kreutzmann founded the Grateful Dead.

Julie Andrews and Christopher Plummer starred as Maria and Georg von Trapp in the film version of *The Sound of Music,* directed by Robert Wise.

Jerzy Kosinski published his autobiographical first novel, *The Painted Bird,* about a homeless child in Nazi-held Europe during World War II.

Richard Burton starred as burnt-out British Cold War spy Alec Leamas opposite Claire Bloom and Oskar Werner in Martin Ritt's film version of John le Carre's 1963 novel *The Spy Who Came In from the Cold.*

The Beatles starred in their second film, *Help!* The associated album included the song "Yesterday." They also issued another album, *Rubber Soul.*

A period of recurrent famines and epidemic diseases that would kill millions began in the Sahel, on the southern verge of the Sahara Desert, as civil wars, population growth, and desertification exacerbated by ill-considered land use schemes created many millions of refugees. During the continuing civil wars in the region, several combatants refused to allow food and medical supplies to reach the sick and starving, greatly intensifying the crises.

Boston Unitarian minister James Reeb, participating in civil rights marches in Selma, Alabama, was severely beaten (Mar. 9) and died two days later. Three Whites were charged with his murder; all were acquitted (Dec.). Detroit civil rights activist Viola Liuzzo was killed while working in a voter registration drive in Selma (Mar. 25). Three Ku Klux Klan members were later imprisoned for conspiracy to murder her.

Massive race riots erupted in the African-American Watts district of Los Angeles; 35 people died, hundreds were injured, and property damage was estimated at $250 million.

In *Griswold v. Connecticut,* the U.S. Supreme Court restated that the right to privacy included the right of Planned Parenthood counselors and doctors in general to provide contraceptive information to married couples and that couples had the right to receive and use that advice without government interference.

With passage of the Mills Act, U.S. president Lyndon B. Johnson established Medicare and Medicaid, both major features of his "Great Society" program.

Cesar Chavez led the California-based United Farm Workers Organizing Committee in the table grape workers' strike (1965-1970), which became La Causa (The Cause); engaging in personal hunger strikes, he gained massive labor and liberal support and mounted a national boycott.

Nicolae Ceausescu became general secretary of the Romanian Communist Party, succeeding Gheorghe Gheorghiu-Dej as national leader (1965-1989). He officially became president in 1967.

The Maldives became an independent state (July 25).

Singapore became an independent state and Commonwealth member (Aug. 9).

d. Winston Leonard Spencer Churchill (1874-1965), World War II British Conservative prime minister (1940-1945; 1951-1953). A notable speaker and prolific writer, he also had been First Lord of the Admiralty (1911-1915; 1939); a major figure in the development of the Cold War.

d. Adlai Ewing Stevenson (1900-1965), Democratic governor of Illinois (1949-1953) and twice unsuccessful Democratic presidential nominee (1952; 1956).

d. Farouk I (1920-1965), the last king of Egypt (1936-1952); deposed by the republican coup (1952), then going into exile.

d. Frances (Fannie Coralie) Perkins (1882-1965), American political figure; Franklin D. Roosevelt's secretary of labor, the first woman cabinet member (1933-1945).

d. Gheorghe Gheorghiu-Dej (1901-1965), communist premier of Romania (1952-1965); a hard-line Stalinist who before his death in office had moved away from Soviet domination.

d. Henry Agard Wallace (1888-1965), American political figure; New Deal secretary of agriculture (1933-1940), vice president (1941-1945), and secretary of commerce (1945-1946); failed presidential nominee of the Progressive Party (1948).

d. Joseph Clark Grew (1880-1965), American diplomat; as ambassador to Japan (1932-1941), he repeatedly warned of Japan's intent to go to war with the United States, and early in 1941 he specifically warned of a possible attack on Pearl Harbor.

cosmic microwave radiation, supporting the "big bang" theory of the development of the cosmos.

Jacques Cousteau published *World Without Sun* and also led an aquanautic team that spent 23 days underwater in a bathyscaphe, studying the Mediterranean Sea. That same year, a U.S. Navy team spent 45 days underwater off California in *Sealab II*.

The first computer language designed for use by the general public, BASIC (beginner's all-purpose symbolic instruction code), was developed by John Kemeny and Thomas Kurtz.

R. D. Laing established pioneer homelike small-group settings for the communal treatment of mental patients in London; his success would lead to the adoption of this approach in other countries, notably in North America.

Soviet agriculturalist Trofim Lysenko finally lost his position as director of the Institute of Genetics, where for a quarter century he had purged any researcher who dissented from his conclusions on inheritance of acquired characteristics (1929).

Insulin was synthesized by American biochemist Robert Bruce Merrifield.

Kevlar, the superstrong synthetic fiber used in bulletproof vests, tires, and spacecraft, was developed by American chemist Stephanie L. Kwolek.

Using the recently invented laser (1960), Americans Emmet N. Leith and Juris Upatnieks developed the first practical holograms, using patterns of light reflections to convey a three-dimensional photograph, originally envisioned by Dennis Gabor (1947). Hard to duplicate,

Rod Steiger starred in the title role in Sidney Lumet's film *The Pawnbroker,* about a Jewish concentration camp survivor in New York's East Harlem who ultimately finds that it may be possible to begin to live again.

Larry Rivers painted and sculpted the large, realistic mural *The History of the Russian Revolution.*

Jim Morrison, Ray Manzarek, Robby Krieger, and John Densmore founded the Doors.

Stanley Kramer's film version of the 1962 Katherine Anne Porter novel *Ship of Fools* starred Vivien Leigh, Simone Signoret, and Oskar Werner.

Richard Kiley starred in the roles of Cervantes and Don Quixote in the Mitch Lee–Joe Darion musical *Man of La Mancha.*

Paul Simon and Art Garfunkel had their first hit album *Wednesday Morning, 3 A.M.* The album included the song "Sounds of Silence," written by Simon.

Soviet novelist Mikhail Sholokhov was awarded the Nobel Prize for literature.

d. T. S. (Thomas Stearns) Eliot (1888-1965), American-born British writer and critic whose work in the 1920s greatly influenced the course of modernism in poetry.

d. Dorothea Lange (1895-1965), leading American photographer, most notably during the Great Depression and World War II.

d. Lorraine Hansberry (1930-1965), American writer; a major figure from the staging of her first play, *A Raisin in the Sun* (1959).

d. Nat "King" Cole (Nathaniel Adams Coles) (1917-1965), American jazz pianist and bandleader; a leading popular singer from the 1940s.

American consumer advocate Ralph Nader published *Unsafe at Any Speed,* his indictment of dangerously or defectively designed cars, emerging as a leading consumer advocate. His exposé helped spark passage of the National Traffic and Motor Vehicle Safety Act (1966), which brought automobile design under federal government regulation.

Massive Bay of Bengal cyclones killed an estimated 40,000 to 45,000 people (June 1-2).

Off Nassau, Bahamas, the American cruise ship *Yarmouth Castle* caught fire and sank (Nov. 13), killing 89 people; tighter inspection of passenger ships resulted.

Satchel (Leroy Robert) Paige appeared in his final major league baseball game with the Cleveland Indians; at approximately 59, he became the oldest man to play in a professional major league game.

An Eastern DC-7B crashed into the Atlantic Ocean after takeoff from New York City's Kennedy airport (Feb. 8); 84 people died.

The United Nations Children's Fund (UNICEF) was awarded the Nobel Peace Prize.

d. Martin Buber (1878-1965), Austrian-born Jewish philosopher and theologian; founder of the German-Jewish periodical *Der Jude* (1916) and best known for his work *I and Thou* (1923); after dismissal from his German university post (1933), he emigrated to Palestine (1938).

d. Bernard Baruch (1870-1965), American stockbroker who became an economic adviser to several presidents, starting with Woodrow Wilson. He chaired World War I's War Industries Board.

d. Edward R. (Roscoe) Murrow (1908-1965), American journalist who broadcast from London during the Blitz (from 1940); he was later noted for

1965 cont.

d. Syngman Rhee (1875-1965), first president of South Korea (1948-1960), who ruled absolutely in the later years of his presidency and was deposed by a pro-democracy rising.

d. Pedro Albizu Campos (1891-1965), Puerto Rican lawyer; head of the Nationalist Party, who was imprisoned for allegedly trying to organize an armed rebellion (1936-1943), after Puerto Rican nationalists tried to assassinate U.S. president Harry S. Truman (1950-1953), and after five congressmen were wounded in the House of Representatives (1954-1964).

holograms would be widely used for credit cards.

American chemist Robert Burns Woodward received the Nobel Prize for chemistry for his synthesis of large organic molecules such as quinine (1944) and chlorophyll (1960).

Jacques Monod, François Jacob, and André Lwoff shared the Nobel Prize for physiology or medicine for their work on gene operation.

Richard Phillips Feynman, Julian S. Schwinger, and Shinichiro Tomonaga shared the Nobel Prize for physics, for their independent contributions to quantum electrodynamics.

d. Albert Schweitzer (1875-1965), German physician, philosopher, and musician best known as a medical missionary in Africa (from 1913).

1966

Massive American forces, numbering more than 400,000 by year's end, fought in alliance with South Vietnamese forces in an unsuccessful guerrilla war in South Vietnam; they were unable even to secure the outskirts of Saigon, while American warplanes attacked North Vietnam and unsuccessfully attacked supply lines to the south through Cambodia. Sharp opposition to the war developed in the United States.

In a failed, disastrous attempt to create an entirely egalitarian society in China, Mao Zedong initiated the Cultural Revolution (1966-1969), creating the Red Guards, millions of youths operating in bands, who attacked China's educators, artists, intellectuals, and dissenters, in the process destroying much of China's remaining artistic and cultural artifacts. Mao's wife, Jiang Qing, played a major role in organizing and directing the attack.

American sex researchers William Masters and Virginia Johnson published *Human Sexual Response,* their controversial and best-selling report based on laboratory study of human sexual activity at their Reproductive Biology Research Foundation in St. Louis, Missouri. The work exposed many misconceptions about human sexual activity and sparked a reevaluation of human sexuality, especially over the role of women, previously often seen as passive, subservient, and pleasureless.

The French Academy of Medicine first developed and used a clinical definition of death: not heart stoppage, but absence of electrical activity in the brain, as measured on an electroencephalograph (EEG); this concept of "brain death" came to be widely adopted. Because a person's circulatory and respiratory systems

d. (William) Somerset Maugham (1874-1965), popular British writer of novels, plays, short stories, memoirs, and essays; many of his works were later dramatized.

d. Myra Hess (1890-1965), British pianist; a World War II figure for her National Gallery concerts, many of them during the Blitz.

d. Shirley Jackson (1916-1965), American writer best known for her novels and short stories.

d. Dorothy Dandridge (1923-1965), breakthrough African-American film star in the mid-1950s.

his *See It Now* and *Person to Person* television programs and was a key opponent of Senator Joseph McCarthy in the early 1950s.

d. Felix Frankfurter (1882-1965), American legal scholar and U.S. Supreme Court justice (1939-1965); a leading liberal who became one of the leading conservative members of the Court.

d. Malcolm X (Malcolm Little) (1925-1965), African-American militant leader; he was assassinated in New York City (Feb. 21), apparently by rivals in the Nation of Islam (Black Muslims), of which he had been a key leader before leaving to found the Muslim Mosque (1964).

Paul Scofield as Thomas More starred opposite Robert Shaw as Henry VIII in Fred Zinnemann's film version of Robert Bolt's 1960 play, *A Man for All Seasons,* costarring Wendy Hiller, Orson Welles, and Leo McKern.

Franco Zeffirelli's production of Samuel Barber's opera *Antony and Cleopatra* opened Lincoln Center's new Metropolitan Opera House.

Vanessa Redgrave created Edinburgh teacher Jean Brodie in Jay Presson Allen's stage version of the 1961 Muriel Spark novel *The Prime of Miss Jean Brodie.*

Jessica Tandy and Hume Cronyn starred as the couple seeking to maintain their sanity in an unbalanced world in Edward Albee's play *A Delicate Balance.*

In *Miranda v. Arizona,* the U.S. Supreme Court set forth the "Miranda rules," strongly protecting the rights of criminal suspects, requiring that they be represented by counsel, and invalidating evidence obtained without required "Miranda" warnings.

Race riots erupted in several major American cities, including New York, Chicago, and Detroit; in New York, armed clashes occurred between National Guard troops and African-American urban guerrillas.

Ex-Marine Charles Whitman killed his wife and mother (July 31), then killed 16 more people and wounded 30, shooting from the University of Texas observation tower (Aug. 1); he was ultimately killed by police gunfire; an autopsy revealed that he had a brain tumor.

The Tashkent Agreement (Jan. 19) ended the India-Pakistan War; Indian forces withdrew from Pakistan.

Indira Gandhi succeeded Lal Bahadur Shastri as prime minister of India (1966-1977; 1980-1984).

Jean Bédel Bokassa took power by coup in the Central African Republic (1966-1979).

Jonas Savimbi founded the National Union for the Total Independence of Angola (UNITA); it became the third of the guerrilla forces fighting the Portuguese during the Angolan War of Independence (1961-1975) and would later fight the Popular Movement for the Liberation of Angola (MPLA) during the Angolan Civil War (1975-).

The long Namibian War of Independence began (1966-1988), led by the Southwest Africa People's Organization of Namibia (SWAPO), with Angolan, Soviet, and Cuban assistance.

Soviet literary dissenters Andrei Sinyavsky and Yuli Daniel were imprisoned (1966-1970), signaling a hardening of Soviet government attitudes and the end of the "thaw" of the post-Stalin era.

Yakubu Gowon took power by military coup in Nigeria (July) and deposed General Johnson Aguyi-Ironsi, who had earlier taken power by coup (Jan.).

A military coup deposed President Kwame Nkrumah of Ghana, replacing him with General Joseph Ankrah.

The Chad National Liberation Front (Frolinat) was founded, beginning the long guerrilla insurgency that would later become the Chad Civil War (1975-1987).

Edward William Brooke was elected to the U.S. Senate, becoming the first African-American senator in American history (1967-1979).

Joaquin Balaguer became the elected president of the Dominican Republic, defeating Juan Bosch Gaviño and ending the civil war.

might be kept functioning on a minimal level by various external machines, even with the brain dead, this led to complicated questions about the patient's "right to die," especially what limits, if any, should be placed on the use of such extraordinary measures to keep a patient "alive" and who should place those limits: patient (in prior statements), family, or physicians.

The Soviet Union's *Luna 9* satellite made the first "soft" landing on the moon (Feb. 3), as opposed to a "hard" (crash) landing. The U.S. space probe *Surveyor 1* also made its first soft landing on the moon (June 2). The Soviet *Luna 10* was the first craft to orbit the moon (Apr. 3). Numerous American probes would do the same. All would send back detailed photographs of the moon, including the hidden far side.

The U.S. spacecraft *Gemini 8* performed the first space docking with an unpiloted craft (Mar. 16).

Unable to continue nuclear testing in Algeria after that nation gained its independence, France began nuclear weapons testing on Moruroa (1966-1974), in French Polynesia, and to a lesser extent on neighboring Fangataufa, in more than 40 open-air tests contaminating large areas of the Pacific and the Pacific Rim; radioactive fallout from one especially "dirty" test (Sept. 1966) reached Western Samoa, 2,000 miles downwind. After 1974, tests would be conducted underground.

Partial meltdown occurred in a nuclear breeder reactor at the Enrico Fermi nuclear plant on Lake Michigan (Oct. 5); had it not been brought under control, much of the area around Detroit, just 30 miles away, might have been contaminated.

Richard Burton and Elizabeth Taylor starred in Mike Nichols's film version of Edward Albee's 1962 play *Who's Afraid of Virginia Woolf?*

Liv Ullmann starred as the mute actress opposite Bibi Andersson as her nurse in Ingmar Bergman's film *Persona*.

Robert Preston as Henry II and Rosemary Harris as Eleanor of Aquitaine starred in the play *The Lion in Winter* by James Goldman.

Susan Sontag published her influential early essay collection *Against Interpretation*.

Gene Roddenberry's classic science fiction television series *Star Trek* began, starring William Shatner as Captain Kirk and Leonard Nimoy as Spock (1966-1969).

Jill Haworth as Sally Bowles, Joel Grey, and Bert Convy starred in the stage musical *Cabaret* by Fred Ebb and John Kander, based on John Van Druten's 1951 play *I Am a Camera,* itself based on Christopher Isherwood's 1939 novel *Goodbye to Berlin.*

Truman Capote published *In Cold Blood,* his "nonfiction novel" about a Kansas mass murder and the murderers' trial and execution.

Michael Caine became an international star in *Alfie,* Lewis Gilbert's film written by Bill Naughton from his own play.

German-Jewish poet-playwright Nelly Sachs and Galician-Israeli writer Shmuel Yoseph Agnon shared the Nobel Prize for literature.

d. Le Corbusier (Charles Edouard Jenneret) (1887-1966), Swiss-French architect and painter; a key theoretician in 20th-century architecture, whose work often featured geometric forms and rough concrete.

Mass murderer Richard Speck killed eight student nurses in Chicago (July 13-14); a ninth, who hid under a bed, survived. Captured, Speck was imprisoned for life.

Betty Friedan founded and became the first president of the National Organization for Women (NOW), a key organization in the reviving women's movement.

Some Student Nonviolent Coordinating Committee (SNCC) and Congress of Racial Equality (CORE) activists began to call for violent and separatist — rather than peaceful and integrated — civil rights movement tactics, using the slogan "Black Power." Stokely Carmichael became chairman of SNCC.

At Oakland, California, Huey Newton and Bobby Seale founded the Black Panther Party.

American tennis player Billie Jean King won her first of 6 women's singles titles at Wimbledon (1966-1968; 1972; 1973; 1975); she would eventually garner a record 20 Wimbledon titles, including 10 doubles and 4 mixed doubles.

Flooding of the Arno River caused massive damage to irreplaceable artworks and library holdings in Florence, Italy (Nov.).

U.S. president Lyndon B. Johnson appointed Robert Weaver secretary of housing and urban development; Weaver became the first African-American cabinet member.

The U.S. Congress passed the Animal Welfare Act (AWA) to regulate the transportation, handling, and sale of dogs, cats, and some other animals; later amendments would establish humane standards and minimum requirements for food and care. Though unevenly, sometimes indifferently, enforced, it would provide the basis for many animal rights lawsuits.

Prime Minister Milton Obote took power as president and dictator of Uganda (1966-1971).

Suharto succeeded Sukarno as president and sole ruler of Indonesia (1966-).

Botswana (Republic of Botswana) became an independent state and Commonwealth member; its president was Seretse Khama (1966-1980).

Guyana became an independent state and Commonwealth member (May 26).

Lesotho, formerly Basutoland, an enclave surrounded by South Africa, became an independent state and Commonwealth member (Oct. 4).

Barbados became an independent state and Commonwealth member (Nov. 30).

d. Chester William Nimitz (1885-1966), American admiral who took command of the Pacific Fleet after the Japanese attack on Pearl Harbor and led it throughout World War II.

d. Lal Bahadur Shastri (1904-1966), Congress Party prime minister of India (1964-1966).

John von Neumann's *Theory of Self-Reproducing Automata*, a groundbreaking discussion of cybernetics and robots, was published posthumously.

Jacques Cousteau created his influential television documentary series *The World of Jacques Cousteau* (1966-1968).

d. Sergei Korolev (1906-1966), Soviet aeronautical engineer; the preeminent Soviet rocket fuel and spacecraft designer.

d. Georges Edouard Lemaître (1894-1966), Belgian priest and astronomer who posited the "big bang" theory (1927).

d. Anna Akhmatova (Anna Andreyevna Gorenko) (1889-1966), Russian poet; suppressed during the Stalin period, she emerged as a major figure in the 1960s.

d. Alberto Giacometti (1901-1966), Swiss sculptor and painter who moved from cubism to surrealism to the elongated figures that marked his mature work.

d. Nicolai Cherkassov (1903-1966), Soviet stage and screen star best known abroad for his title roles in *Alexander Nevsky* (1938) and *Ivan the Terrible* (1944; 1946).

d. André Breton (1896-1966), French writer and editor; from his *Manifesto of Surrealism* (1924), the leading theoretician and organizer of the surrealist movement.

d. Buster (Joseph Francis) Keaton (1895-1966), American actor, writer, and director; a leading comedian of the silent film era.

d. Jean Arp (Hans Arp) (1877-1966), German painter and sculptor; a noted abstractionist and experimentalist of the interwar period.

d. Sophie Tucker (Sonia Kalish) (1884-1966), American vaudeville and variety star whose signature song was "Some of These Days" (1910).

d. Walt (Walter Elias) Disney (1901-1966), American film animator; with Ib Iwerks, the cocreator of Mickey Mouse; he became a leading entertainment industry figure.

The Boston Celtics won an unprecedented 8th National Basketball Association championship in a row, having won 9 titles in 10 years; coach Red Auerbach retired to become the team's general manager.

A U.S. C-14 transport carrying American servicemen crashed near Binh Thai, South Vietnam (Dec. 24); 129 people died.

An Air India 707 crashed into Mont Blanc, near Geneva, Switzerland (June 24), killing 117 people.

An All-Nippon 727 crashed into the bay while landing in Tokyo, Japan (Feb. 4), killing 133 people.

British-American jockey Johnny Longden retired after a 40-year career, having won a then-record 6,032 races.

Near Mount Fuji, Japan, a BOAC 707 crashed into a mountainside in heavy wind (Mar. 5); 124 people died, many of them salespeople from Minnesota.

The Greek ferry *Iraklin* sank in the Aegean Sea, off Greece (Dec. 8), after partly flooding, killing 241 people.

British designer Mary Quant introduced the miniskirt, which set a major fashion trend.

d. Margaret Louise Higgins Sanger (1879-1966), American public health nurse who was a key leader in the fight for legal access to birth control information and techniques.

Israeli forces mounted successful surprise air and ground attacks on Egypt, Jordan, Syria, and Iraq in the Six-Day War (Third Arab-Israeli War) (June 5-10), destroying most of their opponents' air forces on the ground and completely defeating their ground forces, taking the Sinai Peninsula, the Jordanian-held portions of Jerusalem, the West Bank, and the Golan Heights, which they continued to occupy; no peace treaty ended the war. Egyptian forces were withdrawn from Yemen after the war.

Civil war began in Nigeria (1967-1970), as the Christian and animist Ibos of Biafra seceded from Muslim-dominated Nigeria. The war would result in the loss of 1.5 million to 2 million lives, many of them children and most noncombatants, who died of famine and famine-induced disease while government forces blocked international relief supplies.

The European Community (EC) was founded, as provided by the 1965 Brussels Treaty, joining the European Economic Community (Common Market), European Coal and Steel Community, and European Atomic Energy Community; the original members were Belgium, France, West Germany, Italy, Luxembourg, and the Netherlands. The EC included the Council of Ministers, Commission, Parliament, and Court of Justice.

American forces in Vietnam had grown to nearly 500,000 by year's end, but the guerrilla war continued.

At the Glassboro (New Jersey) Summit, U.S. president Lyndon Baines Johnson and Soviet premier Aleksei N. Kosygin discussed a possible nuclear nonproliferation treaty.

New York congressman Adam Clayton Powell was refused seating by the U.S. House of Representatives because of alleged financial irregularities. He was seated after winning a special election (1968); the U.S. Supreme Court later ruled the House's 1967 action unconstitutional (1969).

Congo (Zaire) government forces defeated an insurrection in Katanga; both sides employed foreign mercenaries.

The first successful transplant of a human heart was performed by South African surgeon Christiaan Barnard (Dec. 3); the patient, Louis Washansky, died of pneumonia 18 days later. After learning open-heart surgery in America, Barnard had developed the technique working on dogs. The technique would be improved and spread worldwide, but the survival rate would be low, and by the 1980s emphasis would be placed on devices to assist, rather than replace, the heart. That same year, American surgeon Michael De Bakey implanted an artificial heart to supplement that of the patient, who survived four days, while American surgeon Rene Favalaro pioneered the coronary bypass operation to "reroute" blood around a clogged artery.

American physicist Steven Weinberg developed the electroweak theory, attempting to reconcile electromagnetism with the "weak" force that produces radioactive decay. Pakistani physicist Abdus Salam and American physicist Sheldon Lee Glashow independently contributed.

Space exploration's first deaths occurred when a fire broke out in an Apollo spacecraft during a countdown rehearsal (Jan. 27). The three astronauts aboard were killed: Virgil (Gus) Grissom, Edward H. White II, and Roger Bruce Chaffee. Soviet cosmonaut Vladimir Mikhaylovich Komarov was the first person killed during an actual space mission (Apr. 24), on an emergency reentry of his *Soyuz 1*, the new Soviet spacecraft.

Cambridge graduate student Jocelyn Bell first discovered and named the pulsar, a rapidly spinning neutron star that emits regular bursts (pulses) of radiation, confirming predictions of its existence (1938). Bell's supervisor, Anthony Hewish, who had developed the three-acre array of radio telescope receivers used in the

The Beatles released *Sergeant Pepper's Lonely Hearts Club Band,* one of the best-known albums of the rock era, containing, in addition to the title song, "Lucy in the Sky with Diamonds," "With a Little Help from My Friends," "When I'm 64," and the concluding "A Day in the Life." They also issued the classic countercultural songs "All You Need Is Love" and "Strawberry Fields Forever," all by John Lennon and Paul McCartney.

Gabriel Garcia Marquez emerged as a world literary figure with the publication of his surreal, multi-generational novel *One Hundred Years of Solitude.*

Faye Dunaway as Bonnie Parker and Warren Beatty as Clyde Barrow became international film stars as the real-life Depression era outlaws in Arthur Penn's film *Bonnie and Clyde,* produced by Beatty.

Sidney Poitier as Mr. Tibbs starred opposite Rod Steiger as the small-town southern sheriff in Norman Jewison's film *In the Heat of the Night.*

Spencer Tracy, in his last film, starred opposite Katharine Hepburn, Sidney Poitier, and Katharine Houghton in Stanley Kramer's pro-integration film *Guess Who's Coming to Dinner.*

William Styron published the novel *The Confessions of Nat Turner,* about the 1831 Virginia slave rebellion led by Turner.

Dustin Hoffman in the title role, Katharine Ross, and Anne Bancroft starred in Mike Nichols's film comedy *The Graduate.*

Marshall McLuhan and Quentin Fiore published *The Medium Is the Message,* calling the world a "global village" in which books would be replaced by electronic works.

Mick Fleetwood, John McVie, Peter Green, and Jeremy Spencer founded Fleetwood Mac.

Summer race riots erupted in several American cities (July), most notably in Detroit, where 43 people died and almost 5,000 regular U.S. Army troops were sent in to restore order, and in Newark, where 26 people died before the riot was suppressed by National Guard units and police. Some African-Americans, including H. Rap Brown and Stokely Carmichael, called for more violence, with Brown calling violence "as American as cherry pie."

The National Organization for Women (NOW) began a major, failed campaign to pass the Equal Rights Amendment (ERA).

The Green Bay Packers defeated the Kansas City Chiefs in the first Super Bowl, played after the National Football League and American Football League had agreed to merge. It was the first of two back-to-back Super Bowl wins for the Packers under coach Vince Lombardi.

At age 65, British yachtsman Francis Chichester completed the first solo voyage around the world (1966-1967), sailing 29,600 miles in his *Gipsy Moth III,* in a record 226 days, with a 7-week layover in Australia.

U.S. president Lyndon B. Johnson appointed Solicitor General Thurgood Marshall, formerly head of the legal staff of the National Association for the Advancement of Colored People (NAACP) and the leading American civil rights lawyer, to the Supreme Court. Marshall became the first African-American Supreme Court justice.

Some of the extraordinary and illegal penetration of the Central Intelligence Agency (CIA) into American life came to light when the National Student Association revealed that it had received at least $3 million from the CIA over a 15-year period.

Svetlana Alliluyeva, the daughter of former Soviet dictator Joseph Stalin, left the Soviet Union, defecting to the West with great media attention.

d. Che Guevara (Ernesto Guevara de la Serna) (1928-1967), a leader of the Cuban Revolution; he was killed by Bolivian forces after his capture (Oct. 7). He had been attempting to build a guerrilla insurrection in Bolivia on the Cuban model.

Indonesia, Malaysia, the Philippines, Singapore, and Thailand founded the noncommunist Association of Southeast Asian Nations (ASEAN); Brunei joined in 1984.

South Yemen won its independence (Nov. 30). Egyptian troops had been withdrawn after the Third Arab-Israeli War (June).

Zulfikar Ali Bhutto founded the socialist and Islamic Pakistan People's Party, which would later be led by his daughter, Benazir Bhutto.

Swaziland became an independent state and Commonwealth member (Sept. 6).

d. Albert John Luthuli (1898-1967), South African Zulu chief; an apostle of nonviolence who was president of the African National Congress (1952-1967). While in internal exile, he was awarded the 1960 Nobel Peace Prize.

d. Arthur William Tedder (1890-1967), British air marshal; Allied air commander in the Mediterranean theater and later in western and southern Europe during World War II, then British air chief of staff (1946-1950).

d. Clement Richard Attlee (1882-1967), British Labour prime minister (1945-1951) who shaped Labour's postwar rule, abandoning much of the British Empire, initiating the National Health Service, and nationalizing basic industries.

d. Hsüan T'ung (Henry P'u Yi) (1906-1967), the last Manchu (Ch'ing) emperor of China, who ruled briefly as a child (1908-1912) and was later Japanese puppet ruler of Manchukuo (Manchuria).

discovery, would receive the Nobel Prize for physics (1974); she would not.

Dian Fossey began studying mountain gorillas at the Karisoke Research Centre in Rwanda's Parc des Volcans in the Virungas Mountains (1967-1985), encouraged (like Jane Goodall) to do so by Louis Leakey.

R. Buckminster Fuller's geodesic dome, a solidly built, easily erected structure of lightweight metal tetrahedrons, was a hit at the Montreal Exposition; the American engineer had originally developed it in the 1950s.

The existence of biofeedback — assertion of voluntary control over normally involuntary biological processes, such as heart rate and blood pressure — was scientifically demonstrated by Neal Miller and Jay Towill.

The last major epidemic of smallpox occurred, in India and Pakistan; the World Health Organization (WHO) mounted a successful inoculation campaign to eliminate the disease.

The West Indian (Florida) manatee, the Florida panther, the gray and red wolves, the Caribbean monk seal, the American alligator, the California condor, the bald eagle, the Eskimo curlew, the Cape Sable and dusky seaside sparrows, four species of trout, and four species of cranes were among the animals listed as endangered.

Active DNA was first synthesized by a team led by Arthur Kornberg; other research showed that DNA and RNA, carriers of the "genetic code," are common to all living forms.

Results of a 20-year study in Evanston, Illinois, showed that fluoridation of the water supply sharply decreased dental decay. By the 1990s,

Guatemalan writer Miguel Asturias was awarded the Nobel Prize for literature.

d. Carl Sandburg (1878-1967), one of America's most notable 20th-century poets and a leading Abraham Lincoln biographer.

d. Edward Hopper (1882-1967), American painter; a leading realist whose works used stark contrasts to emphasize social isolation.

d. Spencer Tracy (1900-1967), American film star; a major international star from the mid-1930s through the year of his death; long the companion and costar of Katharine Hepburn.

d. Vivien Leigh (Vivian Mary Hartley) (1913-1967), British stage and film actress; among her film roles were Scarlett O'Hara in *Gone With the Wind* (1939) and Blanche Du Bois in *A Streetcar Named Desire* (1951).

d. Basil Rathbone (1892-1967), British stage and screen star; a screen "heavy," later the definitive Sherlock Holmes in 14 films (1939-1946).

d. (James) Langston Hughes (1902-1967), African-American poet of the 1920s Harlem Renaissance; creator of the "Simple" short stories.

d. Carson McCullers (1917-1967), American writer; a major figure from her first novel, *The Heart Is a Lonely Hunter* (1940).

d. Dorothy Parker (1893-1967), American writer and critic; a notable and often acerbic wit.

d. Claude Rains (1889-1967), British actor; a film star of Hollywood's golden age from his title role in *The Invisible Man* (1933).

d. John Masefield (1878-1967), British writer; a very popular poet from the publication of his poetry collection *Salt Water Ballads* (1902).

World heavyweight boxing champion Muhammad Ali was stripped of his title by the U.S. government and sentenced to prison for refusing to serve in the U.S. Army on religious grounds; the Supreme Court would later reverse the action (1970).

British racer Donald Malcolm Campbell was killed while attempting to better his own water speed record (1964), his hydroplane crashing at a speed over 300 miles per hour.

Dominant center Bill Russell became player-coach of the Boston Celtics basketball team (1967-1969); a trailblazing African-American coach in major professional American sports.

Coached by John Wooden and led by high-scoring center Lew Alcindor (later Kareem Abdul-Jabbar), the University of California at Los Angeles (UCLA) Bruins won the National Collegiate Athletic Association (NCAA) basketball championships for the first of three years in a row (1967-1969).

French skier Jean Claude Killy won the first World Cup for Men, coming in first in every downhill race in which he competed.

American jockey Willie Shoemaker won both the Belmont Stakes and the Preakness, two races in the Triple Crown.

Teamsters Union president James Hoffa began a 13-year prison term after convictions for jury tampering, mail fraud, and financial malfeasance in office.

At Brussels, Belgium, fire engulfed the department store L'Innovation (May 22), killing 322 people.

The Silver Bay suspension bridge over the Ohio River at Point Pleasant, West Virginia, collapsed during the evening rush hour (Dec. 15), killing more than 35 people.

d. Konrad Adenauer (1876-1967), German lawyer and Christian Democratic politician; first chancellor of the Federal Republic of Germany (1949-1963).

d. John Nance "Cactus Jack" Garner (1868-1967), Texas Democratic politician; a 15-term congressman (1903-1933) who was Franklin D. Roosevelt's rather conservative vice president (1933-1941).

d. Mohammed Mossadeq (1880-1967), Iranian politician; Iranian National Front Party premier (1951-1953); he was deposed by an army coup (1953), imprisoned (1953-1956), and then held in house arrest until his death.

d. Shigeru Yoshida (1878-1967), Japanese politician and diplomat; Japan's first postwar foreign minister (1945-1946) and later prime minister (1948-1954).

the rate of tooth decay in children and adults would drop 50 percent. Concerns persisted about fluoridation increasing the risk of cancer, but most long-term studies found no evidence for such a connection. Some critics maintained that better care, rather than fluoridation, was largely responsible for the lower rate of decay.

LSD (lysergic acid diethylamide) was found to cause genetic damage, in addition to psychological problems.

China exploded its first hydrogen bomb in the Lop Nor desert.

The tanker *Torrey Canyon* ran aground off Cornwall, England (Mar. 18), and later broke up (Mar. 26-27); most of its 118,000 tons of crude oil spilled into the sea and washed ashore, fouling 120 miles of seashore in Britain and 55 miles in France, in a major ecological disaster.

Element 105, named hahnium for Otto Hahn, was discovered.

British zoologist Desmond Morris published *The Naked Ape,* a best-selling book exploring human behavior in light of primate behavior.

d. J. (Julius) Robert Oppenheimer (1904-1967), American nuclear physicist who led the American effort to build the atomic bomb (1942-1945); later denied security clearance (1953). He died of cancer, as did many who worked on the atomic bomb project.

d. Charles Burchfield (1893-1967), American painter; a leading realist who focused on surreal landscapes late in his career.

d. Paul Muni (Muni Weisenfreund) (1895-1967), American stage and screen star; a leading dramatic actor of Hollywood's golden age from *Scarface* (1931) and *I Am a Fugitive from a Chain Gang* (1932).

d. Woody (Woodrow Wilson) Guthrie (1912-1967), leading American Depression era composer, folksinger, and guitarist.

d. Zoltán Kodály (1882-1967), Hungarian composer and teacher working largely in Hungarian folk themes.

d. Elmer Rice (Elmer Reizenstein) (1892-1967), American writer who emerged as a major playwright in the 1920s.

d. G. W. (Georg Wilhelm) Pabst (1885-1967), Austrian-born German film director; a leading figure of the silent film era.

d. Mary Garden (1874-1967), Scottish-American soprano; one of the leading opera singers of the century.

d. Paul Whiteman (1890-1967), popular American bandleader of the 1920s and 1930s.

The USS *Forrestal* exploded in the South China Sea off South Vietnam (July 29), killing 134 people.

d. Henry John Kaiser (1882-1967), American industrialist; World War II builder of Liberty ships and postwar automaker; his Kaiser-Permanente Plan (1942) was a model for later large group health plans.

d. Alfred (von Bohlen und Halbach) Krupp (1907-1967), German industrialist; heir to the Krupp business empire, built on steel and munitions. A Nazi supporter, he was imprisoned after the war but released in 1951 at American recommendation to help rebuild German industry.

North Vietnamese forces mounted the Tet Offensive (Jan.-Feb.) throughout South Vietnam, even attacking the American embassy in Saigon. Although the military offensive completely failed, it decisively turned American public opinion against the war, for there was clearly no "light at the end of the tunnel." The My Lai Massacre (Mar. 16), in which Lieutenant William L. Calley's platoon murdered 150 unarmed women, children, and old men, was an atrocity that further turned Americans against the war. U.S. president Lyndon Johnson announced that he would not run for another term (Mar. 31). Paris peace negotiations began (May 10), and President Johnson ordered a stop to all attacks on North Vietnam (Oct. 31).

d. Robert Francis Kennedy (1925-1968), a brother of President John F. Kennedy and Senator Edward M. Kennedy; he was shot in Los Angeles by Sirhan Sirhan (June 5) while campaigning for the Democratic presidential nomination; he died on June 6.

Hubert H. Humphrey became his party's presidential candidate at the tumultuous Chicago Democratic National Convention, while Chicago police attacked thousands of anti–Vietnam War demonstrators outside the convention hall. Republican Richard M. Nixon defeated Humphrey to become the 37th president of the United States (1969-1974).

Alexander Dubček's Czech government initiated the series of major democratic reforms called the Prague Spring (Jan.-Aug.); the Soviet Union reasserted imperial domination, and invasion forces numbering 400,000 retook Czechoslovakia (Aug. 20), beginning a new period of repression. In an attempt to justify the invasion, Soviet premier Leonid Brezhnev stated the Brezhnev Doctrine, an assertion that Soviet intervention in the affairs of any other communist state was justified when the existence of communism was threatened in that state.

Massive student protests, joined by millions of workers, paralyzed Paris and many other French cities after the students, led by Daniel Cohn-Bendit, had closed the Sor-

The U.S. ship *Glomar Challenger* began drilling into ocean beds, notably in the Red Sea, the Galápagos Rift, and the Falkland Plateau, removing core samples for analysis, as part of the Deep Sea Drilling Project (DSDP) (1968-1983) seeking geological information on the earth's geological history and resources. Evidence produced supported the theory of plate tectonics — that the earth's crust is composed of numerous movable "plates" — and also indicated likely underwater oil deposits.

Assured of their safety, former inhabitants were allowed to return to Bikini, in the Pacific's Marshall Islands, the site of atomic and later hydrogen bomb tests (1946-1958); they would be removed again (1978) after reassessment of the continuing hazards from radioactive fallout.

Werner Arber discovered that bacteria produce restriction enzymes, substances that split genes naturally.

Astronomer Thomas Gold theorized that pulsars were rotating neutron stars — small but dense, and with powerful magnetic fields. Observations that pulsars gradually slow their rotation and pulsation, presumably from loss of energy, would support the theory.

After years of experiments, American physicists Frederick Reines and Clyde Lorrain Cowan — who had discovered atomic particles called antineutrinos (1956) — finally found evidence of neutrinos, whose existence had been posited by Wolfgang Pauli (1931). However, they detected far fewer neutrinos being produced by the sun than had been predicted, raising the perplexing question of missing neutrinos, and indeed missing mass in the universe.

James Earl Jones as African-American prizefighter Jack Johnson starred opposite Jane Alexander as his White lover in Howard Sackler's trailblazing play *The Great White Hope.*

Joseph Wiseman starred as the witch-hunted American nuclear scientist in Heinar Kipphardt's play *In the Matter of J. Robert Oppenheimer.*

Stanley Kubrick cowrote with Arthur C. Clarke and directed the classic science fiction film *2001: A Space Odyssey,* starring Keir Dullea, Gary Lockwood, William Sylvester, and Daniel Richter.

Walter De Maria painted two parallel lines on the desert floor, titling his painting *Mile Long Drawing;* it was a key work of "conceptual art," also called land art, earth art, and earthworks.

Albert Finney made his directorial debut and starred in *Charlie Bubbles,* screenplay by Shelagh Delaney. Billie Whitelaw, Colin Blakeley, and Liza Minnelli costarred.

Anthony Harvey's film version of James Goldman's 1966 play *The Lion in Winter* starred Katharine Hepburn as Eleanor of Aquitaine opposite Peter O'Toole as Henry II.

Arthur Kennedy and Pat Hingle starred as two feuding brothers opposite Kate Reid in Arthur Miller's play *The Price.*

David Crosby, Stephen Stills, Graham Nash, and Neil Young founded Crosby, Stills, Nash, and Young (1968-1971).

Mia Farrow starred as the pregnant victim of a group of deceptive-looking devil worshipers in Roman Polanski's seminal modern horror film *Rosemary's Baby,* based on Ira Levin's 1967 novel.

Ludwig Mies van der Rohe designed Berlin's Gallery of the Twentieth Century, a leading artifact of the International Style.

d. Martin Luther King, Jr. (1929-1968), American civil rights leader; he was assassinated by James Earl Ray in Memphis, Tennessee (Apr. 4). The African-American minister was a key leader of the mid-century American civil rights movement and a world figure as an apostle of nonviolence. Following his death, arson and rioting broke out in many American cities.

Arthur Ashe was the first African-American tennis player to win the men's singles title at the U.S. Open; he also won the U.S. Amateur title.

At the Mexico City Olympics, American track star Bob Beamon set a new world and Olympic record with a long jump of 29 feet 2½ inches, almost 2 feet beyond the previous record. Czech gymnast Vera Caslavska, who had trained in hiding from Soviet invasion troops, won four gold and two silver medals. African-American runners Tommy Smith and John Carlos, first and third in the 200 meters, were suspended for giving "Black Power" salutes while accepting their medals.

U.S. president Lyndon B. Johnson nominated liberal Abe Fortas to succeed Earl Warren as chief justice of the Supreme Court, but he was forced to withdraw the nomination because of conservative opposition in the Senate.

Ralph Abernathy led the Poor People's Campaign, which marched on Washington, D.C., and set up a tent settlement called Resurrection City.

The Civil Rights Act of 1968 legally established open housing, but covert discrimination continued in many areas.

Eldridge Cleaver published *Soul on Ice;* he also fled the United States after a gunfight between Black Panthers and police in Oakland, California.

French skier Jean Claude Killy duplicated the feat of Toni Sailer (1956) in taking all three Alpine

bonne (May); civil war was averted by President Charles de Gaulle, with army and widespread moderate support.

Led by the United States, the Soviet Union, and Britain, but not including the nuclear powers France and the People's Republic of China, more than 60 countries signed the Nuclear Nonproliferation Treaty, pledging not to acquire or help others to acquire nuclear weapons. Although more than 100 nations ultimately signed the agreement, many nations went on to acquire nuclear weapons.

Andreas Baader and Ulrike Meinhof led the German anarchist-terrorist Red Army Faction (Baader-Meinhof Group) in a long series of bombings, robberies, and murders (1968-1972).

Civil war recommenced in Yemen, with South Yemeni forces joining the Yemeni republican rebels and Saudi Arabia again supporting the government.

The USS *Pueblo* and its 83-man crew were seized by North Korea in the Sea of Japan (Jan. 23) and held for 11 months; one crew member died in captivity.

The Ba'ath Party (Arab Socialist Renaissance Party) took power by coup in Iraq (July).

In Peru, a military coup deposed President Fernando Belaunde Terry; he was replaced by General Juan Velasco Alvarado.

French troops intervened on behalf of the government against Arab rebel forces in the Chad Civil War.

French-Canadian Liberal Party leader Pierre Elliot Trudeau became prime minister (1968-1979; 1980-1984); during his tenure, he successfully resisted Quebec separatism and developed the concept of a bilingual, binational Canada.

René Lévesque founded the separatist Parti Québécois, Quebec's ruling party (1976-1985).

The first supersonic airliner, the Tupolev TU-144, capable of traveling faster than the speed of sound, was unveiled in the Soviet Union.

The U.S. spacecraft *Apollo 8*, with Frank Borman, James A. Lovell, Jr., and William S. Anders aboard (Dec. 21-27), circled the moon 10 times; it was the final U.S. Apollo flight before the moon landing (1969).

The Soviet space probe *Zond 5*, with no crew, circled the moon (Sept. 17).

Using improved electron microscopes, American paleontologist Elso Sterrenberg Barghoorn first recognized in fossilized material from ancient rocks simple-celled life forms such as bacteria, called *microfossils*. Since some dated back 3.5 billion years, this discovery suggested that life began on earth within the first billion years after its formation.

American molecular biologist James D. Watson published *The Double Helix*, describing his codiscovery of the structure of DNA (1953).

René Dubos published *So Human an Animal*, his Pulitzer Prize–winning work on humans and their environment.

Soviet nuclear physicist and dissenter Andrei Sakharov published *Progress, Coexistence and Intellectual Freedom*, becoming an international figure, in disfavor with the Soviet government.

American physicist Luis Walter Alvarez received the Nobel Prize for physics for his work on subatomic particles with the bubble chamber (much improved by him) and linear accelerators.

d. Lise Meitner (1878-1968), Austrian-born physicist who first described and named nu-

Joanne Woodward starred as the repressed school-teacher and Paul Newman made his directorial debut in the film *Rachel, Rachel.*

George Dunning's innovative film *Yellow Submarine* combined animation with a score and characters from the Beatles, who introduced the title song and also released their *White Album,* including "Hey, Jude."

Mart Crowley's pioneering play about a group of gay men, *The Boys in the Band,* starred Kenneth Nelson, Leonard Frey, Peter White, and Robert La Tourneaux.

Yves Montand and Irene Papas starred in Constantin Costa-Gavras's film *Z,* an attack on the Greek military dictatorship of the time.

Jimmy Page, John Bonham, Robert Plant, and John Paul Jones founded Led Zeppelin.

Neil Simon's linked one-act plays *Plaza Suite* starred Maureen Stapleton and George C. Scott; it would be the basis of the 1971 film.

Britain's Royal Ballet introduced *The Enigma Variations,* Frederick Ashton's ensemble ballet to Edward Elgar's 1899 work.

Norman Mailer published his Pulitzer Prize–winning Vietnam War essays, *Armies of the Night.*

Blues singer Janis Joplin issued her album *Cheap Thrills.*

Japanese novelist Yasunari Kawabata was awarded the Nobel Prize for literature.

d. John Steinbeck (1902-1968), American writer best known for his Depression era novels, most notably *The Grapes of Wrath* (1939); he was awarded the 1962 Nobel Prize for literature.

medals — the downhill, slalom, and giant slalom — at the Grenoble Olympics.

Barbara Jane Mackle was kidnapped in Atlanta, Georgia (Dec. 17); three days later, after a $500,000 ransom had been paid, she was found alive, buried in a wooden box. Caught and convicted, Gary Steven Krist received a life sentence and Ruth Eisenmann-Schier seven years; most of the ransom was recovered.

The report of the Kerner Commission (National Advisory Commission on Civil Disorders) called racism and living conditions the chief causes of the Watts and other 1965-1968 race riots.

The U.S. Congress passed the Wild and Scenic Rivers Act, under which free-flowing rivers with outstanding scenic, geologic, recreational, cultural, or other attributes would be protected from dams and other water projects, as well as development and logging. Also, the National Trails System Act established a network of scenic, historic, and recreation trails, the first two being the Appalachian and Pacific Crest Trails.

Walter Reuther led the United Automobile Workers (UAW) out of the AFL-CIO; he had led his union and the entire CIO into the merged labor federation in 1955. The UAW later rejoined the federation.

The U.S. nuclear submarine *Scorpion* sank in the Atlantic Ocean, near the Azores (May 21), killing 99 people.

The hovercraft (hydrofoil) was put into regular commercial service across the English Channel.

Automated check clearing among major banks was pioneered in Britain, soon spreading to New York City (1970). Electronic transfer of funds, rather than physical transfer of paper checks, would lead to the development of automated teller machines, to

Practicing "ping-pong diplomacy," the Chinese invited a U.S. ping-pong team to visit China, beginning an attempt to resume U.S.-Chinese relations.

The Republic of Equatorial Guinea became an independent nation (Oct. 12) led by President Francisco Macías (later Macie Naguema Biyuogo Negue Ndong), who became a notably murderous dictator in 1969.

Vice President Albert-Bernard Bongo (El Hadj Omar) succeeded to the presidency of Gabon after the death of President Léon M'ba, turning Gabon into a one-party state.

Mauritius became an independent state and Commonwealth member (Mar. 12).

Nauru became an independent state and Commonwealth member (Jan. 31).

d. Husband Edward Kimmel (1882-1968), American Pacific Fleet commander at Pearl Harbor (Dec. 7, 1941).

d. Karl Barth (1886-1968), Swiss Protestant theologian; a leading pacifist and anti-Nazi activist during the interwar period and an antinuclear leader during the Cold War.

d. Konstantin Konstantinovich Rokossovski (1896-1968), Soviet field marshal; commander at the defense of Moscow (1941) and at Stalingrad (1942-1943).

d. Norman Mattoon Thomas (1884-1968), American socialist politician; six times the presidential candidate of the Socialist Party (1928-1948).

d. Trygve Halvdan Lie (1896-1968), Norwegian diplomat; first secretary-general of the United Nations (1946-1953).

clear fission (1939) after she left Nazi Germany for Sweden (1938). She opposed the building and use of the atomic bomb and after Hiroshima (1945) ceased work on nuclear fission.

d. George Gamow (1904-1968), Russian-American physicist; a leading exponent of the "big bang" theory of the universe's origin (1948) and author of *One, Two, Three . . . Infinity* (1947), who first posited that nucleic acids (in DNA and RNA) work in groups of three (1954).

d. Otto Hahn (1879-1968), German chemist whose experiments with Lise Meitner led her to posit nuclear fission; he, but not she, won the Nobel Prize for chemistry (1944) for their work.

d. Yuri Alekseyevich Gagarin (1934-1968), Soviet pilot; the world's first astronaut, in *Vostok I* (1961); he died in an air accident.

d. Marcel Duchamp (1887-1968), French artist, an early abstractionist and pioneering absurdist whose cubist *Nude Descending a Staircase No. 2* (1912) became a landmark work after its reception at the 1913 Armory Show.

d. Upton Sinclair (1878-1968), American writer and socialist; best known for his classic muckraking novel *The Jungle* (1906).

d. Conrad Richter (1890-1968), major American writer from the publication of his novel *The Trees* (1937).

d. Alice Guy-Blaché (1875-1968), prolific French director and producer of the silent film era; the first woman film director and director of perhaps the first story film (1896).

d. Ruth St. Denis (Ruth Dennis) (1878-1968), American dancer, choreographer, and teacher; a founder of the modern dance movement; cofounder of the Denishawn school and dance company (1915-1931).

d. Edna Ferber (1887-1968), popular American novelist and playwright; many of her works became hit stage musicals and films.

d. Carl Dreyer (1899-1968), Danish film director, most notably of the silent film epic *The Passion of Joan of Arc* (1928).

personal banking on home computers, and theoretically, to a future checkless society.

George Halas, founder and longtime coach of the Chicago Bears and cofounder of the National Football League (1920), retired, having won a then-record 321 regular-season games; he was responsible for innovations such as the T formation, introduced in the 1930s.

Paul Ehrlich and Anne Howland Ehrlich published *The Population Bomb,* on the world's population explosion.

Drilling for oil began in the North Sea.

In Mannington, West Virginia, 68 people died in a coal mine explosion (Nov. 20).

d. Helen Adams Keller (1880-1968), American speaker and campaigner for blind, deaf, and mute people; herself blind and deaf from 19 months, she learned to communicate with a manual alphabet (1887), aided by teacher Annie Sullivan, and later graduated from Radcliffe College (1904).

American forces build-up in Vietnam reached 700,000, as peace negotiations proceeded. American troop withdrawals began (June), although bombing of North Vietnam resumed. Intense secret bombing of North Vietnamese and Khmer Rouge forces in Cambodia began (1969-1973).

Anti–Vietnam War American military adviser Daniel Ellsberg took the top-secret Pentagon Papers, on Southeast Asian policy, secret decisions, and lies, to the *New York Times,* which published large portions after the Supreme Court ruled against a government attempt to stop publication. Attempted prosecutions of Ellsberg and Daniel Russo resulted in mistrials because of illegal wiretapping and the burgling of Ellsberg's psychiatrist's office by the same "plumbers" unit that would conduct the Watergate break-in (1972).

A Khmer Rouge insurgency against the Cambodian government quickly became full-scale civil war (1969-1975) that would end with Khmer Rouge victory and the Cambodian Holocaust.

Massive Catholic demonstrations developed in Northern Ireland, as Provisional Irish Republican Army forces ("Provos") began a guerrilla insurgency. British occupying forces were sent to Northern Ireland (Aug.).

As French student demonstrations and economic problems grew, Charles de Gaulle resigned the French presidency.

At Chappaquiddick Island, off Martha's Vineyard, Massachusetts, U.S. senator Edward M. Kennedy drove his car off a bridge, drowning passenger Mary Jo Kopechne; Kennedy left the scene and reported the accident nine hours later (July). This "Chappaquiddick incident" so completely compromised Kennedy that he was, in essence, forever barred from running for president, although he became a longtime senator.

Chinese and Soviet forces repeatedly skirmished on the Manchurian border (Mar.).

Neil Armstrong and Edwin (Buzz) Aldrin, Jr., were the first people to walk on the surface of the moon (July 20) after landing their *Apollo 11* lunar module, while Michael Collins remained in lunar orbit aboard the command module. On landing, Armstrong said, "That's one small step for a man, one giant leap for mankind." Other Apollo landings would follow, yielding information, lunar samples, and experimental results.

The first docking of piloted spacecraft and exchange of crews in space was performed when the Soviet *Soyuz 4* and *Soyuz 5* linked together (Jan. 14).

The first temporary implant of an artificial heart to replace a human heart was made by American cardiologist Denton Cooley, with Domingo Liotta. Five days later, after a human donor was found, it was replaced by a human heart transplant, but the patient, Haskell Karp, died three days later.

Jonathan Beckwith and others first isolated a gene.

After a well blew out in an oil rig off Santa Barbara, California, an estimated 800,000 gallons (approximately 2,700 tons) of crude oil spilled into the sea (Jan. 31-Feb. 8), coming ashore to foul 20 miles of heavily populated California coastline and damaging shore life. Four oil companies eventually paid $4.5 million in property damage claims, as well as token fines on criminal charges. Already controversial, offshore drilling became a major target of conservationists seeking an end to unrestricted drilling.

British geneticist C. D. (Cyril Dean) Darlington published *The Evolution of Man and Society,* an exploration of the genetic and cultural inter-

In the classic countercultural event of the era, at least 400,000 people gathered at the Woodstock (Bethel), New York, music festival (Aug. 15-17) to peacefully hear many of the most celebrated rock and folk musicians of the 1960s.

Luchino Visconti explored the lives, commitments, and fall of a rich German industrial family during the Nazi period in his film *The Damned*, starring Dirk Bogarde, Ingrid Thulin, Helmut Griem, Helmut Berger, and Charlotte Rampling.

Arlo Guthrie's song "Alice's Restaurant" (1966) generated Arthur Penn's film *Alice's Restaurant*, set in the Massachusetts restaurant of that name and starring Guthrie, Pat Quinn as Alice, and James Broderick.

Joni Mitchell's album *Clouds* included the title song and "Songs to Aging Children Come," used in the film *Alice's Restaurant*.

Genevieve Bujold starred in the title role as Anne Boleyn, opposite Richard Burton as Henry VIII, in the film version of Maxwell Anderson's 1948 play *Anne of the Thousand Days*.

Kurt Vonnegut published his partly autobiographical novel *Slaughterhouse-Five, or The Children's Crusade*, set during the World War II bombing of Dresden, with its accompanying firestorm.

Maggie Smith starred as Edinburgh teacher Jean Brodie in Ronald Neame's film version of Muriel Spark's 1961 novel *The Prime of Miss Jean Brodie*.

Paul Newman as Butch Cassidy, Robert Redford as the Sundance Kid, and Katharine Ross starred in George Roy Hill's classic Western outlaw film *Butch Cassidy and the Sundance Kid*.

Ashley Hutchings, Maddy Prior, Gay Woods, Terry Woods, and Tim Hart founded Steeleye Span.

American gays, reacting to a police raid on New York City's Stonewall Inn (June 28), created the new gay liberation movement; tens of thousands of male and female homosexuals "came out of the closet" to demand equal legal and social rights, with worldwide social and political resonance and impact far beyond their numbers.

The U.S. National Environmental Policy Act, sometimes called the "national charter for protection of the environment," was the first major American law to call for government to consider the environmental consequences of federal government decisions.

At Beverly Hills, California, devil-worshiping cult leader Charles Manson and four of his followers murdered five people (Aug. 9), including actress Sharon Tate and her unborn child, and then two more people, Leno and Rosemary La Bianca (Aug.); captured and convicted, Manson, Charles (Tex) Watson, Patricia Krenwinkel, Susan Atkins, and Leslie Van Houten were imprisoned for life.

Abe Fortas was the first justice to resign from the U.S. Supreme Court because of possibly irregular, though not illegal, financial conduct.

President Richard M. Nixon appointed Warren Burger chief justice of the U.S. Supreme Court (1969-1986), succeeding Chief Justice Earl Warren.

President Richard M. Nixon's nomination of conservative Clement Haynesworth to the U.S. Supreme Court was defeated 55–45 in the Senate.

The New York Mets scored a remarkable upset, winning the World Series over the favored Baltimore Orioles. Among the stars was fastball pitcher Tom Seaver, who won the Cy Young Award with 25 regular-season wins.

American educational psychologist Arthur R. Jensen claimed that Blacks have lower intelligence (IQ)

Yasir Arafat became head of the Palestine Liberation Organization (PLO) (1969-   ).

Fatah (Palestine Liberation Movement) merged with the Palestine Liberation Organization (PLO); PLO cross-border attacks into Israel intensified, as the PLO developed guerrilla bases in Lebanon.

Muammar al-Qaddafi took power in Libya by coup, ruling as dictator (1969-   ).

U.S. president Richard M. Nixon unilaterally renounced the use of biological weapons and the first use of chemical weapons.

Quebec Liberation Front terrorists mounted a series of bombings and kidnappings, among them the murder of Quebec labor minister Pierre La Porte.

Students for a Democratic Society splintered; one of those splinters was the terrorist Weathermen group, which went underground, its members committing several random terrorist acts into the early 1980s.

Shirley Chisholm became the first African-American woman to serve in the U.S. Congress (1969-1983).

The Chicago Seven were convicted and sentenced on charges arising from the 1968 Democratic National Convention antiwar demonstrations; they and their lawyers received more than 100 contempt citations from Judge Julius Hoffman.

General Agha Mohammed Yahya Khan took power as military dictator in Pakistan after the resignation of Mohammad Ayub Khan.

General Mohammed Siad Barre took power by coup in Somalia, ruling as dictator (1969-1991).

Iranian and Iraqi forces fought an undeclared border war, largely over control of the Shatt-al-Arab waterway.

actions underlying human history. The book was controversial because of what critics charged were racist implications.

Astronomers observed the first optical pulsar star, giving off waves of visible light as well as microwaves.

Bell Laboratories invented an imager computer chip, leading to the development of ever-smaller handheld television cameras.

Designed by Jacques Piccard for long-term underwater use, the bathyscape *Ben Franklin* carried a six-person crew on a 1,650-mile journey along the Gulf Stream.

The U.S. spacecraft *Mariner 6* and *Mariner 7* flew by Mars, sending back photos of craters on the planet's surface.

Elisabeth Kubler-Ross published *On Death and Dying*, bringing new openness and understanding to the needs of the dying and their survivors.

A partial meltdown occurred in a Saint-Laurent, France, nuclear reactor (Oct. 17).

In a nuclear accident in Lucens Vad, Switzerland, radiation leaked into a cavern (Jan. 21), which was then sealed.

The U.S. Air Force's Project Blue Book (1947-1969), established to gather data on sightings of unidentified flying objects (UFOs), ended with a report by Edward U. Condon; like previous interim reports (1952; 1966; 1968), it rejected the idea of extraterrestrial visitations.

Salvador Edward Luria, Max Delbrück, and Alfred Day Hershey shared the Nobel Prize for

Jon Voight as male prostitute Joe Buck and Dustin Hoffman as Ratso Rizzo starred in John Schlesinger's classic, harshly realistic film *Midnight Cowboy*.

The Beatles issued the albums *Yellow Submarine* and *Abbey Road,* and, as the group began to split apart, John Lennon and the Plastic Ono Band recorded the Lennon–Paul McCartney song "Give Peace a Chance."

Joan Ganz Cooney's gentle, landmark children's television series *Sesame Street* began its very long run (1969-   ).

Glenda Jackson, Alan Bates, Oliver Reed, and Eleanor Bron starred in Ken Russell's film *Women in Love,* based on D. H. Lawrence's once-daring 1920 novel.

Duane Allman, Gregg Allman, Butch Truchs, Dicky Betts, Berry Oakley, and Jai Johanny Johanson founded the Allman Brothers Band.

Kenneth Tynan's nude musical *Oh, Calcutta!* began its long set of New York runs.

Peter Townshend's rock opera *Tommy* was premiered in a concert version by the Who.

Graham Chapman, John Cleese, Eric Idle, Terry Jones, Michael Palin, and Terry Gilliam created the British television series *Monty Python's Flying Circus,* which was a worldwide success for its offbeat humor, seen also in several later films.

Maurice White and Verdine White founded Earth, Wind, and Fire.

Irish writer Samuel Beckett was awarded the Nobel Prize for literature.

d. Ludwig Mies van der Rohe (1886-1969), German architect; a leading theoretician of the International

scores than Whites because they are genetically inferior. His dismissal of environmental influences on human development caused enormous controversy in the middle of the civil rights movement.

The Boston Women's Health Collective was established; it would be a model for many other women's health information centers.

Thor Heyerdahl and his crew sailed across the Atlantic in an early Egyptian-style reed boat, *Ra II* (1969-1970); the 56-day voyage from Morocco to Barbados was undertaken to support the hypothesis that there had been early Egyptian contacts with the Americas. An attempt in the original *Ra,* earlier in the year, had been cut short.

The specially built ice-breaking oil tanker *Manhattan* made the first commercial journey on the Northwest Passage, the Arctic sea route north of North America, after the discovery of oil in northern Alaska.

Led by quarterback Joe (Joseph William) Namath, the New York Jets of the American Football League defeated the National Football League's favored Baltimore Colts in the Super Bowl.

Scottish auto racer Jackie (John Young) Stewart won the first of his three world driving championships (1969; 1971; 1973).

Michel Foucault published *The Archaeology of Knowledge* as part of his attempt to develop a historical sequence of basic thought structures.

Hurricane Camille struck the Gulf Coast and devastated several states, killing an estimated 250 people, injuring thousands, and causing damage estimated at $1 billion to $2 billion.

d. Tom (Thomas Joseph) Mboya (1930-1969), Kenyan political leader; thought to be Jomo Kenyatta's heir apparent, he was assassinated in Nairobi.

George Habash founded the terrorist Popular Front for the Liberation of Palestine.

A military coup in Sudan deposed Prime Minister Mohammed Ahmed Mahgoub; he was replaced by Colonel Gafaar Mohammed al-Nimeiry.

Golda Meir became prime minister of Israel (1969-1973).

d. Eduardo Mondlane (1920-1969), Mozambican guerrilla leader; assassinated by the Portuguese.

d. Dwight David Eisenhower (1890-1969), American supreme commander of Allied forces in Europe during World War II and 34th president of the United States (1953-1961).

d. Ho Chi Minh (Nguyen That Thanh) (1890-1969), Vietnamese communist and independence movement leader; first president of the Democratic Republic of Vietnam (1945-1969).

d. Harold Rupert Leofric George Alexander (1891-1969), British field marshal; commander at Dunkirk (1940), of the Italian invasion (1943-1944), and of the Mediterranean theater (1944).

d. Liu Shaoqi (Liu Shao-chi) (1899-1969), leading Chinese communist theoretician; imprisoned (1968) during the Cultural Revolution. He died in prison and was later "posthumously rehabilitated."

physiology or medicine for their work with viruses.

Murray Gell-Mann received the Nobel Prize for physics for his classification scheme for fundamental particles.

Style; head of the Bauhaus (1930-1933) and later (a refugee from the Nazis) a leading American modernist.

d. Walter Gropius (1883-1969), German architect, designer, and teacher; as director of the Bauhaus (1919-1928), a leading figure in 20th-century design.

d. B. Traven (probably Ret Marut) (1890?-1969), German-born writer, long resident in Mexico.

d. Jack Kerouac (1926-1969), leading "Beat Generation" American writer after his autobiographical novel *On the Road* (1957).

d. Judy Garland (Frances Gumm) (1922-1969), American actress and celebrated popular singer; she was Dorothy in the 1939 movie *The Wizard of Oz.*

d. Boris Karloff (William Henry Pratt) (1887-1969), British actor; a leading horror film star beginning with *Frankenstein* (1931).

d. Josef von Sternberg (1894-1969), Vienna-born American film director, most notably for *The Blue Angel* (1930) and his six subsequent Marlene Dietrich films.

d. Ben Shahn (1898-1969), American painter, printmaker, and photographer, a leading Depression era realist.

d. Robert Taylor (Spangler Arlington Brugh) (1911-1969), American film star of Hollywood's golden age.

Soviet chess player Boris Vasselievich Spassky defeated Tigran Petrosian to become world champion (1969-1972).

Australian tennis player Rod Laver won a grand slam, taking the men's singles titles at Wimbledon and the U.S., French, and Australian Opens.

The French-British Concorde supersonic airliner made its first flight, at Toulouse, France.

A Viasa DC-9 crashed on takeoff from Maracaibo, Venezuela (Mar. 16); 155 people died, 71 of them on the ground.

d. John L. (Llewellyn) Lewis (1880-1969), American labor leader; United Mine Workers (UMW) president and a founder and first president of the Committee for Industrial Organizations (1935).

d. Karl Jaspers (1883-1969), German psychiatrist and philosopher; an anti-Nazi whose work was basic to the development of 20th-century existentialism; after World War II, he focused on moral questions, such as that of German guilt for the crimes of the Nazi period.

Escalating antiwar protests in the United States forced withdrawal of American and South Vietnamese forces from Cambodia (Apr.-June); peace negotiations and American troop withdrawals continued.

Ohio National Guard troops fired on unarmed antiwar demonstrators at Kent State University (May 4), killing 4, wounding 10, and generating further massive nationwide antiwar protests.

A Cambodian military coup deposed Norodom Sihanouk, replacing him with Lon Nol. Sihanouk went into Chinese exile; the civil war intensified.

Biafra surrendered (Jan. 12) in the Nigerian Civil War (1967-1970); the war had cost 1.5 million to 2 million lives, most of them civilian victims of famine and famine-induced disease.

Conservative Party leader Edward Heath became British prime minister (1970-1974), replacing Labour's Harold Wilson; Heath would take Britain into the European Community (1973).

After prolonged Chinese-Malay rioting, Tunku Abdul Rahman resigned as Malaysian prime minister; he was succeeded by Tun Abdul Razak (1970-1976).

Jordanian forces defeated and expelled most Palestine Liberation Organization (PLO) forces, throwing back allied Syrian forces. PLO forces resettled in Lebanon and increased cross-border attacks on Israel, which responded with heavy attacks on PLO bases.

Mujibur Rahman's Awami League won the Pakistani general elections (Dec.), but the military government held power and outlawed the league when it generated an East Pakistani disobedience campaign.

Socialist Party candidate Salvador Allende Gossens was elected president of Chile (1970-1973) and quickly moved toward land redistribution and nationalization of much of the economy.

The Asiatic lion, the Mediterranean monk seal, the golden-headed tamarin, the Brazilian three-toed sloth, the Andean condor, the vicuña, the brown pelican, the American and Arctic peregrine falcons, the Atlantic and Pacific sea turtles, the Galápagos and Madagascar tortoises, and various species of gorillas, crocodiles, tigers, leopards, tapirs, cranes, rhinoceroses, wallabies, monkeys, parrots, whales, and pheasants were among those animals listed as endangered.

The first restriction enzyme, a substance that naturally splits genes, was found by American microbiologists Hamilton Othanel Smith and Daniel Nathans; this would make genetic engineering possible.

Indian-born American biochemist Har Gobind Khorana led the first team to synthesize a gene directly from chemicals; he would later insert a synthesized gene in a living cell and show that it functioned (1976).

(Sri Lankan)–American biochemist Cyril Ponnamperuma discovered in a recent meteorite five amino acids needed to make proteins, support for the theory that life might have begun naturally from compounds present on earth.

Fiber-optic technology was developed, using light waves passing through clear glass fibers; less expensive and able to carry more information, the new technology made possible much-expanded telecommunications.

A capsule from the Soviet space probe *Venera 7* landed on the surface of Venus, transmitting back information for 23 minutes before the hostile atmosphere destroyed it; it was the first soft (as opposed to crash) landing on another planet.

Documentarian Marcel Ophüls released *The Sorrow and the Pity*, a powerful, revealing, and, for some, acutely embarrassing film about France during the German occupation.

John Gielgud and Ralph Richardson starred as quite sane insane asylum inmates in David Storey's play *Home*, the playwright's comment on modern British life.

Maya Angelou emerged as a major African-American literary figure with her autobiography *I Know Why the Caged Bird Sings*.

Robert Altman emerged as a major film director with *M*A*S*H*, starring Donald Sutherland and Elliott Gould as Korean War doctors; the very popular black comedy would be the basis for a long-running television series (1972-1983).

George C. Scott starred as U.S. general George Patton in Franklin Schaffner's biographical film *Patton*; he would later refuse the Academy Award for best actor.

Judy Collins introduced her widely popular version of "Amazing Grace" in the album *Whales and Nightingales*.

Paul Simon and Art Garfunkel released their album *Bridge Over Troubled Water*; the title song, by Simon, would be widely recorded by others, notably Willie Nelson.

John Ashbery published his Pulitzer Prize–winning poetry collection *Self-Portrait in a Convex Mirror*.

The Grateful Dead released three albums: *Live Dead*, *Workingman's Dead*, and *American Beauty*, pleasing their fans, called Deadheads.

Dustin Hoffman starred in *Little Big Man*, opposite Faye Dunaway and Chief Dan George. Arthur

The earth's population was estimated at 3.6 billion to 3.7 billion, now growing at enormous speed, with more than half a billion people added in a decade and a terrifyingly large world population of 6 billion or more in clear sight before the end of the century.

A cyclone and accompanying massive sea wave killed 150,000 to 200,000 people in eastern Pakistan (later Bangladesh); one of the worst disasters of the century.

U.S. president Richard M. Nixon established the Environmental Protection Agency (EPA), charging it with administering the National Environmental Policy Act of 1969 and other federal laws affecting the environment. Among the 1970 laws it would administer were the U.S. Resource Recovery Act, which provided funds for recycling valuable materials and began to establish government control over management of hazardous substances; the Water Quality Improvement Act, which focused on the cleanup of ocean spills and pesticide drainage, notably in the Great Lakes region; and the Clean Air Act, under which the EPA would monitor air quality and set emissions standards for air pollutants, requiring less-polluting catalytic converters on American cars starting with the 1973 model year (1974 for cars from abroad).

The first Earth Day was celebrated (Apr.), an indication of the strength of the growing environmental movement; that same year, David Brower and others founded the environmental organization Friends of the Earth.

In northern Peru, a massive earthquake (May 31), which included the Mount Huascarán avalanche, killed 50,000 to 70,000 people.

Brazil won its unprecedented third World Cup in four contests, defeating Italy four games to one.

Wladyslaw Gomulka's Polish government fell as renewed antigovernment rioting broke out (Dec. 15-20); he was replaced by Edward Gierek.

Quebec separatists ended their "October crisis" terror campaign under heavy military and police pressure.

Syria's Ba'ath Party split; General Hafez al-Assad took power by coup.

Argentine anti-Perónist military officer Pedro Aramburu was assassinated by Perónist terrorists.

Fiji became an independent state and Commonwealth member.

Tonga became an independent state and Commonwealth member (June 4).

d. Charles André Joseph Marie de Gaulle (1890-1970), French officer; Free French organizer and head of the French government-in-exile during World War II; head of the first postwar French government (1945-1946), premier again (1958), and president of the Fifth Republic (1959-1969).

d. Gamal Abdel Nasser (1918-1970), Egyptian officer; leader of the 1952 coup that ended the monarchy and president of Egypt (1956-1970); he was succeeded by Anwar al-Sadat.

d. Lazaro Cardenas Del Rio (1895-1970), Mexican general; the Depression era reform president of Mexico (1933-1940), especially notable for his acceleration of land redistribution and expropriation of foreign-owned oil companies.

d. Sukarno (1901-1970), Indonesian independence movement leader; the first president of Indonesia (1949-1966).

d. William Joseph Slim (1891-1970), British general; World War II commander in Burma (1942-1945).

The Soviet Union's *Luna 19* satellite (Sept. 12) landed a remote-controlled roving vehicle on the moon's surface.

After the rupture of an oxygen tank supplying the *Apollo 13* spacecraft, U.S. astronauts James A. Lovell, Jr., Fred W. Haise, Jr., and John L. Swigart, Jr., were forced to abort a mission to the moon (Apr. 11-17) but were able to return safely by using the oxygen in the lunar module.

British physicist Stephen Hawking theorized that black holes had a temperature and so, in a cooler environment, could evaporate and grow smaller, producing "baby black holes."

Jacques Monod published *Chance and Necessity,* positing that no plan exists for the universe and that evolution has proceeded from pure chance; though he sought pure scientific objectivity, Monod's view had links with the existentialism of Albert Camus and others.

Removable "floppy disks" were introduced to make storage of computer data more flexible and expandable.

American biochemist Linus Pauling proposed that large amounts of vitamin C could prevent the common cold, an idea lacking hard evidence that still caused millions to increase their vitamin C intake.

The Minuteman III was introduced in the United States, the first intercontinental ballistic missile (ICBM) with multiple independently targeted reentry vehicles (MIRVs), warheads directed toward different targets.

Norman Borlaug was awarded the Nobel Peace Prize for his contributions to feeding the world's people in the Green Revolution.

Penn's satirical Western film was based on the 1964 Thomas Berger novel.

The Beatles' final album, *Let It Be*, appeared after the group had split up.

Soviet writer Alexander Solzhenitsyn was awarded the Nobel Prize for literature.

b. Mariah Carey (1970-), American singer; widely popular from the release of her first album, *Mariah Carey* (1990).

d. E. M. (Edward Morgan) Forster (1879-1970), British writer and critic; a leading 20th-century cultural figure for his novels, short stories, and immensely influential essays.

d. Erich Maria Remarque (1898-1970), major German writer from his first novel, *All Quiet on the Western Front* (1929).

d. Nelly Sachs (1891-1970), German-Jewish poet and playwright whose major theme was the Holocaust; she shared the 1966 Nobel Prize for literature.

d. Shmuel Yoseph Agnon (Samuel Yosef Czackzkes) (1888-1970), Galician-Israeli writer, largely of pre–World War II Eastern European Jewish life; he shared the 1966 Nobel Prize for literature.

d. Yukio Mishima (Hiraoka Kimitake) (1925-1970), prolific Japanese writer; a fascist, he committed ritual suicide after leading a failed attack on Japan's armed forces headquarters.

d. Janis Joplin (1943-1970), American blues singer; personally troubled, she died after an overdose of heroin.

d. Jimi Hendrix (1942-1970), American rock guitarist and singer whose death was probably caused by substance abuse.

Bernard Cornfeld's Swiss-based International Overseas Services (IOS) mutual fund empire collapsed when investors realized that their far-too-high rates of return masked massive losses of their money and tried to withdraw what little was left. Even that proved difficult when financier Robert Vesco bought control of IOS from Cornfeld, allegedly looted more than $224 million of what remained, and avoided fraud and bribery charges by allegedly buying refuge in Costa Rica (1972), other countries (1978-1983), and finally Cuba.

Canadian ice-hockey star Phil Esposito scored a record 152 points and 76 goals (1970-1971); he led his Boston Bruins to the Stanley Cup championship, the first of his two championships with them (1970; 1972).

In his work *Infallible? An Inquiry*, Swiss theologian Hans Küng became the first modern major Roman Catholic figure to reject the idea of the pope's infallibility; a leading dissenter, he was later disciplined by the Vatican and forbidden to teach theology under Catholic auspices.

A chartered DC-9 carrying Marshall University's football team crashed on approach to Huntington, West Virginia (Nov. 14), killing all 75 people aboard. Six weeks earlier (Oct. 2), 30 people had died when a charter plane carrying Wichita State University's football team crashed into a mountain.

American jockey Willie Shoemaker broke Johnny Longden's career record of wins (6,032), before his own retirement building that to 8,833.

Black Panther Party leaders Fred Hampton and Mark Clark were killed by attacking Chicago police.

Australian tennis player Margaret Smith Court had a grand slam, winning all four major women's singles titles: Wimbledon and the U.S., Australian, and French Opens.

1970 cont.

d. Alexander Fyodorovich Kerensky (1881-1970), Russian Socialist Revolutionary Party leader; premier of the short-lived Russian Provisional Government (Mar.-Nov. 1917).

d. Antonio de Oliviera Salazar (1889-1970), Portuguese fascist dictator (1932-1968).

d. Edouard Daladier (1884-1970), French politician; premier three times in the 1930s (1933; 1934; 1938-1940); a signatory of the Munich Pact. He was imprisoned during World War II, then resumed his political career.

Fuel rods melted in the Savannah River nuclear plant near Aiken, South Carolina (Dec. 27); it was one of a series of incidents not reported publicly until 1988. In Morris, Illinois, the Dresden II nuclear reactor went temporarily out of control (June 5).

1971

The Bangladesh War of Independence began (Mar.-Dec.), as Mujibur Rahman declared East Pakistan independent (Mar. 26). Pakistani forces quickly defeated the rebels, killing tens of thousands; 6 million to 10 million people fled to India, while India-supported insurgents continued a cross-border guerrilla war. Pakistan attacked Indian Kashmir (Dec. 3); India then invaded East Pakistan and quickly took Dacca and 90,000 Pakistani prisoners (Dec. 5), also successfully counterattacking in Kashmir. Bangladesh independence came (Dec. 16), followed by a cease-fire (Dec. 17). Rahman, imprisoned at the start of the insurrection, became the first prime minister of Bangladesh (1971-1975).

While Vietnam War peace negotiations continued, so did American and allied troop withdrawals, although American bombing of North Vietnam resumed (Dec.).

The Soviet-American Seabed Non-nuclearization Treaty provided that nuclear weapons would not be placed on or under the ocean floor.

Ted (Marcian) Hoff of Intel developed the microprocessor chip (microchip), which could contain a computer's central processing unit, formerly a room-size set of heat-producing vacuum tubes and wire circuits; the resulting miniaturization made possible inexpensive personal computers, robots, and small special-purpose computers in products such as cars, telephones, and pocket calculators, the first of which went on sale that year.

The CAT (computerized axial tomography) scan machine was developed by South African–American Allan MacLeod Cormack and British physicist Godfrey N. Hounsfield, using a high-speed X-ray machine and a computer to link pictures in a computer-simulated three-dimensional view, originally providing brain, but later whole body (1974), scans to aid medical diagnosis.

The first space station, *Salyut 1,* was launched (July 30), with various Soyuz craft used to ferry

d. Mark Rothko (Marcus Rothkovich) (1903-1970), American painter; a leading abstract expressionist; he committed suicide.

d. François Mauriac (1885-1970), French writer; a major figure in European literature and winner of the 1952 Nobel Prize for literature.

d. John Dos Passos (1896-1970), American writer; a leading novelist from the mid-1920s.

d. Lawren Stewart Harris (1885-1970), Canadian artist; a leading northern landscape painter and member of the Group of Seven.

d. Richard Neutra (1892-1970), Austrian architect, in America from 1923; a key California-centered modernist.

Colette MacDonald and her two daughters were murdered in their home at Fort Bragg, North Carolina (Feb. 17); charges initially brought against her husband, U.S. Army doctor Jeffrey MacDonald, were dismissed by the Army, but Colette's stepfather led a campaign to bring new murder charges (1975), leading to a conviction (1979).

d. Bertrand Russell (1872-1970), British philosopher, mathematician, educator, writer, radical reformer, and antiwar activist.

d. Walter Philip Reuther (1907-1970), president of the United Automobile Workers (UAW) (1946-1970) and of the Congress of Industrial Organizations (CIO) (1952-1955).

Alexander Solzhenitsyn published his massive novel *August 1914,* on the opening days of World War I.

Glenda Jackson created the role of Elizabeth I of England in the classic television series *Elizabeth R;* Robert Hardy, Ronald Himes, Rachel Kempson, and Bernard Hepton were among her costars.

Jane Fonda starred as New York prostitute Bree Daniels opposite Donald Sutherland in Alan J. Pakula's murder mystery *Klute.*

Lynn Seymour danced the lead in Kenneth MacMillan's ballet *Anastasia,* presented by Britain's Royal Ballet company.

Vittorio De Sica's classic film *The Garden of the Finzi-Continis,* about an Italian-Jewish family destroyed during the fascist period, starred Dominique Sanda, Lino Capolicchio, and Helmut Berger.

The Convention on Wetlands of International Importance, Especially as Waterfowl Habitat, an international agreement to foster cooperation in conserving and protecting key wetland areas around the globe, was adopted in Ramsar, Iran (effective 1975).

Spurred by mainly false reports of atrocities committed against police hostages, 1,500 New York State Police stormed and took Attica Prison from 1,000 inmates who had held the prison for four days; police gunfire killed 28 inmates and 9 hostages.

The environmental organization Greenpeace was founded to use nonviolent action to protect the environment, its first major action being a successful protest against underground nuclear weapons tests on Amchitka, an island off Alaska, which later became a bird sanctuary.

Ms. magazine was founded by a group of feminist writers, led by editor Gloria Steinem; its first issue appeared in January 1972.

The American-Soviet Nuclear Accidents Agreement provided means by which misunderstandings leading to nuclear war might be averted.

Zimbabwe African National Union (ZANU) and Zimbabwe African People's Union (ZAPU) forces began cross-border guerrilla attacks into Rhodesia from their bases in neighboring countries.

Saddam Hussein became ruler of Iraq, suppressing all opposition.

A military coup deposed the government of Bolivian general Juan José Torres, who was replaced by Colonel Hugo Banzer Suárez (Aug.).

Sri Lankan government forces defeated a People's Liberation Front revolt (Apr.-June).

A military coup deposed Ugandan leader Milton Obote, who was replaced by General Idi Amin; Amin began a reign of terror.

The United Nations ratified the Biological Warfare Ban Treaty.

Erich Honecker succeeded Walter Ulbricht as East German Communist Party general secretary and government leader.

Hungarian Catholic cardinal Jozsef Mindszenty left Budapest's American embassy, where he had taken refuge (1956) after the defeat of the Hungarian Revolution. He had earlier been imprisoned and then placed under house arrest (1949-1956). He would die four years later.

Qatar became an independent state (Sept. 1).

The United Arab Emirates was established, consisting of Abu Dhabi, Sharjah, Ajman, Umm al Qaiwain, Fujairah, and Dubai.

Bahrain became an independent state; its absolute ruler was Sheikh Salman ibn Hamad Al Khalifa.

Soviet cosmonauts to and from earth. Three astronauts launched aboard the *Soyuz 10* were the first to dock with the *Salyut 1* (Apr. 24). The three-man *Soyuz 11* crew — Georgi T. Dobrovolsky, Vladislav N. Volkov, and Viktor I. Patsayev — died after a failure of pressurization on reentering the earth's atmosphere (June 30).

The crew of the U.S. spacecraft *Apollo 14* (Jan. 31-Feb. 9) landed on the moon (Feb. 5), gathering rocks for analysis. The crew of *Apollo 15* (July 26-Aug. 7) used a land vehicle, the lunar rover, to travel 17 miles on the moon, gathering more rocks.

The first successful pancreas transplant was performed by Swiss surgeons, based on work by University of Minnesota researchers.

The Soviet spacecraft *Mars 1* and *Mars 2* were launched into orbit around Mars, landing capsules on its surface and briefly transmitting television signals. The U.S. spacecraft *Mariner 9* also was put into orbit around the planet, transmitting data.

The U.S. observational and research satellite *Pioneer 10* was launched; after flying by and transmitting information on the planets Jupiter (1973) and Neptune (1983), it would become the first human-made object to leave the solar system, still transmitting.

Soviet biologist Zhores Medvedev and his twin brother, historian Roy Medvedev, published *A Question of Madness,* about Zhores's imprisonment in a psychiatric hospital for his dissent from Trofim Lysenko's false, but government-sponsored, genetics. The work exposed widespread use of psychiatric detention for dissenters.

John Schlesinger's film *Sunday, Bloody Sunday* starred Glenda Jackson, Peter Finch, and Murray Head.

Andrew Lloyd Webber became a major musical theater figure with his rock opera *Jesus Christ Superstar,* starring Ben Vereen and Jeff Fenhold.

Daniel Berrigan's anti–Vietnam War play *The Trial of the Catonsville Nine,* starring Sam Waterston and Michael Moriarty, was based on the real-life trial of Catholic priests Daniel and Philip Berrigan and other war protesters.

Herman Wouk published the novel *The Winds of War,* set in World War II before Pearl Harbor; it would be the basis of the 1983 television series.

E. L. Doctorow published the novel *The Book of Daniel,* his view of the trial and 1953 execution of Julius and Ethel Rosenberg.

Max von Sydow and Liv Ullmann starred in Jan Troell's film *The Emigrants,* about 19th-century Swedish immigrants to the American Midwest.

Peter Bogdanovich's film *The Last Picture Show,* starring Timothy Bottoms, Jeff Bridges, Cloris Leachman, and Ben Johnson, explored 1950s Texas small-town life; based on the 1966 Larry McMurtry novel.

Paul McCartney founded the rock group Wings.

Chilean poet and diplomat Pablo Neruda was awarded the Nobel Prize for literature.

d. Igor Stravinsky (1882-1971), Russian composer; a leading figure in 20th-century music, most notably in ballet, beginning with *The Firebird* (1910).

d. Louis "Satchmo" Armstrong (1901-1971), American trumpeter, cornetist, singer, and bandleader

Kareem Abdul-Jabbar won the first of his six National Basketball Association Most Valuable Player Awards (1971; 1972; 1974; 1976; 1977; 1980).

Austrian skier Annemarie Moser-Proell won the first of what would be a record 6 World Cup championships (1971-1975; 1979) and 62 individual victories, a total not surpassed until a decade later, by Ingemar Stenmark (1982).

Elizabeth Janeway published *Man's World, Woman's Place,* a landmark work of the newly reinvigorated women's rights movement.

In a criminal exploit that captured the public imagination, airplane hijacker D. B. Cooper parachuted out of a plane over the state of Washington, carrying with him a $200,000 ransom; Cooper disappeared, but some of the money was later found in a riverbank.

Seeking to safeguard children, the U.S. Lead-Based Paint Poisoning Prevention Act required that paint containing lead be removed from federally subsidized housing; insufficient funds were allocated, however, and experts could not agree on how to handle the job safely.

Soviet historian Roy Medvedev published *Let History Judge,* a notable attack on Stalinism.

The prison sentence of Teamsters Union president James Hoffa was commuted by President Richard M. Nixon.

Jesse Jackson founded People United to Save Humanity (PUSH).

An Alaskan 727 crashed in the mountains near Juneau, Alaska (Sept. 4), killing 109 people.

An F-86 Sabrejet piloted by a student collided with an All-Nippon 727 near Morioha, Japan (July 30); 162 people died.

d. Nikita Sergeyevich Khrushchev (1894-1971), leader of the Soviet Union (1955-1964); most notable for his 1956 "secret speech" on the crimes of the Stalin period and for bringing the world to the brink of nuclear war during the 1962 Cuban Missile Crisis.

d. Dean Gooderham Acheson (1893-1971), American lawyer and diplomat; Truman administration secretary of state (1949-1953). Although he played a major role in developing such Cold War strategies as the Truman Doctrine and the Marshall Plan, he was attacked by Senator Joseph McCarthy as being "soft" on communism.

d. François "Papa Doc" Duvalier (1907-1971), Haitian dictator (1957-1971); he was succeeded by his son, Jean Claude, dubbed "Baby Doc" (1971-1986).

d. Jacobo Arbenz Guzmán (1913-1971), Guatemalan soldier and politician; president of Guatemala (1950-1954) who fled into exile after losing to U.S.-backed forces in the Guatemalan Civil War.

d. Lin Biao (1907-1971), Chinese political leader who had been Mao Zedong's heir apparent; he was reportedly killed in an airplane crash in flight after leading an aborted coup.

d. Ralph Johnson Bunche (1904-1971), African-American diplomat and civil rights movement leader; chief United Nations mediator for Palestine (1948) and winner of the 1950 Nobel Peace Prize.

d. Thomas Edmund Dewey (1902-1971), American lawyer, prosecutor, and Republican politician; governor of New York (1942-1954) and twice unsuccessful Republican presidential candidate (1944; 1948).

The U.S. Food and Drug Administration banned DES (diethylstilbestrol), a synthetic estrogen prescribed for many pregnant women from 1940, citing evidence of damage to their children, especially rare cancers of the reproductive organs in their daughters.

The Canadian government's Hydro-Québec began building the James Bay hydropower project, planned as the world's largest hydropower project, with more than 200 dams and dikes, 23 power stations, and diversion of 19 rivers, sparking continuing local and environmental opposition.

An invisible X-ray source — Cygnus X-1, in the Cygnus constellation — believed to be a black hole paired with a visible star, was discovered by Canadian astronomer C. T. Bolt.

Unpaved roads of Times Beach, Missouri, were covered with thousands of gallons of an oil meant to control dust; in fact, it was waste from a chemical plant that made the defoliant Agent Orange, containing highly toxic dioxin, and would create a major chemical disaster. By 1974, the deaths of many local animals were linked to the chemical, but no action was taken until 1982, in the mistaken belief that the chemical would quickly break down in the environment.

The Northern States nuclear reactor released 50,000 gallons of radioactive water into the Mississippi River, near Monticello, Minnesota (Nov. 19).

d. William Lawrence Bragg (1890-1971), Australian physicist who, with his father, William Henry Bragg, did key work in X-ray crystallography.

from the early 1920s; as the first leading jazz soloist, a seminal figure in jazz history.

d. Lil (Lillian) Hardin Armstrong (1898-1971), American jazz pianist, singer, and bandleader; a notable figure in early jazz; the first wife and musical colleague of Louis Armstrong.

d. George Seferis (Georgios Seferiades) (1900-1971), Greek poet and diplomat; a major literary figure from his first poetry collection, *Turning Point* (1931), and winner of the 1963 Nobel Prize for literature.

d. Margaret Bourke-White (1906-1971), American photographer; one of the world's leading photojournalists from the early 1930s.

d. Thomas Beecham (1869-1971), celebrated British conductor; founder of several major orchestras, including the Royal Philharmonic Orchestra (1946).

d. Jim Morrison (1943-1971), American lead singer of the Doors; his death was probably due to substance abuse.

d. Tyrone Guthrie (1900-1971), British director and actor; founder of Minneapolis's Guthrie Theater (1963).

d. Paul Lukas (Pal Lukàcs) (1894-1971), Hungarian-American actor; a leading Hollywood character actor from 1928; he starred on stage and screen in Lillian Hellman's *Watch on the Rhine* (1941; 1943).

d. Stevie (Florence Margaret) Smith (1902-1971), British poet, novelist, and illustrator; a noted poet from the late 1930s.

d. David Sarnoff (1891-1971), Russian-American engineer who built the Radio Corporation of America (RCA), as its chairman helping to shape the development of radio and television.

d. Coco (Gabriel Bonheur) Chanel (ca. 1883-1971), French fashion designer who pioneered the loose, low-waisted, unconstricted women's clothes of the 1920s, such as the chemise dress (1920), and perfumes such as her Chanel No. 5 (1922).

d. John Charles Walsham Reith (1889-1971), British administrator who directed the British Broadcasting Corporation (BBC) in its formative years (1922-1938).

d. Bobby (Robert Tyre) Jones (1902-1971), American amateur golfer; the first to win the British and U.S. Opens in the same year (1926), winning them again in 1930, along with two other major tournaments.

d. Hugo LaFayette Black (1886-1971), American lawyer; Democratic Alabama senator (1927-1937) and U.S. Supreme Court justice (1937-1971); a leading liberal on the Court despite his 1920s membership in the Ku Klux Klan.

d. Reinhold Niebuhr (1892-1971), American Protestant theologian, educator, and writer; a pacifist who became a leading antifascist in the 1930s.

d. Cyril Lodowic Burt (1883-1971), British psychologist; a key figure in shaping Britain's modern educational system. His influential twin studies, supporting his view that intelligence was largely inherited, were later discredited, found after his death to have been faked.

President Richard M. Nixon visited China (Feb.); his historic "Opening to China" ended more than two decades of almost complete estrangement, dating back to U.S. support of Nationalist forces during the Chinese Civil War.

During the U.S. presidential campaign, five burglars employed by the Republican National Committee were arrested after breaking into Democratic National Committee headquarters in Washington's Watergate apartment complex (June 17), beginning the Watergate scandal, which would result in the 1974 resignation of President Richard M. Nixon.

Incumbent Republican Richard M. Nixon defeated Democrat George McGovern to win a second term as U.S. president.

By year's end, fewer than 50,000 American and allied troops remained in Vietnam, but the North Vietnamese Easter Offensive failed. While peace negotiations continued, President Richard Nixon ordered the massive "Christmas bombing" of Hanoi and Haiphong and the mining of North Vietnamese harbors.

In Burundi, Tutsi-dominated armed forces massacred 100,000 to 250,000 Hutus after a failed Hutu insurrection.

At Laurel, Mississippi (May 15), former Alabama governor and presidential candidate George Wallace was wounded in an assassination attempt.

Austrian diplomat Kurt Waldheim became the fourth secretary-general of the United Nations (1972-1982).

British troops killed 13 unarmed Catholic demonstrators in Londonderry, Northern Ireland (Jan. 30). As guerrilla war intensified, Britain imposed direct rule on Northern Ireland (Mar.).

The Chicago Seven convictions (1969) were reversed on appeal; Judge Julius Hoffman was censured for prejudicial behavior during the trial.

The pesticide DDT (dichlorodiphenyltrichloroethane) was banned in the United States, following recognition that it concentrated to toxic levels in the food chain, causing birth defects and reproduction problems, especially thinning the shells of birds' eggs and bringing some species close to extinction. Many other countries followed suit, allowing for the revival of some species. However, in some parts of the world, DDT would continue to be used even in the 1990s.

Dennis L. Meadows of the Massachusetts Institute of Technology prepared for the Club of Rome a highly influential report, *The Limits of Growth*, employing computer modeling to forecast a world in which unchecked economic expansion, waste, pollution, and population growth could deplete natural resources and cause a disastrous decline in the provision of food and services for the world's population.

American paleontologists Stephen Jay Gould and Niles Eldredge posited the controversial theory of punctuated evolution, suggesting that evolutionary change takes place not steadily, as had long been assumed, but in rapid spurts when environmental pressures force a species to change, with species otherwise being relatively stable.

A second capsule was landed on the planet Venus, this one from the Soviet spacecraft *Venera 8*.

Apollo 17 was launched (Dec. 7), the last American mission to land on and explore the moon.

The Soviet space probe *Luna 20* landed on the moon, took soil samples, and returned safely to earth.

Marlon Brando created Mafia family head Don Vito Corleone in Francis Ford Coppola's classic film *The Godfather*, costarring Al Pacino, Robert Duvall, James Caan, and Diane Keaton; based on the 1969 Mario Puzo novel, as adapted by Puzo and Coppola.

Twenty years after having been blacklisted and expelled from the United States, Charles Chaplin returned to accept a special Academy Award for his whole body of work, effectively an apology from the American film industry for its appalling McCarthy era treatment of one its greatest figures.

E. M. Forster's fifth novel, *Maurice*, was published posthumously; completed in 1914, Forster had not published the work because of its then-taboo openly homosexual themes.

Luis Buñuel cowrote and directed the often-bitter film satire *The Discreet Charm of the Bourgeoisie*, set at a rather surreal dinner party, his metaphor for part of contemporary French society; Fernando Rey, Delphine Seyrig, and Stephane Audran led a large cast.

Edward Durell Stone, moving beyond the International Style, designed Washington's John F. Kennedy Center for the Performing Arts.

Zoë Caldwell and George Grizzard starred as Eve and Adam in Arthur Miller's allegorical play *The Creation of the World and Other Business*.

Steve Goodman introduced his classic folk-rock song "The City of New Orleans," written during the 1972 presidential campaign; it would be widely recorded by others, notably Judy Collins and Arlo Guthrie.

Harriet Andersson, Ingrid Thulin, Liv Ullmann, and Erland Josephson starred in Ingmar Bergman's classic film *Cries and Whispers*.

A landmark antidiscrimination law, Title IX of the 1972 Education Act Amendments, banned discrimination in most federally assisted educational programs and related activities, including sports.

Chess player Bobby Fischer defeated Russian master Boris Spassky to become the first American world champion; he then refused to defend his title, which was finally stripped from him by the International Chess Federation (1975).

At Managua, Nicaragua, a massive earthquake destroyed most of the city center, killing 5,000 people (Dec. 23).

At the Munich Olympics, American swimmer Mark Spitz won a record seven gold medals. Soviet gymnast Olga Korbut won three gold medals, two for the floor exercise and balance beam events, one as part of a team.

"Black September" Palestinian terrorists attacked Israeli athletes at the Munich Olympics (Sept.), killing two and taking nine hostages; during a failed rescue operation, all nine hostages and five terrorists were killed.

The Convention Concerning the Protection of the World Cultural and Natural Heritage was signed in Paris, providing an international framework for identifying and protecting "world heritage" sites — cultural or natural areas of "outstanding universal value."

The Convention on the Prevention of Marine Pollution by Dumping of Waste and Other Matter, an international agreement covering deliberate disposal of waste at sea, was adopted (effective 1975).

The Equal Rights Amendment (ERA) was passed by the Senate; the long, failed campaign for ERA enactment ensued (1972-1982).

1972 cont.

Ferdinand Marcos took full power as military dictator in the Philippines, imprisoning Benigno Aquino and other opposition leaders.

Minister and Southern Christian Leadership Conference (SCLC) leader Andrew Young became the first African-American congressman from Georgia since Reconstruction.

Mississippi Freedom Democratic Party delegates were seated as the Mississippi delegates to the Democratic National Convention.

The Strategic Arms Limitation Agreements of 1972 (SALT I) halted further deployment of intercontinental ballistic missiles (ICBMs) for five years and limited the use of antiballistic missiles (ABMs).

Democratic senator Thomas Eagleton was obliged to withdraw as vice-presidential candidate after the disclosure of previous nervous exhaustion and shock treatments.

Labour Party leader Edward Gough Whitlam became prime minister of Australia (1972-1975).

West German terrorists Andreas Baader and Ulrike Meinhof were captured and imprisoned.

Ahmed Kérékou took power in Dahomey; in the three years that followed, he set up a Marxist-Leninist state and changed the country's name to Benin (1975).

A military coup in Ecuador deposed the elected government of President José Maria Velasco Ibarra (Feb.), replaced by General Guillermo Rodriguez Lara.

d. Harry S. Truman (1884-1972), 33rd president of the United States (1945-1953); his decision to use atomic bombs on Hiroshima (Aug. 6, 1945) and Nagasaki (Aug. 9, 1945) marked the beginning of a new, terror-filled era in human history.

American physicist Murray Gell-Mann developed the theory that atomic particles called quarks exist in what he called three "colors" — red, blue, and green — which, as with true colors, produce a lack of property (white) when all three are present; this founded the new field of quantum chromodynamics.

American chemist Robert Burns Woodward first synthesized the complicated vitamin B_{12} molecule.

For his work on superconductivity (1951), American electrical engineer and physicist John Bardeen won the second of his two Nobel Prizes in physics (1956; 1972), the first person ever so honored; this one was shared with Leon Cooper and John Schrieffer.

The U.S. *Landsat I* satellite was launched to take wide-scale photographs of the earth, providing an unprecedented view of global resources.

A team of laser-wielding physicists led by Kenneth M. Evenson obtained the most precise measurement yet for the speed of light: 186,282.3959 miles per second.

Barbara Ward and René Dubos published *Only One Earth,* an influential cautionary work about the globe's limited resources.

The snow leopard was listed as an endangered species.

d. Louis Seymour Bazett Leakey (1903-1972), British anthropologist and paleontologist who made key discoveries of early hominid remains in East Africa, notably at Olduvai Gorge, in Tanzania (from 1959), with his wife, Mary Leakey, who succeeded him as director at Olduvai, and their son Richard Leakey. He also

Wole Soyinka published *The Man Died: Prison Notes of Wole Soyinka*.

Yves Montand starred in the Constantin Costa-Gavras political murder film *State of Siege*, set in Uruguay.

David Bowie released the album *The Rise and Fall of Ziggy Stardust and the Spiders from Mars*, touring America.

Christo won worldwide publicity for a massive artwork, covering a section of Australian coastline with 1 million square feet of plastic sheeting.

Stevie Wonder had a major hit with "You Are the Sunshine of My Life" and released two albums, *Music of My Mind* and *Talking Book*.

London's Tate Gallery made a controversial purchase: unconnected stacks of bricks, which minimalist creator Carl Andre called "land art."

German writer Heinrich Böll was awarded the Nobel Prize for literature.

d. Mahalia Jackson (1911-1972), leading African-American gospel singer of the century, and a prominent civil rights movement activist.

d. Ezra Pound (1885-1972), American poet, critic, and translator; a noted literary figure early in the century. In Italy from 1924 through World War II, he was a bigot who broadcast for the Fascists. He escaped a postwar treason conviction by being placed in an insane asylum (1946-1958).

d. Bronislava Nijinska (1891-1972), Russian dancer with Sergei Diaghilev's Ballets Russes company (1909-1914); a leading choreographer from the early 1920s; she was the sister of Vaslav Nijinsky.

d. Asta Nielsen (1883-1972), Danish actress; a major silent film star in Germany, she went home to Denmark after the Nazis won power.

Baseball pitcher Steve Carlton won his first of four Cy Young Awards (1972; 1977; 1980; 1982).

Richard Lee Petty won his fourth stock-car-racing national championship (breaking the record of his father, Lee Petty) and passed 100,000 miles of competition, becoming the first stock-car racer with career earnings of more than $1 million.

Norwegian philosopher Arne Naess coined the phrase *deep ecology*, referring to exploration of the relationship between human beings and nature, in particular affirming the value of all life forms.

The Dallas Cowboys won the first of their four Super Bowl titles (1972; 1978; 1993; 1994).

The first major Great Lakes Water Quality Agreement was signed, aimed at reducing sewage discharge into the lakes, at a time when Lake Erie was described as "dead" and Lakes Ontario and Michigan were little better.

The government of India, working with the World Wildlife Fund, set up 11 reserves to help save the threatened Indian tiger.

The United Nations Conference on the Human Environment in Stockholm, Sweden, produced a declaration outlining ideal international efforts to protect the environment, especially representative natural ecosystems. It also called for a 10-year moratorium on whaling that was not adopted, but marked intensification of the worldwide campaign to save the endangered whales. That same year, the United States passed the Marine Mammal Protection Act.

When the Canyon Lake Dam broke, flooding Rapid City, South Dakota (June 9), 200 people died.

Alex Comfort's best-selling book *The Joy of Sex* both exemplified and helped speed changes in sexual attitudes, with a focus on learning how to maximize

d. Kwame Nkrumah (1909-1972), Ghanian independence movement and pan-African movement leader; Gold Coast prime minister (1951-1957), prime minister of Ghana (1957-1960), and first president of Ghana (1960-1966).

d. Duke of Windsor (1894-1972), who had been Britain's King Edward VIII until his abdication (Dec. 1936), forced after he announced his intention to marry American divorcée Wallis Simpson, later the Duchess of Windsor.

d. Adam Clayton Powell (1908-1972), the first African-American member of the New York City Council (1941-1945) and a longtime Harlem Democratic congressman (1945-1971).

d. Franz Halder (1884-1972), German general and chief of staff (1938-1942); imprisoned (1944) after the failed Hitler assassination attempt.

d. James Francis Byrnes (1879-1972), American politician; South Carolina Democratic congressman (1911-1925) and senator (1931-1941); U.S. secretary of state (1945-1947).

d. Lester Bowles Pearson (1897-1972), Canadian politician and diplomat; while Canada's minister of external affairs (1948-1957), he played a major role in resolving the Suez Crisis, receiving the 1957 Nobel Peace Prize. He was later prime minister (1963-1968).

d. Paul-Henri Spaak (1889-1972), Belgian politician; three times premier (1938-1939; 1946; 1947-1950) and president of the United Nations General Assembly (1946).

encouraged many young scientists working in Africa, including Jane Goodall and Dian Fossey.

d. Maria Goeppert Mayer (1906-1972), German-American nuclear physicist who developed the shell theory of nuclear structure (1948); the second woman to receive the Nobel Prize for physics (1963).

d. Harlow Shapley (1885-1972), American astronomer who first described the shape of the Milky Way (1918); also known for his popular writings.

d. Igor Ivan Sikorsky (1889-1972), Russian-American aeronautical engineer whose helicopter became the 20th-century standard.

d. Richard Courant (1888-1972), German-American mathematician; after key early work in Germany, long associated with New York University (1934-1958), where he founded (1953) the institute named, at his retirement, the Courant Institute of Mathematical Sciences.

d. Edmund Wilson (1895-1972), prolific American writer, critic, and editor; a highly influential figure in American letters.

d. John Berryman (1914-1972), leading American poet from the publication of his collection *Homage to Mistress Bradstreet* (1956); he committed suicide.

d. John Grierson (1898-1972), British filmmaker; a noted figure in British and Canadian documentary film who created classics such as *Song of Ceylon* (1935) and *Night Mail* (1936).

d. Marianne Moore (1887-1972), leading objectivist American poet from the publication of her first collection, *Poems* (1921).

d. Ted Shawn (1891-1972), leading American dancer and choreographer; cofounder of the Denishawn school and dance company (1915-1931) and founder of the All-Male Dance Company (1932) and Jacob's Pillow Dance Festival (1933).

d. Maurice Chevalier (1888-1972), French singer; a star in variety, opposite Mistinguett, from 1909 and on screen from 1929.

sexual pleasure and a new recognition of masturbation and homosexuality as acceptable sexual alternatives.

An explosion at a coal mine in Wankie, Rhodesia (June 6), killed 427 people.

An Eastern L-1011 landed in a swamp in Florida's Everglades (Dec. 29), killing 101 of 176 people aboard.

Rock slides struck two trains in the Vierzy Tunnel near Soissons, France (June 16); 107 people died.

d. Jackie (Jack Roosevelt) Robinson (1919-1972), American baseball player who broke the color bar in America's professional athletics, as the first African-American to play major league baseball, with the Brooklyn Dodgers (1947-1957).

d. J. Edgar Hoover (1895-1972), director of the U.S. Federal Bureau of Investigation (FBI) (1924-1972); during his career, he was associated most notably with the Palmer Raids (1920), the fight against criminal "public enemies" in the 1930s, the anticommunist campaigns of the McCarthy era and beyond, and the surveillance of antiwar and other dissidents, including Martin Luther King, Jr., in the 1960s.

d. Rose (Rachel) Schneiderman (1882-1972), Polish-American trade union leader; an organizer of the International Ladies' Garment Workers' Union (ILGWU).

d. Cristóbal Balenciaga (1895-1972), Spanish fashion designer noted for the loose-fitting styles of the 1950s.

Egyptian, Syrian, Iraqi, and Jordanian forces made surprise attacks on Israel on the Jewish holy day of Yom Kippur (Oct. 6), making substantial initial gains at the start of the Yom Kippur War (Fourth Arab-Israeli War). Counterattacking Israeli forces with air superiority retook the Golan Heights and were ready to take Damascus (Oct. 12), simultaneously successfully attacking Egypt across the Suez Canal. Soviet-American war came close, as Soviet forces mobilized to save the Egyptian Third Army from destruction were met by an American ultimatum (Oct. 24). A United Nations–sponsored cease-fire (Oct. 27) brought UN peacekeeping forces to Suez and the Golan Heights. The Arab oil embargo followed, as the Arab states, through the Organization of Petroleum Exporting Countries (OPEC), imposed a crippling oil embargo on the world's industrial states (Oct. 1973-Mar. 1974), resuming shipments only after victorious Israeli forces disengaged following the war.

After the five Watergate burglars and E. Howard Hunt and G. Gordon Liddy pleaded guilty to Watergate-related charges, many Nixon administration illegal actions were exposed, despite sustained cover-up attempts that broke down late in 1973, when President Richard Nixon fired special prosecutor Archibald Cox and Deputy Attorney General William Ruckelshaus (in the "Saturday night massacre") in an attempt to conceal the contents of the "Watergate tapes." President Nixon instead destroyed his own public credibility, and was forced to appoint a new prosecutor, Leon Jaworski.

The Paris Peace Accords on Vietnam (Jan. 27) ended the Vietnam War, providing for complete American withdrawal, a truce, and the return of American prisoners of war; American forces completed their withdrawal (Mar. 29), although air attacks on Cambodia continued until congressional action forced their stop (Aug.). Civil war continued in Vietnam and Cambodia. Peace negotiators Henry Kissinger and Le Duc Tho shared the Nobel Peace Prize, which Kissinger accepted and Le Duc Tho refused.

A Chilean military coup led by General Augusto Pinochet and backed by the U.S. Central Intelligence Agency (CIA)

Genetic engineering began when Stanley Cohen and Herbert Boyer became the first scientists to "cut and paste" DNA, using previously discovered restriction enzymes (1968; 1970) to split and transfer genes in *Escherichia coli* bacteria, creating altered genes.

The magnetic resonance imager (MRI) or nuclear magnetic resonance (NMR) imager was developed in Britain; like the CAT scan (1971), the medical diagnostic device used a computer to convert pictures of the body at different planes into three-dimensional simulations, measuring proton density rather than using radiation. MRI pictures were not as sharp as CAT scan pictures, but could provide doctors with more medically useful information about the biological and chemical state of body tissues.

John Vincent Atanasoff and Clifford E. Berry were effectively recognized as builders of the world's first fully electronic computer (1942), after a patent suit filed by others over royalties on the ENIAC, the first patented electronic computer. A judge found that Atanasoff's computer had contributed significantly to the ENIAC's development and so voided the ENIAC's patent.

In Kenya, physical anthropologist Richard Leakey discovered a hominid skull some 2.9 million years old and with a larger brain capacity than expected for that age. With discoveries by Donald Johanson (1974), this would spark a reevaluation of when hominids diverged from *Australopithecus*, a date pushed back to 3 million to 4 million years ago.

Skylab, a U.S. orbital space station designed for scientific experiments, was launched (May 14); damaged on takeoff, it was repaired by the first three-man crew during their 28-day stay (from May 25). The year also saw two other *Skylab* missions, the longest for 84 days.

Alexander Solzhenitsyn left the Soviet Union after publication abroad of the first volume of *The Gulag Archipelago,* his classic exposé of the Soviet prison system (1973-1975).

Peter Pears as von Aschenbach sang the lead in Benjamin Britten's opera *Death in Venice,* libretto by Myfanwy Piper; based on Thomas Mann's celebrated 1912 story.

Barbra Streisand and Robert Redford starred in Sydney Pollack's film *The Way We Were,* a retrospective look at some of the artists and intellectuals of the Depression era college generation that matured in the late 1930s, taking them through World War II and the McCarthy period.

Barnard Hughes in the title role and Brian Murray as his son starred in Hugh Leonard's Ireland-set play *Da.*

Edward Fox starred as the failed assassin in Fred Zinnemann's film *The Day of the Jackal,* the story of an unsuccessful attempt to murder Charles de Gaulle; the character was based on that of "Carlos," the long-sought terrorist finally taken two decades later (1994).

Liv Ullmann and Erland Josephson starred as a wife and husband whose marriage is disintegrating in Ingmar Bergman's *Scenes from a Marriage,* made as a television series, then recut into a theatrical film.

Douglas Turner Ward starred in the Negro Ensemble Company's production of Joseph A. Walker's play *The River Niger,* a meditation on some aspects of the African-American experience.

George Roy Hill's film *The Sting,* starring Paul Newman and Robert Redford as 1920s Chicago con men, revived interest in the music of Scott Joplin.

Len Cariou and Glynis Johns starred in Stephen Sondheim's musical *A Little Night Music,* based on

In its landmark *Roe v. Wade* decision, the U.S. Supreme Court clearly established the legality of abortion in the United States, a decision that was to trigger a massive, decades-long fight and be substantially weakened by future decisions, but that would, in 1994, be sharply and unequivocally restated by the Court. In *Roe v. Wade,* the Court recognized the right of women to choose abortion, within stated limits, allowing unrestricted abortions during the first trimester of pregnancy but allowing states to regulate abortion in the second trimester and to regulate or prohibit abortion in the third trimester, except when the mother's life or health was endangered.

Buffalo Bills running back O. J. (Orenthal James) Simpson was the first professional football player to rush for more than 2,000 yards in a season, gaining 2,003 yards.

Environmentalists seeking to protect the world's species won two important victories. The first and most successful major international wildlife conservation treaty, the Convention on International Trade in Endangered Species of Wild Fauna and Flora (CITES), was designed to identify and protect endangered or threatened plants and animals from trade and overexploitation. Also, the U.S. Congress passed the Endangered Species Act; though not strongly enforced, it established the principle and provided a basis for legal action.

American Indian Movement (AIM) activists occupied the Wounded Knee Massacre site in South Dakota, focusing media attention on their program.

American Telephone and Telegraph (AT&T) signed a landmark anti–sex segregation Equal Employment Opportunity Commission consent decree.

Coached by Don Shula, the Miami Dolphins posted the only perfect season in National Football League history (17-0), going on to win the Super Bowl twice in succession (1973; 1974).

deposed the elected government of socialist President Salvador Allende Gossens (1908-1973), who was killed during the coup, probably by the military. Martial law and a reign of terror began.

A cease-fire (Feb.) ended the Laotian Civil War, with a Pathet Lao victory and a Pathet Lao coalition government.

Deng Xiaoping was "rehabilitated"; he had been "purged" during China's Cultural Revolution.

Juan Perón returned to become president of Argentina (1973-1974); his vice president was Isabel Perón, his second wife.

U.S. vice president Spiro Agnew resigned after pleading "no contest" to a charge of income tax evasion. He was succeeded by House Republican minority leader Gerald R. Ford.

A military coup deposed Greek dictator George Papadopoulos (Nov. 25); he was replaced by General Phaidon Gizikis.

A republican coup deposed King Mohammed Zahir Shah of Afghanistan, setting up the Republic of Afghanistan (1973-1978).

The United Kingdom, Denmark, and Ireland joined the European Community; Britain and Denmark withdrew from the European Free Trade Association, which continued as an organization of small European countries.

Tuparamos (National Liberation Front) guerrilla forces were decisively defeated and dispersed by the Uruguayan army.

The Bahamas (Commonwealth of the Bahamas) became an independent country and British Commonwealth member.

d. Jeanette Pickering Rankin (1880-1973), the first elected congresswoman; a socialist and pacifist who

The U.S. observational and research satellite *Pioneer 10* passed within 81,000 miles of the planet Jupiter (Dec.), exploring its magnetic field and moons and transmitting data about its composition. Aboard was a message from earth, including drawings of a man, a woman, and the spacecraft itself (to scale), as well as information about the solar system.

The U.S. space probe *Mariner 10* was launched toward Mercury.

Subatomic particles called quarks were theorized as having the strongest attraction to each other at the *farthest*, rather than the nearest, distance.

Konrad Lorenz, Nikolaas Tinbergen, and Karl von Frisch shared the Nobel Prize for physiology or medicine for their work on animal behavior.

d. Paul Dudley White (1886-1973), American cardiologist; a founder of the American Heart Association, long associated with Harvard Medical School, who pioneered in the use of the electrocardiograph (ECG or EKG) to record the heart's electrical activity and in emphasizing the roles of diet, stress, and exercise in the heart's health.

Ingmar Bergman's 1955 film *Smiles of a Summer Night*.

Edward G. Robinson and Charlton Heston starred in the prophetic and despairing science fiction film *Soylent Green*, portraying the evil end of massive population growth, based on Harry Harrison's 1966 novel *Make Room! Make Room!*

Federico Fellini's bittersweet autobiographical film *Amarcord* was set in the fascist 1930s Italy of his youth.

Rita Mae Brown published the autobiographical novel *Rubyfruit Jungle*, a trailblazing radical lesbian novel.

François Truffaut starred in his own film about filmmaking, *Day for Night*, along with Jacqueline Bisset, Jean-Pierre Leaud, Valentina Cortese, and Jean-Pierre Aumont.

Glenda Jackson and George Segal starred in Melvin Frank's film *A Touch of Class*.

Thomas Pynchon published *Gravity's Rainbow*, which won a National Book Award; he would not publish his next novel, *Vineland*, until 1989.

Wole Soyinka published the novel *Season of Anomy*.

Australian writer Patrick White was awarded the Nobel Prize for literature.

d. Pablo Ruiz Picasso (1881-1973), extraordinarily prolific Spanish artist; a towering figure in 20th-century art who, with Georges Braque, originated cubism early in the century.

d. Pablo Casals (1876-1973), leading Spanish cellist, composer, and conductor; for seven decades, a major figure in music.

d. Edward (Edouard Jean) Steichen (1879-1973), leading American photographer for six decades.

In tune with the times, the militant 9 to 5, National Association of Working Women, was founded.

American tennis player Billie Jean King successfully defended her women's singles title at Wimbledon; she also won a highly publicized "battle of the sexes" match against 1939 Wimbledon and U.S. men's champion, Bobby Riggs, at the Houston Astrodome.

Labor contractor Juan Corona was convicted of the murders of 25 Mexican migrant workers in Yuba County, California (1970-1971), and sentenced to 25 terms of life imprisonment.

The Agreement on Conservation of Polar Bears made the world's largest carnivore an internationally protected species, sharply restricting polar bear hunting, primarily to traditional Eskimo hunters.

The bar code, a series of black and white stripes read by a laser scanner and decoded by a computer, was first put into use in the U.S. grocery industry, soon expanding to other areas.

President Richard Nixon appointed Robert Bork U.S. solicitor general.

The Consumer Product Safety Commission was established in the United States to set safety and performance standards, issue warnings, and call for recalls or bans where necessary for the public's protection.

American Exxon executive Victor E. Samuelson was kidnapped by guerrillas in Campana, Argentina (Dec. 6); he was later freed after payment of a record $14.2 million ransom.

In a major insurance industry scandal, top executives of the Equity Funding Corporation were found to have fraudulently created and sold to reinsurance companies billions of dollars' worth of false insur-

voted against U.S. entry into both world wars. Hers was the only congressional vote against entry into World War II, and it ended her political career.

d. Lyndon Baines Johnson (1908-1973), 36th president of the United States (1963-1969), who succeeded to the presidency after the assassination of John F. Kennedy, won a full term (1964), became identified with the Vietnam War in spite of his work on civil rights and domestic social concerns, and did not run again in 1968.

d. David Ben-Gurion (David Green) (1886-1973), Polish-Israeli politician; founder of the socialist Mapai Party (1930), leader of the Israeli and world Zionist movements (1935-1948), and first prime minister of Israel (1948-1953; 1955-1963).

d. Fulgencio Batista y Zalvidar (1901-1973), Cuban soldier and politician; president of Cuba (1940-1944) and dictator (1952-1958), until his corrupt government fell to Fidel Castro's guerrilla forces.

d. Ismet Inönu (1884-1973), Turkish prime minister (1923-1938; 1961-1965) and president (1938-1950).

d. Louis Stephen St. Laurent (1882-1973), Canadian lawyer and politician; the second French-Canadian prime minister (1948-1958).

d. J. R. R. (John Radford Reuel) Tolkien (1892-1973), British writer; a unique literary figure for *The Hobbit* (1937) and the trilogy "The Lord of the Rings" (1954-1955).

d. W. H. (Wystan Hugh) Auden (1907-1973), British-American poet and dramatist; a leading 20th-century poet.

d. John Ford (Sean Aloysius O'Feeney) (1895-1973), American film director, a leading figure in world cinema from the early 1930s through the mid-1960s.

d. Noël Coward (1899-1973), prolific British writer, actor, composer, and director who emerged as a major playwright with *The Vortex* (1924).

d. Pablo Neruda (Ricardo Neftali Reyes Basualto) (1904-1973), Chilean; winner of the 1971 Nobel Prize for literature.

d. Jacques Lipchitz (Chaim Jacob Lipschitz) (1891-1973), Lithuanian-Jewish sculptor; a major figure in 20th-century art.

d. Mary Wigman (1886-1973), German dancer, choreographer, and teacher; a central figure in the modern dance movement.

d. Pearl Sydenstricker Buck (1892-1973), China-born American writer; a major figure from the publication of her novel *The Good Earth* (1931) and winner of the 1938 Nobel Prize for literature.

d. Anna Magnani (1908-1973), Italian actress who became an international film star in *Open City* (1945).

d. Edward G. Robinson (Emmanuel Goldenberg) (1893-1973), American actor; a film star from his creation of the title role in *Little Caesar* (1931).

d. William Inge (1913-1973), American writer who emerged as a major playwright with *Come Back Little Sheba* (1950).

ance policies; total losses to those companies and others with Equity stock came to more than $1.75 billion.

Marian Wright Edelman founded and became first president of the Children's Defense Fund (1973-).

Scion of the oil-rich Getty family, 17-year-old J. Paul Getty III was kidnapped in southern Italy (July 10); he would be released after a $2.8 million ransom was paid (Dec. 15).

The Great Dismal Swamp, on the Virginia–North Carolina border south of Norfolk, was established as a national wildlife refuge.

A British jet crashed on landing during a snowstorm at Basel, Switzerland (Apr. 10); 104 people, many of them women shoppers, were killed.

A Delta DC-9 crashed short of the runway in fog in Boston, Massachusetts (July 31); 88 of 89 people aboard died.

A ferry off Rangoon, Burma, collided with the Japanese freighter *Bombay Maru* and sank (Feb. 1), killing more than 200 people.

A Jordanian 707 crashed on landing in fog in Kano, Nigeria (Jan. 23); 176 people died, most of them Muslim pilgrims.

d. Chic (Murat Bernard) Young (1901-1973), American cartoonist who created Blondie and Dagwood.

d. Walt Kelly (1913-1973), American cartoonist who created *Pogo*.

In *United States v. Nixon,* the Supreme Court directed President Richard M. Nixon to produce the Watergate tapes for special prosecutor Leon Jaworski; their contents made impeachment certain. Facing three counts of impeachment, Nixon resigned (Aug. 9). Vice President Gerald R. Ford became the 38th president of the United States (1974-1977); he appointed Nelson Rockefeller to the vice-presidency. As president, Ford pardoned Nixon, who was thereby shielded from prosecution.

A military coup deposed Emperor Haile Selassie I of Ethiopia; coup leader Haile Mariam Mengistu took power, ruling as dictator.

British Labour Party leader Harold Wilson was again prime minister, leading a Labour-Liberal coalition government (1974-1976).

Industrialist and Liberal Democratic Party leader Kakuei Tanaka resigned as Japanese prime minister (1972-1974) because of alleged financial misconduct while in office. He was later convicted (1983) of bribe taking in the Lockheed scandal (1975), but until his death (1993) would remain a "kingmaker" in Japanese politics.

The Portuguese Armed Forces Movement took power in a bloodless coup that ended the dictatorship, established democracy, and freed Portugal's colonies.

The Republic of Guinea-Bissau became an independent state (Sept. 10), ending the long guerrilla war of independence against Portugal. Luis de Almeida Cabral was its first president.

The U.S. Senate ratified the Geneva Protocol of 1925, which banned the use of chemical and biological warfare, and the supplementary 1972 Biological Warfare Ban Treaty.

French conservative Valéry Giscard d'Estaing became president of France (1974-1981).

Social Democratic Party leader Helmut Schmidt became West German chancellor (1974-1982).

Depletion of the ozone layer (ozonosphere), high in the earth's upper atmosphere, which partly shields humans from ultraviolet radiation, was recognized (by 1974); key culprits were identified as chlorofluorocarbons (CFCs), chlorofluoromethanes (CFMs), and Freons; calls began for restrictions and bans on these chemicals, commonly used as spray propellants and refrigerants.

The tomb of Qin Shih Huang Di (Ch'in Shih Huang Ti), the first emperor and unifier of China, who died in 210 BC, was discovered near Xian (Sian), containing thousands of life-size terra-cotta statues of soldiers.

Working in East Africa, American physical anthropologist Donald Carl Johanson discovered much of a fossilized skeleton he named Lucy, which he believed represented a new humanlike species, *Australopithecus afarensis,* one that had already — 4 million years ago — begun to walk on two feet.

Responding to public concerns about the danger from the release or escape of genetically engineered forms, the U.S. government issued stringent guidelines for deliberate manipulation of DNA. Several researchers who failed to follow the guidelines had their experiments stopped; rules were later relaxed somewhat (1980).

Discovery of the J/psi particle was a notable event in particle physics, tending to support the existence of quarks with the "flavor" called "charm," originally posited by Sheldon Lee Glashow (1964).

American physicist Martin L. Perl found evidence for a new variety of atomic particle, called the *tau electron,* or *tauon.*

Al Pacino, Robert De Niro, Diane Keaton, Robert Duvall, John Cazale, and Lee Strasberg starred in Francis Ford Coppola's second classic Mafia film, *The Godfather, Part II,* a Corleone family "prequel" and sequel to *The Godfather* (1972); Coppola and Mario Puzo again wrote the script.

Washington Post reporters Robert Woodward and Carl Bernstein, who had played a major role in exposing the Watergate scandal, published *All the President's Men,* a landmark in investigative journalism.

John le Carré published *Tinker, Tailor, Soldier, Spy,* the first of the three novels in his George Smiley trilogy; it would be the basis for a 1977 television miniseries.

Burt Lancaster starred opposite Silvana Mangano and Helmut Berger in Luchino Visconti's classic film *Conversation Piece.*

Gordon Bunshaft designed Washington's Hirshhorn Museum.

Maya Angelou published the novel *Gather Together in My Name.*

Prominent defectors from the Soviet Union included cellist-conductor Mstislav Rostropovich and singer Galina Vishnevskaya, husband and wife, and ballet star Mikhail Baryshnikov.

Roman Polanski's film *Chinatown,* starring Jack Nicholson, Faye Dunaway, and John Huston and written by Robert Towne, explored incest and greed in 1920s Los Angeles.

Louis Kahn's Yale Center for British Art was completed posthumously.

d. Karen Gay Silkwood (1946-1974), whistle-blowing American atomic plant worker employed at Kerr-McGee's Cimarron plutonium-producing plant near Oklahoma City, Oklahoma. She died in a suspicious automobile accident, possibly forced off the road, while en route to meet a union official and a *New York Times* reporter (Nov. 13); documents she was carrying to support her charges of atomic safety hazards at the plant were never found. Her story was told in the film *Silkwood* (1983).

In what became an unfolding drama before a worldwide audience, Patty (Patricia) Hearst, granddaughter of publisher William Randolph Hearst, was kidnapped by members of a small terrorist group, the Symbionese Liberation Army (SLA) (Feb. 4); she then joined them in a San Francisco bank robbery (Apr. 15) and was captured with them after a gunfight with the Federal Bureau of Investigation (FBI) that cost the lives of six SLA members (Sept. 18, 1975). Kidnappers William and Emily Harris were sentenced to 10 years to life (1978) and later paroled (1983). Hearst was sentenced to 7 years (Mar. 20, 1976) and later released by executive clemency (Feb. 1, 1979).

American tennis player Chris Evert won the women's singles title at the French Open, her first of six, and at Wimbledon, her first of three (1974; 1975; 1981).

American tennis player Jimmy (James Scott) Connors won the men's singles titles at Wimbledon (his first of two), the U.S. Open (his first of five), and the Australian Open, beginning a record 159 weeks (July 29, 1974-Aug. 16, 1977) as the top-ranked men's player.

Baseball player Hank (Henry Louis) Aaron hit his 715th home run (Apr. 8), breaking Babe Ruth's long-standing record for career homers, which Aaron would build to 755 by his retirement (1976).

Turkish forces took most of northern Cyprus (July-Aug.), establishing the Turkish Republic of Northern Cyprus.

Grenada became an independent state and Commonwealth member.

d. Georges Pompidou (1911-1974), French politician closely associated with Charles de Gaulle during and after World War II; he was premier (1962-1968) and succeeded de Gaulle to the presidency (1969-1974).

d. Georgi Konstantinovich Zhukov (1896-1974), Soviet general whose Far Eastern Army forces defeated Japan's Kwangtung Army in an undeclared border war (1939) and whose forces probably later saved Moscow (1941). As Soviet chief of staff, he took the German surrender in Berlin (1945).

d. Haj Amin al Husseini (1893-1974), Palestinian Arab politician; British-appointed grand mufti of Jerusalem (1921-1937), a leader of the Palestinian Arab Revolt (1936-1939), and a German ally during World War II; for several decades, a leader of anti-Israeli forces in the Arab world.

d. Juan Domingo Perón (1895-1974), Argentine president; he was succeeded by Isabel Perón, his vice president and wife.

d. Mohammad Ayub Khan (1907-1974), Pakistani officer; military dictator of Pakistan (1960-1969).

d. U Thant (1909-1974), Burmese diplomat; third secretary-general of the United Nations (1961-1971), who worked from a nonaligned, pro–Third World position during his tenure.

Sheldon Lee Glashow and Howard M. Georgi produced notable work toward a grand unification theory (GUT), attempting to reconcile the main forces of the universe, including gravitation and electromagnetism.

British physicist Stephen Hawking proposed that black holes, apparently formed by the gravitational collapse of stars, could emit radiation, called Hawking radiation.

The U.S. spacecraft *Mariner 10* flew by Venus, transmitting data on that planet before moving on into an orbit that brought it close to Mercury, flying by that planet several times and transmitting data on its composition, including an unsuspected magnetic field.

A Soviet spacecraft crashed during an attempted landing on Mars.

American astronomer Charles T. Kowall discovered a 13th satellite of Jupiter, named Leda.

An explosion occurred at a breeder reactor plant in Shevchenko, in the Soviet Union.

d. Vannevar Bush (1890-1974), American electrical engineer, inventor, and educator who developed the analog computer (1930); during World War II, he headed the U.S. Office of Scientific Research and Development (1941-1945).

d. Virginia Apgar (1909-1974), American physician and anesthesiologist who developed the Apgar score for evaluating newborns (1952).

Swedish writers Eyvind Johnson and Harry Martinson shared the Nobel Prize for literature.

d. Vittorio De Sica (1902-1974), Italian director and actor who emerged as a major international figure with his neorealist films *Shoeshine* (1946) and *The Bicycle Thief* (1948).

d. Duke (Edward Kennedy) Ellington (1899-1974), American composer, pianist, and orchestra leader; a major jazz figure from the mid-1920s.

d. Louis Kahn (1901-1974), who emerged as a leading American architect with his Yale Art Gallery (1954).

d. Marcel Pagnol (1895-1974), French writer, director, and producer for the stage and screen from the late 1920s, beginning with the "Marius" trilogy (1929-1936).

d. David Alfaro Siqueiros (1896-1974), Mexican painter and communist organizer; a leading 20th-century muralist.

d. Alexander Young Jackson (1882-1974), Canadian painter; a leading northern landscape painter and a founder of the Group of Seven.

d. Darius Milhaud (1892-1974), prolific French composer; a leading modernist.

d. Jack Benny (Benjamin Kubelsky) (1894-1974), American comedian; the star of his own radio and then television show for more than three decades (1932-1965).

d. David Oistrakh (1908-1974), leading Soviet violinist who became a world figure during the postwar period.

d. Katharine Cornell (1893-1974), American actress-manager; a leading figure in the American theater from the mid-1920s.

Frank Robinson became the manager of the Cleveland Indians; he was the first African-American manager in major league baseball.

The U.S. Freedom of Information Act mandated greater access to federally held information and procedures for contesting federal secrecy rules.

Muhammad Ali regained the world heavyweight boxing title by defeating George Foreman.

The U.S. Safe Drinking Water Act (strengthened in 1986) authorized the Environmental Protection Agency (EPA) to set minimum national standards for drinking water systems serving 25 or more people.

Near Paris, France, a Turkish DC-10 crashed when a cargo door burst open in midair (Apr. 3), killing 346 people.

In São Paulo, Brazil, an office building fire killed 189 people.

An express train derailed near Zagreb, Yugoslavia (Aug. 30), killing 153 people.

d. Earl Warren (1891-1974), American politician and judge; Republican governor of California (1943-1953) appointed by President Dwight D. Eisenhower to be chief justice of the U.S. Supreme Court (1953-1969). A liberal, he became a major figure in American history for a series of landmark decisions during his tenure, including *Brown v. Board of Education of Topeka,* which he wrote.

d. Charles Augustus Lindbergh (1902-1974), American aviator and inventor who made the first solo transatlantic flight (1927) and codeveloped an external blood-pumping machine (1936); the kidnapping and murder of his child (1932) received worldwide attention.

North Vietnamese forces took Hue (Mar. 25) and Danang (Apr. 1). South Vietnam surrendered (Apr. 30). Final evacuation of remaining Americans and some Vietnamese was by air from Saigon, as North Vietnamese forces moved on the city; more than 2,000 people left from the American embassy in Saigon, as television cameras broadcast the event to the world.

Phnom Penh fell (Apr. 16); Cambodia surrendered to the Khmer Rouge, ending the Cambodian Civil War. The Cambodian Holocaust began (1975-1978), in which an estimated 2 million to 3 million Cambodians died, partly in the course of mass relocation of millions from city to country.

After Portuguese forces were withdrawn from Angola (Nov. 10), the Soviet-backed Popular Movement for the Liberation of Angola (MPLA) set up the People's Republic of Angola (Nov. 11). Angola's other guerrilla armies, the National Front for the Liberation of Angola (FNLA) and the National Union for the Total Independence of Angola (UNITA), did not accept the new government; the Angolan Civil War began (1975-).

Cambodian forces seized the American merchant ship *Mayaguez* in international waters off Cambodia. American forces responded with a rescue mission and air attacks on Cambodian targets, forcing the release of the ship and crew (May 12-14).

Indira Gandhi declared an India-wide state of emergency, had the leaders of the opposition arrested, and ruled by decree (1975-1977).

Pathet Lao forces reopened the Laotian Civil War, taking Vientiane (May) and then the rest of the country.

After the assassination of President N'Garta (François) Tombalbaye, the Chad Civil War (1975-1987) began between northern forces backed by Libya and southern forces backed by France and other Black African countries.

Personal computers (PCs), compact but capacious devices designed and priced for home, school, and small business use, were introduced, the first being the Altair, sold in kit form. Prepackaged "plug-in" computer programs (software) also began to appear, especially for personal computers, where previously users had to write programs for each new task. Also that year, IBM introduced the first laser printer, which produced higher-quality images and were quieter and faster than earlier typewriter-style printers.

American surgeon Henry J. Heimlich introduced the Heimlich maneuver, a thrust of pressure to the upper abdomen of a choking victim to dislodge the food or object stuck in the windpipe. Although some physicians initially questioned whether the maneuver could be performed by laypeople, that proved to be no problem. It would be widely publicized, with many restaurants soon being required to display posters showing the maneuver, which saved many thousands of lives.

A small freshwater fish, the snail darter, first discovered in the Little Tennessee River (1973), was declared an endangered species. Since its habitat was to be flooded by the Tennessee Valley Authority's Tellico Dam, a series of federal court actions ensued, resulting in a 1978 Supreme Court decision that completion of the dam would violate the 1973 Endangered Species Act. The U.S. Congress then passed a law making an exception of the Tellico Dam, which was completed. Transplanted, the snail darter survived, and new populations were later found nearby.

The continuing drilling project by the U.S. ship *Glomar Challenger* uncovered evidence of substantial oil and gas deposits in the North Sea, off northern Norway. Drilling in the Mediter-

Ellen Burstyn in the title role starred opposite Jodie Foster and Kris Kristofferson in Martin Scorsese's film drama *Alice Doesn't Live Here Anymore,* about a struggling, independent woman, her life emblematic of the times.

Robert Altman directed and Joan Tewkesbury wrote the screenplay for *Nashville,* set in that country music capital. The large cast included Lily Tomlin, Ronee Blakley, Henry Gibson, Keith Carradine, Barbara Harris, Keenan Wynn, Karen Black, and Gwen Welles.

Sixty-four years after its composition, Scott Joplin's 1911 folk opera *Treemonisha* received its first full staging, at the Houston Opera.

Jack Nicholson starred as the quite sane insane asylum inmate destroyed by his life in the institution in Milos Forman's film version of Ken Kesey's 1962 novel *One Flew Over the Cuckoo's Nest;* Louise Fletcher costarred.

Robert LuPone and Donna McKechnie starred in *A Chorus Line;* the musical, directed and choreographed by Michael Bennett, would run for 15 years.

John Gielgud and Ralph Richardson starred in Harold Pinter's play *No Man's Land.*

Al Pacino and John Cazale starred as the trapped, crazed, hostage-taking bank robbers in Sidney Lumet's film *Dog Day Afternoon.*

Ruth Prawer Jhabvala published the India-set novel *Heat and Dust,* its parallel 1970s and 1920s love stories her vehicles for commenting on massive changes and enduring patterns in Indian society.

Roger Daltrey, Elton John, Tina Turner, and Eric Clapton starred in Ken Russell's screen version of Peter Townshend's 1969 rock opera *Tommy.*

At Sacramento, California (Sept. 5), Charles Manson follower Lynette Alice "Squeaky" Fromme tried to assassinate U.S. president Gerald R. Ford, but her gun would not fire. Later, in San Francisco (Sept. 22), Sara Jane Moore fired on and missed President Ford. Both were captured and later sentenced to life imprisonment.

The Lockheed kickback scheme exploded in the news, tarnishing some powerful international figures, especially in Japan, West Germany, the Netherlands, and Italy, who were found to have been paid heavy bribes by Lockheed for plane contracts (from the 1950s).

Desmond Tutu became the first Black Anglican dean of Johannesburg and the general secretary of the South African Council of Churches, further emerging as a leader of the South African freedom movement and a proponent of nonviolence.

Arthur Ashe was the first African-American tennis player to win the men's singles title at Wimbledon.

Australian animal rights philosopher Peter Singer published *Animal Liberation,* a key work in the animal rights movement, exploring human-animal relationships; he popularized the idea of *speciesism,* a bias toward one's own species and against others.

Edward Abbey published the novel *The Monkey Wrench Gang,* focusing on a group of direct-action environmentalists who set out to blow up the Glen Canyon Dam, on the Colorado River near the Grand Canyon. Radical environmentalists such as Dave Foreman and other leaders of Earth First! would be much influenced by Abbey's work, dubbing as "monkey-wrenching" their direct, often illegal actions to save the environment.

d. James Riddle Hoffa (1913-1975), American leader of the International Brotherhood of Teamsters (1957-1975); he disappeared and is thought to

The Lebanese Civil War (1975-1991) began with Phalange Christian militia and Palestine Liberation Organization (PLO) clashes in Beirut; other militias were soon involved in what was to become a long, extraordinarily damaging set of conflicts.

Prime minister Mujibur Rahman of Bangladesh was assassinated with his wife and five children during a failed army coup (Aug. 15).

Former Nixon administration attorney general John Newton Mitchell was convicted on several Watergate scandal charges (Jan. 1); he was imprisoned for 19 months.

The Soviet Union, the United States, Canada, and all the nations of Europe except Albania signed the Helsinki Accords (Aug. 1), affirming the principles of civil liberties, freedom of expression, and other human rights. With no enforcement mechanism, human rights continued to be violated with impunity by the nations of the Soviet bloc.

The new Portuguese democratic government defeated two attempted coups — one from the Right (Mar. 11) and the other from the Left (Nov. 25-28).

Conservative Party leader Robert David Muldoon became prime minister of New Zealand (1975-1984).

Liberal Party leader Malcolm Fraser became Liberal–National Country coalition prime minister of Australia (1975-1983).

The Comoro Islands (Federal Islamic Republic of the Comoros) became an independent state.

Indonesia annexed East Timor (Nov. 29); resistance to Indonesian occupying forces continued.

Papua New Guinea became an independent nation (Sept. 16).

ranean Sea, indicated that for a long period the Mediterranean had been cut off from the Atlantic Ocean, which later breached the Strait of Gibraltar.

In the first joint U.S.-Soviet space mission, the Soviet spacecraft *Soyuz 19* docked with the U.S. spacecraft *Apollo 18* (July 19); both had been launched on July 15.

The Soviet spacecraft *Venera 9* and *Venera 10* landed capsules on Venus and transmitted the first pictures of its surface.

The U.S. space probes *Viking 1* and *Viking 2* were launched toward Mars; although a battery charger on *Viking 2* failed, a backup successfully operated, and the two would arrive on schedule in 1976.

American zoologist Edward O. Wilson published *Sociobiology: The New Synthesis*, effectively founding a new interdisciplinary science focusing on the genetic roots of social behavior.

Dutch-American physician Willem J. Kolff developed a portable "artificial kidney" for home dialysis.

The organism that causes leprosy (Hansen's disease) was cultured by Olaf K. Skinsnes at the University of Hawaii Medical School, raising the possibility of developing a vaccine against the disease, which had already begun to develop some resistance to bacterial treatment.

Endorphins, substances released by the body's nervous system to alleviate pain, were first discovered. Painkillers such as morphine and codeine are believed to work by mimicking the work of these endorphins.

On his album *Redheaded Stranger,* Willie Nelson revived Fred Rose's 30-year-old song "Blue Eyes Cryin' in the Rain."

E. L. Doctorow published the novel *Ragtime,* set in the United States at the turn of the century.

Johnny Rotten, Paul Cook, Steve Jones, and Glen Matlock founded the Sex Pistols.

Paul Simon created a new standard with "Still Crazy After All These Years," on his album of the same name.

Robert Redford, Faye Dunaway, and Max von Sydow starred in Sydney Pollack's CIA assassination thriller *Three Days of the Condor.*

British rock singer Rod Stewart's album *Atlantic Crossing* included the haunting "Sailing."

Italian poet Eugenio Montale was awarded the Nobel Prize for literature.

d. Dmitri Shostakovich (1906-1975), prolific Soviet composer; a massive figure in 20th-century music.

d. Fredric March (Ernest Frederick McIntyre Bickel) (1897-1975), leading American dramatic actor; a stage and screen star for half a century.

d. Ivo Andric (1892-1975), Yugoslav writer best known for his "Bosnian" trilogy (1945); he received the 1961 Nobel Prize for literature.

d. (Jocelyn) Barbara Hepworth (1903-1975), British sculptor; from the early 1930s, a leading abstractionist.

d. Josephine Baker (1906-1975), African-American singer, dancer, and actress; a star in France from her 1925 Paris appearance in *La Revue Nègre.*

have been kidnapped and murdered (July 30), although his body was never found.

Martina Navratilova defected to the West; the Czech national champion would become the world's top-ranked woman tennis player.

Soviet chess player Anatoly Karpov became world champion, winning a Candidates Series of tournaments held after American chess champion Bobby Fischer refused to defend his world championship title. The 23-year-old Karpov defeated previous world champion Boris Spassky, among others.

The Great Barrier Reef, consisting of more than 400 different types of coral and running 1,250 miles along Australia's northeast coast, became a protected area; the world's largest marine reserve, it covers more than 85 million acres (133,000 square miles) on the continental shelf, along with associated islands, themselves rich in wildlife.

The Pittsburgh Steelers defeated the Minnesota Vikings to win Super Bowl IX, the first of their four Super Bowl wins (1975; 1976; 1979; 1980).

Chris Evert became a force in tennis with her first of six women's singles titles at the U.S. Open (1975-1978; 1980; 1981).

Sony introduced the first videocassette recorder (VCR) for home use.

In Dhanbad, India, at least 350 people, and perhaps as many as 700, died after an explosion and flooding at the Chasnala mine (Dec. 27).

Two triple-decker excursion boats collided during a storm in the West River near Canton, China (Aug. 3), killing 500 people.

A U.S. Air Force plane crashed near Saigon, Vietnam (Apr. 4); 172 people died, many of them Vietnamese children en route to the United States.

1975 cont.

São Tomé and Principe became an independent nation (July 12).

Suriname became an independent state (Nov. 25).

d. Chiang Kai-shek (1887-1975), Chinese soldier and politician; commander of the Kuomintang army (1926-1927); leader of the Republic of China on the mainland (1928-1949) and on Taiwan after Communist victory (1949-1975).

d. Eamon De Valera (1881-1975), Irish independence movement leader; first president of the Irish Republic (1919-1921), founder of the Fianna Fail Party, president of the Irish Free State executive council (1932-1937), three times prime minister of Ireland (1937-1948; 1951-1954; 1957-1959), and, late in his career, holder of the largely ceremonial presidency of the republic (1959-1973).

d. Francisco Franco (1892-1975), Spanish fascist dictator (1939-1975); the victor in the Spanish Civil War (1936-1939). At his death, Juan Carlos became king of Spain, and democracy was quickly restored.

d. Haile Selassie I (Ras Tafari) (1892-1975), Ethiopian regent and king (1916-1930), then emperor (1930-1974).

d. Eisaku Sato (1901-1975), Japanese politician; prime minister (1964-1972) and with Sean McBride corecipient of the 1974 Nobel Peace Prize for his contribution to the 1968 Nuclear Nonproliferation Treaty.

d. Jacques Duclos (1896-1975), French communist politician; general secretary of the French Communist Party (1931-1964); head of French Communist Resistance forces after the German invasion of the Soviet Union.

d. Nikolai Aleksandrovich Bulganin (1895-1975), Soviet politician; premier (1955-1958) who retired after losing a power struggle to Nikita Khrushchev.

The U.S. Environmental Protection Agency approved the first fungicide to attack the fungus *Ceratocystis ulmi,* which causes Dutch elm disease. The fungus had wiped out most American elms (from the 1930s). In the 1980s, a disease-resistant variety, the American Liberty elm *(Ulmus americana libertas),* would be developed.

Cardiac pacemakers, electronic devices implanted to regulate heartbeat (from 1958), were found to be disrupted by exposure to radiation from microwave ovens.

The first whooping crane bred in captivity was hatched in the U.S. Fish and Wildlife Service's project to save the species from extinction.

The American crocodile was listed as an endangered species.

Fire dangerously lowered coolant levels in the Brown's Ferry nuclear reactor (Mar. 22) near Decatur, Alabama.

Soviet nuclear physicist and dissenter Andrei Sakharov was awarded the Nobel Peace Prize; because he was barred from leaving the country, the award was accepted by his wife, Elena Bonner.

d. Alice Evans (1881-1975), American microbiologist who identified the cause of brucellosis (undulant fever) and its cure: pasteurization of milk (1917).

d. Julian Sorell Huxley (1887-1975), British biologist and writer; the first director general of UNESCO (United Nations Educational, Scientific, and Cultural Organization) (1946-1948). He was the son of biologist Thomas Henry Huxley, an early supporter of Darwin's theories of evolution, and the brother of novelist Aldous Huxley.

d. St.-John Perse (Alexis Saint-Léger Léger) (1887-1975), French poet and diplomat; a major poet from the publication of his epic poem *Anabasis* (1924) and winner of the 1960 Nobel Prize for literature.

d. Thornton Wilder (1897-1975), leading American novelist from the publication of his second novel, *The Bridge of San Luis Rey* (1927), and a leading playwright from *Our Town* (1938).

d. P. G. (Pelham Grenville) Wodehouse (1881-1975), British writer; a humorist whose best-known creations were Jeeves and Bertie Wooster in the "Jeeves" novels.

d. Noble Sissle (1899-1975), African-American singer, composer, and bandleader; often Eubie Blake's collaborator in the 1920s.

d. R. C. (Robert Cedric) Sherriff (1896-1975), British writer who emerged as a major playwright with *Journey's End* (1928).

d. Susan Hayward (Edythe Marrener) (1918-1975), American film star of the 1940s and 1950s.

d. Thomas Hart Benton (1889-1975), American painter; a realist who worked largely in southern and western historical themes.

The Federation of Feminist Women's Health Centers (FFWHC) was founded as a national umbrella for a network of local women's health clinics, focusing on reproductive rights and self-help.

A Czechoslovak Ilyushin-62 crashed in the desert near Damascus, Syria (Aug. 20), killing 126 people.

An Eastern 727 crashed on landing at New York City's Kennedy airport during a thunderstorm (June 24); 113 people died.

Fire from a cooking stove flashed through a Muslim pilgrims' tent city at Mecca, Saudi Arabia (Dec. 12), killing 138 people.

Former Black Panther Party leader Eldridge Cleaver returned to the United States as a born-again Christian lecturer, having fled in 1968.

d. Hannah Arendt (1906-1975), German-American political philosopher and writer, noted for her explorations of freedom and totalitarianism.

Democrat Jimmy Carter defeated Republican incumbent Gerald Ford to become the 39th president of the United States (1977-1981).

d. Mao Zedong (1893-1976), undisputed leader and chief theoretician of Chinese communism from the mid-1930s until his death; leader of the People's Republic of China (1949-1976). After his death, the moderate faction led by Deng Xiaoping took effective control of China, and Deng emerged as leader of the People's Republic of China.

Four Maoist leaders of China's Cultural Revolution — Jiang Qing (Mao Zedong's widow), Zhang Chunqiao, Wang Hongwen, and Yao Wenhuan — were arrested (Oct.) and later convicted as the "Gang of Four" for plotting a coup and many other crimes against the state.

South Africa's government tried to force the use of Afrikaans as the official language in the country's schools, generating rioting in Soweto that spread throughout the country; more than 600 were killed by the police.

A military coup deposed Argentine president Isabel (Maria Estela) Perón (Mar. 24), initiating the "dirty war," a reign of terror in which tens of thousands were murdered and disappeared (the *desaparacios*).

After Spanish forces were withdrawn from Western Sahara, the new Saharan Arab Democratic Republic, Morocco, and Mauritania fought for control of the country.

Israeli parachute troops freed 98 Jewish hostages held by hijackers at Uganda's Entebbe airport (July 4).

Syrian forces took partial control of northern Lebanon; heavy fighting continued in the south, as did the Palestine Liberation Organization (PLO)–Israeli border war.

Chilean secret police murdered former Allende government official Orlando Letelier del Solar in Washington, D.C. (Sept. 21).

Lyme disease — a tick-borne bacterial disease that, if untreated or unresponsive to antibiotics, can cause arthritis and serious neurological and cardiological problems — was identified by Allen Steere and a Yale medical team, alerted by a concerned mother to an unusual incidence of childhood arthritis in Lyme, Connecticut. Its effects had been known in Europe and the northeastern United States since at least the 19th century.

Legionnaire's disease (Legionellosis), a severe pneumonia, was discovered when more than 180 American Legion members contracted it at a convention in Philadelphia, Pennsylvania (July 21-24), and 29 of them died. Researchers later identified the bacillus responsible, often found in water tanks and ventilation systems, and learned that it had been responsible for other previous mysterious pneumonia outbreaks.

PCBs (polychlorinated biphenyls), highly toxic compounds that form even more toxic compounds at high temperatures, were banned by the United States and the European Community (EC), except in totally enclosed electrical equipment. They proved extremely persistent in the environment, however; by the mid-1980s, the Environmental Protection Agency estimated that virtually every U.S. inhabitant carried at least traces of PCBs in their bodies.

Two American spacecraft, *Viking 1* and *Viking 2*, went into orbit around Mars and then successfully landed on its surface, with *Viking 1* broadcasting data for more than five years.

Przewalski's horse, the wild Asian horse from which the domestic horse is believed to have developed, was declared an endangered species. By the 1990s, the horse would be extinct in the wild, with only 200 to 300 surviv-

Alex Haley published the novel *Roots,* about his African-American family history; the Pulitzer Prize–winning best-seller would be the basis for two widely popular television series (1977; 1979).

Robert Redford and Dustin Hoffman starred as *Washington Post* reporters Robert Woodward and Carl Bernstein in Alan J. Pakula's Watergate film *All the President's Men,* based on the 1974 Woodward-Bernstein book.

Philip Glass emerged as a major opera composer with the innovative, minimalist "portrait" opera *Einstein on the Beach,* its central figure Albert Einstein.

Bernardo Bertolucci's multigenerational film *1900* starred Burt Lancaster, Robert De Niro, Gerard Depardieu, Donald Sutherland, and Dominique Sanda.

The celebrated North American rock group called The Band (1967-1976) gave their farewell concert at San Francisco on Thanksgiving Day. They were joined by Joni Mitchell, Bob Dylan, and many others; the event was filmed by Martin Scorsese as *The Last Waltz.*

Sidney Lumet's bitterly prophetic fantasy *Network,* set in a frenetic, amoral television world, starred William Holden, Faye Dunaway, and Peter Finch.

Kermit the Frog and Miss Piggy became television stars on Jim Henson's *The Muppet Show* (1976-1981).

American novelist Saul Bellow was awarded the Nobel Prize for literature.

d. (Edward) Benjamin Britten (1913-1976), British composer; a leading 20th-century opera composer; he composed many of his works for his longtime companion, singer Peter Pears.

A massive earthquake destroyed much of Tangshan, China, reportedly killing at least 242,000 people and injuring 164,000, in what was probably one of the worst disasters of the century.

In a landmark "right to die" decision, the Supreme Court let stand the New Jersey Supreme Court ruling allowing removal of comatose Karen Anne Quinlan's life support systems, as requested by her parents. Quinlan survived until 1981.

In *Gregg v. Georgia,* the U.S. Supreme Court restored the legality of capital punishment; while debate raged over the death penalty, no executions had been carried out in the United States since 1967; after *Gregg,* the killing of prisoners on death row would resume, the first of them being murderer Gary Gilmore (1977).

An earthquake in central Guatemala (Feb. 4) killed 20,000 to 25,000 people, destroying much of Guatemala City.

In *Planned Parenthood v. Danforth,* the U.S. Supreme Court overturned a Missouri law that required a married woman to obtain her husband's consent for an abortion.

The first commercial genetic engineering firm, Genentech, was founded near San Francisco, California.

Romanian gymnast Nadia Comaneci was the star of the Montreal Olympics, winning three gold medals; for two of the events — the uneven bars and the balance beam — she received perfect scores of 10, the first ever given in Olympic gymnastics.

Swedish tennis player Björn Borg won the first of his five consecutive men's singles titles at Wimbledon (1976-1980).

Serial murderer David Berkowitz, who claimed demonic possession, calling himself the "Son of Sam,"

During her trial, German Red Army Faction leader Ulrike Meinhof was found dead in her cell, allegedly a suicide (May).

Socialist and army chief of staff António Ramalho Eanes became president of Portugal (1976-1986).

The Seychelles became an independent state and Commonwealth member (June 29).

d. Zhou Enlai (1898-1976), after Mao Zedong the second leader of Chinese Communism through the civil war; the first premier of the People's Republic of China (1949-1976).

d. Bernard Law Montgomery (1887-1976), British field marshal; commander of British forces at El Alamein (1942) and in the following North African, Italian, and western European campaigns.

d. James Aloysius Farley (1888-1976), American politician; a key political adviser and presidential campaign organizer for Franklin D. Roosevelt (1932; 1936).

d. Zhu De (1886-1976), Chinese general; founder and commander in chief of the Red Army (1926-1954).

d. Mitsuo Fuchida (1902-1976), Japanese aviator; commander of the Japanese naval air forces at Pearl Harbor (Dec. 7, 1941).

d. Tun Abdul Razak (1922-1976), Malaysian lawyer and politician; second prime minister of Malaysia (1970-1976).

ing in captive breeding programs. Also declared endangered that year were the Asian elephant, the mountain zebra of South Africa, the Hawaiian monk seal, two species of tamarins, and nine species of monkeys.

Hoffman–La Roche's Givaudan chemical plant in Seveso, Italy, exploded (July 10), releasing a cloud of gases containing extremely toxic dioxin over an area of seven square miles. Hundreds of animals were killed, and the townspeople were evacuated.

The tanker *Urquiola* ran aground, exploded, and sank en route to the port of La Coruña (May 12), spilling 60,000 to 70,000 tons of crude oil, which fouled 50 to 60 miles of Spain's northwestern coast.

IBM introduced the ink-jet computer printer.

d. Trofim Denisovich Lysenko (1898-1976), Soviet agricultural scientist whose adherence to the theory of the inheritance of acquired characteristics (1929) crippled Soviet agricultural science.

d. Werner Karl Heisenberg (1901-1976), German physicist who developed the uncertainty principle (1927) and matrix algebra (1925).

d. Jacques Lucien Monod (1910-1976), French biochemist noted for his work on genes and his book *Chance and Necessity* (1970).

d. André Malraux (1901-1976), French writer best known for the novel *Man's Fate,* set during the Shanghai Massacre that began the Chinese Civil War. He also was French minister of culture (1958-1969).

d. Paul Robeson (1898-1976), African-American actor and singer; a leading stage figure from his starring role in Eugene O'Neill's *All God's Chillun Got Wings* (1924), a concert singer from the mid-1920s, and a notable figure on the political Left from the late 1930s.

d. Luchino Visconti (1906-1976), Italian director who directed several major works in the 1960s.

d. Agatha Christie (1890-1976), British mystery novelist; the creator of Jane Marple and Hercule Poirot.

d. Lotte Lehmann (1888-1976), German soprano; one of the leading opera singers of the interwar period.

d. Alexander Calder (1898-1976), American sculptor and painter who began to create "mobiles" and "stabiles" in the early 1930s.

d. Busby Berkeley (1895-1976), leading 1930s American film choreographer.

d. Edith (Mary) Evans (1888-1976), British actress; a leading theater figure from the early 1920s.

d. Sybil Thorndike (Agnes Sybil Thorndike) (1881-1976), leading British stage actress from the early 1920s.

was arrested for six murders and seven attempted murders in New York City (1976-1977). In response to his case, New York enacted the "Son of Sam law," specifying that convicted criminals could not profit, as from book or movie rights, from their crimes, but that money instead should be paid to their victims.

Swedish skier Ingemar Stenmark won the first of his three consecutive World Cup championships (1976-1978).

The first regularly scheduled supersonic airliner, the Anglo-French Concorde, went into service.

In the world's worst cable car disaster, 42 people died when a cabin plunged into a valley after a cable snapped (Mar. 9) near Cavalese, Italy.

The commuter ferry *George Prince* and the Norwegian tanker *Frosta* collided in the Mississippi River (Oct. 20), near Luling, Louisiana, killing 74 people.

d. Howard Robert Hughes (1905-1976), American entrepreneur, airplane designer, aviator, and film producer; a recluse from the 1950s.

d. Roy Herbert Thomson (1894-1976), Canadian-British communications mogul who built an empire of radio stations, newspapers, and publishing firms; best known as the publisher of *The Times* of London (from 1967).

d. Martin Heidegger (1889-1976), German philosopher associated with existentialism; best known for his *Being and Time* (1927).

Somali forces invaded Ethiopia's Ogaden region (July), besieging Harar (Sept.). Both nations were Soviet Cold War clients, but Soviet and Cuban forces backed Ethiopia; the Somalis broke with the Soviets, becoming American Cold War clients.

In Pakistan, a military coup toppled the government of Zulfikar Ali Bhutto; General Mohammad Zia Ul-Haq took power.

West German forces rescued 86 hostages held by the Red Army Faction (Baader-Meinhof Group) at Mogadishu, Somalia (Oct. 18).

Andreas Baader and two other imprisoned German Red Army Faction leaders were found dead in their cells, allegedly suicides (Oct.).

Enver Hoxha's Albania broke with China after Chinese-American rapprochement began, thereafter independently pursuing hard-line Stalinist policies until Hoxha's death (1985), coincident with the beginning of the end of the Cold War.

Border clashes between Vietnamese and Cambodian forces intensified.

Central African Republic dictator Jean Bédel Bokassa proclaimed himself Emperor Bokassa I (Dec. 4).

Haile Mariam Mengistu took full power as dictator in Ethiopia (1977-1991).

The Republic of Djibouti became an independent state (June 17); formerly French Somaliland and then the Territory of the Afars and Issas (1967-1977).

d. Anthony Eden (1897-1977), British Conservative politician; foreign secretary (1935-1938; 1940-1945; 1951-1954) and prime minister (1955-1957) who retired from public life after falling from power in the wake of the Suez Crisis (1956).

Smallpox became the first disease to be totally eradicated by medical intervention. The last new case was reported (Oct.), and the last death occurred, in Somalia, except for a British photographer who would die (1978) after being inadvertently infected in a British laboratory.

Two men in New York City were discovered to have a rare form of cancer; these were among the earliest cases of the disease later identified (1981) as AIDS (acquired immunodeficiency syndrome).

British gynecologist-obstetrician Patrick Steptoe first successfully used the technique of *in vitro* (in glass) fertilization, in which the mother's extracted egg is mixed with the father's sperm in a laboratory dish or test tube, and the resulting fertilized egg is implanted into the womb. It laid the basis for a range of reproductive technologies allowing infertile couples to bear children — and for controversy about the proper limits of human intervention in life processes.

Superhot underwater springs, called hydrothermal vents or "chimneys," were first discovered deep under oceans, the first in the Galápagos Rift, near the East Pacific Rise; they were found to yield masses of sulfurous metallic ores and shelter many previously unknown life forms, living virtually without oxygen, light, or photosynthesis.

Balloon angioplasty, a nonsurgical treatment for clogged arteries, was developed in Germany by Andreas R. Gruentzig.

The U.S. spacecraft *Voyager 1* and *Voyager 2* were launched toward Jupiter and Saturn.

Apple introduced the Apple II, the first fully assembled personal computer, developed by

Rudolf Nureyev and Margot Fonteyn danced the leads in *Romeo and Juliet,* choreographed by Kenneth MacMillan to Sergei Prokofiev's music for an earlier (1938) version of the ballet.

Steven Spielberg wrote and directed the classic science fiction film *Close Encounters of the Third Kind,* about a peaceful first contact between humans and aliens, starring Richard Dreyfuss, Melinda Dillon, François Truffaut, and Cary Guffey.

Alex Haley's 1976 novel *Roots* became the basis for an extraordinarily popular 12-hour television miniseries.

George Lucas wrote and directed the very popular science fiction film *Star Wars,* starring Mark Hamill, Harrison Ford, Carrie Fisher, and Alec Guinness. A special effects triumph, the film accentuated the move toward spectacle in American filmmaking.

Jane Fonda starred as Lillian Hellman opposite Jason Robards as Dashiell Hammett and Vanessa Redgrave in *Julia,* Fred Zinnemann's film version of Lillian Hellman's 1973 book *Pentimento.*

Fleetwood Mac introduced Christine McVie's song "Don't Stop (Thinkin' About Tomorrow)," later a 1992 presidential campaign theme.

Spanish poet Vicente Aleixandre was awarded the Nobel Prize for literature.

d. Charles Spencer Chaplin (1899-1977), British actor, director, writer, composer, and producer; as the "Tramp," the world's foremost film comedian, and a major figure in cinema history.

d. Elvis Presley (1935-1977), American singer and actor; from the mid-1950s, a leading rock star and one of the world's leading celebrities.

d. Roberto Rossellini (1906-1977), Italian film director noted for his postwar neorealist classics *Open City* (1945) and *Paisan* (1946).

After a 10-year hiatus in capital punishment in the United States, with vigorous arguments being made for and against the death penalty, the killing of prisoners resumed, the first of them being Utah murderer Gary Gilmore. His life and execution was the subject of Norman Mailer's *The Executioner's Song* (1979) and his brother Mikal Gilmore's *A Shot to the Heart* (1994).

Amnesty International received the Nobel Peace Prize for its worldwide work on behalf of prisoners of conscience.

In the world's worst air disaster, 583 people died when two 747s — one American, one Dutch — collided on a runway at Tenerife, Canary Islands (Mar. 27).

In what was dubbed Koreagate, a South Korean influence-peddling scheme was exposed, spearheaded by businessman Tongsun Park and involving bribes paid to U.S. congressmen, most of whom escaped indictment, though one pleaded guilty.

Known as the "Hillside Stranglers," Angelo Buono and Kenneth Bianchi terrorized the Los Angeles area; posing as policemen (from Oct. 1977), they tortured, raped, and strangled 10 girls and young women. When eventually apprehended, Bianchi pleaded guilty and testified against Buono (1983), both receiving life sentences.

Many of California's 1970s "trash bag murders" — in which bodies were dismembered and the parts wrapped in plastic trash bags and dispersed — were solved with the confession of Patrick Kearney to 21 of the 28 murders.

Saudi Arabian Princess Misha' was stoned to death as a punishment for adultery; a controversial television documentary, *Death of a Princess,* gave worldwide publicity to the event, intended as secret.

1977 cont.

d. Steve Biko (1946-1977), Black South African leader; he died while in police custody, in circumstances that strongly suggested that he had been murdered by the police (Sept. 12).

d. Alexander Bustamente (1884-1977), Jamaican labor leader and politician; first prime minister of independent Jamaica (1962-1967).

d. Alice Paul (1885-1977), founder of the National Woman's Party (1916) and initiator of the first proposed Equal Rights Amendment (1923).

d. Kurt von Schuschnigg (1897-1977), Austrian politician; chancellor and dictator of Austria (1934-1938).

d. Tom Campbell Clark (1899-1977), U.S. Supreme Court justice (1949-1967); he resigned to preclude any conflict of interest that might seem to arise when his son, Ramsey Clark, became U.S. attorney general.

Steven Jobs and Stephen Wozniak. William Gates and Paul Allen founded Microsoft, which would become a giant in producing software programs for personal computers.

Fiber-optic technology was first tested in communications systems. By 1988, it would be used in transoceanic cables.

The magnetic resonance imager (MRI) was introduced for medical use by Raymond V. Damadian.

d. Wernher Magnus Maximilian von Braun (1912-1977), German-American rocket expert who developed the V-1 and V-2 bombs for Germany during World War II and later was a key figure in the U.S. intercontinental ballistic missile (ICBM) and space programs.

1978

Egyptian president Anwar al-Sadat and Israeli prime minister Menachem Begin signed the Camp David Accords (Sept. 17), mediated by U.S. president Jimmy Carter, providing for a coming peace treaty and normalization of relations between Egypt and Israel. Begin and Sadat shared the 1978 Nobel Peace Prize.

A military coup overthrew the Afghan government; civil war began, and antigovernment Mujaheddin forces took much of the country (1978-1979). Assassinated during the coup was Sardar Mohammad Daud Khan, premier of Afghanistan (1953-1963), leader of the republican revolution of 1973, and president of the Afghan republic (1973-1978).

At Love Canal, near Niagara Falls, New York, some 240 families, and later 500 more, were evacuated after high rates of illness and birth defects were linked to the estimated 21,000 to 22,000 tons of chemical waste, including dioxin, dumped by the Hooker Chemical Company (1942-1953). A school was built after the company donated the property to the local school district (1953), while attempting to forestall any liability for damage resulting from the dump, from which chemicals oozed for decades. It would become the first federal environmental disaster site (1980), resettled after

1977 cont.

d. Bing (Harry Lillis) Crosby (1904-1977), American singer and actor; a popular figure worldwide from the early 1930s.

d. Ethel Waters (1896-1977), African-American singer and actress; her signature song was "Stormy Weather" (1933).

d. Groucho (Julius Henry) Marx (1890-1977), American comedian; the oldest of the Marx Brothers, worldwide stars from the mid-1920s.

d. Robert Lowell (Traill Spence, Jr.) (1917-1977), American poet; a major figure from his *Lord Weary's Castle* (1946).

d. Vladimir Nabokov (1899-1977), Russian-American writer, who suddenly became a leading popular novelist with *Lolita* (1955).

d. Howard Hawks (1896-1977), American film director, writer, and producer; a leading figure in Hollywood from the early 1930s.

d. James Jones (1921-1977), American writer, who emerged as a major figure with his first novel, *From Here to Eternity* (1951).

Smoke inhalation and panic-related injuries resulted in 164 deaths in Kentucky's Beverly Hills Supper Club fire (May 28).

Eric Heiden won the world speed-skating championship, the first American to do so.

In *Beal v. Doe,* the U.S. Supreme Court ruled that states could not use public funds to pay for abortions.

The Soviet icebreaker *Arktika* was the first surface vessel to reach the North Pole.

Colorado mother Ann Moore patented the Snugli baby carrier, inspired by carriers she had seen while with the Peace Corps in West Africa.

The Surface Mining Control Reclamation Act (SMCRA) required companies to restore the land after mining, including replacing topsoil, restructuring, revegetation, and burial of toxic materials.

d. Fannie Lou Hamer (1917-1977), African-American civil rights movement leader; cofounder of the Mississippi Freedom Democratic Party (1964).

1978

With many people in the United States still trying to come to terms with the enormous abrasions caused by the Vietnam War, Jane Fonda and Jon Voight, both of whom had been leading opponents of the war, starred opposite Bruce Dern in Hal Ashby's film drama *Coming Home,* which focused on the postwar problems faced by Vietnam veterans.

Michael Cimino's classic Vietnam War film *The Deer Hunter* starred Robert De Niro, Christopher Walken, Meryl Streep, John Savage, and John Cazale.

At Jonestown, Guyana, People's Temple cult leader Jim (James Warren) Jones committed suicide, and 911 of his followers also died, most of them suicides by poisoning but some murdered when they refused to commit suicide (Nov. 18); most were Americans, and 200 were children. Cult members had previously ambushed and murdered U.S. congressman Leo Ryan and 4 other people in his investigative party, wounding 10 others. Very few of the cult members escaped death; one, Larry John Layton, was later convicted of the Ryan party murders (1986).

Fighting intensified in Lebanon, as the multifactional civil war progressed. Israeli forces invaded southern Lebanon (Mar.), withdrawing (June) after establishing a buffer zone there.

Vietnamese forces invaded Cambodia, decisively defeated Khmer Rouge forces, and set up a puppet regime. The Khmer Rouge fought on, largely as cross-border guerrillas operating out of bases in Thailand, with the tacit approval of the Thai government.

Massive antigovernment demonstrations in Iran threatened the government of Shah Mohammed Reza Pahlevi; he named democratic leader Shahpur Bakhtiar premier (Dec. 25). Islamic fundamentalism and powerful anti-Western sentiment were gaining strength, led by Ayatollah Ruhollah Khomeini, then in exile.

Somali forces were decisively defeated by Ethiopian, Cuban, and Soviet forces at Diredawa-Jijiga (Mar. 2-5), then withdrew from the Ogaden region and left the war.

Soviet-backed Cuban and Ethiopian forces scored successes in Eritrea but did not defeat Eritrean guerrilla forces, which disappeared into the countryside, later emerging to retake most of Eritrea.

Senator Harrison A. Williams, Jr., and Congressmen John W. Jenrette, Jr., Raymond F. Lederer, Michael O. Myers, John M. Murphy, and Frank Thompson, Jr., were all caught and ultimately convicted on charges generated by the Federal Bureau of Investigation (FBI) "sting" operation called Abscam (Arab scam); they had accepted bribes from FBI agents posing as rich Arab businessmen.

Former Italian prime minister Aldo Moro was assassinated by Italian Red Brigades terrorists, who intensified their actions.

Daniel Arap Moi succeeded Jomo Kenyatta to the Kenyan presidency (1978-).

being declared safe (1988), a controversial decision.

In England, the first "test-tube baby," Louise Brown, was born (July 25); she had been conceived (late 1977) through the technique of in vitro fertilization, developed by Patrick Steptoe.

Chlorofluorocarbons (CFCs), chlorofluoromethanes (CFMs), and Freons were banned for use in aerosol sprays in the United States, in an attempt to prevent further depletion of the protective ozone layer.

Toxic shock syndrome, a rare but severe and sometimes fatal bacterial infection, was first recognized as a distinct disease; in the worst year (1980), 69 of 819 people diagnosed with the disease in the United States died. Occurring most often in menstruating women, the disease was found to be linked with the use of super-absorbent tampons (1981), and the number of cases declined sharply after they were taken off the market.

American pediatric surgeon Michael Harrison founded the fetal treatment program at the University of California, there developing pioneering operations on the fetus, performed with the fetus partly removed from the womb for surgery, then replaced for the continuation of normal development; lifesaving procedures developed included unblocking a urethra and correcting a diaphragmatic hernia.

The supertanker *Amoco Cadiz* ran aground off Portsall, Brittany, France, during a storm (Mar. 17); its entire 226,000 tons of crude oil were spilled, fouling the waters and some 200 miles of the French coast with a slick some eight times the size of the later *Exxon Valdez* spill

Sam Wanamaker, Michael Moriarty, and Meryl Streep led a large cast in the television miniseries *Holocaust,* about a German-Jewish family during the German mass murder of at least 6 million Jews. The film had considerable impact when shown in Germany.

Nell Carter and Andre De Shields starred on Broadway in the African-American musical *Ain't Misbehavin',* a revue based on the work of jazz composer Fats Waller.

Glenda Jackson starred as poet Stevie Smith, opposite Mona Washbourne, Trevor Howard, and Alec McCowen, in Hugh Whitemore's film *Stevie,* based on his own play.

I. M. Pei designed the monumental East Building of Washington's National Gallery of Art.

Ugo Tognazzi and Michel Serrault starred as the gay couple in Edouard Molinaro's film *La Cage aux Folles.*

Henry Fonda and Jane Alexander starred as Supreme Court justices in the play *First Monday in October* by Jerome Lawrence and Robert E. Lee.

Ingrid Bergman and Liv Ullmann starred as mother and daughter in Ingmar Bergman's film *Autumn Sonata.*

Judy Chicago created *The Dinner Party,* her feminist artwork showing, through "place settings," major women's achievements.

John Irving published his novel *The World According to Garp,* which would be the basis for George Roy Hill's 1982 film.

Polish-American writer Isaac Bashevis Singer was awarded the Nobel Prize for literature.

In *Regents of the University of California v. Bakke,* the U.S. Supreme Court outlawed as discriminatory college admission quota systems openly favoring minority students.

In San Francisco, former city supervisor Dan White killed Mayor George Moscone and Supervisor Harvey Milk (Nov. 27), a homosexual, triggering protests against mistreatment of gays. Dianne Feinstein succeeded Moscone as mayor. White was ultimately convicted of manslaughter.

After being denied landing permission by Malaysia and towed out to sea, a ship overloaded with Vietnamese "boat people" sank in the South China Sea (Nov. 22); 200 people died. In similar incidents, 145 people (Dec. 2) and 100 people (Apr. 3, 1979) died.

At Abadan, Iran, Shi'ite Muslim extremists set fire to a movie theater (Aug. 19), killing 377 people.

Czech-American tennis player Martina Navratilova won her first of what would be a record nine women's singles titles at Wimbledon (1978; 1979; 1982-1987; 1990).

Fran (Francis Asbury) Tarkenton ended his football career where he had begun, with the Minnesota Vikings, having set National Football League records for total number of passes (6,467), total passes completed (3,686), total passing yards (47,003), and total touchdown passes (342).

Striking down local ordinances and overruling lower courts, the U.S. Supreme Court upheld the constitutional right of American Nazis to march in Skokie, Illinois, a decision supported by the American Civil Liberties Union, which lost a substantial portion of its membership for taking the stand, although many later returned. In the end, the Nazis did not march, but the principle had been restated for yet another generation of Americans.

1978 cont.

The Commonwealth of Dominica became an independent state and Commonwealth member (Nov. 3).

The Solomon Islands became an independent state (July 7).

Tuvalu, formerly the Ellice Islands, became an independent state and Commonwealth member (Oct. 1).

d. Jomo Kenyatta (1890-1978), anthropologist and leader of the Kenyan independence movement; first prime minister and then president of independent Kenya (1963-1978); for almost half a century, a leading figure in pan-African and worldwide anticolonial movements.

d. Golda Meir (Golda Meyerson) (1898-1978), Russian-born, American-raised Israeli politician; prime minister (1969-1973).

d. Hubert Horatio Humphrey (1911-1978), American politician; Minnesota Democratic Senator (1949-1965; 1971-1978), U.S. vice president (1965-1969), and defeated presidential candidate (1968).

d. Robert Gordon Menzies (1894-1978), Australian politician; United Australia Party prime minister (1939-1941) and Liberal prime minister (1949-1966); a Korean War and Vietnam War American ally.

d. Houari Boumedienne (Mohammed Boukharouba) (1927-1978), Algerian guerrilla general who took power by coup (1965) and ruled Algeria (1965-1978). He was succeeded by General Chadli BenJedid.

(1989); Amoco was later ordered to pay $85 million to French claimants (1988).

Two U.S. spacecraft in the Pioneer series were launched toward Venus; two Soviet spacecraft, *Venera 11* and *Venera 12*, landed on the planet. From these probes, scientists confirmed that Venus rotates "backward," disproved the theory that it is covered with water, and gained increasing information about the planet's surface from radar waves able to pass through the heavy clouds shrouding the planet.

The African elephant was listed as an endangered species; in the succeeding decade (1979-1989), its population would fall from approximately 1.3 million to a little over 600,000.

Apple introduced the first disk drive to accompany its personal computers; the "floppy disk" had been developed in 1970.

d. Kurt Gödel (1906-1978), Austrian-American mathematician who demonstrated Gödel's proof (incompletability theorem) (1931).

d. Margaret Mead (1901-1978), American anthropologist long associated with the American Museum of Natural History (1926-1945); best known for her *Coming of Age in Samoa* (1928).

1979

Shah Mohammed Reza Pahlevi fled Iran (Jan. 16), appointing Shahpur Bakhtiar prime minister of a new democratic government. But Ayatollah Ruhollah Khomeini returned to Iran (Feb. 1) and quickly took power. Iran took 66 Americans hostage at the Tehran embassy (Nov. 7) and held 52 of them for 444 days, winning several con-

At the Three Mile Island nuclear plant near Middletown, Pennsylvania, a partial core meltdown occurred (Mar. 28, starting 4 AM) after equipment failures and human errors caused overheating of the reactor. A major containment-breaching explosion (like that later at Cher-

d. Tamara Platonovna Karsavina (1885-1978), Russian ballerina; one of the century's most celebrated dancers as prima ballerina of Sergei Diaghilev's Ballets Russes company in its early years (1909-1922), often dancing opposite Vaslav Nijinsky.

d. Giorgio De Chirico (1888-1978), Italian painter; an early modernist whose "metaphysical art" prefigured surrealism; he later became a thoroughgoing traditionalist.

d. Aram Khachaturian (1903-1978), major Armenian composer of the Soviet period, who often worked in Armenian folk themes.

d. Norman Rockwell (1894-1978), American artist noted for his magazine illustrations, many for the *Saturday Evening Post* (1916-1969).

d. Charles Boyer (1897-1978), French actor; an international romantic star during Hollywood's golden age.

d. Sylvia Townsend Warner (1893-1978), British novelist, poet, and short story writer; her 1926 novel *Lolly Willowes* was the first selection of the Book-of-the-Month Club.

The U.S. Pregnancy Discrimination Act outlawed discrimination against women because of pregnancy in firms with 15 or more employees.

d. Paul VI (Giovanni Battista Montini) (1898-1978), Italian priest (1920-1978) and pope (1963-1978); succeeding Pope John XXIII, he completed Vatican II (1965) and then sought to put into practice its ecumenical and social goals, while pursuing a far more conservative course on birth control and church reform.

d. John Paul I (Albino Luciani) (1912-1978), Italian priest who briefly succeeded Paul VI as pope (Aug. 26-Sept. 18) before dying of a heart attack. He was succeeded by Polish cardinal Karol Wojtyla (1918-   ), who became Pope John Paul II, the first Polish pope and the first non-Italian pope for several centuries. A conservative, he would hold fast to traditional positions on matters such as abortion and the role of women in the Catholic Church, also resisting the participation of priests in liberal and radical movements.

Jane Fonda as the television reporter starred opposite Jack Lemmon as the nuclear plant operator and Michael Douglas as the photographer who captures a near-nuclear-meltdown event in James Bridges's film *The China Syndrome*. The coincidental parallel to the near-catastrophe at the Three Mile Island nu-

In a notable National Collegiate Athletic Association (NCAA) championship, Earvin "Magic" Johnson's Michigan State team defeated Larry Bird's Indiana University team; during the 1980s the friendly rivalry between the two, playing for the Los Angeles Lakers and Boston Celtics, respectively,

cessions from the United States and greatly harming American prestige and the Carter presidency.

Soviet forces numbering 130,000 invaded and took Afghanistan; airborne forces took Kabul (Dec. 25). Afghan premier Hafizullah Amin died during the invasion; the Soviets installed Babrak Karmal as premier.

As Sandinista forces took control of Nicaragua, Anastasio Somoza Debayle fled into exile (July 17). Guerrilla civil war continued, with those formerly in power becoming the Contras (Againsts).

At the Vienna Summit (June), U.S. president Jimmy Carter and Soviet president Leonid Brezhnev signed the Strategic Arms Limitation Agreement of 1979 (SALT II), limiting the numbers of intercontinental ballistic missiles (ICBMs), multiple independently targeted reentry vehicles (MIRVs), and missile launchers.

Conservative Party leader Margaret Thatcher became Britain's first woman prime minister (1979-1990); she would be her country's longest-serving prime minister of the century.

Guerrilla civil war intensified in El Salvador between the U.S.-backed government and Cuban- and Nicaraguan-backed guerrilla forces.

Ian Smith stepped down in Rhodesia; the succeeding government, led by Bishop Abel Muzorewa, was not accepted by the insurgents or abroad; British-supervised elections were scheduled for 1980.

Invading Tanzanian forces deposed Libyan-supported Ugandan dictator Idi Amin, taking Kampala (Apr. 11); Amin fled abroad. Former president Milton Obote became Uganda's elected president; his new reign of terror would generate yet another civil war.

d. Louis Mountbatten (1900-1979), World War II British naval officer, Allied Southeast Asia commander (1943-1946), and the last British viceroy of India. Great-

nobyl, in 1986) was averted, although the accident's full seriousness was not reported until 1984. Some radiation was released (in disputed amounts), and the state ordered the evacuation of pregnant women and children nearby; thousands of others fled the area on their own, as the world watched the events unfold. Later (Aug. 7), radioactive uranium released from an Erwin, Tennessee, nuclear plant exposed 1,000 people. The effect was clear: After Three Mile Island, no new U.S. orders for nuclear plants were placed, and those ordered after 1973 were canceled.

The largest recorded oil spill (though perhaps eclipsed by the 1983 Persian Gulf spill) took place when the *Ixtoc I* well blew (June 3), spilling an estimated 600,000 tons of crude oil into the Bay of Campeche, off southern Mexico, causing massive environmental damage. The Sedco company settled Mexican and U.S. claims for some $2 million each (1983).

The largest known shipping oil spill occurred in the Caribbean Sea off Tobago when the *Atlantic Empress* and the *Aegean Captain* collided (July 19); 27 people died, and an estimated 370,000 tons of oil spilled, although environmental damage was relatively small, as most of the oil moved away from the islands and out to sea. The *Atlantic Empress* sank off Barbados (Aug. 2) while being towed.

An electrical transformer at a feed-processing firm leaked fluid containing highly toxic PCBs (polychlorinated biphenyls) (June); in the next few months, 1.9 million pounds of PCB-contaminated feed was sent to farms in Minnesota, Montana, Idaho, Washington, North Dakota, and Utah. By mid-September, more than 1 million eggs, 400,000 chickens, and the products of many bakeries and other food plants had to be destroyed.

clear plant near Middletown, Pennsylvania, was seen as shockingly cautionary.

Sally Field starred as a southern textile worker, rank-and-file union organizer, and free woman in the title role of *Norma Rae,* costarring Ron Liebman and Beau Bridges and directed by Martin Ritt.

Francis Ford Coppola directed *Apocalypse Now,* a Vietnam War film starring Marlon Brando as a rogue American officer who has "gone native" in classic, antique terms and is leading a private indigenous army, opposite Martin Sheen as the American officer assigned to find and kill him; partly and tenuously based on Joseph Conrad's 1902 novel *Heart of Darkness.*

Len Cariou in the title role starred opposite Angela Lansbury as his very willing accomplice in Stephen Sondheim's stage musical *Sweeney Todd, the Demon Barber of Fleet Street.*

Mickey Rooney and Ann Miller starred on Broadway in the popular musical *Sugar Babies,* by Ralph Allen and Harry Rigby.

Norman Mailer published *The Executioner's Song,* a "nonfiction novel" about condemned murderer Gary Gilmore.

Robert Benton's film *Kramer vs. Kramer* starred Dustin Hoffman and Meryl Streep as an affluent New York couple embroiled in a nasty child custody battle.

The Andrew Lloyd Webber–Tim Rice musical *Evita* starred Patti LuPone in the title role, as Argentine politician Evita Perón, wife of dictator Juan Perón.

William Styron published the novel *Sophie's Choice,* about a concentration camp survivor and her life in postwar America.

would greatly increase national and international interest in professional basketball.

Moses Malone won the first of his three National Basketball Association Most Valuable Player Awards (1979; 1982; 1983).

In *Bellotti v. Baird,* the U.S. Supreme Court ruled that states could not require teenagers to obtain a parent's consent for an abortion without providing an alternative, such as obtaining consent from a judge.

National attention was focused on the murders of 28 African-American children in Atlanta, Georgia (1979-1981); Wayne B. Williams was eventually convicted (Feb. 17, 1982) of two murders and sentenced to life imprisonment.

American tennis player John McEnroe won the first of his four U.S. Open men's singles titles (1979-1981; 1983).

U.S. Army doctor and Green Beret captain Jeffrey MacDonald was convicted of murdering his wife, Colette MacDonald, and their two daughters (1970); he had been exonerated after a 1970 Army court-martial, but the case had been reopened in 1975.

Black Panther Party cofounder Huey Newton, who had fled the United States (1974) to escape a murder charge, returned to face trial on the charge and was exonerated.

Cellular phone networks were introduced, first in Tokyo, Japan, and then in Chicago, Illinois. They would go into regular use by 1983.

Philips and Sony began to sell videodisks; not immediately successful, they would spark somewhat more interest in the 1990s.

Mother Teresa was awarded the Nobel Peace Prize for her work as founder of the Missionaries of Charity (1950).

grandson of Queen Victoria, he was assassinated by Irish Republican Army terrorists off the coast of Ireland (Aug. 28).

d. Park Chung Hee (1917-1979), South Korean dictator; he was assassinated by the head of the South Korean CIA (Oct. 26). The South Korean general had taken power by coup (1961) and ruled as dictator (1971-1979).

The Egyptian-Israeli peace treaty (Mar. 26), based on the Camp David Accords, provided for normalization of relations and Israeli withdrawal from the Sinai Peninsula.

The West German Green Party was organized; stressing ecological preservation and antinuclear issues, it spurred the formation of other "green" parties and similar organizations throughout the world.

d. Zulfikar Ali Bhutto (1928-1979), Pakistani lawyer and politician; he was executed by the government of dictator Zia Ul-Haq, allegedly for murder (Apr. 4). Father of Benazir Bhutto, he founded the Pakistan People's Party (1967) and was prime minister (1972-1977) until deposed by the army coup that brought Zia Ul-Haq to power.

British art historian and Soviet spy Anthony Blunt, secretly pardoned in 1964, lost his knighthood after his espionage became a matter of public knowledge, although he continued to work as an art historian.

Central African Republic emperor Bokassa I (Jean Bédel Bokassa) was deposed by the French-backed forces of former president David Dacko (Sept.).

Maurice Bishop took power by coup in Grenada.

Saddam Hussein, in power since 1971, formally became president of Iraq (1979-   ).

In Equatorial Guinea, dictator Macie Nguema Biyuogo Negue Ndong was deposed by coup and later executed by the government led by his nephew, Teodoro Obiang Nguema Mbasogo.

The first human-powered flight across the English Channel was made by California biologist Bryan Allen, pedaling to work the propeller in the tail of his specially built aircraft, the *Gossamer Albatross*.

British atmospheric scientist James Lovelock published *Gaia: A New Look at Life on Earth*, popularizing the theory, developed by Lovelock and American microbiologist Lynn Margulis (late 1960s), that the global ecosystem is best seen as a single living, creative system, called Gaia (after the Greek goddess of the earth).

Physicists from Hamburg, Germany, first observed gluons, subatomic particles that bind together other particles, called quarks.

The U.S. spacecraft *Voyager 1* and *Voyager 2* (both launched in 1977) flew by the planet Jupiter. These flybys revealed information about the planet's turbulent atmosphere and possible volcanic activity on its moon Io, and also discovered a ring and some previously unknown satellites. *Pioneer 11* reached the region near Saturn, revealing previously unknown moons.

The Soviet spacecraft *Soyuz 34* was launched without a crew (June 6), docked with the *Salyut 6* space station, and carried the cosmonauts back to earth.

The first European Space Agency (ESA) rocket, the Ariane, was launched successfully from French Guiana, serving both the ESA and commercial users.

A new study linked lead in children's blood, even at low levels, with lower intelligence scores. A ban on lead-containing paint (1980) and successively lower maximum acceptable lead blood levels followed.

Michael Weller's play *Loose Ends* starred Kevin Kline, Roxanne Hart, and Jay O. Sanders.

I. M. Pei designed the John F. Kennedy Library in Dorchester, Massachusetts.

Woody Allen's film comedy-drama *Manhattan* starred Allen, Diane Keaton, Michael Murphy, Mariel Hemingway, and Meryl Streep as affluent young New Yorkers.

Frances Sternhagen and Tom Aldredge starred as the aging couple in Ernest Thompson's play *On Golden Pond*.

Bob Marley released his most celebrated album, *Survival*, including his song "Zimbabwe," honoring African freedom fighters.

Greek poet Odysseus Elytis was awarded the Nobel Prize for literature.

d. Jean Renoir (1894-1979), French film director; a major figure in French cinema from *La Chienne* (1931) and in world cinema from his classics *Grand Illusion* (1937) and *The Rules of the Game* (1939). He was the son of painter Pierre-Auguste Renoir.

d. John Wayne (Marion Michael Morrison) (1907-1979), American action film star of Hollywood's golden age. He emerged as an international star in John Ford's *Stagecoach* (1939), also starring in Ford's "Cavalry Trilogy" (1948-1950).

d. Leonid Massine (1895-1979), Russian dancer and choreographer; a major figure in world ballet as a leading dancer with Sergei Diaghilev's Ballets Russes company (from 1914) and as a choreographer with the company (from 1917 with *Parade*).

d. Mary Pickford (Gladys Marie Smith) (1893-1979), leading American silent film actress, often in

The Convention on Long-Range Transboundary Air Pollution (LRTAP) was adopted (effective 1983), under which various countries, mostly from Europe and North America, agreed to cooperate to combat air pollution and acid rain.

Lane Kirkland succeeded George Meany as president of the American Federation of Labor–Congress of Industrial Organizations (AFL-CIO).

Reverend Jerry Falwell founded the conservative Moral Majority political organization (June).

Yachts participating in the Fastnet Race between southern England and Ireland were struck by a sudden gale (Aug. 14); at least 23 boats and 18 sailors were lost.

An American Airlines DC-l0 crashed on takeoff from Chicago, Illinois (May 25), killing 273 people, many of them publishers and booksellers en route to a convention.

A New Zealand DC-10 crashed into Mount Erebus, in Antarctica (Nov. 28), killing 257 people.

A Pakistani jet crashed in a mountainous region after takeoff from Jidda, Saudi Arabia (Nov. 26), killing 156 people.

An oil-drilling rig collapsed in a storm off China, in the Gulf of Bohai (Chili), killing 72 people.

d. A. (Asa) Philip Randolph (1889-1979), African-American labor and civil rights organizer; founder and first president of the Brotherhood of Sleeping Car Porters (1925-1968), leader of the successful fight to establish the World War II Fair Employment Practices Commission (FEPC), and organizer of Martin Luther King, Jr.'s 1963 "March on Washington."

d. Erich Fromm (1900-1980), German-American psychoanalyst and social critic, in the United States

The Republic of Kiribati became an independent state and Commonwealth member (July 12).

Saint Lucia became an independent state and Commonwealth member (Feb. 22).

Saint Vincent and the Grenadines became an independent state and Commonwealth member (Oct. 27).

d. Nelson Aldrich Rockefeller (1908-1979), American politician; grandson of John D. Rockefeller; he was four-term governor of New York (1958-1973), U.S. vice president (1974-1977), and three times failed candidate for the Republican presidential nomination (1960; 1964; 1968).

d. Augustinho Neto (1922-1979), leader of the Popular Movement for the Liberation of Angola (MPLA) (1957-1979); first president of the People's Republic of Angola (1974-1979).

d. John George Diefenbaker (1895-1979), Canadian Conservative politician; prime minister (1957-1963).

d. Ludvik Svoboda (1893-1979), Czech soldier and communist politician; president of Czechoslovakia (1968-1975).

d. Mustafa al-Barzani (1901-1979), leader of the Iraqi portion of the Kurdish national movement and of the continuing Kurdish insurrection in Iraq (1960-1970; 1974-1979).

d. Victor Raúl Haya de la Torre (1895-1979), Peruvian liberal politician; founder and leader of the American Popular Revolutionary Alliance (APRA) (1924-1979).

VisiCalc (Visible Calculator) became the first microcomputer "spreadsheet" program, for business applications.

A study indicated a link between exposure to extremely low frequency (ELF) magnetic fields, found in any electricity flow, and increased risk of childhood cancers, especially leukemia. The controversy raised by this report would rage for years, as some studies confirmed these results and others did not.

American scientists developed a hydrogen maser clock, designed to run 50 million years without losing a second.

d. Immanuel Velikovsky (1895-1979), Russian-American physician, psychologist, and astronomer best known for his controversial theories of cosmic collisions with the earth (1950).

children's roles; dubbed "America's Sweetheart," she tried adult roles, without much popular success.

d. Richard Rodgers (1902-1979), American composer; a massive figure in the musical theater, in collaboration with Lorenz Hart and, most notably, Oscar Hammerstein II, for *Oklahoma!* (1943), *Carousel* (1945), *The Sound of Music* (1959), and much more.

d. Arthur Fiedler (1894-1979), American conductor and violinist; as head of the Boston Pops Orchestra (1930-1979), a leading popularizer of classical music.

d. Charles Mingus (1922-1979), American jazz composer and bandleader; a leading jazz bassist from the early 1940s.

d. Dorothy Arzner (1900-1979), one of the earliest American women film directors, from the mid-1920s, and a leading screenwriter and film editor.

d. Jean Rhys (1894-1979), a leading British feminist writer in the 1930s who reemerged with *The Wide Sargasso Sea* (1966).

d. Emmett Kelly (1898-1979), the leading American circus clown of his time, most notably as Weary Willie, whom he created in 1931.

d. Gracie Fields (Grace Stansfield) (1898-1979), British singer, comedian, and actress in music halls from the mid-1920s and on radio in the 1930s.

d. Elizabeth Bishop (1911-1979), American writer; a leading poet from the publication of her first collection, *North and South* (1946).

from 1934, who stressed cultural over biological factors in the shaping of the individual, exploring wide social concerns in works such as *Escape from Freedom* (1940).

d. Charles Edward Coughlin (1891-1979), American Catholic priest; a leading anti-Semitic and pro-fascist figure in the 1930s, through his publication *Social Justice* and as a Detroit-based radio broadcaster.

d. Al Capp (1909-1979), American cartoonist who created *L'il Abner*.

d. Herbert Marcuse (1898-1979), German philosopher, in the United States from 1934; a Marxist whose thinking considerably influenced many of the New Left activists of the 1960s.

d. Cyrus Stephen Eaton (1883-1979), Canadian-American financier; a leading post–World War II anti–nuclear weapons and antiwar figure.

Republican Ronald Reagan defeated Democratic incumbent Jimmy Carter to become the 40th president of the United States (1981-1989).

In Gdansk, 17,000 workers struck at the Lenin Shipyard (Aug. 14), triggering strikes throughout Poland. Lech Walesa led the committee that quickly settled the strike (Aug. 30), then led in the formation of Solidarity (Sept. 18), which became the main vehicle of the Polish freedom movement.

Fighting intensified and terrorism grew in El Salvador, including the murders of four American nuns by death squads (Dec. 3). José Napoleon Duarte became the military-backed leader of El Salvador (Dec.).

Protesting the Soviet invasion of Afghanistan, the United States boycotted the Moscow Olympics, embargoed American grain shipments to the Soviet Union, and massively supplied the Afghan resistance. An estimated 2 million to 3 million Afghan refugees poured into Pakistan, while Afghan guerrillas fought from bases in that country.

In Operation Desert One, American airborne forces engaged in an aborted attempt to rescue the Iran hostages (Apr. 24-25).

Iraq attacked Iran (Sept.), beginning the Iran-Iraq War (1980-1988), which would ultimately cost an estimated 1 million lives, as the war developed into a long stalemate, much like the western front trench warfare of World War I.

d. Anastasio Somoza Debayle (1925-1980), former Nicaraguan dictator; he was assassinated at Asunción, Paraguay (Sept. 17).

The Zimbabwe African National Union (ZANU) won the British-supervised elections in Zimbabwe (Rhodesia); Robert Mugabe led the new government, while ZANU and Zimbabwe African People's Union (ZAPU) forces began an intermittent guerrilla war.

American physicist Luis Walter Alvarez and his son, geologist Walter Alvarez, theorized that dinosaurs and other species became extinct after the earth was hit by a huge meteorite some 65 million years ago, at the end of the Cretaceous period, suggesting that volcanic eruptions, earthquakes, fires, tidal waves, and heavy sun-blocking clouds of debris so changed conditions that many species could not survive.

Chinese scientists produced the first clone of a fish — an organism genetically identical to and produced from a single ancestor, rather than two parents. Previously, only plant and animal tissues had been successfully cloned, although popular works had claimed the cloning of a human during the 1970s.

Among the first substances to be genetically engineered was the virus-fighting protein interferon, which was then used to combat conditions such as herpes infections, warts, and tumors.

Atomic physicist Frederick Reines conducted experiments suggesting that atomic particles called neutrinos, long thought massless, had some mass and positing that they might make up part of the "missing mass" in astronomers' calculations of the mass of the universe.

The U.S. space probes *Voyager 1* and *Voyager 2* (launched 1977) flew by the planet Saturn, photographing its rings and discovering new moons (1980-1981).

France exploded a neutron bomb in the South Pacific (June).

Carl Sagan hosted the television series *Cosmos*, bringing questions about the universe to wide audiences.

Robert De Niro created his celebrated role as Jake LaMotta in *Raging Bull*, Martin Scorsese's film biography of the prizefighter.

Satyagraha, focusing on Mahatma Gandhi, was the second of Philip Glass's three "portrait" operas.

Phyllis Frelich as the deaf student and John Rubinstein as her teacher starred in Mark Medoff's play *Children of a Lesser God*.

Akira Kurosawa directed the late-medieval Japanese epic film *Kagemusha*, starring Tatsuya Nakadai, Tsutomu Yamazaki, and Kenichi Hagiwara.

Daniel Mann's television film *Playing for Time*, set at the Auschwitz German death camp, starred Vanessa Redgrave and Jane Alexander; based on the Fania Fenelon autobiography.

Reflecting the times, Jane Fonda, Lily Tomlin, and Dolly Parton starred as feminist office workers in Colin Higgins's film *Nine to Five*.

Robert Redford debuted as a film director with *Ordinary People*, starring Donald Sutherland, Mary Tyler Moore, and Timothy Hutton.

Peter Shaffer's play *Amadeus*, basis of the 1984 film, starred Paul Scofield as Salieri and Ian McKellan as Mozart; McKellan later won a Tony playing Salieri on Broadway.

William Atherton, Joan Copeland, and John Randolph starred in Arthur Miller's play *The American Clock*.

Lanford Wilson's Pulitzer Prize–winning play *Talley's Folly*, his second on the Talley family, starred Judd Hirsch and Trish Hawkins.

d. Jean-Paul Sartre (1905-1980), French writer and philosopher; a key popularizer of existentialism who

In *Diamond v. Chakrabarty*, the U.S. Supreme Court ruled that genetically engineered biological organisms could be patented under U.S. federal law. Genetic engineering firms applauded, but many warned of potential problems resulting from the patenting of life forms.

In his first year as a professional, Earvin "Magic" Johnson, teamed with veteran Kareem Abdul-Jabbar, led the Los Angeles Lakers to the first of what would be five National Basketball Association championships (1980; 1982; 1985; 1987; 1988).

The U.S. "Superfund" law — Comprehensive Environmental Response, Compensation and Liability Act (CERCLA) — provided funds for the containment and cleanup of spills or abandoned disposal sites containing hazardous substances.

The world's largest solar energy plant, Solar One, was built in California's Mojave Desert (1980-1982).

Weather Underground leaders Bernardine Dohrn and Cathlyn Wilkerson gave themselves up after years in hiding.

A massive Mount St. Helens, Washington, volcanic eruption (May 18), killed 40-60 people.

After a fire began in the plane's cabin, a Saudi Lockheed L-1011 made an emergency landing near Riyadh, Saudi Arabia (Aug. 19), but all 301 people aboard died when the doors could not be opened.

American speed skater Eric Heiden became the first athlete to win five gold medals at the Winter Olympics, at Lake Placid winning the 500-meter, 1,000-meter, 1,500-meter, 5,000-meter, and 10,000-meter races.

Swedish skier Ingemar Stenmark won the first of what would be a record three consecutive world

1980 cont.

Samuel K. Doe took power by coup in Liberia (Apr. 12).

Vanuatu became an independent nation and Commonwealth member (July 30).

The Cape Verde Islands (Republic of Cape Verde) became an independent state (Sept. 7).

d. Shah Mohammed Reza Pahlevi (1919-1980), the last shah of Iran (1941-1979); he had fled into Egyptian exile after being deposed.

d. Tito (Josip Broz) (1892-1980), Yugoslav Communist Party leader, anti-Nazi partisan leader, and head of state (1945-1980). After Tito, and as the Soviet Union turned away from its Eastern European empire, suppressed ethnic tensions reappeared in Yugoslavia, and the country began to fall apart.

d. Seretse Khama (1921-1980), Bamanwato hereditary chief, Botswana independence movement leader, and first president of Botswana (1966-1980), which he built as a multiracial democracy.

d. William O. (Orville) Douglas (1898-1980), American lawyer; chair of the Securities and Exchange Commission (1936-1939) and Supreme Court justice (1939-1975); a leading liberal on the Court, very notably in defense of the Bill of Rights.

d. Luis Munoz Marín (1898-1980), Puerto Rican politician; founder of the Puerto Rican Popular Democratic Party (1938); first appointed governor (1947) and later three-term elected governor (1952-1964) of the island.

d. Helen Gahagan Douglas (1900-1980), American actress; a liberal Democratic California congresswoman (1945-1951) who was defeated by Richard M. Nixon's witch-hunting tactics in a senatorial campaign (1950).

d. Oswald Mosley (1896-1980), British racist; founder of the British Union of Fascists (1932).

The black rhinoceros of sub-Saharan Africa was listed as an endangered species; by the 1990s, only 2,000 to 3,000 would remain.

Soviet nuclear physicist and dissenter Andrei Sakharov and his wife, Elena Bonner, were sent into internal exile at Gorky (1980-1986), but they continued to protest for human rights.

d. Jean Piaget (1896-1980), Swiss psychologist; director of Geneva's International Center for Epistemology (1955-1980), who in experiments with children outlined the regular stages by which they develop basic concepts about the world around them, such as space, causation, and time.

d. Edwin Way Teale (1899-1980), American naturalist and nature writer best known for his works about journeying across America through the seasons, beginning with *North with the Spring* (1951).

d. Willard Frank Libby (1908-1980), American chemist who developed the radiocarbon dating technique (1947).

d. Joseph Banks Rhine (1895-1980), American psychologist; founder of the Parapsychology Laboratory at Duke University (1930), where he studied claims of extrasensory perception (ESP).

was awarded, but declined, the 1964 Nobel Prize for literature; longtime companion of Simone de Beauvoir.

d. John Lennon (1940-1980), British singer, composer, and guitarist; a world figure as a member of the Beatles (1958-1970); he was murdered by deranged Mark David Chapman in New York City.

d. C. P. (Charles Percy) Snow (1905-1980), British novelist, essayist, and scientist, whose literary works often dealt with the intertwining worlds of science, culture, and government.

d. Alfred Hitchcock (1899-1980), British director and producer; a leading director of thrillers from the mid-1930s, such as *The 39 Steps* (1935), *Rear Window* (1954), and *North by Northwest* (1959).

d. Barbara Stanwyck (Ruby Stevens) (1907-1980), American film star of the 1930s and 1940s; later a television star.

d. Marshall McLuhan (1911-1980), Canadian writer, most notably of *The Medium Is the Message*, who contended that, with new electronic media, a fully integrated "global village" had come into being.

d. Katherine Anne Porter (1890-1980), American short story writer and novelist best known for her only full-length novel, *Ship of Fools* (1962).

d. Mae West (1892-1980), American actress and writer; a leading sex symbol from the mid-1920s who often dealt in self-parody.

d. Lewis Milestone (1895-1980), leading American film director, most notably for *All Quiet on the Western Front* (1930).

d. Marc (Marcus Cook) Connelly (1890-1980), prolific American writer and director; a leading playwright from the mid-1920s.

slalom championships (1980-1982), also winning two gold medals at the Lake Placid Olympics.

In *Harris v. McRae*, the U.S. Supreme Court upheld the Hyde Amendment, which allowed the states to ban Medicaid payment for abortions, even if medically necessary.

In the "Scarsdale Diet" murder, Jean Harris, headmistress of an exclusive Virginia private school, killed her erstwhile lover, Dr. Herman Tarnower (Mar. 10), famed for originating the Scarsdale Diet.

The first American infertility clinic opened, using the new technique of in vitro fertilization (1977).

d. George Meany (1894-1980), American labor leader; president of the American Federation of Labor (AFL) (1952-1955) and first president of the AFL-CIO (1955-1979).

d. Dorothy Day (1897-1980), American Catholic pacifist, journalist, feminist, and socialist; cofounder of the Catholic Worker Movement (1932) and its newspaper, *Catholic Worker* (1933).

d. Edith Clara Summerskill (1901-1980), British physician, women's rights advocate, socialist, and politician, a key figure in the post–World War II Labour Party.

d. Joy Gessner Adamson (1910-1980), Austrian-British conservationist and writer, best known for her book *Born Free* (1960).

1980 cont.

1981

The American Iran hostages were released the day President Ronald Reagan took office (Jan. 20).

John W. Hinckley shot and wounded U.S. president Ronald Reagan in Washington, D.C. (Mar. 30). No deaths resulted, and President Reagan recovered completely; presidential press secretary James Brady, who later became a leading gun control advocate, was permanently paralyzed, and others were wounded.

d. Anwar al-Sadat (1918-1981), Egyptian president (1970-1981); assassinated by Islamic fundamentalists in Cairo (Oct. 6), he was succeeded by Vice President Hosni Mubarak, formerly armed forces commander in chief.

A military stalemate developed in Afghanistan, with massive Soviet armored and air forces unable to defeat American-supplied Mujaheddin guerrilla forces, operating from cross-border bases in Pakistan.

The American-Libyan confrontation intensified; two Libyan warplanes were downed by two American warplanes over the Mediterranean (Aug. 19).

Backed by the Soviet Union, General Wojciech Jaruzelski took power as first secretary of the Polish Communist Party (Oct.), declaring martial law (Dec.) and arresting Lech Walesa and many other dissidents.

Organization of African Unity peacekeeping forces replaced Libyan forces that had invaded Chad; Chad Civil War factional fighting was only temporarily halted.

At the 31st Pugwash (Canada) anti–nuclear weapons meeting, a worldwide "nuclear freeze" movement was born, calling for the freezing of all nuclear weapons at current levels.

AIDS (acquired immunodeficiency syndrome) was first recognized as a distinct disease in the United States. The deadly disease leaves the body defenseless against other diseases (such as pneumonia and cancers) by attacking the immune system. Researchers traced the earliest American cases back to 1977. The virus that causes it — HIV (human immunodeficiency virus) — was thought to have originated in Africa.

Columbia, the first reusable spacecraft, went into service (Apr. 12); other U.S. space shuttles (formally the Space Transportation System, or STS), would include *Challenger, Atlantis, Discovery,* and *Endeavour.*

Swiss scientist Karl Illmensee produced clones (identical, single-parent copies) of several mice, the first mammals known to have been cloned. American researchers Allan Wilson and Russell Higuchi also cloned genes from an extinct species, the zebralike quagga.

The first genetically engineered vaccine, against hoof-and-mouth disease, was made available by Genentech. Interferon, synthesized by genetically altered bacteria, was first used in cancer patients.

The U.S. National Cancer Institute branded as "ineffective" for treating cancer the drug laetrile, made from apricot pits; even so, some cancer patients traveled to other countries, notably Mexico, for the treatment.

The IBM PC (personal computer), using DOS (Disk Operating System), was introduced, as

1980 cont.

d. Oskar Kokoschka (1886-1980), Austrian artist who began to emerge as a leading European expressionist before World War I.

1981

Warren Beatty directed and starred as American journalist John Reed in the Bolshevik Revolution and Russian Civil War epic film *Reds,* costarring Diane Keaton as his wife and colleague, Louise Bryant.

Ben Cross and Ian Charleson starred as champion runners in Hugh Hudson's film *Chariots of Fire,* set before and during the 1924 Olympics.

Henry Fonda, Katharine Hepburn, and Jane Fonda starred in Mark Rydell's film version of Ernest Thompson's 1979 play *On Golden Pond.*

Natalia Makarova and Mikhail Baryshnikov danced the leads in Kenneth MacMillan's ballet *The Wild Boy.*

Harrison Ford was Indiana Jones in Steven Spielberg's hit adventure film *Raiders of the Lost Ark;* he would reprise the role in two sequels (1984; 1989).

John Updike published the third novel in his "Rabbit" trilogy, *Rabbit Is Rich.*

Mary Beth Hurt and Mia Dillon starred in Beth Henley's Pulitzer Prize–winning play *Crimes of the Heart.*

After 42 years at the Museum of Modern Art, Pablo Picasso's *Guernica* (1937) was returned to Spain, to the Prado, as he had directed be done only after Spain once again had a democratic government.

MTV, the music television cable channel, was introduced.

Judge Sandra Day O'Connor was appointed to the U.S. Supreme Court by President Ronald Reagan, becoming the first woman associate justice.

The Castro government allowed an estimated 114,000 people to flee Cuba through the port of Mariel and go to the United States; they became known as the "Mariel boat people."

Mehmet Ali Agca shot Pope John Paul II in St. Peter's Square, Rome; the pope was seriously wounded but survived the attempted assassination.

British skaters Jayne Torvill and Christopher Dean won the first of their three successive European and World ice-dance championships (1981-1983).

Canadian hockey star Wayne Gretzky was the National Hockey League's leading scorer, his first of seven consecutive years in the top spot (1981-1987).

Race rioting erupted in Brixton, in south London, as Britain began to encounter problems generated by its changing ethnic and racial mix.

American tennis player John McEnroe defeated Swedish champion Björn Borg at Wimbledon, ending Borg's streak of five straight titles (1976-1980). McEnroe also won the U.S. Open for the third straight time.

In Britain, Jack Sutliffe (the "Yorkshire Ripper") was sentenced to life imprisonment; he had murdered at least 13 women in his attack on alleged prostitutes.

Communications mogul Rupert Murdoch purchased the highly respected *Times* of London, spark-

Socialist François Mitterrand was elected president of France (1981-1995).

President Ziaur Rahman of Bangladesh was assassinated in a failed coup attempt.

Solidarity was outlawed by the Polish government (Dec.), then went underground.

Datuk Seri Mahathir bin Mohammad became prime minister of Malaysia (1981-   ).

Tamil United Liberation Front forces went over to armed insurrection in Sri Lanka, beginning the long Sri Lankan Civil War (1981-   ).

Antigua and Barbuda became an independent country and a member of the Commonwealth.

Belize (formerly British Honduras) became an independent state and a member of the Commonwealth (Sept. 21).

d. Ch'ing-ling Soong (Madame Sun Yat-sen) (1892-1981), widow of Sun Yat-sen and a major figure in the People's Republic of China. She had broken with the Kuomintang after the Shanghai Massacre (1927).

d. Moshe Dayan (1915-1981), Israeli Haganah general and politician; commander of Israeli forces during the 1956 Sinai-Suez War (Second Arab-Israeli War) and later defense minister (1977-1979).

d. Omar Bradley (1893-1981), American general who commanded the First Army during the Normandy invasion (1944) and the 12th Army Group during the drive into Germany. He was the first chairman of the Joint Chiefs of Staff (1949-1953).

was the Osborne, the first computer made in a single box. The Osborne would not survive, but the PC would, from IBM or from competitors who produced IBM-style machines, called clones.

IBM researchers Gerd Binnig and Heinrich Rohrer invented the scanning tunneling microscope, which can produce images of things as small as individual atoms.

At the Sequoyah nuclear plant, near Chattanooga, Tennessee, eight workers were exposed to radioactive water (Feb. 11), as a core was nearly exposed; it was one of a series of such accidents.

At a Tsuruga, Japan, nuclear plant, radioactive material from a cracked pipe contaminated 100 people (Jan. 24-27; Mar. 8).

d. Harold Clayton Urey (1893-1981), American chemist who discovered deuterium and heavy water (1931) and, in the Manhattan Project, played a key role in extracting uranium isotopes needed for nuclear fission. He later urged nuclear disarmament and turned to geophysics, notably exploring how life emerged on earth (1953).

1981 cont.

Bulgarian-British author Elias Canetti, who wrote in German, was awarded the Nobel Prize for literature.

d. Abel Gance (1889-1981), French film director whose 1927 silent film epic, *Napoleon,* was later reconstituted by Kevin Brownlow, reshown first in 1979, and given a landmark new premiere at Radio City Music Hall, with a new score by Carmine Coppola, shortly before Gance's death.

d. William Wyler (1902-1981), German-American director; a leading director of Hollywood's golden age, for films such as *Dodsworth* (1936), *Dead End* (1937), and *The Best Years of Our Lives* (1946).

d. E. Y. (Edgar Yipsel) "Yip" Harburg (1898-1981), American lyricist whose first hit was the Depression era song "Brother, Can You Spare a Dime?" (1932).

d. Hoagy (Howard Hoagland) Carmichael (1899-1981), American composer and musician; noted popular composer from "Stardust" (1931).

d. Lotte Lenya (Karoline Blamauer) (1898-1981), Austrian-born singer and actress; a star in Weimar Germany, most notably in *The Threepenny Opera,* by Bertolt Brecht and Lenya's husband, Kurt Weill.

d. William Holden (William Franklin Beedle) (1918-1981), American film star; in dramatic leads for more than four decades, from *Golden Boy* (1939).

d. Christy Brown (1932-1981), Irish poet and novelist whose lifelong cerebral palsy afforded him use of only his left foot; Daniel Day-Lewis would portray him in the 1989 film *My Left Foot.*

d. A. J. (Archibald Joseph) Cronin (1896-1981), British writer; a leading popular novelist from publication of *The Stars Look Down* (1935).

d. Bob (Nesta Robert) Marley (1945-1981), Jamaican singer, songwriter, and guitarist who became a worldwide figure in reggae.

ing controversy because of his ownership of several sensation-oriented tabloid newspapers.

The oceangoing ferry *Tampomas 2* caught fire and sank in rough waters in the Java Sea, off Indonesia; 580 of the 1,200 people aboard died.

At the Hyatt Regency Hotel in Kansas City, Missouri, the collapse of two interior suspended walkways over an atrium lobby killed 113 people (July 17).

d. Joe Louis (Joseph Louis Barrow) (1914-1981), American boxer called the "Brown Bomber"; the second African-American man to be world heavyweight champion (1937-1949).

d. Roger Nash Baldwin (1884-1981), American social worker, pacifist, and civil libertarian; a founder and first director (1920-1950) of the American Civil Liberties Union.

d. Roy Wilkins (1901-1981), African-American civil rights leader; long a leader of the National Association for the Advancement of Colored People (NAACP) (1931-1981), and its executive secretary (1955-1977).

d. Barbara Ward (1914-1981), British economist and writer whose work focused on rational and equitable use of the world's resources.

1981 cont.

1982

Israel invaded Lebanon (June), encircled and neutralized Palestine Liberation Organization (PLO) and Syrian forces in West Beirut, and drove other Syrian forces into the Bekaa Valley. U.S. mediation and United Nations peacekeeping forces brought about withdrawal of PLO and Syrian forces from Beirut (Aug.). After the assassination of Lebanese president-elect Bashir Gemayel (Sept. 14), Lebanese Maronite Christian Phalange militia murdered at least 400 people in Beirut's Sabra and Shatilla Palestinian refugee camps (Sept. 16-18) without opposition from Israeli forces, drawing worldwide charges of Israeli complicity.

Iraqi peace efforts were rejected, and Iranian forces invaded Iraq, but with little success. The stalemate and extremely costly trench warfare continued. The Iranian-supported Kurdish insurrection in northern Iraq intensified.

Argentine forces took the disputed Falkland Islands (Malvinas) from Britain, beginning the brief Falklands (Malvinas) War (Apr. 2-June 14). British forces made seaborne landings (Apr.) and quickly forced Argentina to surrender (June 14), which was followed by the collapse of the Argentine military government.

Peruvian diplomat Javier Pérez de Cuéllar became the fifth secretary-general of the United Nations (1982-1991).

d. Leonid Ilyich Brezhnev (1906-1982), Communist Party general secretary (1964-1982) and president of the Soviet Union (1977-1982).

Soil tests (Nov.) showed that Times Beach, Missouri (population 2,400), near St. Louis, was heavily contaminated with highly toxic dioxin — 100 to 300 times safe levels — from a dust-controlling oil (actually a chemical plant waste product) that had been placed on the town's dirt roads (1971). The government urged temporary evacuation, then offered (Feb. 1983) to use $33 million of Superfund cleanup money to buy the town and relocate its residents. The town was closed by 1985, but plans to incinerate the soil were dropped after strong local opposition, while disposal discussions continued.

The compact disc (CD) was introduced by Philips and Sony; these thin metal discs contained sounds encoded by tiny indentations, which could be read as digits by the laser beam in a CD player and translated into sounds. Made possible by miniaturization in computers and standardization of technology, CDs quickly established themselves, with 700,000 sold in the first three years in the United States alone. By the mid-1990s, many recording companies had stopped producing long-playing records, instead producing both new works and remasterings of older ones in the CD format.

The first permanent implant of a mechanical heart was made by a team of surgeons under

1981 cont.

d. Marcel Lajos Breuer (1902-1981), Hungarian architect and designer; a leading International Style architect and teacher at the Bauhaus and (from 1937) in the United States.

d. William Saroyan (1908-1981), Armenian-American writer, a major literary figure from his play *The Time of Your Life* (1939).

1982

Maya Lin designed Washington's Vietnam Veterans Memorial, which very quickly became an attraction on a par with the Lincoln Memorial, Washington Monument, and Arlington National Cemetery.

Richard Attenborough directed and produced the epic film biography *Gandhi*, starring Ben Kingsley in the title role, leading a cast that included Saeed Jaffrey, Edward Fox, John Gielgud, Ian Charleson, John Mills, and Candice Bergen.

Steven Spielberg's gentle, entirely nonviolent science fiction film *E.T.*, an enormous worldwide hit, was the story of an alien spaceship crew member, stranded on earth and befriended by a young boy; Henry Thomas and Dee Wallace starred.

Alec Guinness starred as British spy George Smiley in the television miniseries *Smiley's People*, based on the 1980 John le Carré novel.

Meryl Streep starred in the title role, opposite Kevin Kline and Peter MacNicol, in Alan J. Pakula's film *Sophie's Choice*, based on William Styron's 1979 novel.

Alice Walker published the Pulitzer Prize–winning novel *The Color Purple*, the life-and-times story of a southern African-American woman.

Harvey Fierstein wrote and starred in the three one-act plays of his *Torch Song Trilogy*, trailblazing in

Cyanide inserted into Tylenol capsules killed seven people in Chicago, Illinois; the murders remained unsolved, as did some of the many copycat poisonings that followed throughout the United States. Following one such death (Feb. 1986), Johnson & Johnson halted production of Tylenol capsules. The first person to be convicted in such a tampering death was Stella Nickell (1988), of Auburn, Washington, found to have killed her husband and a stranger who bought some of her cyanide-laced Excedrin capsules in a store.

Led by quarterback Joe Montana, the San Francisco 49ers won the first of four Super Bowls (1982; 1985; 1989; 1990).

The Convention on the Law of the Sea, or Law of the Sea Convention (LOSC), was adopted at Montego Bay, Jamaica, providing a comprehensive international legal framework — a "constitution for the oceans" — covering use of the oceans, marine life, and other resources.

The International Whaling Commission adopted a worldwide ban on whaling (fully effective 1986), which sharply cut the world whale kill, though it was partially circumvented by several countries, including Japan and the Soviet Union.

A fuel truck explosion in Afghanistan's Salang Tunnel sent fire through an army convoy (Nov. 2); 700 or more people died, many of smoke inhalation.

Yuri Andropov became general secretary of the Soviet Communist Party and leader of the Soviet Union (1982-1984). He formally became president in 1983.

Panamanian officer Manuel Antonio Noriega became de facto dictator of Panama, continuing to work with the U.S. Central Intelligence Agency (CIA) and at the same time with international drug cartels.

A major Muslim Brotherhood insurrection at Hama (Feb.) was defeated by the Syrian army.

Christian Democratic Party leader Helmut Kohl succeeded Helmut Schmidt as chancellor of West Germany.

A massive Central Park (New York City) nuclear freeze demonstration drew 500,000 to 1 million people.

A military coup in Bangladesh brought General Hussein Mohammad Ershad to power.

General André-Dieudonne Kolingba took power in a Central African Republic military coup, replacing David Dacko.

Liberal Democratic Party leader Yasuhiro Nakasone became Japanese prime minister (1982-1987).

Alva Reimer Myrdal and Alfonso García Robles were corecipients of the Nobel Peace Prize.

Jamaica became an independent state and Commonwealth member (Aug. 6).

Senegal and Gambia joined in the confederation of Senegambia (1982-1989).

d. Mohammed Abdullah (1905-1982), Kashmiri independence leader known as the "Lion of Kashmir"; leader of Kashmir as part of India (1948-1953), then imprisoned for leading the Kashmiri independence movement (1953-1973); again leader of Indian Kashmir after his release.

William De Vries; the patient, Barney Clark, lived for 112 days with the polyurethane Jarvik-7 device, designed by Robert K. Jarvik and Willem J. Kolff.

The U.S. Food and Drug Administration (FDA) approved the first genetically engineered commercial product, human insulin produced by bacteria.

Underwater archaeologists raised the *Mary Rose*, Henry VIII's flagship, from the floor of Britain's Portsmouth harbor, where it had sunk in 1545; the remains were preserved and later displayed.

On its fifth flight, the U.S. space shuttle *Columbia* was used to launch the first satellite from a shuttle.

Willy Burgdorfer first isolated the bacteria *Borrelia burgdorferi*, responsible for causing Lyme disease.

American physical anthropologist Donald Carl Johanson published *Lucy: The Beginnings of Human Kind*, his popular but controversial book about the primitive hominid skeleton he had found in East Africa (1974).

Compaq was the first computer manufacturer to produce a "clone," or virtually identical copy, of a mainstream computer, the IBM PC (personal computer).

The Soviet space probes *Venera 13* and *Venera 14* landed on Venus.

Radioactive steam was released after a pipe rupture in the Ginna nuclear plant near Rochester, New York (Jan. 25).

d. Vladimir Kosma Zworykin (1889-1982), Russian-American electrical engineer and in-

that they dealt openly with the life of a gay man; they were *The International Stud, Fugue in a Nursery,* and *Widows and Children First.*

Jack Lemmon starred as an American father trying to fight through the wall of silence created by American officials and the Chilean military to find his missing son in the Constantin Costa-Gavras political film *Missing.* Sissy Spacek costarred.

Julie Andrews as a female impersonator in 1930s Paris, Robert Preston as a gay man working as an entertainer and manager, and James Garner starred in Blake Edwards's musical comedy film *Victor/Victoria.*

Michael Jackson released *Thriller,* containing "Billie Jean" and "Beat It"; produced by Quincy Jones, it became the best-selling album ever.

The television miniseries *Brideshead Revisited,* adapted by John Mortimer from Evelyn Waugh's 1945 novel, starred Jeremy Irons, Anthony Andrews, Laurence Olivier, Claire Bloom, and Diana Quick.

Colombian writer Gabriel Garcia Marquez was awarded the Nobel Prize for literature.

d. Henry Fonda (1905-1982), American stage and screen star who became a world figure in cinema as Tom Joad in *The Grapes of Wrath* (1940); father of actress Jane Fonda and actor Peter Fonda.

d. Artur Rubinstein (1887-1982), Polish pianist; one of the leading pianists of the century; father of American actor John Rubinstein.

d. Ingrid Bergman (1915-1982), Swedish actress; an international film star from her role in *Casablanca* (1942).

d. John Cheever (1912-1982), American short story writer and novelist; a major figure from his novel *The Wapshot Chronicle* (1957).

After a 10-year campaign led by the National Organization for Women, the states failed to ratify the U.S. Equal Rights Amendment (ERA).

Communications giant American Telephone and Telegraph settled a federal antitrust suit by agreeing to a breakup, divesting itself of its massive local telephone systems and ending its American telephone monopoly.

In the course of his work, Venezuelan-American cardiologist Hacib Aoun became infected with HIV, the virus that causes AIDS. Removed from his post at Johns Hopkins Hospital because of the infection, he became until his death (1992) a public spokesman for people, especially health care workers, with AIDS.

American tennis player Jimmy Connors defeated American rival John McEnroe for his long-sought second Wimbledon men's singles title.

New York Giants defensive linebacker Lawrence Taylor was named to his first Pro Bowl; he would become the first player in the National Football League ever to be so honored nine years in a row (1982-1990).

The United Nations Environment Programme (UNEP) and the Food and Agriculture Organization (FAO) published a landmark global assessment of tropical rain forest resources, using satellite information.

The United Nations General Assembly adopted the World Charter for Nature, an international declaration of conservation principles designed to guide human actions affecting the environment.

Unification Church head Sun Myung Moon was convicted of tax evasion; he was imprisoned for 18 months.

1982 cont.

d. Wladyslaw Gomulka (1905-1982), Polish communist politician; leader of Poland (1945-1949; 1956-1970). Advocating the "Polish road to socialism," he was imprisoned (1951-1955), returned to power as a liberal after the Polish October of 1956, turned much more conservative and even anti-Semitic during the late 1960s, and was removed again by the Soviets when he was unable to quell unrest.

d. Eduardo Frei Montalva (1911-1982), Christian Democratic president of Chile (1964-1970).

d. Philip John Noel-Baker (1889-1982), British pacifist and socialist; longtime Labour member of Parliament (1929-1931; 1936-1950; 1950-1970); a leading advocate of multilateral nuclear disarmament; awarded the 1959 Nobel Peace Prize.

d. Pierre Mendès-France (1907-1982), French socialist premier (1954-1955) who ended the Indochina War.

ventor who built the first all-electronic television, laying the basis for modern television (1924; 1932).

d. René Jules Dubos (1901-1982), French-American bacteriologist and ecologist long associated with the Rockefeller Institute; the first to find naturally occurring antibiotics in the soil (1939); also noted for his writings on humans and their environment, such as *So Human an Animal* (1968).

d. Helene Deutsch (1884-1982), Polish-American Freudian psychoanalyst, director of the Vienna Psychoanalytic Institute (1925-1933), who focused on the psychology of women.

1983

Israeli forces withdrew from Beirut; United Nations peacekeeping forces were ineffective, as civil war flared throughout Lebanon. Palestine Liberation Organization (PLO) forces defeated by the Syrian-backed Lebanese army were evacuated by sea from Tripoli (Oct.). In Beirut, Arabs on suicide missions drove bomb-laden trucks into American and French barracks, killing 241 Americans and 58 French (Oct. 23).

Irish Republican Army (IRA) forces stepped up terrorist attacks in England and Northern Ireland, among them the bombing of Harrod's department store in London (Dec. 17), in which six died.

In probably the world's worst oil spill, during the Iran-Iraq War, a well in the Nowruz oil field off Iran blew out (Feb.), and Iraqi sea and air attacks damaged other wells (Mar. 2) there and at the Kharg Island oil facility. By the end of April, at least 225,000 barrels of heavy crude oil had spilled. Oil continued flowing in massive amounts and, when the winds shifted (late May), came ashore on the coasts of Saudi Arabia, Bahrain, and other southern Persian Gulf nations, causing major environmental damage throughout the summer, until the wells were finally capped.

d. Archibald MacLeish (1892-1982), American poet and playwright; a noted literary figure from his long poem *Conquistador* (1932).

d. Celia Johnson (1908-1982), British stage and screen actress best known for her role in the film *Brief Encounter* (1945).

d. Louis Aragon (1897-1982), French writer; a leading surrealist in the 1920s and, from 1931, a leading communist literary figure.

d. Rainer Werner Fassbinder (1946-1982), German film director; a major figure on the Left with *The Bitter Tears of Petra von Kant* (1972).

d. Thelonious Sphere Monk (1917-1982), American musician, who became a major jazz composer and pianist in the mid-1940s.

An Air Florida 737 crashed after takeoff from Washington's National Airport, hitting a bridge over the Potomac River and landing in the icy water (Jan. 13); 78 people died, 7 of them on the bridge.

Britain's Ian Botham became the first cricketer to score 3,000 runs and take 250 wickets in test matches.

A CH-47 Chinook helicopter crashed at a Mannheim, West Germany, air show (Sept. 11); 46 people died.

A Pan Am 727 crashed during a storm at New Orleans, Louisiana (July 9); 153 people died, 8 of them on the ground.

d. Abe Fortas (1910-1982), American lawyer; the first U.S. Supreme Court justice (1965-1969) to resign because of possibly irregular, though not illegal, financial conduct.

d. David Dubinsky (1892-1982), American labor leader; president of the International Ladies' Garment Workers' Union (ILGWU) (1932-1966).

Meryl Streep starred as doomed atomic plant whistle-blower Karen Silkwood in Mike Nichols's film *Silkwood,* costarring Cher and Kurt Russell.

James Ivory's film *Heat and Dust* starred Julie Christie as a visitor to modern India and Greta Scacchi as her grandmother, whose similar story is told in flashbacks; based on Ruth Prawer Jhabvala's 1975 novel, it costarred Shashi Kapoor and Madhur Jaffrey.

Philip Johnson and John Burgee designed New York's American Telephone and Telegraph Building, a centerpiece of postmodernist architecture.

Martina Navratilova won tennis's grand slam, taking the women's singles championships at Wimbledon, the U.S. Open (her first of four: 1983; 1984; 1986; 1987), and the French and Australian Opens, with a record tally of 86–1; in the process, she set a yearly earnings record for women athletes ($1.4 million).

Vanessa Williams became the first African-American "Miss America" (Sept. 17); she would be forced to relinquish her title (July 23, 1984) after *Penthouse* magazine published nude photographs previously taken of her. Williams went on to build a major career as a singer and actress.

1983 cont.

North Korean agents assassinated South Korea's President Chun Doo Hwan, 4 cabinet members, and 13 other South Koreans in a bombing during a state visit to Burma (Oct. 9).

Philippines opposition leader Benigno Aquino was assassinated while returning from exile; Corazon Aquino then replaced her husband as head of the Liberal Party and would go on to win the Philippine Revolution (1986).

President Ronald Reagan proposed the "Star Wars" (Strategic Defense Initiative, or SDI) nuclear defense, receiving large initial funding from Congress.

U.S. forces, with token assistance from some Caribbean countries, invaded and in three days took Marxist-dominated Grenada, encountering significant resistance only from a group of Cuban combat engineers (Oct.).

Jesse Jackson, campaigning for the Democratic presidential nomination, emerged as the first serious African-American presidential contender in American history.

Australian Labour Party leader Bob Hawke won the first of his four terms as prime minister (1983-1991), moving Australia away from its very close Cold War American alliance into a considerably more independent and antinuclear position.

French intervention in Chad (Aug.) brought a cease-fire and another round of peace negotiations after Libyan-assisted Chad National Liberation Front (Frolinat) forces had taken much of northern Chad.

Hard-line Herut Party leader Yitzhak Shamir succeeded Menachem Begin as Israeli prime minister (1983-1984; 1986-1992).

Neil Gordon Kinnock became leader of the British Labour Party (1983-1992), taking it in a centrist political direction.

Soviet warplanes shot down Korean Air Lines Flight 007 (Sept. 1) after the civilian airliner had strayed into Soviet

Researchers found the first "genetic markers" linked with specific diseases, for Duchenne's muscular dystrophy and Huntington's disease. This resulted from recognition (early 1970s) that genetic engineering techniques could be used to identify parts of the DNA molecule linked with a specific disease or defect. More such discoveries would follow, raising the hope of developing specific treatments or producing genetic alterations to correct the defect and identify carriers.

Cyclosporine was approved as an immunosuppressive drug, proving a breakthrough in controlling transplant rejection.

Sparked by Luis and Walter Alvarez's theory (1980) of possible mass extinctions from a meteorite, an interdisciplinary group of scientists, including Carl Sagan, developed the theory that a war with atomic weapons could produce a "nuclear winter," with atmospheric debris blocking the sun's rays and leading to global cooling, crop failures, and extinctions.

As personal computers continued to develop, Apple offered the Lisa, the first computer to have a mouse and to use icons, rather than memorized multiword commands. IBM offered the PC-XT, the first to have a built-in hard disk. Computer viruses — self-replicating programs designed to be intrusive and often damaging — began causing trouble.

Physicists at the European Center for Nuclear Research (CERN), in Geneva, Switzerland, discovered the two W and Z particles predicted by the electroweak theory of particle physics.

The second U.S. space shuttle, *Challenger*, was first launched (Apr. 4); on its second flight (June 18), it carried the first American woman astronaut in space, Sally Ride; on its third flight

Shirley MacLaine, Debra Winger, and Jack Nicholson starred in James L. Brooks's film *Terms of Endearment*, based on Larry McMurtry's 1975 novel.

Herman Wouk's 1971 novel *The Winds of War* became a massive television miniseries, following Robert Mitchum as Pug Henry from the beginning of World War II through Pearl Harbor; Wouk's sequel, *War and Remembrance* (1978), would be dramatized in 1989, again with Mitchum.

William Kennedy published *Ironweed*, the Pulitzer Prize–winning third novel in his "Albany Trilogy."

Angela Lansbury starred in the title role of Jerry Herman's stage musical *Mame*, based on *Auntie Mame*, the 1956 play from Patrick Dennis's book.

Madonna emerged as a major popular music star with her album *Madonna*, followed by *Like a Virgin* (1984).

British writer William Golding was awarded the Nobel Prize for literature.

d. Tennessee (Thomas Lanier) Williams (1911-1983), American playwright; a massive figure in the American theater, from his early classics *The Glass Menagerie* (1945) and *A Streetcar Named Desire* (1947).

d. George Balanchine (Georgi Melitonovich Balanchivadze) (1904-1983), leading Russian-American choreographer and ballet director; founder of the American Ballet (1935), later the New York City Ballet.

d. Joan Miró (1893-1983), Spanish artist; a surrealist in the mid-1920s; a noted fantasist, working in painting, sculpture, and ceramics.

d. Luis Buñuel (1900-1983), Spanish director and writer; early in his life, a surrealist and social critic; from the late 1920s, a leading cinema figure.

Sixty volumes of "Hitler diaries," for which the West German magazine *Stern* paid $3.7 million, were revealed as frauds, after the *Sunday Times* of London had paid $400,000 for the right to print excerpts.

The *Australia II* won yachting's prestigious America's Cup, defeating the American yacht *Liberty;* it was the first Australian win in the history of the contest.

Martin Luther King Day was established as an American federal holiday; a long state-by-state dispute over who would honor the day intensified.

After hitting a railroad bridge over the Volga River, near Ulyanovsk, the Soviet passenger ship *Aleksandr Suvorov* was hit by a freight train (June 5), killing more than 100 people.

The Nile steamer *10th of Ramadan* sank in Lake Nasser, Egypt, after a fire (May 25), killing at least 196 people.

A Colombian 747 crashed near the airport at Madrid, Spain (Nov. 23), killing 183 people.

A fire in a Turin, Italy, movie house killed 64 people (Feb. 13).

In Madrid, Spain, a fire in a discotheque killed 83 people (Dec. 17).

d. Raymond Claude Aron (1905-1983), French philosopher, writer, historian, and sociologist; editor of *La France Libre* during World War II, then a leading French centrist; a prolific writer claimed variously by the Left and Right.

d. George Halas (1895-1983), American sports figure; founder of the Chicago Bears and cofounder of the National Football League (both 1920); a leader in the development of professional football. He was

airspace off Sakhalin Island over the Sea of Japan, killing all 269 people aboard.

Raúl Alfonsin Foulkes became president of Argentina (1983-1989); his administration brought economic reforms and a revival of democracy.

Southern Sudanese Christian and animist rebels intensified their guerrilla war against the Muslim-dominated north after government imposition of Islamic law on the entire country.

Polish freedom movement leader Lech Walesa was awarded the Nobel Peace Prize.

Federation of Saint Kitts and Nevis became an independent state and Commonwealth member (Sept. 19).

d. Balthazar Vorster (1915-1983), South African fascist who was imprisoned for Nazi activities (1942-1944); a National Party leader who was justice minister (1961-1966), prime minister (1966-1978), and president (1979) of South Africa.

d. Georges Bidault (1889-1983), French politician; leader of the French Resistance (1943-1944), twice prime minister (1946; 1949-1950), and leader of the opposition to Algerian independence.

d. Anthony Blunt (1907-1983), British art historian and Soviet spy.

d. Miguel Alemán Valdés (1903-1983), Mexican lawyer and politician; president of Mexico (1946-1952).

d. Keith Jacka Holyoake (1904-1983), New Zealand National Party conservative prime minister (1957; 1960-1972).

(Aug. 30), it carried the first African-American astronaut in space, Guion Bluford, Jr.

The U.S. research satellite *Pioneer 10* passed Neptune, becoming the first human-made object to leave the solar system.

Dian Fossey published *Gorillas in the Mist*, about her work with mountain gorillas in Rwanda.

d. R. (Richard) Buckminster Fuller (1895-1983), American engineer, architect, teacher, and designer known for his geodesic dome developed in the 1950s (popularized 1967).

d. Ralph Richardson (1902-1983), British stage and screen star; a leading figure on the British stage from the early 1930s.

d. Gloria Swanson (Gloria Josephine Swenson) (1897-1983), American silent film star of the 1920s who made an extraordinary comeback as the aging silent film star in *Sunset Boulevard* (1950).

d. Raymond Massey (1896-1983), Canadian-British actor and director, notably in the title role in *Abe Lincoln in Illinois* (1938 on stage; 1940 on screen); the father of actors Daniel Massey and Anna Massey.

d. Eubie (James Hubert) Blake (1883-1983), African-American composer and pianist; a leading figure in ragtime; composer of "I'm Just Wild About Harry" (1921).

d. George Cukor (1899-1983), leading American director of Hollywood's golden age.

an active player (1920-1929) and then coach of the Bears until his retirement (1968); one of his many innovations was the T formation.

Incumbent Republican president Ronald Reagan won a second term, defeating Democrat Walter Mondale, who won only his home state of Minnesota and the District of Columbia.

Indian army forces killed Sikh fundamentalist leader Jarnail Singh Bhindranwale and hundreds of followers during an assault on the Sikh Golden Temple (June 5-6).

d. Indira Gandhi (1917-1984), Indian prime minister; she was assassinated by two Sikh members of her personal guard (Oct. 31). The daughter and political heir of Jawaharlal Nehru, she had been prime minister (1966-1977; 1980-1984). She was succeeded by her son, Rajiv Gandhi (1984-1989).

Muslim terrorists in Lebanon began to take Western hostages. William Buckley, Central Intelligence Agency (CIA) station chief in Beirut, was kidnapped and would later be tortured and murdered (1985).

d. Yuri Vladimirovich Andropov (1914-1984), Soviet Communist Party general secretary (1982-1984) and president (1983-1984); former head of the KGB (secret police) (1967-1982). He was succeeded by Konstantin Chernenko (1984-1985).

Civil war and accompanying terrorism and death squad murders continued in El Salvador, while the United States and President José Napoleon Duarte continued to foster peace negotiations and some measure of reconciliation. Five Salvadoran National Guardsmen were convicted of the 1980 murders of four nuns (May).

Iraqi forces in northern Iraq used poison gas against Kurdish dissidents; both Iran and Iraq also used poison gas on their main battlefront, failing to break the stalemate in the Iran-Iraq War.

Peacekeeping forces were withdrawn from Beirut, Lebanon (Feb.-Mar.), as the civil war continued.

Progressive Conservative Party leader Martin Brian Mulroney became prime minister of Canada (1984-1993).

In Bhopal, India, a Union Carbide pesticide-producing plant released a cloud of deadly methyl isocyanate over a densely populated area (Dec. 3). Safety devices failed or had been turned off; no emergency plans existed; the city had not been warned of potential danger. More than 2,000 people died immediately, with as many as 10,000 deaths directly related to the poison cloud; at least 200,000, and perhaps 500,000 (the number of compensation claims filed), were injured.

Researchers identified HIV (human immunodeficiency virus), which causes AIDS (acquired immunodeficiency syndrome), allowing for the development of tests for HIV and research on vaccines and treatments. After a lawsuit, Luc Montagnier of Paris's Pasteur Institute and Robert Gallo of the U.S. National Cancer Institute agreed (1987) to share credit for the discovery, but Montagnier maintained that Gallo had only "discovered" the virus specimens Montagnier had sent him. Gallo later admitted that was so, saying it was by inadvertence; after a government investigation, Gallo was said to have engaged in "scientific misconduct" (1992), but charges against him would be dropped (1993).

Alec Jeffreys developed the technique of "genetic fingerprinting," analyzing tissue or body fluids for each person's unique repetitive sequences of DNA. Used first to gain a conviction in Britain (1987), its long-term value remained to be determined, as extreme precision and skill — not always available — are required in testing.

Physicists at the European Center for Nuclear Research (CERN) found the predicted and long-sought atomic particle called the top quark, further supporting the electroweak theory of particle physics.

David Lean directed *A Passage to India,* an epic film adapted from E. M. Forster's more modestly proportioned 1924 novel; Alec Guinness, Judy Davis, Victor Bannerjee, James Fox, Peggy Ashcroft, and Nigel Havers starred.

August Wilson emerged as a major playwright with *Ma Rainey's Black Bottom,* set in African-American life and starring Theresa Merritt and Charles Dutton; Lloyd Richards directed.

Gabriel Garcia Marquez published the novel *Love in the Time of Cholera.*

Paul Esswood sang the title role in Philip Glass's third "portrait" opera, *Akhnaten,* its central figure the Egyptian ruler.

John Hurt and Richard Burton starred in Michael Radford's film version of George Orwell's antibureaucratic novel *1984* (1949).

Bob Geldof organized the massive international rock music benefit Band Aid to aid the victims of war and famine in Ethiopia.

Jack Nicholson and Meryl Streep starred in Hector Babenco's film version of William Kennedy's 1983 novel *Ironweed.*

Alison Lurie published the Pulitzer Prize–winning novel *Foreign Affairs,* her late-20th-century view of Americans abroad.

The Jewel in the Crown, the acclaimed television miniseries based on Paul Scott's "Raj Quartet" (1966-1973), was set in India on the eve of independence; its large cast included Art Malik, Susan Wooldridge, Tim Piggott-Smith, Geraldine James, Charles Dance, and Peggy Ashcroft.

Milan Kundera published *The Unbearable Lightness of Being,* his novel set in Czechoslovakia after

A national debate over self-defense, vigilante action, and gun control was sparked when Bernhard Goetz, dubbed the "subway vigilante," shot four young African-Americans with an illegal handgun while in a threatening situation on a New York City subway (Dec. 22), paralyzing one of them. Ultimately, Goetz was acquitted of all major charges (1987) but convicted of carrying a concealed weapon (1989) and sentenced to one year in prison.

Cellular radios — mobile radio communication systems using microwave transmitters to cover areas called cells — were introduced commercially in 20 major American cities.

An epic contest between two Soviet chess players, world champion Anatoly Karpov and challenger Gary Kasparov, ended inconclusively after a record 5 months and 48 games (1984-1985) because Karpov, just one game short of victory, suffered from nervous exhaustion. In a later rematch (1985), Kasparov took the title, at age 22 the youngest world champion ever; he would successfully defend it against challenges by Karpov (1986; 1987; 1990).

At the Sarajevo Olympics, skaters Jayne Torvill and Christopher Dean won the ice-dancing gold medal, with a perfect 6 points across the board from every judge for their extraordinary and trailblazing modern dance interpretation of Ravel's *Bolero.*

American stock-car racer Richard Lee Petty won his last championship, a record 200th, at the Daytona International Speedway; the car he drove was put on display at the Smithsonian Institution.

American track star Carl (Frederick Carleton) Lewis won four gold medals at the Los Angeles Olympics: in the 100 meters, 200 meters, long jump, and 4 × 100-meter relay, helping set a world record. In so doing, he matched the achievements of Jesse Owens at the 1936 Olympics.

His period in office would be marked by massive economic problems, the unresolved question of French separatism, and the Canada-U.S. trade treaty of 1988.

Labour Party leader David Russell Lange became prime minister of New Zealand (1984-1989), leading New Zealand toward a strongly antinuclear position, refusing entry to an American ship that would not certify itself nuclear weapons free (1985), and prosecuting French agents who had sunk the Greenpeace antinuclear ship *Rainbow Warrior* in Auckland harbor (1985).

The Nobel Peace Prize was awarded to Desmond Tutu, the Anglican bishop of Johannesburg and a leader of the South African freedom movement.

Brunei legally became an independent state (Jan. 1) but remained a de facto British protectorate.

d. Ahmed Sékou Touré (1922-1984), Guinean Democratic Party leader; the first president of Guinea (1958-1984) and a major pan-African movement figure.

d. Souvanna Phouma (1901-1984), Laotian politician; a Western-oriented moderate who was head of government (1951-1958; 1959-1975) through much of the Laotian Civil War and later an adviser to the Pathet Lao government.

On the fourth flight of the U.S. space shuttle *Challenger* (launched Feb. 3), two astronauts took the first untethered space walk, moving about using jet-propelled backpacks.

The Macintosh computer was introduced by Apple, drawing on its Lisa technology (1983), with icons, pull-down menus, and a mouse. IBM introduced the PCjr., a family-oriented version of its PC computer. Laptop, or notebook, computers first appeared, from various companies.

The CD-ROM (compact disc, read-only memory) was introduced; similar to a music compact disc but designed to carry data of various kinds, it would become a popular text and multimedia form in the 1990s.

The British tanker *Alvenus* grounded in the Gulf of Mexico off Lake Charles, Louisiana (July 30), leaking an estimated 1.8 million gallons (approximately 6,000 tons) of heavy crude oil and causing substantial environmental damage to the Louisiana and Texas coasts.

The giant panda was listed as an endangered species.

d. Paul Adrien Maurice Dirac (1902-1984), British mathematical physicist who first predicted the existence of antimatter (1928).

the Soviet invasion; it would be the basis of a 1988 film.

Angela Lansbury created the role of mystery writer Jessica Fletcher in what would become the long-running television drama series *Murder, She Wrote* (1984-).

Bruce Springsteen released *Born in the U.S.A.,* his major hit album.

Jaroslav Seifert was awarded the Nobel Prize for literature.

d. François Truffaut (1932-1984), French "new wave" director and critic; a major figure from his first feature film, *The 400 Blows* (1959).

d. Lillian Hellman (1905-1984), leading American playwright, most notably for *The Little Foxes* (1939) and *Watch on the Rhine* (1941).

d. Richard Burton (Richard Walter Jenkins) (1925-1984), Welsh-British actor; a leading stage figure from the late 1940s and a major film star from the early 1960s, most notably in *Becket* (1964) and, opposite Elizabeth Taylor, in *Who's Afraid of Virginia Woolf?* (1966).

d. Ansel Easton Adams (1902-1984), American landscape and nature photographer; a noted figure from his *Taos Pueblo* (1930).

d. Mikhail Sholokhov (1905-1984), Soviet novelist noted for his Russian Civil War tetralogy *The Quiet Don* (1928); he was awarded the 1965 Nobel Prize for literature.

d. Ethel Merman (Ethel Zimmerman) (1909-1984), American actress; a Broadway star from her "I Got Rhythm" in *Girl Crazy* (1930).

d. J. B. (John Boynton) Priestley (1894-1984), British writer and critic; a popular novelist and playwright from the early 1930s.

Chicago Bears running back Walter Payton broke Jim Brown's records for career rushing yards (12,312), total career yards (15,549), and total games rushing for 100 yards or more (58). Eric Dickerson broke O. J. Simpson's single-season rushing record, with 2,105 yards.

Kareem Abdul-Jabbar became professional basketball's all-time leading scorer; he would have 38,387 points by the end of his career (1969-1989).

Larry Bird won the first of his three National Basketball Association Most Valuable Player Awards (1984-1986).

A gasoline truck explosion set off larger explosions in a Mexico City natural gas plant (Nov. 19), killing an estimated 450 people and leaving 31,000 homeless.

d. Martin Niemöller (1892-1984), German Protestant minister; a leading antifascist who, with Karl Barth, formed the anti-Nazi Synod of Barmen. After eight years in concentration camps (1937-1945), he emerged to resume his ministry and become a leading West German pacifist.

d. Michel Foucault (1926-1984), French philosopher and historian noted for his work on human attitudes toward subjects such as insanity, punishment, and sexuality and for his analysis of the development of knowledge, as in *The Archaeology of Knowledge* (1969).

d. George Horace Gallup (1901-1984), American public opinion pollster and analyst; originator of the Gallup Poll (1935).

d. Konstantin Ustinovich Chernenko (1911-1985), general secretary of the Communist Party and leader of the Soviet Union (1984-1985). He was succeeded by Mikhail Gorbachev.

Mikhail Gorbachev became general secretary of the Communist Party of the Soviet Union (Mar.). Internally, he quickly introduced glasnost (openness), a major set of democratic reforms, and perestroika, a major set of economic reforms. He also initiated the historic changes in Soviet policy that would result in the end of the Cold War, the end of the war in Afghanistan and many regional wars, the end of the Soviet empire, and ultimately the dissolution of the Soviet Union, although he would resist the last.

At the Geneva Summit, Soviet Communist Party general secretary Mikhail Gorbachev and U.S. president Ronald Reagan began the process that would ultimately end the Cold War and many regional conflicts.

The Reagan administration tried to trade arms sales to Iran for American hostages held in Lebanon and to circumvent Congress's prohibition of aid to the Nicaraguan Contras by using arms sales profits to buy and send arms to the Contras. The plan involved, among others, White House staff members Oliver North, Robert McFarlane, and John Poindexter and Central Intelligence Agency (CIA) chief William Casey, and had Israeli support. At least 2,000 TOW missiles were shipped to Iran (1985-1986), and covert Contra supply operations were mounted.

In Colombia, 95 of 300 hostages died, including 11 Supreme Court justices, when the Colombian military stormed the Palace of Justice in Bogota (Nov. 9), where 300 hostages were being held by M-19 guerrillas.

Civil war intensified in Sudan, as northern fundamentalist Muslims took an even harder Islamic line after General Abdul Rahman Siwar el-Dahab took power by coup (Apr. 6).

British scientists found that depletion of the upper atmosphere ozone layer had proceeded so far that a seasonal "hole" developed over Antarctica, which later analysis showed had begun several years earlier.

Some 14,000 citizens in the area of Fernald, Ohio, on the Great Miami River, 18 miles northwest of Cincinnati, began a landmark legal action against the National Lead Company, former operator of the Fernald nuclear weapons plants, which had for decades secretly released radioactive uranium dust into the water and air and stored highly concentrated liquid radioactive waste in leaking concrete tanks. The Department of Energy eventually settled the suit for $78 million (1989) under a new government policy, but it could not undo the damage to the people and their environment.

The United States banned the herbicide 2,4,5-T (2,4,5-trichlorophenoxyacetic acid) after it was found to cause cancer and birth defects. It and another herbicide, 2,4-D (2,4-dichlorophenoxyacetic acid), had become notorious as a 50-50 mixture called Agent Orange, used as a defoliant during the Vietnam War, with disastrous effects, not least on the soldiers working with it.

Harry W. Kroto and Robert F. Curl posited the existence (confirmed in 1990) of a huge soccer ball–shaped 60-atom carbon molecule (C_{60}) resembling R. Buckminster Fuller's geodesic dome and so named buckminsterfullerene, or the "bucky ball."

Computer innovations included PageMaker, the first desktop publishing program for personal computers, and Windows, a program that allowed IBM-style PCs to have a Macintosh-style format.

Akira Kurosawa created *Ran,* his epic Japanese version of *King Lear;* Tatsuya Nakadai, Satoshi Terao, Jinpachi Nezu, Daisuke Ryu, and Mieko Harada starred.

James Ivory directed the film *A Room with a View,* adapted by Ruth Prawer Jhabvala from E. M. Forster's 1908 novel; Maggie Smith, Helena Bonham Carter, Denholm Elliott, and Daniel Day-Lewis starred.

Claude Lanzmann created the massive, extraordinarily powerful documentary *Shoah,* on the Holocaust.

Meryl Streep starred as writer Isak Dinesen, opposite Robert Redford and Klaus Maria Brandauer, in Sydney Pollack's film *Out of Africa,* based on Dinesen's Africa-set books.

Robert Penn Warren became the first U.S. poet laureate.

Bob Geldof organized the massive rock benefit concert Live Aid, two 16-hour simultaneous concerts in Philadelphia and London broadcast worldwide, again to aid African victims of war and famine.

"We Are the World," written by Michael Jackson and Lionel Richie, was sung by a star ensemble, many of whom also contributed songs for an album, all to benefit U.S.A. for Africa (American Band Aid).

August Wilson's play *Fences,* set in African-American life, starred James Earl Jones and was directed by Lloyd Richards.

Danny Glover and Whoopi Goldberg starred in Steven Spielberg's film *The Color Purple,* based on Alice Walker's 1982 novel.

John Huston directed the Brooklyn Mafia family comedy *Prizzi's Honor,* based on Richard Condon's

Massive earthquakes (Sept. 19-20) that destroyed part of the center of Mexico City and caused much damage in southern Mexico killed 5,000 to 10,000 people and left hundreds of thousands homeless.

A Bay of Bengal cyclone struck Bangladesh, killing at least 10,000 people and leaving 200,000 to 300,000 homeless. The worst damage was on low-lying islands off the coast, many of them new delta lands on which settlement had been encouraged by the government of the overcrowded country.

As the environmental organization Greenpeace had been protesting against French atmospheric nuclear weapons tests on the Pacific atoll of Moruroa, French secret agents bombed and sank Greenpeace's ship *Rainbow Warrior* in the harbor at Auckland, New Zealand, killing a Greenpeace photographer aboard and triggering an international incident between France and New Zealand. The agents were convicted of manslaughter in New Zealand but later freed after United Nations mediation and French payment of $7 million.

German tennis player Boris Becker became the first unseeded player to win the men's singles title at Wimbledon, and also the youngest, at 17. He would win it again in 1986 and 1989.

In Philadelphia, Pennsylvania, police attempting to evict occupants of the radical group MOVE's headquarters dropped a bomb intended to force evacuation (May 13), instead setting the building afire, killing 11 people and destroying 61 homes.

An Air India 747 exploded in midair over the Irish Sea, off Ireland (June 23), probably caused by a bomb; 329 people died.

Cincinnati Reds player-manager Pete Rose broke the major league record for most career hits, 4,191, set by baseball great Ty Cobb (1928); before his retirement (1987), Rose would build that to 4,256.

1985 cont.

Islamic Holy War terrorists hijacked an Athens-to-Rome TWA airliner with 153 passengers; murdered 1 passenger, U.S. Navy diver Robert Stethem; secured the release of 300 Shi'ite Muslim Israeli prisoners; and escaped into Beirut, Lebanon (June 14-30).

Palestinian terrorists hijacked the Italian ship *Achille Lauro* (Oct. 7), murdering disabled American passenger Leon Klinghoffer (Oct. 8); an Egyptian airplane carrying the hijackers to safety after a negotiated withdrawal was forced down by American warplanes (Oct. 10), and the hijackers were then held by the Italian government.

Brazilian vice president José Sarney Costa succeeded to the presidency (1985-1990) on the death of president-elect Tancredo de Almeida Neves; he was later elected on his own (1988).

General Ibrahim Babangida took power by coup in Nigeria (Aug. 17).

Karen guerrillas in Burma bombed a Rangoon-Mandalay train (July 14), killing more than 60 people, as the Karen insurgency strengthened.

President Milton Obote was once again deposed by coup in Uganda, by the forces of General Tito Okello (July 27-29).

Sandinista leader Daniel Ortega Saavedra became president of Nicaragua.

The United States applied economic sanctions to South Africa (July 31), adding to increasing world pressure on that country.

Elie Wiesel was awarded the Nobel Peace Prize, largely for his work on the Holocaust.

d. Enver Hoxha (1908-1985), Albanian hard-line Communist Party and government leader (1944-1985).

d. Linden Forbes Sampson Burnham (1923-1985), Guyanese politician; prime minister of colonial Guyana

The first crew change in space occurred at the Soviet space station *Salyut 7*.

Lasers were first used in medicine to help clear deposits from clogged arteries.

DNA was extracted from a 2,400-year-old Egyptian mummy, and parts of it were cloned.

An implantable defibrillator, a battery-powered device to keep the heart from beating too rapidly or quivering (fibrillating), was approved for use.

In a medical first, a robot — actually a computer-operated arm — was used to drill a surgical hole in a patient's head during brain surgery.

The U.S. International Cometary Explorer (ICE) flew through the tail of Comet Giacobini-Zinner (Sept. 11), confirming Fred Whipple's "dirty snowball" theory of comet composition (1949).

A Three Mile Island–type accident was prevented by technicians at the Davis-Besse nuclear plant (June 9), near Oak Harbor, Ohio.

Zebra mussels from Eurasia were unintentionally introduced into the Great Lakes in ballast water (ca. late 1985); in just a few years, they would spread widely, their massive clusters causing problems for ships and water systems and disrupting the food chain.

The fourth U.S. space shuttle, *Atlantis*, was first launched.

d. Dian Fossey (1932-1985), American primatologist in Rwanda (1967-1985) who wrote *Gorillas in the Mist* (1983), the basis of the 1988 movie *Gorillas in the Mist*. Her unsolved murder may have resulted from her fight to

1982 novel; Jack Nicholson, Kathleen Turner, and Anjelica Huston starred.

Larry McMurtry published his Pulitzer Prize–winning novel *Lonesome Dove,* set in the Old West, which would be the basis for a 1989 television miniseries.

Judy Chicago's artwork *The Birth Project* celebrated the role of women in the creation of life.

Raul Julia and William Hurt starred in Hector Babenco's film *The Kiss of the Spider Woman,* the basis for a 1992 stage musical.

Rita Dove published the Pulitzer Prize–winning poetry collection *Thomas and Beulah*.

French writer Claude Simon was awarded the Nobel Prize for literature.

d. Orson Wells (George Orson Welles) (1915-1985), American director, actor, writer, and producer; a major cinema figure who created *Citizen Kane* (1941) and *The Magnificent Ambersons* (1942).

d. Marc Chagall (1887-1985), protean Russian-Jewish painter; a fantasist painter, book illustrator, muralist, stained glass creator, and ballet designer.

d. Michael Redgrave (1908-1985), British stage and screen star; from the 1940s, one of the leading figures on the British stage; the father of Vanessa, Lynn, and Corin Redgrave, and the husband of Rachel Kempson, all also in the theater, as were a third generation.

d. Robert Graves (1895-1985), British poet, novelist, and critic; a major figure in poetry for almost six decades, he was best known for his historical novels, most notably *I, Claudius* (1934).

d. Rock Hudson (Roy Scherer) (1925-1985), American film star from the mid-1950s. He was one of

Los Angeles Raiders running back Marcus Allen was named the National Football League's Most Valuable Player, scoring 14 touchdowns and setting records for total yards (rushing and receiving), with 2,314, and consecutive games in which he gained more than 100 yards (11).

Florida-based ESM Government Securities, a government bond dealer, was found to have defrauded hundreds of banks, municipalities, and other institutions by paying high returns that were in actuality the principal of later investors. In Ohio, a run on banks not federally insured resulted.

Whaling in the region of Antarctica was prohibited under an international moratorium, although Japanese and Soviet whalers would continue activities there into the late 1980s.

In the world's worst single-plane air disaster, 520 of 524 people died when a Japan Air 747 crashed into Mount Ogura, Japan (Aug. 12).

With miniaturization, video cameras as small as paperbacks were produced for home use.

Returning from Europe, 248 soldiers of the U.S. 101st Airborne Division and 8 crew members were killed when an Arrow Air DC-8 crashed on takeoff at Gander, Newfoundland, Canada (Dec. 12).

d. Fernand Braudel (1902-1985), French historian; the leading member of the Annales school, whose work, which studied whole societies and their structures, included *Civilization and Capitalism, 15th-18th Century* (1979).

1985 cont.

(1964-1966) and independent Guyana (1966-1980); president of Guyana (1980-1985).

d. Samuel James Ervin, Jr. (1896-1985), North Carolina Democratic senator (1954-1975); chair of the Senate's Watergate committee (1973-1974).

d. Tage Erlander (1901-1985), Swedish Social Democratic Party leader; premier (1946-1969) of Sweden and architect of much of the country's social services network.

protect Rwanda's mountain gorillas from poachers.

1986

The Iran-Contra Affair unfolded, beginning with the confession of American pilot Eugene Hasenfus, shot down on a covert mission over Nicaragua (Oct. 5), followed by published reports in Beirut, Lebanon. Televised congressional hearings followed, as did the dismissal of Lieutenant Colonel Oliver North from his White House National Security Council position and the resignation of Admiral John Poindexter as national security adviser.

Corazon Aquino was elected president of the Philippines (Feb. 7); civil war threatened when incumbent Ferdinand Marcos tried to deny her the election by falsifying election returns. Facing American and armed forces opposition, Marcos resigned.

U.S. president Ronald Reagan and Soviet Communist Party general secretary Mikhail Gorbachev met at the seemingly failed Reykjavik Summit (Oct.), ultimately disagreeing on limitation of the American Star Wars program but laying the basis for future nuclear agreements.

American forces mounted air and sea attacks on Tripoli and Benghazi; among their targets were the home and headquarters of Libyan president Muammar al-Qaddafi.

The world's worst nuclear accident occurred at the Chernobyl power station, near Kiev, in the Ukraine, when human error during a safety-system test led to meltdown in a nuclear reactor (Apr. 25-May 1); fires and explosions broke through the concrete containment shell and sent a massive radioactive cloud across Europe. The disaster was publicly announced only after Scandinavian sources began to report heavy radioactive fallout (Apr. 28), with the Soviet Union then requesting foreign help for the first time since World War II. The fire was finally put out only after helicopter pilots dumped sand and concrete on it, the reactor later being encased in concrete and metal. How many people were killed immediately or severely sickened by radiation is unclear. Some 130,000 were evacuated days after the accident, followed by 200,000 more, and then 120,000 more (1991); large areas were severely contaminated, although many continue to be farmed, and the rest of the Chernobyl plant resumed operation. Chernobyl made clear that nuclear power was not the cheapest, but by far the

1985 cont.

the first celebrities to state publicly that he had AIDS, helping to demystify the illness and bring wider acceptance of those who were its victims.

d. Simone Signoret (Simone Kaminker) (1921-1985), French actress; an international film star from the early 1950s; she was married to actor Yves Montand.

d. Yul Brynner (1915-1985), Russian-American actor and director best known for his role as the king in *The King and I* (1951).

d. Emil Grigoryevich Gilels (1916-1985), Soviet pianist; one of the world's leading soloists.

1986

Margaret Atwood published the feminist science fiction novel *The Handmaid's Tale*, warning against the dangers of a future world in which fertile women are treated as breeders of babies for people who cannot have their own.

Marlee Matlin as the deaf student and William Hurt as her teacher starred in Randa Haines's film version of Mark Medoff's 1980 play *Children of a Lesser God*.

Andrew Wyeth showed 240 previously unknown paintings and drawings — the "Helga" pictures — of his neighbor Helga Testof.

Claude Berri made two sequential films based on Marcel Pagnol's 1952 novel *Manon of the Spring*. The first, *Jean de Florette,* starred Yves Montand and Gerard Depardieu; the second, *Manon of the Spring,* starred Montand and Emmanuelle Beart.

Stockard Channing, Swoosie Kurtz, and John Mahoney starred in John Guare's play *The House of Blue Leaves.*

A major "inside information" stock market trading scandal broke; to many emblematic of the greed-driven 1980s, the scandal would ultimately involve speculator Ivan Boesky; Dennis Levine and his Drexel Burnham Lambert firm; Michael Milken; and many other Wall Street figures. Levine and Boesky implicated others, many of whom pleaded guilty to misuse of confidential information for personal gain and agreed to fines and repayment, with some receiving prison terms.

As researchers came to better understand the dangers of lead, especially to fetal and child intellectual development, and the pervasiveness of lead poisoning, the U.S. government banned the use of lead solder and lead materials in public water systems, the first of several major moves against lead in the environment. Many other contaminants and pollutants in public water systems also were regulated.

American aviators Richard Rutan and Jeana Yeager made the first nonstop flight around the world, taking nine days to travel 25,012 miles in the *Voyager,* a tiny, specially built, extremely light airplane.

Civil war flared in South Yemen (Jan.) after President Ali Nasser Mohammed al-Hasani used assassins to murder dissident ruling Socialist Party leaders at a cabinet meeting. Al-Hasani fled after a week of fighting that cost an estimated 4,000 lives.

Former United Nations secretary-general Kurt Waldheim became president of Austria (1986-1992) and at the same time became a highly controversial figure because of allegations, which he denied, that he had been involved in Nazi atrocities in Greece and Yugoslavia during World War II.

Jean Claude "Baby Doc" Duvalier fled Haiti as his government fell (Feb. 7).

Pro-democracy student demonstrations in China generated a conservative backlash and the fall from power of reformer Hu Yaobang.

d. Olaf Palme (1927-1986), Swedish Social Democratic Party leader and premier (1969-1976; 1982-1986); a leading international peace negotiator; he was assassinated in Stockholm (Feb. 28).

Yoweri Musaveni took power in Uganda (Jan. 29); former government forces went over to a guerrilla insurgency.

At Soviet direction, Afghan puppet ruler Babrak Karmal was deposed by coup and replaced by Mohammed Najibullah.

Former Central African Republic dictator Bokassa I (Jean Bédel Bokassa), who had been sentenced to death in absentia, returned home (Oct.) and received another death sentence, later reduced to life imprisonment.

Spain and Portugal joined the European Community.

d. (Maurice) Harold Macmillan (1894-1986), British Conservative politician; as a member of Parliament (1924-1929; 1931-1964), he opposed appeasement in the

most costly, kind of energy; public resistance to nuclear power grew dramatically.

The U.S. space shuttle *Challenger*, launched on its fifth flight from Cape Canaveral, Florida (Jan. 28, 11:38 AM), exploded in the air a minute after liftoff. All seven people aboard died: Francis R. Scobee, Michael J. Smith, Gregory B. Jarvis, Ronald E. McNair, Ellison S. Onizuka, Judith A. Resnick, and S. Christa McAuliffe, who was to have been the first teacher in space. The problem was later found to be cold-weather failure of the seals (O-rings) joining the rockets to the shuttle — demonstrated to the investigative commission by physicist Richard Feynman, who simply placed an O-ring in ice water and showed the resulting inelasticity. The American space program would be set back for years.

At least 30 tons of mixed toxic chemicals, some including mercury, were washed into the Rhine River upriver from Basel, Switzerland, as water was poured onto a fire at the Sandoz AG warehouse 956 (Nov. 1), which contained some 840 tons of pesticides and other toxic chemicals. Much river life was killed, and many cities faced a water crisis. During an investigation, other companies were found to have dumped toxic materials into the Rhine, notably 100 gallons of highly toxic atrazine spilled into the Rhine by Ciba-Geigy (Oct. 30). Green movements, especially in Germany, received much additional support.

IBM researchers Karl Alex Müller and J. Georg Bednorz discovered new ceramic materials that become superconductive — that is, lose resistance to electricity — at temperatures more moderate than the extreme cold required for previous superconductive materials.

The Soviet Union launched the space station *Mir (Peace)* (Feb. 20), built under the direction

Paul Simon drew on South African musical sources in his acclaimed album *Graceland,* on which he was joined by the group Ladysmith Black Mambazo.

Sean Connery starred in Jean-Jacques Annaud's Middle Ages-set mystery film *The Name of the Rose,* based on Umberto Eco's 1981 novel.

Whitney Houston made a major musical debut with her album, *Whitney Houston,* its multiple hits including "Didn't We Almost Have It All?", "The Greatest Love of All," and "Saving All My Love for You."

In his own film *Hannah and Her Sisters,* Woody Allen starred opposite Mia Farrow, Dianne Wiest, Barbara Hershey, and Michael Caine.

The New York City headquarters building for Equitable Life, designed by Edward Larrabee Barnes, also included Roy Lichtenstein's *Mural with Blue Brushstroke.*

Robert Lindsay and Maryann Plunkett starred in a notable Broadway revival of the Noel Gay–L. Arthur Rose–Douglas Furber 1937 musical *Me and My Girl,* with Lindsay reprising his role in the 1984 London revival.

Toni Morrison published her Pulitzer Prize–winning novel *Beloved.*

Black Nigerian writer Wole Soyinka was awarded the Nobel Prize for literature.

d. Georgia O'Keeffe (1887-1986), one of the leading American artists of the century and a world figure; a unique figurative painter whose work also embodied abstraction, defying restrictive classification.

d. Cary Grant (Archibald Alexander Leach) (1904-1986), British actor; a Hollywood star, largely in comedy, from the late 1930s.

At Lake Nios, Cameroon, toxic gases rising from the volcanic crater beneath the lake killed at least 1,700 people (Aug. 21).

Desmond Tutu became archbishop of Johannesburg and the trailblazing first Black leader of the Anglican Church in South Africa.

In a series of fights (1986-1988), American boxer Mike Tyson defeated three opponents who held world heavyweight championship titles proclaimed by rival boxing organizations, uniting the titles to become the undisputed sole world heavyweight champion (1988-1990), at 22 the youngest ever.

Oklahoma mail carrier Patrick Sherrill, apparently despondent over a poor job appraisal, killed 14 coworkers and wounded 7 others in the Edmond Post Office (Aug. 20) before killing himself.

President Ronald Reagan nominated Robert Bork to the U.S. Supreme Court; after a major, televised nomination fight, the Senate rejected the nomination.

The U.S. Gramm-Rudman Act (Dec.) mandated across-the-board budget cutting when budgets were not met, with the stated goal of reaching a balanced budget by 1991; in practice, massive deficits continued to accelerate.

American cyclist Greg Le Mond won his sport's most prestigious race, the Tour de France, his first of three victories (1986; 1989; 1990).

The U.S. Congress established a far-too-small trust fund to help pay the massive costs of cleaning up sites into which petroleum products and other toxic chemicals had been leaking, as under gas stations.

A nighttime collision between the freighter *Pyotr Vasev* and the cruise ship *Admiral Nakhimov* in the Black Sea, near Novorossisk (Aug. 31), killed 398 people.

1930s; he served in Winston Churchill's World War II cabinet and in several postwar cabinets, and was Conservative prime minister (1957-1963).

d. Alva Reimer Myrdal (1902-1986), Swedish teacher, social planner, politician, diplomat, and peace activist who shared the 1982 Nobel Peace Prize with Alfonso García Robles. She was a United Nations social welfare official (1949-1956), Swedish ambassador to India (1956-1961), and Swedish minister for disarmament and church affairs (1966-1973). Her sometimes collaborator and husband was economist Gunnar Myrdal.

d. Roy Marcus Cohn (1927-1986), American lawyer; a prosecutor of Ethel and Julius Rosenberg (1951) and Owen Lattimore (1952); chief assistant to Senator Joseph McCarthy (1953-1954). Later a highly controversial corporate lawyer, he was disbarred in 1986.

d. Vyacheslav Mikhailovich Molotov (1890-1986), chief Soviet foreign policy aide (1939-1953) to Joseph Stalin, who lost power in the factional struggles that followed Stalin's death.

d. Rudolph Hess (1894-1986), Nazi leader who drew world attention with his failed peace proposal flight to Britain (1941); a war criminal, he died at Spandau Prison.

d. Samora Machel (1933-1986), Mozambican independence leader, head of the Mozambican National Liberation Front (FRELIMO) (1970-1986), and the first president of Mozambique (1975-1986). He was succeeded by Joaquim Alberto Chissanó.

d. (William) Averell Harriman (1891-1986), American Democratic politician and diplomat, whose many posts included ambassador to the Soviet Union (1943-1946) and governor of New York (1955-1959); he was an adviser to five Democratic presidents.

of Valentin Glushko; cosmonauts Vladimir Solovyev and Leonid Kizim boarded it later (May 5).

The U.S. spacecraft *Voyager 2* flew by the planet Uranus, transmitting photographs of its rings and discovering new satellites.

A container of nuclear material burst (Jan. 6) in Kerr-McGee's Sequoyah Fuels plant in Gore, Oklahoma. One person was killed and more than 100 injured; the area was contaminated by uranium-bearing gas emissions.

Halley's comet, which had returned late in 1985, became brightly visible, sparking much popular interest; the United States, Soviet Union, and European Space Agency all sent space probes to pass through the comet's tail.

The first genetically engineered virus was introduced — a vaccine against herpes in swine. Also, genetically engineered organisms were first used in field trials, which had been previously blocked in court.

Digital audiotape (DAT) technology was developed in Japan.

Louis Kunkel and his team discovered the defective gene that causes Duchenne's muscular dystrophy

d. Helen Brooke Taussig (1898-1986), American pediatric cardiologist who learned how to correct infant heart defects (1944) and was among the first to warn of the dangers of thalidomide (1961-1962).

d. Henry Moore (1898-1986), British sculptor; a world figure from the late 1920s.

d. Alan Jay Lerner (1918-1986), American lyricist and writer, long the collaborator of composer Frederick Loewe, most notably in *My Fair Lady* (1956).

d. Benny (Benjamin David) Goodman (1909-1986), American clarinetist and leading jazz bandleader of the "swing" era.

d. Bernard Malamud (1914-1986), American novelist and short story writer, most of whose work was set in Jewish-American life.

d. Jean Genet (1910-1986), French writer; a leading playwright of the "theater of the absurd," from *The Maids* (1947).

d. Robert Preston (Robert Preston Meservey) (1918-1986), American actor who emerged as an international film star in the 1960s.

d. Harold Arlen (Hyman Arluck) (1905-1986), American songwriter and composer; a noted figure in popular music and in the musical theater.

d. Jorge Luis Borges (1899-1986), Argentine writer; a leading poet, short story writer, and essayist.

d. James Cagney (1899-1986), American film star from his gangster lead in *Public Enemy* (1930).

Near Dhaka, Bangladesh, a double-decker riverboat sank (May 25), killing 500 people.

d. Simone de Beauvoir (1908-1986), French writer, philosopher, and feminist; a worldwide women's movement figure and with her longtime companion, Jean-Paul Sartre, a leading existentialist; most notably the author of *The Second Sex* (1949).

d. Wallis Warfield Simpson, Duchess of Windsor (1896-1986), American wife of the former Edward VIII of Britain; he succeeded to the throne, but abdicated (1936) rather than give up their planned marriage; they then married, becoming the Duke and Duchess of Windsor.

d. L. Ron (Lafayette Ronald) Hubbard (1911-1986), American writer and founder of the Church of Scientology (1952).

d. Tenzing Norgay (1914-1986), Sherpa mountaineer who, with climber Edmund Hillary, first reached the top of Mount Everest (1953).

At the Washington Summit, U.S. president Ronald Reagan and Soviet Communist Party general secretary Mikhail Gorbachev worked out the terms of the Intermediate Nuclear Forces (INF) Treaty, for the first time agreeing to destroy a category of nuclear weapons (Dec. 8). The Cold War began to recede, and with it the threat of humanity-destroying nuclear war.

Costa Rican president Oscar Arias Sánchez proposed the Arias Plan (Feb.), which helped end the Nicaraguan Civil War and brought him the Nobel Peace Prize.

The report of the Tower Commission (John Tower, Edmund Muskie, and Brent Scowcroft) sharply criticized the Reagan administration for its conduct regarding the Iran-Contra Affair.

Jonathan J. Pollard, an employee of the U.S. Naval Intelligence Support Center, was convicted of having spied for Israel and sentenced to life imprisonment. Anne Henderson Pollard, his wife, also was convicted and received a five-year sentence.

Klaus Barbie, the Nazi World War II "Butcher of Lyon," was sentenced to life imprisonment in France; he had been captured in Bolivia (1983).

Li Peng succeeded Zhai Ziyang as Chinese prime minister, emerging as a major leader of the conservative faction in Chinese communism.

Liberal Democrat Noboru Takeshita became prime minister of Japan (1987-1989); he would be forced to resign because of his involvement in the Recruit stock scandal.

Southern Chadian forces scored major civil war victories, taking the Libyan base at Faya-Largeau and its massive stores of weapons, as well as the Libyan air base at Ouadi Doum, then invading Libya and forcing Libya to negotiate a truce.

Saudi Arabian police fought Iranian fundamentalist pilgrims at Mecca's Grand Mosque (July 1), killing hundreds.

The Environmental Protection Agency (EPA) issued the landmark report *Unfinished Business: A Comparative Assessment of Environmental Problems,* attempting for the first time to assess "the relative risks to human health and the environment posed by various environmental problems," from ozone layer depletion and loss of wetlands to air pollution and toxic chemicals, as a guide for future public policy.

In a controversial move, the last California condors were brought in from the wild to a captive breeding program aimed at saving North America's largest bird from extinction. The total number of condors at that time was 27: 13 males and 14 females.

Astronomers Oscar Duhalde and Ian Shelton were the first to discover a new supernova (1987A) (Feb. 24), the brightest in centuries, for some months visible to the naked eye; the star's core was found to be emitting neutrinos, the first detected outside the solar system.

British physicist Stephen Hawking published his surprise best-seller *A Brief History of Time,* becoming an international celebrity, despite being constricted (from 1962) by amyotrophic lateral sclerosis (Lou Gehrig's disease).

An advanced telecommunications network, the Integrated Services Digital Network (ISDN), using microelectronics to handle voice, data, facsimile, and video through high-speed digital transmissions, was being tested in the United States and elsewhere. New signaling systems also allowed telephone companies to offer new services such as the caller's phone number, call forwarding, and selective call blocking.

For the first time in U.S. history, nuclear power was more expensive than power produced by coal; nuclear energy had always been touted as

Bernardo Bertolucci's epic film *The Last Emperor,* about the last Manchu emperor of China, the child emperor Hsüan T'ung (Henry Pu Yi), starred John Lone in the title role opposite Joan Chen and Peter O'Toole.

Norman Jewison's film *Moonstruck,* set in Italian-American New York family life, starred Cher, Nicolas Cage, Danny Aiello, Olympia Dukakis, and Vincent Gardenia.

Stephen Sondheim wrote the music and lyrics for the musical *Into the Woods,* based on a book by James Lapine, who also directed the musical, starring Bernadette Peters and Tom Aldredge.

Steven Spielberg's film *Empire of the Sun* was set in Shanghai's European community immediately after the onset of World War II, and starred Christian Bale and John Malkovich.

Peter Brooks directed his massive nine-hour stage version of the Indian epic *Mahabharata.*

John Boorman directed his autobiographical film *Hope and Glory,* set in World War II London and starring David Hayman, Sarah Miles, Sammi Davis, and Ian Bannen.

Martin Scorsese directed *The Last Temptation of Christ,* his controversial film based on Nikos Kazantzakis's 1955 novel, starring Willem Dafoe and Harvey Keitel.

Louis Malle wrote and directed his autobiographical film *Au Revoir Les Enfants,* set in World War II occupied France.

Russian-American poet Joseph Brodsky was awarded the Nobel Prize for literature.

d. Fred Astaire (Frederick Austerlitz) (1899-1987), American dancer and actor; a stage star in vaude-

On "Black Monday" (Oct. 19), the Dow Jones industrial average dropped a record 508.32 points (22.6 percent) on a record New York Stock Exchange trading volume of 604.33 million shares, climaxing a slide of 984 points, from 2,722 to 1,738; although many people lost a great deal of money, the crash did not trigger a recession or depression.

Protestant fundamentalist minister Jim Bakker, a star television evangelist, resigned from his own Praise the Lord (PTL) network (Mar.) after newspapers reported that he had had sex with secretary Jessica Hahn (1980) and had subsequently bought her silence with PTL money. Bakker and his wife, Tammy Faye Bakker, left PTL, which went bankrupt. Bakker was later convicted on various federal charges and imprisoned.

At Howard Beach, Brooklyn, a group of White youths beat up two African-Americans (Dec. 21); while fleeing along a highway, one of the victims, Michael Griffith, was struck by a vehicle and died. A major New York City racial confrontation ended when four of the attackers — Scott Kern, Jason Ladone, Jon Lester, and Michael Pirone — were convicted and imprisoned.

In the century's worst peacetime marine disaster, 1,750 to 3,000 people died when the interisland ferry *Dona Paz* sank after colliding with the oil tanker *Victor* off the Philippines (Dec. 20).

Off Zeebrugge, Belgium, the British Channel ferry *Herald of Free Enterprise* capsized (Mar. 6), killing 188 people.

Steffi Graf won the French Open, emerging as a leading woman tennis player, with 66 consecutive victories.

The U.S. Patent and Trademark Office ruled that genetically engineered animals, including vertebrates, could be patented.

1987 cont.

Substantial Indian peacekeeping forces arrived in Sri Lanka after Indian mediation of the increasingly bitter and widespread civil war had failed.

Iraqi missiles killed 37 sailors aboard the USS *Stark* in the Persian Gulf (May 17).

New Zealand declared its waters a nuclear-free zone.

Michael K. Deaver, a former long-term personal assistant to Ronald Reagan (1967-1985), was convicted of perjury regarding his post–White House lobbying activities.

Senator Joseph Biden withdrew from the Democratic presidential race after the staff of Democratic candidate Michael Dukakis charged that Biden had plagiarized the speeches of British Labour leader Neil Kinnock and others.

Lieutenant Colonel Sitiveni Rabuka took power by coup in Fiji.

d. Camille Chamoun (1900-1987), Lebanese Maronite Christian politician (1952-1958) who became president by coup (1952) and left the presidency as part of the peace agreement settling the Lebanese Civil War (1958).

d. Hans Speidel (1897-1987), German general who, with Allied forces nearing Paris, refused direct orders to destroy the city (late Aug. 1944). Later he was NATO central European commander (1957-1963).

d. William Joseph Casey (1913-1987), American lawyer and politician; head of the Central Intelligence Agency (CIA) (1981-1987), who was probably a key figure in the aborted Iran-Contra arms-for-hostages swap. He resigned on February 2 and died three months later (May 6).

cheaper, even though that was clearly only a very short-term comparison.

Genetic researchers reported discovering a genetic marker linked with manic depression (bipolar disorder).

Soviet cosmonaut Yuri Romanenko spent a record 326 days aboard the space station *Mir* before returning to earth.

Using analysis of genetic material called mitochondrial DNA (mDNA), Allan Wilson and others proposed a common African ancestor, "Eve," for all modern humans; the analysis sparked widespread controversy and intensified the debate between scientists favoring an "out of Africa" origin and those theorizing that humans developed elsewhere or in several locations.

d. Louis de Broglie (Prince Louis-Victor Pierre Raymond; Duc de Broglie) (1892-1987), French physicist who first posited the wave nature of particles (1923).

d. Peter Brian Medawar (1915-1987), Brazilian-born British-Lebanese zoologist best known for his discovery of the mechanism by which the body rejects transplants (1944).

ville and the musical theater with his sister Adele (1906-1931), then the leading dancer in cinema history, most notably for the 10 classic musical films he did with Ginger Rogers.

d. Fritz Lang (1890-1987), Austrian director of several classic silent films in Weimar Germany, notably *Metropolis* (1927) and *M* (1931).

d. John Huston (1906-1987), American director, actor, and writer; a major figure from his directorial debut, *The Maltese Falcon* (1941); he was the son of Walter Huston and the father of Anjelica Huston, who starred in his last film, *The Dead* (1987), based on a James Joyce short story.

d. Andrés Segovia (1893-1987), Spanish guitarist; one of the leading classical guitarists of the century.

d. James Arthur Baldwin (1924-1987), African-American writer; a noted author from his first novel, *Go Tell It on the Mountain* (1953).

d. Andy Warhol (Andrew Warhola) (1930-1987), a leading American pop artist in the 1960s; also an experimental filmmaker.

d. Jascha Heifetz (1901-1987), Russian-American violinist; from the early 1920s, one of the world's leading violinists.

d. Bob Fosse (1927-1987), American dancer, choreographer, and director; a leading figure in the musical theater who also worked in film.

d. Rita Hayworth (Margarita Carmen Cansino) (1918-1987), American dancer and actress; a film star and 1940s sex symbol.

A Korean Air jet crashed into the jungle near the Thailand-Burma border, probably after the explosion of a bomb placed by North Korea (Nov. 29); 115 people died.

British golfer Nick Faldo won his first of three British Opens (1987; 1990; 1992).

Economist Alan Greenspan succeeded Paul Volcker as chairman of the Federal Reserve Board (June).

Fire raging through China's Heilungkiang province (May-June) killed more than 190 people and burned nearly 2.5 million acres.

The Montreal Protocol on Substances That Deplete the Ozone Layer was signed, an international agreement to phase out substances damaging to the earth's ozone layer, notably chlorofluorocarbons (CFCs) and halons; 93 nations signed an amended version in 1990.

The United Nations World Commission on Environment and Development, chaired by Norwegian leader Gro Harlem Brundtland, published its influential Brundtland Report, *Our Common Future,* serving as a basis for international policy regarding the environment and development.

The first conviction based on "genetic fingerprinting" occurred in Britain.

d. (Karl) Gunnar Myrdal (1898-1987), Swedish economist and sociologist; a major figure in international economics for more than half a century, he shared the 1974 Nobel Prize for economics with Friedrich von Hayek. He was the husband of sociologist and diplomat Alva Myrdal.

At the Moscow Summit (May), Soviet Communist Party general secretary Mikhail Gorbachev and U.S. president Ronald Reagan signed the Intermediate Nuclear Forces (INF) Treaty and resolved a considerable range of remaining Cold War–related regional conflicts.

Republican George Bush defeated Democrat Michael Dukakis to become the 41st president of the United States (1989-1993).

The Afghan-Soviet War ended with the Geneva Agreement (Apr. 14), providing for Soviet withdrawal, although the Afghan Civil War continued; Soviet troop withdrawals began (May).

Angola, Cuba, and South Africa made an Angolan peace agreement, mediated by the superpowers. Cuban troops were withdrawn from Angola, South African aid to the National Union for the Total Independence of Angola (UNITA) was ended, and Namibia was to be free. UNITA did not sign the agreement, and the civil war continued.

A United Nations–mediated cease-fire (Aug. 20) was followed by Geneva peace negotiations that ended the Iran-Iraq War (1980-1988). Iraqi forces then attacked Kurdish insurgents in northern Iraq, using poison gas to kill tens of thousands.

A cease-fire (Mar. 24) ended the Nicaraguan Civil War (1978-1988); democratic elections were to follow.

Burmese military dictator Ne Win resigned (July 23) because of the massive antigovernment demonstrations, called the "Burmese Spring" (Mar.-Sept.). U Nu led a short-lived democratic government, which was deposed by a military coup led by General Saw Maung (Sept. 18). Democratic leader and international figure Daw Aung San Suu Kyi was placed under house arrest (1988-1995).

As Soviet peacekeeping efforts failed, Azerbaijan and Armenia went to war over the disputed Armenian Nagorno-Karabachi enclave within Azerbaijan (1988-   ).

RU-486 (Mifepristone) was developed by Etienne-Emile Baulieu, of France's Groupe Roussel Uclaf. The "abortion pill" operates by preventing implantation of a fertilized egg in the uterus, a process safer and cheaper than surgical abortion, though carrying a risk of hemorrhage. After antiabortion protests, the firm withdrew the pill, but the French government ordered that it be put back into distribution. Other European countries also began using it, although religious-political considerations would keep it out of the United States, even for testing, until 1994.

Soviet cosmonaut Vladimir Lyakhov and Abdul Ahad Mohmand of Afghanistan were stuck in earth orbit for 25 hours, their air supply growing short, before they were able to crash-land safely (Sept. 7). Later that year, cosmonauts Vladimir Titov and Musa Manarov, along with France's Jean-Loup Chrétien, returned to earth (Dec. 21), the two Russians having spent a record 365 days aboard the space station *Mir*.

An Ashland Oil storage tank collapsed (Jan. 2), spilling 700,000 to 750,000 gallons (2,400 to 2,500 tons) of diesel fuel into the Monongahela River, which spread to Pittsburgh, Pennsylvania, 20 miles downriver, and then on down the Ohio River, creating a 100-mile oil slick that caused water supply emergencies in many cities along the river, exacerbated when the oil-covered river froze, and killed much wildlife. Ashland was later fined $2.25 million (1989) for environmental law violations and settled legal claims for approximately $30 million (1990).

The Environmental Protection Agency recommended that all homes and lower-floor apartments be checked for levels of the colorless, odorless radioactive gas radon, part of a recog-

Salman Rushdie published the novel *The Satanic Verses,* attacked by many Muslims for allegedly slandering Islam. Despite riots, book burnings, murders, and a "death sentence" proclaimed in early 1989 by Ayatollah Ruhollah Khomeini, the book became a worldwide best-seller, while Rushdie went into hiding, protected by Scotland Yard.

Jodie Foster starred as the woman who fights to win vindication and the conviction of the men who gang-raped her in Jonathan Kaplan's film *The Accused,* based on a real-life case. Kelly McGillis costarred as the prosecutor.

Marcel Ophüls created the classic documentary film *Hotel Terminus: The Life and Times of Klaus Barbie,* exploring a wide range of questions involving SS officer and war criminal Barbie, the Holocaust for which he and some of those who later shielded him shared guilt, and some wider questions involving wartime and postwar France.

Charles S. Dutton and S. Epatha Merkerson starred in August Wilson's play *The Piano Lesson,* directed by Lloyd Richards and set in Depression era African-American family life in Pittsburgh.

Daniel Day-Lewis, Juliette Binoche, Lena Olin, Derek de Lint, and Erland Josephson starred in Philip Kaufman's film *The Unbearable Lightness of Being,* based on Milan Kundera's 1984 novel, set in 1960s Czechoslovakia.

Gene Hackman and Willem Dafoe starred in Alan Parker's film *Mississippi Burning,* about the real-life 1964 murders of civil rights activists James Chaney, Andrew Goodman, and Michael Schwerner in Neshoba County, Mississippi.

John Lithgow and B. D. Wong starred in David Henry Hwang's play *M. Butterfly,* directed by John Dexter and based on the true story of a French diplomat in love with a Chinese opera star he be-

A massive earthquake struck Soviet Armenia, killing an estimated 55,000 people and leaving 500,000 homeless, with many towns, including Leninakan (a city of 290,000) almost totally destroyed (Dec. 7). Further signaling the end of the Cold War, Soviet Communist Party general secretary Mikhail Gorbachev welcomed disaster relief and medical aid from abroad.

Pan Am's Flight 103, en route from London to New York, exploded in midair over Lockerbie, Scotland (Dec. 21), blown up by a bomb planted in the luggage compartment by Islamic terrorists; 259 people on board died, including 35 from Syracuse University, and 11 on the ground.

Medical waste washing ashore, including some materials infected with viruses causing diseases such as AIDS and hepatitis, caused the closing of numerous American beaches, notably in New York and New Jersey, and public outcry, leading to two new federal laws: the Ocean Dumping Reform Act and the Infectious Waste Tracking Act.

A school bus carrying 30 Soviet children was taken by 5 Soviet hijackers in Ordzhonikidze, in the Caucasus Mountains (Dec. 3); the children were released in exchange for $3 million and a cargo plane, which the hijackers flew to Israel. On landing, they were arrested and returned to the Soviet Union (Dec. 3), in an unprecedented example of Israeli-Soviet cooperation.

In a cause célèbre, Chico Mendez (Francisco Mendes Filho), president of the Brazilian rubber tappers union, was killed, apparently because of attempts to halt clearing of the already much-devastated Amazon rain forest for cattle ranches; three ranchers were convicted of his murder.

Kohlberg Kravis Roberts and Co. won a long and bitter takeover battle for RJR Nabisco, the purchase price of $25.07 billion being the largest to date in

d. Mohammad Zia Ul-Haq (1924-1988), Pakistani dictator (1977-1988); killed in an airplane crash (Aug. 17). He was succeeded by democratic leader Benazir Bhutto, daughter of Zulfikar Ali Bhutto, who had been executed by the Zia Ul-Haq government.

The Intifada (Uprising) began in the West Bank and Gaza Strip; unarmed groups of Palestinian teenagers stoned Israeli occupation forces.

In Burundi, the Tutsi-controlled armed forces defeated a Hutu insurrection, then massacring at least 5,000 Hutus.

Augmented Indian forces numbering more than 50,000 unsuccessfully attacked Tamil Liberation Tiger forces in Sri Lanka; the guerrilla civil war continued.

Hungary became a free nation. Imre Nagy, leader of the 1956 Hungarian Revolution, was reburied with honors; 300,000 attended the burial.

The United States refused to admit Yasir Arafat into the country to address the United Nations. The UN General Assembly then moved its meeting to Geneva, where Arafat spoke.

Muslim terrorists in Lebanon kidnapped and murdered American lieutenant colonel William Higgins, head of the United Nations Lebanon truce team.

A missile fired from the USS *Vincennes* in the Strait of Hormuz destroyed an Iranian civilian airliner, killing all 290 aboard (July 3).

U.S. attorney general and key Ronald Reagan aide Edwin Meese III resigned before the special prosecutor's report on the Wedtech case was made public; although the report found no basis for criminal prosecution, it stated that Meese had "probably violated the criminal law" four times while in office.

Colorado Democratic senator Gary Hart was forced out of the race for his party's presidential nomination by the

nition of the hazards of indoor air pollution, with its concentrations of volatile organic chemicals.

Radiocarbon dating showed that the Shroud of Turin, which many believed to be the burial sheet of Jesus, carrying his image, had actually been woven of linen produced by plants only seven centuries ago.

The bending of radio waves and other electromagnetic radiation by gravity, predicted by Albert Einstein (1936), was confirmed by American astronomer Jacqueline Hewitt's team, using the Very Large Array telescope in New Mexico.

A major study indicated that a single aspirin taken every other day helped reduce the risk and severity of heart attacks; previous studies had shown that regular low aspirin intake reduced the risk of a second attack.

The Adriatic Sea was struck by extraordinarily heavy summer blooms of algae (1988; 1989) that depleted oxygen supplies and threatened marine life, already made vulnerable by heavy pollution.

The first California condor was born in captivity, part of a captive breeding program to save the nearly extinct species.

The first genetically engineered vertebrate, a mouse, was patented in the United States.

The Soviet spacecraft *Phobos 1* and *Phobos 2* were launched toward Mars, but both failed (early 1989) before reaching the planet.

The U.S. space shuttle *Discovery* was launched, the first NASA space flight since the loss of *Challenger* (1986); seals and joints on the

lieves to be a woman; it would be the basis for a 1993 film.

Max von Sydow created the role of the father of Pelle Hvenegaard in Bille August's film *Pelle the Conqueror,* based on Martin Andersen Nexö's four-volume novel (1906-1910).

Bob Dylan, George Harrison, Tom Petty, Jeff Lynne, and Roy Orbison founded the folk-rock group the Traveling Wilburys.

Dustin Hoffman as the autistic brother and Tom Cruise starred in Barry Levinson's film *Rain Man.*

Joan Allen as Heidi starred in Wendy Wasserstein's Pulitzer Prize–winning play *The Heidi Chronicles,* about the world and development of a woman trying to find herself.

Oscar Hijuelos published the Pulitzer Prize–winning novel *The Mambo Kings Play Songs of Love.*

Ray McAnally starred as the radical Labour prime minister opposite Alan MacNaughton as his bitter opponent, the Tory national security chief, in Mick Jackson's television miniseries *A Very British Coup.*

The Andrew Lloyd Webber and Charles Hart musical *Phantom of the Opera* starred Michael Crawford and Sarah Brightman, with Harold Prince directing.

Harvey Fierstein starred in *Torch Song Trilogy,* Paul Bogart's film based on Fierstein's own 1982 one-act plays.

Egyptian writer Naguib Mahfouz was awarded the Nobel Prize for literature.

d. Frederick William Ashton (1904-1988), British dancer, choreographer, and ballet director; a major choreographer and a key figure (1935-1970) in the companies that ultimately became the Royal Ballet.

American history. The battle was depicted in the 1993 telefilm *Barbarians at the Gate.*

As the price of facsimile machines dropped under $1,000, the fax suddenly became a standard business machine, with more than a million sold in a single year in the United States alone.

Middletown, Ohio, hospital orderly Donald Harvey admitted to killing 24 people, most of them by poisoning, and possibly 30 more.

The Drexel Burnham Lambert securities firm was charged with huge securities frauds, most of them in Michael Milken's "junk bond" department.

The Wellington Convention, an international agreement, would have allowed mining and oil drilling in Antarctica, until then banned under the Antarctic Treaty. Marine explorer and environmentalist Jacques Cousteau almost single-handedly led a successful fight (1988-1991) to repudiate the treaty, notably in France and the United States, preserving Antarctica's protected status.

At the Seoul Olympics, American track star Jackie Joyner-Kersee won the gold medal in the two-day, seven-event heptathlon — the 100-meter hurdles, high jump, shotput, 200 meters, long jump, javelin, and 800 meters — with a record 7,291 points. She would be the first to win two consecutive gold medals in the event, repeating at the Barcelona Olympics (1992).

The Occidental Petroleum Company's North Sea oil rig *Piper Alpha,* off Aberdeen, Scotland, exploded into a massive fire that destroyed the rig (July 6), killing 167 people aboard.

An earthquake measuring 7.6 on the Richter scale struck China's Yunnan province (Nov. 6), killing some 1,000 people.

1988 cont.

massive adverse media coverage following an accusation that he had had an extramarital affair with Donna Rice.

Daniel Arap Moi became dictator of Kenya, having been "reelected" to the presidency without a popular vote.

d. Georgi Maksimilianovich Malenkov (1902-1988), Soviet political figure; an aide to Joseph Stalin who succeeded Stalin to the leadership of the Soviet Union (1953-1955); he was defeated in an intraparty leadership fight and succeeded by Nikita Khrushchev.

d. Kim (Harold Adrian Russell) Philby (1912-1988), British double agent; a Soviet mole in British intelligence who became the principal figure in one of the century's most notable spy stories. He had escaped to the Soviet Union in 1963.

d. Takeo Miki (1907-1988), Japanese Liberal Democratic Party prime minister (1974-1976); he succeeded Kakuei Tanaka as prime minister during a financial scandal, and in 1976 pursued the Lockheed scandal (1975) and the subsequent prosecution of Tanaka.

rocket booster, responsible for that crash, had been redesigned.

d. Raymond A. Dart (1893-1988), Australian–South African anatomist and physical anthropologist who discovered *Australopithecus africanus* (1924) and posited an African origin for humans.

d. Luis Walter Alvarez (1911-1988), American physicist who codeveloped the theory that some species extinctions were caused 65 million years ago by a meteorite colliding with the earth (1980).

d. Nikolaas Tinbergen (1907-1988), Dutch-British zoologist; a founder of ethology, the scientific study of animal behavior.

d. Richard Phillips Feynman (1918-1988), American physicist who in the late 1940s developed quantum electrodynamics to describe the behavior of electrons with mathematical precision.

1989

d. Hu Yaobang (1915-1989), Chinese communist politician; a protégé of Deng Xiaoping who while Communist Party chairman (1981-1986) became the leading reformer of his time. His death occasioned the massive pro-democracy student demonstrations that ended with the Tienanmen Square massacre.

Massive pro-democracy student-led demonstrations erupted in China; world attention was focused on the student occupation of Beijing's Tienanmen Square. Chinese troops killed hundreds of students as they were evacuating the square (June 4); the hard-line government then mounted a countrywide reign of terror.

Ethnic conflicts and independence movements shook the Soviet Union, as that country and its empire began to dis-

America's worst oil spill occurred when the supertanker *Exxon Valdez,* carrying oil from the Alyeska Pipeline, ran aground on Bligh Reef, 25 miles off Valdez, Alaska (Mar. 24, 12:04 AM), releasing more than 11 million gallons (approximately 260,000 barrels, or 37,000 tons) of oil into Prince William Sound. Promised oil-industry emergency containment and cleanup plans were nonexistent or ineffective, leading Alaska and local communities to take over the cleanup, at Exxon's expense. Some vital salmon hatcheries were saved, but the oil slick eventually grew to 50 miles; more than 350 miles of shoreline, including wildlife breeding grounds, had major short- and long-term environmental damage, some from the

d. Robert Joffrey (Abdullah Jaffa Anver Khan) (1930-1988), American dancer who emerged as a leading choreographer in the early 1950s; founder of the Joffrey Ballet Company (1956).

d. Louise Nevelson (Louise Berliawsky) (1900-1988), American sculptor; a leading modernist from the 1950s.

d. Trevor Howard (1916-1988), British actor who became a film star with *Brief Encounter* (1945).

d. Beatrice Lillie (1894-1988), Canadian-British actress and singer; a theater star from *Charlot's Revue* (1924); later a radio star.

As a major cyclone struck the coast of Bangladesh and northeastern India (Nov. 29), at least 1,000 people died and tens of thousands lost their homes.

Caribbean hurricane Gilbert (Sept. 12-14) killed hundreds and left 500,000 homeless in Jamaica and 100,000 homeless in Mexico.

A ferry capsized in the Ganges River near Kathir, India (Aug. 6), killing 400 people.

In Lashio, Burma, a fire started in a kitchen raged through more than 2,000 buildings (Mar. 20), killing 113 people.

The inter-island ferry *Dona Marilyn* sank in a typhoon off the Philippines (Oct. 24), killing 360 people.

d. Charles Addams (1912-1988), American cartoonist; creator of the "Addams Family" cartoons, which from 1935 appeared in *The New Yorker* and were later published in several collections.

Daniel Day-Lewis starred as the astonishingly productive Irish writer and cerebral palsy victim Christy Brown in Jim Sheridan's film *My Left Foot,* based on Brown's 1954 autobiography.

I. M. Pei unveiled his acclaimed and controversial *Pyramid* sculpture, leading to the entrance to the Louvre.

Jessica Tandy in the title role starred opposite Morgan Freeman and Dan Aykroyd in Bruce Beresford's film *Driving Miss Daisy,* adapted by Robert Uhry from his own 1987 play.

Oliver Stone's anti–Vietnam War film *Born on the Fourth of July* starred Tom Cruise as paralyzed, to-

In Stockton, California's Cleveland Elementary School yard, five children — all refugees from Southeast Asia — were killed and some 30 children and adults wounded by Patrick Edward Purdy (West) (Jan. 17), who fired 110 rounds from his AK-47 semiautomatic assault rifle before committing suicide. Largely sparked by this event, the federal government banned the import of such rifles (Mar. 14), and public support grew for restrictions on their manufacture, sale, and possession.

A massive earthquake measuring 7.1 on the Richter scale struck northern California (Oct. 17), killing more than 60 people and injuring thousands. Occurring a few minutes before the start of the third game of the World Series, it was televised worldwide.

solve. The Armenian-Azerbaijani guerrilla war intensified; Sunni-Shi'ite Muslim conflict flared in Uzbekistan; Uzbeks and Kirghiz fought in Kirghizia. Latvian, Lithuanian, and Estonian independence movements strengthened.

Czechoslovakia became a free nation, with dissident playwright Vaclav Havel its new president and 1968 Prague Spring leader Alexander Dubček chairman of the democratic parliament.

d. Nicolae Ceausescu (1918-1989), Romanian dictator, and his wife, Elena Ceausescu (1918-1989); they were deposed and executed (Dec. 25) during the Romanian Revolution (Dec. 16-28), quickly concluded when the army joined revolutionary forces and defeated internal security forces.

Massive pro-democracy demonstrations swept East Germany, and large numbers of East German emigrants moved into the West through Hungary. Early hard-line East German government resistance crumbled; the Honecker government fell (Oct. 18). Free emigration and the opening of the Berlin Wall quickly followed (Nov.). A new day began for Germany and Europe.

The trade union Solidarity was legalized in Poland, and a series of major democratic and economic reforms was introduced (Apr. 5). Poland became a free nation, the Polish Republic, rather than the Polish People's Republic (Dec. 29).

American forces attacked Panama, quickly taking the country (Dec. 20-24) and deposing the government of General Manuel Noriega.

Civil war reintensified in Lebanon, as General Michel Aoun's Lebanese army forces unsuccessfully attacked Muslim forces in Beirut (Mar.-Dec).

Japanese prime minister Noboru Takeshita (1987-1989) resigned because of his involvement in the Recruit stock scandal, which had revealed a pattern of corruption in-

cleanup efforts themselves. Out-of-court settlements collapsed, and in the mid-1990s most claims and suits were still pending.

The National Institutes of Health performed a landmark gene therapy experiment involving extraction of a patient's cells, which were then modified and reinserted into the patient, in this first instance not as therapy, but as a tracking test; the hope was that the approach could be used to treat conditions such as cancer, with modified cells "reversing" the problems caused by the defective cells.

Genetic researchers Lap-Chee Tsui, John Riordan, and Francis Collins announced that they had located the defective gene that causes cystic fibrosis, leading to hopes for a prenatal test and gene therapy.

B. Stanley Pons of the University of Utah and Martin Fleischmann of Britain's University of Southampton announced that they had achieved the long-elusive nuclear fusion at room temperature, so-called cold fusion. The report generated enormous excitement, since success could provide long-sought cheap power for the world, but other scientists were unable to duplicate the claimed results.

Magellan became the first spacecraft launched from a space shuttle, *Atlantis* (May 4), starting a 15-month, 795-million-mile voyage toward Venus. With the easing of the Cold War, Soviet space scientists had shared with their American colleagues data from their earlier Venus probes. Later, the spacecraft *Galileo* was shuttle-launched (Oct. 18) toward Jupiter, its arrival pegged for 1995.

The U.S. spacecraft *Voyager 2,* having flown 7 billion miles since its 1977 launching, flew by Neptune (Aug. 25), sending back data on that

tally disillusioned Vietnam veteran and antiwar activist Ron Kovic, who cowrote the screenplay with Stone; based on Kovic's autobiography.

A blues star of the 1970s, Bonnie Raitt made a major comeback with her album *Nick of Time,* with its celebrated title song, and with her duet version of the 1951 song "I'm in the Mood," sung with John Lee Hooker on his album *The Healer.* In a year of comebacks, Bob Dylan toured with his album *Oh Mercy,* and Paul McCartney made his first world tour in 13 years.

Maya Lin's Civil Rights Memorial in Montgomery, Alabama, quickly became a national shrine.

Gabriel Garcia Marquez published the novel *The General in His Labyrinth.*

Phil Alden Robinson wrote and directed the film *Field of Dreams,* starring Kevin Costner as an Iowa farmer who brings back the ghosts of the scandal-doomed 1919 Chicago White Sox, led by Ray Liotta as "Shoeless Joe" Jackson; James Earl Jones, Amy Madigan, Burt Lancaster, and Gaby Hoffman costarred.

James Naughton starred as the writer in 1940s Hollywood in the musical *City of Angels* by Larry Gelbart, Cy Coleman, and David Gippel.

Spanish writer Camilo José Cela was awarded the Nobel Prize for literature.

d. Irving Berlin (Isadore Baline) (1888-1989), American songwriter; a major figure in the history of American popular music and musical theater.

d. Laurence Olivier (1907-1989), British actor, director, and producer; a noted actor from the mid-1930s, he became one of the century's leading stage and screen stars.

A Soviet government commission reported that tens — perhaps even hundreds — of thousands of people purged during the Stalin era were buried in mass graves near Kiev.

Episcopal priest Barbara Clementine Harris, an African-American, became the first woman bishop of the Episcopal Church and of the worldwide Anglican Communion.

Art Shell, long a defensive tackle and then line coach of the Los Angeles Raiders football team, was named the Raiders' coach, the first African-American National Football League coach in 60 years.

In an effort to save the African elephant, whose number had halved in a decade to some 600,000, the Convention on International Trade in Endangered Species (CITES) proclaimed a worldwide ban on the ivory trade; despite international efforts, several African countries continued to export, and Asian countries to import, ivory.

In *Webster v. Reproductive Health Services,* a bitterly divided U.S. Supreme Court upheld a Missouri law banning abortions at public hospitals and clinics (except where the mother's life was endangered), especially affecting women of limited means.

Pro-choice demonstrators, numbering an estimated 300,000 to 600,000, held a massive rally in Washington, D.C. (Apr. 9), as the abortion rights debate raged.

The U.S. federal government passed a law providing a massive bailout for the failed savings and loan industry; bailout funds would ultimately run into the $250 billion to $300 billion range.

At Chelyabinsk, in the Urals, on the Trans-Siberian railroad, 600 to 650 people died, most of them children, when two trains were caught in a gas pipeline explosion and fire (June 3).

volving many high government officials and the Recruit Cosmos real estate company; Takeshita's finance, economics, and justice ministers also resigned.

Oliver North was convicted on three felony counts related to the Iran-Contra Affair. All charges against North were later dropped (Sept. 1991).

Soviet forces completed their withdrawal from Afghanistan (Feb. 15).

The Tesoro Beach Accords (Feb. 14) formally ended the Nicaraguan Civil War, providing for democratic reforms, free elections, and the dissolution of Contra forces.

General Andres Rodriguez took power by coup in Paraguay (Feb. 2-3), ending the dictatorship of Alfredo Stroessner (1954-1989).

d. Ayatollah Ruhollah Khomeini (Ruhollah Kendi) (1900-1989), Iranian fundamentalist Shi'ite cleric; political and religious leader of Iran (1979-1989). Ali Akbar Hashemi Rafsanjani succeeded him as political leader.

d. Ferdinand Edralin Marcos (1917-1989), Philippine politician; president (1965-1986) and dictator (1971-1986) until forced into exile.

d. Hirohito (1901-1989), emperor of Japan (1926-1989); revered in Japan but without power, as evidenced by his inability to stop the Japanese military from taking his country into World War II.

d. Oliver Edmund Clubb (1901-1989), American diplomat and author; an "old China hand" who became a victim of McCarthyism (1951); formally cleared (1952), but his diplomatic career ended, he became a leading author on east Asia.

d. Josef Cyrankiewicz (1911-1989), Polish communist politician; prime minister (1947-1952; 1954-1970).

planet, its moon, Triton, and its satellites, discovering six new ones, before moving beyond Pluto and heading out of the solar system.

After three astronauts returned to earth (Apr. 27), the Soviet space station *Mir* was for the first time left empty, perhaps because of budget constraints or technological problems.

In a pioneering liver transplant operation performed at Wyler Children's Hospital at the University of Chicago, 21-month-old Alyssa Smith received a section of a liver from a living donor, her mother.

The hairy-eared dwarf lemur, the smallest of all the primates and one thought to be extinct, was discovered surviving on Madagascar.

The U.S. Cosmic Background Explorer (COBE) was launched to provide information on radiation in space and the universe's origin.

d. Andrei Dmitriyevich Sakharov (1921-1989), Soviet nuclear physicist, dissenter, and human rights advocate; winner of the 1975 Nobel Peace Prize; in his last year, a member of the new Soviet congress.

d. Konrad Zacharias Lorenz (1903-1989), Austrian zoologist and psychiatrist; cofounder of ethology, the study of animal behavior.

d. Valentin Glushko (1908-1989), Soviet engineer who built the rockets that launched the first intercontinental ballistic missile (ICBM) and the first space satellite, *Sputnik 1* (both 1957), and helped build the *Mir* space station.

d. Samuel Beckett (1906-1989), multifaceted Irish writer; one of the century's most noted playwrights from his first play, *Waiting for Godot* (1953), a central work of the "theater of the absurd." He was awarded the 1969 Nobel Prize for literature.

d. Robert Penn Warren (1905-1989), American writer and critic; a celebrated poet from the 1940s; best known for his novel *All the King's Men* (1946). He was the first U.S. poet laureate (1985).

d. Bette (Ruth Elizabeth) Davis (1908-1989), American actress; a star in such golden age film classics as *Of Human Bondage* (1934), *The Petrified Forest* (1936), *Dark Victory* (1939), *The Little Foxes* (1941), *Now Voyager* (1942), and *All About Eve* (1950). She won best actress Academy Awards for *Dangerous* (1935) and *Jezebel* (1938).

d. Vladimir Samoylovich Horowitz (1904-1989), Soviet-American pianist; one of the world's leading pianists from the late 1920s.

d. Lucille Ball (1911-1989), American film and television star; one of the world's leading comedians from her creation of television's "Lucy" (1951).

d. Salvador Dali (1904-1989), Spanish painter; a leading surrealist whose work featured the grotesqueries that, with a talent for self-promotion, also made him a leading celebrity.

d. Alvin Ailey (1931-1989), African-American dancer and choreographer; founder of the Alvin Ailey American Dance Theater (1958).

d. Georges Simenon (1903-1989), prolific Belgian-French novelist and short story writer best known for the more than 100 mystery novels starring Inspector Maigret, which began in 1930.

d. Herbert von Karajan (1908-1989), Austrian conductor; a major musical figure in Nazi Germany,

Hurricane Hugo, with 138-mile-per-hour winds, swept across the Caribbean, causing great damage and more than a score of deaths before striking Charleston, South Carolina, and surrounding areas (Sept. 22), where tens of thousands of people were left homeless and damage was estimated at $2 billion to $3 billion.

Reverend Jim Bakker was convicted on 24 counts of fraud and conspiracy and sentenced to a 45-year prison term; he would be released in 1994.

The Vatican issued a statement that the Catholic Church condemned apartheid, anti-Semitism, and all other forms of racism (Feb. 10).

Washington lawyer Ronald H. Brown was named chairman of the Democratic National Committee (Feb. 10), becoming the first African-American to lead a major U.S. political party.

At Hillsborough, near Sheffield, England, 95 people died and hundreds were injured when a crowd stampeded in panic at a soccer stadium (Apr. 15), crushing many against steel control fences.

d. Sugar Ray Robinson (Walker Smith) (1920-1989), American boxer who won both welterweight (1946-1951) and middleweight (1951 twice; 1955; 1957; 1958) world titles.

d. Barbara Wertheim Tuchman (1912-1989), American historian and writer, best known for *The Guns of August* (1962).

1989 cont.

1990

Iraqi forces invaded Kuwait (Aug. 2), quickly taking the country and beginning the Persian Gulf War. Backed by a United Nations condemnation of the action, American and allied forces quickly built a massive armed presence in the area and prepared to retake Kuwait and invade Iraq.

Mikhail Gorbachev's program of political and social reform faltered, as the Soviet economic system began to break down and ethnic and separatist pressures pulled the Soviet Union apart. Boris Yeltsin became president of the Russian Federation (May), acting as a focus of discontent. Soviet forces began their withdrawal from Eastern Europe, Soviet arms and political commitments to regional allies were discontinued, and the Warsaw Pact effectively dissolved.

The release of Nelson Mandela (Feb. 11) was followed by an African National Congress–South African government cease-fire agreement (Aug. 7), the release of many political prisoners, and the beginning of decisive negotiations aimed at ending apartheid and creating a multiracial, majority-ruled South Africa.

Christian Lebanese army forces led by General Michel Aoun were decisively defeated by Christian Phalangist militia and the Syrian army.

Former Panamanian ruler Manuel Noriega, granted sanctuary in the Vatican embassy, surrendered to U.S. forces (Jan. 3) and was taken to the United States for trial on drug trade charges.

Bacteria genetically engineered to clean up oil spills, patented a decade earlier (1980), were first used in the field off Galveston, Texas, after two separate accidents. The first was an explosion and fire on the Norwegian supertanker *Mega Borg* during off-loading, which killed four crew members and burned out of control for a week (June 8-15), spilling an estimated 4.3 million gallons (15,000 tons) of light crude oil; the second was a spill of an estimated 500,000 gallons (1,700 tons) of heavy crude oil after two oil-carrying barges collided with the Greek tanker *Shinoussa* (July 28), causing closure of the Houston Ship Channel (July 29-31). Other notable 1990 spills included an estimated 400,000 gallons (1,400 tons) (Feb. 7) that fouled the California coast near Huntington Beach (from Feb. 15) and five oil spills, three of them major, in New York harbor (Jan.-June), totaling an estimated 1,045,000 gallons (3,600 tons), which temporarily reversed the ecological comeback of the lower Hudson River.

The Hubble Space Telescope, perhaps the costliest scientific instrument in history, at $1.5 billion, was launched into space by the space shuttle *Discovery* (Apr. 24-29); despite a defect in its main mirror, it still sent back higher-resolution images than previously obtained.

Previously unknown vents and species were discovered at the bottom of Lake Baikal, more

then internationally in the postwar period, notably as director of the Berlin Philharmonic (1954-1989).

d. Robert Mapplethorpe (1947-1989), American photographer and filmmaker; a victim of AIDS; some of his sexually explicit work was attacked as obscene after his death.

Conductor Mstislav Rostropovich and his wife, singer Galina Vishnevskaya returned to the Soviet Union for the first time, as did many other artists and intellectuals who had left for the West during the communist period.

A major controversy about censorship of the arts erupted when performance artist Karen Finley's work was labeled obscene and she was denied a National Endowment for the Arts (NEA) grant.

Barbet Schroeder's film *Reversal of Fortune,* based on the Claus von Bulow murder trial, starred Jeremy Irons as von Bulow, Glenn Close as his wife, and Ron Silver as his lawyer, Alan Dershowitz.

Gary Sinise, Lois Smith, and Terry Kinney starred in the play *The Grapes of Wrath,* adapted from John Steinbeck's 1939 novel and directed by Frank Galati.

John Guare's play *Six Degrees of Separation,* directed by Jerry Zaks, starred Stockard Channing, John Cunningham, and Courtney Vance.

Garth Brooks released his enormously popular debut album *Garth Brooks;* with five more albums in the next three years, he quickly established himself as a major country music star.

Kevin Costner directed and starred in the film *Dances with Wolves,* the story of a post–Civil War soldier who joins the Sioux Nation.

Natasha Richardson, Robert Duvall, and Faye Dunaway starred in Volker Schlöndorff's film version of

The ballooning population of the earth was estimated at 5.3 billion, more than three times (330 percent) the 1.61 billion in 1900. As fears increased about the earth's ability to support such increasing numbers of people without disastrous and permanent damage to the environment, the United Nations estimated that by 2025 the world's population would be 7.6 billion to 9.4 billion, with most of the increase coming in developing countries. India alone was projected to go from 853 million in 1990 (nearly double its 1960 population of 442 million) to 1.445 billion in 2025.

A massive Bay of Bengal cyclone killed 125,000 to 150,000 people in southern Bangladesh.

A powerful earthquake measuring 7.7 on the Richter scale struck northwestern Iran, killing at least 40,000 people, injuring at least 60,000 and leaving 400,000 to 450,000 homeless.

After a widespread anti–drift net campaign (from the 1970s), including a tuna boycott, major American tuna canners announced that they would no longer use tuna caught by drift nets set over dolphins, the two species often swimming together. Some 3 million to 6 million dolphins and other species had been killed "incidentally" by drift net fishing (1960s-1980s), which fishing vessels of many countries continued, despite multinational restrictive agreements (1988) and a United Nations call for a worldwide moratorium on drift net use (1990).

An internationally mediated cease-fire and the presence of West African peacekeeping forces failed to stop the Liberian Civil War.

Massive demonstrations in Nepal (Apr.) forced King Birenda Bir Bikram Shah Deva to end his autocratic rule and accept democratic elections.

Populist Catholic priest Jean-Bertrand Aristide became the elected president of Haiti (Dec. 17).

Responding to growing insurrection in the province of Assam, India took over direct rule of the province. Muslim separatist insurrections grew in other northern provinces, including Kashmir.

Sam Nujoma was elected the first president of the new nation of Namibia.

Violeta Chamorro was elected president of Nicaragua (Feb. 25); both sides accepted her free election.

Margaret Thatcher, who had been the century's longest-serving British prime minister (1979-1990), was succeeded by John Major (1990-).

Lech Walesa became the elected president of Poland.

Mikhail Gorbachev was awarded the Nobel Peace Prize.

d. Bruno Kreisky (1911-1990), Austrian socialist politician; foreign minister (1959-1966) and chancellor (1970-1983).

d. Dolores Ibarruri ("La Pasionara") (1895-1990), Spanish Communist Party leader; a major Republican figure during the Spanish Civil War (1936-1939); she returned to Spain after the death of Francisco Franco (1975).

d. José Napoleon Duarte Fuentes (1926-1990), Salvadoran politician; a moderate Christian Democrat who headed the governing junta (1980-1984) and was president (1984-1989).

than a mile deep, in southern Siberia, intensifying concerns about pollution from the industrial sites on its shores.

A four-year-old girl with SCID (severe combined immunodeficiency) became the first patient to receive gene therapy — with injection of genes modified to supply those she lacked. In failing health before the therapy, she was later able to go to school (1992).

After describing his "suicide machine" on national television, physician Jack Kevorkian helped a woman with Alzheimer's disease commit suicide. First-degree murder charges were brought against Kevorkian, then later dropped, as debate raged over the case.

Continuing out into interstellar space, the U.S. spacecraft *Voyager 1* sent back the first photograph of the entire solar system. *Voyager 2* flew by Saturn, sending back pictures of its rings and confirming the existence of an 18th moon. Also, *Magellan* completed its 15-month, 795-million-mile voyage to Venus, moving into orbit around the planet and sending back information until it expired and fell onto the planet (1994).

Wolfgang Krätschmer and Donald R. Huffman confirmed the existence of the 60-atom carbon molecule (C_{60}), buckminsterfullerene (the "bucky ball"), predicted in 1985; others soon found a whole class of "fullerenes," some with potential as superconductors.

A new species, the lion tamarin monkey, was discovered on an island off Brazil. The Madagascar serpent eagle, believed extinct for nearly six decades, was sighted alive.

Margaret Atwood's 1986 novel *The Handmaid's Tale,* adapted for film by Harold Pinter.

Still facing an Islamic fundamentalist death sentence (1988) and in hiding, Salman Rushdie published *Haroun,* a book of children's stories.

The Sistine Chapel, noted for its glorious Italian Renaissance murals, reopened after 10 years of restoration work, which had removed accumulated grime to reveal surprisingly brilliant colors.

With his album *Please Hammer Don't Hurt 'Em,* (M. C.) Hammer became the first notable rap artist to cross over, becoming a popular music star.

Mexican writer Octavio Paz was awarded the Nobel Prize for literature.

d. Greta Garbo (Greta Louise Gustafsson) (1905-1990), Swedish actress; an international star from her first Hollywood film, *The Torrent* (1926), who became a legendary figure in world cinema.

d. Leonard Bernstein (1918-1990), American composer, conductor, and pianist; a leading figure in classical music from the mid-1940s; he also worked in the musical theater.

d. Rex (Reginald Carey) Harrison (1908-1990), British actor known worldwide as Henry Higgins in *My Fair Lady* (1956 on stage; 1964 on screen).

d. Aaron Copland (1900-1990), American composer whose work often featured American folk themes, most notably his ballets *Billy the Kid* (1938), *Rodeo* (1942), and *Appalachian Spring* (1944).

d. Mary Martin (1913-1990), American singer and actress; a leading musical theater star from the mid-1940s.

d. Alberto Moravia (Alberto Pinchale) (1907-1990), Italian writer.

Throwing a record five touchdowns, with no interceptions, quarterback Joe Montana took football's San Francisco 49ers to their fourth Super Bowl win under his leadership.

A massive earthquake measuring 7.7 on the Richter scale struck the Philippines, its center near Manila; 1,500 to 2,000 people died, at least 3,000 were injured, and more than 100,000 were left homeless.

Still in mid-career, hockey great Wayne Gretzky scored his 2,000th goal (Oct. 26), a total even he had once thought unreachable.

At Mecca, Saudi Arabia, 1,426 people died when crowded Muslim pilgrims panicked in a pedestrian tunnel (July 3).

An estimated 200 million people in 140 countries celebrated the 20th annual Earth Day (Apr.).

With increasing population density in urban slums, a new epidemic of cholera — a disease once thought nearly eradicated — began in Lima, Peru, killing more than 8,000 people out of some 200,000 cases in Peru alone.

d. Harry Bridges (1901-1990), Australian-American labor leader; leader of the San Francisco General Strike (1934) and founder and first president (1937-1977) of the International Longshoremen's and Warehousemen's Union (ILWU).

d. Alice Marble (1913-1990), American tennis player; a dominant figure in the late 1930s, she introduced the serve-and-volley style to women's tennis.

d. Ralph David Abernathy (1926-1990), African-American Baptist minister; with Martin Luther King, Jr., a leader of the historic Montgomery bus boycott (1955-1956); a founder and the first secretary-treasurer of the Southern Christian Lead-

1990 cont.

d. Tunku Abdul Rahman (1903-1990), Malaysian lawyer and politician; first prime minister of independent Malaya (1957-1963) and first prime minister of the Federation of Malaysia (1963-1970).

Through captive breeding, the number of California condors in the world was increased to 40.

d. B. F. (Burrhus Frederic) Skinner (1904-1990), American psychologist; a key exponent of behaviorist theory from the late 1930s.

d. Bruno Bettelheim (1903-1990), Austrian-American child psychologist noted for his work with severely disturbed children.

1991

In the Persian Gulf War, allied forces successfully attacked Iraq (Operation Desert Storm; Jan. 17-Feb. 28), quickly disabling the Iraqi air force and partly destroying Iraqi SCUD missile capability. The Iraqi army was decisively defeated by a massive combined armored envelopment and frontal attack (Operation Desert Sabre; Feb. 24-28); southern Iraq was taken and Kuwait retaken, with allied casualties of fewer than 1,000 and Iraqi dead and wounded of at least 100,000; 60,000 to 65,000 Iraqi prisoners were taken. Saddam Hussein was left in power, with significant forces.

After the Iraqi defeat in the Persian Gulf War, Kurdish national forces unsuccessfully rebelled in northern Iraq, as did Iranian-supported Shi'ites equally unsuccessfully in southern Iraq.

In the wake of a failed right-wing Communist coup (Aug. 19-21), the Soviet Union dissolved. President Mikhail Gorbachev, captured while on holiday in the Crimea, refused to resign. Russian president Boris Yeltsin gathered

During the Persian Gulf War, a major environmental disaster resulted from two acts. First, Iraqis began deliberately discharging oil from two island terminals (from Jan. 23) and several tankers off the coast of Kuwait. American planes bombed pipelines feeding the terminals (Jan. 27), attempting to halt the flow. The resulting massive spill, at least 70,000 tons and perhaps multiples larger, caused an ecological disaster for bird and marine life in the shallow, vulnerable upper Persian Gulf. Second, the retreating Iraqis set fire to an estimated 1,000 oil wells (late Feb.) in Kuwait, creating a pall of black, oily smoke over the Gulf and southwest Asia. International crews were brought in (Apr.) but required months to put out all the fires (Nov. 5). Predictions of a "nuclear winter" created by the smoky pall were not realized, but short-term environmental effects were disastrous and long-term effects unknown.

d. Gordon Bunshaft (1909-1990), American architect; a leading modernist whose glass-walled Lever House (1952) helped define a major turn in modern architecture.

d. Irene Dunne (1901-1990), American actress; a leading film star of Hollywood's golden age.

d. Jim (James Maury) Henson (1937-1990), American puppeteer; in the mid-1950s, the creator of the Muppets.

d. Ava Gardner (1922-1990), American film star; a reigning sex symbol from the mid-1940s through the mid-1950s.

ership Conference (SCLC), he became its president after King's 1968 assassination (1968-1977).

Jodie Foster as an FBI agent starred opposite Anthony Hopkins as a cannibalistic psychopath in Jonathan Demme's horror film *The Silence of the Lambs,* based on Thomas Harris's novel.

Kevin Costner as New Orleans district attorney Jim Garrison, Tommy Lee Jones, Sissy Spacek, and Jay O. Sanders starred in Oliver Stone's film *JFK,* Stone's highly controversial conspiracy-theory view of the assassination of U.S. president John F. Kennedy.

John Avnet cowrote and directed the film *Fried Green Tomatoes,* starring Jessica Tandy and Kathy Bates; based on Fannie Flagg's novel *Fried Green Tomatoes at the Whistle Stop Cafe.*

Keith Carradine starred in the title role of the Broadway musical *The Will Rogers Follies* by Cy Coleman, Betty Comden, and Adolph Green.

Rudolf Nureyev created the Aschenbach role in the ballet *Death in Venice,* choreographed by Flemming Flindt and based on the 1912 Thomas Mann story.

Law professor Anita Hill and U.S. Supreme Court nominee Clarence Thomas contested her allegations that he had sexually harassed her while she was his assistant at the Office of Civil Rights of the U.S. Education Department and at the U.S. Equal Employment Opportunity Commission in the early 1980s. After a historic set of hearings before the Senate Judiciary Committee and a worldwide television audience (Oct. 11-13), Thomas's nomination was ultimately confirmed by the Senate (Oct. 15), and the lagging American women's rights movement was galvanized.

As civil wars and regional wars continued to grow in the wake of the Cold War, refugee populations continued to rise, to an estimated 17 million worldwide, with the largest single group the 6 million Afghan Civil War refugees in Pakistan and Iran, but with many millions more in the several countries of eastern Africa.

hundreds of thousands of supporters at the Russian Federation White House, and the armed forces refused to join the coup. When capital district paratroops and armor arrayed in defense of the government, the coup collapsed. But so then did the Soviet state; Yeltsin took the lead as head of the sovereign Russian nation and was followed by the leaders of most of the other former Soviet republics. Russia, Belarus, and Ukraine formed the Commonwealth of Independent States.

Croatia and Slovenia formally declared their independence (June 25) as Yugoslavia fell apart. Slovenia became an essentially unchallenged independent state, but Serbia and Croatia went to war, with Serbian forces ultimately taking approximately one-third of Croatia.

A military coup deposed Haitian president Jean-Bertrand Aristide (Sept. 29-30), who fled abroad; international efforts to restore Haitian democracy were not successful until the 1994 American intervention.

Eritrean and rebel Ethiopian forces took Addis Ababa, as the Ethiopian army disintegrated and dictator Haile Mariam Mengistu fled abroad (May), ending the Ethiopian-Eritrean War and related conflicts (1962-1991).

Former Panamanian dictator Manuel Noriega, who described himself as a political prisoner, was convicted on drug-related charges in Florida and sentenced to a 40-year term of imprisonment.

In South Africa, a continuing low-level Inkatha–African National Congress guerrilla civil war intensified, as Inkatha forces unsuccessfully attempted to create the conditions for the emergence of a separate Zulu nation.

Irish Republican Army (IRA) terrorist actions grew; they included a mortar attack on the British prime minister's quarters at 10 Downing Street, London (Feb. 7).

Nine of eleven Western hostages still held in Lebanon were freed, the last of them journalist Terry Anderson

In defiance of judicial bans, Jack Kevorkian helped two more women commit suicide; charges of murder would be dropped. As the debate continued, Kevorkian's *Prescription: Medicide: The Goodness of Planned Death,* on physician-assisted suicide, and Derek Humphry's *Final Exit,* a guide to suicide for terminally ill people, both became best-sellers. Physician Timothy Quill also wrote about assisting a terminally ill patient commit suicide, in the prestigious *New England Journal of Medicine.*

After a derailed tanker car plunged into the Sacramento River (July 14), rupturing and leaking some 19,500 gallons of the pesticide metam sodium (Vapam), a half-mile-long chemical blob flowed down the river, destroying "every living thing in the river," and then into Shasta Lake, California's largest reservoir. The nearby town of Dunsmuir was evacuated; the long-term effects on the people and region were unknown.

In the controversial Biosphere 2 project, four men and four women went to live in a sealed glass-and-steel environment (Sept. 26) near Tucson, Arizona, along with hundreds of other species of animals living in habitats representative of those on earth ("Biosphere 1"). The venture, funded by multimillionaire Edward Bass, was designed as a continuing experiment, with teams of humans staying for two years at a time and being replaced by others. It was not fully isolated, however, with power and carbon dioxide–removing devices operating. By 1994, Bass had separated all of the original Biospherians from the project, some involuntarily. It continued to function as a scientific research laboratory with new teams and as a tourist attraction.

Paul McCartney's first classical work, the *Liverpool Oratorio,* written with Carl Davis, premiered at the Liverpool Anglican Cathedral, performed by the Royal Liverpool Philharmonic.

Susan Sarandon and Geena Davis starred as feminist road buddies on the run in Ridley Scott's film *Thelma and Louise.*

Michael Jackson released a new hit album, *Dangerous.* One of its hits, "Heal the World," was the theme for his accompanying world tour.

Mark Blum and Mercedes Ruehl starred in Neil Simon's autobiographical play *Lost in Yonkers,* directed by Gene Saks.

Natalie Cole released the album *Unforgettable.* The popular title song was an electronically engineered duet combining her voice with an early recording by her father, Nat "King" Cole.

South African writer Nadine Gordimer was awarded the Nobel Prize for literature.

Russian-born Joseph Brodsky became U.S. poet laureate.

d. Frank Capra (1897-1991), American director; a leading figure of Hollywood's golden age, beginning with *It Happened One Night* (1934).

d. Graham Greene (1904-1991), British writer who emerged as a major 20th-century novelist in the 1940s.

d. Isaac Bashevis Singer (1904-1991), Jewish-Polish-American writer; a major 20th-century novelist and short story writer from the mid-1930s; he won the 1978 Nobel Prize for literature.

d. Martha Graham (1893-1991), American choreographer and dancer; a massive figure in the modern dance movement from the late 1920s.

A huge Bay of Bengal cyclone struck Bangladesh, depopulating many coastal islands; at least 135,000 people died, and millions were left homeless.

The international agreement protecting Antarctica from exploitation was renewed; Jacques Cousteau had led the international fight against approval of the Wellington Convention (1988), which would have allowed mining and oil drilling, now banned under a 50-year moratorium.

A powerful volcanic eruption at Mount Pinatubo in the Philippines killed more than 400 people; more than 30,000 were evacuated from Clark Air Force Base and surrounding areas. The size and upward thrust of the eruption were to change worldwide weather patterns for several years.

Armed with two semiautomatic handguns, George Hennard murdered 23 random victims at Luby's Cafeteria in Killeen, Texas, wounding 20 more; he later committed suicide. National pressure to regulate handguns continued to grow.

Basketball star Earvin "Magic" Johnson, starting his 12th season with the Los Angeles Lakers, retired after learning that he carried HIV, the virus that causes AIDS, thereafter using his celebrity to educate others about the dangers of the disease. He would return for the All-Star Game and America's "Dream Team" at the Barcelona Olympics (both 1992) and play basketball around the world with a touring team.

After 17 years of imprisonment and on their third appeal, six Irish men (the "Birmingham Six") gained a reversal of their 1974 convictions for killing 21 people in two pub bombings in Birmingham, England.

In the landmark case *Automobile Workers v. Johnson Controls, Inc.,* the U.S. Supreme Court ruled that employers could not refuse to place pregnant

(Dec. 4), who had been held for almost seven years and was the longest held of the American hostages. The final two Western hostages were freed in 1992.

Racist antiforeign Nazi rioting grew in Germany, much of it directed against Turkish immigrants; weak in its early response but supported by massive German anti-Nazi demonstrations, the government took some steps to block the spread of "neo-Nazism."

d. Rajiv Gandhi (1944-1991), Indian politician and prime minister (1984-1989); he was assassinated by a bomb at Sriperumbudur, Tamil Nada, in southern India, while campaigning; grandson of Jawaharlal Nehru; son and political heir of Indira Gandhi, whom he had succeeded after her own assassination (1984).

Somali dictator Mohammed Siad Barre was deposed by rebel coalition forces, which took Mogadishu; he fled the country as fighting developed within the victorious coalition. Mass starvation and disease, much of it due to factional blocking of international relief shipments, threatened millions and began to draw international attention.

The Soviet Union formally accepted the independence of Latvia, Lithuania, and Estonia.

The Treaty of Paris (Oct. 23) ended the guerrilla war in Cambodia; it provided for a cease-fire, substantial United Nations peacekeeping forces, the return of refugees, and the development of a democratic state.

The Warsaw Pact was formally dissolved.

d. Klaus Barbie (1913-1991), the Nazi "Butcher of Lyon," who had been sentenced to life imprisonment in France (1987).

d. Vijaya Lakshmi Pandit (Madame Pandit) (1900-1991), Indian Congress Party leader; the often-jailed sister of Jawaharlal Nehru. After India won its independence, she became Indian ambassador to the Soviet Union (1947-

Two hikers in the Tyrolean Alps found the naturally mummified body of a man who had been frozen in a glacier after his death, some 5,200 to 5,300 years ago, along with his clothing and equipment, including a stitched fur robe, leather shoes, kits with food and probably herbal medicines, the oldest known quiver, and various tools, all yielding an unprecedented picture of late Neolithic life.

In a major scandal, four top French government health officials were charged with knowingly distributing, from mid-1985, blood possibly contaminated with HIV, the virus that causes AIDS. More specifically, they were accused of failing to test blood for HIV and of distributing untreated blood supplies, rather than using American blood that had been treated with heat to kill the virus. At least 1,200 people, perhaps many more, were infected with HIV from tainted blood.

A fire at the Chernobyl nuclear plant threatened a repeat of the 1986 accident. The fire blew the roof off a power turbine building but was kept from spreading to the reactor. Public pressure increased to shut down the plant, still supplying 20 percent of Ukraine's power.

Britain opened a wave-power station on the island of Islay, using an air chamber open to the sea; as waves surge into the chamber, air is pushed into turbines, and as the waves recede, they suck air back through the turbines, both generating electricity.

The U.S. space shuttle *Atlantis* released into orbit the Gamma-Ray Observatory (GRO) (Apr. 7), while the space shuttle *Columbia* carried aloft the Space Life Science-1 laboratory (June). *Atlantis* later performed the first night landing at Kennedy Space Center (Aug. 11).

d. Margot Fonteyn (Peggy Hookam) (1919-1991), British dancer who emerged in the mid-1930s as the leading British ballerina of the century; in her late career, she was often partnered with Rudolf Nureyev.

d. Rudolf Serkin (1903-1991), Austrian-American pianist; one of the world's leading pianists; he was the father of pianist Peter Serkin.

d. Peggy Ashcroft (Edith Margaret Emily Ashcroft) (1907-1991), British actress; one of the leading figures of the British stage from the early 1930s.

d. Rufino Tamayo (1899-1991), Mexican painter; a leading abstractionist, much of whose work was on folk and ethnic themes.

d. Giacomo Manzù (1908-1991), Italian artist who emerged as a leading sculptor in the mid-1930s.

d. Robert Motherwell (1915-1991), American modernist painter; a leading abstract expressionist from the late 1940s.

d. Yves Montand (Ivo Livi) (1921-1991), French actor and singer; a star in cabaret from the late 1930s and in films from the mid-1940s.

d. Joseph Papp (Joseph Papirovsky) (1921-1991), American producer and director; founder of the New York Theater Workshop (1954), which would become the New York Shakespeare Festival.

d. Colleen Dewhurst (1926-1991), American actress; a stage star from her role as Mary Follett in *All the Way Home* (1960).

women in specific jobs because of possible danger to their unborn children.

Massive sexual harassment and open sexual assaults by scores of active and retired U.S. Navy aviators were reported by women attending the annual convention of the Tailhook Association at the Hilton Hotel in Las Vegas, generating the "Tailhook scandal" and drawing media attention to sexual discrimination in the Navy.

d. (Ian) Robert Maxwell (Jan Ludwig Hoch) (1923-1991), Czech-British entrepreneur; after his mysterious death, in a fall from a yacht off the Canary Islands, his publishing empire collapsed, proving to have been greatly overextended, perhaps worth less than the debt it was carrying; in succeeding years, it would be sold piecemeal to pay off creditors.

The Texas Rangers' 44-year-old Nolan Ryan pitched an astonishing seventh career no-hitter (May 3), striking out 16 batters, some of whom had not even been born when he began his baseball career.

Duke University's Blue Devils basketball team won the National Collegiate Athletic Association (NCAA) tournament; they would repeat twice more (1992; 1994), for three championships in four years.

Former corporate takeover figure and banker Charles Keating was found guilty in California on state charges of criminal fraud in the Lincoln Savings and Loan Association case; he would be sentenced to a 10-year prison term and fined $250,000 (1992).

In a major soccer scandal, Argentine star Diego Maradona tested positive for drug use and was banned from the sport for 15 months. He had played in Spain and then Italy (from 1982) and had led his national team to a World Cup victory (1986). He would resume play with his national team in 1993.

1991 cont.

1949), the United States (1949-1951), and Great Britain (1954-1961). She was the first woman president of the United Nations General Assembly (1953-1954).

The National Institutes of Health launched the Women's Health Initiative, acknowledging that women had been understudied in key health areas.

The Navajo Generating Plant, which had been spewing clouds of pollutants over the Grand Canyon, was ordered by the Environmental Protection Agency to cut its emissions by 70 percent. Ironically, the coal-burning plant had been built after environmentalists had succeeded in blocking two electricity-generating dams on the Colorado River (1960s).

d. John Bardeen (1908-1991), American electrical engineer and physicist who won two Nobel Prizes for physics (1956; 1972).

1992

U.S. president George Bush and Russian president Boris Yeltsin, meeting in Washington (June 16-17), agreed on a series of nuclear weapons reductions, as the Cold War receded further.

Arkansas Democratic governor Bill Clinton defeated incumbent Republican president George Bush and independent candidate H. Ross Perot (Nov. 3) to become the 42nd president of the United States. Clinton's electoral college landslide (380 to 168 for Bush and none for Perot) was not matched by his popular vote (43 percent to 38 percent for Bush and 19 percent for Perot).

Bosnia and Herzegovina seceded from Yugoslavia; Serbian-Muslim fighting spread throughout the country, and the long siege of Sarajevo began. By year's end, the Serbians held 65 to 70 percent of the country, and Croatian forces had joined the war, creating a three-way conflict with shifting alliances. Although Serbian aggression was condemned by the United Nations, which applied economic sanctions, the war continued, with peacekeeping forces ineffective and unable to stop Serbian genocidal "ethnic cleansing."

Drawing on analysis of data sent back by the Cosmic Background Explorer (COBE) satellite (launched in 1989), George Smoot and his team announced that they had detected minute variations in the temperature of the universe almost immediately after its origin, some 15 billion years ago. These "ripples" in the space-time fabric were taken as strong evidence supporting the "big bang" theory of the universe's origin.

A cave near Marseilles, France, which because of a rise in sea level can be reached only by a deep underwater entrance, was found to contain engravings and late Pleistocene paintings, later dated (1993) to 27,000 years ago.

Researchers aboard the U.S. deep-diving submersible *Alvin* discovered a new type of invertebrate, amphipod crustaceans swimming in

Led by Michael Jordan, the Chicago Bulls won the National Basketball Association championship over the Los Angeles Lakers; it would be their first of three consecutive titles (1991-1993).

Massive hillside brushfires at Berkeley and Oakland, California, killed at least 25 people and destroyed thousands of dwellings (Oct. 19-20).

d. Richard Benjamin Speck (1941-1991), American mass murderer who died in prison; he had been sentenced to eight consecutive terms of life imprisonment for the murders (July 13-14, 1966) of eight women students at the South Chicago Community Hospital School of Nursing.

Philip Glass's opera *The Voyage*, libretto by David Henry Hwang, celebrating the 500th anniversary of the Columbus voyage, opened the new season at New York's Metropolitan Opera House.

James Ivory's film version of E. M. Forster's 1910 novel *Howards End*, screenplay by Ruth Prawer Jhabvala, starred Vanessa Redgrave, Emma Thompson, Helena Bonham Carter, and Anthony Hopkins.

Alice Walker attacked the worldwide practice of ritual genital mutilation of women in *Possessing the Secret of Joy*. With filmmaker Pratibha Parmar, she would attack the practice more directly with a film, *Warrior Marks*, and an accompanying book (1993).

August Wilson's play *Two Trains Running* opened on Broadway, directed by Lloyd Richards and starring Larry Fishburne, Roscoe Lee Browne, Al White, and Cynthia Martells; set in a Pittsburgh restaurant in 1969, it was Wilson's sixth play based on African-American life.

In South Central Los Angeles, massive race rioting, accompanied by widespread rioting and looting, followed the acquittal (Apr. 29) of four Los Angeles police officers who had been charged with the 1991 beating of African-American Rodney King, a beating that had been recorded on videotape, shown again and again worldwide. The rioting was ultimately contained by U.S. Marine and Army forces. Two of the four police officers were later convicted on federal charges of violating King's civil rights and sentenced to brief prison terms (1993).

American boxer Mike Tyson's attempts to regain the world heavyweight title (lost in 1990) were ended when he was convicted (Feb.) of raping a Miss Black America contestant (July 1991); Tyson was jailed, and later paroled.

In *Planned Parenthood v. Casey*, the U.S. Supreme Court delivered a mixed message on abortion, reaffirming that abortion was legal, as established by *Roe v. Wade* (1973), but also reaffirming that abortion could be restricted by the states.

Russia moved to reassert its influence on several small former Soviet republics, as when President Boris Yeltsin sent Russian peacekeeping forces to Georgia, at the same time encouraging Russian secessionists in Georgia's Abkhazia province; encouraged Russian minority insurgency in western Moldova; kept Russian troops in the Baltic countries; and kept Russian border forces in action on the Tajikistan-Afghanistan border.

With United Nations approval and in a humanitarian role, American and allied forces entered Somalia, quickly being drawn into an unsuccessful peacekeeping role.

In Algeria, an Islamic fundamentist guerrilla insurrection began; tens of thousands of prisoners were taken by the army, scheduled elections were canceled, and the Islamic Front was outlawed. President Muhammad Boudiaf was assassinated (June 29).

Civil war resumed in Angola (Oct. 30) after Jonas Savimbi's National Union for the Total Independence of Angola (UNITA) refused to accept the reported electoral victory of the rival Popular Movement for the Liberation of Angola (MPLA).

Israeli-Arab peace negotiations resumed after Yitzhak Rabin became Israeli Labor prime minister.

Nationwide Hindu-Muslim rioting flared in India after fundamentalist Hindus destroyed the Babri Mosque in Ayodha, Uttar Pradesh (Dec. 6). Guerrilla wars continued in northern India.

The Mozambican Civil War (1975-1992) ended with a cease-fire and peace treaty aimed at establishing a multi-party democracy.

As the Georgian Civil War intensified, former Soviet foreign minister Eduard Shevardnadze, a Georgian, became head of state.

President Alberto Fujimori of Peru took power as dictator (Apr. 5). Although Sendoro Lumino leader Abimeal

dense swarms along the hot water vents in the Pacific Ocean's Galápagos Rift near the East Pacific Rise.

Russian cosmonaut Sergey Krikalev returned to earth after an unexpectedly long mission in space (Mar. 25); he had been launched toward the space station *Mir* (May 1991) for an expected five-month stay, but the breakup of the Soviet Union and arguments between Russia and Kazakhstan about payment for launching spacecraft to retrieve him left him in space an additional five months, for a total of 313 days.

Replacing *Challenger* (lost in 1986), the U.S. space shuttle *Endeavour* was sent on its first mission (May 7-16). Astronauts Thomas Akers, Richard Heib, and Pierre Thuot performed the first three-person space walk, to repair manually an *Intelsat* 6 communications satellite that they had been unable to fix with their high-tech tools.

As nuclear energy continued on the wane, especially in the United States, the Shoreham nuclear plant on New York's Long Island was dismantled by public agreement, having cost $5.5 billion but operated for only 30 hours. Two venerable nuclear plants elsewhere, the Yankee Rowe in Massachusetts and the San Onofre I in California, chose to close rather than spend the money necessary to meet current safety standards.

Researchers discovered a cancer-fighting compound in broccoli, possibly responsible for part of the anticarcinogenic effect observed from it and other cruciferous vegetables, such as cabbage, cauliflower, and brussels sprouts.

Two captive-bred California condors were released into the wild (Jan.), but one died after

Denzel Washington starred in the title role in Spike Lee's biographical film *Malcolm X,* about the Black Muslim leader, based on *The Autobiography of Malcolm X* (1965).

Geena Davis, Tom Hanks, Lori Petty, and Madonna starred in Penny Marshall's women's baseball film *A League of Their Own.*

Whitney Houston made her film debut opposite Kevin Costner in Mick Jackson's *The Bodyguard*; her version of Dolly Parton's 1974 song "I Will Always Love You" from the soundtrack became one of the bestselling songs of the century.

Mona Van Duyn became U.S. poet laureate.

Stockard Channing and James Naughton starred in John Guare's *Four Baboons Adoring the Sun,* directed by Peter Hall.

Clint Eastwood, Gene Hackman, and Morgan Freeman starred in Eastwood's bleak Western film *Unforgiven.*

With her album *Ingenue,* including the hits "Constant Craving" and "Miss Chatelaine," k. d. lang moved from country to mainstream music.

Regis Wargnier cowrote and directed the film *Indochine,* starring Catherine Deneuve and set in colonial French Indochina.

Controversy was sparked by violent lyrics in *Body Count,* the first album by Ice-T (Tracy Marrow) and his hard-core rap group, Body Count. The song "Cop Killer" includes the lines "I'm 'bout to dust some cops off . . . die, pig, die."

Paul Simon was the first major artist to perform in South Africa after international sanctions were lifted. His tour was filmed for the conclusion of the biographical video documentary *Born at the Right Time.*

In the landmark *Franklin v. Gwinnett County Public Schools* sexual harassment case, the U.S. Supreme Court unanimously ruled that a student could collect damages from a school district after she had been sexually harassed by a teacher-coach.

The United Nations Conference on Environment and Development, dubbed the Earth Summit, was held in Rio de Janeiro, Brazil (June); the main treaty resulting from it was the biodiversity convention: the Convention on Protecting Species and Habitats.

Atlantic hurricane Andrew smashed into the Bahamas, South Florida, and Louisiana, killing more than 40 people and causing an estimated $20 billion in damage (Aug. 23-26).

Baseball commissioner Fay (Francis) Vincent was forced out of office by the team owners, in what many feared was the end of nonpartisan control of baseball, as would be amply confirmed during the 1994 baseball strike.

At the Barcelona Olympics, America's basketball team, dubbed the "Dream Team," for the first time included professional players, many of them international stars.

Canada's huge Olympia and York Developments, Ltd., went into bankruptcy; among the projects threatened were London's massive Canary Wharf.

Mafia leaders John Gotti and Frank Locascio were convicted on a wide range of counts, including murder, and sentenced to life imprisonment without parole.

The Anglican Churches of England and Australia voted to allow the ordination of women priests; women began to be ordained in 1994.

The Toronto Blue Jays, under manager Cito Gaston, won baseball's World Series; they would repeat in

Guzmán Reynoso was captured (Sept. 12), guerrilla war continued in many areas.

In Egypt, Islamic fundamentalists attacked tourists and bombed historic sites, as their guerrilla insurrection continued.

d. Alexander Dubček (1921-1992), Czechoslovak communist leader of the Prague Spring (Jan.-Aug. 1968) and 21 years later chairman of his country's democratic parliament (1989-1992).

d. Jiang Qing (1914-1992), Mao Zedong's third wife; a leader of China's Cultural Revolution (1966-1969) who was later stigmatized as part of the "Gang of Four" and imprisoned; she reportedly committed suicide in prison.

d. Menachem Begin (1913-1992), Polish-Israeli politician; a leader of the terrorist Irgun Zvai Leumi (1943-1948) who ultimately became Likud prime minister of Israel (1977-1983). He shared the 1978 Nobel Peace Prize with Anwar al-Sadat of Egypt for their work on the 1978 Israeli-Egyptian peace treaty.

d. Willy Brandt (Carl Herbert Frahm) (1913-1992), German Social Democratic Party leader; mayor of West Berlin (1957-1966), West German foreign minister (1966-1969) and chancellor (1972-1974), and winner of the 1971 Nobel Peace Prize for his moves toward East-West rapprochement.

drinking antifreeze; another six were released later (Dec.).

Pediatric researchers confirmed that babies do not grow continuously, but in spurts of as much as an inch in a day.

Off La Coruña, Spain, the Greek tanker *Aegean Sea* grounded on rocks in a storm (Dec. 3), breaking apart and catching fire; the resulting oil slick contaminated some 60 miles of coastline.

d. Grace Brewster Murray Hopper (1906-1992), American mathematician and computer pioneer, long serving in the U.S. Navy (1944-1983), who developed the first computer compiler language (1952) and the COBOL programming language (1959).

d. Barbara McClintock (1902-1992), American geneticist, long associated with the Carnegie Institution's Cold Spring Harbor Laboratory (1941-1992), who was noted for her work on the transposition of genetic fragments (1951).

Caribbean writer Derek Walcott was awarded the Nobel Prize for literature.

d. Marlene Dietrich (1901-1992), German actress who emerged as a film star in *The Blue Angel* (1930); at first a leading Hollywood sex symbol, later a highly regarded character actress.

d. Satyajit Ray (1921-1992), Indian film director; a towering figure who brought Indian films to worldwide audiences, beginning with the "Apu" trilogy (1955-1959).

d. Alex Palmer Haley (1921-1992), African-American writer best known for his family history, *Roots* (1976).

d. Judith Anderson (Frances Margaret Anderson) (1898-1992), Australian actress; a noted figure on the American stage from the early 1930s.

d. Olivier Messiaen (1908-1992), French composer, teacher, and organist; an influential figure in European music.

d. Sidney Robert Nolan (1917-1992), leading Australian painter who worked largely in historical themes.

1993, making them the first back-to-back winners since the New York Yankees (1977; 1978).

An El Al cargo plane crashed into an apartment building complex in Amsterdam; the crash and resulting fire killed all four crew members and at least 70 people on the ground (Oct. 4).

At Guadalajara, Mexico, a gasoline pipeline leak fed gasoline fumes into the city's sewer system, causing a series of massive explosions that killed at least 200 people (Apr. 22).

At New York City's La Guardia airport, a US Air Fokker-28 crashed on takeoff during a snowstorm (Mar. 22); 27 people died.

d. John Joseph Sirica (1904-1992), American judge; chief judge in the Watergate trials (1973-1975), from the original Watergate burglars trials through the series of Watergate tapes proceedings that led directly to the resignation of President Richard M. Nixon.

d. Friedrich August von Hayek (1899-1992), Austrian economist; a conservative whose book *The Road to Serfdom* (1944) strongly influenced many antistatist conservative thinkers and politicians in the decades that followed.

b. Helen Pennell Joseph (1905-1992), South African activist, a key White anti-apartheid leader.

d. Petra Kelly (1947-1992), founder of the West German Green Party (1979), reportedly murdered by companion Gerd Bastian, who then reportedly committed suicide (Oct. 19). Their colleagues and many others strongly suggested that both had been assassinated.

d. Joseph Shuster (1914-1992), American cartoonist who was cocreator of *Superman*.

An insurrection was mounted in Moscow by parliament supporters, opponents of Boris Yeltsin's strong rule; led by Vice President Alexandr Rutskoi and parliamentary speaker Ruslan Khasbulatov, rebels fired on police at the Russian White House and attacked the mayor's office and the broadcasting center (Oct. 3). The Russian military shelled and stormed the White House (Oct. 4), ending the rebellion, which did not spread into the military or into other areas.

The Mideast peace process began, with Israeli and Palestinian agreement in principle to some form of Palestinian self-rule and continuing negotiations on the specifics. In an attempt to impede the process, Iranian-backed Hezbollah forces increased cross-border attacks from Lebanon; Israeli forces responded with substantial cross-border air and artillery attacks that killed hundreds; an estimated 200,000 fled north to safety.

Muslim terrorists bombed New York's World Trade Center (Feb. 26); 6 people died, and more than 1,000 were injured. Among the Muslim activists convicted or charged but not tried at year's end was Egyptian Islamic fundamentalist cleric Omar Abdel Rahman.

d. Chris (Martin Thembisile) Hani (1942-1993), general secretary of the South African Communist Party; he was assassinated by right-wing terrorists (Apr. 10); African National Congress leaders were able to avert massive rioting that might have stopped the peace process.

Despite continuing Inkatha–African National Congress (ANC) clashes, the ANC, the National Party, and 19 other parties agreed on a new constitution establishing "fundamental rights" for all South Africans during the transition to majority rule (Nov.); national elections were scheduled for April 27, 1994. Willem De Klerk and Nelson Mandela shared the Nobel Peace Prize.

Canada's Liberal Party won a sweeping general election victory over the Progressive Conservative (Tory) Party, the Tories losing all but 2 of their 153 House of Commons seats in the debacle. Tory Party leader Kim Camp-

British mathematician Andrew Wiles announced (June) that he had solved a key problem in number theory by developing a proof for Fermat's last theorem, which had eluded mathematicians for centuries, ever since Pierre de Fermat noted in the margin of his book (1637) that he had a proof for the theorem but no room to write it. A snag in Wiles's approach was soon reported; he later announced (1994) that the problem had been resolved, but that remained to be confirmed.

Astrophysicists reported confirmation of the idea that observable matter, including stars and dust, makes up less than 10 percent of the universe's mass, the rest being "dark matter," as yet undetected; wide disagreement existed as to what form it might take.

A new mammal, the first discovered in more than five decades, was reported in Vietnam; the vu quang ox (Pseudoryz nghetinhensis) has a cowlike body and long antelopelike horns. Among the animals thought extinct for some years but rediscovered were the giant ibis in Laos, the Bulmer's fruit bat in Papua New Guinea, and the Cebu woodpecker in the Philippines.

As the world watched on television, astronauts Story Musgrave and Jeffrey Thornton, on a mission with the space shuttle *Endeavour*, worked to correct problems with the Hubble Space Telescope, notably its flawed main mirror; early indications were that their repairs were successful. In a major disappointment for the U.S. space program, the *Mars Observer* ceased communicating with earth (Aug. 21) just three days before it was scheduled to go into orbit around Mars.

Genetic researchers announced success in locating the defective genes that cause Hunting-

Toni Morrison was awarded the Nobel Prize for literature; she was the first African-American woman to be so honored.

Steven Spielberg directed and produced the classic Holocaust film *Schindler's List.* He also directed the blockbuster special effects science fiction film *Jurassic Park,* a worldwide commercial hit.

Maya Angelou was the first American inaugural poet since Robert Frost (at the John F. Kennedy inauguration), reading her new poem "On the Pulse of Morning."

James Ivory directed the film *The Remains of the Day,* adapted by Ruth Prawer Jhabvala from the 1989 Kazuo Ishiguro novel and set in an exceedingly class-conscious segment of 1930s British society; Anthony Hopkins, Emma Thompson, and James Fox starred.

Eugene Perry sang the title role, opposite Elizabeth Futral as Eurydice, in Philip Glass's chamber opera *Orphée,* adapted by Glass from the 1949 Jean Cocteau film.

Harold Pinter made a major comeback with his first full-length play in 15 years — *Moonlight,* starring Ian Holm, Claire Skinner, and Anna Massey.

Martin Scorsese directed and cowrote the film *The Age of Innocence,* starring Daniel Day-Lewis, Winona Ryder, and Michelle Pfeiffer, a comedy of manners set in 1870s New York society and based on the 1920 Edith Wharton novel.

Jeremy Irons as the French diplomat starred opposite John Lone as the transvestite Chinese opera star in David Cronenberg's film *M. Butterfly,* adapted by David Henry Hwang from his 1988 play.

President Bill Clinton appointed actress Jane Alexander to head the National Endowment for the Arts (NEA).

Near Waco, Texas, after a 51-day siege, federal armored forces attacked the compound of the Branch Davidian sect, led by David Koresh (Apr. 19). During the attack and subsequent massive fire, 86 Branch Davidians died, including 17 children and Koresh; no firefighting equipment was at the scene. Four federal agents had been killed in the failed attack that preceded the siege (Feb. 26).

After immense law enforcement and popular pressure, Congress enacted the Brady Handgun Control Law, a rare, quite limited attempt to curb the acquisition and use of handguns; this was a triumph for Sarah Kemp Brady, who had become the nation's most effective gun control advocate, and her husband, James Brady, who had been shot and partially paralyzed during the 1981 assassination attempt on U.S. president Ronald Reagan.

At the peak of his power and career, after winning three straight National Basketball Association championships (1991-1993) and seven straight scoring titles (1987-1993), Michael Jordan stunned the sports world by retiring from basketball. The following year, he began his try for a baseball career, spending much of the year in the minor leagues.

The "flood of the century" struck the Mississippi and Missouri River basins, killing at least 50 people and driving millions from their homes, 70,000 or more permanently. In the wake of the massive disaster, federal government aid began to be directed toward removal of population centers to higher ground rather than return of people to their riverside homes.

A massive earthquake in India's Maharashtra state, measuring 6.4 on the Richter scale, shook apart and shattered tens of thousands of unreinforced mudbrick homes, killing approximately 10,000 people.

In the landmark *Harris v. Forklift Systems* decision, the U.S. Supreme Court ruled unanimously that in

bell, who had succeeded Brian Mulroney to become briefly Canada's first woman prime minister, was succeeded by Liberal Party leader Jean Chrétien.

Benazir Bhutto again became prime minister of Pakistan, leading a coalition government after her Pakistan People's Party won an electoral plurality.

Low-level civil war continued in Northern Ireland, but substantial progress toward peace was reported for the first time in many years, as secret and then public direct peace talks developed between the British government and the Irish Republican Army.

The three-way war in Bosnia continued, although the combatants spent much time at the internationally mediated bargaining table, while the major powers threatened armed intervention.

United Nations peacekeeping forces failed to contain the Somali Civil War, themselves coming under repeated attack. Mohammed Farah Aidid's forces attacked American and UN forces.

In Angola, National Union for the Total Independence of Angola (UNITA) forces retook much of the territory they had held before the cease-fire, then went on to take several major cities, as the very costly Angolan Civil War continued.

Tajik and allied Afghan forces made cross-border attacks into Tajikistan; they were ultimately repelled by reinforced Russian border forces.

U.S. president Bill Clinton won ratification of the North American Free Trade Agreement.

Georgian leader Eduard Shevardnadze was forced to take Georgia into the Russian-dominated Commonwealth of Independent States, in return for Russian support in the Georgian Civil War.

Escaped Medellin drug cartel leader Pablo Escobar was captured and killed by the Colombian military (Dec.).

ton's disease and certain inherited forms of diabetes, neurofibromatosis, amyotrophic lateral sclerosis (Lou Gehrig's disease), and cancer (von Hippel–Lindau disease), as well as a gene strongly associated with the risk of breast and ovarian cancers.

New studies from Australia and New Zealand confirmed previous indications that the risk of sudden infant death syndrome (SIDS, crib or cot death) was increased if babies were put to sleep on their stomachs; pediatricians increasingly began to suggest that babies be placed on their backs or sides for sleeping.

The crew of the Russian space station *Mir* affixed a docking mechanism to their craft in preparation for a planned visit by the U.S. space shuttle *Atlantis,* as part of a joint American-Russian effort (1995). The Americans canceled plans for their own space station, and the Europeans canceled a space shuttle program because of budget problems.

The World Health Organization estimated that by the year 2000, some 30 million to 40 million people would be infected by HIV, the virus that causes AIDS, and that people under age 25 accounted for half of all new infections.

In both a tragedy and a scandal, the German pharmaceutical company UB Plasma was accused of failing to screen blood products for HIV, the AIDS-causing virus. People in Germany and several neighboring countries who had received transfusions or blood products back to the early 1980s were being urged to be tested for HIV infection. Several UB Plasma employees were arrested, and charges were pending.

Key conservation groups jointly published the *World Zoo Conservation Strategy,* outlining

Rita Dove became poet laureate of the United States.

d. Federico Fellini (1920-1993), Italian director and screenwriter; a historic figure in world cinema; he was the husband of Giulietta Masina, who starred in several of his most notable films.

d. Marian Anderson (1897-1993), African-American contralto who had what Arturo Toscanini called "the voice that comes once in a hundred years." Her Easter Sunday 1939 Lincoln Memorial concert also made her a central figure in the American civil rights struggle.

d. Rudolf Nureyev (Rudolf Nureyev Hametovich) (1938-1993), Russian dancer and choreographer; a leading Soviet dancer until his flight to the West (1961); he then emerged as a world figure and one of the leading dancers of the century, often partnered with Margot Fonteyn.

d. Myrna Loy (Myrna Adele Williams) (1905-1993), American actress who emerged as a film star as Nora Charles opposite William Powell in *The Thin Man* (1934); she went on to become a major figure, most notably in the classic *The Best Years of Our Lives* (1946).

d. William Gerald Golding (1911-1993), British novelist who became a major literary figure with his first novel, *The Lord of the Flies* (1954); he won the 1983 Nobel Prize for literature.

d. Audrey Hepburn (1929-1993), Belgian-born British actress and dancer who became an American stage star in *Gigi* (1951) and a film star in *Roman Holiday* (1953). From the 1980s, she was a noted humanitarian, as goodwill ambassador for the United Nations Children's Fund (UNICEF).

d. Dizzy (John Birks) Gillespie (1917-1993), American jazz trumpeter and bandleader; a leading figure in jazz for half a century; his signature work was "A Night in Tunisia."

sexual harassment cases, the rule of "workplace equity" was to be applied, rather than compelling complainants to prove psychological damage or inability to perform their workplace tasks.

President Bill Clinton appointed Judge Ruth Bader Ginsburg, former director of the American Civil Liberties Union Women's Rights Project, to the U.S. Supreme Court; she became the second woman justice.

The International Whaling Commission reaffirmed its ban on commercial whaling. Norway openly defied the ban, killing 296 minke whales (136 for "research"); Japan proposed to do the same.

The Dallas Cowboys, led by quarterback Troy Aikman and running back Emmitt Smith, defeated the Buffalo Bills in football's Super Bowl. They would repeat in 1994, for the Cowboys' second straight Super Bowl win and the Bills' third straight loss.

d. Thurgood Marshall (1908-1993), American lawyer; head of the National Association for the Advancement of Colored People (NAACP) legal staff (1940-1962) and the leading civil rights lawyer of his time, most notably for *Brown v. Board of Education of Topeka* (1954). He was the first African-American Supreme Court justice (1967-1991) and a leading liberal member of the Court.

d. Arthur Robert Ashe, Jr. (1943-1993), African-American tennis player who was forced to retire prematurely (1979) after heart attacks; he died of AIDS, probably contracted by blood transfusions in heart operations (1979; 1983) before blood was routinely tested for the HIV virus.

d. Cesar Estrada Chavez (1927-1993), founder of the United Farm Workers of America, who led the table grape workers' strike (1965-1970), winning union recognition and national support for La Causa (The Cause).

1993 cont.

Tansu Çiller became Turkey's first woman prime minister.

d. Bob (Harry Robbins) Haldeman (1926-1993), American politician; White House chief of staff (1969-1973) and a major figure in the Watergate scandal, who resigned (1973) and was ultimately imprisoned for 18 months on Watergate-related charges.

d. Oliver Tambo (1917-1993), South African freedom movement leader; president of the African National Congress (1967-1993).

d. John Bowden Connally (1917-1993), governor of Texas (1962-1968) and U.S. treasury secretary (1971-1972); he was wounded during the assassination of President John F. Kennedy (Nov. 22, 1963).

d. Jimmy (James Harold) Doolittle (1896-1993), American air general who led the first U.S. bombing raid on Japan during World War II (1942).

the increasing role of zoos in the survival of species, through captive breeding programs and reintroduction into the wild, as well as research and public education.

Off Scotland's southern Shetland Islands, between Fair Isle and Sumburgh Head, the Liberian-registered tanker *Braer* lost power and was dashed onto rocks after rescue efforts failed; its cargo of 85,000 tons of light crude oil, plus 5,000 tons of heavier oil, spilled into Quendale Bay, damaging coastal areas and salmon farms.

Carolyn Shoemaker, Eugene Shoemaker, and David Levy discovered a new comet, unusual in that it looked like a string of beads; it would spectacularly crash into Jupiter (1994).

1994

In the republic of Chechnya, which was attempting to break away from Russia, fighting intensified between pro-Russian and Chechnyan government forces (Sept.). Russian armored forces invaded (Dec. 11), meeting strong resistance as they moved toward the capital, Grozny, which they assaulted at year's end (Dec. 31). The conflict brought with it heightened fears that Boris Yeltsin's weak reform government would be succeeded by a hard-line government in Russia, still in possession of a nuclear arsenal large enough to destroy much or all of humanity.

Genocide came to Rwanda after Rwandan president Juvénal Habyarimana and Burundi president Cyprien Ntaryamira, both Hutus, died in a plane shot down while landing at Kigali, the Rwandan capital. Hard-line Rwandan Hutus organized attacks on the Tutsi minority and on moderate Hutus, killing an estimated 500,000 to 1 million, and forcing hundreds of thousands more to flee Rwanda. Civil war followed; Tutsi Rwandan Patriotic

As directed by Secretary of Energy Hazel O'Leary, the U.S. Energy Department began a major investigation into radiation experiments involving humans, including deliberate exposure to radiation and injection with radioactive materials, generally with no informed consent or no consent at all, from the mid-1940s into at least the 1970s. The experiment involved an estimated 16,000 people including pregnant women, mentally retarded children, prisoners, and military personnel. The investigation sparked a powerful debate on scientific ethics and comparisons with German experiments during the Nazi period.

In a gorge near France's Ardèche River, explorers found a huge cavern, named the Chauvet cave, with more than 300 Paleolithic cave paintings and possible human footprints, apparently undisturbed for millennia after a rock-

d. Anthony Burgess (John Anthony Burgess Wilson) (1917-1993), prolific British writer and composer best known for his 1962 novel *A Clockwork Orange*.

d. John Richard Hersey (1914-1993), American writer; a journalist who became a major figure with the publication of the Pulitzer Prize–winning novel *A Bell for Adano* (1944).

d. Sam Wanamaker (1919-1993), American actor and director whose promising American career was ended by his blacklisting during the McCarthy period; moving to Britain, he built a stage and screen career, also leading the campaign to rebuild Shakespeare's Globe Theatre.

d. Norman Vincent Peale (1898-1993), American Protestant clergyman; a leading radio minister from the early 1930s and author of the perennial bestseller *The Power of Positive Thinking* (1951).

Tom Hanks starred in the title role of the contemporary fantasy film *Forrest Gump,* which would win six Academy Awards, including those for best picture, best actor for Hanks, and best director for Robert Zemeckis.

After almost two decades of critical disfavor, playwright Edward Albee made a powerful return to the New York stage with his acclaimed, Pulitzer Prize–winning autobiographical play *Three Tall Woman.* The play had premiered in Vienna in 1991 and in London in 1993.

Michelangelo's restored fresco *The Last Judgment* was unveiled by Pope John Paul II in Rome's Sistine Chapel after a four-year restoration project.

Elton John wrote the music and Tim Rice the lyrics for the animated film musical *The Lion King,* directed by Roger Allers and Rob Minkoff, with

The population of the earth was estimated at 5.6 billion; it had been estimated at 1.61 billion in 1900 and had more than tripled during the course of the century.

Antiabortion activists in the United States stepped up attacks on birth control and pro-abortion activists. Defensive Action founder Paul J. Hill shot and killed Dr. John Bayard Britton and James Barrett in Pensacola, Florida, and was later in the year sentenced to death for the murders. Also in Pensacola, Michael J. Griffin was sentenced to life imprisonment for the 1993 murder of Dr. David Gunn.

In the landmark case *Madsen v. Women's Health Center,* the U.S. Supreme Court ruled that the activities of antiabortion activists demonstrating outside a Florida clinic could be restricted, upholding the major part of an injunction.

Front forces defeated the Rwandan military, which, with an estimated 2 million Hutus, fled into neighboring countries.

U.S. president Bill Clinton suffered a massive legislative defeat when his health care reform proposals were rejected by Congress, forcing their withdrawal. He and the Democratic Party also suffered a massive defeat in the midterm elections, as the Republican Party gained control of the House of Representatives for the first time since 1954 and the Senate for the first time since 1986, and also won many gubernatorial elections.

Historic Israeli-Palestinian peace accords (May 4), which called for Palestinian self-rule in the Gaza Strip and Jericho, were followed by the establishment of a Palestinian government, led by Palestine Liberation Organization (PLO) chairman Yasir Arafat. Jordan and Israel signed a peace treaty (Oct. 26), formally ending their 46-year state of war. Israeli prime minister Yitzhak Rabin, Arafat, and Israeli foreign minister Shimon Peres shared the Nobel Peace Prize.

African National Congress (ANC) leader Nelson Mandela became the first president of the new multiracial South Africa (May 10) after ANC victory in South Africa's first fully free elections (Apr. 26-29); he formed a government of national unity, calling for racial and political reconciliation.

Destabilization began in Mexico with a rural insurrection in the southern state of Chiapas (Jan.). Mexico's ruling Institutional Revolutionary Party (PRI) presidential candidate, Luis Colosio Murrieta, was assassinated (Mar. 23). He was succeeded by economist Ernesto Zedillo Ponce de Leon, who was elected to the presidency (Aug. 21); shortly after taking office (Dec. 1). The new president was caught in a major financial and political crisis that would fully unfold in 1995.

With U.S. invasion forces already in the air, peace negotiators, led by former U.S. president Jimmy Carter, persuaded Haitian general Raoul Cedras's military gov-

fall had sealed off the main entrance. They were dated at over 30,000 years old, making them the world's oldest known cave paintings. Rock carvings from the same period were reported on isolated cliffs along Portugal's Côa River, already partly covered by water from a dam.

Comet Shoemaker-Levy 9 broke into fragments and crashed into the planet Jupiter (July 16-22), sending up plumes and fireballs. Information sent back to earth by *Galileo* and other space probes was expected to yield valuable insights about the composition of the planet.

Despite increased security concerns, the number of people connected on the international web of computer networks called the Internet swelled to an estimated 15 million; it had begun with a few linked computers in the 1960s. Even scientists in Antarctica began communicating with the outside world over the Internet, via satellite.

Anthropologists found the oldest known remains from the human evolutionary line, a hominid, *Australopithecus ramidus,* dated at 4.4 million years old, placing the divergence of humans and apes earlier than previously thought.

Researchers at the Center for Heavy Ion Research in Darmstadt, Germany, announced the discovery of two new elements, 110 and 111, both extremely short-lived, with the highest atomic numbers yet known. Disputes raged over what to name these and elements 101-109.

In the *Visible Man* project, thousands of digital images of the body of a convicted killer who had left his body to science were assembled into a three-dimensional computerized cadaver, available from the National Library of Medi-

James Earl Jones as the voice of Mufasa, the Lion King, and the Academy Award–winning song "Can You Feel the Love Tonight?"

Japan's Kansai International Airport opened, on an island built on landfill in Osaka Bay, its terminal building designed by architect Rienzo Piano.

Quentin Tarantino wrote and directed the film *Pulp Fiction,* starring John Travolta, which won the Palme d'Or as best film at the 1994 Cannes International Film Festival.

"Streets of Philadelphia," the Grammy Award–winning song composed and sung by Bruce Springsteen for the sound track of the 1993 AIDS-discrimination film *Philadelphia,* became the first rock work to win an Academy Award as best original song.

Jules Verne's novel *Paris in the 20th Century* — rejected by his publisher in 1863 for its "unlikely" depiction of a 1960s world with subways, gas-driven cars, "electronic concerts," and devices such as telephones, faxes, calculators, and computers — was finally published in France.

Steven Spielberg, David Geffen, and Jeffrey Katzenberg announced that they were organizing a major new Hollywood studio.

Japanese novelist Kenzaburō Oe was awarded the Nobel Prize for literature.

d. Burt (Burton Stephen) Lancaster (1913-1994), an international film star for more than four decades whose most notable roles included *Come Back Little Sheba* (1952), *Elmer Gantry* (1960; best actor Academy Award), *Birdman of Alcatraz* (1962), *Seven Days in May* (1964), *Conversation Piece* (1975), *1900* (1976), and *Atlantic City* (1980).

d. Madeleine Renaud (1900-1994), leading actress of the French theater for seven decades. In 1946,

A powerful earthquake struck the Los Angeles area (Jan. 17), measuring 6.8 on the Richter scale. More than 60 people were killed, and an estimated 9,000 to 10,000 were injured, with damages estimated at $15 billion to $20 billion.

Former professional football star and national celebrity O. J. Simpson was accused of the murders of his former wife, Nicole Brown Simpson, and her friend Ronald L. Goldman, both found dead outside her Los Angeles home (June 13). The case drew enormous worldwide media attention; an audience of hundreds of millions followed a long, complicated series of prosecution and defense moves throughout the year, with the actual trial starting in 1995.

The Church of England ordained its first women priests (Mar.); by year's end, more than 1,000 women had been ordained.

In the landmark case *Board of Education of Kiryas Joel v. Grumet,* the U.S. Supreme Court ruled that a special New York State school district set up for the disabled children of a Jewish Hasidic sect violated the constitutional separation of church and state.

U.S. Supreme Court justice Henry A. Blackmun retired from the Court after 24 years; he was replaced by Justice Stephen G. Breyer.

Major league baseball players went on strike (Aug. 11); baseball owners canceled the rest of the season and, for the first time in 90 years, the World Series (Sept. 14). Despite White House intervention, the strike would not be settled until the spring of 1995.

Unranked boxer George Foreman scored an extraordinary upset at 45 defeating 26-year-old Michael Moorer to win back the world heavyweight championship title he had lost two decades earlier; he became the oldest fighter at any weight to win a title (Nov. 6).

ernment to leave power (Sept. 18). American forces occupied Haiti; elected president Jean-Bertrand Aristide returned to Haiti and formed a new government.

Peace talks, under way since early 1993, bore fruit in Northern Ireland; a cease-fire came (Aug. 31), followed by formal peace negotiations.

In one of the major spy stories of the century, Central Intelligence Agency (CIA) counterintelligence officer Aldrich (Rick) Ames was exposed as having been a Soviet mole within the CIA since 1986 or even earlier. He and his wife, Rosario Ames, pleaded guilty to espionage; he was sentenced to life imprisonment and she to a lesser term.

d. Richard Milhous Nixon (1913-1994), 37th president of the United States (1969-1974). A California Republican, he was a congressman (1947-1951), senator (1951-1953), and vice president (1953-1961); after losing his first presidential bid to John F. Kennedy (1960), he defeated Hubert Humphrey in 1968 and George McGovern in 1972. His career and reputation were destroyed by the Watergate scandal, which began with break-ins at the Democratic National Committee headquarters (June 17, 1972) and ended with Nixon's resignation to avoid impeachment. He was succeeded by Vice President Gerald Ford (Aug. 9, 1974), who later pardoned him (Sept. 1974).

d. Jacqueline Bouvier Kennedy Onassis (1929-1994), wife of U.S. president John F. Kennedy. Although she later married Greek shipping magnate Aristotle Onassis (1968) and pursued a publishing career, she was to the world "Jackie" Kennedy, covered with the blood of her murdered husband in Dallas (Nov. 22, 1963).

d. Kim Il Sung (Kim Jong Ju; 1912-1994), Korean communist leader; hard-line dictator of the Democratic People's Republic of North Korea (1948-1994). Kim initiated the Korean War (1950-1953) and until the end of his life pursued an aggressive Cold War policy toward South Korea, coming into conflict with the United States and

cine over the Internet to students and other interested parties. A *Visible Woman* project also was under way.

The antidepressant Prozac, introduced in 1987, began to be more widely used for treatment of other disorders and was the subject of widespread discussion in the media, much of it focusing on concerns about overuse of the mood-altering drug for "personality engineering," treating conditions such as shyness and irritability.

Among the new genetic markers linked with heritable disorders were two associated with breast cancer and others associated with colon cancer, polycystic kidney disease, achondroplasia (responsible for dwarfism), fragile-X syndrome, and bone density, key to the risk for osteoporosis.

Research on the vulnerability of amphibian eggs to ultraviolet (UV) radiation suggested that decreases in the ozone layer, which protects the earth against UV rays, were implicated in a worldwide decline of amphibian populations.

Two new species of mammals were discovered: the black-and-white tree kangaroo in Indonesia and the muntjac, or barking deer, in Vietnam. The California gray whale was removed from the list of endangered species.

d. Linus Carl Pauling (1901-1994), American chemist who did key work on bonds between atoms and suggested that protein molecules have a helical (spiral) form, adopted by Francis Crick and James Watson in their model of DNA. Pauling was a nuclear disarmament campaigner from the 1960s. He later theorized that vitamin C could prevent the common cold (1970).

she and her husband, Jean-Louis Barrault, founded the Renaud-Barrault repertory company, which became the Théâtre de France (1958). She also was a film star, most notably creating the title role in Julien Duvivier's *Maria Chapdeleine* (1934).

d. Jean-Louis Barrault (1910-1994), French actor, director, and theater company manager; a central figure in the French theater from the mid-1940s. On-screen, he created the role of the mime Deburau in Marcel Carné's classic *Children of Paradise* (1945).

d. Cab(ell) Calloway (1907-1994), African-American singer, bandleader, and songwriter; one of the central figures in jazz, beginning with his recording of his own "Minnie the Moocher" (1931), his signature song.

d. Giulietta (Giulia Anna) Masina (1920-1994), Italian actress who became a world figure with her creation of Gelsomina in *La Strada* (1954), directed by her husband, Federico Fellini; she also starred in other classic films, such as his *Nights of Cabiria* (1956) and *Juliet of the Spirits* (1965).

d. Helen Hayes (Helen Hayes Brown) (1900-1994), American actress, whose career spanned much of the century. Her most notable stage role was in *Victoria Regina* (1937); she won a best actress Academy Award in *The Sin of Madelon Claudet* (1931).

d. Jessica Tandy (1909-1994), celebrated British-American classical actress who created the Blanche Du Bois role onstage in Tennessee Williams's *A Streetcar Named Desire* (1947). Late in her career, she became an international film star, winning a best actress Academy Award for *Driving Miss Daisy* (1989).

d. Elias Canetti (1905-1994), Bulgarian-born writer who wrote in German and lived in England from 1939; he was awarded the 1981 Nobel Prize for literature.

U.S. ice-skating champion Nancy Kerrigan was attacked and injured (Jan.), then forced to withdraw from the national championships, won by Tonya Harding. The attack was later traced to Harding's former husband and others; Harding denied prior knowledge of the attack, but pleaded guilty on related charges and was fined, put on probation, stripped of her title, and banned from U.S. Figure Skating Association events for life. Ukrainian skater Oksana Baiul won the Olympic gold medal, with Kerrigan winning the silver and Harding out of the running.

The Dallas Cowboys defeated the Buffalo Bills 32–13 to win their second consecutive Super Bowl (Jan. 30).

d. John Anthony Curry (1949-1994), British ice-skater who won five British national championships (1970; 1972-1975) and the world, Olympic, and European championships (1976), then turning professional and becoming one of the world's leading dancers; his work merged ballet and modern dance into ice dancing.

d. Ezra Taft Benson (1899-1994), American religious leader; president of the Mormon Church (1985-1994) and a leading American conservative from the late 1930s.

d. Menachem Mendel Schneerson (1902-1994), the seventh grand rabbi of the Lubavich Hasidim, who had been proclaimed the Messiah by many of his 200,000 followers.

d. Wilma Glodean Rudolph (1940-1994), African-American athlete who, at the 1960 Rome Olympics, was the first woman to win three Olympic gold medals: in the 100 meters, 200 meters, and 400 meter relay.

the United Nations again in the 1990s, as he attempted to acquire nuclear weapons capability.

d. Erich Honecker (1912-1994), East German communist leader (1971-1989); he was arrested and released several times after being deposed and ultimately went into exile in Chile, where he died.

d. Dorothy Mary Crowfoot Hodgkin (1910-1994), Egypt-born British chemist; a pioneer in using X-ray crystallography and computers to study organic molecules, notably penicillin (1949) and vitamin B_{12} (1955).

d. John James Osborne (1929-1994), British playwright and actor, whose early play *Look Back in Anger* (1956) established him as the leading British "angry young man" of his generation.

d. Eugène Ionesco (1912-1994), Romanian writer, in France from 1939; he became a leading early absurdist playwright with plays such as *The Bald Soprano* (1950), *The Chairs* (1952), *Jack, or the Submission* (1952), and *Rhinoceros* (1959).

d. Karl Raimund Popper (1902–1994), Austrian-British philosopher, much of whose work focused on questions of determinism and free will.

d. Randy Shilts (1951–1994), American journalist, who played a major role in developing public awareness of AIDS during the early years of the epidemic, himself dying of AIDS.

Index

Aaron, Hank, 365
Abbey, Edward, 369
Abbey Road (album), 339
Abbey Theatre (Dublin), 19, 31, 105, 109, 117, 145
Abboud, Ibraham, 278
Abd el-Krim, 96, 116, 306
Abdul Hamid II, sultan of Turkey, 34, 38
Abdul-Jabbar, Kareem, 225, 327, 349, 393, 413
Abdullah, Mohammed, "Lion of Kashmir," 24, 254, 402
Abdullah ibn Hussein, king of Transjordan, 136, 246
Abegg, Richard Wilhelm Heinrich, 18
Abel, Rudolph, 272, 300
Abe Lincoln in Illinois (Sherwood), 171
  film version, 183
Abelson, Philip Hauge, 180
Abernathy, Ralph David, 118, 119, 263, 271, 331, 441
abortion issue
  Supreme Court on, 37, 359, 375, 381, 387, 395, 435, 449
  Church and, 385
  "abortion pill," 428
  antiabortion activity, 459
Abplanalp, Robert H., 256
Abraham Lincoln (Borglum sculpture), 167
Abraham Lincoln (French sculpture), 103
Abraham Lincoln: The Prairie Years (Sandburg), 117
Abscam (FBI operation), 382
absolute zero, 26
"absurdism," 191, 311. *See also* theater ("of the absurd")
Abu Dhabi, 348
Academy Awards. *See* Oscars
Academy of Motion Picture Arts and Sciences, 121
Accused, The (film), 429
acetylcholine, 58, 98
Achebe, Chinua, 133, 277
Acheson, Dean, 350
Achille Lauro (ship), 416
acid rain, 389
Acousticon, 8
ACTH (adrenocorticotropic hormone), 268
Actor Prepares, An (Stanislavsky), 161
Actor's Studio (New York), 221
Adair v. United States, 35
Adams, Ansel Easton, 13, 131, 201, 285, 413
Adams, Henry, 83
Adams, John Quincy, 83
Adams, Maude, 23, 259
Adams, Sherman, 276, 278
Adamson, Joy Gessner, 45, 289, 395
Addams, Charles, 53, 433
Addams, Jane, 13, 43, 64, 86, 93, 136, 159

Adding Machine, The (Rice play), 107
Adelaide News (Australia), 137
Adenauer, Konrad, 328
Adkins v. Children's Hospital, 105
Adler, Alfred, 10, 46, 168
Admiral Nakhimov (cruise ship), 421
adrenaline, 6
Adriatic Sea, 430
Advise and Consent (film), 299
Aegean Captain (oil tanker), 386
Aegean Sea (oil tanker), 452
aerosol sprays, 256, 382
Affluent Society, The (Galbraith), 279
Afghanistan, 60, 84, 148, 360
  Civil War, 128, 380, 428, 443
  -Soviet War, 386, 392, 396, 414, 420, 428, 436
AFL-CIO, 263, 273, 333, 389
African-Americans
  in sports, *see below*
  in government office, 36, 110, 120, 321, 338, 354
  "Back to Africa" movement, 69, 87, 93, 105
  in theater and films, 97, 107, 111, 201, 283, 359, 411, 415, 429, 449
  in opera, 123, 265
  voting by, 310, 314
  on Supreme Court, 325
  "inferiority" of, 339 (*see also* racism)
  in the Church, 368, 421, 435
  in space, 408
  in politics, 437
  win Nobel Prize, 455
African-Americans in sports
  boxing, 35, 167, 235, 241, 247, 313, 325, 367
  football, 69, 91, 359, 413, 435
  baseball, 89, 101, 209, 225, 227, 365, 367, 445
  basketball, 121, 193, 223, 271, 277, 287, 301, 327, 349, 393, 413, 445
  tennis, 121, 239, 245, 277, 307, 331, 369
  at Olympics, 161, 287, 289, 331, 431, 445
  track events, 331
African-American 10th Cavalry, 48
African anti-colonial movement, 2
African National Congress (ANC), 50, 286, 288, 298, 326, 438, 444, 454, 460
African Queen, The (film), 245
African Republic, 93
Afternoon of a Faun, The (ballet), 51
After the Fall (Miller play), 311
Against Interpretation (Sontag), 321
Agar, Milton, 87
Agassiz, Elizabeth Cary, 33
Agca, Mehmet Ali, 397

Agee, James, 41, 187, 245, 265, 273, 289
"Agent Orange," 208, 350, 414
Age of Innocence, The (Wharton), 91
  film version, 455
Agnew, Spiro Theodore, 82, 360
Agnon, Shmuel Yoseph, 321, 345
Agon (ballet), 273
Agricultural Adjustment Act, 144, 161
Agricultural Adjustment Administration (AAA), 161
Agriculture, U.S. Department of, 125, 132
Aguinaldo, Emilio, 2, 6, 312
Aguyi-Ironsi, Johnson, 320
Ahidjo, Ahmadou, 110
Ahmad Mirza, shah of Iran, 38, 98
Ah, Wilderness! (O'Neill play), 149
Aidid, Mohammed Farah, 456
AIDS, 296, 378, 396, 429, 445, 456
  activity against, 143, 199
  deaths from, 225, 403, 417, 463, 465
  HIV identified, 410
  European scandals, 446, 456
Aiello, Danny, 425
Aiglon, L' (Rostand), 5
Aiken, Howard, 202
Ailey, Alvin, 139, 279, 287, 437
Ain't Misbehavin' (revue), 383
Air America, 282
air conditioner, 14
aircraft carriers, 102
Air Force, U.S., 223, 224, 337, 338
airlift to Berlin, 228
airmail, 79, 85
airplane crashes
  (1935-1946), 159, 211, 219
  (1951-1960), 247, 257, 269, 279, 283, 287, 289
  (1961-1970), 293, 301, 317, 323, 341, 345
  (1971-1980), 349, 357, 363, 371, 373, 379, 380, 393
  (1982-1985), 405, 407, 415, 417
  (1987-1992), 427, 429, 453
  world's worst, 379, 417
  Lockerbie, Scotland, 429
airplane hijacking, 349, 374, 416
airplanes, 45, 48, 51, 113
  Wright brothers, 4, 14
  airplane industry, 27, 51, 183
  helicopters, 32, 106, 176
  military, 50, 56, 64, 172
  four-engine, 56
  German, 64, 178
  transatlantic and transcontinental, 85, 93, 119, 133, 143, 163, 177
  commercial air service, 87, 93, 261
  around-the-world flights, 135, 149, 167, 419
  World War II, 162, 163
  pressurized, 172

jet, 178, 249
  supersonic, 332, 341, 377
airships (dirigibles), 2, 143
  disasters involving, 99, 113, 127, 147, 165
Akers, Thomas, 450
Akhmatova, Anna, 309, 323
Akhnaten (opera), 411
Akins, Zoë, 87
Akron (dirigible), 147
Alaska border claims, 16
Albania, 42, 174, 180, 216, 370
  nation established, 54, 112
  and China, 272, 378
Albanian Woman with Headcloth (Hine photograph), 23
Albee, Edward, 299, 311, 319, 459
Albéniz, Isaac, 27, 41
Albert Herring (opera), 223
Alcock, John William, 85
Alcoholics Anonymous (AA), 157
Alda, Alan, 295
Alder, Kurt, 124
Aldredge, Tom, 389, 425
Aldrin, Edwin "Buzz" Jr., 336
Aleichem, Sholem, 31, 71, 311
Alekhine, Alexander, 121, 229
Aleksandr Suvorov (passenger ship), 407
Alemán Valdés, Miguel, 16, 408
Alexander I, king of Yugoslavia, 96, 128, 154
Alexander, Grover Cleveland, 63
Alexander, Harold Rupert Leofric George, 340
Alexander, Jane, 179, 331, 383, 393, 455
Alexander Nevsky (film), 171, 323
"Alexander's Ragtime Band" (song), 47
Alexandra, czarina of Russia, 71
Alexandrovich, Sergei, grand duke of Russia, 24
Alfie (film), 321
Alfonso XIII, king of Spain, 134
algae, heavy blooms of, 430
Algeciras Conference (1906), 28
Algeria, 16, 82, 120, 292, 314
  War of Independence, 234, 258, 268, 276, 280, 286, 298
  as independent state, 298, 320
  insurrection, 450
Algren, Nelson, 235
Al-Hasani, Ali Nasser Mohammed, 420
Ali, Muhammad (Cassius Clay), 193, 313, 327, 367
Alice Doesn't Live Here Anymore (film), 369
Alice's Restaurant (film), 337
Alien Registration Act. *See* Smith (Alien Registration) Act (1940)
All About Eve (film), 239
Allen, Bryan, 388
Allen, Gracie, 143
Allen, Jay Presson, 319

Allen, Joan, 431
Allen, Marcus, 417
Allen, Paul, 380
Allen, Ralph, 387
Allen, Woody, 159, 389, 421
Allenby, Edmund Henry Hynman, 164
Allende Gossens, Salvador, 36, 64, 342, 360
allergy, 12, 28, 42
Allers, Roger, 459
All God's Chillun Got Wings (O'Neill play), 109
Allgood, Sara, 109
Alliance for Progress, inter-American (1961), 294
Allies
    World War I, 58, 62, 68, 72, 76
    World War II, 174, 188, 196
    in Middle East (1950s), 266
Alliluyeva, Svetlana, 325
Allison, Fran, 231
All-Male Dance Company, 357
Allman, Duane and Gregg, 339
Allman Brothers Band, 339
All My Sons (Miller play), 221
    film version, 227
All Quiet on the Western Front (Remarque), 129
    film version, 131
All the King's Men (Warren), 217
    film version, 235
All the President's Men (Woodward and Bernstein), 365
    film version, 375
All the Way Home (Mosel play), 289
All-Union Communist Party, 250. *See also* Bolsheviks; Communist Party
"All You Need Is Love" (song), 325
Alonso, Alicia, 97, 227
alpha particles, 34, 82
Alpher, Ralph, 226
Alpine Ski Club, 49
Alsace-Lorraine, 82
Altman, Robert, 343, 369
Alvarez, Luis Walter, 48, 332, 392, 406, 432
Alvarez, Walter, 392, 406
Alvenus (oil tanker), 412
Alvin (research vessel), 448
Alzheimer, Alois, and Alzheimer's disease, 26
Amadeus (Shaffer play), 393
Amado, Jorge, 53, 277
Amahl and the Night Visitors (opera), 247
Amalgamated Clothing Workers of America, 219
Amanullah Khan, 84, 128
Amarcord (film), 361
"Amazing Grace" (song), 343
Ambartsumian, Viktor Amazaspovich, 262
Ambassadors, The (James), 15
Amchitka island, 347
American Beauty (album), 343
American Broadcasting Corporation (ABC), 229
American Civil Liberties Union (ACLU), 93, 129, 241, 383
    Women's Rights Project, 457
American Clock, The (Miller play), 393
American Dance Theater, 279

American Dilemma, An (Myrdal), 205
American Expeditionary Force (AEF) (World War I), 72
American Federation of Labor (AFL), 77, 111, 253, 263. *See also* AFL-CIO
American Football League, 91, 283, 325, 339
American Gothic (Wood painting), 133
American Heart Association, 360
American Indian Movement (AIM), 359
American in Paris, An (film), 245
American Institute of Public Opinion, 157
American Language, The (Mencken), 87
American Lawn Tennis (magazine), 239
American Lawn Tennis Association, 121, 239
American League, 5, 7, 15, 21
American Marconi Company, 67
American Negro Theater, 201
American Popular Revolutionary Alliance (APRA), 108, 300
American Rolling Mill Company, 103
American Scene (art) movement, 133
Americans for Democratic Action (ADA), 222
American Shakespeare Theater, 305
American Telephone and Telegraph (AT&T), 235, 359, 403, 405
American Tragedy, An (Dreiser), 113
    film version, 137
American Union Against Militarism, 81
American Woman's Peace Party, 64
American Women (1963 report), 305
America's Cup, 407
americium (element 95), 202
Ames, Aldrich and Rosario, 462
Amin, Hafizullah, 386
Amin, Idi, 114, 348, 386
amino acids, 234, 254, 432
Amnesty International, 293, 379
amniocentesis, 250
Amoco Cadiz (supertanker), 382, 384
Ampex Corporation, 227
Amritsar Massacre (India) (1919), 84
Amundsen, Roald Engelbregt, 17, 47, 49, 79, 117, 127
amyotrophic lateral sclerosis. *See* Lou Gehrig's disease
Anabasis (Perse), 373
anaphylaxis, 12
Anarchism and Other Essays (Goldman), 43
Anastasia (ballet), 347
Anastasia (film), 269
Andalusian Dog, An (film), 125
Anders, William S., 332
Andersen, Dorothy Hansine, 170
Anderson, Carl David, 122, 140, 162, 168
Anderson, Elizabeth Garrett, 74
Anderson, Judith, 223, 453
Anderson, Marian, 175, 265, 457

Anderson, Maxwell, 157, 227, 231, 261, 285, 337
Anderson, Robert, 255
Anderson, Sherwood, 87, 191
Anderson, Terry, 444
Andersonville (Kantor), 265
Andersson, Bibi, 157, 267, 271, 321
Andersson, Harriet, 263, 297, 353
Andre, Carl, 159, 355
Andrea Doria (liner), 267
Andrews, Anthony, 403
Andrews, Dana, 215
Andrews, Julie, 59, 157, 267, 315, 403
Andrews, Roy Chapman, 66, 290
Andrews, Tod, 229
Andreyev, Leonid, 89
Andric, Ivo, 209, 295, 371
Andromeda nebula, 92, 104
Andropov, Yuri Vladimirovich, 60, 402, 410
androsterone, 138
Andrzejewski, Jerzy, 229, 279, 287
anemia, 92, 116
    sickle cell, 42, 232
anesthesia, 12
Angelou, Maya, 127, 343, 365, 455
Anglican Church, 368, 421, 435, 451, 461. *See also* religion
Anglo-French Entente Cordiale, 18
Anglo-Russian Entente, 30
Angola, 12, 102
    National Union for the Total Independence of (UNITA), 152, 320, 368, 428, 450, 456
    War of Independence and Civil War, 152, 294, 368, 428, 450, 456
    Popular Movement for the Liberation of (MPLA), 268, 294, 300, 320, 368, 450
    National Front for the Liberation of, 368
"angry young man," 131
Animal Dispersion in Relation to Social Behaviour (Wynne-Edwards), 300
Animal Farm (Orwell), 17, 207
Animal Liberation (Singer), 369
animals
    endangered, *see* endangered or extinct species
    tests on, 120, 122, 284
    animal rights movement, 122, 321, 369
    behavior of (ethology), 156
    new species or types discovered, 440, 448, 454, 462
Animal Welfare Act (1966), 321
Ankrah, Joseph, 320
Anna and the King of Siam (film), 217
Anna Christie (O'Neill play), 95
    film version, 131
Annales (magazine), 129
Anna Lucasta (Yordan play), 201
Annapurna, 239
Annaud, Jean-Jacques, 421
Anne of Green Gables (Montgomery), 35
Anne of the Thousand Days (Anderson play), 231
    film version, 337
Annie Allen (Brooks), 235
Annie Get Your Gun (musical), 217

Anouilh, Jean, 287
Anschluss, the (1938), 170
Antarctica, 129, 460
    expeditions to, 9, 39, 47, 49, 63, 103, 127, 249, 277
    protection of, 42, 272, 280, 431, 445
Antarctic Treaty (1959), 431
Anthony, Susan B., 18, 26
anthropology, 124, 152, 171
antiballistic missiles (ABMs), 354
antibiotics, 124, 176, 188, 202, 275
    penicillin, 124, 160, 182, 186, 210, 230, 234
Anti-Comintern Pact (1940), 162
antidiscrimination law (1972), 353
Antigua and Barbuda, 398
antihistamine, 166
antimatter theory, 140
antiparticle, 152
anti-Semitism, 14, 22, 28, 32, 119, 149, 154, 291. *See also* Jews
antisweatshop laws (1911), 45
antitrust actions, 6, 11, 19, 47, 59, 71, 169, 235, 403
Antonescu, Ion, 182, 218
Antonioni, Michelangelo, 53
Antony and Cleopatra (opera), 319
Anything Goes (musical), 153
Auon, Hacib, 403
Aoun, Michel, 434, 438
Apalachin Conference (1957), 273
Aparajito (Banerji), 99, 243, 269
apartheid, 75, 227, 250, 282, 437. *See also* racism
Apgar, Virginia, and Apgar score, 40, 250, 366
Apocalypse Now (film), 387
Apollinaire, Guillaume, 83
Apollo (ballet), 125
Apollo spacecraft, 332, 336, 344, 348, 352, 370
Appalachian Spring (ballet), 201
Appalachian Trail, 333
    Conference (ATC), 113
Apparitions (ballet), 163
"appeasement" policy (1930s), 170, 420
Apple computers, 378, 384, 406, 412
Appleton, Edward, 108
Applin, Esther, 96
Aqualung, 196
Aquino, Benigno, 354, 406
Aquino, Corazon Cojuangco, 148, 406, 418
Arabia
    Civil War, 10, 84, 112
    conquest of, 108
    pan-Arab movement, 222
    See also Saudi Arabia
Arab independence movement, 92
Arab-Jewish conflicts, 96, 128, 134, 162, 166, 176, 222, 314
    First Arab-Israeli War, 226, 232
    Second Arab-Israeli (Sinai-Suez) War, 266
    Third Arab-Israeli (Six-Day) War, 324, 326
    Fourth Arab-Israeli (Yom Kippur) War, 358
Arab Revolt
    (1916), 68, 136, 148, 158
    (1936-1939), 162

Arafat, Yasir, 128, 280, 314, 338, 430, 460
Aragon, Louis, 405
Aral Sea, 282
Aramburu, Pedro, 344
Arber, Werner, 330
Arbuckle, Roscoe "Fatty," 97
archaeology, 100, 112, 252, 256
    discoveries in China, 18, 364
    dating system and, 90
    Sumerian civilization, 98, 128
    Linear B, 250
    underwater, 402
Archaeology of Knowledge, The (Foucault), 339
Archibald, John, 174
Archipenko, Alexander, 51, 313
architecture
    International Style, 29, 129, 235, 251, 269, 303, 331, 353
    modern, 45, 91, 165, 167, 283, 303
    tallest buildings, 55, 137
    Bauhaus, 87, 141, 341
    geodesic dome, 327
    postmodernist, 405
Arch of Triumph (Remarque), 217
Arctic explorations, 55, 137
    North Pole, 39, 93, 117, 127, 277, 289, 381
Arden, Elizabeth, 39
Arendt, Hannah, 29, 373
Argentina, 122, 216, 264, 344, 408
    "dirty war" in, 374
    and Falkland Islands, 400
Argentina, La (dancer), 165
Arget, Eugène, 123
Arias, Arnulfo, 246
Arias Sánchez, Oscar, 190
    Arias Plan, 424
Aristide, Jean-Bertrand, 440, 444, 462
Ark Royal (aircraft carrier), 186
Arktika (icebreaker), 381
Arlen, Harold, 25, 203, 423
Arletty, 207
Arliss, George, 221
Armas, Carlos Castillo, 260
Armendariz, Pedro, 195, 225
Armenia, 62, 429
    -Azerbaijani wars, 24, 428, 434
    Holocaust in, 70
Armies of the Night (Mailer), 333
Armistice, the, 78
armored vehicles. *See* tanks
Armory Show, 55
arms race, 30, 34, 38
    disarmament sought, 130, 140, 276
Armstrong, Edwin Howard, 78, 146
Armstrong, Henry Jackson "Hurricane Henry," 171
Armstrong, Lillian Hardin, 113, 351
Armstrong, Louis "Satchmo," 9, 113, 197, 349
Armstrong, Neil, 7, 132, 336
Army Alpha Test, 68
Army-McCarthy hearings. *See* McCarthy, Joseph Raymond
Army Medical Corps, U.S., 110
Arnold, Edward, 91
Arnold, Hap, 242
Aron, Raymond Claude, 25, 407

Arosmena, Alcibiades, 246
Arp, Jean, 47, 67, 323
Arrabal, Fernando, 143
Arrowsmith (Lewis), 113
    film version, 137
"arsenal of democracy," 175
Arsenic and Old Lace (Kesselring play), 189
Artaud, Antonin, 233
art deco style, 113
Arthur, Jean, 161, 255
artificial body parts. *See* medicine
"artificial intelligence," 266
Arzner, Dorothy, 391
Asch, Sholem, 275
ascorbic acid, 144. *See also* vitamins
Ashanti War (1901), 8
Ashbery, John, 343
Ashby, Hal, 381
"Ashcan School," 35
Ashcroft, Peggy, 33, 411, 447
Ashe, Arthur Robert Jr., 199, 307, 331, 369, 457
Ashes and Diamonds (Andrzejewski), 229
    film version, 279
Ashmolean Museum (Oxford), 188
Ashton, Frederick William, 21, 137, 163, 229, 239, 271, 333, 431
Asian flu. *See* influenza
aspirin and heart attacks, 430
Asquith, Anthony, 171
Asquith, Herbert Henry, 34, 126
Assad, Hafez al-, 124, 304, 344
assassinations, 340, 388
    U.S., 6, 156, 302, 330, 331
    Russia and Europe, 30, 58, 60, 78, 106, 116, 154, 382
    Latin America, 54, 90, 106, 152, 182, 270, 292, 344, 392
    Japan and China, 96, 126, 134, 140
    Burma, India, Bangladesh, 224, 226, 246, 370, 398, 410, 446
    Middle East, 230, 246, 276, 396
assassinations, attempted, 50, 146, 202, 238, 369, 396, 397
assembly line, 3, 55
Association of Southeast Asian Nations (ASEAN), 326
Astaire, Adele, 111, 427
Astaire, Fred, 49, 111, 141, 145, 157, 281, 425
astatine (element 85), 182
asthma, 42
As Thousands Cheer (musical), 147
"As Time Goes By" (song), 191
Aston, Francis William 84
Astor, Mary, 161, 185
Astor, Nancy Langhorne, 312
astronomy, 92, 116, 222, 262, 302
    discoveries, 20, 24, 34, 48, 58, 130, 230, 234, 264, 424, 458
    stellar evolution theory, 22, 42, 108, 136, 152
    advances in, 50, 76, 104, 128, 246, 310
    classification system, 78, 108
    "dirty snowball" theory, 232
    paleoastronomy, 304
    "missing mass," 392
    "dark matter," 454
    See also black holes; comets; pulsars; telescopes
Asturias, Miguel, 327

Atanasoff, John Vincent, and Atanasoff-Berry Computer, 16, 192, 358
Atatürk (Mustapha Kemal), 90, 100, 104, 172
Athenia (ship), 176
Atherton, William, 393
Atkins, Susan, 337
Atlantic Charter, 188
Atlantic City (film), 461
Atlantic Crossing (album), 371
Atlantic Empress (oil tanker), 386
Atlantis spacecraft, 396, 416, 434, 446, 456
atom
    atomic structure, 18, 34, 44, 54, 66, 112, 124, 134, 140, 156, 228 (*see also* quarks)
    atomic theory, 22, 50, 116
    size, 34
    atomic number, 54, 66, 460
    splitting, 82, 114, 248
    "atom smasher," 136, 140
Atom and the Molecule, The (Lewis), 68
atomic bomb, 28, 129, 174, 180, 182, 184, 190, 192, 194, 264
    first use, 206, 208
    first Soviet, 232, 258
    first British, 250
    first French, 288
    first Chinese, 310
    See also nuclear energy
atomic clock, 230, 260, 310
Atomic Energy Commission, 206, 218, 254, 261, 306
Attenborough, Richard, 401
Attica Prison riot (1971), 347
Attlee, Clement, 156, 326
Atwood, Margaret, 179, 419
Auden, W. H., 33, 175, 363
Audran, Stephanie, 353
Auerbach, Red, 271, 283, 323
August, Bille, 431
Augusta, Lady Gregory, 145
August 1914 (Solzhenitsyn), 347
Aumont, Jean-Pierre, 257, 361
Aung San, 64, 224
Aung San Suu Kyi, Daw, 224, 428
Auntie Mame (Lawrence-Lee play), 269
    musical version, 407
aureomycin, 202. *See also* antibiotics
Au Revoir Les Enfants (film), 425
Auschwitz-Birkenau camp complex, 192. *See also* concentration camps
Austen, Jane, 183
Austin, Herbert, 23
Austin, Mary, 131
Australia, 8, 15, 248, 354, 370, 406
    World War II, 174
    nuclear tests in, 254
    coastline artwork, 355
Australia II (yacht), 407
Australopithecus spp., 108, 280, 358, 364, 460
Austria, 152, 170, 380
Austro-Hungary, 34, 58, 78, 82
"auteur" theory, 143
Autobiography of Alice B. Toklas, The (Stein), 147
Autobiography of an Ex-Colored Man (Johnson), 51

Autobiography of Malcolm X, The (Haley and Malcolm X), 315
    film version, 451
Autogiro, 106
automated teller machines, 333
Automobile Club of America, 3
automobile industry, 3, 17, 329
    Britain, 23, 25, 33, 55, 117
    diesel-powered car, 153
    streamlined design, 153
    Germany (Volkswagen), 161
    emissions standards, 343
automobile racing, 17, 45, 47, 159, 169, 245, 293, 311, 339
    stock-car, 355, 411
Automobile Workers v. Johnson Controls, Inc., 445
Autumn Across America (Teale), 246
Autumn Harvest Uprisings (China) (1927), 118
Autumn Sonata (film), 383
Avanti! (Milan socialist newspaper), 11
Avengers, The (TV series), 173
Avery, Oswald Theodore, 202
Avery, Sewell, 201
Avnet, John, 443
Axis Powers (World War II), 174, 182
Ayckbourn, Alan, 179
Ayer, A. J., 165
Aykroyd, Dan, 433
Ayres, Agnes, 97
Ayres, Lew, 133, 231
Ayrton, Hertha, and Ayrton fan, 64
Ayub Khan, Mohammad, 32, 286, 338, 366
Azerbaijan, 24, 428, 434
Azner, Dorothy, 5

Baade, Walter, 152, 234
Baader, Andreas, and Baader-Meinhof Group, 332, 354, 378
Ba'ath Party, 222, 276, 304, 332, 344
Babangida, Ibrahim, 416
Babbitt (Lewis), 101
Babel, Isaak Emanuilovich, 117, 189
Babenco, Hector, 411, 417
Babes in Toyland (operetta), 17
babies
    "blue," 200
    growth of, 452
    crib death (SIDS), 456
Babi Yar, 149
    poem and symphony on, 291, 299
Bacall, Lauren, 203, 215, 227
"Back to Africa" movement, 69, 87, 93, 105
Backus, John, 268
Bacon, Francis Thomas, 201, 282
Bacon, Lloyd, 145
bacteriophages, 64
Baden-Powell, Robert, 35
Badlands (film), 273
Badoglio, Pietro, 270
Bad Seed, The (Anderson play), 261
Baekeland, Leo Hendrik, 38
Baez, Joan, 189
Bahamas, 360
Bahrain, 348

Bainter, Fay, 153
Baird, John Logie, 104, 108, 116, 124, 172, 218
Baiul, Oksana, 463
Bakelite, 38, 125
Baker, James A. II, 132
Baker, Josephine, 29, 115, 371
Baker, Lee, 135
Baker v. Carr, 298
Bakhtiar, Shahpur, 382, 384
Bakke case, 383
Bakker, Jim, 425, 437
Bakker, Tammy Faye, 425
Balaguer, Joaquin, 32, 320
balanced budget, 421
Balanchine, George, 21, 125, 129, 163, 229, 273, 407
Balch, Emily Greene, 86, 294, 295
Balchen, Bernt, 129
Bald Soprano, The (Ionesco play), 465
Baldwin, James Arthur, 111, 255, 307, 427
Baldwin, Roger Nash, 81, 93, 241, 399
Baldwin, Stanley, 108, 156, 224
Bale, Christian, 425
Balenciaga, Cristóbal, 265, 275, 357
Balfour, Arthur James, 74, 134
Balfour Declaration, 74
Balkan League, 50, 54
Balkan Wars, 10, 38, 42, 50, 54
Ball, Lucille, 47, 245, 437
Balla, Giacomo, 43
ballet, 35, 89, 97, 171
   Ballets Russes, 31, 39, 43, 47, 51, 55, 59, 73, 85, 93, 105, 125, 129, 355
   Bolshoi, 43
   Kirov, 181, 293
   Ballets Russes de Monte Carlo, 193
   Sadler's Wells, 203
   Stuttgart, 305
   Royal, 333, 347
   American (later New York City), 407
   Robert Joffrey Company, 433
Ballívian, Hugo, 246, 250
balloon angioplasty, 378
balloon experiments, 44, 136, 152, 222, 302
balloon pump, 294
ballpoint pen, 171
Balsam, Martin, 257
Baltimore Colts, 277
Baltimore Orioles, 337
Bancroft, Anne, 281, 325
Band, the, 375
Banda, Hastings Kamuzu, 4, 310
Band Aid (rock music benefit), 411
Bandaranaike, Sirimavo Ratwatte, 70, 288
Bandaranaike, Solomon, 288
Bandung (Indonesia) Conference (1955), 262
Banerji, Bibhuti Bhusan, 243
Bangladesh, 94, 370, 398, 402
   cyclones, 343, 415, 433, 439, 445
   War of Independence, 346
Bankhead, Tallulah, 177, 193
"bank holiday" (1933), 144
Banking Act (1933), 145
Bannen, Ian, 425

Bannerjee, Victor, 411
Bannister, Roger, 259
Banting, Frederick, 94, 188
Banzer Suárez, Hugo, 348
Bao Dai, 244
Barbados, 322
Barbara, Joseph Sr., 273
Barbarians at the Gate (telefilm), 431
Barber, Samuel, 319
Barbie, Klaus ("Butcher of Lyon"), 56, 424, 429, 446
barbiturates, 16. *See also* drugs
Barbusse, Henri, 69, 159
bar code, 361
Bardeen, John, 36, 220, 246, 268, 354, 448
Bardot, Brigitte, 149
Barghoorn, Elso Sterrenberg, 332
Barkley, Alben William, 270
Barnack, Oskar, 56
Barnard, Christiaan Neelthing, 102, 324
Barnes, Binnie, 147
Barnes, Edward Larrabee, 421
Barnett, M. F., 108
Barrault, Jean-Louis, 43, 207, 463
Barre, Mohammed Siad, 94, 338, 446
Barrett, James, 459
Barretts of Wimpole Street, The (Besier play), 139
Barrie, James M., 23, 37
Barrie, Wendy, 147
Barrientos Ortuño, René, 310
Barrow, Clyde, 141, 151
Barry, Philip, 177
Barrymore, Ethel, 9, 87, 285
Barrymore, John, 195, 285
Barrymore, Lionel, 227, 285
Barth, Karl, 87, 153, 334
Barthelmess, Richard, 85, 93
Bartók, Béla, 213
Barton, James, 215
Barton, Otis, 130, 154
Baruch, Bernard "Barney," 79, 317
Baryshnikov, Mikhail, 231, 365, 397
Barzani, Mustafa al-, 8, 210, 216, 286, 390
baseball, 7, 13, 91, 455
   Leagues formed, 5, 15
   perfect games, 19, 73, 171, 447
   record-breaking, 47, 63, 121, 137, 171, 187, 217, 231, 293, 365, 415
   Black Sox scandal, 81
   farm system, 87
   African-Americans in, *see* African-Americans in sports
   Hall of Fame, 163, 259
   MVP, 267
   Cy Young Award, 337, 355
   baseball strike, 451, 461
   See also World Series
Basehart, Richard, 259
BASIC (computer language), 316
Basic Laws of Arithmetic (Frege), 10
basketball, 121, 177, 193, 223, 225, 235, 269, 285
   championship, 271, 283, 301, 311, 323, 327, 393, 447
   MVP awards, 277, 287, 349, 387, 413
   "Dream Team," 445, 451

   Jordan retires from, 455
Bass, Edward, 444
Bastian, Gerd, 453
Basutoland, 322
Bataan Death March (1942), 190
Bates, Alan, 91, 153, 311, 339
Bates, Blanche, 23
Bates, Daisy Gatson, 103
Bates, Kathy, 443
Bateson, William, 12
Bathhouse, The (Mayakovsky), 129
bathysphere, bathyscaphe. *See* underwater observation
Batista y Zaldivar, Fulgencio, 8, 250, 280, 362
Batlle y Ordóñez, José, 18
Batman (comic strip), 177
Battisti, Carlo, 251
"Battle Hymn of the Republic," 43
Battle of Britain (World War II), 154, 180
Battle of Jutland (1916), 60, 66, 158
Battle of the Atlantic
   World War I, 60, 62, 72
   World War II, 176, 180, 186, 192, 196
Battle of the Bulge (1944-1945), 200
Battle of the Coral Sea (1942), 190
Battle of Warsaw (1920), 90
Battleship Potemkin (film), 113
Bauhaus school. *See* architecture
Baulieu, Etienne-Emile, 428
Baum, L. Frank, 3, 177
Bavarian Communist Republic, 84
Bavolek, Cecelia, 254
Bawden, Frederick Charles, 166
Baxter, Anne, 239
Baxter, Warner, 145
Bay, Zoltan Lajos, 216
Bayliss, William Maddock, 12
Bay of Pigs (1961), 292
Beadle, George Wells, 186
Beal v. Doe, 381
"Beale Street Blues" (song), 69
Beamon, Bob, 331
Beard, Charles Austin, 55, 121, 233
Beard, Mary Ritter, 55, 121
Beart, Emmanuelle, 419
"Beat" generation, 119, 267, 273
"Beat It" (song), 403
Beatles, the, 183, 193, 199, 277, 307, 309, 315, 325, 333, 339, 345
Beaton, Cecil, 163, 239
Beatty, Warren, 215, 325, 397
"beautiful people," 285, 315
beauty salons, 37, 39
Beauvoir, Simone de, 37, 233, 269, 423
Beaverbrook, Lord, 313
Bechet, Sidney, 285
Beck, Julian, 247
Becker, Boris, 415
Becket (Anouilh), 287
   film version, 309
Beckett, Samuel, 29, 253, 339, 437
Beckman, Max, 87
Beckwith, Jonathan, 336
Bedbug, The (Mayakovsky play), 125
Bednorz, J. Georg, 420
Beebe, Charles William, 130, 154, 302

Beecham, Thomas, 351
Beer Hall Putsch (1923), 104
bees, "dance" of, 84, 122, 222
Beggar's Opera, The (Gay), 125
Begin, Menachem, 56, 198, 214, 380, 406, 452
Begley, Ed, 221
Behavior (Watson), 60
behaviorism. *See* psychology
Behring, Emil von, 8, 16
Being and Time (Heidegger), 121
Belarus, 444
Belasco, David, 3, 19, 23, 43
Belaunde Terry, Fernando, 332
Bel Geddes, Barbara, 265
Belgium, 58, 180, 280
Belize, 398
Bell, Alexander Graham, 102
Bell, James "Cool Papa," 101
Bell, Jocelyn, 324
Bell, Marion, 225
Bell, Thomas, 6
Bellamy, Ralph, 195, 277
Bell for Adano, A (Hersey), 61
   film version, 203
Bell Jar, The (Plath), 309
Bell Laboratories, 136, 220, 314, 338
Belloacq, E. J., 57
Bellotti v. Baird, 387
Bellow, Saul, 65, 375
Bell Telephone Company, 62
Belmondo, Jean-Paul, 283, 293
Beloved (Morrison), 421
Bely, Andrei, 155
Benavente y Martínez, Jacinto, 87, 103
Ben Bella, Ahmed, 82, 298, 314
Benedict, Ruth Fulton, 152, 232
benefit concerts, 411, 415
Beneš, Eduard, 156, 230
Benesch, Alfred A., 61
Benét, Stephen Vincent, 125
Ben Franklin (bathyscape), 338
Bengal, 24, 26
Ben-Gurion, David, 132, 362
Benin, 288, 354
BenJedid, Chadli, 128, 384
Bennett, Arnold, 35, 139
Bennett, Floyd, 117, 127
Bennett, Michael, 369
Bennett, Richard, 91, 157
Benny, Jack, 143, 367
Benson, Ezra Taft, 463
Benton, Robert, 387
Benton, Thomas Hart, 373
Bentsen, Lloyd, 118
Bentz, Melitta, 37
Berenson, Bernard, 285
Beresford, Bruce, 433
Berg, Alban, 159
Bergen, Candice, 217, 401
Bergen, Edgar, 217
Berger, Hans, 128
Berger, Helmut, 337, 347, 365
Berger, Thomas, 345
Berger, Victor Louis, 46, 80, 98, 130
Bergius, Friedrich, 52
Bergman, Ingmar, 81, 131, 157, 173, 263, 267, 271, 281, 285, 297, 321, 353, 361, 383
Bergman, Ingrid, 65, 191, 197, 203, 269, 383, 403
Bergson, Henri Louis, 33, 121, 191

Beria, Lavrenti Pavlovich, 252, 254
beriberi, 6, 162
Berkeley, Busby, 145, 377
Berkeley Free Speech Movement, 310
berkelium (element 97), 234
Berkman, Alexander, 92, 162
Berkowitz, David, 375
Berlin, Irving, 47, 79, 147, 157, 193, 217, 435
Berlin Alexanderplatz (Doblin), 129
Berlin blockade and airlift (1948), 228
Berliner, Emile, 20
Berliner Ensemble, 233
Berliner Gramophone, 5
Berlin Philharmonic, 439
Berlin Wall, 292, 434
Bernadotte, Folke, 230
Bernhardt, Sarah, 5, 107
Bernstein, Carl, 365, 375
Bernstein, Leonard, 81, 203, 273, 293, 441
Berri, Claude, 419
Berrigan, Daniel, 98, 349
Berrigan, Philip, 349
Berry, Clifford E., 192, 358
Berryman, John, 61, 357
Berson, Solomon A., 238
Bertolucci, Bernardo, 183, 375, 425
Besant, Annie, 73
Besier, Rudolf, 139
Best, Charles, 94
Best, Pete, 277
Best Years of Our Lives, The (film), 215
Betancourt, Rómulo, 276
beta rays, 2
Bethe, Hans Albrecht, 28, 176, 226
Bethlehem Steel Company, 179
Bethune, Mary McLeod, 265
Bettelheim, Bruno, 16, 204, 240, 442
Betts, Dicky, 339
Bevan, Aneurin "Nye," 290
Beveridge, William, and "Beveridge Plan," 193
Beverly Hills Supper Club, 381
Bevin, Ernest, 101, 246
Bevis, Douglas, 250
Beymer, Richard, 293
Beyond the Fringe (revue), 299
Beyond the Horizon (O'Neill play), 91
Bhindranwale, Jarnail Singh, 410
Bhopal, India, pesticide disaster, 410
Bhutto, Benazir, 126, 198, 326, 388, 430, 456
Bhutto, Zulfikar Ali, 126, 198, 326, 378, 388, 430
Biafra, 324, 342
Bialik, Hayim Nachman, 15
Bianchi, Kenneth, 379
bicycle racing, 421
Bicycle Thief, The (film), 227
Bicycle Wheel (Duchamp sculpture), 55
Bidault, Georges, 408
Biden, Joseph, 426
Bierce, Ambrose, 61
Bierstadt, Albert, 15
"big bang" theory, 118, 226, 316, 448

"Big Bertha" (World War I), 58
"Big Brother," 233
Big Sky, The (Guthrie), 223
Big Sleep, The (film), 215
Bikel, Theodore, 283
Bikila, Abebe, 287, 311
Bikini nuclear tests, 214, 260, 330
Billboard magazine, 183
billiards, 189
"Billie Jean" (song), 403
Billings, Warren K., 69, 177
Billy Budd, Foretopman (Melville), 109
opera version, 247
Billy Liar (film), 305
Billy the Kid (ballet), 171
Binet, Alfred, 24, 48, 68
Bing Crosby Show, The (radio), 229
Bingham, Hiram, 45, 271
Bini, Lucio, 166
Binoche, Juliette, 429
biochemistry, 20, 26, 52
biofeedback, 326
"biological clock," 120
biological weapons renounced, 338
Warfare Ban Treaty (1971), 348, 364
Biosphere projects, 444
Bird, Larry Joe, 269, 285, 385, 413
Bird in Flight (Brancusi sculpture), 51, 181
Bird in Space (Brancusi sculpture), 117
Birdman of Alcatraz (film), 461
Birdseye, Clarence, 109
Birenda Bir Bikram Shah Deva, king of Nepal, 440
"Birmingham Six" (Irish men), 445
Biro, Lazlo and George, 171
birth control, 59, 63, 67, 71, 79, 97
new methods introduced, 40, 133, 262, 287
Clinical Research Bureau, 105
clinics, 130, 141
government support of, 137, 315
Birth of a Nation, The (film), 63, 69, 205
Birth Project, The (Chicago artwork), 417
birth trauma, 110
Bishop, Elizabeth, 49, 391
Bishop, K. S., 100
Bishop, Maurice, 388
Bismarck (battleship), 186
Bisset, Jacqueline, 361
Bitter Rice (film), 239
Bitter Sweet (musical), 129
Bitter Tears of Petra von Kant, The (film), 405
Bitzer, Billy, 205
Bjerknes, Vilhelm Friman and Jacob Aall Bonnevie, 90
Bjørnson, Bjørnstjerne, 17
Björnstrand, Gunnar, 263, 267, 281, 297
Black, Davidson, 118
Black, Hugo, 351
Black, Karen, 369
Black Dragon Society (Japan), 7
Blackett, Patrick, 114
black holes, 72, 136, 178, 344, 350, 366. *See also* astronomy
blacklisting, 89, 221, 233, 301, 353
See also witch-hunting

"black markets," 207
Black Marxism, 115
Blackmer, Sidney, 241
"Black Monday" (stock exchange) (1987), 425
Blackmun, Harry Andrew, 37, 461
Black Muslims (Nation of Islam), 113, 115, 135, 153, 257, 313, 319
Black Narcissus (film), 223
Black Panther Party, 169, 321, 331, 345, 373, 387
"Black Power," 321, 331
Blacks. *See* African-Americans
"Black September" terrorists, 353
Blackshirts, 94, 98, 128
Black Sox scandal (1919), 83
Black Square (Malevich painting), 63
Black Star Shipping Line, 87, 107
"Black Tuesday" (Wall Street Crash) (1929), 129
Blackwell, Elizabeth, 44
Blair, Mary, 109
Blake, Eubie, 97, 373, 409
Blakeley, Colin, 331
Blakley, Ronee, 369
Blalock, Alfred, 200, 312
Blankers-Koen, Fanny, 229
Blatch, Harriet Stanton, 42
Bledsoe, Jules, 121
Blériot, Louis, 27, 39
Bleyl, Fritz, 23
Bliss, Arthur, 203
Bliss and Other Stories (Mansfield), 93
Blithe Spirit (film), 211
Blitzstein, Marc, 171, 261
Bloch, Felix, 216
Bloch, Konrad Emil, 238, 310
Bloch, Marc, 129, 205
Block, Martin, 266
Blodgett, Katherine, 170
Blok, Alexander, 79, 99
Blondie (comic strip), 135
Blood and Sand (film), 103
Blood Purge (Germany) (1934), 150
blood test, 28
blood types and transfusions. *See* medicine
Bloody Sunday (1905), 22
Bloom, Claire, 315, 403
Bloomer Girl (musical), 203
Bloomsbury Group, 107, 279
"Blowin' in the Wind" (song), 303
Blücher, Vasili Konstantinovich, 172, 272
Blue Angel, The (film), 133
"blue babies," 200
Bluebeard (ballet), 187
Blue Bird, The (Maeterlinck play), 39
Blue Devils, 447
"Blue Eyes Cryin' in the Rain" (song), 371
Blue Rider, The (Kandinsky painting), 17
Blue Rider group, 47, 63
Bluestocking (Japanese magazine), 46
Bluford, Guion Jr., 408
Blum, Léon, 160, 242
Blum, Mark, 445
Blumenthal, Karl Konstantin Albrecht Leonhard von, 4

Blunt, Anthony, 32, 388, 408
Bly, Nellie, 103
Board of Education of Kiryas Joel v. Grumet, 461
Boas, Franz, 194
"boat people"
Vietnamese, 383
Cuban ("Mariel"), 397
Boccioni, Umberto, 43
Bock, Jerry, 311
Body Count (album), 451
Bodyguard, The (film), 451
Boeing 707, 261
Boer War, 2, 4, 6, 12, 52, 86, 102
Boesky, Ivan, 419
Bogarde, Dirk, 305, 313, 315, 337
Bogart, Humphrey, 155, 167, 185, 187, 191, 203, 215, 227, 229, 245, 275
Bogart, Paul, 431
Bogdanovich, Peter, 349
Bohème, La (opera), 111
Bohr, Niels Henrik David, 44, 54, 66, 102, 174, 300
Bokassa, Jean Bédel, 98, 320, 378, 388, 420
Bolam, James, 301
Bolero (Ravel orchestral work), 411
Boles, John, 197
Bolivia, 246, 250, 310, 326, 348
Historical Nationalist Revolutionary Movement, 32, 188
war with Paraguay, 140, 158, 172
Böll, Heinrich, 75, 355
Bolm, Adolphe, 39, 51
Bolsheviks, 14, 30, 50, 72, 78, 90, 96, 108, 250. *See also* Russian revolutions
Bolshoi Ballet, 43. *See also* ballet
Bolt, C. T., 350
Bolt, Robert, 287, 315, 319
Boltwood, Bertram Borden, 32
Bombay Maru (freighter), 363
bombings, 43, 69, 177, 265, 415
wartime, of civilians, 154, 165, 206
wartime targets, 160, 180, 196
terrorist, 211, 214, 239, 303, 332, 338, 406, 427, 429, 445, 446, 454
by police, 415
Bond, Julian, 185
Bondi, Hermann, 226
Bonds of Interest, The (Benavente play), 87
Bongo, Albert-Bernard, 334
Bonham, John, 333
Bonhoeffer, Dietrich, 33, 211
Bonilla, Manuel, 38
Bonjour Tristesse (Sagan), 261
Bonnard, Pierre, 227
Bonner, Elena, 372, 394
"Bonnie and Clyde," 141, 151
Bonnie and Clyde (film), 189, 325
Book of Daniel, The (Doctorow), 349
Book-of-the-Month Club, 119, 385
Boorman, John, 425
Booth, Hubert Cecil, 5
Booth, Shirley, 177, 195, 241
Borel, Emile, 96, 124
Borg, Björn, 375, 397
Borges, Jorge Luis, 423

Borglum, John Gutzon, 133, 163, 167, 177, 191
Bork, Robert Heron, 123, 361, 421
Borlaug, Norman Ernest, 60, 202, 344
Borman, Frank, 332
Bormann, Martin, 4, 210
Born, Max, 116
Born at the Right Time (film), 451
Born Free (Adamson), 289
Born Free and Equal (Adams photographs), 201
Born in the U.S.A. (album), 413
Born on the Fourth of July (film), 433
Born Yesterday (film), 239
Borodin, Alexander, 39
Borodin, Mikhail Markovich, 248
Borzage, Frank, 121, 141, 171
Bosch, Carl, 30
Bosch Gaviño, Juan, 304, 314, 320
Bose, Satyendra Nath, 110
Bose-Einstein statistics, 110, 118
Bosnia, 58, 448, 456
Bosnia-Herzegovina, 34, 80
"Bosnian" trilogy (Andric), 209
Boston Bruins, 345
Boston Celtics, 271, 277, 283, 301, 323, 327, 385
Boston Police Strike (1919), 85, 104
Boston Pops Orchestra, 391
Boston Red Sox, 15, 21, 69, 91
"Boston Strangler," 299
Boston Women's Health Collective, 339
Botha, Louis, 88
Botha, Pieter Willem, 70
Botham, Ian, 405
Botswana, 322
Bottoms, Timothy, 349
Botvinnik, Mikhail, 229
Boudiaf, Muhammad, 450
Boulle, Pierre, 271
Boumedienne, Houari, 120, 314, 384
Bound East for Cardiff (O'Neill play), 69
Bourguiba, Habib, 16, 250, 268
Bourke-White, Margaret, 29, 167, 207, 351
Boutique fantasque, La (ballet), 85
Bovet, Daniele, 160, 166
Bowie, David, 355
Boxer Protocol (1901), 6
Boxer Rebellion (1900), 2, 6
boxing
  (1900-1920), 3, 29, 35, 45, 63, 77, 91
  (1921-1938), 95, 123, 133, 149, 151, 171
  (1947-1956), 223 235, 241, 245, 247, 257, 269
  (1959-1974), 283, 299, 313, 325, 367
  (1986-1994), 421, 461
boycotts
  union-organized, 35
  Chinese, of Japanese goods, 138
  Montgomery bus, 263
  national, of California products, 315
  tuna, 349
  of Moscow Olympics, 392
Boyer, Charles, 203, 385
Boyer, Herbert, 358

Boyle, W. A. "Tony," 281, 289
Boy Scout movement, 35
Boys in the Band, The (Crowley play), 333
Boznesensky, Andrei, 149
Bradley, Omar, 398
Bradman, Donald George, 231
Brady, James, 396, 455
Brady, Sarah Kemp, 455
Brady Handgun Control Law (1993), 455
Braer (oil tanker), 458
Bragg, William Henry, 64, 350
Bragg, William Lawrence, 64, 350
Braille, 141
"brain death," 318, 320
Braine, John, 279
Branagh, Kenneth, 289
Branch Davidian sect, 455
Brancusi, Constantin, 31, 51, 91, 109, 117, 161, 275
Brandauer, Klaus Maria, 415
Brandeis, Louis Dembitz, 69, 189
Brando, Marlon, 111, 221, 245, 259, 353, 387
Brandt, Willy, 56, 452
Braque, Georges, 27, 151, 307
Brasília, 264
Brauchitsch, Walther von, 232
Braudel, Fernand, 13, 129, 237, 417
Braun, Eva, 208
Braun, Karl Ferdinand, 6, 26, 40
Braun, Wernher Magnus Maximilian von, 52, 160, 192, 380
Brave New World (Huxley), 139
Brazil, 132, 264, 429
  insurrections in, 108, 142, 210, 260
  soccer in, 183, 299, 343
Breakfast at Tiffany's (film), 295
Breathless (film), 283
Brecht, Bertolt, 33, 125, 233, 269
breeder reactor, 246
Brennan, William Joseph Jr., 29, 267
Brent, George, 145
Breton, André, 67, 83, 109, 323
Bretton Woods Conference (1944), 201
Breuer, Marcel Lajos, 13, 401
Breuil, Henri Edouard Prosper, 296, 304
Breyer, Stephen G., 461
Brezhnev, Leonid Ilyich, 28, 308, 330, 386, 400
Brezhnev Doctrine, 330
Brian, Donald, 61
Briand, Aristide, 142
bribery, 98, 364, 369, 379, 382
Brice, Fanny, 93, 97, 247, 311
Brideshead Revisited (TV series), 403
bridge (game), 163, 265
Bridge of San Luis Rey, The (Wilder), 373
Bridge on the River Kwai, The (film), 271
Bridge over Troubled Water (album), 343
Bridges, Beau, 387
Bridges, Harry, 9, 151, 167, 171, 441
Bridges, James, 385
Bridges, Jeff, 349

bridges collapse, 183, 327
Brief Encounter (film), 209
Brief History of Time, A (Hawking), 424
Brigadoon (musical), 225
Brightman, Sarah, 431
Bringing Up Father (comic strip), 55
"brinkmanship," 282
Brink's robbery (Boston), 239
Britain
  colonies of, 8, 16
  pact with Japan, 10
  Empire declines, 22
  in India, 24, 26, 84, 140, 194
  World War I, 58, 62, 66, 72, 126
  and China, 112, 228
  in Middle East, 134, 142, 162, 214, 222
  World War II, 174, 176, 180, 182, 184, 190
  in European Community, 342, 360
  See also Conservative Party (Britain); Labour Party (Britain)
British Broadcasting Corporation (BBC), 27, 99, 163, 173
British Commonwealth of Nations, 136, 360
British Medical Association, 35
British National Birth Control Council, 133, 137
British South Africa Company, 12
British Trades Union Congress, 117
British Transport and General Workers Union (TGWU), 101
British Union of Fascists, 142
Brittain, Vera, 147
Brittain, Walter Houser, 220, 268
Britten, Benjamin, 57, 207, 223, 239, 247, 255, 287, 289, 359, 375
Britton, John Bayard, 459
broad and long jump records, 157, 161, 431. *See also* track events
broccoli, 450
Broderick, James, 337
Brodsky, Joseph Alexandrovich, 183, 425, 445
Broglie, Louis de, 104, 152, 426
Broken Blossoms (film), 85
Bron, Eleanor, 339
Brontë, Charlotte, 203
Brontë, Emily, 177
Brooke, Edward William, 320
Brooke, Rupert, 67
Brooke, Sorrell, 295
Brooklyn-Battery Tunnel, 241
Brooklyn Dodgers, 209, 217, 221, 255, 277
Brooks, David, 225
Brooks, Garth, 301, 439
Brooks, Gwendolyn, 75, 211, 235
Brooks, James L., 407
Brooks, Louise, 125, 129
Brooks, Peter, 425
Brooks, Richard, 287, 309
Broonzy, Big Bill, 279
"Brother, Can You Spare a Dime?" (song), 399
Brotherhood of Sleeping Car Porters, 113
Brough, Louise, 229
Brower, David Ross, 53, 251, 343
Brown, Anne, 155

Brown, Arthur, 85
Brown, Christy, 145, 399, 433
Brown, Clarence, 121, 131
Brown, H. Rap, 199, 325
Brown, Jim, 273, 413
Brown, Paul, 239
Brown, Rachel Fuller, 234
Brown, Rita Mae, 361
Brown, Ronald H., 437
Brown v. Board of Education of Topeka, 259, 457
Browne, Roscoe Lee, 449
Brownian motion, 22, 34
Brownie camera, 3
Browning, Tod, 137
Brownlow, Keith, 399
Brown University, 69
Brücke art group, 23
Brumel, Valeri, 295
Brundtland, Gro Harlem, and Brundtland Report, 427
Brunei, 326, 412
Brunhes, Bernard, 28
Brusilov, Aleksei Alekseevich, 118
Brusilov Offensives, 68, 72, 118
Brussels Treaty (1965), 324
Brussels World's Fair (1958), 279
Bryan, William Jennings, 34, 113, 114, 287
Brynner, Yul, 67, 245, 269, 419
bubble chamber, 252, 288, 332
Buber, Martin, 69, 105, 317
Buchalter, Louis "Lepke," 175
Buchan, John, 65
Buchenwald, 146, 192, 207. *See also* concentration camps
Buck, Pearl, 137, 167, 173, 363
Buckley, William, 410
buckminsterfullerene ("bucky ball"), 414, 440
Buck Rogers (comic strip), 131
Buddenbrooks (Mann), 7
Budge, Donald, 171
Buffalo Bill's Wild West Show, 17, 75, 119
Buffalo Bills, 359, 457, 463
Buffalo Pan-American Exposition (1901), 6
Bugsy (biofilm), 215
Bujold, Genevieve, 337
Bukharin, Nicolai Ivanovich, 172
Bulgakov, Mikhail, 185
Bulganin, Nikolai Aleksandrovich, 372
Bulgaria, 10, 50, 58, 78, 80
  war with Greece, 136
bulletproof vests, 316
"Bull Moose" party, 42, 48
Bulow, Bernhard von, 130
Bunche, Ralph Johnson, 20, 240, 350
Bunin, Ivan Gasse, 149
Bunshaft, Gordon, 41, 251, 365, 443
Buntline, Ned, 75
Buñuel, Luis, 5, 125, 353, 407
Buono, Angelo, 379
Burbidge, Margaret, 274
Burch, R. (scientist), 282
Burchfield, Charles, 329
Bureau of National Standards, U.S., 230, 310
Burgdorfer, Willy, 402
Burgee, John, 405
Burger, Warren Earl, 29, 337
Burgess, Anthony, 75, 299, 459

Index

Burgess, Guy, 32, 244
Burke, Martha Jane Cannary (Calamity Jane), 17
Burkina Faso, 290
Burma, 224, 228, 278, 298, 433
  World War II, 190, 196, 202
  Karen War of Independence, 230, 240, 416
  "Burmese Spring" (1988), 428
Burma Road, 176, 190
Burnet, MacFarlane, 200, 234, 288
Burnham, Linden Forbes Sampson, 106, 416
Burns, George, 143
Burns, Tommy, 29, 35
Burns, William J., 63
burns, treatment of, 182
Burnt Norton (Eliot), 163
Burr, Raymond, 197
Burroughs, Edgar Rice, 61, 243
Burstyn, Ellen, 369
Burt, Cyril Lodowic, 351
Burton, Harold Hitz, 313
Burton, Richard, 115, 267, 309, 315, 321, 337, 411, 413
Burundi, 300, 352, 430
Bush, George Herbert Walker, 110, 428, 448
Bush, Vannevar, 112, 186, 366
Bus Stop (film), 269
Bustamente, Alexander, 380
Bustamente, José, 230
Butch Cassidy and the Sundance Kid (film), 337
Butenandt, Adolf Friedrich, 132, 138
Buthelezi, Mangosuthu Gatsha, 124
Butler, Nicholas Murray, 136
Butler, Samuel, 15
Button, Dick, 229, 251
Bye Bye Birdie (musical), 289
Byrd, Richard E., 117, 127, 129, 275
Byrnes, James Francis, 356

Caan, James, 353
Cabaret (musical), 321
Cabell, James Branch, 83
Cabinet of Dr. Caligari, The (film), 85
Cabin in the Sky (musical), 197
Cabiria (film), 61
cablecar disaster, 377
Cabral, Amilcar, 304
Cabral, Luis de Almeida, 364
Cabrini, Francesca (Mother Cabrini), 75, 217
Cacoyannis, Michael, 311
Cadillacs, 47
Caesar and Cleopatra (film), 215
Cage, Nicholas, 425
Cage Aux Folles, La (Molinaro play), 383
Cagney, James, 423
Cahill, Thaddeus, 8
Cain, James M., 153, 187, 201
Caine, Michael, 149, 321, 421
Caine Mutiny, The (Wouk), 247
Calamity Jane, 17
Calder, Alexander, 377
Caldicott, Helen Broinowski, 173
Caldwell, Erskine, 141, 167
Caldwell, Zoë, 353
California, emergence of in American life, 277
California Bruins, 327

California Institute of Technology, 306
California Polytechnic State University football team, 289
californium (element 98), 234
Calkins, Richard, 131
Callaghan, James, 52
Callendar, G. S., 170
Calley, William L., 330
Call for the Dead (le Carré), 293
Call of the Wild, The (London), 15
Calloway, Cab, 33, 463
Calvin, Melvin, 164, 294
Cambodia, 188, 282, 342, 358
  Holocaust, 124, 336, 368
  vs. Vietnam, 378, 382
  war ends, 446
Cambridge, Godfrey, 295
cameras. See photography; television
Camera Work magazine, 15
Cameroon, 110, 294
Camille (film), 163
Camino Real (Williams play), 257
Campaign for Nuclear Disarmament (CND), 276
Campbell, Donald Malcolm, 311, 327
Campbell, Kim, 454
Campbell, Malcolm, 159, 311
Campbell, Mrs. Patrick, 59, 185
Camp David Accords (1979), 380, 388
Campos, Pedro Albizu, 238, 318
Camus, Albert, 57, 191, 269, 275, 289, 344
Canada, 16, 101, 362, 410, 412
  Liberal Party, 88, 454
  World War II, 174
  hydropower project, 350
  development corporation fails, 451
  1993 election, 454
  See also Group of Seven (Canadian artists); Quebec separatist movement
Canal Zone, 18, 59
Canaris, Wilhelm, 210
Canary Wharf (London), 451
cancer, 4, 42, 456, 462
  treatment, 14, 396
  chemically induced, 64
  test for, 146
  radioactivity and, 258, 272, 328
  smoking and, 308
  magnetic fields and, 390
  anticarcinogenic effect of vegetables, 450
Canetti, Elias, 25, 157, 399, 463
Caniff, Milton, 33
Cannery Row (Steinbeck), 211
Cannon, Annie Jump, 78, 108, 188
Cannon, "Uncle Joe," 42, 118
Cannon, Walter Bradford, 116
"Can't Buy Me Love" (song), 309
Cantor, Eddie, 313
Cantos, The (Pound), 113
"Can You Feel the Love Tonight?" (song), 461
Capa, Robert, 57, 161, 261
Capablanca y Graupera, José Raúl, 97, 121
Capek, Karel, 97
Cape Verde Islands, 394
capital punishment issue, 375, 379
  See also crime (executions for)

Capolicchio, Lino, 347
Capone, Al, 129, 137, 225
Capote, Truman, 295, 321
Capp, Al, 41, 153, 391
Capra, Frank, 161, 175, 187, 217, 445
Captain Jinks of the Horse Marines (Fitch play), 9
Captive, The (Proust), 109
Cardenas Del Rio, Lazaro, 344
cardiac catheterization, 128, 186
Cardiff, Jack, 289
Cardin, Pierre, 103, 241
Cardinale, Claudia, 305
Cardozo, Benjamin Nathan, 173
Carducci, Giosue, 29
CARE (Cooperative for American Remittance to Europe), 207
Caretaker, The (Pinter play), 153, 287
Carey, Mariah, 345
Caribbean Conservation Corporation, 261
Cariou, Len, 359, 387
Carissan, Eugene Olivier, 92
Carlos, king of Portugal, 36
"Carlos" (terrorist), 359
Carlos, John, 331
Carlson, Chester Floyd, 170, 230
Carlton, Steve, 355
Carmichael, Hoagy, 137, 399
Carmichael, Stokely, 189, 321, 325
Carmina Burana (Orff cantata), 167
Carné, Marcel, 171, 207
Carnegie, Andrew, 7, 21, 42, 89
Carnegie Endowment for International Peace, 42, 89
Carnegie Institution, 452
Carnegie Steel Company, 7, 89, 179
Carnival of the Animals (Saint-Saëns orchestral work), 31
Carnovsky, Morris, 305
Carol II, king of Romania, 132, 182, 256
Caron, Leslie, 245, 257, 277
Carothers, Wallace Hume, 172
Carousel (musical), 39, 211
Carpentier, Georges, 91, 95
Carr, Emily, 213
Carradine, Keith, 369, 443
Carranza, Venustiano, 60, 64, 90
Carrel, Alexis, 22, 52, 58, 68, 160, 204
Carrel-Dakin treatment, 68
Carrier, Willis, 14
Carroll, James, 2
Carson, Rachel Louise, 32, 246, 296, 312
Carter, Helena Bonham, 415, 449
Carter, Hodding, 310
Carter, Howard, 100
Carter, James Earl "Jimmy," 110, 374, 380, 386, 392, 460
Carter, Nell, 383
cartoons, 61
  with sound, 125
  theater drawings, 131
  full-length animated, 167
  See also comic strips
Caruso, Enrico, 11, 41, 43, 99
Carver, George Washington, 198
Casablanca (film), 191
Casals, Pablo, 361
Casement, Roger David, 70

Casey, William Joseph, 56, 414, 426
Cash, Johnny, 143
Caslavska, Vera, 331
Cassatt, Mary, 119
cassettes, 307
  VCR, 371
Castello Branco, Humberto de Alencar, 310
Castro, Bernard, and Castro convertible, 211
Castro Ruz, Fidel, 8, 116, 250, 254, 268, 276, 280, 397
catalytic action, 56
Catcher in the Rye, The (Salinger), 245, 253
Catch-22 (Heller), 293
caterpillar tractor, 20, 68
Cather, Willa, 55, 81, 227
Cathleen ni Houlihan (Butler and Gregory play), 11
cathode-ray tubes, 26, 30, 108
Catholic Church. *See* Roman Catholic Church
Catholic Worker (newspaper), 395
Cat on a Hot Tin Roof (Williams play), 265
CAT scan, 346, 358
Catt, Carrie Chapman, 18
Cavell, Edith Louisa, 64
Cavendish Laboratory (England), 84, 152, 310
cave paintings, 182, 304, 448, 458
Cazale, John, 365, 369, 381
CD, CD-ROM, 400, 412
Ceausescu, Elena, 434
Ceausescu, Nicolae, 82, 316, 434
Cedras, Raoul, 460
Cela, Camilo José, 435
cellular phones, 387
cellular radios, 411
censorship, 85, 123, 133, 201, 439
Census, U.S. Bureau of, 13
Central African Republic, 288, 320, 388, 402, 420
Central Intelligence Agency (CIA), 56, 222, 282, 284, 325, 358, 402
  station chief kidnapped, 410
  and Iran-Contra, 414
  espionage within, 462
Central Powers (World War I), 58, 68
Cepheid variables, 50, 76, 104
ceramic materials, 420
Cerlutti, Ugo, 166
Cermak, Anton J., 146
Cézanne, Paul, 29
Chabelska, Maria, 73
Chaco War (1930s), 140, 158, 172
Chad, 2, 288
  National Liberation Front (Frolinat), 320, 406
  Civil War, 320, 332, 368, 396, 406, 424
Chadwick, Florence, 241, 251
Chadwick, James, 96, 138, 158
Chadwick, John, 250
Chaffee, Roger Bruce, 324
Chagall, Marc, 417
Chain, Ernst Boris, 182, 210
chairlift, 169
Chairs, The (Ionesco play), 465
Chakiris, George, 293
Chaliapin, Feodor Ivanovich, 43, 173

Challenger spacecraft, 396, 406, 412, 430, 450
disaster, 420
Chalmers, Thomas, 135
Chamberlain, Neville, 170, 180, 184
Chamberlain, Owen, 264
Chamberlain, Wilt, 287, 301
Chambers, Whittaker, 228
Chamorro, Violeta, 178, 440
Chamoun, Camille, 4, 250, 276, 426
Chance, Frank, 33
Chance and Necessity (Monod), 344
Chandler, Raymond, 201, 203, 215
Chandrasekhar, Subrahmanyan, and "Chandrasekhar limit," 136
Chanel, Coco, 53, 93, 101, 351
Chaney, James, 309
Chaney, Lon, 105, 115
Chang Hsüeh-liang, 126, 160
Chang Tso-lin, 120, 126
Channing, Carol, 237, 307
Channing, Stockard, 419, 439, 451
Chaplin, Charles, 85, 113, 137, 161, 181, 223, 249, 379
blacklisted, 253, 353
Chaplin, Sidney, 311
Chapman, Graham, 339
Chapman, Mark David, 395
Chappaquiddick Island, 336
Chariots of Fire (film), 397
Charles, Ezzard, 241
Charleson, Ian, 397, 401
Charlie Bubbles (film), 331
Charlot's Revue (musical), 111
Charpentier, Gustave, 3
Chase, Mary, 201
Chasing Rainbows (film), 87
Chatterton, Ruth, 161
Chavez, Cesar Estrada, 121, 315, 457
Chayevsky, Paddy, 257
Cheap Thrills (album), 333
Chechnya, 458
"Cheek to Cheek" (song), 157
Cheever, John, 53, 273, 403
Cheka (Soviet secret police), 74, 118
Chekhov, Anton, 7, 19, 283
chemical weapons renounced, banned, 338, 364
chemise dress, 93
chemotherapy, 32
Chen, Joan, 425
Chennault, Claire, 278
Ch'en Tu-hsiu, 90, 96
Cher, 217, 405, 425
Cheribon Agreement (1946), 214
Cherkassov, Nicolai, 17, 201, 323
Chernenko, Konstantin Ustinovich, 48, 410, 414
Chernobyl, 384, 418, 446
Cherry Orchard, The (Chekhov play), 19
chess, 97, 121, 189, 199, 229, 341, 353, 371, 411
computer, 238
Chessman, Caryl, 287
chestnut blight, 21
Chetnik army (Yugoslavia), 218
Chevalier, Maurice, 277, 357
Chiang Kai-shek, 108, 160, 198, 278, 372

Chiang Kai-shek, Madame, 120
Chicago, Judy, 383, 417
Chicago Bears, 91, 141, 181, 335, 415
Chicago Bulls, 449
Chicago Cubs, 33
Chicago gang wars (1929, 1937), 129, 167
Chicago Poems (Sandburg), 69
Chicago Seven (1968-1969), 338, 352
Chicago White Sox, 83, 435
Chichester, Francis, 133, 289, 325
Chienne, La (film), 389
Chifley, Joseph Benedict, 248
Child, Julia McWilliams, 53
Childe, Vere Gordon, 112, 274
Childhood and Society (Erikson), 238
Child of Our Time, A (Tippett), 187
children
laws protecting, 11, 349
child labor, 49, 171
See also babies
Children of a Lesser God (Medoff play), 393
film version, 419
Children of Paradise (film), 43, 207
Children's Bureau, U.S., 51
Children's Defense Fund, 179
Children's Hour, The (Hellman play), 153
Chile, 46, 342, 358
China
Boxer Rebellion, 2, 6
Republic of (Nationalist), 6, 44, 48, 54, 60, 176, 232, 234
archaeological discoveries in, 18, 364
People's Republic of, 20, 232, 262, 374, 398
Civil War, 20, 44, 47, 118, 122, 145 (*see also* Kuomintang)
student demonstrations and dissent, 88, 268, 420, 432
Communism in, *see* Communist Party
earthquakes and floods, 91, 141, 175, 375, 431
Northern Expedition, 106, 116, 122
antiforeign feeling, 112
vs. Japan, 160, 164, 170, 176, 182
World War II, 174, 176, 182, 196, 202
-U.S. relations, 234, 334, 352, 378
in Tibet, 238, 260, 282
in Korean War, 238, 244
industrialization campaign, 276
border wars, 298, 336
nuclear weapons, 310, 328, 332
Cultural Revolution, 318, 340, 360
Red Guards, 318
"Gang of Four," 374
See also Mao Zedong
China Syndrome, The (film), 385
Chinatown (film), 365
Chinese Exclusion Act (1902), 10
Ch'ing. *See* Manchu dynasty
Chirac, Jacques, 142
Chisholm, Shirley Anita St. Hill, 110, 338

Chissanó, Joaquim Alberto, 178, 422
chlorofluorocarbons and chlorofluoromethanes (CFCs, CFMs), 364, 382, 427
chlorophyll, 24, 288
cholera epidemic, 441
cholesterol, 246
Chomsky, Noam Avram, 125, 275
Chorus Line, A (musical), 369
Chrétien, Jean-Loup, 428, 456
Christian X, king of Denmark, 224
Christianity. *See* religion
Christians, Mady, 187
Christian Science movement, 45
Christie, Agatha, 377
Christie, Julie, 189, 305, 315, 405
Christina's World (Wyeth painting), 227
Christo (artist), 355
chromosomes. *See* genetics
Chrysler Airflow, 153
Chun Doo Hwan, 404
Church, Alonzo, 160
Church, the. *See* religion
Churchill, Winston, 46, 108, 208, 246, 257, 264, 316
in World War II, 180, 188, 196, 198, 202, 206, 422
"iron curtain" speech, 214
Church of England. *See* Anglican Church
Church of Scientology, 251
Church of the Foursquare Gospel, 107
Ciano, Galeazzo, 16, 204
Ciba-Geigy (Germany), 420
Cierva, Juan de la, 106
Çiller, Tansu, 458
Cimino, Michael, 381
Cincinnati Reds, 83, 171, 177, 415
Cinderella (ballet), 229
"Cineorama," 3
Cities of the Plain (Proust), 95
Citizen Kane (film), 185
Citizens Party, 74
Citröen Traction Avant, 153
City and Suburban Electric Carriage Company (London), 25
City College (New York), 181
City Lights (film), 137
City of Angels (musical), 435
"City of New Orleans, The" (song), 353
Civic Repertory Theater (New York), 117
Civilian Conservation Corps (CCC), 144, 147
Civilization and Capitalism (Braudel), 417
Civil Rights Acts, 285, 309, 331
Civil Rights Memorial (Alabama), 435
civil rights movement, 55, 75, 271, 285
violence against, 299, 303, 309, 315
separatist tactics demanded, 321
Civil Works Administration (CWA), 147
Clapton, Eric, 211, 369
Clark, Arthur C., 208
Clark, Barney, 402
Clark, Mark, 345
Clark, Ramsey, 122
Clark, Tom Campbell, 380

Clarke, Arthur, 331
Classical symphony (Prokofiev), 73
Claude, Georges, 42
Claudine at School (Colette), 3
Clay, Cassius. *See* Ali, Muhammad
Clayton, Jack, 279
Clayton, Jan, 211
Clean Air Act (1970), 343
"clear and present danger," 86
Cleaver, Eldridge, 159, 331, 373
Cleese, John, 339
Clemenceau, Georges Eugene Benjamin (The Tiger), 130
Cleopatra (ballet), 35
Cleveland Browns, 181, 239, 273
Cleveland Indians, 217, 227, 317, 367
Clifford, Clark McAdams, 28
Clift, Montgomery, 193
Clinton, Bill, 448, 455, 456, 457, 460
Clinton, Hillary Rodham, 224
Cliveden Set, 312
Cloak, The (opera), 81
Clockwork Orange, A (Burgess), 299
cloning, 392, 396, 398, 402, 416
Close, Glenn, 439
Close Encounters of the Third Kind (film), 379
Clouds (album), 337
cloud seeding, 216
Clubb, Oliver Edmund, 8, 436
Club of Rome, 352
Clurman, Harold, 137
Cobb, Lee J., 233, 259
Cobb, Ty, 163, 415
COBOL (computer language), 282
Cock, The (Brancusi sculpture), 109
Cockcroft, John Douglas, 140, 248
Cockerell, Christopher, 264
Cocoanut Grove fire (1942), 193
Cocteau, Jean, 73, 307, 455
code-breaking, 194
Cody, Buffalo Bill, 17, 75
coelacanth, 170
coenzymes. *See* enzymes
Coffin, William Sloane Jr., 111
Cohan, George M., 19, 73, 149, 195
Cohen, Stanley, 358
Cohn, Roy Marcus, 122, 253, 422
Cohn-Bendit, Daniel, 330
Cointelpro operation, 268
Colbert, Claudette, 25
Cold War, 206, 214, 232, 264, 294, 378, 462
intensified, 220, 270, 281, 292, 306
and blacklisting, 233
U.S. policy, 262
ends, 414, 424, 429, 434, 448
Cole, Nat "King," 75, 317, 445
Cole, Natalie, 445
Coleman, Cy, 435, 443
Colette, 3, 261, 277
Collazo, Oscar, 238
Collected Poems (Frost), 133
Collected Poems (MacLeish), 251
Collins, Francis, 434
Collins, Judy, 179, 343, 353
Collins, Michael (astronaut), 336
Collins, Michael (IRA leader), 100
Colman, Ronald, 137, 279
Colombia, 228, 256, 414, 456

"Colombo Plan" (Asian aid), 239
colonialism. *See* imperialism
Colony Club (New York), 25
Color Purple, The (Walker), 401
   film version, 415
Colosio Murrieta, Luis, 460
Columbia Broadcasting System
      (CBS), 69, 137, 182, 187, 301
Columbia Records, 37
Columbia spacecraft, 396, 402, 446
Columbia University, 304
Comaneci, Nadia, 375
Comden, Betty, 203, 443
Come Back Little Sheba (Inge
      play), 241
   film version, 461
comets, 238
   Halley's, 40, 422
   Giacobini-Zinner, 416
   Shoemaker-Levy 9, 458, 460
   See also astronomy
Comfort, Alex, 355
comic strips
   (1908-1918), 37, 43, 55, 61, 81
   (1924-1934), 111, 131, 135,
      137, 153
   (1938-1939), 173, 177
   (1950), 243
   See also cartoons
Cominform (Communist Informa-
      tion Bureau), 222, 230
Coming Home (film), 381
Coming of Age in Samoa (Mead),
      124
Comintern. *See* Communist Party
Committee for Industrial Organiza-
      tions, 157
Commoner, Barry, 74
Common Market. *See* European
      Economic Community (EEC)
*Common Sense Book of Baby and
      Child Care, The* (Spock), 215
Commonwealth of Independent
      States (Russia, Belarus,
      Ukraine), 455, 456
communications, 137. *See also*
      films; journalism; radio; tele-
      phone; television
Communism, 20
   U.S. anti-communist activities,
      171 (*see also* McCarthy,
      Joseph Raymond; Red Scare)
Communist Party
   Soviet Union, 48, 120, 250
   Germany, 84
   worldwide (Comintern), 86, 156,
      160, 222
   U.S., 86, 244, 296
   China, 90, 96, 116, 118, 130,
      146, 150, 156, 188, 228
   China, vs. Kuomintang, *see*
      Kuomintang
   China, Yenan Period, 156
   Italy and France, 168, 372
   "flip-flops," 174, 186
   Eastern Europe, 228, 316, 396
Comoro Islands, 370
compact disc (CD), 400, 412
Compaq Company, 402
Comprehensive Environmental Re-
      sponse, Compensation and Li-
      ability Act (CERCLA) (1980),
      393
Compton, Arthur Holly, and
      "Compton effect," 104, 300
computers, 26, 266, 376

early models, 112, 162, 164,
      186, 192, 194, 202, 250
   ENIAC, 214, 238, 358
   "machine language," 220, 268,
      282, 316
   checkers-playing, 224
   chess-playing, 238
   UNIVAC, 240, 244, 249
   computer chips, 288, 338, 346
   disks ("hard," "floppy"), 298,
      344, 384
   personal (PCs), 368, 378, 384,
      396, 402, 406, 414
   software, 368, 380
   "spreadsheet" program, 390
   cloned, 402
   computer viruses, 406
   laptop, 412
   innovations in, 414
   Internet, 460
COMSAT (communications satel-
      lite), 286
concentration camps, 4, 6, 70, 201
   death camps, 146, 192, 196, 197,
      207, 212, 249
"conceptual art," 331
Concorde airliner, 341, 377
conditioning, 18, 54
Condon, Edward U., 338
Condon, Richard, 415
condors, 424, 430, 442, 450
Confederation of Mexican Workers
      (CTM), 163
Confessions of Nat Turner, The
      (Styron), 325
Congo (Zaire), 284, 288, 290, 292,
      304, 308, 314, 324
Congress of Industrial Organiza-
      tions (CIO), 157, 169, 253,
      341
   becomes AFL-CIO, 263
Congress of Racial Equality
      (CORE), 193, 291, 293, 321
Congress of Zionist Organizations,
      20
Congress Party (India), 4, 20, 24,
      26, 75, 80, 128, 182, 194
Conklin, Peggy, 155, 255
Connally, John Bowden, 76, 458
Connelly, Marc, 297, 395
Connery, Sean, 135, 299, 421
Connolly, James, 54, 68
Connolly, Maureen, 249
Connor, Eugene "Bull," 303
Connors, Jimmy, 365, 403
Conqueror, The (film), 244, 258
Conquistador (MacLeish), 405
Conrad, Joseph, 3, 33, 387
conscientious objectors, 81, 84
conservation. *See* endangered or ex-
      tinct species; environment
Conservative Party
   Nicaragua, 38, 112, 120, 152
   Britain, 156, 207, 264
   New Zealand, 370
Constantinople, 50, 90
constructivism (architecture), 91
Consumer Product Safety Commis-
      sion, 361
consumer protection, 6, 132, 155,
      289, 317, 361
contact lenses, 162, 241
Conti, Piero, 32
continental drift, 48, 112, 284
Contras. *See* Nicaragua
Convention on International Trade

in Endangered Species
      (CITES), 359, 435
Convention on the Law of the Sea
      (1982), 277
Conversation Piece (film), 365
convoy system, 72
Convy, Bert, 321
Cook, Barbara, 273
Cook, Elisha Jr., 149
Cook, Frederick A., 39
Cook, Paul, 371
Cook, Peter, 299
cooking, 11, 125
Cooley, Denton Arthur, 92, 262,
      336
Coolidge, Calvin, 85, 104, 108,
      120, 148
Coony, Joan Ganz, 339
Cooper, D. B., 349
Cooper, Gary, 9, 141, 147, 161,
      187, 197, 251, 295
Cooper, Leon, 354
Cooper, Merian D., 147
Cooper, Miriam, 63
Copeland, Joan, 393
"Cop Killer" (song), 451
Copland, Aaron, 5, 171, 193, 201,
      441
Coppola, Carmine, 399
Coppola, Francis Ford, 179, 353,
      365, 387
Coq d'or, Le (opera and ballet), 39,
      59
Corbett, James J., 3
Cori, Carl Ferdinand and Gerty,
      and Cori cycle, 224
Cormack, Allan MacLeod, 346
Cornell, Katharine, 139, 367
Cornfeld, Bernard, 105, 345
Corn Is Green, The (Williams play),
      171
Cornu, Paul, 32
Corona, Juan, 361
Corregidor, 190
Correns, Karl, 4
Cortese, Valentina, 361
cortisone, 154, 162, 228, 246
Corydon (Gide), 109
Coryell, Charles DuBois, 208
Cosby, Bill, 169
Cosmic Background Explorer
      (COBE), 436, 448
cosmic egg, 118
cosmic rays, 44, 114
Cosmos (TV series), 392
Costa-Gavras, Constantin, 333,
      335, 403
Costa Rica, 30, 190
Costello, Dolores, 193
Costello, Frank, 129
Coster, Dirk, 106
Costner, Kevin, 435, 439, 443, 451
Cotten, Joseph, 177, 193, 203, 233
Cotton Club Parade, The (revue),
      147
Coubre, La (freighter), 291
Coughlin, Charles Edward, 161,
      391
Council for Mutual Economic As-
      sistance (COMECON), 236
Council of Europe, 234, 255
Courageous (aircraft carrier), 176
Courant, Richard, and Courant In-
      stitute, 356
Cournand, André Frédéric, 186,
      268

Courrèges, André, 295
Court, Margaret Smith, 307, 345
Courtenay, Tom, 301, 305, 313
Cousteau, Jacques, 42, 196, 228,
      316, 322, 431, 445
Cousy, Bob, 271
Cowan, Clyde Lorrain, 266, 330
Cowan, Marie, 15
Coward, Noel, 129, 133, 147, 209,
      211, 363
Cox, Archibald, 52, 358
Cox, James Middleton, 90, 93, 274
Cradle Will Rock, The (Blitzstein
      play), 171
Craig, Gordon, 127
Crane, Hart, 145
Crater, Joseph Force, 169
Crawford, Broderick, 167, 235,
      239
Crawford, Cheryl, 137, 221
Crawford, Joan, 209
Crawford, Michael, 431
*Creation of the World and Other
      Business, The* (Miller play),
      353
Creative Evolution (Bergson), 33
credit cards, 222, 241, 318
Crete, 24
Crichton, Charles, 245
Crick, Francis Harry Compton, 70,
      202, 252, 300
cricket, 231, 405
Cries and Whispers (film), 353
crime, 153
   executions for, 65, 108, 146,
      161, 375, 379
   unsolved, 101
   national crime syndicate, 129,
      147, 175, 215, 217, 273, 451
   Bonnie and Clyde, 141, 151
   Prohibition and, 147
   "public enemy No. 1," 151
   war criminals, 210, 218, 223,
      293, 341
   Brink's robbery, 239
   poisonings, 401, 431
   conviction on "genetic finger-
      printing," 427
   See also hijacking; kidnapping;
      lynchings; murder; terrorism
Crimes of the Heart (Henley play),
      397
Crippen, Hawley Harvey, 43
Cripps, Stafford, 252
Crisis, The (NAACP journal), 43
Crisp, Donald, 85
Croatia, 80, 444, 448
Croce, Benedetto, 253
crocodile, 372
Crome Yellow (Huxley), 307
Cromwell, John, 183, 187, 217
Cronenberg, David, 455
Cronin, A. J., 399
Cronin, Hume, 319
Cronkite, Walter Leland Jr., 69, 301
Crosby, Bing, 21, 141, 193, 381
Crosby, David, 331
Crosby, Stills, Nash, and Young,
      331
Cross, Ben, 397
"Cross of Gold" speech (Bryan),
      114
crossword puzzles, 55
Crowley, Mart, 333
Crozier, Eric, 247
Crucible, The (Miller play), 253

Cruel Sea, The (film), 255
Cruise, Tom, 301, 431, 433
Cry, The (Munch painting), 205
Cry, the Beloved Country (Paton), 227
Crystal Night ("Kristallnacht") (1938), 170
"crystal sets," 6
Cuba, 250, 254, 428
 as U.S. protectorate, 10, 14, 28, 38, 74, 152
 Revolution (1956-1959), 124
 excluded from OAS, 246
 under Castro, 280
 Bay of Pigs invasion, 292
 Missile Crisis, 296, 309
 "boat people" from, 397
cubism, 27, 267, 313, 323
Cukor, George, 163, 183, 203, 239, 409
Culbertson, Ely, 265
Cullen, Countee, 17, 219
cults, 381, 455
Cultural Revolution. *See* China
"culture shock," 3
cummings, e. e., 303
Cunningham, John, 439
Cunningham, Merce, 89
Cuomo, Mario, 142
Curaçao (cruiser), 193
Curie, Marie Sklodowska, 6, 14, 30, 48, 59, 150, 306
Curie, Pierre, 6, 14, 30, 150
curium (element 96), 202
Curl, Robert F., 414
Currie, Finley, 217
Curry, John Anthony, 237, 463
Curtis, Heber Doust, 90
Curtis, Tony, 281
Curtiss, Glenn Hammond, 13, 37, 45, 48, 85, 132
Curtiz, Michael, 191, 209
cybernetics, 226, 322
Cybernetics (Wiener), 226
cyclamate, 240
cyclones
 Bay of Bengal, 193, 217
 Bangladesh, 343, 415, 433, 439, 445
cyclosporine, 406
cyclotron, 136. *See also* synchrocyclotron
Cygnus galaxy, 262, 350
Cyprus, 248, 268, 280, 304
Cyrankiewicz, Josef, 48, 436
cystic fibrosis, 170, 434
cytochrome, 110
Czech Legion, 78
Czechoslovakia, 80, 86, 156, 168, 174, 299, 390
 Munich Pact and, 170
 Communist coup in, 230, 256, 330
 Prague Spring, 330
 becomes free nation, 434
Czolgosz, Leon, 6

Da (Leonard play), 359
Dacko, David, 288, 388, 402
Dacron (terylene), 188
dada movement, 67
Dafoe, Willem, 425, 429
Dahlbeck, Eva, 263
Dahomey. *See* Benin
Daily Mail (Britain), 85, 103, 133
Dakin, Henry, 68

Daladier, Edouard, 346
Dalai Lama, 238, 282
Dale, Henry Hallett, 58, 98
Dali, Salvador, 21, 125, 437
Dallas Cowboys, 289, 355, 457, 463
Dalmatia, 80
Daltrey, Roger, 311, 369
Daly, Mary, 125
Dam, Henrik, 156
Damadian, Raymond V., 380
Damned, The (film), 337
dams collapse, 125, 355
Dan, Takuma, 140
"Danbury Hatters" case (1908), 35
Dance, Charles, 411
dance, modern, 65, 121, 123, 363, 411. *See also* ballet
Dances with Wolves (film), 439
Dandridge, Dorothy, 107, 319
Dangerous (album), 445
Dangerous (film), 437
Daniel, Yuli, 320
Daniels, Bebe, 145
D'Annunzio, Gabriele, 86, 172
Daphnis and Chloe (ballet), 51
Darclée, Hericles, 3
Dardanelles, 46
Darío, Rubén, 83
Darion, Joe, 317
Darkness at Noon (Koestler), 181
Dark Victory (film), 437
Darling (film), 315
Darlington, C. D., 336
Darrow, Clarence Seward, 31, 43, 109, 113, 287
Dart, Raymond A., 108, 432
Dartmouth College, 266
Darwell, Jane, 181
Darwin, Charles, 46, 372
dating methods, 32, 90
 radiocarbon, 220, 238, 290, 430
Daud Khan, Sardar Mohammad, 380
Daugherty, Harry Micajah, 191
Daughters of Ireland, 2
Daughters of the American Revolution, 175
Davalos, Richard, 263
Davies, Arthur, 35
Davies, Emily, 99
Davis, Angela, 205
Davis, Bette, 37, 187, 197, 239, 437
Davis, Carl, 445
Davis, Dwight F., 5
Davis, Geena, 445, 451
Davis, John W., 108
Davis, Judy, 411
Davis, Marguerite, 56
Davis, Ossie, 77, 295
Davis, Sammi, 425
Davis Cup. *See* tennis
Davison, Emily Wilding, 56
Dawes, Charles, and Dawes Plan, 109, 247
Dawn of European Civilization, The (Childe), 112
Day, Dorothy, 395
Dayan, Moshe, 64, 398
Day for Night (film), 361
Day-Lewis, Daniel, 279, 415, 429, 433, 455
Day of the Jackal, The (film), 359
D-Day (June 6, 1944), 200
DDT, 176, 230, 296, 352

Dead, The (film), 427
Dead End (Kingsley play), 157
 film version, 167
Dead End Kids, 167
Dead Sea Scrolls, 221
Dean, Christopher, 397, 411
Dean, Dixie, 125
Dean, James, 139, 265
Dean, John Wesley III, 172
Dean, Man Mountain, 169
De Angelis, Anthony "Tino," 307
Dearborn Independent, 119
death, clinical definition of, 318
Death (Kollwitz lithographs), 151
death camps. *See* concentration camps
Death in the Family, A (Agee), 273
 stage version, 289
Death in Venice (Mann), 359
 opera version, 359
 ballet version, 443
Death of a Loyalist Soldier (Capa photograph), 161
Death of a Princess (TV documentary), 379
Death of a Salesman (Miller play), 233
death penalty. *See* crime (executions for)
Deaver, Michael K., 426
De Bakey, Michael Ellis, 34, 310, 324
De Banzie, Brenda, 259
de Bort, Léon-Philippe Teisserenc, 10
Debs, Eugene Victor, 8, 23, 50, 80, 90, 118
Debussy, Claude, 11, 51, 55, 83
Debye, Peter, 50, 72, 164
De Chirico, Giorgio, 385
Decker, George, 286
Declaration of Sentiments and Resolutions (women's rights), 12
Declaration of the Rights of Women, 12
Déclassé (Akins play), 87
Decline of the West (Spengler), 100
Dee, Ruby, 283, 293, 295
"deep ecology," 355
Deep Sea Drilling Project (DSDP), 330
Deer Hunter, The (film), 381
Defensive Action (antiabortion group), 459
De Forest, Lee, 26, 41, 62, 152, 296
Degas, Edgar, 77
De Gasperi, Alcide, 260
de Gaulle, Charles André Joseph Marie, 180, 248, 276, 280, 332, 336, 344, 359, 366
De Havilland, Geoffrey, 113
de Havilland, Olivia, 229
De Klerk, Willem, 454
De la Beckwith, Byron, 115, 305
Delaney, Shelagh, 277, 295, 331
Delbrück, Max, 214, 338
Deledda, Grazie, 117
De Leon, Daniel, 23, 62
Delicate Balance, A (Albee play), 319
de Lint, Derek, 429
Delon, Alain, 305
Del Rio, Dolores, 195, 225
Demarçay, Eugène-Anatole, 8

De Maria, Walter, 331
Dement, William Charles, 252
Demian (Hesse), 85
De Mille, Agnes, 193, 195, 203, 227
De Mille, Cecil B., 59, 61, 249
Demme, Jonathan, 443
Democracy and Social Ethics (Addams), 13
Democracy in Education (Dewey), 69
Democratic National Committee, 352, 437
Democratic National Conventions, 114, 138, 310, 330, 338, 354
Democratic Party, 310, 460
Demoiselles d'Avignon, Les (Picasso painting), 27
Dempsey, Jack, 85, 95, 117, 123
Dempster, Arthur Jeffrey, 156
Demy, Jacques, 305
Dench, Judi, 153
dendrochronology, 90
Deneuve, Catherine, 197, 305, 451
Deng Xiaoping, 20, 360, 374
Denikin, Anton, 82, 224
De Niro, Robert, 199, 365, 375, 381, 393
Denishawn dance company, 65
Denman, Gertrude, 133
Denmark, 180, 224, 360
Dennett, Mary, 87, 129
Dennett Bill, 87
Dennis, Patrick, 407
Dennis v. United States, 244
Densmore, John, 317
Depardieu, Gerard, 419
Dern, Bruce, 381
Dershowitz, Alan, 439
DES (synthetic estrogen), 182
De Salvo, Albert, 299
de Santis, Guiseppe, 239
desegregation. *See* segregation/desegregation issue
Desert Years, The (Krutch), 252
De Shields, André, 383
De Sica, Vittorio, 13, 215, 227, 251, 293, 347, 367
Design for Living (Coward play), 147
Desire Under the Elms (O'Neill play), 111
de Sitter, Willem, 72
Desolation (Mistral), 275
Destinn, Emmy, 43
Destroyed City, The (Zadkine sculpture), 247
Detroit Lions, 181
deuterium ("heavy hydrogen"), 136
Deutsch, Helene, 110, 114, 204, 404
De Valera, Eamon, 84, 142, 372
Devil's Dictionary, The (Bierce), 61
Devil's Disciple, The (Shaw play), 33
Devil's Tower (Wyoming), 27
Devol, George, 216, 287, 293
De Vries, Hugo, 4, 8
De Vries, William, 402
De Wet, Christiaan Rudolph, 102
Dewey, John, 69, 251
Dewey, Thomas Edmund, 12, 175, 202, 226, 350
Dewhurst, Colleen, 119, 289, 447
de Wilde, Brandon, 255
de Wolfe, Elsie, 25

D'Hérelle, Félix-Hubert, 64
diabetes, 94, 100, 456
Diaghilev, Sergei, 39, 47, 51, 55, 59, 73, 85, 93, 105, 129, 131
dial telephone, 24
dialysis machines, 196, 370
Diamond v. Chakrabarty, 393
diamonds, synthetic, 264
"Diamonds Are a Girl's Best Friend" (song), 237
Diamond Sutra (book), 18
Dianetics (Hubbard), 243
Diary of a Lost Girl (film), 129
Diary of Anne Frank, The (Goodrich-Hackett play), 263
Diary of a Young Girl, The (Frank), 249
Díaz, Porfirio, 40, 44, 66
Dick, George and Gladys, and Dick skin test, 106
Dickens, Charles, 217
Dickerson, Eric, 413
Dickey, James, 107
Dick-Read, Grantly, 144
Dickson, J. T., 188
Dick Tracy (comic strip), 137
Didion, Joan, 155
Diefenbaker, John George, 390
Diels, Otto Paul Hermann, 124
Diels-Alder reaction, 124
Diem, Ngo Dinh, 264, 302
diene synthesis, 124
Dies, Martin, and Dies Committee, 170
Dietrich, Marlene, 9, 133, 293, 341, 453
Dieudonné, Albert, 119
Digges, Dudley, 87, 107, 215
digital audiotape technology (DAT), 422
Dillinger, John, 153
Dillon, Melinda, 379
Dillon, Mia, 397
DiMaggio, Joe, 187
Dimitrov, Georgi Mikhailovich, 156, 236
Diners Club, 241
Dinesen, Isak, 151, 303, 415
Dinner at Eight (Kaufman-Ferber play), 143
Dinner Party, The (Chicago artwork), 383
dinosaurs, theories about, 392
Dior, Christian, 25, 223, 241, 275
dioxin, 400
diphtheria, 8, 54
dipole moments, 50
Dirac, Paul Adrien Maurice, 14, 118, 122, 140, 146, 412
dirigibles. *See* airships
disarmament. *See* arms race
disc jockeys, 287
Discovery space shuttle, 430, 438
Discreet Charm of the Bourgeoisie, The (film), 353
discus-throwing, 267
disease
 vaccines against, 8, 60, 138, 168, 208, 248, 256, 259, 266, 274, 370, 396, 422
 epidemics, 23, 69, 77, 191, 273, 315, 326, 441
 drug-resistant, 294

"genetic markers" linked with, 406
 See also drugs; *entries for individual diseases*
Disney, Walt, 11, 183, 323
Disneyland, 263
distress signal, 35
Ditte, Daughter of Man (Nexö), 73
Divided Self, The (Laing), 286
Dixie Clipper (airplane), 177
Djibouti, 378
Djilas, Milovan, 46, 272
Dmytryk, Edward, 203
DNA. *See* nucleic acids
Doblin, Alfred, 129
Dobrovolsky, Georgi T., 348
Dobzhansky, Theodosius, 168
Doctorow, E. L., 349, 371
Doctor Zhivago (Pasternak), 263, 279
 film version, 315
Documentation Centers, 223, 293
Dodds, Johnny, 113
Dodsworth (Lewis), 129, 153
 film version, 161
Doe, Samuel K., 394
Doering, William von Engers, 200
Dog Day Afternoon (film), 369
Dohrn, Bernardine, 393
Doisy, Edward Adelbert, 132, 178
Dolce Vita, La (film), 285
Dole, Robert Joseph, 106
Dolin, Anton, 187
Dollfuss, Engelbert, 152
dolphins, 439
Domagk, Gerhard, 140
Dome of Many-Coloured Glass, A (Lowell), 51
Dominica, 384
Dominican Republic, 132, 304, 320
 U.S. intervention, 10, 70, 108, 314
Dona Marilyn (ferry), 433
Dona Paz (ferry), 425
Donen, Stanley, 251
Donovan, William Joseph "Wild Bill," 284
Don Quichotte (opera), 43
"Don't Stop Thinkin' About Tomorrow" (song), 379
Doolittle, James, 190, 458
Doors, the, 317
Dorn, Friedrich Ernst, 4
Dorsey, Tommy, 183
Dos Passos, John, 347
Dostoevsky, Fyodor, 73
Double Helix, The (Watson), 332
Double Indemnity (film), 201
Double Life, A (film), 279
Douglas, Dorothea, 17
Douglas, Helen Gahagan, 4, 394
Douglas, Kirk, 205, 223, 311
Douglas, Michael, 205, 385
Douglas, William O., 394
Douglass, Andrew Ellicott, 90, 300
Dove, Rita, 417, 457
Dove's Nest, The (Mansfield), 107
Dovzhenko, Alexander, 271
Dowling, Eddie, 179, 209
Downing, Joseph, 157
Doyle, Arthur Conan, 11, 135, 177
Drabble, Margaret, 179
Dracula (film), 137
Drake, Edwin, 195, 229
Dreadnaught battleships (Britain), 28

Dreiser, Theodore, 3, 113, 137, 213
Drew, Charles Richard, 20, 180, 184, 240
Drexel Burnham Lambert firm, 419, 431
Dreyer, Carl, 125, 335
Dreyfus, Alfred, 28, 158
Dreyfuss, Richard, 231, 379
drift net fishing, 439
Driving Miss Daisy (film), 433
Dr. Jekyll and Mr. Hyde (film), 141
Dr. Mabuse, the Gambler (film), 107
Dr. No (film), 299
Dr. Strangelove (film), 309
drugs
 barbiturates, 16
 harmful medication, 23, 167, 274, 292
 "sulfa," 34, 140, 160
 immunosuppressive, 52, 200
 antibiotics, 124, 160, 176, 182, 186, 188, 196, 202, 210, 230, 275
 psychedelic, 196
 tranquilizers, 256, 260, 268
 disease resistance to, 294
 aspirin, 430
 Prozac, 462
drug trafficking, 402, 438, 444, 447, 456
Drury, Allen, 299
Druse insurrections (Syria), 112, 120, 256
Duarte Fuentes, José Napoleon, 118, 392, 410, 440
Dubai, 348
Dubček, Alexander, 98, 330, 434, 452
Dubinsky, David, 405
Dubliners (Joyce), 59
Du Bois, W. E. B., 2, 17, 43, 210, 223, 307
Dubos, René Jules, 10, 176, 332, 354, 404
Dubrovska, Felia, 129
Duchamp, Marcel, 51, 55, 67, 335
Duck Soup (film), 149
Duclos, Jacques, 372
Dugar, Benjamin Minge, 202
Duhalde, Oscar, 424
Dukakis, Michael Stanley, 148, 426, 428
Dukakis, Olympia, 425
Duke, Patty, 281
Duke University, 311, 447
Dullea, Keir, 331
Dulles, John Foster, 262, 282
Dumas, Alexandre, 163
Dumbarton Oaks Conference (1944), 204
Dunant, Henri, 2
Dunaway, Faye, 189, 325, 343, 365, 371, 375, 441
Dunbar, Paul Laurence, 31
Duncan, Isadora, 123
Duncan, Todd, 155
Dunham, Katherine, 45
Dunne, Irene, 9, 161, 217, 443
Dunning, George, 333
Dunnock, Mildred, 233
Dunton, John C., 24
Du Pont Company, 172
Duras, Marguerite, 61, 281

Durkheim, Emile, 77
Durrell, Gerald, 282
Durrell, Lawrence, 273
d'Usseau, Arnaud, 195
Dust Bowl (1933-1939), 145
Dutch elm disease, 372
Dutch imperialism, 34, 214, 234
Dutton, Charles, 411, 429
Duvalier, François "Papa Doc," 32, 270, 310, 350
Duvalier, Jean Claude "Baby Doc," 350, 420
Duvall, Robert, 353, 365, 441
Duvivier, Julien, 463
dye, bacteria-killing, 32
dye, synthetic, 12
Dyer, Reginald, 84
Dying Swan, The (ballet), 31
Dylan, Bob, 189, 303, 375, 431, 435
Dzerzhinsky, Felix Edmundovich, 118

Eagle, Harry, and Eagle's growth medium, 284
Eagleton, Thomas, 354
Eakins, Thomas, 71
Earhart, Amelia, 143, 167
Earle, Willie, 221
Early Bird satellite, 314
"early warning" system, 306
Earp, Wyatt, 131
Earth (Soviet film), 271
Earth Day, 343, 441
Earth First! (organization), 225, 369
earthquakes
 California, 27, 433, 469
 Sicily, 37
 theories regarding, 38, 46, 58
 China, 91, 141, 375, 431
 Japan, 105
 Richter scale, 156
 Turkey and Armenia, 177, 429
 Latin America, 229, 233, 343, 353, 415
 Iran, 299, 439
 Philippines, 441
 India, 455
Earth Summit (1992), 451
Earth, Wind, and Fire, 339
Easter Rising (Ireland) (1913), 54, 67, 68, 70
Eastland (liner), 65
Eastman Kodak, 3
East Timor, 370
Eastwood, Clint, 135, 451
EAT (Indiana poster), 311
Eaton, Cyrus Stephen, 133, 391
Ebb, Fred, 321
Ebert, Friedrich, 114
Echegaray, José, 19
Echo satellite, 286
Eckert, John Presper, 214, 244
Eco, Umberto, 421
E. coli bacteria, 358
economic conditions. *See* finance; Great Depression; inflation
Economic Consequences of Peace, The (Keynes), 87
Economic Interpretation of the Constitution, An (Beard and Beard), 55
Economics (Samuelson), 231
economic theories, 53
Ecuador, 222, 229, 233, 354

Eddington, Arthur Stanley, 58, 82, 108, 204
Eddy, Mary Baker, 45
Edelman, Marian Wright, 179, 363
Eden, Anthony, 264, 378
Ederle, Gertrude, 117
education, 31, 69, 99, 109, 253
    special, 461
Education Act Amendments (1972), 353
Edward VII, king of England, 34, 42, 162
Edward VIII, Duke of Windsor, 162, 355
Edwards, Blake, 295, 403
Ego and the Id, The (Freud), 106
Egoist, The (magazine), 47, 59
Egypt, 18, 68, 102, 260, 452
    1952 Revolution, 82
    and UAR, 278
    in Six-Day War, 324
    in Yom Kippur War, 358
    Camp David Accords, 380, 388
Ehrlich, Anne Howland, 335
Ehrlich, Paul, 32, 40, 66, 335
Eichmann, Adolf, 30, 286, 302
Eight, The ("Ashcan School"), 35
8½ (film), 305
Eighteenth Amendment. See Prohibition
eight-hour workday, 85
Eijkman, Christiaan, 6
Einstein, Albert, 2, 34, 46, 68, 110, 120, 264, 300, 430
    relativity theory, 22, 30, 62, 72, 82, 90
    awarded Nobel Prize, 98
    leaves Germany, 146
einsteinium (element 99), 248
Einstein on the Beach (opera), 375
Einthoven, Willem, 14
Eisenhower, Dwight David, 206, 248, 249, 262, 266, 278, 340
    appointments by, 255, 267
Eisenhower Doctrine, 270
Eisenmann-Schier, Ruth, 333
Eisenstein, Sergei, 83, 113, 123, 171, 201, 232
Ekerot, Bengt, 267
Eldredge, Niles, 352
Eldridge, Florence, 193, 267
electoral apportionment, 298, 305
electrical inventions, early
    typewriter, hearing aid, 8
    washing machine, 27
    self-starter, 47
    refrigerator, mixer, 81
electric chair, 94
electricity, 32, 46, 56
electrocardiograph (ECG or EKG), 14, 360
electroconvulsive therapy (ECT), 166
electroencephalograph (EEG), 128, 318
electronics, 26, 46, 220, 333. See also computers; television
electronic watches, 294
electron microscope. See microscope
electrons, 2, 18, 26, 46, 66, 70, 120
    and positron, 123, 140
    resonance between, 138
electron tubes, 6, 26, 62
Elegy to the Spanish Republic (Motherwell paintings), 235

Elektra (opera), 39
elephant population, 384, 435
Elgar, Edward, 7, 155, 333
Eliot, T. S., 43, 47, 101, 231, 317
Elizabeth II, queen of England, 116, 248, 255
Elizabeth R (TV series), 347
Elk Hills oil scandal, 98, 120
Ellice Islands, 383
Ellington, Duke, 103, 139, 367
Elliott, Denholm, 255, 415
Ellis, Charles, 111
Ellis, Henry Havelock, 122
Ellis Island, 3, 30
Ellis Island Madonna (Hine photograph), 23
Ellison, Ralph, 251
Ellsberg, Daniel, 336
Ellsworth, Lincoln, 117, 137, 249
Elmer Gantry (Lewis), 121
    film version, 287, 461
El Salvador, 28, 286, 386, 392, 410
Eluard, Paul, 67, 253
Elvehjem, Conrad Arnold, 166
Elytis, Odysseus, 389
embargoes, 392
embryo transplants, 234, 240
Emerson, John, 97
Emery, Katherine, 153
Emigrants, The (film), 349
Eminent Victorians (Strachey), 79
Emperor Jones, The (O'Neill play), 91
Empire of the Sun (film), 425
Empire State Building (New York), 137
    hit by plane, 211
Empress of Ireland (liner), 59
endangered or extinct species, 59, 326, 342, 354, 372, 374, 394, 412, 436
    protection of, 15, 101, 157, 217, 261, 295, 355, 363, 368, 439, 456
    international agreements, 47, 359, 361, 435, 451
    whales, 113, 217
    captive-breeding programs, 260, 282, 376, 424, 430, 442, 450
    elephants, 384, 435
    dinosaurs, theories about, 392
    dolphins, 439
Endangered Species Act (1973), 359, 368
Endeavour spacecraft, 396, 450, 454
Enders, John Franklin, 230
Endless Column (Brancusi sculpture), 91
endorphins, 370
Endurance (ship), 63
Energy, U.S. Department of, 414, 458
Engel v. Vitale, 299
Engelberger, Joe, 287, 293
engineering failures, 125, 183, 327, 355, 399
English Opera Group, 223
ENIAC computer. See computers
Enigma Variations, The (ballet), 333
Eniwetok, 202, 214, 248
Enola Gay (bomber), 208
Entertainer, The (Osborne play), 273
Entwistle, John, 311

environment
    conservation of, 6, 11, 231, 311
    pollution of, 96, 176, 192, 216, 352, 380, 420, 429, 440, 448
    cleanup of, 218, 393, 421
    protection of, 223, 333, 337, 352, 371, 388
    international agreements on, 231, 353, 355, 389
    water problems, 282, 304, 350, 419
    Greenpeace and, 347, 412, 415
    radical environmentalists, 369
    UN program, 403
    See also endangered or extinct species; environmental disasters
environmental disasters, 192, 380, 386, 400, 410, 414, 418, 420, 442, 444. See also earthquakes; floods; nuclear accidents; oil spills; storms
Environmental Protection Agency (EPA), 343, 374, 424, 428, 448
enzymes, 100, 116, 156
    coenzymes, 20, 222
    restriction, 330, 342, 358
Epic of American Civilization, An (Orozco murals), 151
epidemics. See disease
Epistemology, International Center for, 394
Epistle to the Romans, The (Barth), 87
epoxy resins, 196
Epsom Derby, 56
Epstein, Jacob, 35, 51, 283
Equal Employment Opportunity Commission (EEOC), 309
    AT&T and, 359
Equal Rights Amendment (ERA), 106, 326, 353, 403
Equatorial Guinea, 388
Equitable Life Insurance building (New York), 421
Equity Funding Corporation, 361
ERA, 325
Eric, Elspeth, 157
Erikson, Erik, 238
Eritrea, 186, 298, 382, 444
Erlander, Tage, 10, 418
Ernst, Max, 67
Eros and Civilization (Marcuse), 265
Ershad, Hussein Mohammad, 402
Ervin, Samuel James Jr., 418
Escape from Freedom (Fromm), 183
Escobar, Pablo, 456
Escoffier, Georges Auguste, 125, 159
ESM Government Securities, 417
espionage, 224, 228, 235, 244, 300, 306, 388
    convictions for, 216, 254, 424, 462
    false accusations, 233, 240
    within CIA, 462
Espionage Act (1917), 74
Esposito, Phil, 345
Esswood, Paul, 411
Estenssoro, Victor Paz, 32, 188, 246, 250, 310

Estimé, Dumarsais, 216, 240
Estonia, 84, 92, 174, 434, 446
estrone, 132
E.T. (film), 401
Ethan Frome (Wharton), 47
Ethiopia, 80, 124, 132, 364
    Italian invasion of, 152, 154, 156, 160
    World War II, 186
    -Eritrean War, 298, 382, 444
    vs. Somali, 378, 382
"ethnic cleansing," 448. See also genocide
Etiquette (Post), 291
Eucken, Rudolf, 37
eugenics, 139
Euler, Ulf Svante von, 216
European Atomic Energy Community (Euratom), 278, 324
European Coal and Steel Community (ECSC), 250, 324
European Commission of Human Rights, 255
European Community (EC), 238, 278, 286, 324, 342, 360, 374
    Spain and Portugal join, 420
European Court of Human Rights, 255
European Economic Community (EEC) (Common Market), 278, 324
European Free Trade Association (EFTA), 286, 360
European Space Agency (ESA) rocket, 388
europium (element 83), 8
Evans, Alice, 72, 372
Evans, Arthur John, 188, 250
Evans, Edith, 305, 377
Evans, Herbert McLean, 100
Evans, Walker, 187
"Eve" (common ancestor), 426
Evening Standard (Britain), 103
Evenson, Kenneth M., 354
Everglades National Park, 223
Evers, Charles, 310
Evers, Johnny, 33
Evers, Medgar Wiley, 115, 305
Evert, Chris, 311, 365, 371
Evita (musical), 387
Evolution of Man and Society, The (Darlington), 336
evolution theories, 352, 372
Ewing, Maurice, 256
exclusion principle, 112
Executioner's Song, The (Mailer), 379, 387
executions. See crime
Existence and Being (Heidegger), 129
existentialism, 129, 269, 344
Existentialism and Humanism (Sartre), 217
Explorer satellites, 276, 282
explosions
    (1900-1920), 5, 28, 29, 55, 73, 74
    (1921-1940), 99, 117, 169
    (1942-1951), 193, 203, 211, 225, 231, 247
    (1953-1960), 257, 269, 273, 291
    (1962-1975), 301, 313, 327, 335, 357, 371
    (1976-1992), 376, 401, 413, 431, 453
expressionism, 23, 127

extrasensory perception (ESP), 132
Exxon Valdez (oil tanker), 382, 432
Eysenck, Hans Jürgen, 70

Fabian Society, 2, 26, 241
Fabrizi, Aldo, 207
Fabry, Charles, 56
Facade (ballet), 137
Face the Music (musical), 143
Facing Mount Kenya (Kenyatta), 171
factoring machine, 92
Fail-Safe (film), 311
Fairbanks, Douglas, 85, 179
"Fair Deal," 234
Fair Employment Practices Commission (FEPC), 187
Fair Labor Standards Act (1938), 171, 187
Faisal I, king of Iraq, 68, 92, 98, 136, 142, 148, 158
Faisal II, king of Iraq, 276
Falange (Spanish Fascist Party), 146
Falconetti, Maria, 125
Faldo, Nick, 427
Falkenhayn, Erich von, 104
Falkland Islands (Malvinas), and Falklands War, 400
Fall, Albert M., 98, 120, 128
Falla, Manuel de, 85, 221
fallout. *See* radioactivity
Fall River Legend (ballet), 227
Falwell, Jerry, 149, 389
Family Limitation (Sanger), 59
Family of Man (photo exhibition), 263
Family Planning Association (Britain), 133
famines, 315, 324, 342, 446
Fancy Free (ballet), 203
Fangio, Juan Manuel, 245
Fanny (musical), 261
Fanon, Frantz Omar, 115, 295
Fantasia (film), 183
Farben, I. G., 162, 231
Farewell My Lovely (film), 203
Farewell to Arms, A (Hemingway), 93
film version, 141
Farley, James Aloysius, 376
Farmer, Fannie, 11
Farmer, James Leonard, 93, 193, 293
Farnum, Dustin, 59
Farouk I, king of Egypt, 94, 248, 316
Farrar, David, 223
Farrell, Charles, 121
Farrell, James T., 143
Farrow, Mia, 331, 421
fascism, 24, 94, 100, 139, 156
in Italy, 98, 108, 128, 166, 168
Vatican recognizes, 128
in Spain, 146, 156, 160, 170, 174
in France, 152, 161
Fascists, British Union of, 142
fashion design, 107, 241, 265, 275, 277, 295
Chanel, 53, 93
"New Look," 223
miniskirts, 323
Fassbinder, Rainer Werner, 219, 405
Fastnet Race (1979), 389
Fatah. *See* Palestine Liberation Movement

Father and Mother (Kollwitz sculpture), 103
Faubus, Orval, 281
Faulkner, William, 129, 135, 229, 237, 301
Favalaro, René, 324
Fawcett, E. W., 146
fax machines, 431
Fay, Frank, 201
February Revolution. *See* Russian revolutions (1917)
Febvre, Lucien, 129
Federal Bureau of Investigation (FBI), 37, 151, 153, 233, 268, 365
"sting" operation, 382
Federal Communications Commission (FCC), 151, 187
Federal Deposit Insurance Corporation (FDIC), 145
Federal Emergency Relief Administration (FERA), 144, 145
Federal Insecticide, Fungicide, and Rodenticide Act (1947), 223
Federal Reserve System, 59, 110, 427
Federal Trade Commission (FTC), 61
Federation of Feminist Women's Health Centers (FFWHC), 373
feedback, 116, 228
biofeedback, 326
Feinstein, Dianne, 383
Felix the Cat (cartoon), 61
Feller, Bob, 217
Fellini, Federico, 93, 95, 215, 259, 267, 285, 305, 315, 361, 457
Fellowship of the Ring, The (Tolkien), 259
Female Eunuch, The (Greer), 179
Feminine Mystique, The (Friedan), 305
feminism, 3, 5, 56, 57, 63, 80, 125. *See also* women
Fences (Wilson play), 415
Fenelon, Fania, 393
Feng Yu-hsiang, 232
Fenhold, Jeff, 349
Ferber, Edna, 121, 143, 297, 335
Fermat, Pierre de, and Fermat's last theorem, 454
Fermi, Enrico, 8, 116, 150, 172, 174, 180, 190, 192, 262
Fermi Award, 306
Fermi-Dirac statistics, 118
fermium (element 100), 248
Fernald nuclear weapons plants, 414
Fernandez, Emilio, 195
Ferrer, José Figueres, 30
Ferrer, Mel, 257
Fessenden, Reginald Aubrey, 2, 26, 30
fetal surgery, 382
Feydeau, Georges, 99
Feynman, Richard Phillips, 78, 230, 308, 318, 420, 432
fiber-optic technology, 342, 380
Fick, Adolf Eugen, 241
Fickett, Mary, 277
Fiddler on the Roof (musical), 311
Fiedler, Arthur, 391
Field, Betty, 277
Field, Sally, 387
Field Guide to the Birds (Peterson), 154

Field of Dreams (film), 435
Fields, Gracie, 391
Fields, W. C., 221
Fierstein, Harvey, 401, 431
Fifth Amendment, 272
figure skating. *See* skating
Fiji, 344, 426
films
experimental, 5
first features, 11, 15
epic, 51, 61, 63, 69, 119, 125, 393, 425
serials, 59
film industry, 85
Indian, 99
documentary, 101, 151
"new wave," 103, 283
Italian, 107
"talkies," 119, 125, 131, 152
censorship of, 123, 133, 201
film musicals, *see* musicals
propaganda, 157
Depression era, 161, 181
antiwar, 165
full-length cartoon, 167
special effects, 379
International Film Festival winner, 461
new studio organized, 461
Final Exit (Humphry), 444
finance, 7, 71
"panic of 1907," 31
World War I funding and reparations, 73, 109
financial scandals, 85, 141, 143, 307, 343, 345, 361, 417, 419, 424, 431, 432, 434, 447
Wall Street crashes, 129, 152, 425
"bank holiday" (1933), 144
balanced budget, 421
"Black Monday" (1987), 425
hostile takeover, 429, 431
savings and loan failures, 435, 447
Finch, Peter, 349, 375
Finian's Rainbow (musical), 223
Finland, 74, 78, 92, 248
Soviet Union invades, 176, 180
Finlandia (Sibelius orchestral work), 275
Finley, Karen, 439
Finnegans Wake (Joyce), 175, 292
Finney, Albert, 305, 331
Finsen, Niels Ryberg, 4
Fiore, Quentin, 325
Firebird, The (ballet), 43
Fire Next Time, The (Baldwin), 307
fires
(1900-1910), 5, 15, 21, 37, 41, 43
(1911-1920), 45, 79
(1929-1939), 131, 133, 153, 177
(1943-1949), 193, 203, 217, 235
(1961-1983), 293, 327, 373, 381, 407
(1987-1993), 427, 431, 433, 449, 455
"fireside chats," 144
First Abstract Watercolor (Kandinsky painting), 41
First Amendment, 221, 273
First Men on the Moon, The (Wells), 7
First Monday in October (Lawrence-Lee play), 383

Fischer, Bobby, 199, 353, 371
Fischer, Emil Hermann, 12, 16
Fish, The (Brancusi sculpture), 109
Fish and Wildlife Service, U.S., 372
Fishburne, Larry, 449
Fisher, Alva J., 27
Fisher, Bud, 37
Fisher, Carrie, 379
Fitch, Clyde, 9
Fitzgerald, Barry, 109, 295
Fitzgerald, Ella, 81
Fitzgerald, F. Scott, 113, 149, 185
Five-Year Plans. *See* Soviet Union
Flagg, Fannie, 443
Flagstad, Kirsten, 303
Flaherty, Robert J., 101, 151, 249
Flash Gordon (comic strip), 153
Flatiron Building (New York), 19
Steichen photograph, 23
Fleetwood, Mick, 325
Fleetwood Mac, 325, 379
Fleischmann, Martin, 434
Fleming, Alexander, 100, 124, 210
Fleming, John Ambrose, 18
Fleming, Victor, 97, 177
Fleming, Williamina Paton Stevens, 42, 48
Flesh and the Devil (film), 121
Fletcher, Louise, 369
Flindt, Flemming, 443
floods, 123, 125, 165, 175, 245, 321, 355
"of the century," 455
"floppy disks," 344
Florey, Howard Walter, 182, 210
Flotsam (Remarque), 187
Floyd, Charles Arthur "Pretty Boy," 151
fluoridation, 211, 326
Flying Down to Rio (film musical), 145
Flying Tigers (World War II), 278
Foch, Ferdinand, 130
Focke, Heinrich, 162
Fokine, Mikhail, 31, 35, 39, 42, 45, 51, 59, 187, 195
Follies. See Ziegfeld Follies
Fonda, Henry, 25, 169, 181, 225, 229, 299, 311, 383, 397, 403
Fonda, Jane, 169, 347, 379, 381, 385, 393, 397
Fonda, Peter, 403
Fontaine, Joan, 77, 203
Fontanne, Lynn, 95, 125, 147
Fonteyn, Margot, 89, 163, 193, 277, 293, 379, 447
food, frozen, 109. *See also* cooking; nutrition
Food and Drug Administration (FDA), U.S., 125, 167, 171, 182, 402
Food, Drug, and Cosmetic Act (1938), 167, 171, 296
football, 79, 141, 239, 247, 269, 277, 285
Rose Bowl, 11, 69
rule changes, 23
Super Bowl, 91, 325, 339, 355, 359, 371, 401, 441, 457, 463
records set, 109, 181, 273, 359, 383, 403, 413, 417, 441
college draft system, 109
AFL founded, 283
Dallas Cowboys founded, 289
T formation, 335
teams killed in plane crashes, 345

foot-binding, Chinese, 47
Ford, Ford Madox, 127, 179
Ford, Gerald Rudolph, 56, 201, 360, 364, 374
  assassination attempts, 369
Ford, Glenn, 187
Ford, Harrison, 193, 379, 397
Ford, Henry, 3, 17, 35, 55, 119, 225
Ford, John, 157, 177, 181, 225, 229, 235, 239, 363
Ford, Wallace, 167
Ford Motor Company, 17, 189
Foreign Affairs (Lurie), 411
Foreign Affairs magazine, 220
Foreman, David, 225, 369
Foreman, George, 461
Forester, C. S., 245
Forman, Milos, 369
Formosa (Taiwan), 262, 372
Forrestal, James Vincent, 236
Forrestal, USS, 329
Forrest Gump (film), 459
Forssmann, Werner Theodor Otto, 128, 188, 268
Forster, E. M., 35, 41, 59, 109, 247, 345, 353, 411
Forster, Rudolph, 125
Forsythe Saga, The (Galsworthy), 27
Fort Apache (film), 229
Fortas, Abe, 45, 331, 337, 405
For the Union Dead (Lowell), 311
FORTRAN (computer language), 268
42nd Street (film musical), 145
For Whom the Bell Tolls (Hemingway), 181
  film version, 197
Fosse, Bob, 123, 427
Fossey, Dian, 142, 326, 408, 416
fossils. *See* paleontology
Foster, Jodie, 301, 369, 429, 443
Foster, William Zebulon, 83, 296
Foucault, Michel, 119, 293, 339, 413
Foulkes, Raúl Alfonsin, 122, 408
Four Baboons Adoring the Sun (film), 451
"Four Freedoms," 188
"Four Horsemen" (football), 79
Four Horsemen of the Apocalypse, The (Ibanez), 69
  film version, 97
400 Blows, The (film), 413
Four Quartets (Eliot), 163
"Fourteen Points," 80
fourth dimension, 30, 62
Fourth of July, The (Ives orchestral work), 55
Fowler, William, 274
Fox, Edward, 359, 401
Fox, Fontaine, 37
Fox, James, 305, 411, 455
Foyt, A. J., 293
France, Anatole, 97
France, 3, 364
  in North Africa, 2, 16, 46, 50, 96, 116, 258, 292, 370
  World War I, 58, 66, 72, 130
  in Middle East, 92, 120, 216
  Third Republic, 152, 161, 218
  Popular Front, 156, 160
  World War II, 174, 176, 180
  French Resistance movement, 176, 205, 372, 408
  in Indochina, 214, 238, 240, 244, 258

Fourth Republic, 218, 276
  Malagasy rising against, 222
  nuclear program, 230, 320, 332, 392, 415
  Fifth Republic, 276, 280, 286
  AIDS scandal, 446
France Libre, La (journal), 407
Franciosa, Anthony, 265
Francis Ferdinand, archduke of Austria, 58
francium (element 87), 178
Franco, Francisco, 146, 160, 164, 372
Franco-Prussian War, 4
Frank, Anne, 249
Frank, Hans, 210
Frank, Leo, 63
Frank, Melvin, 361
Frankenheimer, John, 311
Frankenstein (film), 137
Frankenthaler, Helen, 127
Frankfurter, Felix, 319
Franklin, Kenneth Linn, 264
Franklin, Rosalind Elsie, 92, 252, 278, 300
Franklin, Sidney, 137, 167
Franklin v. Gwinnett County Public Schools, 451
Franks, Robert, 109
Fraser, Malcolm, 134, 370
Fraser, Peter, 242
fraud. *See* finance (financial scandals); hoaxes
Frazer, James George, 31, 189
Freedom of Information Act (1974), 367
"freedom rides," 291
Freedom 7 (spacecraft), 106, 292
Free French forces (World War II), 180, 199
Freeman, Morgan, 173, 433, 451
"free radicals," 4, 74
Free Yemen Republic, 298
Frege, Gottlieb, 10
Freikorps militia (Germany), 84, 92
Frelich, Phyllis, 393
FRELIMO. *See* Mozambique
French, Daniel Chester, 103, 139
French Chef, The (TV series), 53
French Legion of Honor, 125
Frend, Charles, 255
Freon, 132, 256, 364, 382
Freud, Anna, 114
Freud, Sigmund, 10, 18, 22, 46, 50, 70, 106, 114, 178
  ideas rejected, 186
Frey, Leonard, 333
Frick, Henry Clay, 162
Frick, Wilhelm, 210
Friedan, Betty Goldstein, 99, 305, 321
Fried Green Tomatoes (film), 443
Friedman, Milton, 53
Friendship 7 spacecraft, 298
Friends of the Earth, 343
Frisch, Karl von, 84, 122, 222, 360
Frisch, Otto, 174, 180
From Here to Eternity (Jones), 245
  film version, 255
Fromm, Erich, 5, 183, 389
Fromme, Lynette Alice "Squeaky," 369
Frontier in American History, The (Jackson), 143
Frost, Robert, 59, 105, 133, 307, 455

Frosta (tanker), 377
frozen food, 109
Fuchida, Mitsuo, 12, 376
Fuchs, Klaus, 240
Fuchs, Vivian, 277
fuel cells, 282
Fugard, Athol, 145
Fugate, Carol Ann, 273
Fugitive, The (film), 225
Fujairah, 348
Fujimori, Alberto, 450
Fulbright, James, and Fulbright Act, Fulbright Scholarships, 215
Fuller, Richard Buckminster, 326, 408
fundamentalism
  Christian, 113, 287, 425
  Islamic, 128, 382, 414, 424, 441, 450
  Sikh, 410
  Hindu, 450
  See also religion
Funk, Casimir, 52
Funny Girl (musical), 311
Funny Thing Happened on the Way to the Forum, A (musical), 301
Furber, Douglas, 421
Futral, Elizabeth, 455
futurists, 43

Gabin, Jean, 171
Gable, Clark, 9, 15, 155, 175, 289
Gabo, Naum, 91
Gabon, 288, 334
Gabor, Dennis, 220, 316
Gabriela, Clove and Cinnamon (Amado), 277
Gagarin, Yuri Alekseyevich, 154, 290, 334
Gaia: A New Look at Life on Earth (Lovelock), 388
Gaitskell, Hugh, 28, 308
Galati, Frank, 439
Galbraith, John Kenneth, 279
"Galen" (Soviet adviser), 172
Galileo spacecraft, 434, 460
Gallipoli, 46, 54, 62, 66
Gallo, Robert, 410
Gallup, George Horace, 9, 157, 413
Gallup Poll, 157
Galsworthy, John, 27, 143, 151
Gambia, 306, 402
Gambler, The (opera), 73
game theory, 96, 124
Gamma Ray Observatory (GRO), 446
gamma rays, 2
Gamow, George, 20, 224, 226, 262, 334
Gance, Abel, 83, 119, 399
Gandhi (film), 401
Gandhi, Indira, 74, 204, 320, 368, 410
Gandhi, Mohandas (Mahatma), 26, 50, 60, 75, 86, 102, 140, 226, 393
  nonviolence campaigns, 84, 90, 130
Gandhi, Rajiv, 74, 204, 410, 446
gangsters, 159. *See also* crime
Gapon, Georgy, 22
Garbo, Greta, 25, 97, 121, 131, 163, 177, 441

Garcia, Jerry, 315
García Lorca, Federico, 165, 305
García Márquez, Gabriel, 127, 325, 403, 411, 435
García Robles, Alfonso, 402
Garden, Mary, 11, 329
Gardenia, Vincent, 425
Garden of the Finzi-Continis, The (film), 347
Garden Party, The (Mansfield), 103
Gardner, Ava, 103, 281, 443
Gardner, Erle Stanley, 197
Garfield, John, 223
Garfunkel, Art, 317, 343
Garland, Hamlin, 73
Garland, Judy, 19, 103, 177, 341
Garner, James, 403
Garner, John "Cactus Jack," 328
Garrison, Jim, 443
Garson, Greer, 183, 191
Garth Brooks (album), 439
Garvey, Marcus, 61, 69, 87, 93, 105, 121, 185
gas chamber, 108
Gaslight (film), 203
gasoline, 52, 96
Gasoline Alley (comic strip), 81
Gassman, Vittorio, 239
Gaston, Cito, 451
Gates, William, 380
Gather Together in My Name (Angelou), 365
Getty, Harold, 135
Gaudí, Antonio, 119
Gauguin, Paul, 17, 87
Gaul, George, 101
Gautier, Dick, 289
Gaviño, Juan Bosch, 40
Gay, John, 125
Gay, Noel, 421
Gay Divorce, The (musical), 141
Gaynor, Janet, 121
gay rights movement, 337, 383. *See also* homosexuality
Gazzara, Ben, 265
Gazzo, Michael V., 265
Gbenye, Christophate, 308
Gebhardt, Paul H., 254
Gee, Lottie, 97
Geffen, David, 461
Gehrig, Lou, 17, 137, 189
Geiger, Hans, 44
Geiger, Johannes Hans Wilhelm, and Geiger counter, 54, 210
Gelbart, Larry, 435
Geldof, Bob, 411, 415
Gell-Mann, Murray, 130, 214, 256, 292, 308, 340, 354
Gemayel, Bashir, 400
Gemayel, Pierre, 162
Gemini spacecraft, 314, 320
Genentech, 375, 396
General Agreement on Tariffs and Trade (GATT), 221, 305
General Electric Company, 181, 207, 216
General in His Labyrinth, The (García Márquez), 435
General Motors Corporation, 35, 161, 167, 207, 293
General Slocum (steamer), 21
General Theory of Employment, Interest, and Money, The (Keynes), 157
Genet, Jean, 45, 423
gene therapy, 434, 440

genetics, 4, 34, 107, 186, 230, 232, 330, 336, 342
mutations, 8, 120, 168, 208, 218
chromosomes, 12, 22, 40, 42, 52
DNA and RNA, *see* nucleic acids
genetic engineering, 214, 358, 364, 375, 392, 393, 396, 402, 406, 422, 425, 430, 438
genetic counseling, 250
Soviet-sponsored, 316, 348
"genetic code," 326
"genetic markers," 406, 426, 462
"genetic fingerprinting," 410, 427
Genetics and the Origins of Species (Dobzhansky), 168
Geneva Accords on Vietnam (1954), 258
Geneva agreements (1988), 428
Geneva conference on naval limitation (1927), 120
Geneva Protocol (1925), 364
"Geneva summit" (1955), 262
Geneva Summit (1985), 414
genocide, 139, 170, 188, 192, 279, 458
"ethnic cleansing," 448
See also concentration camps (death camps)
Genovese, Kitty, 313
"Gentleman's Agreement" (U.S.-Japan) (1907), 31
Gentleman's Agreement (film), 71, 223
Gentlemen Prefer Blondes (musical), 237
film version, 257
geodesic dome, 326, 414
George, Chief Dan, 343
George V, king of England, 42, 56, 162
George VI, king of England, 162, 248
George Prince (ferry), 377
George Washington (Borglum sculpture), 133
George White's Scandals (revue), 85
Georgi, Howard M., 366
Georgian Civil War, 450, 456
geothermal energy, 32, 56
Germany
imperialism/militarism, 18, 30, 82, 87, 146, 170
World War I, 56, 58–78
Revolution (1917), 78
war reparations, 82, 87, 104, 109
and Soviet Union, 100, 156, 172
World War II, 110, 174, 176, 180–202, 206–208
repudiates treaties, 112, 154, 160
Nazi, emigration from, 141
automobile and aircraft industries, 161, 172
Anti-Comintern Pact (with Japan), 162
partition of, 234
Federal Republic of (West), 234, 364, 378, 434
Democratic Republic of (East), 234, 240, 254, 292, 434
antiforeign rioting in, 446
AIDS scandal, 456
See also Nazis
Geronimo (Apache leader), 40

Gershwin, George, 79, 109, 117, 137, 155, 169
Gershwin, Ira, 109, 117, 137, 189
Gesell, Arnold, 46, 296
Gestalt approach, 50
Gestapo, 146. *See also* Nazis
Getty, J. Paul III, 363
Ghana, 272
Gheorghiu-Dej, Gheorghe, 8, 316
Ghiorso, A. (physicist), 294
Giacometti, Alberto, 9, 323
Gianni Schicchi (opera), 81
Giap, Vo Nguyen, 52
Gibbon, John H. Jr., 254
Gibbon, Lewis Grassic, 141
"GI Bill of Rights," 201
Gibran, Khalil, 107
Gibson, Althea, 121, 239, 245, 277
Gibson, Henry, 369
Gibson, Josh, 49, 225
Gibson, Reginald, 146
Gibson, William, 281
Gide, André, 41, 109, 225, 247
Gideon v. Wainwright, 307
Gielgud, John, 21, 127, 223, 311, 343, 369, 401
Gierek, Edward, 344
Gigi (Colette): film and stage versions, 277, 457
Gilbert, Cass, 55
Gilbert, John, 121
Gilbert, Lewis, 321
Gilbert, Ronnie, 231
Gilels, Emil, 71, 419
Gilgamesh (Sumerian epic), 98
Gillespie, Dizzy, 75, 457
Gillette-Brown murder case, 113
Gilliam, Terry, 339
Gilman, Charlotte Perkins, 17, 65
Gilmore, Gary, 375, 379, 387
Gilmore, Mikal, 379
Gilpin, Charles S., 91
Gingold, Hermione, 277
Ginsburg, Alan, 267
Ginsburg, Ruth Bader, 148, 149, 457
Gipp, George, 79
Gippel, David, 435
Giraudoux, Jean, 205
Girl Crazy (musical), 413
Girl from Utah, The (musical), 61
Girl of the Golden West, The (Belasco play), 2
opera version, 43
Girl on a Chair (Manzú), 147
Girton College (Cambridge, England), 99
Giscard d'Estaing, Valéry, 116, 364
Gish, Dorothy, 79, 101
Gish, Lillian, 63, 79, 85, 93, 101
Gitanjali (Tagore), 49
"Give My Regards to Broadway" (song), 19
"Give Peace a Chance" (song), 339
Gizikis, Phaidon, 360
Gjellerup, Karl Adolph, 73
Glackens, William, 35
Glaser, Donald, 252, 288
Glasgow, Ellen, 213
Glashow, Sheldon Lee, 308, 324, 364, 366
Glaspell, Susan, 63
glass, nonreflecting, 170
Glass, Philip, 169, 375, 411, 449, 455

Glassboro (New Jersey) Summit (1967), 324
Glass Menagerie, The (Williams play), 209
Glen Canyon Dam, 304, 369
Glenn, John Herschel Jr., 98, 298
Glenville, Peter, 309
"global village," 325
Glomar Challenger (research ship), 292, 330, 368
Gloriana (opera), 255
Glover, Danny, 415
Glushko, Valentin, 36, 270, 422, 436
Goa, 294
Godard, Jean-Luc, 283
"God Bless America" (song), 79
Goddard, Paulette, 161
Goddard, Robert Hutchings, 82, 116, 210
Godden, Rumer, 223, 245
Gödel, Kurt, and Gödel's proof, 28, 40, 134, 384
Godfather, The (film), 179, 183, 353, 365
Godfree, Kitty, 111
Goebbels, Joseph, 116, 212
Goering, Hermann, 142, 210
Goethals, George Washington, 19, 59, 127
Goetz, Bernhard, 411
Gold, Thomas, 226, 330
Goldberg, Whoopi, 415
Goldberg, Joseph, 64, 114
Goldberger, Joseph, 64, 114
Golden Bough, The (Frazer), 31
Golden Bowl, The (James), 19
Golden Boy (film), 399
Golden Gate International Exposition (1939-1940), 175
Golden Notebook, The (Lessing), 301
Goldfine, Bernard, 278
Golding, William Gerald, 47, 261, 407, 457
Goldman, Emma, 43, 92, 162, 184
Goldman, James, 321, 331
Goldman, Ronald L., 461
Goldmark, Peter, 182, 228
Gold Rush, The (film), 113
gold standard, U.S., 3
Goldwater, Barry Morris, 308
golf, 201, 235, 427
Bobby Jones, 107, 117, 131
U.S. Open, 107, 117, 229, 239, 247, 251, 277, 299
Ben Hogan, 229, 239, 251, 255
women in, 247, 277
Gombert, Moses, 4
Gompers, Samuel, 111
Gomulka, Wladyslaw, 24, 268, 344, 404
Gone With the Wind (Mitchell), 161
film version, 57, 175
Gonne, Maud, 2, 11, 256
Goodall, Jane, 154, 286, 326
Goodbye, Mr. Chips (Hilton), 151
Goodbye to Berlin (Isherwood), 177
musical version, 321
Good Earth, The (Buck), 137
film version, 167
Good Fairy, The (Molnar), 253
Goodman, Andrew, 309
Goodman, Benny, 41, 423
Goodman, Steve, 353

Good Neighbor Policy, 144, 150
"Good Night Irene" (song), 241
Goodpasture, Ernest William, 138
Goodrich, Frances, 263
Good Soldier Schweik, The (Hasek), 94
Gorbachev, Mikhail Sergeyevich, 48, 136, 178, 414, 418, 429, 438, 440, 442
and INF treaty, 424, 428
Gordimer, Nadine, 107, 445
Goren, Charles, 163
Gorgas, William Crawford, 19, 92
Gorillas in the Mist (Fossey), 408
Goring, Marius, 231
Gorky, Maxim, 11, 33, 165
Gorman, Margaret, 99
Gorney, Jay, 141
Gossamer Albatross (aircraft), 388
Gösta Berling's Saga (film), 97
Go Tell It on the Mountain (Baldwin), 255
Gotham Book Mart (New York), 93
Gotti, John, 451
Gottwald, Klement, 256
Goudsmit, Samuel, 112
Goulart, João, 310
Gould, Chester, 137
Gould, Elliott, 343
Gould, Morton, 227
Gould, Stephen Jay, 352
Gow, James, 195
Gowland, Gibson, 111
Gowon, Yakubu, 154, 320
Goyescas (opera), 71
GPU (Soviet secret police), 74, 118
Graceland (album), 421
Graduate, The (film), 325
Graf, Steffi, 425
Graf Spee (battleship), 176
Graf Zeppelin (dirigible), 143
Graham, Billy, 81, 241
Graham, Martha, 121, 201, 223, 445
Graham, Otto, 239
grammar, 275
Gramm-Rudman Act (1986), 421
Grammy Award, 461
Gramsci, Antonio, 168
Granados, Enrique, 71
Grandcamp (freighter), 273
Grand Canyon, 37, 448
Grand Canyon National Park, 304
Grand Coulee Dam, 189
Grand Illusion (film), 165
grand unification theory (GUT), 366
Grange, Red, 109
Grant, Cary, 21, 183, 421
Grapes of Wrath, The (Steinbeck), 145, 175
film version, 181
stage version, 439
Grass, Günter, 211
Grateful Dead, the, 315, 343
Graves, Robert, 71, 153, 417
Gravity's Rainbow (Pynchon), 361
Gray, Harold, 111
Grayson, Kathryn, 229
Graziano, Rocky, 223
Great Barrier Reef, 371
Great Depression, 23, 45, 129, 131, 147, 181
songs, books, and movies of, 141, 157, 161, 181

photographs of, 167
recovery from, 175
Great Dictator, The (film), 181
Great Dismal Swamp, 363
"Great Dissenter," 159
Great Expectations (film), 217
Great Gatsby, The (Fitzgerald), 113
"Great Idaho Fire" (1910), 43
Great Lakes, 416
Water Quality Agreement, 355
"Great Leap Forward" (China), 276
"great paradox" (mathematics), 10, 40
Great Powers, 10, 54
Great Purge (Soviet Union) (1930s), 122, 146, 150, 160, 166, 172, 173, 181, 189, 260
"Great Society," 308, 315
Great Train Robbery, The (film), 15
"Great White Fleet," 33
Great White Hope, The (Sackler play), 35, 331
Greece, 42, 136, 162
Greek-Turkish War, 50, 86, 90, 96, 100
World War I and postwar, 58, 72, 86, 164
independence guaranteed, 174
World War II, 180, 182, 184
civil war in, 214, 220, 230, 234
U.S. aid to, 220
war with Cyprus, 248
Greed (film), 111
Green, Adolph, 203, 443
Green, Hetty, 71
Green, Peter, 325
Green, William, 253
Green Bay Packers, 285, 325
Greene, Graham, 21, 235, 445
greenhouse effect, 170
Greenland, 13, 43
Greenlease, Bobby, 255
Green Party (West Germany), 225, 388
Greenpeace, 347, 412, 415
Green Revolution, 60, 74, 202, 344, 420
Greenspan, Alan, 427
Greenstein, Jesse, 304
Greenstreet, Sydney, 185
Greenwood, Joan, 305
Greer, Germaine, 179
Gregg, Everley, 147
Gregg v. Georgia, 375
Gregory, Lady, 11, 19
Grenada, 366, 388, 406
Gretsky, Wayne, 397, 441
Grew, Joseph Clark, 316
Grey, Edward, 22
Grey, Joel, 321
greyhound racing, 25
Grieg, Edvard, 35
Griem, Helmut, 337
Grierson, Benjamin Henry, 48
Grierson, John, 357
Griffin, Michael J., 459
Griffith, D. W., 59, 61, 63, 69, 79, 85, 93, 101, 233
Griffith, Hugh, 305
Griffith, Michael, 425
Grignard, Victor, 8
Grijns, Gerrit, 6
Grissom, Virgil "Gus," 292, 314, 324
Griswold v. Connecticut, 315

Grizzard, George, 353
Gromyko, Andrei, 40
Gropius, Walter, 87, 341
Groupe Roussel Uclaf, 428
Group of Seven (Canadian artists), 77, 93, 105, 347, 367
Group Theater (New York), 137
group therapy, 236, 316
Groves, Leslie, 190
Grunetzig, Andreas R., 378
Guadalcanal, 192, 224
Guam, 202
Guantanamo, 14
Guare, John, 173, 419, 439, 451
Guatemala, 28, 260, 350, 375
Guazzoni, Enrico, 51
Guderian, Heinz, 260
Guermantes Way, The (Proust), 91
Guernica (Picasso painting), 165, 397
Guess Who's Coming to Dinner (film), 325
Guest of Honor, A (opera), 15
Guevara, Che, 124, 326
Guffey, Cary, 379
Guillet, Leon, 20
Guinea, 102, 278, 334
Guinea-Bissau, 304, 364
Guinness, Alec, 61, 217, 245, 271, 289, 299, 379, 401, 411
Gulag Archipelago, The (Solzhenitsyn), 359
Gulf War. *See* Persian Gulf War
gun control, 396, 411, 433, 445
Brady Law, 455
Gunn, David, 459
Guns of August, The (Tuchman), 299
Gustav Line, 202
Gutenberg, Beno, and Gutenberg discontinuity, 58
Guthrie, A. B., 223
Guthrie, Arlo, 337, 353
Guthrie, Tyrone, 5, 307, 351
Guthrie, Woody, 53, 329
Guthrie Theater (Minneapolis), 307
Guyana, 106, 256, 322, 381
Guy-Blaché, Alice, 11, 335
Guzmán, Jacobo Arbenz, 56, 260, 350
Guzmán Reynoso, Abimael, 452
gymnastics, 353, 375
Gypsy (musical), 283
Gypsy Moth III (yacht), 325

Haakon VII, king of Norway, 274
Habash, George, 340
Haber, Fritz, 30, 78
Haber-Bosch process, 30, 52
Habibullah Khan, 84, 128
Habyarimana, Juvénal, 458
Hackett, Albert, 263
Hackman, Gene, 429, 451
Hadassah (women's organization), 51
Hadden, Britton, 107
hafnium (element 72), 106
Haganah (paramilitary group), 92
Hagen, Uta, 299
Hagenbeck-Wallace Circus, 81
Hägg, Gunder, 211
Hagiwara, Kenichi, 393
Hagman, Larry, 311
Hague Peace Conference (1907), 30
Hahn, Jessica, 425

Hahn, Otto, 74, 174, 192, 328, 334
hahnium (element 105), 328
Haig, Douglas, 126
Haile Mariam Mengistu, 364, 378, 444
Haile Selassie I (Ras Tafari), king of Ethiopia, 80, 124, 132, 364, 372
Haines, Randa, 419
Haise, Fred W. Jr., 344
Haiti, 216, 240, 270, 310, 420, 440
U.S. intervention, 64, 152, 444, 460, 462
Halas, George, 91, 335, 407
Haldane, J. B. S., 124, 312
Haldeman, Bob, 116, 458
Halder, Franz, 356
Hale, George Ellery, 72, 228
Hale telescope, 228
Haley, Alex Palmer, 99, 315, 375, 379, 453
half-life, 10
Hall, Carl Austin, 255
Hall, Edward Wheeler, and Hall-Mills case, 101
Hall, Frances Stevens, 101
Hall, Peter, 293, 451
Hall, Radclyffe, 123
Hall, Willie, 305
Halley's comet, 40, 422. *See also* comets
Halsey, William Frederick Jr., 282
Hamburger, Christian, 250
Hamer, Fannie Lou, 75, 310, 381
Hamill, Mark, 379
Hamilton, Alice, 112
Hamilton, Patrick, 203
Hamlet (ballet), 193
Hamlet (film), 231
Hammarskjöld, Dag, 24, 254, 292
Hammer (music star), 441
Hammerstein, Oscar, 121, 195, 211, 235, 245, 283, 291
Hammett, Dashiell, 153, 185, 197, 295
Hammond, Kay, 211
Hampden, Walter, 255
Hampton, Fred, 345
Hamsun, Knut, 93, 253
Handmaid's Tale, The (Atwood), 419
film version, 441
Handy, W. C., 61, 69, 281
Hanford Nuclear Reservation, 200
hang gliding, 230
Hani, Chris, 194, 454
Hanks, Tom, 451, 459
Hannah and Her Sisters (film), 421
Hansberry, Lorraine, 135, 283, 317
Hanson, Lars, 97
Hansson, Per Albin, 218
"Happy Days Are Here Again" (song), 87
Hapsburg monarchy ended, 82
Hara, Takashi, 96
Harada, Mieko, 415
Harburg, E. Y. "Yip," 141, 203, 223, 399
Hard Day's Night, A (film), 309
Harden, Arthur, 20
Hardie, James Keir, 66
Harding, Tonya, 463
Harding, Warren G., 104
Harding-Cox election, 90, 93

Hardy, Godfrey Harold, and Hardy-Weinberg law, 34
Hardy, James D., 308
Hardy, Robert, 347
Hardy, Thomas, 127
Hare, David, 225
Hari, Mata, 76
Harkins, William Draper, 62
Harlem Globetrotters, 121, 193, 223
Harlem Renaissance, 17, 232
Harmon, Tom, 181, 183
Haroun (Rushdie), 441
Harp-Weaver and Other Poems, The (Millay), 105
Harriman, Averell, 422
Harris, Barbara (actress), 369
Harris, Barbara Clementine (bishop), 435
Harris, Elmer, 231
Harris, Jean, 395
Harris, Julie, 241
Harris, Lawren Stewart, 347
Harris, Louis, 99
Harris, Paul Percy, 23
Harris, Rosemary, 321
Harris, Thomas, 443
Harris, William and Emily, 365
Harris v. Forklift Systems, 455
Harris v. McRae, 395
Harrison, George, 199, 277, 431
Harrison, Harry, 361
Harrison, Michael, 382
Harrison, Rex, 37, 59, 211, 217, 231, 267, 441
Harron, Robert, 79
Harroun, Ray, 47
Hart, Brooke, 147
Hart, Charles, 431
Hart, Gary, 166, 430
Hart, Lorenz, 163
Hart, Marvin, 29
Hart, Moss, 163, 189, 267, 297
Hart, Roxanne, 389
Hart, Tim, 337
Hartnell, Norman Bishop, 107
Harvard Observatory, 48
Harvard University, 181
Harvey, Anthony, 331
Harvey, Donald, 431
Harvey, Laurence, 279, 315
Harvey (Chase play), 201
Hasek, Jaroslav, 93
Hasenfus, Eugene, 418
Hatfield, Mark Odum, 102
Hatful of Rain, A (Gazzo play), 265
Hauptmann, Bruno Richard, 139, 161
Hauptmann, Gerhart, 53
Havel, Vaclav, 163, 434
Havers, Nigel, 411
Hawke, Bob, 130, 406
Hawking, Stephen William, 198, 344, 424
and Hawking radiation, 366
Hawkins, Gerald Stanley, 126, 302
Hawkins, Jack, 255, 271
Hawkins, Trish, 393
Hawkins, William Draper, 96, 138
Hawks, Howard, 137, 203, 223, 257, 381
Haworth, Jill, 321
Haworth, Walter Norman, 144, 168

Hay, John, 24
Haya de la Torre, Victor, 108, 234, 300, 390
Hayakawa, Sessue, 271
Hayden, Melissa, 239
Hayden, Sterling, 309
Haydon, Julie, 179, 209
Hayek, Friedrich August von, 203, 427, 453
Hayes, Helen, 5, 137, 141, 269, 277, 463
hay fever, 42
Hayman, David, 425
Haynes, Marques, 223
Haynesworth, Clement, 337
Hays, Lee, 231, 235
Hays, Will H., and Hays Office, 133
Hayward, Susan, 81, 258, 373
Haywood, William Dudley "Big Bill," 23, 31, 126
Hayworth, Rita, 81, 427
Hazardous Substances Act (1960), 289
Hazen, Elizabeth, 234
Head, Murray, 349
Head Start program, 311
Heady, Bonnie Brown, 255
health care, 215, 329, 339, 373
    Clinton reform proposals rejected (1994), 460
"Heal the World" (song), 445
Hearst, Patty, 365
Hearst, William Randolph, 249, 365
heart
    artificial, 274, 336, 400
    heart defibrillator, 416
    heart surgery, see medicine
Heart of Atlanta Motel, Inc. v. United States, 309
Heart of Darkness (Conrad), 387
Hearts of the World (film), 79
Heat and Dust (Jhabvala), 369
    film version, 405
Heath, Edward Richard George, 70, 342
Heaviside, Oliver, 10
Heaviside layer, 108
"heavy hydrogen," 136
Heavy Iron Research, Center for (Germany), 460
"heavy water," 136, 176
Hebb, Donald O., 234
Heckart, Eileen, 255
Heckel, Eric, 23
Hedin, Sven, 253
Heezen, Bruce Charles, 256
Heflin, Van, 177, 255, 263
Heib, Richard, 450
Heidegger, Martin, 121, 129, 377
Heiden, Eric, 381, 393
Heindenstam, Verner von, 71
Heidi Chronicles, The (Wasserstein play), 431
Heifetz, Jasha, 9, 427
Heimlich, Henry J., and Heimlich maneuver, 368
Heisenberg, Werner Karl, 10, 112, 116, 120, 140, 192, 376
Heisman Trophy (football), 181
Heitler, Walter, 120
helicopters. See airplanes
helium, 152, 167, 170
Heller, Joseph, 107, 293
Hellerman, Fred, 231

Hellman, Lillian, 25, 153, 167, 177, 187, 379, 413
Hello Dolly! (musical), 305
Help! (film), 315
Helpmann, Robert, 163, 193, 203
Helsinki Accords (1975), 370
Hemingway, Ernest, 93, 117, 141, 181, 203, 261, 277, 295
Hemingway, Mariel, 389
hemoglobin and myoglobin, 288
Hench, Philip Showalter, 228, 240
Henderson, Fletcher, 253
Henderson, Florence, 261
Henderson, Leon, 185
Hendrix, Jimi, 195, 345
Henie, Sonja, 123
Henley, Beth, 397
Hennard, George, 445
Henri, Robert, 35
Henry Draper Catalogue, The (astronomy), 108
Henry V (film), 209
Henslow House (Britain), 99
Henson, Jim, 169, 375, 443
Henson, Matthew Alexander, 39, 267
Henze, Hans Werner, 277
Hepburn, Audrey, 131, 295, 457
Hepburn, Katharine, 33, 177, 181, 183, 209, 225, 245, 325, 327, 331, 397
Hepburn Act (1906), 27
Hepton, Bernard, 347
Hepworth, Barbara, 17, 371
Herald of Free Enterprise (ferry), 425
Herbert, George, earl of Carnarvon, 100
Herbert, Victor, 17
herbicides, 208, 350, 414
Herbig, George Howard, 364
Herblock (cartoonist), 41
heredity, laws of, 4. See also genetics
Herland (Gilman), 65
Hermanas, Las (ballet), 305
Herrick, James Bryan, 42
Herriman, George, 43, 205
Hersey, John Richard, 61, 215, 239, 459
Hershey, Alfred Day, 208, 214, 338
Hershey, Barbara, 421
Hersholt, Jean, 111
Hertzog, James, 54, 108, 194
Hertzsprung, Ejnar, 22, 54
Hertzsprung-Russell diagram, 54
Herzegovina, 38, 80, 448
Herzog, Maurice, 239
Herzog, Werner, 195
Hess, Henry H., 284
Hess, Myra, 175, 319
Hess, Rudolph, 184, 422
Hess, Victor, 44, 162
Hesse, Hermann, 85, 101, 121, 217, 301
Heston, Charlton, 361
Hevesy, Georg, 106, 152
Hewish, Anthony, 324
Hewitt, Jacqueline, 430
Heyerdahl, Thor, 61, 221, 339
"Hey, Jude" (song), 333
Heyse, Paul von, 43
Heyward, Dubose, 155
Higgins, Colin, 393
Higgins, William, 430

High Flyer (freighter), 273
High Noon (film), 251
High Sierra (film), 187
Higuchi, Russell, 396
hijacking, 349, 374, 416, 429
Hijuelos, Oscar, 431
Hilbert, David, 6, 198
Hill, Anita Faye, 269, 443
Hill, Arthur, 299
Hill, George Roy, 337, 359, 383
Hill, James Jerome, 19, 71
Hill, Joe, 65
Hill, Paul J., 459
Hillary, Edmund Percival, 89, 255, 277
Hiller, Wendy, 53, 59, 171, 209, 289, 319
Hillier, James, 184
Hillman, Sidney, 219
Hillquit, Morris, 148
"Hillside Stranglers," 379
Hilton, James, 147, 151
Himes, Ronald, 347
Himmler, Heinrich, 4, 128, 146, 212
Hinckley, John W., 396
Hindemith, Paul, 309
Hindenburg, Paul von, 154
Hindenburg (dirigible), 143, 165
Hindenburg Line, 72, 78
Hindu-Muslim rioting (1992), 450
Hine, Lewis Wickes, 23, 185
Hingle, Pat, 289, 331
Hiratsuka, Raicho, 46
Hirohito, emperor of Japan, 8, 116, 436
Hiroshima, 206, 208
Hiroshima (Hersey), 215
Hiroshima, Mon Amour (film), 103, 281
Hirsch, Elroy Leon, 247
Hirsch, Judd, 393
Hirschfeld, Albert, 131
Hirschfeld, Nina, 131
Hirshhorn Museum (Washington), 365
Hiss, Alger, 228, 238
Histoire du Soldat, L' (ballet), 79
History of the Russian Revolution, The (Rivera mural), 317
History of the Standard Oil Company (Tarbell), 19
Hitchcock, Alfred, 65, 395
Hitchcock, Henry-Russell, 141
Hitler, Adolf, 4, 92, 94, 104, 161
    in power, 146, 150, 156
    "appeasement" of, 170
    in World War II, 180
    film caricaturing, 181
    plot against, 202, 204, 210, 211, 356
    death of, 208
"Hitler Diaries," 407
hoaxes, 46, 78, 407. See also finance (financial scandals)
Hobbit, The (Tolkien), 167
Hobson, Valerie, 217
Hobson (minesweeper), 251
Hobson's Choice (film), 259
Ho Chi Minh, 74, 108, 188, 210, 214, 244, 340
Ho Chi Minh Trail, 282
hockey, 109, 203, 267, 285, 345, 397, 441
Hodgkin, Dorothy Mary Crowfoot, 42, 234, 262, 310, 464

Hoff, Marcian (Ted), 346
Hoffa, James Riddle, 57, 273, 327, 349, 369
Hoffman, Dustin, 169, 325, 339, 343, 375, 387, 431
Hoffman, Gaby, 435
Hoffman, Julius, 338, 352
Hoffman-La Roche chemical plant, 376
Hoffman, P. Erich, 22
Hofmannsthal, Hugo von, 39, 47
Hogan, Ben, 53, 229, 239, 251, 255
Holden, William, 81, 239, 257, 271, 375, 399
Holiday Inn (film), 193
Holidays Symphony (Ives orchestral work), 55
Holliday, Billie, 67, 283
Holliday, Judy, 239
Hollywood. See films
"Hollywood Ten" (blacklisted in 1947), 221
Holm, Celeste, 195, 203, 223, 239
Holm, Ian, 455
Holmes, John, 147
Holmes, Oliver Wendell, 13, 86, 159
Holmes, Phillips, 137
Holocaust (TV series), 383
Holocausts
    Armenian, 70
    Cambodian, 124, 336, 368
    Jewish, 154, 174, 188, 192, 415, 416, 429
holography, 222, 316, 318
Holst, Gustav, 69
Holt, Benjamin, 20
Holt, Tim, 193, 229
Holyoake, Keith Jacka, 20, 408
Homage to Catalonia (Orwell), 171
Homage to Mistress Bradstreet (Berryman), 357
Home (Storey play), 343
Home, The: Its Work and Influence (Gilman), 17
Home and the World, The (Tagore), 69
Homeier, Skippy, 195
Home of the Brave (Laurents), 209
homeostasis, 116
Home Owners Loan Corporation (HOLC), 147
Homer, Winslow, 45
hominids, 280, 358, 460
homosexuality, 337
    attitude toward, 59, 123, 353, 357, 383
Honduras, 28, 38, 50
Honecker, Erich, 52, 348, 434, 464
Hong Kong, 186
Hong Kong (steamer), 99
Hooker, John Lee, 75, 435
Hooker Chemical Company, 192, 380
Hoover, Herbert Clark, 87, 120, 124, 140, 141, 312
Hoover, J. Edgar, 268, 357
Hope and Glory (film), 425
Hopkins, Anthony, 443, 449, 455
Hopkins, Frederick G., 26
Hopkins, Harry, 145, 157, 219
Hopkins, Miriam, 147
Hopper, Edward, 327
Hopper, Grace Brewster Murray, 28, 250, 282, 452

hormones, 6, 12, 100, 132, 138, 154, 158, 162, 228, 268
Horne, Lena, 75, 197
Hornet (aircraft carrier), 224
Horney, Karen, 186
Hornsby, Ruston, 20
Horowitz, Vladimir Samoylovich, 21, 437
horse racing, 133, 197, 241, 261, 283, 289, 323, 327, 345
Horthy, Miklós, 92, 274
hospice movement, 278
hostages
    Iran, 392, 396
    Lebanon, 410, 414, 444
    Colombia, 414
hostile takeover, 429, 431
Hotchkiss, Hazel, 41
Hotel Terminus (film), 429
Hot Five, The (jazz group), 113
Hot Line Agreement (U.S.-Soviet), 304
Houghton, Katharine, 325
"Hound Dog" (Song), 267
Hound of the Baskervilles, The (Doyle), 11
    film version, 177
Hounsfield, Godfrey N., 346
Houphoüt-Boigny, Felix, 288
House for Mr. Biswas, A (Naipaul), 293
Houseman, John, 171
House of Bernardo Alba (Garcia Lorca), 305
House of Blue Leaves, The (Guare play), 419
House of Mirth, The (Wharton), 23
House of Tears (Orozco painting series), 53
House Un-American Activities Committee (HUAC), 170, 221, 233, 272
housing
    loans for, 147
    shortages, 195
    rent control, 229
    Levittown, 235
    discrimination in, 331
Houssay, Bernardo A., 224
Houston, Whitney, 307, 421, 451
Houston Opera, 369
hovercraft (hydrofoil), 264, 283, 333
Howard, Ebenezer, 15
Howard, Leslie, 59, 155, 171, 199
Howard, Sidney Coe, 129, 153, 161, 179
Howard, Trevor, 71, 209, 233, 289, 383, 433
Howards End (Forster), 41
    film version, 449
"How Are Things in Glocca Morra?" (song), 223
Howe, Julia Ward, 44
Howe, Louis McHenry, 164
Howl and Other Poems (Ginsburg), 267
Hoxha, Enver, 36, 216, 272, 378, 416
Hoyle, Fred, 64, 226, 274
Hs'en Feng, emperor of China, 34
Hsüan T'ung, emperor of China, 28, 34, 48, 140, 326, 425
Hubbard, L. Ron, 49, 243, 251, 423

Hubble, Edwin Powell, 104, 128, 258
Hubble's law, Hubble's constant, 128
Hubble Space Telescope, 438, 454
Huchinson, Miller Reese, 8
Hudson, Hugh, 397
Hudson, Rock, 115, 417
Hudson River, 438
Hudson River school of painting, 15
Huerta, Victoriano, 54, 60
Huffman, Donald R., 440
Hughes, Barnard, 359
Hughes, Charles Evans, 23, 66, 231
Hughes, Howard Robert, 25, 377
Hughes, Langston, 13, 239, 327
Hukbalahap insurgency (Philippines), 260
Hull, Albert Wallace, 74, 96
Hull, Cordell, 264
Hull, Josephine, 163, 189, 201
Hull House (Chicago), 159
Hülsmeyer, Christian, 20
human-powered flight, 388
human rights, 234, 255, 293, 394
    "right to die," 318
    Helsinki Accords, 370
    South Africa, 454
    See also civil rights movement
Human Sexual Response (Masters and Johnson), 318
Humphrey, Doris, and Humphrey-Weidman school, 379
Humphrey, Hubert Horatio, 48, 330, 384
Humphry, Derek, 444
Hunchback of Notre Dame, The (film), 105
Hundred Flowers Campaign (China), 268
Hungary, 92, 216, 222
    Socialist Republic of, 86
    rebellion suppressed (1956), 266, 278, 348
    becomes free nation (1988), 430
Hunt, E. Howard, 358
Hunt, Lamar, 283
Hunter, Kim, 221
Huntington's disease, 406, 454, 456
Hurricane Andrew, 451. *See also* storms
Hurston, Zora Neale, 9, 167, 291
Hurt, John, 411
Hurt, Mary Beth, 397
Hurt, William, 417, 419
Hussein, Saddam, 166, 348, 388, 442
Hussein I, king of Jordan, 158, 250
Husseini, Haj Amin al, 96, 366
Hussein Ibn Ali, king of the Hejaz, 68, 84, 112, 136, 148
Huston, Anjelica, 251, 417, 427
Huston, John, 29, 185, 227, 245, 251, 365, 415, 427
Huston, Walter, 111, 153, 161, 229, 243, 251
Hutchings, Ashley, 337
Hutton, Timothy, 393
Huxley, Aldous Leonard, 139, 183, 307, 372
Huxley, Julian Sorell, 215, 372
Huxley, Thomas Henry, 372
Hu Yaobang, 64, 420, 432
Hwang, Henry David, 429, 449, 455

Hyakutake, Haruyoshi, 224
Hyatt Regency Hotel disaster, 399
Hyde Amendment, 395
hydrofoil. *See* hovercraft
hydrogen, 52, 62, 66, 136
hydrogen bomb, 34, 176, 192, 248, 256, 260, 272, 328
hydrogen maser clock, 390
hydroplane, 311, 327
hydropower project (Canada), 350
hydrothermal vents, 378
Hyman, Earle, 201

I Am a Camera (Van Druten play), 321
I Am a Fugitive from a Chain Gang (film), 329
I and Thou (Buber), 105
Ibáñez, Vicente Blasco, 69, 97
Ibarruri, Dolores ("La Pasionara"), 440
Iberian Suite (Albéniz piano work), 27
Ibn Saud, king of Saudi Arabia, 10, 84, 108, 112, 147, 256
Ibsen, Henrik, 29
Icarus (asteroid), 234
ice cream cone, 21
Iceland, 224
Iceman Cometh, The (O'Neill play), 215
Ice-T, 451
Ickes, Harold LeClaire, 252
I, Claudius (Graves), 153
iconoscope, 172
Ideal Marriage (Van de Velde), 117
Idle, Eric, 339
Idlewild (later Kennedy) Airport, 231
"If I Had a Hammer" (song), 235
I. F. Stone's Weekly, 257
"I Got Rhythm" (song), 413
I Know Where I'm Going (film), 209
I Know Why the Caged Bird Sings (Angelou), 343
Illmensee, Karl, 396
"I'll Never Smile Again" (song), 183
"I'll See You Again" (song), 129
Illuminations (ballet), 239
I Love Lucy (TV series), 245
"I'm in the Mood" (song), 435
"I'm Just Wild About Harry" (song), 97
immigrants, 23, 75
    at Ellis Island, 3, 30
    laws concerning, 10, 31, 73
immunology, 234
immuno-suppressive drugs, 52, 200
Imo (Belgian steamer), 73
imperialism
    European, 2, 16, 18, 30, 34, 46, 214, 234 (*see also* India)
    American, 6, 10, 50, 168 (*see also* Cuba; Philippines)
    Japanese, 8, 10, 30, 42
impressionism, 29, 53, 119
imprinting, 156
In Cold Blood (Capote), 321
income tax, 69, 110, 195
"incompletability theorem," 40, 134
indanthrene blue, 12
Independent Labour Party (Britain), 2, 26

Independent People (Laxness), 153
India, 16, 298, 355, 368
    British rule, 24, 26, 84, 140, 192
    independence, 128, 214
    partition, 182, 220
    war with Pakistan, 220, 314, 320, 346
    population, 439
    insurrections, 440, 450
    See also Congress Party (India)
Indiana, Robert, 311
Indianapolis auto races, 47, 293. *See also* automobile racing
Indian head penny, 41
Indian National Congress. *See* Congress Party (India)
Indochina
    in World War II, 176, 182
    France and, 214, 238, 240, 244, 258
    Indochina War, 258, 261, 404
Indochine (film), 451
Indonesia, 8, 34, 190, 314, 322, 326
    War of Independence, 210, 214, 234
    vs. Dutch forces, 272, 300
    annexes East Timor, 370
Indus Civilization, The (Wheeler), 256
Industrial Poisons in the United States (Hamilton), 112
Industrial Workers of the World (IWW), 23, 31, 51, 55, 62, 65, 74, 111
Infallible? An Inquiry (Küng), 345
Infectious Waste Tracking Act (1988), 429
inferiority complex, 46
infertility clinic, 395
inflation, 215, 229
influenza
    pandemic, 77, 273
    vaccine, 60, 256
Informer, The (film), 157
Inge, William, 57, 241, 255, 269, 363
Ingenue (album), 451
Ingram, Rex, 97
Ingstad, Helge, 286
Inherit the Wind (Lawrence-Lee play), 287
    film version, 113
Inkatha movement (Zulu), 124, 444
Inkishinikov, Valery, 125
Inönu, Ismet, 362
Inquisitors, The (Andrzejewski), 287
Institute for Advanced Studies (Princeton, N.J.), 146
insulin, 82, 100, 316, 402
Insull, Samuel, 141
insurance industry scandal, 361
Integrated Services Digital Network (ISDN), 424
intelligence ("IQ") tests, 24, 68, 339
    lead blood levels and, 388
Intelsat (communications satellite system), 308, 314
Intercollegiate Athletic Association, 29
intercontinental ballistic missiles (ICBMs), 258, 270, 300, 344
    detection of, 306
    deployment limited, 354, 386

interferometer, 90
interferon, 274, 392, 396
Intermediate Nuclear Forces (INF) Treaty, 424, 428
International Atomic Energy Agency (IAEA), 275
International Brigades (Spain), 160
International Brotherhood of Teamsters, 273, 327
International Business Machines (IBM), 271, 368, 376, 420
PCs, 396, 398, 402, 406, 412, 414
International Chess Federation, 353
International Cometary Explorer (ICE), 416
International Council for Bird Preservation (ICBP), 101
International Criminal Police Organization (INTERPOL), 107
International Fellowship of Reconciliation (IFOR), 86
International Finance Corporation (IFC), 267
International Geophysical Year (IGY), 272, 277, 280
International Labor Organization (ILO), 87
International Ladies' Garment Workers' Union (ILGWU), 39, 357, 405
International Longshoremen's and Warehousemen's Union (ILWU), 167
International Longshoremen's Association, 151, 281
International Monetary Fund (IMF), 201
International Overseas Services (IOS), 343
International Psycho-Analytical Association, 10
International Style. See architecture
International Style, The (Johnson and Hitchcock), 141
International Union for Conservation of Nature and Natural Resources (UCN), 231
International Woman Suffrage Alliance (IWSA), 18
International Women's Day, 43
Internet, 460
Interstate Commerce Commission (ICC), 27
In the Heat of the Night (film), 325
In the Matter of J. Robert Oppenheimer (Kipphardt play), 331
In the Penal Colony (Kafka), 83
Intifada (Uprising) (Palestine), 430
Intolerance (film), 69, 205
Into the Woods (musical), 425
intrauterine device (IUD), 40, 133
Introduction to Mathematical Philosophy (Russell), 84
Intruder in the Dust (Faulkner), 229
Invisible Man, The (Ellison), 251
Invisible Man, The (Wells), 147
film version, 327
in vitro fertilization, 378, 382, 395, 419
Ionesco, Eugène, 53, 465
ionosphere, 12, 108
Iraklin (ferry), 323
Iran, 46, 132, 210, 216, 347, 383

revolution, 4, 88, 382
oil, 38, 244
National Front Party, 244
earthquakes, 299, 439
wars with Iraq, 338, 392, 400, 410, 428
hostages, 392, 396
civilian airliner shot down, 430
refugees in, 443
Hezbollah forces, 454
Iran-Contra Affair, 414, 418, 424, 426, 436
Iraq, 92, 98, 282, 294, 348, 388
Kurdish risings in, 132, 142, 286, 400, 410, 428, 442
vs. Israel, 226, 324, 358
Ba'ath Party coup, 332
wars with Iran, 338, 392, 400, 410, 428
U.S. sailors killed by, 426
invades Kuwait, 438
in Persian Gulf War, 442
Shi'ite rebellion, 442
Ireland
Civil War, 54, 68, 96, 100, 352, 456
War of Independence, 68, 84, 96, 100
partitioned, 94, 100
Republic of, 100, 372
in Economic Community, 360
cease-fire in, 462
See also Abbey Theatre (Dublin); Irish Free State; Irish Republican movement and Army
Irgun Zvai Leumi (Palestine), 134, 198, 214
Irish Free State, 96, 100, 142
Irish Republican movement and Army
Sinn Fein, 24, 80, 84
Volunteers and Citizen Army, 54, 68
guerrilla actions by, 96, 336, 388, 404, 445
Provisional ("Provos"), 336
peace talks, 456
"iron curtain" speech (Churchill), 214
Irons, Jeremy, 403, 439, 455
Ironweed (Kennedy), 407
film version, 411
Iroquois Theater fire, 15
Irving, Henry, 27, 127
Irving, John, 383
Isaacs, Alick, 274
Is America Safe for Democracy? (McDougall), 99
Isherwood, Christopher, 177, 321
Ishiguro, Kazuo, 455
Islam
"Nation of," see Black Muslims
fundamentalist, 128, 382, 414, 424, 441, 450
extremists, 383
in Sudan, 408
conflict within, 434, 440
Islamic Front (Algeria), 450
"Isn't This a Lovely Day?" (song), 157
isolationism, 174, 256. See also pacifism
isotopes, 50, 54, 84, 98, 156
Israel, 340
army of, 92
state established, 226, 250

Arab-Israeli Wars, see Arab-Jewish conflicts
Camp David Accords (1979), 380, 388
-Soviet cooperation, 429
peace treaty (1994), 460
Italy
laws protecting women and children, 11
and Libya, 46, 50, 106, 136
World War I and postwar, 58, 62, 68, 72, 86, 94, 98
and Ethiopia, 152, 154, 160
Communist Party of, 168
and Albania, 174
World War II, 174, 180, 184, 186, 192, 196, 200, 206, 215
postwar, 222, 260
flood damage in Florence, 321
See also fascism; Mussolini, Benito
It Happened One Night (film), 151
Ito, Hiroboumi, 40
It's a Wonderful Life (film), 217
Ivan the Terrible, Part I (film), 201
Ives, Burl, 111, 265
Ives, Charles, 55, 261
Ivory, James, 35, 41, 405, 415, 449, 455
Ivory Coast, 288
ivory trade, 435
"I Want to Hold Your Hand" (song), 307
Iwerks, Ib, 323
"I Will Always Love You" (song), 451
Iwo Jima, 206

J'Accuse (film), 83
Jack Benny Show (radio), 143
Jack, or the Submission (Ionesco play), 465
Jackson, Alexander Young, 367
Jackson, Glenda, 91, 165, 309, 339, 347, 349, 361, 383
Jackson, Jesse Louis, 190, 349, 406
Jackson, Jonathan, 205
Jackson, Mahalia, 49, 355
Jackson, Michael, 279, 403, 415, 445
Jackson, Mick, 431, 451
Jackson, Robert Houghwout, 261
Jackson, Shirley, 71, 235, 319
Jackson, "Shoeless Joe," 81, 435
Jacob, François, 318
Jacob's Pillow Dance Festival, 357
Jacobs, Aletta, 130
Jacobs, Helen Hull, 141
Jacobsson, Ulla, 263
Jaffrey, Madhur, 405
Jaffrey, Safeed, 401
Jagan, Cheddi, 256
Jagger, Mick, 299
Jamaica, 230, 380, 402, 433
James, Geraldine, 411
James, Henry, 13, 15, 19, 45, 71
James, William, 13, 33, 45
Jane Eyre (film), 203
Janeway, Elizabeth, 57, 349
Jannings, Emil, 85, 133, 243
Jansky, Karl Guthe, 136
Japan
militarism of, 8, 10, 18, 42, 96, 134, 140, 160

pacts and agreements, 10, 30, 31, 162
and Russia/Soviet Union, 30, 74, 100, 176 (see also Japanese-Russian wars)
U.S. immigration restricted, 31
World War I, 58, 74
disasters in, 79, 105, 153
feminism in, 80
and Manchuria/Manchukuo, 134, 138, 146
army coup fails, 160
war with China, 164, 170, 176
World War II, 176, 182-190 passim, 196-202 passim, 206, 208
U.S. embargo on, 181
postwar recovery, 211
"kingmaker" in, 364
stock scandal, 424, 434
Japanese-Americans interned, 194, 201
Japanese-Russian wars, 18, 22, 40, 52, 170
Jaruzelski, Wojciech, 396
Jarvik, Robert K., 274, 402
Jarvis, Gregory B., 420
Jaspers, Karl, 341
Jaurès, Jean, 60
Jaworski, Leon, 358, 364
jazz. See music
Jazz Singer, The (film), 119
Jean Christophe (Rolland), 19
Jean de Florette (film), 419
Jeans, James Hopwood, 90, 220, 226
"Jeeves" novels (Wodehouse), 373
Jeffers, Robinson, 223, 303
Jeffreys, Alec, 410
Jeffries, Jim, 3, 29, 45
Jehovah's Witnesses, 197
Jellicoe, John Rushworth, 158
Jenkins, Charles Francis, 104
Jenrette, John W. Jr., 382
Jensen, Arthur R., 107, 337
Jensen, Carl Oluf, 14
Jensen, Hans Daniel, 228, 306
Jensen, Johannes V., 203
Jericho excavations, 252
Jerusalem, 96, 324
Jesus Christ Superstar (opera), 349
jet planes, 178, 249
jet propulsion, 38, 228
jet stream, 206
Jeux (ballet), 55
Jewel in the Crown, The (TV series), 411
Jewish Documentation Centers, 223, 293
Jewison, Norman, 325, 425
Jews
atrocities against, 14, 22, 32, 39, 90, 146, 170
in government office (U.S.), 27, 69
homeland for, 74
See also anti-Semitism; Holocausts; Israel
Jezebel (film), 437
JFK (film), 443
Jhabvala, Ruth Prawer, 35, 41, 369, 415, 449, 455
Jiang Qing, 60, 318, 374, 452
Jiménez, Juan Ramón, 269

Jinnah, Mohammad Ali, 26, 182, 214, 230
"jitterbugging," 197
Job Corps, 311
Jobs, Steven, 380
Jodl, Alfred, 210
Jodrell Bank Experimental Station (Britain), 274
Joffre, Joseph, 136
Joffrey Ballet, 433
Joffrey, Robert, 133, 433
Johannsen, Wilhelm Ludvig, 40
Johanson, Donald Carl, 198, 358, 364, 402
Johanson, Jai Johanny, 339
Johansson, Ingemar, 283
John XXIII (pope), 279, 297, 307, 385
John, Augustus, 297
John, Elton, 369, 459
John Birch Society, 278
John Brown's Body (Benét), 125
Johnny Belinda (film), 231
John Paul I (pope), 53, 385
John Paul II (pope), 93, 385, 397, 459
Johns, Glynis, 359
Johnson, Amy, 133
Johnson, Ben, 349
Johnson, Celia, 37, 209, 405
Johnson, Earvin "Magic," 269, 285, 385, 393, 445
Johnson, Eyvind, 367
Johnson, Jack, 35, 45, 65, 219
Johnson, James Weldon, 51, 173
Johnson, J. Rosamond, 263
Johnson, Lyndon Baines, 36, 302, 308, 324, 330, 362
  programs of, 311, 315
  appointments by, 321, 325, 331
Johnson, Nunnally, 269, 273
Johnson, Philip, 29, 141, 235, 303, 311, 405
Johnson, Rafer Lewis, 287
Johnson, Virginia, 318
Johnson & Johnson, 401
Johnson Space Center, 292
Joint Chiefs of Staff, 398
Jokes and Their Relation to the Unconscious (Freud), 22
Joliot-Curie, Frédéric, 6, 150, 156, 174, 230, 270, 278
Joliot-Curie, Irène, 59, 150, 156, 174, 268
Jolson, Al, 79, 119, 243
Jones, Allan, 161
Jones, Bobby, 15, 107, 117, 131, 351
Jones, Brian, 299
Jones, James (author), 99, 245, 255, 381
Jones, James Earl (actor), 139, 331, 415, 435, 461
Jones, Jennifer, 89
Jones, Jim, 381
Jones, John Paul, 333
Jones, Quincy, 403
Jones, Shirley, 287
Jones, Steve, 371
Jones, Terry, 339
Jones, Tommy Lee, 443
Joplin, Janis, 199, 333, 345
Joplin, Scott, 15, 47, 77, 359, 369
Jordan, Michael, 449, 455
Jordan, 216, 252, 342
  vs. Israel, 226, 324, 358

signs peace treaty, 460
Jorgenson, Christine (formerly George), 250
Joseph (Nez Percé chief), 20
Joseph, Helen Pennell, 25, 453
Joseph and His Brothers (Mann), 151
Josephson, Erland, 353, 359, 429
Jourdan, Louis, 277
journalism, 61, 93, 257
  muckraking, 19, 27
  investigative, 365
Journey into Summer (Teale), 246
Journey's End (Sherriff), 373
Joyce, James, 59, 69, 77, 99, 175, 189, 292, 427
Joyner-Kersee, Jackie, 301, 431
Joy of Sex, The (Comfort), 355
J/psi particle, 364
Juan Carlos, king of Spain, 372
Juárez, Benito, 66
Jude, Der magazine, 69
Judgment at Nuremberg (film), 293
Judith of Bethulia (film), 59
jujitsu, 21
jukebox, 24, 189
Julia, Raul, 417
Julia (film), 379
Julian, Rupert, 115
Juliet of the Spirits (film), 315
June Bug (airplane), 37
Jung, Carl, 10, 50, 96, 296
Jungle, The (Sinclair), 335
Juno and the Paycock (O'Casey play), 109
Jupiter (planet), 58, 348, 360, 366, 378, 388, 434
  hit by comet, 458, 460
Jurassic Park (film), 455
Jurgen (Cabell), 83
Justice Department, U.S., 120
Justine (Durrell), 273

Kádár, János, 266
Kafka, Franz, 63, 83, 111, 113
Kagemusha (film), 393
Kahn, Louis, 11, 259, 365, 367
Kaiser, Henry John, 329
Kaiser-Permanente Plan, 329
Kaiser Wilhelm der Grosse (liner), 5
Kaltenbrunner, Ernst, 210
Kamenev, Lev, 116
Kammerer, Paul, 78
Kander, John, 321
Kandinsky, Wassily, 17, 41, 47, 205
Kane, Robert, 71, 177
Kanin, Garson, 239
Kansai International Airport (Japan), 461
Kansas City Chiefs, 325
Kantor, MacKinlay, 215, 265
Kapitza, Peter, 152, 170, 218
Kaplan, Jonathan, 429
Kapoor, Shashi, 101, 405
Kapp, Wolfgang, and Kapp Putsch, 92
Kapteyn, Jacobus Cornelis, 20, 116
Karajan, Herbert von, 37, 437
Karamanlis, Constantine, 32
Karas, Anton, 235
Karen War of Independence. See Burma
Karloff, Boris, 137, 189, 341
Karmal, Babrak, 386, 420

Kármán, Theodore von, 306
Karp, Haskell, 336
Karpov, Anatoly, 371, 411
Karrer, Paul, 136, 156, 168, 172
Karsavina, Tamara, 43, 45, 51, 55, 85, 93, 385
Kasavubu, Joseph, 284, 314
Kasebier, Gertrude Stanton, 155
Kashmir, 220, 232, 254, 314, 346, 440
Kasparov, Garry, 411
Kassem, Abdul Karim, 276, 306
Katanga, 290, 324
Katmai National Park and Preserve, 51
Katzenberg, Jeffrey, 461
Kaufman, George S., 137, 143, 163, 295
Kaufman, Irving R., 244
Kaufman, Philip, 429
Kaunda, Kenneth David, 110, 312
Kawabata, Yasunari, 333
Kazakhstan, 282, 450
Kazan, Elia, 221, 223, 225, 245, 259
Kazantzakis, Nikos, 265, 275
KDK (Pittsburgh), 93
Keane, George, 225
Kearney, Patrick, 379
Keating, Charles, 447
Keaton, Buster, 323
Keaton, Diane, 353, 365, 389, 397
Kedrova, Lila, 311
Keel, Howard, 229
Keeler, Christine, 306
Keeler, Ruby, 145
Kefauver, Estes, and Kefauver Committee, 240
Keilin, David, 110, 176
Keitel, Harvey, 425
Keitel, Wilhelm, 210
Keller, Helen Adams, 17, 21, 93, 281, 335
Kellogg-Briand Pact (1928), 124, 142
Kelly, Emmett, 391
Kelly, Gene, 53, 179, 245, 251, 287
Kelly, George "Machine Gun," 147
Kelly, Petra, 225, 453
Kelly, Walt, 57, 363
Kelvinator, 81
Kemeny, John, 316
Kempson, Rachel, 169, 347
Kendall, Edward Calvin, 58, 154, 240
Kendrew, John Cowdery, 288
Kennan, George Frost, 220
Kennedy, Arthur, 221, 233, 255, 331
Kennedy, Edward Moore, 112, 142, 152, 336
Kennedy, John Fitzgerald, 74, 152, 257, 284, 292-299 passim, 305, 455
  assassination of, 302, 443, 458, 462
Kennedy, Joseph P., 152
Kennedy, Robert Francis, 112, 142, 152, 330
Kennedy, William, 407
Kennedy Center for the Performing Arts, 353
Kennedy Library, 389
Kennelly, Arthur E., 10
Kennelly-Heaviside layer, 108
Kenney, Annie, 30

Kent State University, 342
Kenya, 250, 306, 310, 358, 432
  Kenya African Union, 216
Kenyatta, Jomo, 171, 210, 216, 310, 340, 382, 384
Kenyon, Kathleen, 252
Kérékou, Ahmed, 354
Kerensky, Alexander Fyodorovich, 72, 346
Kerensky Offensive, 72, 118
Kern, Jerome, 61, 73, 93, 121, 147, 213
Kern, Scott, 425
Kerner Commission (1968), 333
Kerouac, Jack, 119, 273, 341
Kerr, Deborah, 197, 223, 245, 255, 269
Kerr, John, 255
Kerrigan, Nancy, 463
Kerr-McGee, 365, 422
Kert, Larry, 273
Kesey, Ken, 369
Kesselring, Joseph, 189
Kevlar fiber, 316
Kevorkian, Jack, 440, 444
Key Largo (film), 227
Keynes, John Maynard, 87, 157, 219
Keystone Kops, 51
KGB (Soviet secret police), 118
Khachaturian, Aram, 17, 385
Khalifa, Salman ibn Hamad Al, 348
Khama, Seretse, 98, 322, 394
Khasbulatov, Ruslan, 454
Khmer Rouge guerrillas, 124, 244, 336, 368, 382
Khomeini, Ayatollah Ruhollah, 4, 382, 384, 429, 436
Khorana, Har Cobind, 342
Khouri, Bishara al-, 250
Khrushchev, Nikita, 262, 266, 272, 296, 308, 350, 372
Kiangsi Soviet, 130, 136, 146, 150
Kiangya (steamer), 231
Kiche Maru (steamer), 53
kidnapping, 147, 161, 255, 333, 361, 363, 410
  Lindbergh case, 139
  Hearst case, 365
  See also hijacking; hostages
Kikuyu people, 171, 250
Kiley, Richard, 317
Killy, Jean Claude, 327, 331
Kilmer, Joyce, 83
Kim (Kipling), 9
Kimberley, relief of, 2
Kimberly Clark Corporation, 111
Kim Il Sung, 52, 462
Kimmel, Husband Edward, 334
Kimura, Heitaro, 230
King, Billie Jean Moffitt, 199, 321, 361
King, Charles, 124
King, Coretta Scott, 123
King, Ernest Joseph, 270
King, Frank O., 81
King, Martin Luther Jr., 131, 331, 357
  activities of, 86, 263, 271, 303
  awarded Peace Prize, 309
  holiday honoring, 407
King, Rodney, 449
King, Stephen, 225
King, William Lyon Mackenzie, 242

Index

King and Country (film), 313
King and I, The (musical), 245
 film version, 269
Kingdom of Serbs, Croats, and
 Slovenes, 80, 94, 96
King Kong (film), 147
King Lear (Japanese film version),
 415
Kingsley, Ben, 401
Kingsley, Sidney, 157, 167
Kingston, Arthur, 162
Kinney, Terry, 439
Kinnock, Neil Gordon, 406, 426
Kinsey, Alfred, and Kinsey Reports,
 194, 226, 254, 270
Kipling, Rudyard, 9, 33, 165
Kipphardt, Heinar, 331
Kirchner, Ludwig, 23
Kirghizia, 434
Kiribati, 390
Kirkland, Joseph Lane, 389
Kirov, Sergei, 150
Kirov Ballet, 181, 293
Kishinev massacres, 15
Kissinger, Henry, 106, 358
Kiss Me, Kate (musical), 229
Kiss of the Spider Woman, The
 (film), 417
Kizim, Leonid, 422
Klee, Paul, 47, 185
Kleenex, 111
Klein-Rogge, Rudolf, 107
Klem, Bill, 259
Klimt, Gustav, 83
Kline, Kevin, 225, 389, 401
Klinghoffer, Leon, 416
Klute (Pakula film), 347
Knight, Esmond, 245
Knipper, Olga, 283
Knudsen, William S., 187
Koch, Robert, 24
Kodály, Zoltán, 329
Koestler, Arthur, 181
Koffka, Kurt, 50
Kohl, Helmut, 132, 402
Kohlberg Kravis Roberts and Co.,
 429
Köhler, Wolfgang, 50
Kokoschka, Oskar, 397
Kolchak, Alexander, 78, 82, 90, 94
Kolehmainen, Hannes, 51
Kolff, Willem Johan, 196, 274,
 294, 370, 402
Kolingba, André-Dieudonné, 402
Kollwitz, Käthe, 103, 151, 213
Komarov, Vladimir Mikhaylovich,
 324
Kon-Tiki (Heyerdahl), 221
Kopechne, Mary Jo, 336
Korbut, Olga, 353
Korda, Alexander, 147, 271
Korea, 18, 22, 30, 40, 42
 Democratic People's Republic of
  (North), 52, 230, 238, 332
 Republic of (South), 230, 238,
  318
Koreagate, 379
Korean Air Lines flight 007 shot
  down, 406
Korean War, 238, 244, 254, 462
Korematsu v. United States, 201
Koresh, David, 455
Kornberg, Arthur, 326
Korolev, Sergei, 30, 290, 322
Kosinski, Jerzy, 315
Kosygin, Aleksei N., 324

Koussevitsky, Sergei, 249
Kovic, Ron, 435
Kowall, Charles T., 366
Kramer, Stanley, 281, 287, 293,
 317, 325
Kramer v. Kramer (film), 387
Krätschmer, Wolfgang, 440
Krauss, Werner, 85
Krazy Kat (comic strip), 43
Krebs, Hans Adolf, 142, 166
Krebs cycle, 166
Kreisky, Bruno, 440
Kreisler, Fritz, 303
Krenwinkel, Patricia, 337
Kreuger, Ivar, 143
Kreutzmann, Bill, 315
Krieger, Bobby, 317
Krikalev, Sergey, 450
Krist, Gary Steven, 333
Kristin Lavransdatter (Undset), 93
Kristofferson, Kris, 369
Kroto, Harry W., 414
Krupp, Alfred, 33, 197, 245, 329
Krupskaya, Nadezhda, 178
Krutch, Joseph Wood, 252
Kubitschek, Juscelino, 264
Kubler-Ross, Elisabeth, 118, 338
Kubrick, Stanley, 309, 331
Kuhn, Thomas Samuel, 103, 298
Kuiper, Gerard Peter, 222, 230, 234
Kukla, Fran and Ollie (TV show),
 231
Ku Klux Klan (KKK), 63, 113, 309,
 315, 351
Kun, Béla, 86, 178
Kundera, Milan, 411, 429
Küng, Hans, 125, 345
Kunkel, Louis, 422
Kuomintang (China), 398
 founded, reorganized, 60, 100,
  106
 on Northern Expedition, 106,
  116, 120, 122
 vs. Communists, 118, 130, 136,
  146, 188, 196, 210, 214, 222,
  226
 Soviet advisers to, 172, 248
kurchatonium (element 104), 308
Kurchatov, Igor Vasilevich, 218,
 308
Kurdish national movement, 8,
 102, 112. *See also* Iraq
Kurosawa, Akira, 43, 95, 239, 259,
 271, 393, 415
Kurtz, Swoosie, 419
Kurtz, Thomas, 316
Kuwait, 294, 438, 442
Kwajalein, 202
Kwolek, Stephanie L., 316

La Bianca, Leo and Rosemary, 337
labor unions, 35, 189, 219, 253
 strikes by, 11, 39, 83, 161, 167
 founded, 23, 101, 113, 315
 Wagner Act and, 155, 167, 223,
  258
 Mexican, 163
 wartime controls, 201
 Taft-Hartley Act and, 221, 223
 teamsters, 273, 327
 See also AFL-CIO; Industrial
  Workers of the World (IWW);
  strikes
Labour Party (Australia), 354
Labour Party (Britain), 2, 26, 66,
 156, 395, 406

and Labour government, 193,
 207, 208, 215, 246
 initiates Health Service, 215, 231
 Labour-Liberal coalition, 364
La Cage aux Folles, 383 (film)
Lachaise, Gaston, 51
Ladd, Alan, 255
Ladenburg, Mrs. Adolph, 13
Ladies' Home Journal, 23
Ladone, Jason, 425
Lady, Be Good (musical), 109
Lady Chatterley's Lover
 (Lawrence), 123
Lady in the Dark (musical), 189
Ladysmith, siege of (Boer War), 2,
 52
Ladysmith Black Mambazo, 421
laetrile, 396
La Follette, Robert Marion, 108,
 114
Lagerkvist, Pär, 247
Lagerlöf, Selma, 41, 97, 125, 185
La Guardia, Fiorello H., 197, 224
Laing, R. D., 286, 316
Lamotta, Jake, 245
Lancaster, Burt, 57, 227, 245, 255,
 259, 285, 293, 305, 311, 365,
 375, 435, 461
Lanchester, Elsa, 147
Land, Edwin Herbert, 40, 142, 222
Land and Water Conservation Fund
 Act (1964), 311
"land art," 355
Landis, Kenesaw Mountain, 83
"Land of Hope and Glory, The"
 (anthem), 7
Landon, Alfred M., 160
Landon, Margaret, 217
Landowska, Wanda, 285
Landru, Charles, 223
Landry, Tom, 289
Landsat satellite, 354
Landsteiner, Karl, 2, 122, 180,
 198
Lang, Fritz, 107, 117, 137, 427
Lang, k. d., 451
Lang, Walter, 269
Lange, David Russell, 412
Lange, Dorothea, 161, 317
Langevin, Paul, 62
language
 human, 97, 275
 computer, *see* computers
Language (Sapir), 97
Language, Truth, and Logic (Ayer),
 165
Lansbury, Angela, 387, 407, 413
Lansky, Meyer, 129
Lanzmann, Claude, 415
Laos, 238, 282, 286
 Civil War, 300, 360, 368
Lapine, James, 425
La Pasionara, 440
La Porte, Pierre, 338
Largo Caballero, Francisco, 218
Larkin, James, 54
Larned, William A., 41
Larrimore, Earle, 135
Lascaux cave paintings, 182, 304
lasers, 72, 284, 316, 416
 laser printer, 368
Lasker, Emanuel, 97, 189
Lasky, Jesse, 59
Last Emperor, The (film), 425
Last Judgment, The (Michelangelo
 fresco), 459

Last Picture Show, The (film), 349
Last Temptation of Christ, The
 (Kazantzakis), 265
 film version, 425
Last Waltz, The (film), 375
Las Vegas, Nevada, 215
Late George Apley, The (Mar-
 quand), 290
Lateran Treaty, 128, 179
Lathrop, Julia, 51
La Tourneaux, Robert, 333
Lattimore, Owen, 240, 422
Latvia, 78, 84, 92, 434
 World War II, 174, 200
 granted independence, 446
Laue, Max von, 50, 60, 290
Laughton, Charles, 147, 155, 259,
 303
Laurents, Arthur, 209
Laurier, Wilfrid, 88
Laval, Pierre, 212
Lavender Hill Mob, The (film),
 245
Laver, Rod, 299, 313, 341
Lavrovsky, Leonid, 181
lawn mower, 13
Law of the Sea Convention
 (LOSC), 401
Lawrence, Carol, 273
Lawrence, D. H., 55, 63, 91, 123,
 135
Lawrence, Ernest Orlando, 8, 136,
 278, 294
Lawrence, Gertrude, 111, 117, 133,
 189, 209, 245, 253
Lawrence, Jerome, 269, 287, 383
Lawrence, Thomas Edward ("of
 Arabia"), 68, 158
Lawrence of Arabia (film), 143,
 299
lawrencium (element 103), 294
Lawson, Ernest, 35
Laxness, Haldor, 153, 265
Layton, Larry John, 381
Lazear, Jesse William, 2
LD_{50} (median lethal dose) test, 120
Leach, Bernard Howell, 183
Leachman, Cloris, 349
lead
 gasoline containing, 96
 laws banning, 349, 388, 419
Leadbelly, 237, 241
League of Nations, 80, 82, 87, 91,
 92
 mediation by, 136
 protests by, 154
League of Their Own, A (film), 451
League of Women Voterse (LWV),
 90
Leakey, Louis Seymour Bazett, 16,
 108, 204, 280, 286, 326, 354
Leakey, Mary, 204, 280, 354
Leakey, Richard Erskine Frere, 204,
 354, 358
Lean, David, 109, 209, 211, 217,
 259, 271, 299, 315, 411
Leaud, Jean-Pierre, 361
Leavitt, Henrietta Swan, 50, 76,
 104
Lebanon, 216, 338, 430
 Maronite Phalange Party, 162,
  250, 276, 370, 400
 vs. Israel, 226, 342, 382, 400,
  404, 454
 Civil War, 276, 370, 410, 434,
  438

Syria vs., 374, 438
  holds hostages, 410, 414, 444
le Carré, John, 139, 293, 305, 365, 401
Leclerc, Jacques Philippe, 12, 224
Le Corbusier, 251, 321
Leda (satellite of Jupiter), 366
Lederer, Raymond F., 382
Le Duc Tho, 358
Led Zeppelin, 333
Lee, Gypsy Rose, 283
Lee, Harper, 287
Lee, Jennie, 290
Lee, Mitch, 317
Lee, Robert E., 269, 287, 383
Lee, Spike, 315, 451
Lee, Tsung-Dao, 266
Le Gallienne, Eva, 117
Léger, Alexis St.-Léger. See Perse, St.-John
Leger, Fernand, 267
legionnaire's disease, 374
Legion of Honor, 14
Lehar, Franz, 23
Lehman, Herbert Henry, 197, 306
Lehmann, Lotte, 377
Leigh, Vivien, 57, 175, 215, 245, 317, 327
Leith, Emmet N., 316
Lemaître, Georges, 118, 226, 322
Lemmon, Jack, 281, 385, 403
Le Mond, Greg, 421
lemur, dwarf, 436
Lemus, José Maria, 286
Le Neve, Ethel, 43
Lenglen, Suzanne, 85, 173
Lenihan, Winifred, 105
Lenin, Vladimir Illich, 72, 97, 108
  forms party, 14, 50, 86
  portrait destroyed, 145
  colleagues of, 172, 178
Leningrad, Siege of, 185, 186, 187, 200
Lennon, John, 183, 277, 307, 309, 325, 339, 395
Lenya, Lotte, 125, 261, 399
Leonard, Hugh, 359
Leonard, Robert Z., 183
Leonov, Aleksei, 314
Leopard, The (film), 305
Leopold, Nathan, 109
leprosy (Hansen's disease), 370
lepton, 216
Lerner, Alan Jay, 81, 225, 277, 423
Lesage, Jean, 288
Lescot, Elie, 216
Lesh, Phil, 315
Lesotho, 322
Lessing, Doris, 87, 301
Lester, Jon, 425
Lester, Richard, 309
Letchworth community, England, 17
Letelier del Solar, Orlando, 374
Let History Judge (Medvedev), 349
Let It Be (album), 345
"Let's Have Another Cup of Coffee" (song), 143
Let Us Now Praise Famous Men (Agee), 187
leukemia, 150, 390
Levene, Phoebus Aaron Theodor, 38, 128
Lever House (New York), 251
Lévesque, René, 332
Levi-Montalcini, Rita, 40

Levin, Ira, 331
Levine, Dennis, 419
Levinson, Barry, 431
Lévi-Strauss, Claude Gustave, 276
Levitt, William, and Levittown, 235
Levy, David, 458
Lewin, Albert, 87
Lewis, Carl, 411
Lewis, Gilbert Newton, 68
Lewis, John Llewellyn, 157, 341
Lewis, Ralph, 63
Lewis, Robert, 221
Lewis, Sinclair, 91, 101, 113, 121, 129, 133, 137, 153, 247, 287
Leyte (aircraft carrier), 257
Leyte Gulf, 202
Li, Choh Hao, 268
Liaquat Ali Khan, 246
Libby, Willard Frank, 36, 220, 290, 394
libel case (1964), 311
Liberia, 394, 440
Liberty (yacht), 407
Liberty Bell 7 spacecraft, 292
Liberty Loan Act (1917), 73
Libya
  Italy in, 46, 50, 106, 136
  independent state, 246
  Qaddafi takes, 338
  Chad vs., 368, 424
  -U.S. confrontation, 396
Lichtenstein, Roy, 421
Liddy, G. Gordon, 358
Lie, Trygve Halvdan, 214, 334
Liebman, Ron, 387
Liebnecht, Karl, 84
Liebowitz, Samuel S., 135
lie detector. See polygraph machine
Lifar, Serge, 125, 129
Life and Death of Colonel Blimp, The (film), 197
Life of the Bee, The (Maeterlinck), 8
Like a Virgin (album), 407
L'il Abner (comic strip), 153
Lili (musical), 257
Liliom (Molnar play), 39, 211
Lillie, Beatrice, 111, 433
"Limehouse Blues" (song), 111
Limelight (film), 249
Limits of Growth, The (Meadows), 352
Lin, Maya, 401, 435
Lin Biao, 32, 350
Lincoln head penny, 41
Lincoln Memorial, 103
Lindbergh, Anne Morrow, 133, 139
Lindbergh, Charles Augustus, 15, 119, 133, 139
Lindbergh, Charles Augustus Jr., 139, 161
Lindbergh machine (perfusion pump), 160, 254
Lindblad, Bertil, 116
Lindblom, Bunnel, 285
Lindemann, Jean, 274
Lindsay, Robert, 421
Linear B, 250
linguistics. See language
Lion in Winter, The (Goldman play), 321
  film version, 331
Lion King, The (film), 459
"Lion of Kashmir," 24
Liotta, Domingo, 336
Liotta, Ray, 435

Lipchitz, Jacques, 363
Li Peng, 124, 424
Lipmann, Fritz Albert, 222
"Liquid Paper," 268
Liston, Sonny, 299, 313
Liszt, Franz, 163
Li Ta-chao, 90
literacy tests, 73
Lithgow, John, 429
Lithuania, 78, 84, 106, 174, 434
  granted independence, 446
Littérature magazine, 83
Little, Arthur D., 12
Little, Malcolm. See Malcolm X
Little Big Man (film), 345
Little Caesar (film), 363
Little Foxes, The (Hellman play), 177
  film version, 187
Little House on the Prairie (Wilder), 157
Little Johnny Jones (musical), 19
Little Night Music, A (musical), 359
Little Orphan Annie (comic strip), 111
Little Prince, The (St.-Exupéry), 197
Little Review, The magazine, 77
Little Rock (Ark.) schools, 103, 281
Little White Bird, The (Barrie), 23
Litvak, Anatole, 229, 269
Litvinov, Maksim Maksimovich, 248
Liu Shaoqi, 340
Liuzzo, Viola, 315
Live Aid (rock music benefit), 415
Live Dead (album), 343
Liverpool Oratorio (McCartney orchestral work), 445
Livesey, Roger, 197, 209
Livingstone, Mary, 143
Living Theater, The, 247
Lloyd, Frank, 155
Locarno Treaties. See Treaties
Locascio, Frank, 451
Lockheed scandal, 364, 369, 432
Lockwood, Belva Bennett, 76
Lockwood, Gary, 331
Loden, Barbara, 311
Loeb, Richard, 109
Loewe, Frederick, 225, 277
Loewe v. Lawlor, 24
Loewi, Otto, 98
Logan, Ella, 223
Logan, Joshua, 269
logical positivism, 163
Lolita (Nabokov), 265
Lolly Willowes (Warner), 385
Lomax, John, 241
Lombardi, Vince, 285, 325
London, Fritz, 120
London, Jack, 15, 71
London Naval Conference (1930), 130, 132
London Society of Psychical Research, 50
Lone, John, 415, 455
Loneliness of the Long Distance Runner, The (film), 301
Lonesome Dove (McMurtry), 417
Long, Huey Pierce, 156, 217
Long, John Luther, 3, 19
Long Day's Journey into Night (O'Neill play), 267

Longden, Johnny, 197, 323, 345
Long March (China), 150, 156
long-playing records, 228, 400
Long-Range Transbondary Air Pollution (LRTAP), Convention on, 389
Longstreet, James, 20
Long Voyage Home, The (O'Neill play), 73
Lon Nol, 342
Look Back in Anger (Osborne play), 267
Look Homeward, Angel (Wolfe), 129
Loos, Anita, 97
Loose Ends (Weller play), 389
Lopokova, Lydia, 137
Lord, Pauline, 95
Lord Jim (Conrad), 3
Lord of the Flies, The (Golding), 261
Lord of the Rings, The (Tolkien), 259, 263
Loren, Sophia, 111, 155, 293
Lorenz, Konrad Zacharias, 16, 156, 304, 360, 436
Lorin, René, 38
Loring, Eugene, 171
Lorre, Peter, 137, 185, 191
Los Angeles Lakers, 283, 285, 301, 385, 393, 445, 449
Los Angeles Raiders, 417, 435
Los Angeles Rams, 247
Los Angeles Times building, 43
Losey, Joseph, 305, 313
Lost Horizon (Hilton), 147
  film version, 279
Lost in Yonkers (Simon play), 445
Lost Weekend, The (film), 211
Lottery, The (Jackson), 235
Lou Gehrig's disease, 189, 424, 456
Louis, Joe, 61, 151, 167, 235, 241, 247, 399
Louise (opera), 3
Louisiana Purchase Exposition. See St. Louis Fair
Love Canal, 192, 380
Love for Three Oranges, The (opera), 97
Love in the Time of Cholera (García Márquez), 411
Love Is Not Enough (Bettelheim), 240
Lovell, James A. Jr., 332, 344
Lovell House (Los Angeles), 129
Lovelock, James, 388
"Love Me Tender" (song), 267
Lowell, Amy, 51
Lowell, Percival, 24, 70, 130
Lowell, Robert, 75, 311, 381
Lowell Observatory (Arizona), 70
Lower Depths, The (Gorky), 11
Loy, Myrna, 25, 153, 215, 457
"loyalty oaths," 220
LSD, 196, 328
Lubavich, Hasidim, 15
Lubitsch, Ernst, 85, 147, 177, 227
Lucas, George, 211, 379
Luce, Claire, 141
Luce, Henry Robinson, 107
Luciano, Charles "Lucky," 129, 217
"Lucy in the Sky with Diamonds" (song), 325
Lucy: The Beginnings of Human Kind (Johanson), 402

Luftwaffe, 180
Lugosi, Bela, 137, 271
Lukas, Paul, 187, 197, 351
Luks, George, 35
Lumet, Sidney, 311, 317, 369, 375
Lumière, Louis, 32
Lumumba, Patrice, 284, 290
Luna spacecraft, 320, 344, 352
Lunik moon probes, 280, 282
Lunn, Arnold, 49, 101
Lunt, Alfred, 147
Lupino, Ida, 187
LuPone, Patti, 387
LuPone, Robert, 369
Luria, Salvador Edward, 192, 208, 338
Lurie, Alison, 411
Lusitania (liner), 33, 64
lutetium (element 71), 32
Luthuli, Albert, 288, 326
Luxemburg, Rosa, 84
Lvov, Prince Georgy, 72
Lwoff, André, 318
Lyakhov, Vladimir, 428
Lyme disease, 374, 402
lynchings, 147, 221, 263
Lynd, Robert Staughton and Helen Merrell, 129
Lynn, Vera, 89
Lynne, Jeff, 431
Lysenko, Trofim, 128, 316, 348, 376
lyzozyme (human enzyme), 100

M (film), 137
McAnally, Ray, 431
MacArthur, Arthur, 2, 52
MacArthur, Douglas, 52, 140, 244, 312
McAuliffe, S. Christa, 420
Macbeth (Japanese film version), 271
McBride, Sean, 372
McCane, Kitty, 111
McCarran Internal Security Act (1950), 238
McCarthy, Eugene Joseph, 70
McCarthy, Joseph Raymond, 36, 274
    McCarthyism, 89, 122, 182, 238, 240, 253, 255, 319, 350, 353, 357, 436
    Army-McCarthy hearings, 258, 290
McCartney, Paul, 193, 277, 307, 309, 325, 339, 349, 435, 445
McClintock, Barbara, 14, 244, 452
McClung, Clarence, 12
McCollum, Elmer, 56
McCormack, John, 69, 213
McCormack, Patty, 261
McCowen, Alec, 301, 383
McCrea, Joel, 141
McCullers, Carson, 75, 241, 327
MacDonald, Colette, 387
MacDonald, James, 105
MacDonald, Jeffrey, 347, 387
MacDonald, Ramsay, 156, 168
McDonald, Richard and Maurice, and McDonald's chain, 183
McDougall, William, 99
MacDowell, Edward, 39
Macedonia, 10
McEnroe, John, 387, 397, 403
McFarlane, Robert, 414
McGillis, Kelly, 429

McGinley, Phyllis, 289
McGovern, George Stanley, 102, 352
McGraw, John J., 13, 19
McGuire, Dorothy, 223
Machel, Samora, 148, 422
Machu Picchu, 45
Macias, Francisco, 334
McIndoe, Archibald Hector, 182
Mack, Connie, 7
McKay, Claude, 233
MacKaye, Benton, 113
Macke, August, 47, 63
McKechnie, Donna, 369
McKellan, Ian, 393
MacKellar, Helen, 91
Mackenzie, James, 12
McKern, Leo, 319
McKernan, Ron, 315
Mackinac Bridge (Michigan), 279
McKinley, William, 6
McLaglen, Victor, 157
MacLaine, Shirley, 155, 407
Mackle, Barbara Jane, 333
MacLean, Donald, 32, 244
MacLeish, Archibald, 251, 405
Macleod, John J. R., 94
McLuhan, Marshall, 49, 298, 325, 395
McManus, George, 55
McMillan, Edwin Mattison, 180, 248
Macmillan, Harold, 420
MacMillan, Kenneth, 305, 347, 379, 397
MacMurray, Fred, 201
McMurtry, Larry, 349, 407, 417
McNair, Ronald E., 420
McNally, Stephen, 231
McNamara, James B., 43
McNamara, John J., 43
MacNaughton, Alan, 431
McNeil, Claudia, 283, 293
MacNicol, Peter, 401
McPherson, Aimée Semple, 107, 117, 205
McTeague (Norris), 111
McVie, Christine, 379
McVie, John, 325
Madagascar, 222, 290, 436
Madame Butterfly (play and opera), 3, 19, 111
Madame Dubarry (film), 85
Madero, Francisco, 40, 44, 54
Madigan, Amy, 435
Madison Square Garden (New York), 3, 27
Madness and Civilization (Foucault), 293
Madonna, 279, 407, 451
Madsen v. Women's Health Center, 459
Maeterlinck, Maurice, 8, 39, 47
Mafeking, relief of (Boer War), 2
Mafia, 451
Magallanes, Nicholas, 229, 239
Magee, Patrick, 309
Magellan spacecraft, 434, 440
Maggiorani, Lamberto, 227
"magic bullet," 42
Magician, The (film), 281
Magic Mountain, The (Mann), 111
Maginot Line, 176, 180
Magloire, Paul, 240
Magnani, Anna, 37, 207, 363
magnetic fields, 28

extremely low frequency (ELF), 390
magnetic ("hard") disk, 298
magnetic resonance, 172, 216
    imager (MRI), 358, 380
magnetic tape, 4, 240, 244, 298
magnetron, 96
Magnificent Ambersons, The (Tarkington), 79
    film version, 193
Magnificent Seven, The (film), 259
Magsaysay, Ramón, 16, 256, 274
Mahabharata (film), 425
Mahathir bin Mohammad, Datuk Seri, 398
Mahfouz, Naguib, 431
Mahgoub, Mohammed Ahmed, 340
Mahler, Gustav, 49
Mahoney, John, 419
Maiastra (Brancusi sculpture), 51, 181
Mailer, Norman, 107, 209, 333, 379, 385
Maillol, Aristide, 205
Maiman, Theodore Harold, 284
Main Street (Lewis), 91
Major, John, 440
Makarios III, archbishop of Cyprus, 268, 280
Makarova, Natalia, 397
Make Room! Make Room! (Harrison), 361
Malagasy rising, 222. *See also* Madagascar
Malamud, Bernard, 61, 423
Malan, Daniel, 228, 282
malaria, 19, 142, 232, 294
Malawi, 310
Malaya, 272, 306
    Civil War (1948-1960), 228
Malaysia, 306, 326, 342, 383, 398
Malcolm X, 113, 257, 315, 319
    film about, 451
Malcovich, John, 425
Malden, Karl, 221, 259
Maldives, the, 316
Male and Female (Mead), 236
Malenkov, Georgi Maksimilianovich, 12, 262, 432
Malevich, Kasimir, 63, 77, 159
Mali, 290
Malik, Art, 411
Malina, Judith, 247
Malle, Louis, 425
Mallon, "Typhoid Mary," 60
Malone, Moses, 387
Malraux, André, 9, 145, 161, 377
Malta, 312
Maltese Falcon, The (film), 29, 185
Mambo Kings Play Songs of Love, The (Hijuelos), 431
Mame (musical), 407
Mamet, David, 225
Man and Superman (Shaw play), 23
Manarov, Musa, 428
Man at the Crossroads (Rivera mural), 145
Mancheno, Carlos, 222
Manchu dynasty, 2, 6, 28, 44, 48, 140, 326, 425
Manchukuo. *See* Manchuria
Manchuria, 2, 18, 22, 30
    Japan and (Manchukuo), 134, 138, 140, 146, 326

Manchurian-Soviet border wars, 176, 216, 222, 336
Mandarins, The (Beauvoir), 269
Mandela, Nelson Rolihlahla, 80, 298, 438, 454, 460
Mandela, Winnie Nomzano, 155
Mandelstam, Osip, 173
Man Died, The (Soyinka), 355
Man for All Seasons, A (Bolt play), 287
    film version, 319
Mangano, Silvana, 239, 365
Manhattan (film), 389
Manhattan (oil tanker), 339
Manhattan Project, 52, 174, 180, 182, 190, 194, 254
manic depression, genetic marker for, 426
Manifesto of Surrealism (Breton), 109
Man in the Gray Flannel Suit, The (Wilson), 269
Mankiewicz, Herman J., 185, 239
Mann, Daniel, 393
Mann, Heinrich, 133
Mann, Thomas, 7, 111, 131, 151, 359
Mann ("White Slavery") Act (1910), 41
Mannerheim, Karl Gustaf Emil, 248
Mannerheim Line, 176, 180
Manners, J. Hartley, 53
Man of Aran (film), 151
Man of La Mancha (musical), 317
Man of Property, A (Galsworthy), 27
Manon Lescaut (opera), 111
Manon of the Spring (Pagnol), 419
Man's Fate (Malraux), 9, 145
Mansfield, Katherine, 93, 103, 107
Man's Hope (Malraux), 161
Man's Most Dangerous Myth (Montagu), 194
Manson, Charles, 337
Man's World, Woman's Place (Janeway), 349
Mantle, Mickey, 267
Man with the Golden Arm, The (Algren), 235
Manzarek, Ray, 317
Manzù, Giacomo, 37, 147, 311, 447
Mao Zedong, 60, 96, 118, 268, 276, 318, 374
Mapai (Socialist) Party, 132
Mapplethorpe, Robert, 225, 439
Maradona, Diego, 447
Ma Rainey's Black Bottom (Wilson play), 411
Marat/Sade (Weiss play), 309
Marble, Alice, 57, 161, 177, 239, 441
Marc, Franz, 47, 71
March, Fredric, 141, 147, 187, 193, 203, 215, 267, 287, 311, 371
Marchand, Nancy, 257
March of Humanity in Latin America, The (Siqueiros mural), 305
"March on Washington" (1963), 303, 389
Marciano, Rocky, 247, 257, 269
Marconi, Guglielmo, 4, 6, 40, 168

Marcos, Ferdinand Edralin, 76, 354, 418, 436
Marcuse, Herbert, 265, 391
Margo (actress), 157
Margulis, Lynn, 388
Maria Candelaria (film), 195
Maria Chapdeleine (film), 463
Mariah Carey (album), 345
Marin, John, 259
Marine Mammal Protection Act (1972), 355
Mariner spacecraft, 298, 314, 338, 348, 360, 366
Marines, U.S., 38, 50, 152, 214
Maris, Roger, 293
"Marius" trilogy (Pagnol plays), 163, 261
Markham, Beryl, 163
Markova, Alicia, 137, 187
Marley, Bob, 213, 389, 399
Marlowe, Gloria, 263
Marlowe, Hugh, 239
Marquand, J. P., 291
Márquez, Gabriel García. *See* García Márquez, Gabriel
Married Love (Stopes), 79
Mars (planet), 222, 314, 338, 366, 374, 430
Mars Observer spacecraft, 454
Mars spacecraft, 347
Marsden, Ernest, 44
Marsh, Howard, 121
Marsh, Mae, 63
Marshall, E. G., 215, 255
Marshall, George C., 214, 220, 282
Marshall, Penny, 451
Marshall, Thurgood, 37, 325, 457
Marshall Plan, 220, 350
Marshall University football team, 345
Martells, Cynthia, 449
martial arts, 21
Martin, Clyde E., 226, 254
Martin, Mary, 23, 57, 197, 235, 283, 441
Martin du Gard, Roger, 101, 167
Martin Luther King Day, 407
Martinson, Harry, 367
Marty (TV film), 257
Marx, Groucho, 381
Marx Brothers, 149
Mary Rose (Henry VIII's flagship), 402
Masaharu, Homma, 218
Masaryk, Jan, 168, 230
Masaryk, Tomás Garrigue, 156, 168
Masefield, John, 327
masers, 260, 284, 390
M*A*S*H (film), 343
Masina, Giulietta, 93, 259, 267, 315, 463
Massachusetts Institute of Technology, 48, 176
Massenet, Jules, 43, 53
Massey, Anna, 409, 455
Massey, Daniel, 409
Massey, Raymond, 171, 183, 225, 409
Massine, Leonid, 73, 85, 93, 389
"massive retaliation," 262
mass spectrometer, 84
Massu, Jacques, 276
Masters, William, 318
"Masters of War" (song), 303

Mastroianni, Marcello, 107, 285, 305
Masur, Kurt, 123
"Match King," the, 143
Matchmaker, The (Wilder play), 305
mathematics, 6, 92, 96, 112, 134, 158, 160
    "great paradox" in, 10, 40
    game theory in, 96, 124
    Fermat's last theorem, 454
Mathias, Bob, 229
Matisse, Henri, 261
Matlin, Marlee, 419
Matlock, Glen, 371
Matsui, Iwane, 232
Matsushita, Konosuke, and Matsushita Electric Industrial Company, 81
Matteotti, Giacomo, 108
Matthau, Walter, 311
Matthews, D. H., 284
Matthews, Thomas, 286
Mauchly, John, 214, 244
Maugham, Somerset, 65, 87, 319
Mau Mau Society (Kenya), 250
Mauriac, François, 251, 347
Maurice (Forster), 59, 353
Mauritania, 290, 374
Mauritius, 334
Maurras, Charles Marie Photius, 250
Maxwell, Robert, 107, 447
May, Alan Nunn, 216
Mayaguez (merchant ship), 368
Mayakovsky, Vladimir, 79, 125, 129, 135
Mayer, Maria Goeppert, 28, 228, 306, 356
May 4th Movement (China), 88
May 30th Movement (China), 112
M'ba, Léon, 288, 334
Mboya, Tom, 134, 340
M. Butterfly (Hwang play), 429
    film version, 455
Mead, Margaret, 10, 124, 236, 384
Meadows, Dennis L., 352
Me and My Girl (musical), 421
Meany, George, 263, 389, 395
Meat Inspection Act (1906), 27
Medawar, Peter Brian, 66, 200, 234, 288, 426
Medea (Jeffers adaptation), 223
medical waste, 429
Medicare and Medicaid, 315, 395
medicine
    blood types and transfusions, 2, 122, 180
    organ and tissue transplants, 14, 22, 52, 200, 230, 258, 302, 308, 348, 406, 436
    heart surgery, 22, 34, 58, 160, 200, 254, 262, 274, 294, 310, 324, 336
    artificial parts, 24, 274, 336, 370, 400
    wartime, 68
    women in, 74
    animal experiments, 120, 122, 284
    cardiac catheterization, 128, 186
    antihuman experiments, 146, 458

burn treatment, 182
    CAT and MRI scans, 346, 358, 380
    balloon angioplasty, 378
    fetal surgery, 382
    lasers used in, 416
    robot used in, 416
    See also allergy; disease; drugs; X ray
Mediterranean, The . . . (Braudel), 237
Medium Is the Message, The (McLuhan and Fiore), 325
Medoff, Mark, 393, 419
Medvedev, Roy, 348, 349
Medvedev, Zhores, 272, 348
Meeker, Ralph, 255
Meese, Edwin III, 430
"Meet Me in St. Louis" (song), 19
Mega Borg (supertanker), 438
Meinhof, Ulrike, 332, 354, 376
Mein Kampf (Hitler), 104
Meir, Golda, 340, 384
Meitner, Lise, 74, 174, 182, 332, 334
Melbourne (aircraft carrier), 313
Melford, George, 97
Méliès, Georges, 5, 11, 31
Melitta coffee filters, 37
Mellon, Andrew William, 166
Melotte, Philibert Jacques, 34
meltdowns. *See* nuclear accidents
Melville, Herman, 109
Member of the Wedding, The (McCullers play), 241
Memoirs of Hecate County (Wilson), 215
Memorial Day Massacre (Chicago) (1937), 167
memory, theory of, 234
Mencken, H. L., 87, 287
Mendel, Gregor, and Mendelian theory, 4, 128
Mendel, Lafayette, 56
mendelevium (element 101), 264
Mendeleyev, Dmitri, 264
Mendelson, Mira, 209
Mendès-France, Pierre, 32, 404
Mendez, Chico, 429
Menken, Helen, 101
Men of Good Will (Romains), 141
Menotti, Gian Carlo, 49, 247
Menten, Maud Lenora, 56
Menuhin, Yehudi, 71
Menzies, Robert Gordon, 384
Mercedes-Benz, 153
Mercury (planet), 360, 366
Meredith, Burgess, 157
Meredith, George, 41
Meredith, James, 297
Merkerson, S. Epatha, 429
Merman, Ethel, 41, 153, 217, 283, 415
Merrifield, Robert Bruce, 316
Merrill, Gary, 239
Merritt, Theresa, 411
Merry Widow, The (opera), 23
Mesopotamia, 62, 72, 98, 128
Messiaen, Olivier, 37, 453
Metaxa, Georges, 129
Metaxas, Ioannis, 162, 190
meteorology, 10, 90, 92, 206, 216, 238
    satellite, 282, 286, 288
    weather patterns altered, 445
Metesky, George, 239

"method" acting, 221
Method of Reaching Extreme Altitudes, A (Goddard), 82
Metropolis (film), 117
Metropolitan Museum of Art (New York), 57
Metropolitan Opera (New York), 43, 71, 81, 265, 319, 449
Mexico, 344, 433
    Revolution and Civil War, 40, 44, 54, 60, 64, 68, 88, 90
    Church suppressed, 116
    destabilization, 460
Meyerhold, Vsevolod, 185
Miami Dolphins, 359
Michaelis, Leonor, 56
Michaelis-Menten equation, 56
Michelangelo Buonarroti, 459
Michelson, Albert Abraham, 32, 90, 138
Michener, James, 35, 223
Mickey Mouse, 125, 323
microchips, 288, 346
microfossils, 96, 332. *See also* paleontology
microscope
    electron, 146, 184, 192, 332
    field-emission, 160
    scanning tunneling, 398
Microsoft, 380
microwave oven, 208
microwaves, 338
Mid-Atlantic Ridge, 112
Middleton, Ray, 147
Middletown (Lynd and Lynd), 129
Midgley, Thomas Jr., 96, 132
Midnight Cowboy (film), 339
Midsummer Night's Dream, A (opera), 287
Midway Island, 190
Mies van der Rohe, Ludwig, 133, 269, 331, 339
Mifune, Toshiro, 95, 271
Migrant Mother (Lange photograph), 161
Mihajlovic, Draza, 218
Miki, Takeo, 32, 432
Milankovich, Milutin, 92
Mildred Pierce (Cain), 187
    film version, 209
Mile Long Drawing (De Maria painting), 331
Miles, Sarah, 425
Milestone, Lewis, 133, 395
Milhaud, Darius, 367
militarism
    Japanese, 8, 18, 22, 134, 140, 160
    European, 9, 18, 82, 146, 170
    See also arms race
Milk, Harvey, 383
Milken, Michael, 419, 431
Milky Way galaxy, 20, 76, 106, 246
Milland, Ray, 211
Millay, Edna St. Vincent, 105, 243
Miller, Ann, 387
Miller, Arthur, 65, 221, 233, 263, 331, 353, 393
Miller, Glenn, 21, 205
Miller, Jonathan, 299
Miller, Marilyn, 93, 147, 165
Miller, Neal, 326
Miller, Patsy Ruth, 105
Miller, Stanley, 254
Millett, Kate, 155

Index

Millikan, Robert Andrews, 46, 68, 106, 114, 258
Mills, C. Wright, 267
Mills, Eleanor, 101
Mills, John, 217, 259, 289, 401
Mills, Kerry, 19
Mills Act (1965), 315
Milne, A. A., 117, 269
Milosz, Czeslaw, 49
Mindszenty, József, 348
mine disasters
    (1900-1914), 5, 29, 41, 55, 61
    (1942-1962), 193, 247, 269, 289, 301
    (1968-1975), 335, 357, 371
Mingus, Charles, 103, 391
Minh, Duong Van, 304
minimalism, 159
minimax theory, 124
minimum wage laws, 35, 95, 171
Mining Control Act (1977), 381
miniskirt, 323
Minkoff, Rob, 459
Minkowski, Hermann, 30, 62
Minnelli, Liza, 331
Minnelli, Vincente, 197, 245, 277
Minnesota Mining and Manufac-turing, 125
Minnesota Vikings, 371, 383
"Minnie the Moocher" (song), 463
Minot, George, 116
Minuteman (ICBM), 300, 344
Mir (*Peace*) space station, 420, 426, 428, 436, 450, 456
Miracle in the Gorbals (ballet), 203
Miracle Worker, The (Gibson play), 281
Miranda (satellite of Uranus), 230
Miranda v. Arizona and "Miranda rules," 319
Miró, Joan, 407
Misha' (Saudi Arabian princess), 379
Mishima, Yukio, 115, 345
"Miss America" and "Miss Black America," 89, 99, 211, 405, 449
Missing (film), 403
"missing link," 108
Missionaries of Charity, 45, 241, 387
Missionary Sisters of the Sacred Heart, 75
Mississippi Burning (film), 309, 429
Mississippi Freedom Democratic Party, 310, 354
Missouri (battleship), 208
Mistinguett, 271
Mistral, Frédéric, 19
Mistral, Gabriela, 211, 275
Mitchell, Cameron, 233
Mitchell, John Newton, 370
Mitchell, Joni, 197, 337, 375
Mitchell, Margaret, 5, 161, 237
Mitchell, Reginald Joseph, 162, 163
Mitchell, William "Billy," 112, 164
Mitchom, Morris, 11
Mitchum, Robert, 75, 407
Mitscher, Marc Andrew, 224
Mitterrand, François, 70, 398
Mobutu Sese Seko (Joseph), 134, 284, 314
modernism, 13, 303, 313, 317, 367
    postmodernism, 29
Modern Times (film), 161

Modigliani, Amedeo, 95
Mohammad Ali, shah of Iran, 38
Mohammed Zahir Shah, 60
Mohmand, Abdul Ahad, 428
Mohole Project, 292
Mohorovičić, Andrija, 38
Mohorovičić discontinuity, 38, 292
Moi, Daniel Arap, 382, 432
Molinaro, Edouard, 383
Moller, C. (physicist), 216
Molnar, Ferenc, 39, 211, 253
Molotov, Vyacheslav Mikhailovich, 422
Mommsen, Theodor, 13
Mondale, Walter Frederick, 124, 410
Mondlane, Eduardo, 94, 300, 340
Mondrian, Piet, 73, 205
Monet, Claude, 119
Mongolia, 96
    Outer, 52, 82
    People's Republic, 110
    Inner, 146
Monk, Thelonious Sphere, 75, 405
monkey, new species, 440
"monkey trial," 113, 287
Monkey Wrench Gang, The (Abbey), 369
Monod, Jacques Lucien, 44, 318, 344, 376
Monroe, Marilyn, 119, 257, 269, 281, 301, 311, 313
Monsieur Verdoux (film), 223
Montagnier, Luc, 410
Montagu, Ashley, 26, 194, 238
Montale, Eugenio, 371
Montalva, Eduardo Frei, 46, 404
Montana, Joe, 269, 401, 441
Montand, Yves, 99, 333, 355, 419, 447
Mont Blanc (ammunition ship), 73
Montenegro, 58, 80
Montessori, Maria, 31, 251
Montgomery, Bernard Law, 376
Montgomery, L. M., 35
Montgomery (Ala.) bus boycott, 55, 263
Montgomery Ward, 201
Montreal Canadiens, 203, 267, 285
Montreal Exposition (1967), 326
Montreal Protocol (on ozone layer), 427
Monty Python's Flying Circus (TV series), 339
Monument to the Third Interna-tional (Tatlin design), 91
Mood Indigo (Ellington orchestral work), 139
Moody, Helen Wills, 111, 117
Moog, Robert Arthur, and Moog electronic synthesizer, 154, 310
Moon, Keith, 311
Moon, Sun Myung, 259, 403
    and "Moonies," 259
moon
    distance to, calculated, 216
    landings on, 292, 310, 314, 320, 336, 344, 348, 352
    new moons discovered, 392
    See also space flight
Moon and Sixpence, The (Maugham), 87
Mooney, Thomas J., 69
Moonlight (Pinter play), 455
Moon of the Caribees, The (O'Neill play), 79

Moonstruck (film), 425
Moore, Ann, 381
Moore, Archie, 269
Moore, Dudley, 299
Moore, G. E., 279
Moore, Henry, 315, 423
Moore, Marianne, 357
Moore, Mary Tyler, 393
Moore, Sara Jane, 369
Moorer, Michael, 461
Moorhead, Agnes, 258
Moral Majority, 149, 389
Morante, Elsa, 35
Moravia, Alberto, 35, 293, 441
Moreau, Jeanne, 127
Moreno, Rita, 293
Morenz, Howie, 109
mores, changing, 277
Morgan, Helen, 121, 161
Morgan, J. Pierpont, 7, 31, 57, 71
Morgan, Michelle, 171
Morgan, Thomas Hunt, 42, 64, 148, 210
Morgan Library (New York), 57
Morgenstern, Oskar, 204
Moriarty, Michael, 349, 383
Morison, Patricia, 229
Mormon Church, 463
Moro, Aldo, 382
Morocco, 22, 28, 30, 44, 46, 374
    France in, 16, 50, 96, 116
    Spain and, 116, 160
morphine, 23
Morris, Desmond, 328
Morris, Mary, 111
Morris, William, and Morris Mo-tors, 55, 117
Morrison, Jim, 199, 317, 351
Morrison, Toni, 139, 421, 455
Morro Castle (liner), 153
Mortimer, John, 403
Morton, James, 12
Morton, Jelly Roll, 117, 191
Moscone, George, 383
Mosconi, Willie, 189
Moscow Art Theater, 7, 11, 19, 39, 283
Moscow Summit (1988), 428
Mosel, Tad, 289
Moseley, Henry Gwyn-Jeffreys, 54, 66
Moser-Proell, Annemarie, 349
Moses, Anna Mary Robertson "Grandma Moses," 297
Moslem League (India), 26, 182
Moslems. *See* Islam
Mosley, Oswald, 142, 394
Mossadeq, Mohammed, 244, 254, 328
Mostel, Zero, 301, 311
Mother (Gorky), 33
Motherwell, Robert, 67, 235, 447
Motion Picture Production Code, 133
Mott, Lucretia, 12
Mottel, the Cantor's Son (Ale-ichem), 31
Mountbatten, Louis, 4, 386
Mount Everest, 89, 255
Mount Palomar telescope, 228
Mount Pelée erupts, 13
Mount Rushmore sculptures, 133, 163, 167, 177
Mount Wilson telescope, 72, 76, 104, 228

Mourning Becomes Electra (O'Neill play), 135
    film version, 225
MOVE (radical group), 415
movies. *See* films
Moyne, Lord, 204
Mozambique, 94, 148, 178, 450
    National Liberation Front (FRE-LIMO), 300, 310
Mr. Deeds Goes to Town (film), 161
Mrs. Miniver (film), 191
Mr. Smith Goes to Washington (film), 175
Ms. magazine, 347
MTV, 397
Mubarak, Mohammed Hosni, 124, 396
muckrakers, 19, 27
Mueller, Erwin Wilhelm, 160
Mugabe, Robert Gabriel, 110
Muhammad V, sultan of Turkey, 38
Muhammad, Elijah, 153
Muhammad, W. D. Fard, 135, 153
Muir, John, 47, 63
Mujibur Rahman, 92
Mukden Incident (China) (1931), 134
Mukerjee, Suprova, 245
Mukhtar, Omar, 106, 136
Muldoon, Robert David, 370
Muller, Hermann Joseph, 120
Müller, Karl Alex, 420
Müller, Paul, 176, 230
Muller v. Oregon, 35
Mulligan, Robert, 297
Mulroney, Brian, 410, 456
Munch, Edvard, 205
Muni, Paul, 137, 167, 329
Munich Pact (1938), 156, 170, 346
Munoz Marín, Luis, 394
muon (nuclear particle), 168
Muppet Show, The (TV), 375
Mural with Blue Brushstroke (Lichtenstein mural), 421
murder, 109, 113, 139, 273, 281, 305, 313, 345, 395, 401, 459, 461
    mass or serial, 299, 319, 321, 337, 361, 375, 379, 381, 387, 397, 421, 431, 433, 445
    See also assassinations
"Murder, Incorporated" (crime syn-dicate), 175
Murder, She Wrote (TV series), 413
Murdoch, Iris, 87, 293
Murdoch, Rupert, 137, 397
Murfin, Jane, 183
Murnau, F. W., 97
Murphy, Frank, 167
Murphy, James B., 24, 52
Murphy, John M., 382
Murphy, William, 116
Murray, Brian, 359
Murray, Don, 269
Murray, J. A. H., 67
Murray, John Middleton, 107
Murray, Joseph E., 258
Murray, Philip, 253
Murrow, Edward R., 39, 255, 317, 319
Musaveni, Yoweri, 420
muscular dystrophy, 406, 422
Museum of Modern Art (New York), 283, 397

Musgrave, Story, 454
music
  patriotic, 7, 79
  jazz and ragtime, 9, 15, 95, 103, 113, 117
  orchestral, 55
  rock, folk rock, 157, 267, 277, 299, 303, 411, 415, 431
  atonal, 159, 249
  children's, 163
  London concerts during World War II, 175
  Woodstock, 337
  "swing," 423
  Liverpool Oratorio, 445
  See also ballet; opera; popular songs
musicals
  (1904-1929), 19, 61, 79, 109, 117, 125, 129
  (1930s), 137, 143, 145, 147, 153, 157, 163
  (1940s), 189, 193, 195, 197, 203, 211, 217, 223, 229, 235, 237
  (1950s), 245, 251, 257, 261, 267, 273, 277, 283
  (1960s), 289, 305, 311, 339
  (1970s), 359, 369, 387
  (1980s), 403, 421, 425, 431, 435
  (1990s), 443, 459
  film, 145, 197, 245, 257, 269, 277, 293, 315, 459
  change in trend, 195, 289
  rock, 289
Music Man, The (musical), 273
Music of My Mind (album), 355
Muskie, Edmund, 424
Muslim Brotherhood, 128, 402
Muslim Mosque (New York), 115
Muslims. *See* Islam
Mussolini, Benito, 16, 94, 128, 156, 196, 208
  takes power, 98, 108
Mustapha Kemal. *See* Atatürk
mutations. *See* genetics
Mutiny on the Bounty (film), 155
Mutt and Jeff (comic strip), 37
Muzorewa, Abel, 386
My Antonia (Cather), 81
Myers, Michael O., 382
Myerson, Bess, 211
My Fair Lady (musical), 59, 157, 267
My First Summer in the Sierra (Muir), 47
My Lai Massacre (Vietnam), 330
My Left Foot (film), 433
My Life in Art (Stanislavsky), 109
Myrdal, Alva Reimer, 12, 402, 422
Myrdal, Gunnar, 205, 427
Mysterious Stranger, The (Twain), 69
Mystery-Bouffe (Mayakovsky play), 79
Myth of Sisyphus, The (Camus), 191
My World and Welcome To It (Thurber), 193

Nabokov, Vladimir, 265, 381
Nader, Ralph, 155, 317
Nadir Shah, Mohammed, 128, 148
Naess, Arne, 355
Nagaoka, Hantaro, 18
Nagasaki, 206, 208
Naguib, Mahammed, 248

Nagurski, Bronko, 141
Nagy, Imre, 266, 278, 430
Naipaul, V. S., 293
Najibullah, Mohammed, 420
Nakadai, Tatsuya, 393, 415
Nakano, T. (physicist), 214
Nakasone, Yasuhiro, 402
Naked and the Dead, The (Mailer), 209
Naked Ape, The (Morris), 328
Namath, Joe, 339
Name of the Rose, The (film), 421
Namibia, 18, 92, 130, 282, 428, 440
  War of Independence, 320
Namier, Lewis Bernstein, 291
Nanook of the North (film), 101
Nansen, Fridtjof, 91, 101, 135
Napoleon (film), 119, 399
Nash, Graham, 331
Nashville (film), 369
Nasser, Gamal Abdel, 82, 248, 260, 266, 344
Nathans, Daniel, 342
Nation, Carry Amelia Moore, 49
National Academy of Design, 35
National Advisory Commission on Civil Disorders, 333
National Aeronautics and Space Administration (NASA), 276
  Spacecraft Center, 292
National American Woman Suffrage Association (NAWSA), 12, 90
National Association for the Advancement of Colored People (NAACP), 9, 39, 43, 103, 115, 265, 325
National Association of Working Women, 361
National Basketball Association, 235, 271, 283, 301, 323, 327, 393, 449, 455
  MVP awards by, 277, 287, 349, 387, 413
National Birth Control League, 63
National Book Award, 273, 361
National Broadcasting Company (NBC), 67, 209
National Cancer Institute, 396, 410
National Collegiate Athletic Association (NCAA), 29, 177, 311, 327, 385, 447
National Council of the Churches of Christ, 241
National Defense Mediation Board, 187
National Endowment for the Arts, 179, 439, 455
National Environmental Policy Act (1969), 337, 343
National Equal Rights Party, 74
National Football League, 91, 239, 247, 283, 325, 339
  records broken, 181, 273, 335, 359, 383, 403
  MVP awards, 277, 417
National Gallery of Art (Washington), 383
National Guard
  and strikes, 167
  federalized, 297, 305
  and race riots, 319, 325
  at Kent State, 342
National Health Service (Britain), 215, 231, 326

National Hockey League, 397
National Industrial Recovery Act, 144
National Institutes of Health, 434, 448
National Labor Relations Act (Wagner Act) (1935), 155, 167, 223, 258
National Labor Relations Board (NLRB), 155, 167
National Labor Relations Board v. Jones & Laughlin Steel Corporation, 167
National Lead Company, 414
National League, 5, 13, 15, 19, 33, 217
National Liberation Front (FLN) (Algeria), 258, 268, 276
National Library of Medicine, 460
national monuments, 27, 37, 401, 435
National Negro Committee. *See* National Association for the Advancement of Colored People (NAACP)
National Organization for Women (NOW), 321, 325, 403
National Organization of Negro Women, 265
national parks, 37, 47, 51, 101, 223, 304
National Recovery Administration (NRA), 157
National Student Association, 325
National Symphony Orchestra, 123
National Traffic and Motor Vehicle Safety Act (1966), 317
National Trails System Act (1968), 333
National Wilderness Preservation System, 309
National Wildlife Refuge System, 15
National Woman Suffrage Association, 12
National Women's Party, 106
Nation of Islam. *See* Black Muslims
Native American cultures, 152
Native Son (Wright), 181
Natural Childbirth (Dick-Read), 144
natural selection, 300
Naughton, Bill, 321
Naughton, James, 435, 451
Nauru, 334
Nautilus (nuclear submarine), 260, 277
Navajo Generating Plant, 448
naval growth limited (1930), 130
Naval Intelligence Support Center, 424
Navratilova, Martina, 269, 371, 383, 405
Navy, U.S., 33, 38, 85
  Tailhook scandal, 447
Nazimova, Alla, 135
Nazis, 4, 5, 39, 82, 104, 133
  Nazi Party, 86, 92, 94, 116, 161
  secret police, 128, 146
  groups opposing, 152
  aggression of, 170
  and the Church, 179
  collaboration with, 246, 250
  American, 383
  "neo-Nazism," 446

Nazi-Soviet Nonaggression Pact (1939), 156, 174
Neame, Ronald, 289, 337
Needham, Joseph, 262
Ne'emen, Yuval, 292
Negri, Pola, 85
Negrin, Juan, 270
Negro Ensemble Company, 359
Negroes. *See* African-Americans
Negro World (newspaper), 69
Negulesco, Jean, 231
Nehru, Jawahralal, 4, 20, 75, 128, 204, 312
Neill, A. S., 109
Nelson, Byron, 201
Nelson, George "Baby Face," 153
Nelson, Kenneeth, 333
Nelson, Willie, 151, 343, 371
Neolithic man, 446
neon gas, 42, 50
neoprene, 138
Nepal, 440
Neptune (planet), 348, 408, 434
neptunium (element 93), 180
Nereid (satellite for Neptune), 234
Nernst, Walther Hermann, 26, 92
Neruda, Pablo, 21, 349, 363
Nesmith, Bette, 268
Nestle, Charles, 29
Netherlands New Guinea, 272
Neto, Augustinho, 102, 390
Network (film), 375
Neumann, John von, 16, 96, 124, 202, 214, 220, 238, 274, 322
neurofibromatosis, 456
Neutra, Richard, 129, 347
Neutrality Acts, U.S., 156, 176
neutrinos, 134, 330, 392, 424
  antineutrinos, 266, 330
neutron bomb, 392
neutrons, 82, 138, 162
Nevada Test Site, 244, 258
Nevelson, Louise, 5, 433
Neves, Tancredo de Almeida, 416
Newborn Scoring System, 250
New Class, The (Djilas), 272
New Deal, 23, 138, 144, 234, 252, 296
  agencies of, 141, 145, 152
  opposition to, 256
New England Journal of Medicine, 444
Newfoundland, 286
New Guinea, 190, 202
Newhall, Nancy, 285
New Hampshire (Frost), 105
Ne Win, 48, 278, 298, 428
Newlands Reclamation Act, 11
"New Look," 223
Newman, Paul, 283, 333, 337, 359
Newton, Huey, 321, 387
Newton, Isaac, and Newtonian theory, 300
Newton, Theodore, 157
New Women's Association (Japan), 80
New York City
  public library, 7
  subway system, 21
New York City Ballet, 273
New Yorker, The magazine, 115, 297, 433
New York Giants (baseball), 13, 19, 277

New York Giants (football), 277, 403
New York Jets, 339
New York Knicks, 301
New York Mets, 337
New York Philharmonic, 123
New York Psychoanalytic Institute, 186
New York Shakespeare Festival, 261
New York State Theater (Lincoln Center), 303
New York Stock Exchange, 129, 425
New York Theater Workshop, 261
New York Times, 336, 365
New York Times Company v. Sullivan, 311
New York University, 356
New York World, 55
New York World's Fair
    (1939-1940), 175
    (1964), 311
New York Yankees, 91, 121, 137, 175, 177, 187, 255, 293, 301, 453
New Zealand, 174, 370, 412, 415, 426
Nexö, Martin Andersen, 27, 73, 261
Nezu, Jinpachi, 415
Nguema Biyuogo Negue Ndong, Macie, 388
Nguema Mbasogo, Teodoro Obiang, 388
Nhu, Ngo Dinh, 302
niacin and niacinamide, 166
Nicaragua, 120, 353
    U.S. intervention, 38, 50, 112
    Sandinistas, 152, 292, 386, 416
    Civil War, 292, 386, 424, 428, 436
    Contras, 386, 414, 436
    free election, 440
Nicholas II, czar of Russia, 72, 78
Nichols, Dudley, 225
Nichols, Mike, 321, 325, 405
Nicholson, Jack, 169, 365, 369, 407, 411, 417
Nickell, Stella, 401
Nicklaus, Jack, 299
Nick of Time (album), 435
Nicolle, Charles-Jean-Henri, 38
Niebuhr, Reinhold, 351
Nielsen, Asta, 355
Nielsen, Carl, 49
Niemöller, Martin, 153, 413
Nietzsche, Friedrich Wilhelm, 5
Nieuwland, Julius Arthur, 138
Niger, 278
Nigeria, 16, 288, 320, 416
    Civil War, 324, 342
Night, The (Beckman painting), 87
Night and Day (Woolf), 85
Night Flight (St.-Exupéry), 139
Nightingale, Florence, 43
"Night in Tunisia, A" (song), 457
Night Journey (modern dance), 223
Night Mail (film), 357
Night of the Long Knives (Germany) (1934), 150
Nights of Cabiria, The (film), 267
Nijinska, Bronislava, 355
Nijinsky, Vaslav, 35, 42, 45, 51, 55, 241, 355
Nikolayeva, Valentina Vladimirovna, 168

Nimeiry, Gaafar Mohammed al-, 132, 340
Nimitz, Chester William, 322
Nimoy, Leonard, 321
1900 (film), 375
1914 and Other Poems (Brooke), 67
1984 (Orwell), 233
    film version, 411
Nineteenth Amendment, 26, 90
Nine to Five (film), 393
Ninotchka (film), 177
Nishijima, Kasuhiko, 214
nitrogen fixation, 30, 78
Nivelle, Robert Georges, 110
Nivelle Offensive, 72, 110
Nixon, Richard Milhous, 54, 102, 172, 249, 284, 330, 338, 343, 349, 394, 462
    appointments by, 111, 337, 361
    visits China, 352
    and Watergate, 352, 358, 364, 453, 461
Nkrumah, Kwame, 38, 210, 272, 320, 356
NKVD (Soviet secret police), 118
Nobel, Alfred, 278
nobelium (element 102), 278
Nobel Peace Prize
    (1900-1920), 2, 24, 28, 94
    (1922-1946), 101, 109, 136, 142, 264, 294
    (1950-1960), 240, 252, 272, 282, 288
    (1961-1965), 291, 298, 306, 309, 317
    (1970-1978), 344, 358, 372, 379, 380, 452
    (1979-1985), 387, 402, 408, 412, 416
    (1987-1994), 424, 440, 454, 460
Nobel Prize for economics (1974), 427
Nobel Prize for literature
    (1901-1905), 9, 13, 17, 19, 25
    (1906-1910), 29, 33, 37, 41, 43
    (1911-1915), 47, 53, 57, 65
    (1916-1920), 71, 73, 87, 93
    (1921-1925), 97, 103, 107, 111, 115
    (1926-1930), 117, 121, 127, 131, 133
    (1931-1934), 139, 143, 149, 153
    (1936-1939), 163, 167, 173, 179
    (1944, 1945), 203, 211
    (1946-1950), 217, 225, 231, 237, 241
    (1951-1955), 247, 251, 257, 261, 265
    (1956-1960), 269, 275, 279, 283, 289
    (1961-1965), 295, 301, 307, 313, 317
    (1966-1970), 321, 327, 333, 339, 345
    (1971-1975), 349, 355, 361, 367, 371
    (1976-1979), 375, 379, 383, 389
    (1981-1985), 399, 403, 407, 413, 417
    (1986-1990), 421, 425, 431, 435, 441
    (1991-1994), 445, 453, 455, 461
Nobel Prize for science and medicine
    (1901-1905), 8, 14, 18, 24

    (1906-1910), 28, 32, 34, 40, 138
    (1911-1920), 48, 52, 60, 64, 78, 92, 94
    (1921-1925), 98, 102, 106
    (1931-1935), 140, 146, 148, 156, 158
    (1936-1940), 162, 164, 168, 172
    (1945-1950), 210, 218, 224, 230, 240
    (1951-1955), 244, 248, 256, 264, 298
    (1956-1960), 268, 288, 290
    (1961-1965), 294, 300, 306, 310, 318
    (1968-1973), 332, 340, 354, 360
Nobile, Umberto, 117, 127
Noddack, Ida Tacke, 114, 146
Noddack, Walter, 114
Noel-Baker, Philip John, 282, 404
Noether, Emmy, and "Noether school," 78, 158
Nogi, Maresuke, 52
Noguchi, Isamu, 201, 229
Nolan, Sidney Robert, 77, 453
Nolde, Emil, 23
No Man's Land (Pinter play), 369
Nonaligned Movement (Third World), 294
Noonan, Fred, 167
norepinephrine, 216
Norgay, Tenzing, 61, 81, 89, 255, 423
Noriega, Manuel Antonio, 172, 402, 434, 438, 444
Norma Rae (film), 387
Noronic (cruise ship), 237
Norris, Frank, 15, 111
Norris, George, 42
Norris-La Guardia Anti-Injunction Act (1932), 141, 223
North, Oliver, 414, 418, 436
North Africa
    France in, *see* France
    World War II, 186, 192, 194
North American Free Trade Agreement (NAFTA), 456
North and South (Bishop), 391
North Atlantic Treaty Organization (NATO), 234
North by Northwest (film), 395
Northcliffe, Lord, 103
Northeast Passage, 59, 79, 141
Northern Expedition. *See* China
Northern Securities v. United States, 19, 71
North of Boston (Frost), 59
North Pacific Fur Seal Convention, 47
North Pole. *See* Arctic explorations
Northrop, John H., 218
Northwest Passage, 17, 89, 183, 339
North with the Spring (Teale), 246
Norway, 24, 180, 274, 457
Nosferatu, the Vampire (film), 97
Notre Dame University, 79
Nowlan, Philip, 131
N.O.W., 325
Now Voyager (film), 437
Ntaryamira, Cyprien, 458
Nu, U, 32, 228, 278, 428
nuclear accidents, 264, 278, 284, 294, 320, 338, 350, 366, 372, 398, 402, 422
    first recorded, 250
    Chelyabinsk, 272

    not reported, 346
    U.S.-Soviet Agreement on, 348
    Three Mile Island, 384, 385, 386
    Chernobyl, 384, 418, 446
    prevented, 416
nuclear disarmament, 276, 412, 426
    nuclear "freeze," 396, 402
nuclear energy, 6, 28, 62, 275
    nuclear fission, 84, 140, 146, 156, 162, 174, 192, 246
    chain reaction, 138, 140, 174, 190
    nuclear fusion, 176, 246, 248, 434
    experiments, 206, 244, 258
    reactors, 250, 260
    cost of, 424, 434
    cold fusion, 434
    plants close, 450
    See also atomic bomb; hydrogen bomb
Nuclear Research, European Center for (CERN), 406, 410
nuclear tests, 214, 244, 254, 258, 260, 320, 330
    protested, 294, 347, 415
    banned, 304
nuclear treaties
    Soviet-American-British, 304
    Nonproliferation, 324, 332, 372
    Seabed Non-nuclearization, 346
    Intermediate Nuclear Forces (INF), 424, 428
nuclear war, threat of, 258
"nuclear winter," 406, 442
nucleic acids (DNA and RNA), 38, 166, 202, 326, 358
    DNA discovered, isolated, 128, 162
    DNA structure, 252, 262
    government guidelines on, 364
    cloned, 416
    mitochondrial DNA (mDNA), 426
    See also genetics
Nude Descending a Staircase No. 2 (Duchamp painting), 51, 55
Nugent, Elliott, 197
Nujoma, Sam, 130, 440
"number sieve" technology, 92. *See also* mathematics
Nunn, Trevor, 185
Nuremberg Laws (1935), 154
Nuremberg Nazi Party Congress, 157
Nuremberg Trials (1945-1946), 210, 245, 261
Nureyev Hametovich, Rudolf, 89, 173, 293, 379, 443, 457
Nurmi, Paavo, 105, 109
nutrition, 92, 116
    food inspection and testing, 27, 125, 132
    See also vitamins
Nyerere, Julius Kambarage, 102, 312
nylon, 172
nystatin (fungicide), 234

Oakley, Annie, 119, 217
Oakley, Berry, 339
Oates, Joyce Carol, 173
Oberon, Merle, 147, 177
Oberth, Hermann, 110

Obote, Apollo Milton, 110, 322, 348, 386, 416
Obrégon, Alvaro, 90, 124
"obscenity" issue, 83, 99, 122, 123, 129, 215, 265, 439
  term defined, 273
O'Casey, Sean, 105, 109, 117, 313
Occidental Petroleum Company, 431
Ocean Dumping Reform Act (1988), 429
O'Connor, Donald, 251
O'Connor, Flannery, 115, 313
O'Connor, Sandra Day, 135, 397
October Manifesto (1905), 22
October Revolution. *See* Russian revolutions (1917)
Odets, Clifford, 29, 307
Odria, Manuel, 230
Odyssey, The: A Modern Sequel (Kazantzakis), 275
Oe, Kenzaburö, 461
Oerter, Al, 267
Offenbach, Jacques, 187
Office of Economic Opportunity, 311
Office of Price Administration (OPA), 185
Office of Production Management, 187
Office of Scientific Research and Development, 186
Office of Strategic Services (OSS), 222, 284
Of Human Bondage (Maugham), 65
  film version, 437
O'Flaherty, Liam, 157
Of Mice and Men (Steinbeck), 167
Of Thee I Sing (musical), 137
OGPU (Soviet secret police), 74, 118
Ohain, Hans von, 162
Oh, Boy! (musical), 73
Oh, Calcutta! (musical), 339
"Oh, How I Hate to Get Up in the Morning" (song), 79
Ohio State Penitentiary fire, 133
Oh, Kay! (musical), 117
Oh Mercy (album), 435
oil
  Middle Eastern, 38, 46, 147, 244, 286, 294, 358
  North Sea, 335, 368, 431
  Alaska, 339
oil embargo, 358
oil spills, 328, 336, 376, 382, 386, 428, 452, 458
  cleanup funds, 393, 412
  world's worst, 404
  America's worst, 432
  bacteria used in cleanup, 438
oil wells, U.S., 7
  scandals concerning, 98, 104, 120, 128, 191
Oistrakh, David, 37, 367
Okada, Eiji, 281
okapi, 8
O'Keeffe, Georgia, 23, 421
Okello, Tito, 416
"Okies," 145
Okinawa, 206
Oklahoma! (musical), 195
Oldenburg, Claes, 131, 299
Oldfield, Barney, 17, 45

Old Man and the Sea, The (film), 277
Oldsmobiles, 3
Old Wives Tale, The (Bennett), 35
O'Leary, Hazel Rollins, 225, 458
Olin, Lena, 429
Oliphant, Marcus, 152
Oliver, King, 173
Olivier, Laurence, 33, 177, 183, 209, 231, 273, 287, 403, 435
"Ol' Man River" (song), 121, 161
Olson, Anna Christina, 227
Olympia and York Developments, Ltd. (Canada), 451
Olympics
  (1900-1920), 3, 19, 29, 51
  (1924-1936), 109, 123, 161
  (1948-1960), 229, 249, 251, 267, 287, 289
  (1961-1972), 295, 311, 331, 333, 353
  (1976-1984), 375, 392, 393, 395, 411
  (1988-1994), 431, 445, 451, 463
  women in, 3, 229, 289, 331, 353, 375, 431
  Hitler and, 161
  boycotted, 392
Omaha Beach (Normandy), 200
Oman, 246
On Aggression (Lorenz), 304
Onassis, Aristotle Socrates, 143, 462
Onassis, Jacqueline Lee Bouvier Kennedy, 130, 257, 462
On Death and Dying (Kubler-Ross), 338
Ondine (ballet), 277
One Day in the Life of Ivan Denisovitch (Solzhenitsyn), 299
One Flew Over the Cuckoo's Nest (film), 369
One Hundred Years of Solitude (García Márquez), 325
O'Neill, Eugene, 63, 69, 73, 79, 91, 95, 109, 125, 131, 135, 149, 215, 257, 267, 277
  awards to, 111, 163
One Man Band (film), 5
One Touch of Venus (film), 197
One, Two, Three . . . Infinity (Gamow), 224
On Golden Pond (Thompson play), 389
  film version, 397
Onizuka, Ellison S., 420
Only One Earth (Ward and Dubos), 354
Onnes, Heike Kamerlingh, 46
On the Beach (Shute), 273
  film version, 281
"On the Pulse of Morning" (Angelou poem), 455
On the Road (Kerouac), 273
On the Town (musical), 203
On the Waterfront (film), 259
On Your Toes (musical), 163
Oort, Jan Hendrik, 116, 238
Oparin, Alexander Ivanovich, 100, 254
Open City (film), 207
Open Door policy, 24
opera, 3, 19, 23, 43, 47, 81, 97, 209, 223
  ragtime, 15

folk, 47, 155, 369
  chamber, 223
  rock, 339, 349
  "portrait," 375, 393, 411
Operation Crossroads, 214
Operation Desert One, 392
Operation Desert Sabre, 442
Operation Desert Storm, 442
Ophüls, Marcel, 123, 343, 429
Ophüls, Max, 123
O Pioneers! (Cather), 55
Opium (Cocteau), 307
Oppenheimer, J. Robert, 20, 170, 178, 190, 194, 248, 254, 256, 306, 328
Orbison, Roy, 431
Ordinary People (film), 393
Orff, Carl, 167
Organization of African Unity (OAU), 306, 396
Organization of American States (OAS), 246
Organization of Behavior, The (Hebb), 234
Organization of Petroleum Exporting Countries (OPEC), 286, 358
organ transplants. *See* medicine
Orozco, José Clemente, 53, 151, 237
Orphans of the Storm (film), 101
Orphée (opera), 455
Orpheus (ballet), 229
Ortega y Gasset, José, 133, 265
Orwell, George, 17, 171, 207, 233, 241, 411
Ory, Kid, 113
Osachi, Hamaguchi, 132, 134
Osborne, John James, 131, 267, 273, 465
Osborne, Thomas B., 56
Osburn, Paul, 203
Oscars (Academy Awards), 33, 121, 249, 251, 353, 437, 459, 461, 463
  refused, 343
OSO satellites, 298
osteoporosis, 462
Oswald, Lee Harvey, 302
Otis, Arthur S., and Otis Group Test of Mental Ability, 68
O'Toole, Peter, 143, 299, 309, 331, 425
Our Common Future (UN report), 427
Our Town (Wilder play), 373
Outer Mongolia, 52, 82
Out of Africa (film), 415
"out of Africa" origin of humans, 426
Ovando Candía, Alfredo, 310
Over the Brazier (Graves), 71
"Over There" (wartime song), 73
Owen, Wilfred, 83
Owens, Jesse, 157, 161, 411
Oxford English Dictionary, 67
Oxford Union, 146
ozone layer, 56, 132, 256, 364, 382, 414, 462
  international agreement on, 427

Pabst, G. W., 125, 129, 329
pacemakers, 276, 372
Pacem in Terris (papal encyclical), 307
Pacific Crest Trail, 333

pacifism, 24, 81, 84, 86, 146, 174
Pacino, Al, 183, 353, 365, 369
Paderewski, Ignacy Jan, 191
Page, Frederick Handley, 183
Page, Geraldine, 229, 283
Page, Jimmy, 333
Pagliacci (opera), 11
Paglieri, Marcello, 207
Pagnol, Marcel, 163, 367, 419
Paige, Satchel, 227, 317
Painted Bird, The (Kosinski), 315
painting
  "blue period" (Picasso), 7
  Hudson River school, 15
  abstract/expressionist, 23, 41, 53, 55, 63, 207
  modernism in, 35, 79
  Group of Seven (Canada), 77, 93, 105, 347, 367
  postwar German, 87
  American Scene Movement, 133
  prehistoric (cave), 182, 304, 448, 458
  "pop" art, 313
  See also cubism; surrealism
Pais, Abraham, 216
Paisan (film), 215
Pakistan, 246, 338, 342, 396
  creation of, 26, 182
  People's Party, 126, 326, 456
  war with India, 220, 314, 318, 346
  coups in, 286, 378
  refugees in, 443
Pakula, Alan J., 347, 375, 401
paleoastronomy, 304
paleontology, 46, 66, 96, 118, 332
Palestine
  World War I, 68, 72
  Jewish homeland in, 74
  conflict in, 128, 176, 214, 226
  British occupation of, 134, 214, 222
  partition of, 166, 222
  World War II, 176
  refugees from, 243
  Popular Front for the Liberation of, 340
  uprising in, 430
  self-rule agreement, 454, 460
  See also Arab-Jewish conflicts
Palestine Liberation Movement (Fatah), 280, 314, 338
Palestine Liberation Organization (PLO), 128, 280, 310, 338, 342, 370, 374, 400, 404, 460
Palin, Michael, 339
Palmach (Israeli commando force), 188
Palme, Olaf, 122, 420
Palmer, A. Mitchell, and Palmer Raids, 92, 164
Pan-African Congress, 2, 210
Panama, 14, 18, 162, 246, 402, 434
Panama Canal, 19, 59, 92
Pan American Airways, 177, 303
"*Panay* incident" (1937), 164
panda, 412
Pandit, Vijaya Lakshmi, 4, 256, 446
Pandora's Box (film), 125
"panic of 1907," 31
Pankhurst, Christabel, 14, 30

Pankhurst, Emmeline, 14, 30, 54, 60, 126
Panoram Soundie (jukebox), 189
Panther (German gunboat), 46
"panzer" units, 172
Papadopoulos, George, 360
Papanicolaou, George, 146
Papas, Irene, 333
paper clip, 5
Papp, Joseph, 99, 261, 447
Pap smear, 146
Papua, 190
Papua New Guinea, 370
Parade (ballet), 73
Parade's End (Ford), 127
paradigm, 298
Paraguay, 260, 436
  war with Bolivia, 140, 158, 172
Parapsychology Laboratory (Duke University), 132
Pareto, Vilfredo Frederick Damaso, 107
Paris Expositions (1900, 1925, 1937), 3, 113, 165
Paris in the 20th Century (Verne), 461
Paris Peace Accords on Vietnam, 358
Paris Peace Conference (1919), 80, 82, 110, 130, 164
Paris Peace Congress (1949), 255
Paris Treaty (1951), 250
parity concept (nuclear physics), 120, 266
Park Chung Hee, 74, 292, 388
Parker, Alan, 429
Parker, Alton B., 18
Parker, Bonnie, 141, 151
Parker, Charlie "Bird," 95, 267
Parker, Dorothy, 327
Parker, Eugene Newman, 282
parking lots, 25
Parks, Rosa, 55, 263
Parmar, Pratibha, 449
Parsons, Louella, 61
particle physics, electrowave theory of, 406, 410
Parti Québécois, 332
Parton, Dolly, 219, 393, 451
Pascal, Gabriel, 215
Pasiphaë (satellite of Jupiter), 34
Passage to India, A (Forster), 109
  film version, 411
passenger pigeons, 59
Passgard, Lars, 297
Passion (film), 11
Passion of Joan of Arc, The (film), 125
Passy, Frédéric, 2
Pasternak, Boris, 263, 279, 289
Pasteur Institute (Paris), 410
pasteurization, 72
Pastrone, Giovanni, 61
Patent and Trademark Office, U.S., 425
Paterson (Williams), 215
Pather Panchali (Banerji), 99, 243
  film version, 265
Pathet Lao, 244, 286, 300, 360, 368
Paton, Alan, 227
Patsayev, Viktor I., 348
Patterns of Culture (Benedict), 152
Patterson, A. B., 15
Patterson, Floyd, 269, 283, 299
Patterson, Haywood, 135

Patti, Adelina, 89
Patton (film), 343
Paul, regent of Yugoslavia, 154
Paul VI (pope), 385
Paul, Alice, 106, 380
Pauli, Wolfgang, 6, 112, 134, 266, 278, 330
Pauling, Linus Carl, 8, 138, 232, 298, 306, 344, 462
Paulus, Friedrich, 274
Pavarotti, Luciano, 157
Pavlov, Ivan Petrovich, 18, 70, 164
Pavlova, Anna, 31, 35, 139
Pawnbroker, The (film), 317
Paxinou, Katina, 197, 225
Paxton, John, 203
payola scandal, 287
Payton, Walter, 413
Paz, Octavio, 61, 273, 441
PCBs, 216, 374, 386
Peace Corps, 293, 381
Peale, Norman Vincent, 247, 459
Peanuts (comic strip), 243
Pearl Harbor attack, 12, 184, 186, 187, 316, 334, 376
Pears, Peter, 207, 247, 289, 359, 375
Pearse, Patrick, 54, 68
Pearson, Lester, 272, 356
Peary, Robert Edwin, 39, 93
Peasants, The (Reymont), 19
Pechstein, Max, 23
Peck, Gregory, 71, 221, 267, 281, 297
Peel Commission (Britain), 166
Peenemünde research site, 160, 196
Peg o' My Heart (Manners play), 53
Pei, I. M., 75, 383, 389, 433
Peierls, Rudolph Ernst, 180, 182
Peking Man, 118
Pelé (soccer player), 183, 277
pellagra, 64
Pelléas et Melisande (opera), 11
Pelle the Conqueror (Nexö), 27
  film version, 431
Pemba, 312
penicillin. *See* antibiotics
penis envy, 110, 186
Penn, Arthur, 325, 337, 345
penny, U.S., design change, 41
Pentagon Papers, 336
Penthouse magazine, 405
Pentimento (Hellman), 379
Penzias, Arno H., 314
People United to Save Humanity (PUSH), 349
People, Yes, The (Sandburg), 161
Peppard, George, 295
Peres, Shimon, 460
Perey, Marguerite, 178
Pérez de Cuéllar, Javier, 94, 400
Pérez Jiménez, Marcos, 276
perfusion pump, 160, 254
Perier, Jean, 11
Perils of Pauline, The (film series), 59
Perkins, Anthony, 111, 281
Perkins, Frances, 148, 316, 320
Perl, Martin L., 364
Perlman, Itzhak, 211
"permanent" waves, 29
Perón, Isabel, 360, 366, 374
Perón, Juan Domingo, 88, 216, 264, 360, 366

Perón, Maria Eva "Evita," 88, 216, 252, 387
Perot, H. Ross, 448
Perrin, Jean-Baptiste, 34
Perrine, Charles Dillon, 20
Perry, Eugene, 455
Perry, Fred, 153, 163
Perse, St.-John, 275, 289, 373
Pershing, John Joseph "Blackjack," 231
Persia. *See* Iran
Persian Gulf War, 438, 442
Persona (film), 321
Person to Person (TV program), 319
Perthes, George, 14
Peru, 234, 300, 332, 343, 450
  cholera epidemic, 441
Perutz, Max Ferdinand, 288
Pétain, Henri Philippe, 180, 246
Peter II, king of Yugoslavia, 154
Peter and the Wolf (Prokofiev orchestral work), 163
Peter Grimes (opera), 209
Peter Pan (Barrie play), 23, 259
Peters, Bernadette, 425
Peterson, Roger Tory, 36, 154
Petipa, Marius, 45
Petlyura, Simon, 78, 90, 116
Petrie, Daniel, 293
Petrified Forest, The (Sherwood play), 155
  film version, 437
Petrosian, Tigran, 341
Petrushka (ballet), 45
Pettersson, Birgitta, 285
Petty, Lee, 355
Petty, Lori, 451
Petty, Richard Lee, 355, 411
Petty, Tom, 431
Pevsner, Antoine, 91
Pfeiffer, Michelle, 455
Phagan, Mary, 63
Phantom of the Opera, The
  film, 115
  musical, 431
Philadelphia (film), 461
Philadelphia Athletics, 7
Philadelphia Orchestra, 183
Philadelphia Phillies, 63
Philadelphia Story, The (Barry play), 177
  film version, 183
philanthropy, 7, 89, 169
Philby, Kim, 32, 52, 244, 306, 432
Philippines, 6, 260, 326, 354, 418
  war with America, 2, 52
  World War II, 186, 190, 202, 206
  independent state, 216, 256
  Revolution, 406
  natural disasters, 441, 445
Philips Corporation, 307, 387, 400
Phillips, Margaret, 229
Philosophical Investigations (Wittgenstein), 249
philosophy, 13, 33
Phobos spacecraft, 430
phonograph, 102
"Phony War" (1939), 174
photoelectric effect, 68, 84
photography, 11, 13, 23, 131, 161
  amateur, 3
  color, 32
  miniature cameras, 56, 417
  photojournalism, 57, 167, 207
  Polaroid Land, 222

photons, 104
Photo-Secession Group, 11, 23, 155
photosynthesis, 294
Phouma, Souvanna, 8, 412
physics
  beginning of modern, 2
  first Nobel Award for, 8
  and atomic structure, 18
  symmetry in, 78
  nuclear, parity concept in, 120, 266
  See also atom; Nobel Prize for science or medicine
Piaf, Edith, 67, 307
Piaget, Jean, 394
Piano, Rienzo, 461
Piano Lesson, The (Wilson play), 429
Picabia, Francis, 257
Picasso, Pablo, 7, 23, 27, 73, 85, 147, 165, 255, 361, 397
Piccard, Auguste Antoine, 136, 228, 256, 302
Piccard, Jacques, 228, 256, 288, 338
Piccard, Jean Félix, 152, 302, 306
Pickford, Mary, 59, 85, 179, 389
Picnic (Inge play), 255
"picture brides," 31
Piggott-Smith, Tim, 411
Pigott, Lester Keith, 261, 289
Pilnyak, Boris, 173
Pilsudski, Jósef Klemens, 116, 158
Piltdown Man, 46
Piltz, Marie, 55
Pincus, Gregory, 262, 287
"ping-pong diplomacy," 334
Pinilla, Gustavo Rojas, 256
Pinochet, Augusto, 358
Pinter, Harold, 287, 305, 369, 441, 455
Pinza, Ezio, 235, 261
pion (nuclear particle), 156
Pioneer satellites, 348, 360, 384, 388, 408
Piper, Myfanwy, 359
Piper Alpha (oil rig), 431
Pirandello, Luigi, 69, 153, 165
Pirone, Michael, 425
Pitoëff, Georges, 79
Pitts, ZaSu, 111
Pittsburgh Pirates, 15
Pittsburgh Steelers, 371
Pius X (pope), 63
Pius XI (pope), 179
Pius XII (pope), 241, 279
Place in the Sun, A (film), 113
plagiarism, 426
Planck, Max Karl Ernst Ludwig, 2, 22, 46, 78, 224
Planck's constant, 68
Planets, The (Holst orchestral work), 69
Planned Parenthood Federation of America, 97, 315
  v. Danforth, 375
  v. Casey, 449
Plant, Robert, 333
Plante, Jacques, 267, 285
plastics, 38, 100, 125
  plastic lenses, 162
plate tectonics, 284, 330
Plath, Sylvia, 143, 309
Platt Amendment (1901), 14, 152
Playboy of the Western World, The (Synge play), 31, 39

Playing for Time (TV film), 393
Plaza Suite (Simon plays), 333
Please Hammer Don't Hurt 'Em (album), 441
Plekhanov, Georgi Valentinovich, 88
Plexiglas, 162
Plough and the Stars, The (O'Casey play), 117
Plowright, Joan, 273
"plumbers," 336
Plummer, Christopher, 315
Plunkett, Maryann, 421
Pluto (planet), 24, 70, 130, 436
plutonium (element 94), 180, 200, 206
Podoloff, Maurice, 235
Poems (Moore), 357
poetry, 51, 59, 69, 71, 73, 79, 103
    Indian, 49
    wartime, 67, 175
    modernist, 101
    award-winning, 105, 125, 133, 201, 235
    U.S. poet laureates, 415, 445, 451, 457
Pogo (comic strip), 363
Poincaré, Raymond, 154
Poindexter, John, 414, 418
poison gas, 62, 64, 66, 131, 410, 428
poisonings, 401, 431. *See also* murder
"Poison Squad" (Agriculture Department), 132
Poitier, Sidney, 111, 283, 293, 325
Poland, 80, 82, 90, 116
    German invasion of, 174
    World War II, 200, 229
    government falls, 268, 344
    Solidarity, 392, 398, 434
    Communists take power, 396
    becomes Republic, 434
Polanski, Roman, 331, 365
polarized light, 142
Polaroid Corporation, 40, 142
Polaroid Land Camera, 222
police
    actions by, 415, 424, 449
    song threatening, 451
police, secret
    Soviet, 74, 118
    Nazi, 128, 146
    Haitian, 270
polio, 60, 277
    epidemics, 69, 191, 248, 259
    vaccines against, 248, 266, 274
Pollack, Sydney, 359, 371, 415
Pollard, Anne Henderson, 424
Pollard, Fritz, 69, 91
Pollard, Jonathan J., 423
Pollock, Jackson, 53, 207, 271
poll tax outlawed, 310
pollution. *See* environment
polonium (element 84), 48
Pol Pot, 124
polyethylene, 146
polygraph machine, 12
polymers, 100, 256
Pomeroy, Wardell, 226, 254
Pomp and Circumstance (Elgar marches), 7
Pompidou, Georges, 46, 366
Ponnamperuma, Cyril, 342
Pons, B. Stanley, 434
Pontopidan, Hendrik, 73

Ponzi, Charles, 85
Poor People's Campaign (1968), 331
"pop" art, 313. *See also* painting
Popeye the Sailor (comic strip), 131, 173
Poppe, Nils, 267
Popper, Karl Raimund, 13, 463
Popular Front (France), 156, 160
popular songs
    (1904-1916), 19, 47, 61, 67, 69
    (1917-1929), 73, 79, 87, 97, 111, 117, 129
    (1930s), 137, 143, 147, 153, 157
    World War II, 175, 193
    (1940s), 191, 223, 237
    (1950s), 241, 267, 273
    (1960s), 303, 307-317 *passim*, 325, 333, 337, 339
    (1970s), 343, 353, 355, 371, 379, 389
    (1980s), 413, 415, 421, 435, 439
    (1990s), 445, 451, 461
    countercultural, 325
    See also music; musicals
population, world, 3, 91, 133, 181, 239, 285, 343, 439, 459
    report on, 352
    refugees, 443
Population Bomb, The (Ehrlich and Ehrlich), 335
Porgy and Bess (opera), 155
Porsche, Ferdinand, 161
Portal of Death (Manzú sculpture), 311
Porter, Cole, 141, 153, 229, 313
Porter, Edwin Stanton, 15, 59, 191
Porter, Katherine Anne, 299, 395
Port Huron Statement (SDS), 300
Portman, Eric, 277
Port of Shadows (film), 171
Portrait of the Artist as a Young Man (Joyce), 59, 69
Portugal, 36, 42, 58, 116, 216, 370
    in Angola, 294, 320, 368
    Armed Forces Movement takes power, 364
    joins EC, 420
positron. *See* electrons
Possessing the Secret of Joy (Walker), 449
Post, Emily, 291
Post, Wiley, 149, 159
Postman Always Rings Twice, The (Cain), 153
Post Office murders (1986), 421
Potemkin mutiny (1905), 22, 113
Potsdam Conference (1944), 202
Potter, Beatrix, 3, 199
Potter's Book, A (Leach), 183
Poulsen, Valdemar, 4
Pound, Ezra, 47, 113, 355
Powell, Adam Clayton, 36, 324, 356
Powell, Cecil Frank, 156
Powell, Colin Luther, 166
Powell, Dick, 145, 203, 258
Powell, Michael, 197, 209, 223, 231
Powell, William, 153
Power, Tyrone, 57, 281
Power Elite, The (Mills), 267
Power of Positive Thinking, The (Peale), 247

Powers, Francis Gary, 272, 286, 300
Pragmatism (James), 33
Prague Spring (1968), 98
Praise the Lord (PTL) network, 425
Pravda, 260
Prayer, The (Brancusi sculpture), 31
Prebus, Albert, 184
pre-Columbian settlements, 286
Pregnancy Discrimination Act (1978), 385
pregnancy landmark case, 445
Preminger, Otto, 235, 299
Prendergast, Maurice, 35
Prescription: Medicide (Kevorkian), 444
President's Commission on the Status of Women, 305
Presley, Elvis, 157, 267, 379
press. *See* journalism; radio; television
Press (Ontario weekly), 137
Pressburger, Emeric, 197, 209, 223, 231
Prestes, Luis Carlos, 108
Preston, Robert, 81, 273, 321, 403, 423
Price, Leontyne, 123
Price, The (Miller play), 331
Pride and Prejudice (Austen), 183
Priestley, J. B., 413
Prime of Miss Jean Brodie, The (Spark), 295
    stage version, 319
    film version, 337
Primo de Rivera, José Antonio, 146
Primo de Rivera, Miguel, 106, 146
Prince, Harold, 431
Prince Igor (opera), 39
Prince of Wales (battleship), 188
Princess Sophia (steamer), 81
Principia Mathematica (Whitehead and Russell), 40
Principles of Humane Experimental Technique, The (Russell and Burch), 282
Prior, Maddy, 337
Private Life of Henry VIII, The (film), 147
Private Lives (Coward play), 133
Prizzi's Honor (film), 415
Prodigal Son, The (ballet), 129
Profumo, John, 306
Progress, Coexistence and Intellectual Freedom (Sakharov), 332
Progressive Party, 114, 226
Progressives. *See* "Bull Moose" party
Prohibition, 73, 83, 91
    repealed, 147
Project Blue Book (Air Force), 224, 338
Prokofiev, Sergei, 73, 97, 129, 163, 171, 181, 201, 209, 229, 257
promethium (element 61), 208
Prontosil ("wonder drug"), 160
Prophet, The (Gibran), 107
protactinium (element 91), 74
Protestant Ulster Volunteers, 54
Proust, Marcel, 55, 79, 91, 95, 105, 109, 113, 121
Provincetown Players, 63, 69, 73, 79
Prozac, 462
Prudhomme, René, 9
Przewalski's horse, 374

psychoanalysis, 10, 70, 114
Psychoanalysis, Association for the Advancement of, 186
Psychological Types (Jung), 96
Psychological Wednesday Circle, 10
psychology, 18, 50
    behaviorist school, 18, 54, 60, 70, 228
Psychology as a Behaviorist Views It (Broadus), 54
Psychology of the Unconscious (Jung), 50
Psychology of Women, The (Deutsch), 204
Psychopathology of Everyday Life, The (Freud), 18
psychotherapy, 70
Public Enemy (film), 423
"public enemy No. 1," 151
Public Works Administration (PWA), 144
Puccini, Giacomo, 3, 19, 22, 43, 81, 111
Pudovkin, Vsevolod, 125, 259
Pueblo, USS, seized, 332
Puerto Rico, 238, 318, 394
Pugwash (Canada) meeting (1981), 396
Pulcinella (ballet), 93
Pulitzer Prize
    fiction, 91, 161, 265, 273, 401, 407, 411, 417, 421, 431
    poetry, 105, 125, 133, 201, 235, 251, 269, 289, 343, 417
    plays, 111, 125, 393, 397, 431, 459
    nonfiction, 246, 332, 333, 375
Pulp Fiction (film), 461
pulsars, 170, 324, 330, 338
"pumpkin papers," 228
Purcell, Edward Mills, 216, 244
Purdy, Patrick Edward, 433
Pure Food and Drug Act (1906), 27
Purlie Victorious (Davis play), 295
Puzo, Mario, 353, 365
Pygmalion (Shaw play), 53, 59
    film version, 171
Pynchon, Thomas, 361
Pyotr Vasev (freighter), 421
Pyramid (Pei sculpture), 433

Qaddafi, Muammar al-, 194, 338, 418
Qatar, 348
Qin Shih Huang Di, emperor of China, 364
Quant, Mary, 323
quantum theory, 2, 22, 78, 90, 112, 116, 198, 230, 318
    quantum thermodynamics, 354
quarks, 58, 130, 292, 308, 354, 360, 364, 388, 410
quasars, 286, 304
Quasimodo, Salvatore, 283
Quayle, Dan, 224
Quebec separatist movement, 288, 306, 332, 344, 412
    Quebec Liberation Front, 338
Queen Mary (liner), 193
Question of Madness, A (Medvedev and Medvedev), 348
Quick, Diana, 403
Quiet Don, The (Sholokov), 127
Quill, Timothy, 444
quinacrine (Atabrin), 142
quinine, 200

Quinlan, Karen Anne, 375
Quinn, Anthony, 259, 287, 311
Quinn, Pat, 337
Quisling, Vidkun, 212
Quiz Show (film), 281
quiz show scandals, 281
Quo Vadis (film), 51

Ra, Ra II (reed boats), 339
"Rabbit" trilogy (Updike), 287, 397
Rabi, Isidor Isaac, 172
rabies, 24
Rabin, Yitzhak, 102, 450, 460
Rabuka, Sitiveni, 426
Rachel, Rachel (film), 333
Rachmaninoff, Sergei, 199
racing. *See* automobile racing; bicycle racing; horse racing; track events
racism, 9, 99, 201, 338
in sports, 151, 161
race riots, 195, 285, 291, 315, 319, 325, 331, 333, 397, 449
racial confrontation, 425
Vatican position on, 437
See also anti-Semitism; apartheid; Jews; segregation/desegregation issue
radar, 20, 26, 96, 306
Radcliffe College, 33, 335
Radek, Karl Bernhardovich, 178
Radford, Michael, 411
Radha (actor), 245
radiation, electromagnetic, 2, 18, 44, 50, 120, 246
measurement of, 54
effect of, 150
Hawkings, 366
government experiments with, 458
radiation, ultraviolet (UV), 4, 56, 462
radio, 18
transmission by, 2, 6, 30, 41, 78, 108, 146
first radio program, 26
stations established, 67, 119, 137
first news report, 69
regular broadcasts, 89, 91, 99
as sports medium, 95
first paid advertisement, 101
wavelengths assigned, 119
popular shows, 143, 197
FM, 146
first live broadcast of tragedy, 165
radioactivity
early studies of, 2, 10, 14, 32, 84, 146
artificially induced, 150
tracers, 152, 164
secret release of, from nuclear plants, 200
fallout, 244, 258, 272, 320, 330, 418
Radio Acts (1912, 1927), 51, 121
radiocarbon dating. *See* dating methods
Radio Corporation of America (RCA), 67, 85, 140
Radio Free Europe, 250
radioimmunoassay, 238
radio telescope. *See* telescope
radio waves, 264, 298, 430
radium (element 88), 6, 48

radon, 4, 428
Rafsanjani, Ali Akbar Hashemi, 436
Raging Bull (film), 393
ragtime. *See* music
Ragtime (Doctorow), 371
Rahman, Mujibur, 342, 346, 370
Rahman, Omar Abdel, 454
Rahman, Tunku Abdul, 16, 272, 342, 442
Raiders of the Lost Ark (film), 397
railroad disasters
(1915-1940), 65, 73, 81, 169, 177, 183
(1943-1950), 199, 203, 205, 211, 219, 225, 237, 243
(1951-1960), 247, 251, 257, 261, 265, 269, 275, 291
(1962-1989), 301, 313, 357, 435
railroads, 71
strikes barred, 227, 239
Rainbow, The (Lawrence), 63
Rainbow Bridge (Niagara Falls), 189
Rainbow Warrior (antinuclear ship), 412, 415
Rainer, Luise, 137, 167
Rainey, Ma, 179
rain forest, 403, 429
Rain Man (film), 431
Rains, Claude, 147, 191, 215, 327
Raisin in the Sun, A (Hansberry play), 283
film version, 293
Raitt, Bonnie, 237, 435
Raitt, John, 211
"Raj Quartet" (Scott), 411
Rákosi, Mátyás, 222
Ramalho Eanes, António, 376
Rampal, Jean-Pierre, 103
Rampling, Charlotte, 337
Ran (film), 415
Randolph, A. Philip, 113, 187, 389
Randolph, John, 393
Ranger spacecraft, 310, 314
Rank, Otto, 110
Rankin, Jeanette Pickering, 70, 360
Ransome, James Edward, 13
Rape of Nanking (1937), 164, 232
Raphael, Frederic, 315
Rappe, Virginia, 97
Rashomon (film), 95, 239
Rasmussen, Knud Johan Victor, 13, 43, 97, 149
Rasputin (Russian monk), 71
Ras Tafari. *See* Haile Selassie I
Rathbone, Basil, 177, 327
Rathenau, Walter, 100
Rather, Dan, 137
Rauschenberg, Robert, 115
Ravel, Maurice, 51
Rawlings, Marjorie Kinnan, 171, 259
Rawls, Betsy, 247
Ray, James Earl, 331
Ray, Nicholas, 265
Ray, Satyajit, 99, 265, 269, 453
Rayburn, Samuel Taliaferro, 294
Raymond, Alex, 153
rayon, 12
Razak, Tun Abdul, 102, 342, 376
Reagan, Ronald Wilson, 46, 111, 392, 396, 410, 426, 430
appointments by, 397, 421
and Star Wars, 406, 418

and Iran-Contra, 414, 424
and INF treaty, 424, 428
Realistic Manifesto (Gabo and Pevsner), 93
Rear Window (film), 395
Rebecca of Sunnybrook Farm (Wiggin), 15
Rebellion of the Masses, The (Ortega y Gasset), 133
Rebel Without a Cause (film), 265
Reber, Grote, 166
Reclining Figure (Moore sculpture), 315
Reconstruction Finance Corporation (RFC), 141
recording industry, 5, 11, 20, 37
Recruit stock scandal (Japan), 424, 434
recycling, 343
Red Army Faction (Germany), 332, 378
Red Brigades (Italy), 382
Red Cavalry (Babel), 117
Red Cloud (Oglala Sioux general), 40
Red Cross, 2, 91, 184
Redford, Robert, 169, 337, 359, 371, 375, 393, 415
Redgrave, Corin, 169
Redgrave, Lynn, 169
Redgrave, Michael, 37, 169, 225, 301, 417
Redgrave, Vanessa, 169, 319, 379, 393, 449
Red Guards (China), 318
Redheaded Stranger (album), 371
Red Hot Peppers jazz band, 117
Redman, Joyce, 231, 305
Red Rock Lakes Migratory Waterfowl Refuge (Montana), 157
Reds (film), 397
Red Scare (1917-1918), 74, 84
"red shift" (astronomy), 90
Red Shoes, The (ballet), 231
Reeb, James, 315
Reed, Carol, 233
Reed, John Silas, 83, 95, 123, 397
Reed, Oliver, 339
Reed, Walter, 2
refugees
aid to, 243, 245
population, 443
Regents of the University of California v. Bakke, 383
Rehnquist, William Hubbs, 111
Reichstag Fire (1933), 236
Reichstein, Tadeusz, 144, 162, 240
Reid, Alexander, 120
Reid, Harry Fielding, 46
Reid, Kate, 331
Reines, Frederick, 266, 330, 392
Reinhardt, Max, 199
Reis, Irving, 227
Reith, John Charles Walsham, 99, 351
relativity theory, 22, 30, 62, 72, 82, 90, 98
religion, 241
Christian Science movement, 45
Zen Buddhism, 121
separation of church and state, 227, 461
in schools, 245, 299
Blacks in high office, 368, 421, 435
women's role in, 385, 451, 461

See also fundamentalism; Islam; Roman Catholic Church
Remains of the Day, The (film), 455
Remarque, Erich Maria, 129, 133, 171, 187, 217, 345
Remembrance of Things Past (Proust), 55, 79, 91, 95, 105, 109, 113, 121
REM sleep, 252
Renaud, Madeleine, 5, 461
Renoir, Claude, 245
Renoir, Jean, 165, 245, 389
Renoir, Pierre-Auguste, 89, 389
rent control, 229
Republican National Committee, 352
Republican Party, 104, 460
Republic Steel Company, 133, 167
Repulse (battle cruiser), 188
Requiem (Akhmatova), 309
reserpine, 256
Resnais, Alain, 103, 281
Resnick, Judith A., 420
resonance concept, 138, 172
Resource Recovery Act (1970), 343
Respighi, Ottorino, 85
"Resurrection City," 331
Return of the King, The (Tolkien), 263
Reuther, Walter Philip, 33, 161, 333, 347
Revelations (ballet), 287
Revere, Anne, 153, 223
Reversal of Fortune (film), 439
Revue Nègre, La (revue), 115
Rey, Fernando, 353
Reykjavik Summit (1986), 418
Reymont, Wladyslaw, 19, 111
Reynolds, Debbie, 251
Reynolds v. Sims, 305
Reza Shah Pahlevi, Mohammed, shah of Iran, 88, 98, 255, 382, 384, 394
Rhapsody in Blue (Gershwin orchestral work), 109
Rhee, Syngman, 318
rhenium (element 75), 114
Rhesus (Rh) factor, 180
Rhine, Joseph Banks, 132, 394
Rhine River, pollution of, 420
Rhinoceros (Ionesco play), 465
rhinoceros population, 394
Rhodes, Cecil, 12
Rhodesia, 386. *See also* Zimbabwe
Rhys, Jean, 391
Ribbentrop, Joachim von, 210
riboflavin, 114, 156. *See also* vitamins
ribose, 38, 128
Rice, Donna, 432
Rice, Elmer, 87, 107, 329
Rice, Tim, 387, 459
Rich, Adrienne, 131
Richard, Maurice, 203
Richards, Bob, 251
Richards, Dickinson W., 186, 268
Richards, Donald, 223
Richards, Ellen Swallow, 48
Richards, Gordon, 241
Richards, Keith, 299
Richards, Lloyd, 411, 415, 429, 449
Richards, Theodore William, 54
Richardson, Ian, 309
Richardson, Natasha, 169, 441

Richardson, Ralph, 13, 343, 369, 409
Richardson, Tony, 267, 295, 301
Richet, Charles-Robert, 12
Richie, Lionel, 415
Richter, Charles F., and Richter scale, 156
Richter, Conrad, 225, 335
Richter, Curt Paul, 120
Richter, Daniel, 331
Richter, R. (German physician), 40
Rickey, Branch, 87, 209, 221
Rickover, Hyman, 260
Ride, Sally Kristen, 248, 406
Ridon, Jeannette, 152
Riefenstahl, Leni, 157
Rif (French-Moroccan) War, 96, 116
Rigby, Harry, 387
Rigg, Diana, 173
Riggs, Bobby, 177, 361
"right to die," 320, 375
Riis, Jacob A., 63
Rilke, Rainer Maria, 119
Rimsky-Korsakov, Nikolay, 39, 43, 59
Ring of the Lowenskölds, The (Lagerlöf), 125
Rio Grande (film), 239
Riordan, John, 434
Rioton, Marthe, 3
Rise and Fall of the Third Reich, The (Shirer), 291
Rise and Fall of Ziggy Stardust (album), 355
Rise of American Civilization, The (Beard and Beard), 121
Ritt, Martin, 315, 387
Riva, Emmanuele, 281
River, The (film), 245
Rivera, Chita, 273, 289
Rivera, Diego, 145, 275
River Niger, The (Walker play), 359
Rivers, Larry, 317
RJR Nabisco, 429
RNA, 38, 166. See also nucleic acids
Road to Serfdom, The (Hayek), 203
Robards, Jason, 105
Robards, Jason Jr., 105, 267, 311, 379
Robbins, Jerome, 81, 203, 293
Roberta (musical), 147
Roberto, Holden, 300
Roberts, David, 20
Roberts, Joan, 195
Robertson, Pat, 287
Robeson, Paul, 91, 109, 161, 377
Robin, Leo, 237
Robinson, Bill "Bojangles," 237
Robinson, Edward G., 201, 227, 361, 363
Robinson, Edwin Arlington, 159
Robinson, Frank, 367
Robinson, Jackie, 89, 209, 221, 357
Robinson, Phil Alden, 435
Robinson, Sugar Ray, 93, 217, 245, 437
robots, 216, 287, 293, 322, 416
Robson, Flora, 223
Rockefeller, John Davison, 36, 169
Rockefeller, John Davison Jr., 169
Rockefeller, Nelson Aldrich, 36, 169, 308, 364, 390

Rockefeller Center, 145, 177
Rockefeller Foundation, 60, 202
rocket bombs, 196, 202, 232, 380
Rocket into Interplanetary Space, The (Oberth), 110
rocket science, 82, 116, 160, 192, 208, 232, 306, 388
Rockne, Knute Kenneth, 79, 139
Rockwell, Norman, 385
Rocky (film), 219, 223
Roddenberry, Gene, 321
Rodeo (ballet), 193
Rodgers, Richard, 13, 163, 195, 211, 235, 245, 283, 391
Rodin, Auguste, 77
Rodriguez, Andres, 436
Rodriguez Lara, Guillermo, 354
Roe v. Wade, 37, 359, 449
Roehm, Ernst, 92, 150
Roentgen, Wilhelm, 8
Rogallo, Gertrude and Francis, and Rogallo wing, 230
Rogers, Ginger, 49, 145, 157, 427
Rogers, Will, 159
Rokossovski, Konstantin Konstan-tinovich, 334
Rolland, Romain, 19, 65, 101, 205
"rolling pavement," 3
Rolling Stones, the, 299
Rolls Royce Silver Ghost, 33
Romains, Jules, 141
Roman Catholic Church, 63, 116, 128, 163, 241, 437
Nazi curbs on, 179
reevaluation of, 297, 307
in Ireland, 336
papal infallibility questioned, 345
women's role in, 385
See also Vatican, the
Romanenko, Yuri, 426
Roman Holiday (film), 457
Romania, 58, 68, 72, 86, 132, 316
independence guaranteed, 174
World War II, 182, 200
Revolution in, 434
Rome, Harold, 261
Romeo and Juliet (ballet), 181, 379
Rommel, Erwin ("Desert Fox"), 186, 204
Rooks, Conrad, 101
Room of One's Own, A (Woolf), 129
Room with a View, A (Forster), 35
film version, 415
Rooney, Mickey, 95, 387
Roosevelt, Eleanor, 23, 161, 175, 265, 302
with UN, 209, 217, 228
Roosevelt, Franklin Delano, 64, 87, 150, 161, 167, 175, 328
and New Deal, 23, 138, 144, 152, 296
assassination attempted, 146
appointments by, 152, 166
reelected, 160, 163, 182, 202, 244
advisers to, 164, 219, 265, 270, 376
verbal attacks on, 170
and atomic bomb, 174, 184
and World War II, 181, 185-188 passim, 194-202 passim
death of, 206
Roosevelt, Theodore, 6, 9, 13-27 passim, 31, 37, 40, 50, 88
Teddy bear named after, 11

wins Nobel Peace Prize, 28
Root, Elihu, 168
Roots (Haley), 375
TV series, 379
Roper, Elmo Burns Jr., 149
Roper Research Associates (Roper polls), 149
Rorschach, Hermann, and Rorschach inkblot tests, 96
Rose, Fred, 371
Rose, L. Arthur, 421
Rose, Pete, 415
Rose, William Cumming, 234
Rose Bowl game, 11, 69
Rosemary's Baby (film), 331
Rosenberg, Alfred, 210
Rosenberg, Ethel Greenglass and Julius, 244, 254, 349, 422
Rosenkavalier, Der (opera), 47
"Roses of Picardy" (song), 69
Rose Tattoo, The (Williams play), 247
Rosewall, Kenneth, 257
Rosing, Boris, 30
Ross, Barney, 149
Ross, Diana, 205
Ross, Harold, 115
Ross, Katharine, 325, 337
Rossby, Carl-Gustav Arvid, 206
Rossellini, Roberto, 29, 207, 215, 379
Rossen, Robert, 235
Rossini, Gioacchino, 85
Rossum's Universal Robots (RUR) (Capek play), 97
Rostand, Edmond, 5
Rostropovich, Mstislav, 121, 365, 439
Rotary Club, 23
Roth, Philip, 149
Roth v. United States, 273
Rothko, Mark, 17, 347
Rotten, Johnny, 371
Rous, Francis Peyton, 42
Royal Air Force (RAF), 163, 180
Royal Ballet, 333, 347
Royal Liverpool Philharmonic, 445
Royal Naval Air Service, 64
Royal Oak (battleship), 176
Royal Shakespeare Company, 293, 309
Rubber Soul (album), 315
Rubinstein, Artur, 403
Rubinstein, Helena, 37
Rubinstein, Ida, 43
Rubinstein, John, 393, 403
Ruby, Jack, 302
Rubyfruit Jungle (Brown), 361
Rockelshaus, William, 358
Rudolph, Wilma Glodean, 185, 289, 463
Ruehl, Mercedes, 445
RU-486 (mifepristone), 428
Rule, Janice, 255
Rules of Sociological Method (Durkheim), 75
Rules of the Game (film), 389
running. See track events
Runstedt, Karl Rudolph Gerd von, 256
Runyon, Damon, 133
Rural Electrification Administration (REA), 163
Rushdie, Salman, 225, 429, 441
Ruska, Ernst, 146

Russell, Bertrand, 10, 40, 84, 134, 181, 241, 276, 347
Russell, Bill, 271, 277, 327
Russell, Harold, 215
Russell, Henry Norris, 54
Russell, Jane, 257
Russell, Ken, 91, 339, 369
Russell, Kurt, 405
Russell, Rosalind, 225, 269
Russell, W. (scientist), 282
Russia
war with Japan, 10, 18, 22, 40, 52
Social-Democratic Workers' Party, 14, 50
pact with Japan, 20
World War I and postwar, 58, 62, 68, 72, 74, 76, 88
Civil War, 72, 82, 94, 100, 116
war with Poland, 90, 116
Russian Federation (1990), 438, 444, 450
insurrection (1993), 454
in Commonwealth, 455, 456
vs. Chechnya, 458
See also Soviet Union
Russian revolutions, 76
(1905), 10, 14, 22, 26, 113
(1917) (February and October revolutions, Bolshevik Revolution), 14, 30, 72, 73, 79, 83, 88, 108, 172, 178
Russo, Daniel, 336
Rutan, Richard, 419
Ruth, Babe, 91, 121, 231, 293, 365
Rutherford, Ernest, 10, 34, 44, 58, 82, 168, 310
Rutherford, Margaret, 211
rutherfordium (element 104), 310
Rutskoi, Alexandr, 454
Rwanda, 280, 294, 298, 304, 326, 416, 460
genocide in, 458
Ryan, Leo, 381
Ryan, Nolan, 447
Rydell, Mark, 397
Ryder, Winona, 455
Ryskind, Morie, 137
Ryu, Daisuke, 415

Saarinen, Eero, 43, 243, 295
Saarinen, Eliel, 243, 295
Saavedra, Daniel Ortega, 416
Sabah, 306
Sabin, Albert, 266
Sabotage (film), 33
Sacco, Nicola, 96, 120
Sacco-Vanzetti case, 96, 120, 157
Sachs, Nelly, 321, 345
Sackler, Howard, 331
Sadat, Anwar al-, 82, 124, 344, 380, 396
Sadler's Wells, 203. See also ballet
Sagan, Carl, 154, 392, 406
Sagan, Françoise, 261
Sagrada Familia, Church of the (Barcelona), 119
Sahara, 2, 315
Saharan Arab Democratic Republic, 374
Sahel, the, 315
Said, Nuri al-, 132, 276
Sailer, Toni, 267, 331
sailing. See yachting
"Sailing" (song), 371

Sailor Who Fell from Grace with the Sea, The (Mishima), 115
Saint, Eva Marie, 259
St. Cyr, Johnny, 113
St. Denis, Ruth, 65, 335
St.-Exupéry, Antoine, 139, 197
St. James Conference (London), (1939), 176
Saint Joan (Shaw play), 105
St. Joseph's Hospice (London), 278
Saint Kitts, Federation of, and Nevis, 408
St. Laurent, Louis Stephen, 362
St. Laurent, Yves, 275, 277
St. Lawrence Seaway, 283
"St. Louis Blues" (song), 281
St. Louis Cardinals, 87, 217
St. Louis Fair, 19, 21
St. Louis Stars, 91
St. Roch (ship), 183
Saint-Saëns, Camille, 31, 99
St. Valentine's Day Massacre (1929), 129
Saint Vincent and the Grenadines, 390
Saipan, 202
Sakel, Manfred, 146
Sakharov, Andrei Dmitriyevich, 98, 294, 332, 372, 394, 436
Saks, Gene, 445
salad oil swindle, 307
Salam, Abdus, 324
Salan, Raoul, 292
Salazar, Antonio de Oliviera, 140, 216, 346
Salinger, J. D., 89, 245, 253
Salk, Jonas Edward, 60, 248, 256
Sally (musical), 93
Salomé (opera), 23
Salt Water Ballads (Masefield), 327
Salyut space stations, 346, 388, 416
Samory Touré, 4
Samuel, Arthur L., 224
Samuelson, Paul Anthony, 231
Samuelson, Victor E., 361
Sanctuary (Faulkner), 135
Sanda, Dominique, 347, 375
Sandage, Allan Rex, 286
Sandburg, Carl, 69, 117, 161, 327
Sande, Earl, 133
Sanders, George, 239
Sanders, Jay Olcutt, 257, 389, 443
Sanderson, Julia, 61
Sandinistas. *See* Nicaragua
Sandino, Augusto César, 120, 152
Sands, Diana, 283
San Francisco
   Preparedness Day parade (1916), 69, 177
   General Strike (1934), 151
San Francisco 49ers, 269, 401, 441
San Francisco Giants, 301
Sanger, Margaret Louise Higgins, 59, 67, 73, 97, 105, 323
Sanger, William, 59
Sanjurjo, José, 142
Santa Lucia, 390
São Tomé and Principe, 372
Saperstein, Abraham, 121
Sapir, Edward, 97
Sarajevo, siege of, 448
Sarandon, Susan, 445
Sarava, Aparicio, 18
Sarawak, 306
Sargent, John Singer, 115
Sarney Costa, José, 416

Sarnoff, David, 67, 85, 351
Saroyan, William, 37, 179, 401
Sartoris (Faulkner), 129
Sartre, Jean-Paul, 25, 217, 269, 313, 393
Satanic Verses, The (Rushdie), 429
satellites. *See* spacecraft/satellites
Satie, Erik, 73
Sato, Eisaku, 8, 372
Saturday Evening Post, 385
"Saturday night massacre" (Watergate), 358
Saturn (planet), 378, 388, 392, 440
Satyagraha (opera), 393
Sauckel, Fritz, 210
Saudi Arabia, 142, 147, 332, 424
   crowd disaster, 441
Saussure, Ferdinand de, 57
Savage, John, 381
Savimbi, Jonas, 152, 320, 450
savings and loan industry, 435, 447
Saw Maung, 428
Scacchi, Greta, 405
Scarface (film), 137
scarlet fever, 106
"Scarsdale Diet" murder, 395
Scenes from a Marriage (film), 359
Schaefer, Vincent Joseph, 216
Schaffner, Franklin, 343
Schary, Dore, 277
Schaudinn, Fritz R., 22
Schechter Poultry Corporation v. United States, 157
Schéhérazade (ballet), 43
Schell, Maximilian, 293
Schenck v. United States, 86
Schick, Béla, and Schick test, 54
Schildkraut, Joseph, 263
Schindler's List (film), 455
Schine, David, 253
schizophrenia, 122, 286
Schlesinger, John, 305, 315, 339, 349
Schlieffen, Alfred von, and Schlieffen Plan, 56
Schlöndorff, Volker, 441
Schmeling, Max, 133, 151
Schmidt, Helmut Heinrich, 80, 364, 402
Schmidt, Maarten, 304
Schmidt-Rottluff, Karl, 23
Schnabel, Artur, 249
Schneerson, Menachem Mendel, 15, 463
Schneiderman, Rose, 357
Schoenberg, Arnold, 249
Schollander, Don, 311
School of Contemporary Dance, 121
Schrank, John N., 50
Schrieffer, John, 354
Schrödinger, Erwin, 116, 146, 148, 202, 296
Schrödinger wave equation, 116
Schroeder, Barbet, 439
Schultz, Charles, 103, 243
Schuman, Robert, 238
Schuman, William, 223
Schumann-Heink, Ernestine, 39, 165
Schuschnigg, Kurt von, 380
Schwab, Charles Michael, 179
Schwarzkopf, Elisabeth, 67
Schwarzschild, Karl, 72
Schweitzer, Albert, 56, 262, 318
Schwerner, Michael, 309

Schwinger, Julian S., 230, 318
SCID (severe combined immunodeficiency), 440
Science and Civilization in China (Needham), 262
Science and Ethics (Haldane), 124
Science and the Modern World (Heisenberg), 112
science fiction, 7, 35, 97, 117, 147, 208, 321, 361, 401
Scientific American magazine, 37
Scobee, Francis R., 420
Scofield, Paul, 287, 319, 393
Scopes, John T., and Scopes trial, 113, 287
Scorpion (submarine), 333
Scorsese, Martin, 195, 369, 375, 393, 425, 455
Scotch tape, 125
Scots Quair, A (Gibbon), 141
Scott, George C., 123, 309, 333, 343
Scott, Paul, 411
Scott, Peter, 217
Scott, Ridley, 445
Scott, Robert Falcon, 9, 49, 217
Scottsboro case (1931), 135
Scowcroft, Brent, 423
Scriabin, Alexander Nikolayevich, 67
scuba diving, 196
SCUD missiles, 442
Sculptor's Studio, The (Picasso etchings), 147
sculpture
   "kinetic," 55
   Mount Rushmore, 133, 163, 167, 171
   "soft," 299
   "mobiles" and "stabiles," 377
Sea Around Us, The (Carson), 246, 312
Seaborg, Glenn Theodore, 52, 180, 248, 264
Seagram Building (New York), 269
Seal, The (Brancusi sculpture), 161
Sealab II (bathyscaphe), 302, 316
Seale, Bobby, 169, 321
Seaman, Elizabeth Cochrane (Nellie Bly), 103
Seamarks (Perse), 275
Sea of Grass, The (film), 225
Season of Anomy (Soyinka), 361
Seaver, Tom, 337
Seberg, Jean, 283
"Second Hand Rose" (song), 97
Second Sex, The (Beauvoir), 233
Second Vatican Council, 297, 385
Secret Agent (Conrad), 33
Secret Army Organization (OAS) (France), 292, 298
Securities and Exchange Commission (SEC), 152
Sedition Act (1918), 74, 84
Seeger, Pete, 89, 231, 235
See It Now (TV program), 319
Seferis, George, 5, 307, 351
Segal, George, 361
Segar, Elzie, 131, 173
Segovia, Andrés, 427
Segrè, Emilio, 24, 166, 182, 264
segregation/desegregation issue, 103, 259, 263, 281, 285, 291, 299, 303, 305
Seifert, Jaroslav, 413
Selective Service Act (1940), 182

Self-Portrait in a Convex Mirror (Ashbery), 343
Sellers, Peter, 309
Seneca Falls Convention, 12, 26
Senegal, 28, 288, 402
Senegambia, 402
Senghor, Léopold Sédar, 28, 288
Sennett, Max, 51, 291
Serbia, 34, 50, 58, 62, 80, 444
   "ethnic cleansing," 448
Sergeant Pepper's Lonely Hearts Club Band (album), 325
Sergueyev, Konstantin, 181
Serkin, Peter, 447
Serkin, Rudolf, 17, 447
Serrault, Michel, 383
Servant, The (film), 305
Sesame Street (TV series), 339
Seven Days in May (film), 311
Seven Gothic Tales (Dinesen), 151
700 Club (TV program), 287
Seven Pillars of Wisdom (Lawrence), 158, 299
Seven Samurai, The (Kurosawa), 259
Seventh Heaven (film), 101, 121
Seventh Seal, The (film), 267
"76 Trombones" (song), 273
Severed Head, A (Murdoch), 293
sex-change operation, 250
Sex Factor in Marriage, The (Wright), 133
Sex Pistols, the, 371
sexual attitudes, 117, 122, 124, 226, 287, 318, 355
sexual harassment, 443, 447, 451, 455, 457
   See also homosexuality
Sexual Behavior in the Human Female (Kinsey et al.), 254
Sexual Behavior in the Human Male (Kinsey et al.), 228
Sexual Politics (Millett), 155
Seychelles, the, 376
Seyfert, Carl K., and Seyfert galaxies, 196
Seymour, Lynn, 347
Seyrig, Delphine, 353
Seysenegg, Erich von, 4
Seyss-Inquart, Arthur, 210
Shackleton, Ernest Henry, 9, 39, 63, 103
Shadow of a Gunman (O'Casey play), 105
Shaffer, Peter, 393
Shahn, Ben, 341
Shakespeare's Globe Theater, 89
Shalala, Donna Edna, 189
Shame of the Cities, The (Steffens), 19
Shamir, Yitzhak, 64, 406
Shane (film), 255
Shanghai Massacre (1927), 118, 145
"Shangri-La," 147
Shankar, Ravi, 95
Shannon, Claude Elwood, 238
Shapiro, Karl, 201
Shapley, Harlow, 76, 90, 310, 356
Sharif, Omar, 143, 299, 315
Sharjah, 348
Sharman, Bill, 271
Sharon, Ariel, 126
Sharpe, Albert, 223
Sharpeville Massacre (South Africa) (1960), 286, 298

Shasta Lake (California), 444
Shastri, Lal Bahadur, 20, 320, 322
Shatner, William, 321
Shaw, George Bernard, 23, 33, 59, 105, 115, 171, 215, 241
Shaw, Irwin, 231
Shaw, Robert, 319
Shaw, Wilbur, 169
Shawn, Ted, 65, 357
Shearer, Moira, 229, 231
Sheen, Martin, 387
Sheik, The (film), 97
Shell, Art, 435
Shelley, Mary Wollstonecraft, 137
"She Loves You" (song), 307
Shelton, Ian, 424
Shenandoah (dirigible), 113
Shepard, Alan Bartlett Jr., 106, 292
Sheridan, Jim, 433
Sherriff, R. C., 373
Sherrill, Patrick, 421
Sherwood, Robert, 155, 171, 215
Shevardnadze, Eduard, 450, 456
She Wore a Yellow Ribbon (film), 235
Shi'ite rebellion (Iraq) (1991), 442
Shilts, Randy, 247, 465
Shinn, Everett, 35
Shinoussa (tanker), 438
ship losses
    (1900-1910), 5, 21
    (1912-1918), 49, 53, 59, 65, 73, 81
    (1921-1934), 99, 117, 153
    (1942-1949), 193, 203, 217, 231, 235, 237
    (1952-1956), 251, 257, 261, 267
    (1964-1975), 313, 317, 323, 363, 371
    (1976-1983), 377, 386, 389, 399, 407
    (1986-1992), 421, 423, 425, 433, 452
    worst peacetime disaster, 425
Ship of Fools (Porter), 299
    film version, 317
shipping industry, 143
Shirer, William L., 291
Shoah (film), 415
Shockley, William, 220, 268
"shock" therapy, 146, 166, 260
Shoemaker, Carolyn and Eugene, 458
Shoemaker, Willie, 283, 327, 345
Shoemaker-Levy 9 comet, 458, 460
Shoeshine (film), 215
Shollar, Ludmila, 55
Sholokhov, Mikhail, 25, 127, 317, 413
Shore, Ernie, 73
Shostakovich, Dmitri, 29, 187, 299, 371
Shot Red Marilyn (Warhol work), 313
Shot to the Heart, A (Gilmore), 379
Show Boat (musical), 121
    film version, 161
Shreck, Max, 97
Shroud of Turin, 430
Shuffle Along (musical), 97
Shula, Don, 359
Shuster, Joseph, 61, 173, 453
Shute, Nevil, 241, 273, 291
Sibelius, Jean, 275
Siberia, 28, 82, 100, 440

Sibiriakov (ship), 141
sickle cell anemia, 42, 232
Siddhartha (Hesse), 101
Sidney, Sylvia, 45, 137, 167
Siegel, Bugsy, 215
Siegel, Jerry, 173
Siems, Margarethe, 47
Sienkiewicz, Henryk, 25, 51
Sierra Club, 53, 63, 251
Sierra Leone, 294
Signoret, Simone, 99, 279, 317, 419
Sihanouk, Norodom, 102, 188, 342
Sikh Golden Temple, 410
Sikorsky, Igor, 32, 56, 176, 177, 356
Silence of the Lambs, The (film), 443
Silent Spring (Carson), 296, 312
silicon, 100, 288
Silkwood, Karen Gay, 219, 365, 405
Silkwood (film), 365, 405
Sillanpää, Franz Eemil, 179
Sillitoe, Alan, 301
Sills, Beverly, 131
Silver, Ron, 439
Silvera, Frank, 257
Silvera, Joey, 265
Simenon, Georges, 17, 437
Simmons, Jean, 217, 223, 285
Simms, Hilda, 201
Simon, Claude, 417
Simon, Neil, 123, 333, 445
Simon, Paul, 189, 317, 343, 371, 421, 451
Simon, Théodore, 24
Simple Speaks His Mind (Hughes), 239
Simpson, Nicole Brown, 461
Simpson, O. J., 359, 413, 461
Simpson, Wallis Warfield, later Duchess of Windsor, 162, 356, 423
Sinai Peninsula, 68, 324, 388
Sinai-Suez War (1956), 266
Sinatra, Frank, 65, 183, 235
Sinclair, Harry, 128
Sinclair, Upton, 27, 335
Sinbad (musical), 79
Sinden, Donald, 255
Singapore, 190, 306, 316, 326
Singer, Isaac Bashevis, 21, 383, 445
Singer, Peter, 369
Singin' in the Rain (film), 251
Sinise, Gary, 439
Sinn Fein, 24, 80, 84. *See also* Irish Republican movement and Army
Sin of Madelon Claudet (film), 463
Sino-Japanese War (1937-1945), 164, 170
Sinope (satellite of Jupiter), 58
Sinyavsky, Andrei, 320
Siqueiros, David Alfaro, 305, 367
Sirhan, Sirhan, 330
Sirica, John Joseph, 21, 453
Sissle, Noble, 97, 373
Sister Angelica (opera), 81
Sister Carrie (Dreiser), 3
Sistine Chapel, 441, 459
sit-ins, 285
Sitwell, Edith, 313
Siwar el-Dahab, Abdul Rahman, 414

Six Characters in Search of an Author (Pirandello play), 69
Six-Day War (1967), 324, 326
Six Degrees of Separation (Guare play), 439
Sixteenth Amendment, 56
$64,000 Question (TV show), 281
Sjostrom, Victor, 271
Skate (submarine), 289
skating
    figure, 61, 123, 229, 251, 293, 461, 463
    speed, 381, 393
    ice-dancing, 397, 411, 463
    See also hockey
skiing, 49, 101, 267, 327, 331
    chairlift invented, 169
    World Cup, 349, 377, 393
Skinner, B. F., 20, 228, 442
Skinner, Claire, 455
Skin of Our Teeth, The (Wilder play), 193
Skinsnes, Olaf K., 370
Skoda Works (Austro-Hungary), 58
Skylab spacecraft, 358
skyscrapers, 19
Slabs of the Sunburnt West (Sandburg), 103
Slater, Montagu, 207
Slaughterhouse-Five (Vonnegut), 337
Slaughter on Tenth Avenue (ballet), 163
sleeping sickness, 32
Sleigh, Frederick, 2
Slezak, Walter, 261
Slim, Willia Joseph, 344
Slipher, Vesto Melvin, 90
Sloan, John, 35, 249
Slovenia, 444
smallpox, 326, 378
Small Town Tyrant, The (Mann), 133
Smiles of a Summer Night (film), 263, 361
Smiley's People (le Carré), 401
Smith, Alfred E., 124
Smith, Alyssa, 436
Smith, Bessie, 169
Smith, Bob, 157
Smith, Hamilton Othanel, 342
Smith, Ian, 314, 386
Smith, Lois, 439
Smith, Maggie, 155, 337, 415
Smith, Michael J., 420
Smith, Owen Patrick, 25
Smith, Stevie, 13, 351, 383
Smith, Tommy, 331
Smith, Walter Bedell, 206
Smith (Alien Registration) Act (1940), 182, 244, 272
"Smoke Gets in Your Eyes" (song), 149
smoking, warnings against, 308
Smoot, George, 448
Smoot-Hawley Tariff Act (1930), 129, 131
Smuts, Jan Christiaan, 240
snail darter, 368
Snake Pit, The (film), 229
Snead, Sam, 235
Snell, George, 230
Snow, C. P., 25, 181, 395
Snow White and the Seven Dwarfs (film), 167

Snugli baby carrier, 381
Soares, Mário Alberto Nobre Lopez, 110
soccer, 125
    World Cup, 183, 277, 299, 343, 447
    crowd stampede at match, 437
    drug scandal, 447
Social Democratic Party of America, 8
socialism, 46, 156
Socialist Labor Party, 8, 62
Socialist Party, 8, 50, 80, 86, 90, 111, 334
Social Justice magazine, 391
Social Security, 155, 181, 258
Sociobiology (Wilson), 370
Soddy, Frederick, 10, 54, 84, 98, 270
So Ends Our Night (film), 187
software. *See* computers
So Human an Animal (Dubos), 332
solar energy, 56, 393
solar heating, 176
Solar One energy plant, 393
solar wind, 282
Solidarity. *See* Poland
Solomon Islands, 190, 196, 198, 384
Solovyev, Vladimir, 422
Solzhenitsyn, Alexander, 81, 299, 345, 347, 359
Somalia, 290, 338, 378, 382, 446, 450, 456
Somebody Up There Likes Me (film), 223
Some Like It Hot (film), 281
"Some of These Days" (song), 323
"Someone to Watch Over Me" (song), 117
Sommerfield, Arnold, 66
Somoza Debayle, Anastasio, 340, 386, 392
Somoza Debayle, Luis, 270, 304
Somoza Garcia, Anastasio, 114, 270, 304
sonar, 62, 112
Sondheim, Stephen, 273, 283, 293, 301, 359, 387, 425
Song of Ceylon (film), 357
"Songs to Aging Children Come" (song), 337
sonic boom, 222
"Son of Sam Law," 377
Son of the Middle Border, A (Garland), 73
Sons and Lovers (Lawrence), 55
    film version, 289
Sontag, Susan, 149, 321
Sony Corporation, 371, 387, 400
Soong, Ch'ing-ling, 398
Soong, Mei-ling, 120
Sophie's Choice (Styron), 387
    film version, 301
Sopwith, Thomas Octave Murdoch, 51
Sorrow and the Pity, The (Ophüls), 343
SOS, 35
Soul Enchanted, The (Rolland), 101
Soul on Ice (Cleaver), 331
Souls of Black Folk, The (Du Bois), 17
Sound and the Fury, The (Faulkner), 129

sound barrier, 222
Sound of Music, The (musical), 283
    film version, 315
"Sounds of Silence" (song), 317
Soupalt, Philip, 67
Sousa, John Philip, 145
South Africa, 75, 92, 286, 428
    Boer War, 2, 6, (*see also* Boer War)
    Union of, 42, 88
    ANC founded, 50 (*see also* African National Congress)
    National Party, 54 108, 260, 278, 454
    segregation/apartheid, 54, 75, 227, 250, 282
    Suppression of Communism Act, 240
    Republic of, 294
    language riots, 374
    economic sanctions against, 416
    cease-fire agreement, 438
    "fundamental rights," 454
    free elections, 460
Southern Christian Leadership Conference (SCLC), 271, 354
South Pacific (musical), 223, 235
South Pole. *See* Antarctica
Southwest Africa People's Organization of Namibia (SWAPO), 130, 282, 320
South Yemen, 326, 332
Soviet Union
    collapse of, 78, 136, 414, 434-450 *passim*
    New Economic Policy (NEP), 97
    Germany and, 100, 156, 172, 174 (*see also* World War II, *below*)
    recognized, 100
    and Mongolia, 110
    defections from, 121, 231, 266, 293, 325, 365, 371
    Five-Year Plans, 122, 146, 172
    agricultural policy, 128, 282
    and Spain, 160, 166
    World War II, 166, 174, 176, 180-194 *passim*, 200, 206, 208
    and Japan, 170, 172, 176
    border wars, 176, 216, 222, 336
    and UN, 204
    U.S. policy toward ("containment"), 220
    blockades Berlin, 228
    nuclear power, 232, 258, 260, 294
    Warsaw Pact, 264, 266, 438, 446
    space program, 270, 274, 280, 282, 290, 304, 310, 320-352 *passim*, 366, 370, 384, 388, 402, 416-436 *passim*, 452, 456
    "posthumous rehabilitation" by, 272
    "thaw" ends, 320
    human rights, 370, 394
    war with Afghanistan, *see* Afghanistan
    defectors return, 439
    See also Russia; Stalin, Joseph
Soyinka, Wole, 153, 355, 361, 421
Soylent Green (film), 361
Soyuz spacecraft, 324, 336, 346, 348, 370, 388
Spaak, Paul-Henri, 356

spacecraft/satellites
    Russian, *see* Soviet Union
    U.S., 276, 304, 348, 354, 388, 392, 408, 412, 422
    weather, 282, 286, 288
    communications, 282, 286, 298
    French, 314
    crash of, 366
    shuttles, 396, 402, 406, 416, 420, 430, 434, 446, 456
    research, 436
    See also space flight; *entries for individual craft*
space flight
    predicted, 7, 16, 60, 82
    women in, 168, 304, 406
    "space race," 270
    animals in, 290
    first manned, 290, 292, 310
    space walks, 314, 412, 450
    rendezvous in space, 314, 336, 370, 416, 456
    fatalities, 324, 348, 420
    See also moon; rocket science; spacecraft/satellites
Spacek, Sissy, 404, 443
Space Life Science-1 Laboratory, 446
Space Transportation System (STS), 396
Spain, 77, 94, 116, 134, 166, 372
    fascism in, 146, 156, 160, 170, 174
    joins EC, 420
Spanish Civil War, 136, 146, 154, 161, 165, 166, 170, 174, 372, 440
    events leading to, 142
    books about, 171, 181
"Spanish flu," 77
Spark, Muriel, 81, 295
Spartacist League (Germany), 82
Spassky, Boris Vasselievich, 341, 353
"speciesism," 369
Speck, Richard Benjamin, 189, 321, 449
Spectre de la Rose, La (ballet), 45
speed of light, 354
Speidel, Hans, 426
Spencer, Jeremy, 325
Spengler, Oswald, 100
Spielberg, Steven, 217, 379, 397, 401, 415, 425, 455
Spindletop oil well, 7
Spirit of St. Louis, The (airplane), 119
Spitteler, Carl, 87
Spitz, Mark, 353
Spitzer, Lyman Jr., 246
split skirt, 13
Spock, Benjamin, 215
spray cans, 256, 382
Springsteen, Bruce, 237, 413, 459, 461
Sputnik flights, 270, 274
Spy Who Came in from the Cold, The (le Carré), 305
    film version, 315
Squaw Man, The (film), 59
Sri Lanka, 239, 288, 348
    Civil War, 398, 426, 430
Stagecoach (film), 177
stainless steel, 20
Stalag 17 (film), 257
Stalin, Joseph, 30, 74, 201, 255, 325

takes power, 108, 116, 122
    expels Trotsky, 120, 128, 182
    postwar agreements, 198, 206
    purges under, 248, 252, 435 (*see also* Great Purge)
Stallings, Laurence, 93, 285
Stallone, Sylvester, 219
Stambollisky, Alexander, 106
Standard Oil Company, 147, 169
Standard Oil Company of New Jersey v. United States, 47
Standing Woman (Lachaise painting), 51
Stanford-Binet Intelligene Scale, 68
Stanislavsky, Konstantin, 7, 11, 19, 39, 109, 161, 173, 221
Stanley, Kim, 255, 277
Stanley, Wendell Meredith, 156, 162, 218
Stanley Cup, 111, 267, 345
Stanton, Elizabeth Cady, 12, 26
Stanwyck, Barbara, 33, 187, 201, 395
Stapleton, Maureen, 247, 333
"Stardust" (song), 137
Stark, USS, 426
Starkweather, Charles, 273
Starling, Ernest, 12
Star of Alexandria (ship), 313
Starr, Ringo, 183, 277
Stars Look Down, The (Cronin), 399
Star Trek (TV series), 321
Star Wars (film), 379
"Star Wars" (Strategic Defense Initiative, or SDI), 406, 418
Starzl, Thomas E., 302
"Statement of Race" (UNESCO), 238
State of Siege (film), 355
Staudinger, Hermann, 100, 256
Stauffenberg, Klaus Schenck von, 202
Stavisky, Serge, 152
"steady state" theory, 64, 90, 226
Steamboat Willie (animated cartoon), 125
Steeleye Span, 337
steel industry, 7, 83, 103, 179, 233, 281
Steere, Allen, 374
Stefansson, Vilhjalmur, 55, 303
Steffens, Lincoln, 19
Steichen, Edward, 11, 23, 91, 263, 361
Steiff, Richard, 11
Steiger, Rod, 257, 259, 317, 325
Stein, Gertrude, 147, 219
Stein, Marc Aurel, 18, 198
Steinbeck, John, 13, 145, 157, 167, 175, 181, 211, 301, 333
Steinberg, Saul, 61
Steinem, Gloria, 155, 347
Stella, Joseph, 227
stellarator, 246
stellar evolution. *See* astronomy
Steloff, Ida Frances, 93
Stenmark, Ingemar, 349, 377, 393
Steppenwolf (Hesse), 121
Steptoe, Patrick, 378, 382
stereophonic sound, 183
Sterling, Andrew, 19
Stern, Abraham, and Stern Gang, 182, 204, 230
Stern, Isaac, 95
Stern (magazine), 407

Sternberg, Josef von, 133, 137, 341
Sternhagen, Frances, 389
Stetham, Robert, 416
Steunenberg, Frank, 31
Stevens, George, 181, 255
Stevens, Nettie Maria, 22
Stevenson, Adlai Ewing, 4, 248, 266, 316
Stevenson, Robert, 203
Stevie (film), 383
Stewart, Jackie, 339
Stewart, James, 37, 175, 183, 201, 217
Stewart, Michael, 305
Stewart, Rod, 213, 371
Stieglitz, Alfred, 11, 15, 23, 219
Stijl, De (Dutch art group), 73
"Still Crazy After All These Years" (album), 371
Stiller, Mauritz, 97
Still Life (Coward play), 209
Stills, Stephen, 331
Sting (singer), 247
Sting, The (film), 359
Stockholm (liner), 267
stock market. *See* finance; New York Stock Exchange
Stockwell, Dean, 55, 267, 289
Stoker, Bram, 137
Stokowski, Leopold, 183
Stolypin, Pyotr, 26, 48
Stone, Edward Durell, 283, 353
Stone, Harlan Fiske, 219
Stone, I. F., 257
Stone, Oliver, 219, 433, 443
Stonehenge Decoded (Hawkins), 302
Stopes, Marie Charlotte Carmichael, 79, 97, 279
Storchio, Rosina, 19
Storey, David Malcolm, 149, 343
Storm Over Asia (film), 125
storms, 389
    hurricanes, 5, 123, 261, 283, 339, 433, 437, 451
    typhoons, 79, 203, 279, 433
    See also cyclones; floods; meteorology
storm troopers (SA) (Germany), 92, 150
"Stormy Weather" (song), 147
Story of My Life, The (Keller), 17
Storyville Portraits (Bellocq), 57
Strachey, Lytton, 79
Strada, La (film), 95, 259
Straight, Beatrice, 255
Strait Is the Gate (Gide), 41
Straits Convention (1922), 104
Strange Interlude (O'Neill play), 125
strangeness (of atomic particles), 256
Stranger, The (Camus), 191
Strangers and Brothers (Snow), 181
Strasberg, Lee, 137, 365
Strasberg, Susan, 263
Strategic Arms Limitation Agreements (SALT), 354, 386
Strategic Defense Initiative (SDI), 406, 418
stratosphere, 10
Straus, Oscar S., 27
Strauss, Richard, 23, 39, 47, 237
Stravinsky, Igor, 43, 45, 81, 93, 125, 229, 273, 349

"Strawberry Fields Forever" (song), 325
streamlined design, 153
"stream-of-consciousness" technique, 85, 99
Streep, Meryl, 237, 381, 383, 387, 389, 401, 405, 411, 415
Streetcar Named Desire, A (Williams play), 41, 111, 221
 film version, 245
Street in Bronzeville, A (Brooks), 211
Street Scene (Rice play), 87
"Streets of Philadelphia" (song), 461
Streicher, Julius, 210
Streisand, Barbra, 193, 311, 359
Strijdom, Johannes Gerhardus, 260, 278
strikes, 11, 39, 51, 55, 281
 steel industry, 83, 233, 281
 Boston Police, 85, 104
 British General, 117
 San Francisco General, 151
 sit-down, 161, 167
 and Memorial Day Massacre, 167
 wartime and postwar, 197, 207, 215
 railroad, barred, 227, 239
 grape workers', 315
 Poland, 392
 baseball, 451, 461
Strindberg, August, 53
string galvanometer, 14
Stroessner, Alfredo, 260, 436
Stroheim, Erich von, 111, 187, 239
Strong, Anna Louise, 235
Strong, Austin, 101, 121
Strouse, Charles, 289
Strowger, Almon Brown, 24
Structural Anthropology (Lévi-Strauss), 276
structuralism, 57, 276
Structure of Scientific Revolutions, The (Kuhn), 298
student demonstrations, 304, 330, 336
 China, 88, 420, 432
Student Nonviolent Coordinating Committee (SNCC), 185, 321
Students for a Democratic Society (SDS), 286, 300, 338
Studies in the Psychology of Sex (Ellis), 122
Study of History, The (Toynbee), 153
Study of Instinct, The (Tinbergen), 246
Sturges, John, 259
Sturges, Preston, 277, 285
Styne, Jule, 237, 283, 311
Styron, William, 325, 387
submarines, 24, 260, 277, 289
 disasters, 305, 333
submarine warfare
 World War I, 60, 68, 72
 World War II, 176, 192, 196
"subversive" activity, 92, 253
subway system (New York), 21
"subway vigilante," 411
Sudan, 264, 270, 278, 340, 408, 414
sudden infant death syndrome (SIDS), 456

Suez Canal, 266
suffragists. *See* woman suffrage
Sugar Babies (musical), 387
Suharto, 98, 322
suicide, assisted, 440, 444
Sukarno, 8, 210, 214, 234, 322, 344
"sulfa" drugs, 34, 140, 160
Sullavan, Margaret, 49, 171, 187, 197, 291
Sullivan, Annie, 21
Sullivan, Harry Stack, 236
Sullivan, Jack, 61
Sumatra, 34
Sumerian civilization, 98, 128
Summer and Smoke (Williams play), 229
Summerhill School (England), 109
Summerskill, Edith Clara, 9, 395
Sumner, James Batcheller, 116, 156, 218
Sun Also Rises, The (Hemingway), 117
Sunday, Billy, 159
Sunday, Bloody Sunday (film), 349
Sunday Times (London), 407
Sundback, Gideon, 28
Sunrise at Campobello (Schary play), 277
Sunset Boulevard (film), 239
sunspot activity, 90
Sun Stone (Paz), 273
Sun Yat-sen, 44, 48, 54, 60, 100, 106, 114, 248, 398
Super Bowl. *See* football
superconductivity, 46, 246, 354, 420, 440
superfluidity, 170
"Superfund" cleanup, 393, 400
superheterodyne receiver, 78
Superman (comic strip), 173
superman concept, 5
suprematism, 63
Suprematist Composition (Malevich painting), 77
Supreme Court, U.S.
 women appear before, appointed to, 76, 397, 457
 nominations rejected, 123, 166, 331, 337, 421
 "Great Dissenter" at, 159
 Fortas resigns, 337
 and death penalty, 375
Supreme Court appointments
 (1902-1916), 13, 25, 69
 (1953-1969), 255, 259, 267, 299, 325, 337
 (1981-1993), 397, 443, 457
Supreme Court rulings
 (1904-1927), 19, 35, 71, 86, 98, 120
 (1931-1947), 135, 157, 161, 167, 187, 197, 227
 (1951-1962), 244, 245, 259, 272, 273, 298, 299
 (1963-1970), 305, 307, 309, 311, 313, 319, 324, 327, 336
 (1976-1980), 368, 375, 381, 383, 387, 393, 395
 (1989-1994), 435, 445, 451, 455, 459, 461
Surface Mining Control Reclamation Act (SMCRA) (1977), 381
Suriname, 372
surrealism, 67, 109, 125, 207, 323, 385

Survival (album), 389
Sutcliffe, Stuart, 277
Sutherland, Donald, 343, 347, 375, 393
Sutliffe, Jack ("Yorkshire Ripper"), 397
Suttner, Bertha von, 24
Sutton, May G., 23
Sutton, Walter Stanborough, 12
Suzman, Helen Gavronsky, 75
Suzuki, Daisetsu Teitaro, 121
Svoboda, Ludvik, 390
"Swanee" (song), 79
Swann's Way (Proust), 55
Swanson, Gloria, 239, 409
Swaziland, 326
Sweden, 10, 24, 418
Sweeney Todd (musical), 387
Sweet, Blanche, 59
Sweet Bird of Youth (Williams play), 283
Sweet Cheat Gone, The (Proust), 113
Swigert, John L. Jr., 344
swimming, 109, 117, 241, 251, 311, 353
Swinburne, Nora, 245
Swinton, Alan Campbell, 30
Sydow, Max von, 131, 267, 281, 285, 297, 349, 371, 431
Sylvester, William, 331
Symbionese Liberation Army (SLA), 365
Symphony No. 7 (Shostakovich), 187
synchrocyclotron, 210, 218
Synge, John Millington, 19, 31, 39
Synod of Barmen (1934), 153
Syntactic Structures (Chomsky), 275
syphilis, 22, 28, 42
Syria, 92, 186, 304, 402
 Druse insurrections, 112, 120, 256
 independent state, 218
 vs. Israel, 226, 324, 358, 400
 and UAR, 278
 vs. Lebanon, 374, 438
Systematic Theology (Tillich), 247
Szent-Györgyi, Albert, 124
Szilard, Leo, 140, 174, 180, 190, 206, 312

Tacke, Ida. *See* Noddack, Ida Tacke
Taft, Robert Alphonso, 256
Taft, William Howard, 28, 34, 48, 119, 134, 256
Taft-Hartley Act (1947), 223, 256
Tagore, Rabindranath, 49, 57, 69, 189
Tailhook scandal, 447
Taiping (liner), 235
Taiwan. *See* Formosa
Tajikistan, 456
Takamine, Jokichi, 6
Takeshita, Noboru, 424, 434
Tale of Peter Rabbit, The (Potter), 3
Tales of the South Pacific (Michener), 223
Talking Book (album), 355
Tallal, king of Transjordan, 246, 250
Tallchief, Maria, 229
Talley's Folly (Wilson play), 393
Talmadge, Constance, 97
Tamara, 147

Tamar and Other Poems (Jeffers), 303
Tamayo, Rufino, 447
Tamblyn, Russ, 293
Tambo, Oliver, 76, 458
Tamil forces (Sri Lanka), 398, 430
Tampomas 2 (ferry), 399
Tanaka, Kakuei, 364, 432
Tandy, Jessica, 41, 221, 319, 433, 443, 463
Tanganyika, 102, 294, 312
tanks, 4, 12, 64, 68, 74, 78, 100
 German "panzer" units, 172
Tanzania, 102, 312, 386
Taos Pueblo (Adams photographs; text by Austin), 131
tape recorder, 227
Tarantino, Quentin, 461
Tarbell, Ida Minerva, 19, 205
tariffs, 129, 131
Tarkenton, Fran, 383
Tarkington, Booth, 79, 219
Tarnower, Herman, 395
Tarzan of the Apes (Burroughs), 61
Tashkent Agreement, 320
Taste of Honey, A (Delaney play), 277
 film version, 295
Tate, Sharon, 337
Tate Gallery (London), 355
Tatlin, Vladimir, 91, 259
Tatum, Edward Lawrie, 186
Tatum, Goose, 193, 223
tau electron or tauon, 364
Taussig, Helen, 200, 292, 422
taxes, 69, 73, 110
 poll tax outlawed, 310
Taylor, Elizabeth, 143, 320
Taylor, Laurette, 53, 209, 319
Taylor, Lawrence, 403
Taylor, Maxwell D., 292
Taylor, Robert, 49, 163, 171, 341
Tchaikovsky, Peter Ilich, 193
Tea and Sympathy (Anderson play), 255
Teale, Edwin Way, 246, 394
Teamsters Union, 273, 327
Teapot Dome scandal, 98, 104, 120, 128, 191
technetium (element 43), 166
Technical Manifesto of the Futurist Painters, 43
Tedder, Arthur, 206, 326
Teddy bear, 11
Teflon, 203
Tehomi, Avraham, 134
Tehran agreements, 198
Teilhard de Chardin, Pierre, 265
telegraph, 102
telephone, 24, 102
 long-distance, 62, 64, 65, 245
 new systems, 424
telescope
 Mount Wilson, 72, 76, 104, 228
 radio, 166, 274, 304, 324
 Mount Palomar, 228
 Very Large Array, 430
 Hubble, 438, 454
 See also astronomy
television, 26
 color, 20, 124, 182, 243
 experimental/early, 20, 30, 104, 108, 116, 124, 140, 163, 172, 218
 first programs, 53, 143, 157
 first news programs, 71, 301

television (continued)
   transatlantic, 124, 298
   experimental programming, 149
   first sets go on sale, first pictures
      transmitted, 175
   network begins, 181
   commercial begins, 187
   children's, 231, 339, 375
   number of receivers in use, 235,
      285
   presidential campaigns on, 249,
      284
   quiz show scandals, 281
   satellite, 282, 298
   evangelism on, 287
   cameras, 338
   British, 339
   See also entries for individual
      programs
Teller, Edward, 34, 192, 248, 256
Tellico Dam, 368
Telstar satellite, 298
temperance movement, 49
Temple, Shirley, 39, 229
Ten Days That Shook the World
      (Reed), 83
   film version, 83, 123
Tender Is the Night (Fitzgerald),
      149
Tennessee Valley Authority (TVA),
      147, 368
tennis, 41, 97, 177, 313, 375, 403
   Davis Cup, 5, 307
   women's, see tennis, women's,
      below
   African-Americans in, see
      African-Americans in sports
   U.S., Australian and French
      Opens, 153, 165, 171, 199,
      299, 311, 341, 345, 365, 371,
      387, 397, 405, 425
   youngest player, 415
tennis, women's
   (1903-1924), 17, 23, 41, 85, 111
   (1926-1939), 117, 121, 141,
      161, 177
   (1948-1956), 229, 239, 245,
      249, 269, 271
   (1963-1974), 307, 311, 321,
      345, 361, 365
   (1975-1987), 371, 383, 405, 425
10th of Ramadan (Nile steamer),
      407
Terao, Satoshi, 415
Teresa, Mother, 45, 229, 241, 387
Tereshkova, Valentina, 304
Terman, Lewis M., 68
Terms of Endearment (film), 407
Terriss, Norma, 121
terrorism, 332, 353, 359, 365
   Quebec, 306, 338, 344
   Weathermen group, 338, 393
   Argentina, 344, 374
   IRA, 404, 444
   Muslim, 416, 430
   See also bombings; hostages
Terry, Ellen, 127
Tesoro Beach Accords (1989), 435
Tess of the Storm Country (film),
      59
Testament of Youth (Brittain), 147
testosterone, 158
"test-tube babies." See in vitro fer-
      tilization
Tet Offensive (1968), 330
Tevye's Daughters (Aleichem), 311

Tewkesbury, Joan, 369
Texas City explosions, 273
Texas Rangers, 447
Thailand, 326, 382
thalidomide, 274, 292, 296
Thanh, Nguyen. See Hồ Chi Minh
Thant, U, 40, 292, 366
Thatcher, Margaret Roberts, 52,
      112, 386, 440
Thaw, Evelyn Nesbit, 27
Thaw, Harry Kendall, 27
theater
   "of the absurd," 45, 53, 143,
      233, 253, 287, 311
   experimental, 63
   groups formed, 87, 117, 135,
      221, 261
   Hirschfeld drawings, 131
   regional repertory, 307
   See also Abbey Theatre (Dublin);
      films; Moscow Art Theater;
      musicals; opera; Provincetown
      Players
Theater Guild (New York), 87,
      105, 107, 215
Théâtre de France, 463
Theiler, Max, 168, 248
Their Eyes Were Watching God
      (Hurston), 167
Thelma and Louise (film), 445
Theodore Roosevelt (Borglum
      sculpture), 177
Theory of Games and Economic
      Behavior (Neumann and Mor-
      genstern), 204
Theory of Self-Reproducing Au-
      tomata (Neumann), 322
Theory of the Gene (Morgan), 64
Theosophism, 73
"There'll Always Be an England"
      (wartime song), 175
"There's No Business Like Show
      Business" (song), 217
thermodynamics, 26, 92
"They Didn't Believe Me" (song),
      61
They Knew What They Wanted
      (Howard), 179
thiamine, 6, 162. See also vitamins
Thibaults, The (Martin du Gard),
      101
Things Fall Apart (Achebe), 277
Things of This World (Wilbur), 269
Thin Man, The (film), 153
Third International (Comintern).
      See Communist Party
Third Man, The (film), 235
Third Republic. See France
Third World, 209, 267, 294
Thirty-nine Steps, The (Buchan), 65
This Is the American Earth (Adams
      photographs; text by Newhall),
      285
This Is the Army (armed forces
      show), 193
Thomas, Clarence, 269, 443
Thomas, Dylan, 61, 257
Thomas, Henry, 401
Thomas, Norman Mattoon, 334
Thomas and Beulah (Dove), 417
Thomas Jefferson (Borglum sculp-
      ture), 163
Thompson, Dorothy, 295
Thompson, Emma, 449, 455
Thompson, Ernest, 389
Thompson, Frank Jr., 382

Thomson, George Paget, 120, 184
Thomson, Joseph John, 18, 28, 50,
      84, 184
Thomson, Roy Herbert, 137, 377
Thomson, Tom, 77
Thorndike, Edward Lee, 236
Thorndike, Sybil, 171, 377
Thornton, Jeffrey, 454
Thorpe, Jim, 51, 91, 259
Thorpe & Salter (Britain), 25
Three Comrades (Remarque), 171
Three-Cornered Hat, The (ballet),
      85
Three Days of the Condor (film),
      371
Three Doves (Picasso ceramic), 255
Three Essays on the Theory of Sex-
      uality (Freud), 22
Three Faces of Eve, The (film), 273
Three Mile Island, 384, 385, 386
Threepenny Opera, The (musical),
      125, 261
   film version, 125
Three Sisters, The (Chekhov play),
      7, 283
Three Studies for Figures at the
      Base of a Crucifixion (Bacon
      painting), 201
Three Tall Women (Albee play),
      459
Thresher (submarine), 305
Thriller (album), 403
Throne of Blood, The (film), 271
Through a Glass, Darkly (film),
      297
Thulin, Ingrid, 271, 281, 337, 353
Thuot, Pierre, 450
Thurber, James, 193, 297
Thurmond, J. Strom, 228
Thurmond, Thomas, 147
thyroxine, 58
Tiananmen Square massacre
      (1989), 432
Tibet, 16, 238, 260, 282
Tilden, Bill, 97
Till, Emmett, 263
Tillich, Paul, 247
Tillstrom, Burr, 231
Time magazine, 107
Time of Your Life, The (Saroyan
      play), 179
Time Regained (Proust), 121
Times, The (London), 103, 377,
      397
"Times They Are a-Changin', The"
      (song), 303
Times Three (McGinley), 289
Tinbergen, Nikolaas, 32, 246, 360,
      432
Tin Drum, The (Glass), 121
Tinker, Joe, 33
Tiner, Tailor, Soldier, Spy (le Carré),
      365
Tiny Alice (Albee play), 311
Tippett, Michael, 25, 187
TIROS (weather satellites), 286,
      288
Titanic (liner), 49
Tito, Josip Broz, 46, 210, 218, 294,
      394
Titov, Gherman Stepanovich, 290
Titov, Vladimir, 428
tobacco mosaic virus, 166
Tobacco Road (Caldwell), 141
Togliatti, Palmiro, 312
Tognazzi, Ugo, 383

Togo, 290
Togo, Heihachiro, 154
To Have and Have Not (film), 203
Tojo, Hideki, 188, 230
Tokamak, 246
To Kill a Mockingbird (Lee), 287
   film version, 71, 297
Toledano, Vicente Lombardo, 163
Tolkien, J. R. R., 167, 259, 263,
      363
Tolstoy, Leo, 45
Tombalbaye, N'Garta, 288, 368
Tombaugh, Clyde William, 132
Tom Jones (film), 305
Tomlin, Lily, 369, 393
Tommy (rock opera), 339
   film version, 369
Tomonaga, Shinichiro, 230, 318
Tomorrow the World (Gow-
      d'Usseau play), 195
Tone, Franchot, 171
Tonga, 344
Tongsun Park, 379
Tonkin Gulf Resolution, 308
Toonerville Trolley (comic strip), 37
Top Hat (film), 157
"Top Hat, White Tie, and Tails"
      (song), 157
Torch Song Trilogy (Fierstein),
      401
   film version, 431
Toronto Blue Jays, 451
Torrent, The (film), 441
Torres, Juan José, 348
Torresola, Griselio, 238
Torrey Canyon (tanker), 328
Tortilla Flat (Steinbeck), 157
Torville, Jayne, 397, 411
Tosca (opera), 3
Toscanini, Arturo, 43, 275, 457
Touch of Class, A (film), 361
Touch of the Poet, A (O'Neill play),
      277
Tour de France (bicycle race), 421
Touré, Ahmed Sékou, 102, 278,
      412
Tournament of Roses, 11
Tower, John, and Tower Commis-
      sion, 424
Tower of Babel, The (Canetti), 157
Towill, Jay, 326
Towne, Robert, 365
Townes, Charles Hard, 260
Town Like Alice, A (Shute), 241
town planning, 15
Townshend, Peter, 311, 339, 369
toxic shock syndrome, 382
Toya Maru (ferry), 261
Toynbee, Arnold Joseph, 153
toys, 11
trace minerals, 176
track events, 105, 157, 161, 211,
      259, 431
   Olympics, 109, 229, 249, 251,
      287, 289, 295, 311, 331, 411
tractor, caterpillar, 20
Tracy, Spencer, 5, 181, 225, 277,
      287, 293, 325, 327
traffic lights, 61, 81
tranquilizers. See drugs
transistors, 220, 288
Transjordan, 136, 216, 246
transuranium elements, 180
Trapp, Maria and Georg von, 315
Trapp Family Singers, 283
Trauma of Birth (Rank), 110

Traveling Wilburys, the, 431
Traven, B. (writer), 341
Travers, Henry, 163
Travolta, John, 461
Treasure of the Sierra Madre, The (film), 229
Treaties
  Vereeniging (1902), 12
  U.S.-Panama (1904), 18, 162
  Portsmouth (1905), 22
  Ouchy (1912), 50
  London (1913), 54
  Brest-Litovsk (1918), 76
  Versailles (1919), 80, 82, 88, 110, 112, 154, 160
  Saint-Germain (1919), 82
  Neuilly (1919), 82
  Riga (1921), 90, 92
  Dorpat (1920), 92
  Trianon (1920), 92
  Moscow (1920), 92
  Sèvres (1920), 94, 104
  Rapallo (1920), 94, 100
  Lausanne (1923), 104, 112
  Locarno (1925), 112, 132, 142, 160
  Tirana (1927), 120
  Lateran (1929), 128, 179
  Buenos Aires (1938), 172
  Paris (1951), 250
  Rome (1957), 278
  Brussels (1965), 324
  Biological Warfare Ban (1971), 348, 364
  Canada-U.S. trade (1988), 412
  Antarctic (1959), 431
  Paris (1991), 446
  See also nuclear treaties
Tree, Herbert Beerbohm, 59, 77
Treemonisha (folk opera), 47, 369
Trees, The (Richter), 335
Trevan, J. A., 122
Trevor, Claire, 203
Trial, The (Kafka), 113
Trial of the Catonsville Nine (Berrigan play), 349
Triangle Shirtwaist Company fire, 45
Trieste, 254
Trieste (bathyscaphe), 256
Trinidad and Tobago, 300
Trip to the Moon, A (French film), 11
tritium, 152
Triton (submarine), 289
Triumph of the Will, The (Nazi film), 157
Troell, Jan, 349
troposphere, 10
Trotsky, Leon, 96, 120, 123, 128, 182
Truchs, Butch, 339
Trudeau, Pierre Elliot, 332
Truffaut, François, 143, 361, 379, 413
Trujillo Molina, Rafael Leonidas, 132, 292
Truman, Harry S., 28, 226, 234, 244, 270, 354
  and atomic bomb, 206, 208
  Truman Doctrine, 220, 350
  and railroad strikes, 227, 239
  attempted assassination of, 238
trust-busting. *See* antitrust actions
Tshombe, Moise, 284, 290

Tsiolkovsky, Konstantin Eduardovich, 16
Tsui, Lap-Chee, 434
Tsuyohi, Inukai, 140
tuberculosis, 24
Tubman, Harriet, 56
Tuchman, Barbara Wertheim, 53, 299, 437
Tucker, Sophie, 323
Tukhachevsky, Mikhail Nikolayevich, 96, 150, 166
tuna canning industry, 439
Tunes of Glory (film), 289
Tunisia, 16, 250, 268
Tunney, Gene, 117, 123, 133
Tupolev TU-144, 332
turbojet engine, 132, 160, 178, 188
turboprop engine, 257
Turing, Alan Mathison, and "Turing machine," 52, 160, 164, 194, 262
Turkey, 24, 46
  in the Balkans, 10, 32, 42, 50, 54
  Young Turks, 34, 38, 54
  Greeks vs., 50, 86, 90, 96, 100, 248, 304
  World War I and postwar, 58, 68, 78, 94, 104
  Armenian revolt against, 62, 70
  earthquake in, 177
  U.S. aid to, 220
  Turkish immigrants in Germany, 446
Turkish Republic of Northern Cyprus, 366
Turner, D. A., 110
Turner, Frederick Jackson, 143
Turner, Kathleen, 417
Turner, Tina, 369
Turning Point (Seferis), 351
Tushingham, Rita, 295
Tuskegee Institute, 65, 198
Tutankhamen (King Tut), 100
Tutu, Desmond Mpilo, 139, 369, 412, 421
Tuvalu, 384
Twachtman, John Henry, 15
Twain, Mark, 45, 69
Twelve, The (Blok), 79
Twenty-first Amendment, 147
Twenty-second Amendment, 244
Twenty-fourth Amendment, 310
20,000 Leagues Under the Sea (Verne), 31
Twenty Years at Hull House (Addams), 43
Two Cheeseburgers with Everything (Oldenburg sculpture), 299
Twort, Frederick William, 64
"two-term amendment," 244
2001: A Space Odyssey (film), 331
Two Trains Running (Wilson play), 449
Two Women (film), 293
Tylenol murders, 401
Tynan, Kenneth, 339
Tytus, John B., 103
Tz'u Hsi, empress of China, 2, 34

U-boat, 24. *See also* submarines
UFOs, 224, 338

Uganda, 110, 114, 300, 322, 348, 374, 386, 416, 420
Ugarte, Augusto Pinochet, 64
Uhlenbeck, George Eugene, 112
Uhry, Robert, 433
Ukraine, 76, 78, 90, 116, 444
Ulanova, Galina, 43, 181
Ulbricht, Walter, 240, 348
Ullmann, Liv, 173, 321, 349, 353, 359, 383
ultraviolet (UV) rays, 4, 56, 462
Ulysses (Joyce), 77, 175
Umberto D (film), 251
Umbrellas of Cherbourg, The (film), 305
Umm al Qaiwain, 348
Unbearable Lightness of Being, The (Kundera), 411
  film version, 429
"uncertainty principle," 120, 134, 140
Uncle Vanya (Chekhov play), 283
unconscious, theory of the, 50, 106
Under Fire (Barbusse), 69
Underground Railroad, 56
Under Milk Wood (Thomas play), 257
underwater observation, 130, 154, 228, 256, 288, 316, 338, 448
underwater springs (hydrothermal vents), 378
Undset, Sigrid, 93, 127
undulant fever (brucellosis), 72
unemployment, 147
Unfinished Business (EPA landmark report), 424
Unforgettable (album), 445
Unforgiven (film), 451
Unification Church, 259, 403
"unified field theory," 146
Unimation, 287, 293
Union Carbide Corporation, 410
Unione Femminile (Italy), 11
United Arab Emirates, 348
United Arab Republic (UAR), 278
United Artists, 85
United Auto Workers (UAW), 161, 167, 189, 333
United Farm Workers of America, 315
United Kingdom. *See* Britain
United Mine Workers, 11, 197, 281, 341
United Nations, 4, 87, 201, 204, 207, 214, 267, 275, 352
  Relief and Rehabilitation Administration (UNRRA), 197, 208, 224, 245, 308
  U.S. joins, 208
  Food and Agriculture Organization (FAO), 209
  Commission on Human Rights, 209, 217, 227, 228
  women in, 209, 217, 228, 256
  Declaration of Human Rights, 211, 227, 228
  Educational, Scientific, and Cultural Organization (UNESCO), 215, 238, 372
  Children's Fund (UNICEF), 215, 317, 457
  World Health Organization (WHO), 227, 274, 456
  Convention for the Suppression of Traffic in Persons, 235

  Relief and Works Agency (UNRWA), 243
  High Commission for Refugees (UNHCR), 245
  International Refugee Organization (IRO), 245
  and apartheid, 250
  peacekeeping force, 266, 284, 290, 292, 308, 314, 358, 400, 446, 456
  Law of the Sea Conference, 277
  Conference and Commission on Environment, 355, 427, 451
  Environment Programme (UNEP), 403
  Food and Agriculture Organization (FAO), 403
  condemns aggressors, 438, 448
United States
  imperialism of, *see* imperialism
  demonstrates naval power (1907-1909), 33
  intervenes in Haiti, 64, 152, 444, 460, 462
  enters World War I, 72, 79
  and atomic bomb, 184, 206, 208
  World War II, 186, 187 (*see also* World War II)
  Cold War policy, 262 (*see also* Cold War)
  in space race, 276 (*see also* spacecraft/satellites; space flight)
  takes Grenada, 406
  in Persian Gulf War, 438, 442
  See also Supreme Court, U.S.
United States v. Darby, 187
United States v. Nixon, 364
United States Steel Corporation, 7, 179
United Steelworkers of America, 233, 253, 281
UNIVAC computer. *See* computers
Universal Negro Improvement Association (UNIA), 61, 93
University of California, 308, 311
University of Chicago, 436
University of Texas, 319
Unsafe at Any Speed (Nader), 317
Upatnieks, Juris, 316
Updike, John, 143, 287, 397
Upper Volta, 290
uranium (element 92), 156, 180, 182, 192, 206, 246
Uranium, U.S. Advisory Committee on, 174, 180
Uranus (planet), 422
Urbain, Georges, 32
urea cycle, 142
Urey, Harold C., 136, 254, 393
Urias, Cesar Yanes, 286
Ur of the Chaldees (Woolley), 128
Urquiola (oil tanker), 376
Urschel, Charles F., 147
Uruguay, 18, 360
"U-2 incident," 286, 300
Uzbekistan, 282, 434

Vaaler, Johann, 5
vaccines. *See* disease
vacuum cleaner, 5
Valberg, Birgitta, 285
Valentino, Rudolph, 97, 119
Valéry, Paul, 213
Vallone, Raf, 293

Van Allen, James Alfred, and Van Allen belts, 60, 276
Vance, Courtney, 439
van de Hulst, Hendrik Christoffel, 202, 244
Vandenburgh, Arthur Hendrick, 246
Vander Meer, Johnny, 171
Van de Velde, Theodor H., 117
van Doesburg, Theo, 73
Van Doren, Charles, 281
Van Druten, John, 197, 321
Van Duser, Jane, 201
Van Duyn, Mona, 451
Van Dyke, Dick, 289
Van Dyke, W. S., 153
Van Fleet, Jo, 257
Vanguard (British warship), 73
Vanguard satellites, 276, 282
Van Houten, Leslie, 337
Van Lawick, Hugo, 286
van't Hoff, Jacobus, 8
Vanuatu, 394
Vanzetti, Bartolomeo, 96, 120
Vargas, Getúlio, 132, 142, 210, 260, 264
Vargas, Virgilio Barco, 98
Vargas Llosa, Mario, 163
Varieties of Religious Experience, The (James), 13
Vatican, the, 128, 279, 345, 437
  Vatican II, 297, 385
  See also Roman Catholic Church
Vaughan Williams, Ralph, 279
Veidt, Conrad, 85, 191, 199
Veksler, Vladimir Iosifovich, 210
Vela Hotel (military satellites), 304
Velasco Alvarado, Juan, 332
Velasco Ibarra, José Maria, 222, 354
Velikovsky, Immanuel, 240, 390
Venera spacecraft, 314, 342, 352, 370, 384, 402
Venezuela, 10, 177
Venizelos, Eleutherios, 42, 164
Ventris, Michael, 250
Venus (planet), 314, 342, 352, 366, 370, 384, 402, 434, 440
Vereen, Ben, 349
Verne, Jules, 27, 31, 461
Veronal (anesthetic), 12
Very British Coup, A (TV series), 431
Very Large Array telescope, 430
Vesco, Robert, 345
Vichy government (World War II), 180, 186, 246
Victor (oil tanker), 425
Victor Emmanuel III, king of Italy, 98, 226
Victoria, queen of England, 4, 6, 388
Victoria Regina (play), 463
Victor Records, 5, 11
Victor/Victoria (film), 403
video cameras, 417
videocassette recorder (VCR), 371
videodisks, 387
videotape recorders, 268
Vienna Psycho-Analytical Society, 10, 404
Vienna Psychoanalytic Institute, 114
Vienna Summit (1979), 386
"Vie en Rose, La" (song), 67
Vietnam, 210

Vietminh founded, 188
  War of Independence, 214, 240
  partition of, 258
  Civil War, 258, 358
  vs. Cambodia, 378, 382
  "boat people," 383
Vietnam Veterans Memorial, 401
Vietnam War, 52, 106, 264, 268, 282, 292, 300, 314
  opposition to, 70, 102, 111, 125, 318, 330, 336, 342, 349
  U.S. involvement in, 308, 314, 318, 324, 326
  Tet Offensive, 330
  U.S. troops withdraw, 336, 342, 346, 352
  "Christmas bombing," 352
  ends, 358, 368
  veterans of, 381, 401
View from a Distant Star, The (Shapley), 310
View from the Bridge, A (Miller play), 263
Viking spacecraft, 370, 374
Vilkitski, Boris, 59, 79
Villa, Francisco (Pancho), 60, 64, 68, 106
Villard, Paul Ulrich, 2
Vincennes, USS, 430
Vincent, Fay, 451
Vine, F. J., 284
Vineland (Pynchon), 361
Vinson, Frederick Moore, 259
Virgin Spring, The (film), 285
viruses, 42, 208, 214, 218, 230
  tobacco mosaic, 166
  computer, 406
  genetically engineered, 422
Visconti, Luchino, 305, 337, 365, 377
Vishinsky, Andrei Yanuarievich, 260
Vishnevskaya, Galina, 365, 439
Visible Man, Visible Woman projects, 460, 462
VisiCalc "spreadsheet" program, 390
VISTA program, 311
vitamins, 6, 168, 262
  term coined, 26, 52
  discovered and synthesized, 100, 114, 124, 136, 144, 156, 162, 166, 172, 222, 354
  C and the common cold, 344
Vitya (steamer), 217
V-J Day, 208
V-Letter and Other Poems (Shapiro), 201
Voice of America, 193
Voice of the Turtle, The (Van Druten play), 197
Voight, Jon, 339, 381
volcano eruptions, 13, 51, 393, 421, 445
Volcker, Paul, 427
Volkoff, George, 170
Volkov, Vladislav N., 348
Volkswagen, 161
Volstead Act, 91. *See also* Prohibition
Voluntary Parenthood League, 63, 87
von Bulow, Claus, 439
V-1s, V-2s. *See* rocket bombs
Vonnegut, Kurt, 105, 337
Vorster, Balthazar, 64, 408

Vortex, The (Coward), 363
Voskhod spacecraft, 310, 314
Vostok spacecraft, 290, 304
voting rights
  for women, *see* woman suffrage
  for African-Americans, 310, 314
Voting Rights Act (1965), 314
Voyage, The (opera), 449
Voyage Out, The (Woolf), 65
Voyager (airplane), 419
Voyager (destroyer), 313
Voyager spacecraft, 378, 388, 392, 422, 434, 440

Waco, Texas, siege, 455
Wagner, Robert Ferdinand, 258
Wagner (National Labor Relations) Act (1935), 155, 167, 223, 258
Waiting for Godot (Beckett), 253
Wajda, Andrzej, 229, 279
Waksman, Selman A., 188, 196
Walbrook, Anton, 197, 231
Walcott, Derek Alton, 133, 453
Walcott, "Jersey Joe," 257
Walden Two (Skinner), 228
Waldheim, Kurt, 352, 420
Walesa, Lech, 198, 392, 396, 408, 440
Walken, Christopher, 381
Walker, Alice, 205, 401, 449
Walker, Joseph A., 359
Walking (Archipenko sculpture), 51
Wall, The (Hersey), 239
Wallace, Dee, 401
Wallace, George, 135, 305, 352
Wallace, Henry Agard, 228, 316
Wallach, Eli, 247, 257
Waller, Fats, 21, 199, 383
Wall Street crashes, 129, 152, 425
Walsh, Don, 288
Walsh, Raoul, 187
Walter, Bruno, 303
Walters, Charles, 257
Walters, Patricia, 245
Walthall, Henry B., 63
Walton, Ernest Thomas Sinton, 140, 248
Walton, William, 137
"Waltzing Matilda" (unofficial Australian anthem), 15
Wanamaker, Sam, 89, 383, 459
Wandering Through Winter (Teale), 246
Wang Hongwen, 374
Wannsee Conference (1942), 192
Wapshot Chronicle, The (Cheever), 273
War and Peace (Tolstoy), 45
  opera version, 209
War and Remembrance (Wouk), 407
war bonds, 73
war criminals. *See* crime
Ward, Barbara, 61, 354, 399
Ward, Douglas Turner, 359
Wargnier, Regis, 451
Warhol, Andy, 127, 313, 427
War Industries Board, 73, 79
War in the Air, The (Wells), 35
Warner, Sylvia Townsend, 385
War of the Worlds (radio broadcast), 171
"War on Poverty," 311
war production, U.S. (World War II), 175, 181, 207
Warren, Earl, 255, 259, 331, 337

Warren, Robert Penn, 25, 217, 415, 437
war reparations. *See* World War I
Warrior Marks (film), 449
Warsaw Ghetto rising (1943), 196
Warsaw Pact (1955), 264, 266, 438, 446
Warsley, Wallace, 105
Washansky, Louis, 324
Washbourne, Mona, 305, 383
Washington, Booker T., 9, 65
Washington, Denzel, 451
Washington Conference (1921-1922), 100
Washington Post, 365
Washington Redskins, 181
Washington Senators, 73
Wasp (aircraft carrier), 251
Wassermann, August von, 28
Wasserstein, Wendy, 431
waste-disposal convention, 353
Waste Land, The (Eliot), 101
Watch on the Rhine (Hellman play), 187
  film version, 197
Watergate scandal, 116, 123, 172, 336, 352, 358, 364, 365, 370, 453
  book and film about, 365, 375
Waterhouse, Keith, 305
Water Quality Agreement, Great Lakes, 355
Water Quality Improvement Act (1970), 343
Waters, Ethel, 147, 197, 241, 381
Waterston, Sam, 349
Watkins v. United States, 272
Watson, Charles (Tex), 337
Watson, James Dewey, 124, 202, 300, 332
Watson, John Broadus, 54, 60, 70, 252, 278
Watson, Thomas John, 269
Watson, Thomas John Jr., 271
Watson-Watt, Robert Alexander, 154
Watts, Charlie, 299
Watts riots (1965), 315, 333
Waugh, Evelyn, 403
wave-particle duality, 104, 116, 120
wave-power station (Britain), 446
Way Down East (film), 93
Wayne, David, 223
Wayne, John, 33, 177, 229, 235, 239, 244, 258, 389
Way of All Flesh, The (Butler), 15
Way We Were, The (film), 359
"We Are the World" (song), 415
weather. *See* meteorology; storms
Weathermen terrorist group, 338, 393
Weaver, Robert, 321
Weavers, the, 231, 235, 241
Webb, Beatrice Potter, 199
Webb, Clifton, 147
Webb, Sidney, 199
Webber, Andrew Lloyd, 231, 349, 387, 431
Weber, Carl Maria von, 45
Weber, Max (painter, sculptor), 297
Weber, Max (sociologist), 93
Webster v. Reproductive Health Services, 435
Wedeking, Franz, 125

Wednesday Morning, 3 A.M. (album), 317
Wedtech case (1988), 430
Wegener, Alfred, 48
Weil, Simone, 17, 199
Weill, Kurt, 5, 125, 189, 197, 243
Weimar Republic, 114, 154
Weinberg, Steven, 324
Weinberg, Wilhelm, 34
Weiner, Alexander S., 180
Weir, Julian Alden, 89
Weiss, Carl, 156
Weiss, Peter, 309
Weissmuller, Johnny, 109
Weizmann, Chaim, 250
Welch, Joseph Nye, 290
Welch, Robert, 278
Weller, Michael, 389
Welles, Gwen, 369
Welles, Orson, 65, 79, 171, 185, 193, 203, 319, 417
Wellington Convention (1988), 431, 445
"We'll Meet Again" (wartime song), 175
Well of Loneliness, The (Hall), 123
Wells, H. G., 7, 35, 147, 171, 219
Welty, Eudora, 41
Werner, Oskar, 315, 317
Wertheimer, Max, 50
West Africa, 4
West, Mae, 395
Western Electric Company, 235
Western Federation of Miners, 23
Western Samoa, 302
Westinghouse Corporation, 142
Westley, Helen, 87, 107
Weston, Edward, 281
West Side Story (musical), 273
film version, 293
Wetlands of International Importance, Convention on (1971), 347
Whale, James, 135, 147, 161, 275
Whales and Nightingales (album), 343
whaling, 113, 355
International Commission and moratorium on, 217, 401, 417, 457
Whampoa Military Academy, 106, 108, 112
Wharton, Edith, 23, 47, 91, 169
What Every Woman Knows (Barrie play), 37
What Every Woman Should Know (Sanger), 73
What Is Life? (Schrödinger), 202
What Price Glory? (Anderson-Stallings play), 285
Wheeler, Mortimer, 256
Whinfield, John Rex, 188
Whipple, Fred Lawrence, 232, 416
Whipple, George, 92
whistle-blowing, 365
Whistler, James McNeill, 17
White, Al, 449
White, Byron Raymond "Whizzer," 299
White, Dan, 383
White, Edward Higgins II, 314, 324
White, George (show business), 85
White, George Stuart (British field marshal), 52
White, Maurice, 339
White, Patrick, 361

White, Paul Dudley, 360
White, Pearl, 59
White, Peter, 333
White, Stanford, 27
White, Verdine, 339
White, Walter Francis, 265
White Album (Beatles), 333
"White Christmas" (song), 193
"white dwarfs" (astronomy), 42, 48
Whitehead, Alfred North, 40, 112, 134, 224
Whitelaw, Billie, 331
Whiteman, Paul, 109, 329
White Russians, 78, 82, 90, 96. *See also* Russia
Whitlam, Edward Gough, 354
Whitman, Charles, 319
Whitney Houston (album), 421
Whittemore, Hugh, 383
Whittle, Frank, 132, 160
Who, the, 311, 339
whooping cranes, 260, 372
Who's Afraid of Virginia Woolf? (Albee play), 299
film version, 321
Wichita State University football team, 345
Wide Sargasso Sea, The (Rhys), 391
Widmark, Richard, 293
Wiegel, Helene, 233
Wiene, Robert, 85
Wiener, Norbert, 226, 312
Wier, Bob, 315
Wiesel, Elie, 416
Wiesenthal, Simon, 39, 223, 293
Wiesenthal Center, 293
Wiest, Dianne, 421
Wiggin, Kate Douglas, 15
Wigman, Mary, 363
Wigner, Eugene Paul, 120, 162, 306
Wilbur, Richard, 269
Wilcox, Frank, 163
Wild and Scenic Rivers Act (1968), 333
Wild Boy, The (ballet), 397
Wilde, Oscar, 7, 23, 51
Wilder, Billy, 29, 201, 211, 239, 257, 281
Wilder, Laura Ingalls, 157
Wilder, Thornton, 193, 305, 373
Wilderness Act (1964), 309
Wildfowl and Wetlands Trust (Britain), 217
Wildlife Preservation Trust International, 282
wildlife refuges, 15, 363. *See also* endangered or extinct species
Wild Strawberries (film), 271
Wild Swans at Coole, The (Yeats), 73
Wiles, Andrew, 454
Wiley, Harvey Washington, 132
Wilhelm II, kaiser of Germany, 34, 78, 190
Wilkerson, Cathlyn, 393
Wilkins, Hubert, 137
Wilkins, Maurice Hugh Frederick, 70, 252, 300
Wilkins, Robert Wallace, 256
Wilkins, Roy, 9, 399
Willard, Jess, 65, 85
Williams, Anna Wessel, 24
Williams, Emlyn, 171
Williams, Eric, 300
Williams, Harrison A. Jr., 382

Williams, Robert Runnels, 162
Williams, Robin, 251
Williams, Ted, 187
Williams, Tennessee, 47, 209, 229, 247, 257, 265, 283, 407
Williams, Vanessa, 405
Williams, Wayne B., 387
Williams, William Carlos, 215, 307
Willkie, Wendell, 182
Will Rogers Follies, The (musical), 443
Willson, Meredith, 273
Willstätter, Richard, 24
Wilson, Allan, 396, 426
Wilson, August, 211, 411, 415, 429, 449
Wilson, Bill, 157
Wilson, Charles, 46
Wilson, Dooley, 191
Wilson, Edmund, 215, 357
Wilson, Edward O., 370
Wilson, Harold, 70, 310, 364
Wilson, Lanford, 393
Wilson, Robert W., 314
Wilson, Sloan, 269
Wilson, Woodrow, 48, 66, 69, 80, 94, 110, 119, 317
Winchell, Walter, 175
Winds of War, The (Wouk), 349
TV version, 407
Winesburg, Ohio (Anderson), 87
Winger, Debra, 407
Wings (rock group), 349
Wings of the Dove, The (James), 13
Winnie Mae (airplane), 135
Winnie-the-Pooh, 117
Winning Bridge Made Easy (Goren), 163
Winters, Shelley, 265
Winterset (Anderson play), 157
wireless telegraphy, 4, 6, 42
Wireless World (magazine), 208
wiretapping, 268, 336
Wise, Robert, 293, 315
Wise, Stephen Samuel, 237
Wiseman, Joseph, 331
Wise Parenthood (Stopes), 79
witch-hunting, 170, 220, 228, 233, 394
in film industry, 221, 249, 253
McCarthy and, 240, 253, 255, 258, 272, 357
See also blacklisting; McCarthy, Joseph Raymond
Within a Budding Grove (Proust), 79
Wittgenstein, Ludwig Josef Johann, 249
Wizard of Oz, The (film), 177
WNBT (New York), 187
Wodehouse, P. G., 73, 373
Wolfe, Thomas, 129
Woman Ironing (Picasso painting), 7
Woman of the Year (film), 181
Woman Rebel (magazine), 59
Woman Social and Political Union (WSPU), 54
Woman's Place (film), 97
woman suffrage, 12, 14, 18, 30, 42, 54, 60
Woman Suffrage Amendment (1920), 26
won in Britain, 80, 124
won in U.S., 90

won in France, 204
women
laws protecting, 11, 235
women's rights movement, 12, 18, 26, 305, 443, 457 (*see also* woman suffrage)
"immodesty" of, 13
Nobel Prizes awarded to, 14, 24, 41, 48
in work force, 35, 39, 79, 171, 181, 187, 191, 209
in government office, 70, 74, 338, 383, 458
in medicine, 74
in air travel, 143, 163, 167
in space flights, 168, 304, 406
psychology of, 204
in UN, 209, 217, 228, 256
in sports, 247, 277, 301 (*see also* Olympics; tennis, women's)
sexual role of, 318
health care, 339, 373, 446
role of, in the Church, 385, 451, 461
on Supreme Court, 397, 457
See also feminism
Women in Love (Lawrence), 91
film version, 339
Women's Health Initiative, 446
Women's International League for Peace and Freedom (WILPF), 64, 86
Women's Social and Political Union (WSPU), 14, 60
Women's Zionist Organization of America, 51
Wonder, Stevie, 241, 355
Wonderful Wizard of Oz, The (Baum), 3
film version, 177
Wong, B. D., 429
Wood, Grant, 133, 195
Wood, Natalie, 293
Wood, Peggy, 129
Wood, Sam, 197
wood bison and Wood Buffalo National Park (Canada), 101
Wooden, John, 311, 327
Woods, Gay, 337
Woods, Terry, 337
Woodstock festival (1969), 337
Woodward, Joanne, 209, 273, 333
Woodward, Robert (journalist), 365, 375
Woodward, Robert Burns (chemist), 200, 246, 288, 318, 354
Wooldridge, Susan, 411
Woolf, Virginia, 65, 85, 129, 191
Woolley, Leonard, 98, 128, 290
Woolworth Building (New York), 55
Workingman's Dead (album), 343
Works Progress Administration (WPA), 147, 157
World According to Garp, The (Irving), 383
World and Africa, The (Du Bois), 223
World Bank, 201
World Charter for Nature, 403
World Court, 87, 215
World Cup. *See* skiing; soccer
World Disarmament Conference (Geneva) (1932-1934), 140
World Health Organization. *See* United Nations

"world heritage" convention, 353
World Jewish Congress, 237
World of Apu, The (film), 99
World of Jacques Cousteau, The (TV series), 322
World Series
(1901-1907), 7, 13, 15, 19, 33
(1920), 91
(1946-1969), 217, 227, 255, 301, 337
(1988-1992), 433, 451, 453
See also baseball
Worlds in Collision (Velikovsky), 240
World Trade Center bombing (1993), 454
World War I, 51, 56, 58-78, 85, 104, 130, 158
events leading to, 18, 22, 28, 30, 34, 42
opposition to, 67, 74, 80, 86, 126
U.S. enters, 72, 79
reparations for, 82, 87, 92, 104, 109
veterans of, 140
World War II, 56, 110, 134, 141, 174-176, 180-202, 206-208, 322
new devices and techniques in, 20, 55, 62, 96
Allied bases and routes, 43, 59
fund-raising (taxes) for, 73
events leading to, 129, 160, 174
shortages and rationing during, 138, 172, 191, 197, 207
Battle of Britain, 154
casualties, 174
popular songs of, 175, 193
U.S. prepares for, enters, 182, 186
dissent against, 182
World Wildlife Fund, 295, 355
World Without Sun (Cousteau), 316
World Zoo Conservation Strategy (publication), 456
Worth, Irene, 311
Wouk, Herman, 247, 349, 407
Wounded Knee Massacre site, 359
Wozniak, Stephen, 380
Wrangel, Peter, 90
Wray, Fay, 147
wrestling, 169
Wretched of the Earth, The (Fanon), 115

WRGB (Schenectady, NY), 181
Wright, Frank Lloyd, 45, 101, 167, 283
Wright, Helena, 133
Wright, Mickey, 277
Wright, Orville, 4, 14, 232
Wright, Richard Nathaniel, 37, 181, 291
Wright, Teresa, 215
Wright, Wilbur, 4, 14, 52
Wu, Chien-Shiung, 266
Wuthering Heights (film), 177
Wyeth, Andrew, 75, 227, 419
Wyler, William, 3, 13, 161, 167, 177, 187, 191, 215, 399
Wyler Children's Hospital (Chicago), 436
Wyman, Bill, 299
Wyman, Jane, 211, 231
Wynn, Keenan, 369
Wynne-Edwards, Vero Copner, 300

X chromosome, 12. *See also* genetics
xerography, 170, 230, 283
Xerox Corporation, 170, 283
X ray, 8, 14, 57, 104, 120, 218, 346, 350
fire involving, 131
X-ray crystallography, 50, 60, 64, 70, 74, 252, 262, 310

Yablonski, Joseph, 281, 289
yachting, 221, 289, 325
ships lost, 389
America's Cup, 407
Yahya Khan, Agha Mohammed, 338
Yale Art Gallery, 259
Yale Center for British Art, 365
Yale Clinic of Child Development, 46
Yalow, Rosalyn, 238
Yalta Conference (1945), 206
Yamada, Izuzu, 271
Yamamoto, Gonnohyoe, 148
Yamamoto, Isoroku, 198
Yamashita, Tomoyuki, 218
Yamazaki, Tsutomu, 393
Yamoto (battleship), 206
Yang, Chen Ning, 266
"Yankee Doodle Boy" (song), 19
Yao Wenhuan, 374
Yarmouth Castle (cruise ship), 317

Yates v. United States, 272
Yeager, Charles, 222
Yeager, Jeana, 419
Yearling, The (Rawlings), 171
Yeats, William Butler, 11, 19, 67, 73, 107, 179, 256
Yellen, Jack, 87
yellow-dog contracts, 35, 141
yellow fever, 2, 19, 23, 168, 248
Yellow Submarine (album), 339
Yellow Submarine (film), 333
Yeltsin, Boris Nikolayevich, 136, 438, 442, 448, 450
opposition to, 454, 458
Yemen, 298, 324, 332
"Yesterday" (song), 315
Yesterday, Today, and Tomorrow (film), 107
Yevtushenko, Yevgeny, 149, 291, 299
Yip Yip Yaphank (musical), 79
Yom Kippur War (1973), 358
Yordan, Philip, 201
York, Susannah, 305
Yorktown (aircraft carrier), 192
Yosemite Valley, 47
Yoshida, Shigeru, 328
"You Are the Sunshine of My Life" (song), 355
You Can't Take It with You (Hart-Kaufman play), 163
You Have Seen Their Faces (Bourke-White photographs), 167
Young, Andrew, 354
Young, Chic, 9, 135, 363
Young, Cy, 19, 47
Young, John, 314
Young, Neil, 331
Younghusband, Francis, 16
Young Lions, The (Shaw), 231
Young Lonigan (Farrell), 143
Young Turks. *See* Turkey
Yüan Shih-k'ai, 48, 70
Yudenich, Nikolay Nikolayevich, 148
Yugoslavia, 80, 96, 128, 154, 184, 210, 214, 222, 254
leaves Soviet bloc, 230, 394
breaks up, 444, 448
Yukawa, Hideki, 156

Z (film), 333
Zadir Shah, Mohammed, 148, 360

Zadkine, Ossip, 247
Zaharias, Babe Didrikson, 61, 271
Zale, Tony, 223
Zambia, 312
Zamora, Alcalá, 136
Zangara, Joseph, 146
Zanzibar, 312
Zapata, Emiliano, 46, 60, 64, 88
Zátopek, Emil, 249
zebra mussels, 416
Zedillo Ponce de Leon, Ernesto, 460
Zeferelli, Franco, 319
Zelaya, José Santos, 38
Zemeckis, Robert, 459
Zen Buddhism, 121
Zeppelin, Ferdinand von, 2, 74
zeppelins. *See* airships (dirigibles)
Zhai Ziyang, 424
Zhang Chunqiao, 374
Zhdanov, Andrei, 252
Zhou Enlai, 145, 376
Zhu De, 118, 376
Zhukov, Georgi Konstantinovich, 176, 206, 366
Zia Ul-Haq, Mohammad, 110, 378, 388, 430
Ziaur Rahman, 398
Ziegfeld, Florenz, 31, 145
Ziegfeld Follies, 31, 93, 97, 145
Zimbabwe, 110, 314
African National Union (ZANU), 110, 348, 392
African People's Union (ZAPU), 348, 392
"Zimbabwe" (song), 389
Zinneman, Fred, 251, 319, 359, 379
Zinoviev, Grigori, 116
Zionism, 20, 51, 237, 250
zipper, 28
Zogu, Ahmed Bey, 112
Zola, Emile, 13
Zond spacecraft, 332
"zoot suits," 197
Zorba the Greek (Kazantzakis), 275
film version, 311
Zulus, 26, 124, 444
Zuse, Konrad, 162, 186
Zweig, George, 308
Zwicky, Fritz, 150
Zworykin, Vladimir, 30, 108, 140, 172, 184, 402